HULL CITY

A COMPLETE RECORD

1904 - 1989

HULL CITY

A COMPLETE RECORD 1904 - 1989

CHRIS ELTON

Breedon Books Sport

First published in Great Britain by
The Breedon Books Publishing Company Limited
45 Friar Gate, Derby DE1 1DA
1989

ISBN 0 907969 49 6

Printed by Butler and Tanner Limited, Frome.
Jacket designed by Graham Hales and printed by Arkle Print, Northampton.

CONTENTS

Introduction

IT IS 85 years since the Tigers first did battle with Notts County on the Boulevard and 90 years since the professional club's amateur forerunners came into being as an unrated local outfit called Hull Comet. This is therefore an appropriate time to record the exploits of the pioneers and all those who have delighted or frustrated subsequent generations.

The club was elected to the Second Division in 1905 and holds the same status in the Football League in 1989. The aim of the founders of the professional club was to bring First Division football to the city. That aspiration remains unfulfilled, Hull holding the unwanted distinction of being the largest urban area not to have had a First Division team. In pre-war days the club's match programme carried the motto, 'A fair field and no favour'. The phrase, taken from one of Thomas Carlyle's essays, implied, when transferred to a sporting context, that the accumulation of honest endeavour would bring success. Not surprisingly, the suggestion has not born the desired fruit.

Despite the non-attainment of Hull City's ultimate goal, the club has enjoyed times of success over the years. Ambrose Langley's team was frequently on the brink of the top flight, missing out on goal-average in 1910. It was arguably the best side, in terms of consistent performance, in the club's history. The team with the greatest potential came within one step of a Wembley appearance in 1930, only to suffer relegation and be broken apart before its best was seen. Jack Hill's side stands as the club's first champions, winning the Third Division North in 1933. That success was repeated 16 years later by Raich Carter's team, generating a level of interest and support unmatched before or since, not even by Cliff Britton's 1966 Third Division champions, who carry the palm as the club's most free-scoring line-up.

For the writer, the foregoing are the high-spots of the club's history. Each reader will have his own. So, too, with the relative merits of individual players and it is my hope that this volume will help in providing a factual basis to compare the achievements of teams and individuals of one era against another, as well as helping to recall to mind great moments and matches which have inspired through the years.

Regular readers of this series will know something of the difficulties involved in compiling a statistical volume of this nature. Even the apparently straightforward matter of players' appearances brings its problems. The various football annuals differ from one to another in their seasonal totals. Newspapers, too, contain discrepancies in their match-by-match reporting, especially in the early days, when a scribe might begin his report by listing the sides selected earlier in the week and not always advise his readers of any last-minute changes.

Goalscorers bring even greater problems, particularly in pre-war days when players wore unnumbered shirts and, in an age without floodlights, matches might finish in near-darkness. Nor was there the same degree of communication between Press, club and players to clarify such uncertainties, as there is today. Even where club records have survived, they do not always provide satisfactory answers. For instance, at Southend in April 1962, a Doug Clarke shot cannoned off Dudley Price into the net. Price was credited with the score. However, two years later, against Luton, a Chris Chilton header ricocheted into goal off Ron Rafferty. The club credited this one not to Rafferty but to Chilton.

Perhaps the greatest mystery surrounded the Tigers' match with Leicester Fosse in April 1913. Every journalist went away from the game under the impression that Hull City had won 2-0. Even the Tigers' match programme later contained that scoreline. Football League records, however, show a result of 2-1. Only recently have the researches of the Association of Football Statisticians established Fred Osborn as the scorer of Leicester's 'unseen' goal.

Every effort has been made to ensure that the details in this volume are as accurate as possible. Sometimes, though, whilst concentrating on putting the known statistical discrepancies in order, the obvious simple error sneaks in and manages to elude rigorous checking. The club has played 4,027 first-team games, giving a total of 44,297 players' appearances (excluding substitutes) and 6,425 goals. It is not difficult to realize how great is the scope for error.

That the name of Hull City was used prior to 1904 prompted a thorough investigation of the origins of the club and culminated in a statistical analysis of the Tigers' forerunners. A remarkable amount of material has survived from those days, although there are no official records, no summaries of appearances and scorers against which to check the match-by-match records, save for a list of marksmen for 1901-02. Discrepancies and deficiencies exist. For example, there are no less than three different line-ups recorded for the 1903 Scarborough & East Riding Cup Final. Resolving such problems depended on the internal textual evidence of match reports. I hope that the newness of this material will more than offset its imperfections.

Soccer is a world-wide game. So, too, is the pursuit of soccer statistics and this volume would have been much impoverished without help from many people around the globe. I am particularly indebted to those who helped with the hardest part of the task, the tracking down of foreign tour details. To attempt to list all who have helped would be a lengthy process and would inevitably lead to omit and offend someone. To each of them my sincere thanks. Also to those research establishments whose holdings yielded valuable information. Mention must be made here of the Hull Local Studies Library, whose staff have faced my frequent visits over the years with remarkable patience. I am also indebted to Douglas Lamming, whose pioneer work *A Who's Who of Hull City 1904-1984* has helped to make the section on players' records the more complete, and to Mark Peacock for the loan of photographs from his collection. Bill Walker, sports editor of the *Hull Daily Mail*, readily responded to a late cry for help and I must also acknowledge the kind co-operation of the Football League in allowing me to consult material in their archives. Their attendance records filled in many gaps, particularly for the pre-war period, and a number of appearance queries would otherwise not have been satisfactorily resolved.

Finally, my thanks go to Anton Rippon and his staff at Breedon Books for their patience and diligence in transforming my raw manuscript into the finished article.

Chris Elton
Hull
May 1989

Photographic Acknowledgements

Photographs have been supplied by Colorsport, *Hull Daily Mail*, Illustrated London News Picture Library, Mark Peacock Collection.

Programme for the opening match at Boothferry Park.

THE HULL CITY STORY

IT WAS in 1879 that members of the Hull Town Cricket Club decided to take up soccer during the winter months. 'Lamp' Wallgate, who represented Yorkshire at the summer game, and Frank Summers were leading lights in the new club, also called Hull Town, which played on the cricketers' ground in Argyle Street.

The move stimulated interest in the association game locally and, eventually, footballers took over the running of the soccer club. By 1883, Hull Town had reached the Final of the first local county competition, the Scarborough & East Riding Cup, losing to Hull rivals, Blue Star. However, home defeats by Grimsby Town and Lincoln City in the FA Cup competitions of 1883-4 and 1884-5 emphasized the gulf between the best of the locals and the rest of the soccer world. The club fell into decline thereafter and in 1887, in the phraseology of the day, 'went the way of all flesh'.

Twelve months later it was revived, primarily due to the efforts of Harry Sugden, but this venture lasted scarcely two seasons. In January 1889, Town were thrashed 10-0 at Grimsby Humber Rovers. Only six of the side turned up and the number was made up with spectators. In December 1889 another group of players formed the Hull Association FC. Despite inauspicious beginnings, including a 14-2 home defeat by Barton Town in March 1890, the club survived until 1893.

The game, though, was growing in popularity, especially in the schools of Hull. Local leagues began, although some clubs felt the competitions fitted ill with their amateur ethos and remained aloof. After the demise of the Hull Association FC, the mantle of leading local side passed to an outfit called Kingston Amateurs, who won the Hull & District League in 1895. The side which finished second, Albany, took the next step to putting the game on a higher footing in the town.

The year 1895 was that of the great schism, when a number of northern rugby clubs broke away from the Rugby Union to form what became the Rugby League, amongst them the premier local club, Hull FC. The other major exponents of the handling code, Hull Kingston Rovers, remained loyal to the Union until 1897, but when the entire body of local rugby clubs joined the breakaway *en bloc*, Rovers' second team, members of the local league, were left high and dry and temporarily ceased to function.

Albany, with a number of new recruits, renamed themselves Hull Town and arranged to use Rovers' ground on alternate Saturdays for an ambitious programme of friendly matches against teams from as far away as Leeds and Bradford, along with opponents from Grimsby and Scarborough. Amongst the players were Jack Haller, who later became Hull City secretary, the brothers Robson, who were members of a large and noted local footballing family, and Frank Barnes and Geordie Paton, who made their mark with the Tigers' amateur forerunners.

The new Town club reached the Scarborough & East Riding Cup Final, the best local performance in over a decade, even if Scarborough beat them 4-1. The side also reached the Final of the inaugural Hull Times Cup, putting up a creditable performance in losing by the odd goal in three to a Grimsby All Saints' side which won the trophy in four out of the first five seasons. Grimsby Humber Rovers defeated the Hull men 12 months later, but the crowd of 3,282 who watched the Final on the Boulevard was a local association record. That Hull Town club disbanded in the summer of 1898.

Quite unobtrusively, the seeds were already being sown which were to grow into the Hull City Football Club. In the second division of the local league were two moderate outfits called Harlequins and Brunswick. The latter folded midway through 1898-9. Harlequins finished fifth of the eight who stayed the course. Brunswick's secretary, Ben Crompton, first to hold that office for the professional Hull City, made plans for a new team, to be called Hull Comet. On the eve of the new season, Crompton persuaded Harlequins' secretary-goalkeeper Fred Levitt to join him. Several of his teammates followed and the Harlequins collapsed.

Hull Comet began to rise in a meteoric manner befitting its name and at the end of its first season sat proudly at the head of the second division.

		Pld	*W*	*D*	*L*	*Pts*
1	Hull Comet	14	13	0	1	26
2	Beverley Church Inst.Res	14	10	2	2	22
3	East Hull	14	9	2	3	20
4	Sculcoates Amateurs	14	7	1	6	15
5	St Mark's	14	5	2	7	12
6	Paull Garrison	12	3	1	8	7
7	Dairycoates Reserves	12	3	0	9	6
8	New Holland	14	0	0	14	0

(Driffield Church Mutual folded during the season and their record was deleted. Paull Garrison, Dairycoates Reserves and New Holland failed to complete their fixtures, points being awarded to their opponents for unplayed games.)

Only a surprise home defeat by their nearest rivals deprived the Stars of a 100 per cent record. That summer the club moved to the Bull Lane ground, off Stepney Lane, and maintained the momentum, clinching the Hull & District League first division title with a last match victory over Beverley Church Institute, the only side able to overhaul them.

		Pld	*W*	*D*	*L*	*F*	*A*	*Pts*
1	Hull Comet	8	6	2	0	22	6	14
2	Withernsea	8	5	1	2	17	15	11
3	Beverley Church Institute	8	4	2	2	22	7	10
4	East Hull	8	1	1	6	11	20	3
5	Beverley Barracks	8	1	0	7	4	28	2

During the latter part of the competition the Comet men had considerably strengthened their ranks. New faces included the brothers Moxley plus a trio of players borrowed from the Grimsby All Saints' club, including Ted Bromley and Tommy Blythe, both of whom sampled League soccer with Grimsby Town. The trio were not registered with another Hull & District League club, so there was, technically, nothing amiss. The practice was actually quite common but the Bull Lane men still came in for a deal of criticism for their tactics. It indicated the direction in which the club was moving. In August 1901 an extraordinary general meeting agreed to broaden the club's horizons beyond local confines. A new name was approved, the Hull Association FC. An influx of new players improved the side's playing prospects, including several recruits from the defunct Beverley Church Institute Club.

The new club made an inauspicious start. Its application to join the Hull & District League was submitted too late. The governing body declined to accept it, even though their first division was reduced to a farcical three clubs. The team existed on a diet of friendly matches and Cup ties, still a relatively common occurrence in the area. It was frustrating to be left in the lurch from time to time by opponents who failed to appear, but the season had its highlights. Under the captaincy of Mark Andrews, an uncompromising full-back once given a trial by Doncaster Rovers, the side captured the Beverley Hospital Cup, and also reached the Hull Times Cup

Final. It was a surprise when the Hull men took the lead against the Grimsby West Marsh Social Club in extra-time. In fact the green and white ribbons, the local side's colours, were being fastened to the trophy when the Socialists scored a face-saver. It had been a hard encounter, and the Bull Lane contingent were liberally bandaged for the replay. The Grimbarians consequently won at a canter, by eight clear goals.

Further significant developments took place during the close season. At the club's annual meeting, in the Arts and Sports Club in George Street, the members unanimously decided to change their name to Hull City. A new ground had to be found, Bull Lane being swallowed up by a housing development, and the footballers rented Albert United's cricket ground at Dairycoates.

Reports of the annual meeting of the Midland League showed a 'Hull' amongst the applicants for membership. It was the only one not accepted, primarily because no representative was present at the meeting to state his club's case. The City secretaries penned a hasty disclaimer to the local Press. Who the other party was, no one knew for certain, but there were strong rumours that it was the Hull & District FA themselves. Several of their officials were to play prominent roles in the formation of the professional Hull City.

The amateurs of that name deliberated an invitation to join the Sheffield & Hallamshire League, but one suspects the travelling costs involved influenced them to opt for the East Riding League. It proved a mismatch as the City team walked away with the championship.

		Pld	*W*	*D*	*L*	*F*	*A*	*Pts*
1	Hull City	12	9	1	2	35	8	19
2	Barton St Chad's	12	5	4	3	13	14	14
3	Beverley Barracks	12	6	0	6	16	23	12
4	Withernsea	12	5	1	6	27	20	11
5	Brunswick Wesleyans	12	4	3	5	11	23	11
6	Beverley	12	3	4	5	16	21	10
7	St Mark's	12	1	5	6	11	20	7

They also retained the Beverley Hospital Cup and won through to the Finals of the area's two major cups. Scarborough Raincliffe deprived them of the Scarborough & East Riding trophy, although the Hull men's cause was not helped by the absence of Fred Levitt. The Hull Times Cup Final again ended in a 1-1 draw, against Grimsby St John's, but in the replay City established a three-goal lead and then hung on as their opponents reduced the deficit to 3-2. Hull City was the first north-bank name on the trophy.

At the end of the season it was felt that the time was right to seek admission to the Midland League. The voting, for five vacancies, resulted: Nottingham Forest Reserves 14, Gainsborough Trinity Reserves 14, Rotherham Town 14, Thornhill United 10, Gresley Rovers 8, Hull City 5, Sutton-in-Ashfield 5. The last pair missed out. It was a serious blow to the ambitions of the committee, whose sights were firmly set on having a quality soccer team in the city. On the eve of the 1903-04 season came rumours that several key players were leaving. Then followed the brief announcement that the club had disbanded 'owing to lack of funds'.

Thus the short career of the first Hull City came to an end. The majority of their players joined Hessle, who that term became the first local side to reach the first round proper of the FA Amateur Cup and were also first winners of the East Riding Senior Cup. It was a measure of the strength of Hull City that the Hessle line-up contained no less than nine players who had assisted the City team.

Undaunted by the failure of the first Hull City club, the ambitious faction of its committee, including Mark Andrews, Will Hay, Fred Levitt and Ben Crompton, began to formulate an even bolder scheme: the resuscitation of Hull City as a professional club.

It was altogether remarkable that the whole project got off the ground. One attempt to put Hull City on the footballing map by building on the foundations of local talent had already ended in failure. Despite the progress of soccer in Hull, rugby still dominated the local sporting scene and it was an audacious and risky undertaking to attempt to lure the paying public in sufficient numbers to make professional soccer a paying proposition.

Nevertheless, there were factors which were advantageous. The Rugby League was showing signs of a decline in popularity. First champions, Manningham, folded up, to reappear as Bradford City. The Football League, anxious to break into rugby strongholds, found the new club a place in its ranks. In November 1903, the Hull FC directors visited Bradford. Rumour of a similar switch was rife but the Hull directors contemplated disbanding their financially unprofitable Reserve side in favour of a professional soccer team. The scheme fell through, but as the soccer fraternity progressed towards their own similar objective, the rugby club was sympathetic to their search for a ground.

It was on 28 June 1904 that the Hull City AFC Company Limited finally came into being. Players were recruited through an advertisement in the *Athletic News*, a leading sporting newspaper of the day. There was not enough time to seek admission to a league, so a fixture list of friendlies was arranged, attractive enough considering funds did not extend to inviting the best teams in the land. The club also entered the FA Cup and the disadvantages of ground-sharing were soon apparent. Drawn at home to Stockton, the club found the Boulevard required for rugby. They conceded ground advantage, and after a 3-3 draw had to return to Teesside for the replay. The side's defensive tactics in the first game were ill received by a partisan crowd. The City party left the ground to booing and jeering, which culminated in a shower of stones being thrown at their open wagonette. Goalkeeper Jimmy Whitehouse threatened to take a 'big gun' to the replay.

Crowd trouble reared its ugly head again before the end of that eventful season. Hull FC's Cup defeat at home to Hunslet ended with a 'hostile demonstration' against the referee. The rugby authorities closed the Boulevard for the dates of Hull's remaining games. Thinking they had the city to themselves, the Tigers invited FA Cup holders Manchester City. The day before the game the Rugby League

Hull City (on left) and Notts County players before the Tigers' first match as a professional club in September 1904.

Hull City before the start of the 1907-08 season. Back row (left to right): A.Langley (manager), Hedley, G.Browell, Spendiff, Gordon, Robinson, W.Leach (trainer). Seated: Joe Smith, Jack Smith, G.Wright, Shaw, Temple. On ground: Martin, McQuillan. The signing of Joe Shaw in the close season gave added bite to the Tigers' attack and Jackie Smith netted a club record 31 goals.

ruled the soccer match out of order. It forced the club to seek refuge on the Anlaby Road Cricket Circle. It was here that City's long-term future was established. By March 1906, the Tigers' own enclosure on land adjacent to the main Circle pitch was opened. By then the club had been elected to the Football League.

In readiness for Second Division fare, manager Ambrose Langley scoured the country to increase the strength of his squad, bringing in half-backs Billy Robinson, Davy Gordon and George Browell, outstanding in the early League seasons, together with the two Smiths, Joe and Jackie, in attack. Such a collection of talent blended into a side more than able to hold its own in the Second Division. Of the newcomers, only Chelsea fared better.

The early years were good ones for the Tigers. Langley's ability to pick up quality players at negligible cost, especially from the North-East, ensured that the side was up to standard, whilst Corinthians' winger Gordon Wright had a wonderful influence on his colleagues. It was something of a rarity in the period up to 1912 to see the City side in the lower half of the Second Division.

There were epic encounters in the FA Cup too, which drew attendances far in excess of the 8,000 or so regulars at Anlaby Road. There was the three-match marathon with Southern League side, Spurs. For two games the Tigers stood toe-to-toe with their more illustrious opponents before succumbing to a goal from Herbert Chapman, later managerial genius, and brother of future City boss, Harry.

First Division Woolwich Arsenal provided the Tigers' first big scalp in the tournament. They withstood the loss of Davy Gordon with a broken collarbone and held on for a magnificent draw at Plumstead, then shattered the Gunners with three goals in the first quarter of the replay to reach the second round for the first time. Not until 1911 did the Tigers win through to the third round.

In the League, the acquisition of schoolmaster centre-forward Joe Shaw during the close season of 1907 brought a new forcefulness to the attack, and for much of the opening half of 1907-08, City led the Second Division. Inside-forwards Jackie Smith and Arthur Temple were prolific marksmen, Jackie hitting four past Clapton on his way to a club record haul of 31 goals. But a hat-trick of defeats, against Derby, Barnsley and Burnley, spelled the end of promotion hopes.

Programme for the visit of Chelsea in 1911. Tigers' players McQuillan, Neve and Roughley took the match for their joint benefit.

It was September 1909 before the side headed the table again, reinforced in attack by a third Smith, Wally. (The subsequent signing of Ted made the trio a quartet, to go with three Browell brothers, three Gordons and two Wrights.) By the end of September, City held the only unbeaten record in the Second Division. Then disaster struck — a home defeat by Manchester City and a slump which yielded only two wins in ten games. A 7-0 thrashing of lowly Birmingham revived flagging hopes. In February the Maine Road side completed a double over the Tigers. It was almost as if that second defeat released them from some kind of spell cast by the first, for the City men did not lose again until the final Saturday of the season. Between and including those two defeats, their record read: P19 W7 D5 L7 F32 A26 whereas before and after it was a remarkable: P19 W16 D2 L1 F48 A20.

The Tigers roared back into the promotion race. The spectacular 5-1 defeat of West Brom on the penultimate Saturday hoisted them into second place. In the process, Jackie Smith's hat-trick enabled him to better his own scoring record set two seasons earlier. The side needed only to draw at Oldham to go up. They lost 3-0 and missed out on goal-average, and have never been as close to the First Division.

A remodelled side, with Tommy Browell a sensation at centre-forward and Harry Chapman an astute tactician alongside him, again forged its way to the top of the table in October 1911, only to lose by a record 8-0 margin at Wolves the following Saturday. It was not that set-back which doused hopes, but the sale of 'Boy' Browell to Everton in December, followed a couple of months later by brother Andy and Joe Smith. There was a storm of public protest and rumours of further departures, whilst the team, in fourth place until the end of March, clung to the slender hope of promotion.

The rebuilding process accelerated during 1912-13. First trainer Bill Leach, a great asset in the formative seasons, died in April 1912, to be succeeded by Hull FC's long-serving full-back Harry Taylor. Nick Hendry, Sammy Stevens and Stan Fazackerley began to establish themselves and centre-half Patsy O'Connell was a class pivot. However, the season became an increasing disappointment. Re-election hung like a dark cloud over Anlaby Road. Chairman Alwyn Smith, vice-chairman Ken Wilson and secretary Jack Haller all quit in February 1913; in April, Ambrose Langley returned to Hillsborough, whilst Gordon Wright's long association with the club came to an end. It was not until the penultimate Saturday that safety was reached.

But for the war, the 1914-15 season might have been a good campaign for the Tigers. They reached the quarter-finals of the FA Cup for the first time and even led 2-0 at Bolton. Wanderers levelled before the interval and two harsh penalties took the Trotters through. The FA insisted on Cup ties being played on a Saturday that year, which put the Tigers well behind in League games. After the Cup defeat, they were 15th, 11 points behind second-placed Preston but with no less than six games in hand. The deficit ultimately proved too big. Attendances dwindled away. Around 2,000, paying a mere £44, watched City wind up with a sparkling win against Grimsby. It was the last Second Division match for four long seasons.

Regionalization followed. The fixtures for the Midland section of the League did not fill up the season so a subsidiary competition was arranged. In 1918-19, the Tigers topped their section, the first competition the club had won, although no trophy or medals awaited the winners. The City players survived the hostilities with the exception of Juniors' goalkeeper Guest and full-back Douglas Morgan, who was wounded on the last day of 1916 and died the following day.

Somehow things were never the same at Anlaby Road after the war. It was September 1925 before the name of Hull City figured at the head of the Second Division and that for one week only. There were times of promise. By December

Hull City players of the immediate post-war era, featured on a set of cards.

1919 the side had climbed to third, but a double defeat by Spurs over Christmas destroyed any pretention to honours. Much the same occurred two years later, but the loss of four points to Rotherham was disappointing in the extreme.

The board's policy of balancing the books by selling the club's best players — Jack Lee, Sammy Stevens, David Mercer, Sam Cheetham, Mike Gilhooley, Charlie Flood and others besides — did little to increase public confidence or to help a side whose collective standard reached the sum of its individual parts only in flashes. The undoubted potential was clear from such feats as the 3-0 defeat of Burnley in the FA Cup in 1921, and the 5-0 thrashing of Middlesbrough a year later. A stormy annual meeting in 1922, one of many in the inter-war period, was climaxed by a call for the entire board to resign.

The arrival of Bill McCracken promised better times, but initially the Irishman had little say in team selection and with the board wrangling amongst themselves, the spectre of relegation was not banished until Easter 1924. Despite a deficit of £4,714 on the season, there were no major departures, but a bad start to the 1924-5 season meant that the side struggled to reach mid-table. A barren run of over 650 minutes without scoring, and another of almost 500, highlighted a deficiency in scoring power, despite a forward line which included Paddy Mills, George Martin and exciting young prospect Sammy Hamilton, whose untimely death in the summer of 1925 was a severe loss to the club.

A moderate showing in 1925-6 spelled the end of the 'no-transfer' policy. Mills was sold to Notts County, which only exacerbated the Tigers' scoring problems. The close season of 1926 saw changes at all levels of the club. A new chairman,

Dr C.Durham Pullan, took over from Jim Spring, determined to turn the Tigers into a successful First Division outfit. The signings of Billy Taylor, Ronnie Starling, Harry Scott, Bill Cowan and George Guyan, the latter for a club record fee, showed a determination to realize that ambition.

In October the side led the table. By December they were top again, but a bleak Christmas was costly. The New Year brought a memorable three-match Cup encounter with Everton. Dixie Dean's presence did not deter the Tigers and the man of the tie was George Martin, who made such an impression on the Goodison club that, a year later, he became another of City's big-money sales. As League hopes hung in the balance, the club splashed out a record fee for St Mirren inside-forward Jimmy Howieson, only to finish down in sixth place. Twelve points lost at home were more than the seven which separated City from second-placed Portsmouth.

Off the field there were further indications of boardroom disharmony. And concern at the club's debts of £9,619 led the *Eastern Morning News* to ask sensationally in 1928: 'Will Hull City survive next season?' At last, McCracken found a goalscorer, Bradford's crack-shot centre-forward Ken McDonald. The side soon climbed to second place and continued to hold that coveted promotion place until December 1928. Then the Tigers faltered. McDonald's goals dried up and the side slumped into the bottom half of the table. Another turbulent annual meeting saw the chairman make a scathing attack on his fellow directors. "There is pin-pricking, back-biting and dirtiness behind the scenes instead of manly sportsmanship . . .when we sit in a room here I see one man winking at another man, and I am not going to have winking going on behind my back!"

The season which followed reached new heights in triumph and tragedy. The side reached the semi-finals of the FA Cup for the first and only time — and lost its Second Division status. In the League the Tigers held a comfortable mid-table place until March, with 28 points from 28 games, but the stresses of the Cup, injuries and a backlog of matches put an impossible strain on the players, especially the

The Tigers at the start of 1929-30. Back row (left to right): Rodgers, Goldsmith, Walsh, Howieson, McDonald, H.March, Wilson, Bradford, J.Murray. Third row: Fawcett, Williams, Dixon, Childs, Weaver, Starling, Flannigan, Sansom, J.Lodge (assistant trainer). Second row: W.McCracken (manager), Watson, D.Murray, Turner, Bell, Cartwright, Gowdy, Taylor, J.Beck (trainer). Front row: Alexander, Maddison, Bleakley, Gibson, Duncan.

less experienced ones. Only one win in 12 matches made the situation dire, but a victory in the home game against Bristol City would have brought safety. For an hour the Tigers dominated, then gave away a goal and with it their survival hopes.

Lean times followed as the Cup side broke up and the team attempted to adapt to the Northern Section. Occasional scoring sprees, such as the 10-0 rout of Halifax on Boxing Day 1930, were scant consolation for frequently disappointing performances. Bill McCracken made way for Haydn Green, who built a useful side around former England internationals Jack Hill and Russell Wainscoat. In the summer of 1932 the acquisition of Bill McNaughton added the necessary scoring power for the Tigers to make a return to the Second Division.

With only the champions promoted, it was a long, hard slog. City, in second place from October, hit the front in February with Chester and Wrexham in hot pursuit. Chester overtook them but three days later, over 20,000 packed the Anlaby Road ground to see the Tigers overturn their rivals 2-0 and regain top spot. McNaughton's two goals against York wrapped up the title. The centre-forward went on to accumulate 41 goals, the best individual contribution in the four divisions and an unequalled club record. A century of League goals, hand in hand with the best goal-average in the Football League and an unbeaten home record, including 18 wins and 69 goals scored, were impressive heights not even Raich Carter's great side could reach.

Three years later City were back in the Northern Section. A rapid turnover of players pointed to the increasing difficulty in putting out a team to hold its own in the Second Division. In the summer of 1935 manager Jack Hill attempted further major surgery on the side. His new-look line-up was immediately beset by injuries and illness. By mid-October they propped up the table. More signings, including former England captain Austin Campbell, who joined the ranks of the injured after only three outings, did no more than retard the disintegration of the team. Not one of the last 16 games produced a win. The side eventually finished 12 points adrift, with a disastrous 111 goals conceded. Attendances slumped and only 2,669 watched the draw with Leicester City in February. By April the club was £17,303 in the red. The loss on the season was a colossal £7,905.

Hull City in 1936-7. Back row (left to right): Denby, Annables, Maddison, Tabram, Treanor, J.Beck (trainer). Front row: Woodhead, Mayson, Hubbard, Best, Davies, Wilkinson.

It was an understatement to say that David Menzies, starting his second spell as manager, had limited resources to work with. However, victory over Gateshead in October 1936 meant the Tigers were the only unbeaten side in the Football League. The next day Menzies suffered a fatal heart attack. His successor, Ernie Blackburn, continued the work of rebuilding. With a small squad he made a bold bid for promotion in 1937-8. Cliff Hubbard, Jack Fryer, Jack MacNeill, Dai Davies and Jack Pears formed a free-scoring attack, crashing ten goals past Southport in January 1938. With two games to go, the Tigers led the Northern Section. The visit of second-placed Tranmere turned into a disaster. Eden scored off the crossbar. MacNeill hit the woodwork and the ball bounced out. Such was the narrow margin between success and failure. City had blown their chance.

No sooner was the season over than a financial crisis followed. The resignation of chairman Jim Barraclough and director Revell reduced the board to a quartet — Messrs Dickinson, Shepherd, Acaster and Wallace — guaranteeing an overdraft of some £8,500, a situation the bank could not accept. Only the tactfulness of Harry Dickinson kept the club alive. "The Sheriff's officer was almost in possession at one time," he later admitted. Seven new directors were eventually recruited, but the departures of bright prospects Eddie Goodall and Dave Parker were part of the cost of solvency.

The 1938-9 season was an anticlimax, for all the artistry of Arthur Cunliffe on the left wing and a record League score against Carlisle. Major rebuilding was again the order of the day. On paper Ernie Blackburn had assembled a championship side, but the outbreak of war left the prognosis untested.

For two seasons City kept the flag flying in regional competition. Attendances again fell and for the visit of Barnsley in December 1940 the receipts were a meagre £27. Difficulties of fielding a side strong enough to compete with the rest increased as the months went by. Nor had the ground been spared from the effects of the blitz. At the end of the 1940-41 season City decided to close down for the duration of the war. A brief revival ensued in 1944-5, on the Boulevard. With almost total reliance on guest players, heavy defeats were frequent. The end of the war was the signal for reconstruction.

Amongst those who assisted the Tigers through the 1938 crisis was local accountant Dick Smith. His suggestions for complete reorganization fell on deaf ears. After the war, though, he took up the idea again, approaching persons of influence and wealth to back his proposals. Eventually he found a staunch ally in master builder Harold Needler. Looking for a figure-head for the club, Mr Smith approached Mr R.W.G.Mackay, then MP for North-West Hull. The latter declined, but Mr Needler's suggestion, Kenneth Percival, Sheriff of Hull in 1945, consented to become president of the new Hull City. As the trio negotiated with the old board, they were joined by Harold Needler's brothers, John and Henry. By December 1945 representatives of old and new met under Mr Smith's chairmanship, and finalized a deal. The old company was to be wound up to make way for the new organization. At one stage there was a proposal to use the grandiose title of Kingston-upon-Hull AFC. The Boothferry Park ground was put in order. Major Buckley was appointed secretary-manager, and began to rebuild the team. Shares worth £50,000 went on sale. Shares and donations brought in over £60,000 as public response staggered the new board. Over 20,000 turned up for the return of League soccer, and attendances remained at that level for most of the season.

On the field it was a struggle. When the side failed to maintain a good start in the autumn of 1947, concern grew that the Major was overdoing the experimentation in his quest to improve the team. Matters came to a head in March 1948. As the board negotiated with Derby to sign Raich Carter, Buckley was left in the dark. Two days after the signing the Major resigned. It was left to Carter to reap the

Eddie Burbanks (second from right) puts the Tigers in front at Accrington in September 1948, following a free-kick from Ken Harrison (third from left). The victory gave City a record with nine League wins from the start of the season.

rewards of his predecessor's work. The silver-haired maestro was soon rewriting the League's record book with nine wins off the reel at the start of 1948-9. For the Christmas fixture with leaders Rotherham, 70,000 wanted tickets. Only 55,000 were printed. The Northern Section was a two-horse race between these clubs. The Tigers sat for much of the time in second place, with games in hand due to the additional preoccupation of a giantkilling Cup run, which Manchester United ended in the sixth round, before Boothferry Park's record crowd of 55,019. The team returned to the quest for promotion. The crunch came on the last Saturday of April. Stockport's brave resistence crumbled and City ran out 6-1 winners, whilst Rotherham could only draw at home to Carlisle. With 65 points, 27 wins and only 28 goals conceded, three club records had been achieved.

The upward progress continued. By November 1949 the Tigers were second in Division Two. Don Revie was signed from Leicester City to assist the drive for the First Division. However, defensive frailties began to show and injuries took their toll. Stockport humiliated the Tigers in the FA Cup and only one of the last 15 games yielded a win, ironically against champions Spurs. It was to be nearly 20 years before the Tigers stood again in such close proximity to the top flight. Not even the acquisition of such stars as Neil Franklin, Alf Ackerman and Syd Gerrie could propel the side out of mid-table regions.

On 5 September 1951, Carter penned his resignation. Without his inspiration the team floundered and only avoided relegation when he was persuaded to return as a player. Thereafter it became an increasingly uphill struggle to maintain Second Division status. Injuries frequently took their toll, Franklin being especially unfortunate. The quest for new blood in the transfer market brought endless frustration. Nor could those once great forwards, Wilf Mannion and Stan Mortensen, exert a decisive influence on the field.

The FA Cup success at Old Trafford in 1952 and the gallant display against Tottenham two years later were bright highlights amid the gathering gloom. A measure of relief was provided with the installation of floodlights at Boothferry Park. A series of friendly games thrilled the crowds as the Tigers served up attractive football in the more relaxed atmosphere. In 1955 they even upstaged the mighty Hungarians, Vasas. Bill Bradbury hit a hat-trick as the bottom side in the Second Division bewildered the Magyar Cup-holders. It was paradoxical in the extreme. It was Hull City through and through.

Relegation in 1956 increased the Tigers' problems. For a time during the 1957-8 season there were fears that the side would end up in the new Fourth Division. A good Cup run, which eventually ended with a heart-breaking 4-3 defeat at Hillsborough after Sheffield Wednesday had held a seemingly unassailable 4-1 advantage, played a major part in generating the confidence to pull clear of the dreaded basement. It enabled the Tigers to finish fifth, leaving manager Bob Brocklebank ruing early-season failings. The emergence of Bill Bradbury and Colin Smith as a potent strike-force was never more evident than in the 9-0 thrashing of Oldham. Both hit hat-tricks past helpless ex-Tiger, David Teece.

In 1958-9, City came good after a poor start and a deal of unrest amongst the players. Mr Brocklebank persevered. By November the side had climbed to second place. On their own patch they were unstoppable, stringing together 12 wins. The draw against Norwich in March, which ended the sequence, represented the only point dropped at home for the rest of the season. Bradbury's 30 goals was a post-war best for the club. Victory over Bury on a rain-soaked Boothferry Park clinched promotion. Mr Brocklebank's decision to see how the promotion side fared before strengthening the squad proved fatal. Not even the trio of forward signings — Jackie Sewell, Ralph Gubbins and Roy Shiner — could prevent an instant return to the Third Division.

A long struggle ensued to restore the Tigers' fortunes. At times it seemed the Fourth Division was a likelier prospect than the Second. Much of the excitement

Billy Bly dives at the feet of Len Duquemin during the Tigers' goalless draw before nearly 67,000 fans at White Hart Lane in 1950. Spurs won the Second Division title that season but three days later they lost 1-0 at Boothferry Park.

came from the FA Cup: a five-match marathon with Darlington in 1960-61 which only came about after the referee allowed the Quakers a goal from a shot which 'keeper Bernard Fisher quite obviously had tipped over the bar; a 5-4 win over non-League Crook Town in 1962-3; a 1-1 draw with Everton a year later and a plucky performance in the replay at Goodison.

Where it really mattered, in the League, the pattern was depressingly repetitive until the situation was transformed in January 1963 by chairman Harold Needler's gift to the club of £200,000 worth of shares in his Hoveringham Gravel concern. Their value rocketed to around £500,000. The signings of Ken Wagstaff, Ken Houghton and Ian Butler, blending superbly with Sproatley lad Chris Chilton and John McSeveney (and later Ray Henderson), gave the Tigers a forward line awesome in its power and dazzling in its skill. City entered 1965 in second place and climbed to the top. With a record run of 15 games without defeat they looked good for promotion, but blew their chances over a disastrous Easter weekend which yielded only one point.

In 1965-6 the side roared to the Third Division championship with a record 69 points. The goal tally of 109 was a club best. The five forwards amassed exactly 100 of them. Wagstaff, with 31 goals in League and Cup, edged past Bradbury's 1959 record. And for good measure City reached the quarter-finals of the FA Cup before Chelsea eliminated them at Boothferry Park on General Election day, although not before Wagstaff's brace of goals in the last ten minutes at Stamford Bridge had stunned the Pensioners' complacency.

As defences felt the impact of the Tigers' attack, September 1966 ended with Hull City topping the Second Division for the first time since December 1926. But for an appalling run of injuries, Cliff Britton's men might have bettered Raich Carter's attempt to go straight through to the top flight.

The season 1967-8 fully tested the Tigers' character. For much of the time they struggled to avoid relegation. A similar state of affairs two years later led to the announcement that the board intended to promote Mr Britton to general manager to allow a younger man to take charge of the side. Terry Neill, installed as player-manager in June 1970, soon rekindled enthusiasm on the terraces and his side held Manchester United in the Watney Cup, losing only on penalties. Neill marshalled

Ian Butler (11) scores the goal which gave the Tigers promotion from the Third Division in May 1966. Over 30,000 fans saw Hull beat Southend United 1-0.

Hull City playing staff at the start of the 1971-2 season. Back row (left to right): Knighton, Houghton, Banks, de Vries, Blampey, O'Riley. Middle row: Butler, Greenwood, Beardsley, McKechnie, Walters, Pettit, Simpkin, Tommy Docherty (coach). Front row: Pearson, Wagstaff, Terry Neill (manager), Lord, Wilkinson.

his forces well and victory over Swindon in October carried them to the top. In the course of their rise, the defence had been unbreached for over six hours. A 5-1 defeat at Cardiff was a rude awakening. By January, however, City were top once more.

Their success owed much to Chilton's goals, including a magnificent hat-trick against Sunderland. Like other promotion-chasing Tigers before them, Neill's men becamc involved in a lengthy FA Cup run, this one ending controversially with a home defeat by Stoke. Reinforced by new signings Ken Knighton and Bill Baxter, the side emerged 2-1 winners from a fierce encounter at rivals Sheffield United and looked favourites to go up. Four days later, Oxford took both points from Boothferry Park. City's challenge disintegrated, although a final placing of fifth was still the Tigers' best since 1922.

Not for the first time a Hull City side followed a good season with a battle against relegation. John Kaye proved a tower of strength in avoiding the drop, whilst up front Stuart Pearson emerged as a worthy successor to Chilton. A Houghton goal saw West Ham defeated in the FA Cup in February 1973, a performance which typified the heights the Tigers could reach. Supporters were frustrated by City's inability to infuse their League games with displays of the same calibre.

In May 1974, Pearson left for Manchester United, bringing the Tigers a club record fee of £200,000. It was hardly greeted with enthusiasm after a season in which they had scored only 46 goals in the League. The figure dropped to a new low of 40 in 1974-5, despite the record £75,000 splashed out on Millwall striker Alf Wood. By then Neill had departed for Tottenham. His successor, John Kaye, paid out a similar sum for Oxford's commanding Welsh international defender Dave Roberts. With a measure of stability at the back, the side progressed up the table in the final months of 1974, but never managed to find that vital edge to forge a genuine challenge for promotion.

The Tigers in August 1982. Back row (left to right): Jeff Radcliffe (physiotherapist), Chris Chilton (assistant manager), Skipper, Whitehurst, Davies, Findlay, Norman, Richards, Mutrie, Thompson, Colin Appleton (manager). Seated: D.Roberts, McNeil, Booth, Marwood, G.Roberts Flounders, McClaren, Swann.

Kaye strove hard to improve the Tigers' fortunes, but for three seasons the pattern repeated itself: a promising beginning quickly faded away and left little for dwindling crowds to enthuse over. Even a rare excursion to the fourth round of the League Cup in 1975 ended in a 2-1 debacle at Fourth Division Doncaster. Goalscoring became increasingly difficult. In the transfer market Kaye was repeatedly thwarted in his search for forward power. Nor could former Leeds star Billy Bremner transform the situation, for all his midfield industry.

Kaye remained optimistic, bringing in Bobby Collins as coach and reuniting the once-prolific scoring partnership of 'Smash and Grab' — Bruce Bannister and Alan Warboys. A bleak September in 1977, including five games without a win, sent the Tigers slithering towards the relegation zone. Kaye was axed in favour of Collins, but the latter's initial successes quickly gave way to even greater decline. Collins was sacked in February 1978, but the situation was too far gone for Ken Houghton to avert the end of City's longest uninterrupted run of 12 seasons in Division Two.

Even in the Third Division, it was not easy to put together a winning combination, despite the acquisition of the free-scoring Keith Edwards and the club's costliest signing, £150,000 midfielder Mick Tait. November 1979 ended with the Tigers humbled at home in the FA Cup by Carlisle and staring the Third Division relegation zone in the face. At Brentford the side fell apart completely. The following week Houghton was dismissed, along with coach Wilf McGuinness and chief scout Andy Davidson. Welsh team boss Mike Smith did manage to avert the drop for 12 months, thanks largely to Edwards' goals.

A staggering deficit of £491,888 on the season placed the club £838,721 on the wrong side. As City fell into the Fourth Division for the first time, the personal contributions of chairman Christopher Needler were keeping the club alive. The crash came in February 1982, ironically days after the side's highest League score in nine years. The mysterious Branwick Limited, the finance company through whom Mr Needler's funding was channelled, called in the Receiver. Mike Smith and coach Cyril Lea were sacked as an economy measure, leaving caretaker managers Bobby Brown and Chris Chilton to steer the side through the uncertain weeks of restructuring, and maintain the improvement which Smith had belatedly brought about.

As the confusion cleared, Don Robinson took over as chairman in May 1982, bringing in Colin Appleton as manager. Whilst Mr Robinson worked to put the club's finances in order, Appleton began to get the best out of his squad. An unspectacular draw at Chester clinched promotion. The attacking options of Brian Marwood, Les Mutrie, Andy Flounders and Billy Whitehurst contributed to the club's highest League goals tally since 1967.

The revival continued as the Tigers fought their way amongst the Third Division pace-setters. From the final match at Burnley, they needed a three-goal success to go up, but could manage only a 2-0 win and missed out on goal-difference. The post-match gloom was increased by Appleton's decision to quit. Nine days later even the inaugural Final of the Associate Members' Cup failed to provide consolation as Bournemouth won 2-1 at Boothferry Park, even though full-back Bobby McNeil shot the Tigers ahead with a rare goal.

It fell to Brian Horton to restore Hull City to the Second Division 12 months later. In December 1985, Horton came close to taking the side to the Final of another new competition, the Full Members' Cup. Not until the penultimate stage was the Tigers' progress halted. At Manchester City in the second leg of the semi-final, a late goal was a cruel blow to a side which had battled valiantly against their First Division opponents. There were occasions, too, when further success in the League looked possible, but the side failed to pick up the points when it mattered and had to settle for sixth place.

The search for players to strengthen the team was restricted in no small way by the need to plough huge sums of money into improving ground safety at Boothferry

Hull City at the start of 1988-9. Back row (left to right): K.De Mange, L.Thompson, W.Jacobs, G.Roberts, W.Askew, T.Hotte, A.Payton, R.Daniel. Middle row: T.Wilson (reserve-team manager), S.Terry, N.Brown, A.Saville, A.Norman, G.Kelly, L.Jenkinson, J.Moore, R.Jobson, D.Robinson (chairman), J.Radcliffe (physiotherapist). Front row: N.Buckley, C.Palmer, D.Booth (assistant manager), P.Skipper, E.Gray (manager), A.Dyer, K.Edwards.

Park, following the Bradford City disaster. Nevertheless, a remodelled Hull City side began the 1987-8 season in tremendous form. For ten games they were unbeaten, only Bradford City picking up more points. The Tigers entered 1988, only four points from the top of Division Two. Then, with everything to play for, a nightmare run of 13 games without a win sent the side reeling down the table. Horton began to rebuild again but was dismissed after an experimental line-up lost 4-1 at home to Swindon.

It was June before former Leeds United and Scotland favourite Eddie Gray became Hull City's 22nd manager. Gray speeded up the rebuilding process and first-hurdle exits in the Littlewoods Cup and Simod Cup, coupled with a series of indifferent performances in the League, meant that the side ended 1988 only four points clear of the Second Division relegation places.

December saw Billy Whitehurst return to Boothferry Park, from Sunderland, along with former England Under-21 international goalkeeper Iain Hesford, whilst Tony Norman went in the opposite direction in a club record £400,000 deal. Whitehurst was a success and the big striker's forceful presence did much to revitalize the City line-up. Six wins from eight games followed, with Whitehurst and fellow-striker Keith Edwards combining impressively to score 16 goals between them.

Hull City climbed to mid-table and fought through to an epic fifth-round FA Cup tie against Liverpool. Boothferry Park was buzzing once more and the Tigers had the audacity to hold an interval lead against the Anfield outfit. For a while there were dreams of a Cup sensation, but Liverpool took control and the eventual defeat for Hull burst the bubble.

Six successive reverses followed in the League. The final 18 fixtures yielded a meagre nine points and City slithered uncomfortably close to the Third Division, thankful that the bottom three were sufficient points adrift to prevent the situation becoming even more dire. Survival was ensured at Brighton on May Day, thanks to Edwards' 30th goal of the season, just one less than Ken Wagstaff's post-war best. In the League the striker's 26 goals amounted to exactly half his side's total, an invaluable contribution and a sign of hope for better times.

One man who would not be at Boothferry Park to explore that potential in the 1989-90 season was Eddie Gray. A few days after the Tigers completed their League programme, chairman Don Robinson announced that the club had dispensed with Gray's services. On the heady day when Hull City entertained Liverpool with realistic hopes of overcoming arguably the most powerful English club team in the history of the game, the prospect of Gray's demise was the furthest thing from the minds of Tigers' supporters. Now, of course, the side had courted relegation and the manager inevitably paid the price, along with his assistant, Colin Booth. Former Tigers manager Colin Appleton was invited to take charge once more.

Hull City Association Football Club Co., Ltd.

HULL CITY

VERSUS

ADMIT TO ALL MATCHES

KICK-OFF AT

Admit Bearer to Reserved Portion.

COMPLIMENTARY.

W. McCRACKEN, MANAGER.
A. R. DIXON, SECRETARY.

Retain this portion

HULL v. CITY

ADMIT TO ALL MATCHES

Admit Bearer to Reserved Portion.

This portion to be retained.

Complimentary season ticket signed by manager Billy McCracken.

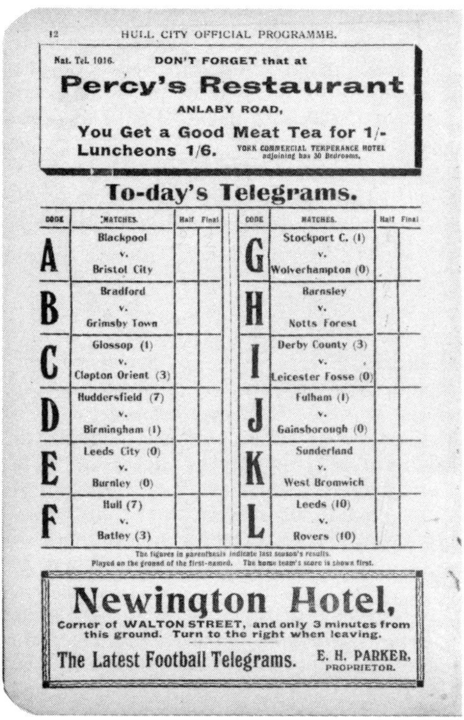

12 HULL CITY OFFICIAL PROGRAMME.

Nat. Tel. 1016. DON'T FORGET that at
Percy's Restaurant
ANLABY ROAD,
You Get a Good Meat Tea for 1/-
Luncheons 1/6. YORK COMMERCIAL TEMPERANCE HOTEL adjoining has 30 Bedrooms.

To-day's Telegrams.

CODE	MATCHES.	Half	Final	CODE	MATCHES.	Half	Final
A	Blackpool v. Bristol City			G	Stockport C. (1) v. Wolverhampton (0)		
B	Bradford v. Grimsby Town			H	Barnsley v. Notts Forest		
C	Glossop (1) v. Clapton Orient (3)			I	Derby County (3) v. Leicester Fosse (0)		
D	Huddersfield (7) v. Birmingham (1)			J	Fulham (1) v. Gainsborough (0)		
E	Leeds City (0) v. Burnley (0)			K	Sunderland v. West Bromwich		
F	Hull (7) v. Batley (3)			L	Leeds (10) v. Rovers (10)		

The figures in parenthesis indicate last season's results.
Played on the ground of the first-named. The home team's score is shown first.

Newington Hotel,
Corner of WALTON STREET, and only 3 minutes from this ground. Turn to the right when leaving.
The Latest Football Telegrams. E. H. PARKER, PROPRIETOR.

In the days before electric score-boards and public-address systems, football spectators had to rely on the half-time score-board where respective goal tallies were placed by hand. This guide printed in a 1911 Anlaby Road programme shows clubs referred to by their original names — Clapton Orient and Leicester Fosse — and two sides which lost their League status, Leeds City (expelled for irregularities) and Gainsborough Trinity.

HULL CITY'S GROUNDS

The Boulevard

FAMED wherever Rugby League is played on account of its timbered 'Threepenny Stand', once the cost of admission, this local sporting arena was built by the Hull Athletic Company in the early 1890s and was named the Athletic Grounds. In the winter months the proprietors allowed the town's rugby clubs to use the stadium. First tenants, on a three-year lease, were Hull Kingston Rovers, who beat Tadcaster 8-4 in their first match there in January 1892. They were succeeded in 1895 by Hull FC, who have remained there ever since. Initially the latter had a ten-year agreement with the owners, but in 1899 purchased the ground for £6,500, renaming it the Boulevard, after the nearby street.

Hull FC regularly allowed local junior soccer cup finals to be played on the ground. In 1897 they even staged an exhibition match between Grimsby Town and Small Heath, which attracted a crowd of around 7,000. It was the Boulevard club who first gave home to Hull City, whose right to use the ground when not wanted for rugby cost £100 a year. The agreement was drawn up for three years. However, the Manchester City fiasco in March 1905 brought home to the soccer club the need for a secure base if they were to realize their ambitions of League status. The Rugby League promptly banned such ground-sharing agreements, but the City directors stuck by their contractual rights and fielded a third team on the Boulevard until the agreement had run its course, occasionally transferring first-team games there when the weather placed a question mark over the fitness of their own ground.

A full survey of the development of the stadium is beyond the scope of this outline. The Threepenny Stand remains, despite ambitious proposals for redevelopment and despite the consequences of the Bradford City fire. The West Stand, which in the early days cost sixpence to enter, suffered extensive damage during World War Two. It was then that Hull FC were once again able to offer a helping hand to the Tigers, allowing them to play on the ground in 1944-5. The following season the Rugby League resumed normal operations and the Hull club was unable to offer lodgings to its homeless neighbour.

Dairycoates

DAIRYCOATES today is a busy industrial area. Ninety years ago it was, for the most part, open fields and a sportsman's paradise on a Saturday. Just beyond the Hessle Road, tram terminus lines crossed the road. A short way beyond the level crossing was Albert United's cricket field. Field it was, with negligible facilities for players or spectators. The nearby Locomotive Inn offered dressing-room accommodation for the participants. It was here that the first Hull City moved after losing their Bull Lane home, spending the 1902-03 season on the cricketers' enclosure. Although the soccer club's activities came to a halt in the summer of 1903, it seems they retained some say in the future use of the ground. When, in 1904, Hull City were unable to entertain Stockton on the Boulevard in the FA Cup, they suggested transferring the tie to Dairycoates. Stockton were agreeable, but the FA declined to allow the switch. Later in the season, the Tigers did entertain Scarborough on the ground. And when negotiating with Hull Cricket Club for the use of the Circle in 1905, the cricket club's existing tenants, the Hull & East Riding RUFC, were induced to exchange the Circle venue for the Dairycoates ground.

The Cricket Circle viewed from the air immediately after World War Two. Soccer matches played on the Circle, before the Tigers moved to Anlaby Road, were staged in front of the pavilion which is at the top of the picture, in front of the trees. The Anlaby Road ground — minus stands — can be seen in the foreground.

Anlaby Road Cricket Circle

HOME of the Hull Cricket Club and used by the Yorkshire County side, the enclosure was but a temporary home for the Tigers — 17 first-team games took place on a pitch laid out in front of the pavilion. The turf was refreshingly smoother and considerably faster than the Boulevard. When the Tigers were elected to the Second Division, the capacity of the ground was increased by adding embankments at either side of the pavilion and improving the accommodation at the ends of the pitch. Crowds of up to 10,000 are recorded in this makeshift setting.

Anlaby Road

HULL City's own ground, on what had previously been the North-Eastern Railway Clerks' cricket pitch, adjacent to the Circle, began to take shape during the 1905-06 season. Drainage and laying of the playing surface were accomplished under the direction of Hull CC groundsman Tom Ford, at a cost of some £300. Embankments for the terracing began to emerge and a grandstand was erected on the west side. Davy Gordon and Billy Robinson had both served their apprenticeships as joiners and assisted in its construction. By mid-March 1906 the initial phase was finished, although the stand offered shelter to only 2,000. The ground was officially opened on the morning of the visit of Blackpool, amid snow and rain. By August 1907 the stand had been extended to hold 8,000 and the remaining terracing was estimated to hold a similar number. The first season passes for a reserved seat cost precisely 21 shillings (£1.05). Subsequently, sections of the North and East Stands were covered over, although on more than one occasion gales removed parts of the roofing. A portion of the North Stand cover was whisked away whilst play was in progress against Leeds in January 1916. Mercifully, no one was in its path.

A disaster of far greater magnitude occurred on Easter Monday 1914, hours after the Tigers had lost at home to Bury to complete a pointless Easter. Fire destroyed the Main Stand. Eyewitnesses claimed the flames appeared simultaneously at both ends of the largely wooden structure. Whether it was arson or simply a cigarette-end tossed carelessly away at the end of the match, no one could say. Some even blamed the suffragettes. At the height of the inferno no one could approach within 40 yards. It was all the fire brigade could do to keep the flames away from the North Stand. Hull CC's new £100 score-board behind the stand was destroyed. The contents of the club's offices were lost. Even the safe burst open in the intense heat. By 3.30am, when the firemen departed, only a tangled mess of girders and corrugated iron was left. During the summer, a new, more substantial structure arose from the ashes, thanks largely to the generosity of director Bob Mungall. It contained 140 tons of iron and 76,000 bricks, and seated over 4,000 spectators.

In 1934 the ground was closed for a fortnight by the FA as punishment for the misbehaviour of a section of the crowd. In the course of Preston's visit in April, the referee, Mr Millward, had come under increasing verbal abuse for some of his decisions. At one stage orange-peel was hurled towards him and at the end of the match a shower of cushions from the grandstand rained down on the official. He reported the matter to the FA, who investigated, without, it must be said, allowing the club to be present at the hearing. The governing body ordered the stadium's closure for the first 14 days of the following season. There was a feeling that the club had been harshly treated and the League sympathetically allowed rearrangement of the fixtures scheduled for the period of the ban.

In 1941 the club decided to suspend operations for the rest of the war. At the height of the blitz, the ground had not been spared the effects of Hitler's bombs.

The Anlaby Road ground pictured in the 1930s. Part of the Cricket Circle can be seen in the bottom left-hand corner of the photograph.

Addressing the annual meeting that year, chairman Alderman Shepherd reckoned that it would cost £1,000 to make good the damage. Moreover, Hull CC, who had retained ownership of the site, served notice to quit on their tenants. Yet, when the football club sought to remove the turnstiles and dismantle the grandstand, the cricketers promptly sought an injunction to prevent them. Eventually the wrangle was resolved. The stands were sold to the cricket club and Hull City's tenancy was officially terminated in 1943.

Play was still possible on the ground and a series of Services matches filled the void left by the dormant professional club. Sometimes sizeable crowds, relatively speaking, turned up for this ersatz football. Three thousand saw the Northern Command beat a Polish Army side 6-1 in November 1942, with Brentford's Tom Cheetham hitting a hat-trick. A month or so earlier, an Army XI had gained a hard-fought 3-2 success over a Civil Defence side. The defenders included a host of ex-Tigers: George Maddison, Cliff Woodhead, Bill Gowdy, Harry Havelock, Alf Jordan, Arthur Bullock, Dick Spivey and George Jacketts. The last-named was then around 56 years old, but had still been playing competitively in local soccer in his 40s.

In 1945, Hull CC started their own soccer side, the Hull Amateurs, playing on the Tigers' former home. For two seasons the team struggled at the foot of the Yorkshire League before folding. At one stage there was a proposal for a speedway track on the ground but the Tigers once more took up residence, using the pitch for training and junior matches.

The Northern Intermediate League fixture against Huddersfield on 20 April 1965 was the last match on the ground. Young George Knutsen's name stands in the record book as the final goalscorer there. Two days later the bulldozers moved in as British Rail put a section of track through the ground to link the west-bound line, to Hessle and beyond, with the East Coast line to Scarborough. It helped to abolish three more of the city's level crossings, a modified version of the scheme which had first been floated 40 years earlier and even then had threatened the Tigers' home.

Boothferry Park

AS long ago as 1925, Hull Corporation had proposed a scheme to abolish all the city's railway level crossings, including the one adjacent to the Anlaby Road complex. The idea involved rerouting the railway over part of the Tigers' enclosure. There were rumours of a move to the 'White City' but, as the colossal cost of the Corporation's plan tempered public enthusiasm, the soccer ground appeared to be safe.

Chairman Dr Pullan, however, was convinced that the club should own its own ground. At the annual meeting of 1929 he declared it was imperative, as the first step to placing the club on a sound financial footing. Whilst the momentous events unfolded on the field during 1929-30, the board negotiated for a site at the junction of Boothferry Road and North Road. It was part of the estate used as a golf course by the Hull Golf Club prior to the latter's removal to Kirkella in 1924. The deal was financed thanks to a loan of £3,000 from the Football Association, at an interest rate of three per cent. Despite relegation, the club were determined to go ahead with the scheme. Architects drew up the plans but an increasingly adverse financial situation meant that it was 1932 before the embankments for the terracing began to take shape. Over the next 12 months the playing area was laid out and part of the terracing put in.

Thereafter, nothing further of note transpired until 1939. That January plans

Boothferry Park in the late 1970s, looking towards the South Stand during the course of a Northern Intermediate League game.

were announced for the development of a multi-purpose sports complex on the site, including a football pitch, at the phenomenal cost, at the time, of £120,000. It seems the primary motivation was the desire for an ice-rink for the city. The Tigers' supporters at once feared the club was about to give up its 'promised land' and the chairman confirmed the possibility. However, the offer received for the site was only around two-thirds of its value. The City directors then resolved to complete their own scheme. During the summer the FA loaned the club an additional £6,600, and Hull City looked forward to moving in the close season of 1940.

A few months later those aspirations were in tatters. The Home Guard was allowed to use the place during the war. At one stage, tanks were repaired there, which explained in part why the pitch waterlogged so easily during 1946-7. When the club decided to resume playing in 1944, the ground was in no fit state. Hence the return to the Boulevard. And when the war ended, problems in obtaining building licences and materials meant that it was impossible to have the stadium ready for the 1945-6 season.

The Boothferry Road ground was finally opened in August 1946, but not before the club had been taken over. The new board planned a super-stadium to hold 80,000, with the grander title of Boothferry Park. Even then it was a race against time to have the ground ready for the visit of Lincoln City. Initially, permission was granted for one grandstand — the West Stand — provided the structure did not cost more than £17,000, and for covering the central third of the North Stand. The old golf club pavilion, on what became the car-park, was carefully dismantled to make use of the timber. The turnstiles were brought from the old ground. No new ones were available. A week before the opening, the club appealed for volunteers to help remove the weeds from the pitch. The Lord Mayor performed the opening ceremony in pouring rain and over 20,000 spectators braved the downpour to watch.

By January 1948 the attendance record had been raised to 40,179 for the FA Cup visit of Middlesbrough. Bulldozers increased the height of the terracing embankments to extend the capacity. Little more than 12 months later, 55,019 witnessed the visit of Manchester United, some of them accommodated in a small temporary stand in the north-west corner of the ground.

The Cup game against Everton in January 1951 marked the start of a railway shuttle service from the main line Paragon Station to Boothferry Park halt. The first of six trains brought 595 fans, who entered the ground through the turnstiles on the platform. At the same time work was being carried out to extend the cover of the North Stand across the full width of the pitch. The covering of the East Stand followed. It was intended as a temporary structure, to make way for a two-tier super-stand incorporating a gymnasium, but remains to this day.

The completion of the East Stand gave the Tigers a suitable set-up for installing floodlights. Although artificial illumination was not approved for competitive games, the progressive clubs went ahead with their lighting systems. The licence for Boothferry Park's lights came through in November 1952. Two gantries, one along the East Stand, the other mounted opposite, housed 96 lamps. At the time the system was reckoned to be among the best in the country. Within a decade its inadequacy was all too apparent.

Part of Harold Needler's gift to the club in 1963 was spent on replacing the lights with a new six-pylon system, unique amongst League clubs. Four of the six towers were switched on for the visit of Barnsley in October 1964. It was hard to tell whether the Oakwell outfit were more dazzled by the lights or City's soccer as Chris Chilton and Ray Henderson hammered in seven goals. The old system later did useful service at Scarborough. A further sum was channelled into the building of a gymnasium behind the South Stand. It was opened in January 1964 by Football League secretary Alan Hardaker, who had assisted Hull City Reserves as an amateur

The old North Stand comes down in February 1982, to make way for a supermarket. As the stand came down, so the club crashed into Receivership.

in the 1930s. The facility, together with the adjoining outdoor training area, proved a timely development in view of the loss of the old ground.

The high bank of open terracing at the south end of the ground, popularly known as Bunkers Hill, gave way to the South Stand during the close season of 1965. The club's efforts to bring the ground up to scratch were rewarded with the staging of representative games between the Football League and the League of Ireland and the Under-23s of England and Austria. Whilst 1966 marked a high point for the club on the field, the state of the nation's economy effectively prevented realization of further stages of the club's proposed redevelopment of the whole stadium.

In June 1979 the board announced plans to build a £1.5 million supermarket-cum-leisure centre on the car-park. The cost of tunnelling beneath the railway line to link the ground directly with alternative parking facilities off nearby Kempton Road forced a radical rethink: demolition of the North Stand to resite the new complex and retain the major part of the existing car-park. The additional income was intended as a financial lifeline for the club but, as the North Stand was demolished early in 1982, so too the football club crashed into Receivership. The supermarket and new club offices went ahead, but the leisure aspects of the scheme were shelved.

The Safety of Sports Ground Act, rigorously implemented in the aftermath of the Valley Parade fire in May 1985, necessitated major work on the ground. For a time, the East Stand was closed. The terracing at the rear of the stand was deemed unsafe and it subsequently reopened with a greatly reduced capacity. In three years, close on £600,000 was spent on bringing the Boothferry Park stadium up to standard.

TIGERS MANAGERS

Ambrose Langley
1905-1913

IT was a bold step when the Tigers appointed Ambrose Langley as team manager in April 1905. Not all League clubs had a manager, let alone a new outfit like Hull City which did not have that degree of status.

Langley's senior career as a player had begun on the other bank of the Humber, when he joined Grimsby Town during the latter's first season in the Football Alliance in 1889-90. In 1891 he moved to Middlesbrough Ironopolis for two seasons. The Teessiders won the Northern League in both of them but, by the time they made their bow in the Football League, Langley had left for First Division Sheffield Wednesday. He stayed with the Owls for 12 years, making nearly 300 League appearances and helping Wednesday to win the FA Cup in 1896. Further honours followed — Second Division champions in 1900 and First Division winners in 1903 and 1904. Ambrose's participation in the last success was restricted to only eight appearances. His career had been disrupted by a serious rib injury sustained at Roker Park.

At 35 his playing days were clearly nearing an end, but the Hull City directors felt he might be a useful player in emergencies and acquired his playing registration too. Langley promptly began the Tigers' League career as first-choice right-back. His playing involvement was effectively over by Christmas and thereafter the Lincolnshire man concentrated on his managerial duties.

It was his ability to discover new talent which marked Ambrose's reign at Anlaby Road. He had a seemingly endless source of supply in the North-East: the Browells, Joe and Jackie Smith, Jack McQuillan, Arthur Temple and many more. Such was Langley's whole-hearted involvement in the Tigers' cause that he and one of his directors, Fred Stringer, rowed across the Tyne to reach Walbottle and secure the signature of Tommy Browell.

Ambrose moulded the Tigers into a quality side. In 1910 he took them closer to the First Division than any of his successors have managed and but for the financial state of affairs which forced the sale of the club's best players, would surely have fulfilled that ambition.

In April 1913 came the shock news of Langley's resignation. He returned to Hillsborough as assistant secretary. After the war he resumed his managerial career with a brief spell in charge of Huddersfield Town prior to Herbert Chapman's appointment at Leeds Road.

Harry Chapman
1913-1914

HARRY Chapman was recruited by Ambrose Langley as a player from the latter's old club, Sheffield Wednesday. He had been 11 seasons with the Owls, a star performer at inside-forward in their 1907 Cup-winning side, as well as being a regular in the championship sides of 1903 and 1904. He was top scorer in the second League success and netted over 100 goals during his Sheffield days.

Chapman headed Wednesday's marksmen again in 1911, even though he left for Anlaby Road in mid-April. Despite being 32, Chapman still had much to offer as a player. Above all, his astute tactical brain was seen by Ambrose Langley as the key factor in leading the Tigers to promotion. The team benefited for little more than a season from Chapman's attacking skills. In September 1912 he broke a kneecap in a Midland League match against Gainsborough and that spelt the end of his playing days.

The following February, secretary Jack Haller tendered his resignation. Three weeks later Chapman was appointed his successor. Scarcely had he settled into his new duties before Ambrose Langley, too, had quit his post. Chapman became secretary and manager, putting together a side which topped the Second Division in January 1914. However, by then Harry was out of action, fighting an even more serious battle against tuberculosis. Jack Haller was pressed into service once more to help with the administrative side. By September 1914, Chapman's worsening health compelled him to resign. He eventually succumbed to the disease in September 1916.

Fred Stringer
1914-1916

WHEN Harry Chapman's health prevented him from carrying out his duties, much of the responsibility fell on the shoulders of one of the club's directors, Frederick George Stringer. Chapman's eventual resignation came shortly after the outbreak of World War One, hardly an appropriate time to be looking for a new manager. Consequently, Mr Stringer resigned his seat on the board and was officially installed as secretary-manager in October 1914. It was a measure intended to keep the wheels turning smoothly until better times allowed a new appointment.

Attendances slumped and Stringer faced a dwindling playing staff as players enlisted in the forces. Yet the club enjoyed a good run in the FA Cup and had a remote chance of promotion. The City manager, who had business commitments locally, steered the club through the first season of regionalized wartime competition and then stood down in July 1916. He continued to be involved in the running of the club until the end of the war.

In his younger days, Stringer had been a keen amateur exponent of the game and had played for the East Riding representative side. It was his enthusiasm for the amateur game which led him to devote much of his time after the war to the administration of the East Riding County FA, eventually becoming its president. He died suddenly in January 1940, at the age of 64.

David Menzies
1916-1921 and 1936

IN June 1914, David Lister Menzies took over as trainer at Anlaby Road, in succession to former Hull FC full-back Harry Taylor. He had previously been trainer to Bradford City. Little more than a month after his arrival, Europe was at war. The situation was further complicated by Harry Chapman's illness, which gave Menzies a greater share of responsibility for the playing side of the club. The Scot became the obvious choice to take over from Fred Stringer.

After the war, Menzies brought a number of quality players into the side, such as Matt Bell, Jackie Crawford, Danny McKinney, Charlie Flood and Paddy Mills. He also assembled the famed half-back line of Collier, Gilhooley and Bleakley.

The great Cup exploit of defeating 'invincible' Burnley marked the high point of Menzies' spell in charge rather than progress in the more important realm of League football.

In July 1921 an offer to take over as manager at Bradford City induced the Scot to return to Valley Parade, where he remained for five years, during which time the West Riding outfit fell from First to Third Division. Doncaster, themselves in the Northern Section, gave Menzies his next opportunity in management. By 1935, Rovers at last succeeded in winning promotion to the Second Division. A more important factor, though, was the £20,000 which their manager had brought into the club through selling players he had discovered and trained.

Such economics did not pass unnoticed at Anlaby Road. When Jack Hill resigned in January 1936, it was to their former manager that the City board turned. The following month David Menzies began his second spell in charge of the Tigers. At the close of one of the worst seasons in the club's history he began to rebuild the side, which was amongst the early pace-setters in the Northern Section. The day after his team beat Gateshead to hold the only unbeaten record in the Football League, tragedy struck. The City manager had stayed away from the game due to a severe chill and on the Sunday afternoon of 11th October 1936 he suffered a fatal heart attack.

As a player he had assisted Raith Rovers, where his father was chairman. Business commitments brought David Menzies to Yorkshire where, along with inter-war Tigers' trainer Joe Beck, he was involved in the formation of the Bradford City club. Menzies continued to turn out for their Reserves before turning to coaching the Valley Paraders, whom he helped to their 1911 FA Cup triumph over Newcastle United.

Harry Lewis
1921-1923

THERE were over 80 applicants to take over from David Menzies in July 1921. The board's choice was Harry Lewis, a man of vast experience at all levels of the game. As a player he had assisted Rotherham Town. As a Football League referee he had once sent off the legendary Billy Meredith in an FA Cup match. As an administrator he had been involved with several leagues and associations in the Sheffield and Rotherham area. In 1911 Mr Lewis was appointed secretary-manager at Stockport. Three years later he returned to Yorkshire to take charge at Barnsley, remaining there for four years. Then pressure of outside business commitments influenced him to quit management, although he retained an involvement with the game, advising Rotherham County during their early League seasons.

The chance of the Anlaby Road managership meant a return to the game on a full-time basis. A genial and unassuming man, Henry Percy Lewis found the Tigers at the foot of the Second Division after half a dozen games. To his credit, the City boss made changes and the side went on to enjoy a successful season, finishing only four points short of a promotion place. However, the sale of such stars as Mike Gilhooley, Charlie Flood and Bobby Hughes made the manager's task of sustaining the upward momentum increasingly difficult. Nor did it help when the board instituted a selection committee to pick the team for him. For the first half of 1922-3, the Tigers languished in the lower half of the Second Division and in January 1923, two days before the side took on West Ham in the first round of the FA Cup, Harry Lewis handed in his resignation.

Bill McCracken
1923-1931

AFTER the departure of Harry Lewis, the board decided to split the duties of secretary and manager. The secretarial duties were thereafter carried out by Archibald Dixon, but as manager the Tigers scooped one of the greats of the game, Bill McCracken.

Born in Belfast on 29 January 1883, he had joined the local Distillery club in 1901, gaining an Irish Cup medal in 1903. By then he had won international honours. In May 1904, Newcastle United, building one of the best teams of the decade, paid £50 for the full-back's services. After 19 years, McCracken had made nearly 400 League appearances for the Geordies, winning three League Championship medals and an FA Cup-winners' medal.

What secured McCracken's place amongst soccer's immortals was his mastery of offside tactics. He did not invent the offside trap, if anyone did that it was Herbert Morley and Jimmy Montgomery of Notts County at the turn of the century. What the Irishman did was to perfect the ploy to such an extent that it was widely copied. Stoppages grew more frequent until in 1925 the laws of the game were changed. McCracken, booed off many a field by frustrated fans, once quipped: "Fortunately, the people who made me must have had some sort of idea that I should eventually become a footballer who would come in for quite a lot of abuse, so they made my hide specially thick." He reckoned the numerous offsides were not the fault of full-backs, but of forwards who did not think what they were doing. When the law was revised, McCracken lamented the change as 'pandering to speed instead of craft'.

When the City directors first approached United, McCracken, despite his 40 years, felt he still had a couple of years of football left in him. Newcastle held on to his registration until the end of the season, so the player joined a select group who qualified for a third benefit. They then asked the Tigers for a totally unrealistic fee and the Irishman's playing career was over.

Arrangements for him to take over at Anlaby Road, on a five-year contract, were completed in February 1923. A fortnight later, Bill McCracken received a final call from his country. He arrived in Hull to find team selection still in the hands of the selection committee. Star winger Jackie Crawford was sold to Chelsea as McCracken came to terms with the financial adversity his predecessors had faced.

The following season the side slumped into the relegation zone. There were rumours of a rift between manager and board. However, by October, the manager had wrested control of team affairs from the directors and the storm was weathered. The sale of the best of the playing staff continued to hamper team-building but, as the decade progressed, there were signs of promise. Twice — in 1926-7 and again in 1928-9 — the team began the season as promotion contenders, only to fall away at the turn of the year.

McCracken's best crop of young players came together at the end of the decade: Ronnie Starling, Sam Weaver, Dally Duncan, Stan Alexander and others. They vindicated their manager's confidence by reaching the FA Cup semi-finals but the side lacked the depth of resources necessary to hold on to the more important asset of Second Division status. The nurturing of their talents was to prove unfruitful for the club as the side gradually broke up. McCracken's own future was also on the line and failure to win promotion at the first attempt cost the Irishman his job. His resignation at the end of the season followed a lengthy meeting with the club chairman.

Not until September 1932 did McCracken have a second chance in management, when Gateshead gave him charge of their team. Eight months later he was on the move again, taking over at Millwall. He managed Aldershot between 1937 and 1949 and scouted for Newcastle and Watford for many years. Bill McCracken died in January 1979, nine days before his 96th birthday.

Haydn Green
1931-1934

HAYDN Green holds a unique place amongst Hull City managers. He stands as the first man to lead the Tigers to promotion. The basis of his success in 1933 was the recruitment of experienced players who knew what was required to achieve success: Russell Wainscoat's brains at inside-forward, Jack Hill's defensive skills and organizational ability and Bill McNaughton's proven marksmanship.

"My managerial experience has been gained in a hard school. I feel sure that it can be turned to good purpose," he commented on his appointment in May 1931. That experience included a spell as assistant at Lincoln, followed by a period in charge of Southern League Ebbw Vale. As a player, he began his League career at Nottingham Forest and he opposed the Tigers in the days before World War One. Subsequently he served Manchester United, Aston Villa and Reading as an inside-forward.

Haydn Green's ability to put together a winning combination brought success to Anlaby Road in two seasons. However, the age of the promotion side set a problem. Rebuilding became a necessity before the side had established itself in the Second Division. Nevertheless, it came as a shock when Green penned his resignation in March 1934.

He did not return to League management until 1939, taking over at Swansea following a spell in charge at Guildford. Haydn Green stayed with the Welsh club until September 1947 and was briefly boss of Watford in the early 1950s. He died in February 1957.

Jack Hill
1934-1936

IN November 1931, Haydn Green caused a sensation by signing former England captain Jack Hill from Bradford City. The centre-half had opposed the Tigers in their 1930 Cup run, when he was in the colours of Newcastle United, whom he joined from Burnley in 1928 for a massive £8,100 fee, five years after the Turf Moor club had paid Plymouth an equally impressive £5,500.

Hill, who between 1925 and 1929 played 11 times for his country, had few peers as a centre-half during those years. His height, 6ft 2in, gave him an ideal qualification for the position and his long legs could make otherwise impossible tackles. The man from County Durham, who had briefly assisted Durham City before joining Plymouth, was never one to miss an opportunity to move forward in support of his attack.

In the summer of 1931, Hill, then 32, left Tyneside for Valley Parade for a more modest £600 but failed to settle in Bradford. The Tigers clinched the deal by allowing Stan Alexander to join the West Riding club. Hill's value to the City defence was readily apparent. In 1930-31 they conceded 55 goals. As Hill led his men into the Second Division two years later, the number had been trimmed to 45. In the four divisions, only Stoke conceded less. The extra pressures of Second Division soccer demanded all Hill's experience and expertise. The departure of Tommy Gardner to Aston Villa in February 1934 prompted Haydn Green to switch Hill to right-half, a role he could play equally well.

Within two months the City captain was facing the new challenge of managing the Tigers. There were many applications to succeed Green but the board, for once, were unanimous in their choice, feeling that Jack Hill knew best the strengths and weaknesses of the players and what was required to make the side successful. During the summer he began rebuilding the team, persuading the board to pay what at the time was the club's second-highest fee, for Port Vale's Billy Tabram, whom Hill saw as his own successor at centre-half. However, there were times when lack of blend and skill were all too apparent in the side as a whole. Further enforced departures due to the worsening financial situation did not make Hill's task easier.

In the summer of 1935 he again attempted a major reconstruction of the team, recruiting a hitherto unparalleled number of Scots, but the new-look line-up, constantly hampered by injuries and illness, flopped. By January 1936, with his team adrift at the foot of the table and his board at loggerheads again, Hill resigned. He left the game to go into business but in 1948 was brought back to supervise Hull City's scouting system until the mid-1950s. From then until his retirement he held a commercial post with Scarborough. He died in April 1972, aged 75.

Ernie Blackburn
1936-1946

FOLLOWING the death of David Menzies, it was not until December 1936 that Hull City appointed a successor. Ernest Blackburn had been manager of Wrexham since 1932 and was under contract to the Welsh club until May 1939.

The City board had interviewed their short-list in November but it was only after lengthy negotiations that Wrexham agreed to part with him. Prior to his appointment at the Racecourse, Blackburn had been in charge at Accrington. As a full-back he played in the First Division with Aston Villa in the seasons immediately after World War One. In the summer of 1922 he moved to Bradford City but injury during the 1923-4 season forced his retirement.

Blackburn brought to Anlaby Road a financial astuteness which was absolutely essential in view of the state of Hull City's finances. In the years leading up to the war he helped reduce the Tigers' debts by some £5,000. His ability to transform non-League recruits, such as Eddie Goodall and Dave Parker, into quality players effectively saved the club from extinction in 1938. On the other hand, he was well aware of the value of experience, bringing in the likes of Jack Pears, Charlie Robinson and Arthur Cunliffe.

During the period up to World War Two, the turnover of playing staff showed Ernie Blackburn's relentless pursuit of a successful blend. He almost achieved his aim in 1938 but the side failed to clinch promotion in the crucial game against Tranmere. And when the additions of the summer did not ensure elevation, the City manager was ruthless enough to break up the side, recruiting no less than 14 new players in the close season of 1939. That squad was reckoned by many as a promotion certainty but the war left its potential unfulfilled. The conflict brought added problems, not least the difficulties of getting together a team during 1944-5, when his own players were scattered far and wide.

When the club was reconstructed after the war, the new board decided not to retain Blackburn's services and his involvement ceased when the affairs of the old regime were wound up in the opening months of 1946. Tranmere appointed him manager that September and he remained at Prenton Park until 1955. He died at his Birkenhead home in July 1964.

Major Frank Buckley
1946-1948

THE choice of Franklin Charles Buckley as first manager of the resuscitated Hull City was guaranteed to arouse the interest of the sporting public, both locally and nationally. Buckley, capped once for England in 1914 as a vigorous, uncompromising centre-half, played for Aston Villa, Brighton, both Manchester clubs, Birmingham, Derby and Bradford City in the decade prior to World War One. He served in the 'Footballers Batallion' during that conflict, rising to the rank of a major, a title he retained with pride for the rest of his life.

After the war he managed Norwich for a brief spell and then left the game to become a commercial traveller. His managerial talent might have been permanently lost to football, had not Blackpool persuaded him to take charge there in 1923. Four seasons later the Major began his remarkable association with Wolves. At Molineux, his ability — unique in its day — for turning young unknowns into stars, was allowed to flourish for 17 years. By the time war again interrupted the course of events, Wolves had risen from a moderate Second Division outfit to be runners-up in the League and FA Cup. Buckley's dealings in the transfer market had brought the club well over £100,000, and possibly nearer £150,000.

Very much the 'major' in his strict disciplinarian's approach, Buckley left Molineux for Notts County in March 1944. The Tigers' approach offered an irresistible challenge to the Major, whose spirit belied his 62 years. "I have come here with one avowed intention," he proclaimed. "And that is to provide First Division football for Hull." He was well aware of the hard work ahead. To trainer George Lax he confided that he thought it would take three years to get out of the Northern Section, a remarkably accurate forecast. In 1946-7 his search for success resulted in the largest number of players turning out for the club in a peacetime League campaign. Over 170 Hull City players were registered with the League in the course of that season. Some of them were given one outing in the first team and then disappeared back into obscurity. Even after the transfer deadline, Buckley's persuasions induced the League to allow the influx of new faces to continue. Hand in hand with recruitment went the trying of players in different positions. Jack Brownsword, who eventually slipped through the Buckley net to make over 700 appearances at full-back for Scunthorpe, found himself on the wing and even at centre-forward.

That the Tigers began to show amongst the Northern Section leaders in the second post-war campaign did not diminish the Major's experimentation, even though the policy appeared to cost the side its chance of promotion. Public concern began to grow and so did the board's. A rift appeared behind the scenes and in October 1947, Buckley almost quit to move to Elland Road. The cracks were patched over temporarily but the final breach came with the signing of Raich Carter. Two days later the Major resigned.

He had made an invaluable contribution in the way of team building but hunger for success on the part of public and board meant that the promised 'free hand' in team affairs was increasingly impinged upon, with the inevitable consequences. Leeds soon made renewed overtures and Buckley signed a three-year contract in May 1948. He moved on to Walsall in April 1953, quitting the Saddlers in June 1956 to go into business at the age of 74. Frank Buckley died in December 1964, aged 81.

Raich Carter
1948-1951

DURING the negotiations with Raich Carter and Derby County in March 1948, one of the Tigers' plusses was the fact that they had an assistant managership to offer. Carter signed as player-assistant manager, little realizing that a month later he would be taking full control following Major Buckley's resignation. The contrast between the two was considerable. Not for the man from County Durham was the relentless experimentation of his predecessor: "I am convinced that once a man has assumed a settled position he should be allowed to make a speciality of it. I am convinced that a minimum of switching and changing will produce the best results," he said. So it proved. The record-breaking start to the 1948-9 season rested on only 12 players.

Carter the manager was the quiet man off the field and a calming influence in the dressing-room, whilst he could lead his men by example out on the pitch. "Our main aim is to play high-class football and let the result take care of itself" was a philosophy which reaped handsome rewards, even to the stage where Carter faced the age-old dilemma of involvement in both League and Cup. The approach led one journalist to tag Hull City the 'couldn't care less club', adding the subtle proviso that the attitude had a deal to do with the success which took the side through to the quarter-finals of the Cup. More important, the greater aim of promotion was not lost amid the dual involvement.

Raich Carter's success as player-manager prompted a number of similar appointments elsewhere. Interestingly, he helped Hull win the Northern Section with only two major additions to Major Buckley's squad — former Sunderland colleague Eddie Burbanks and the 'Great Dane', Viggo Jensen. Carter later confessed that at the start of the season he had not given a serious thought to promotion.

In a bid to take the club into the First Division, Carter brought quality players to Boothferry Park, such as Gerry Bowler, Don Revie and Neil Franklin, whilst bringing out unknowns like Bill Harris.

Raich Carter quit in September 1951, a shock decision to many. "Disagreement on matters of a general nature in the conduct of the club's affairs," he explained in a non-committal manner. The real reasons remained well concealed, despite the stormy scene their non-divulgence produced at the club's annual meeting. It was May 1953 before Leeds gave him a second chance in management. At Elland Road, Carter achieved what everyone in Hull had hoped for. Promotion to the First Division was clinched in 1956, ironically with a 4-1 win at Boothferry Park as the Tigers left the division by the opposite exit. There was general surprise when, in June 1958, Leeds decided not to renew their manager's contract. Subsequently, Carter had spells in charge at Mansfield and Middlesbrough before returning to Hull, at one time running the sports department of a local store. He is still a regular visitor to Boothferry Park.

Bob Jackson
1952-1955

THE man to take over from Raich Carter had to be a man of pedigree. Two unsuccessful moves for Jack Crayston, assistant to Tom Whittaker at Arsenal, indicated the calibre of the man the City board wanted. It was June 1952 before Bob Jackson was appointed to a near-Herculean task. Although in his 50s, Jackson had been in charge of only one League club prior to his move to Boothferry Park, but at Portsmouth he steered the side to the League championship in 1949 and again in 1950.

In a playing career spanning two decades, inside-forward Jackson, had scored some 400 goals, most of them for non-League clubs in Lancashire and Cheshire. He was on Bury's books for a spell but gained his only experience of League soccer at Tranmere, in the shadow of a certain William Ralph Dean.

Jackson was Bolton's chief scout for 11 years, until Worcester City persuaded him to become their secretary-manager in 1945. The following year it was back to scouting, this time with the Fratton Park club. In 1947 he took over from Jack Tinn as Pompey boss.

A pleasant, unassuming Lancastrian, whose bow tie set a new fashion amongst sections of the Boothferry Park regulars, he came to Hull with high hopes of First Division football. The reality, however, was vastly different. An early injury crisis brought its problems. Attempts to strengthen the squad via the transfer market met with little success. The recruiting of a new coach, Johnny Mahon, in the summer of 1953 failed to inject the anticipated new life into the players. The atmosphere became one of permanent struggle against adversity. The board even gave their manager the benefit of their advice by reviving the 'players committee' which had functioned in the months prior to Jackson's appointment.

By March 1955, with the Third Division again all too close, the directors gave Jackson 'leave of absence' and put team affairs in the hands of Bob Brocklebank. Bob Jackson, though, was under contract until June 1957. He eventually took legal action against the club for alleged breach of contract. The case was fixed for June 1956 but, five minutes before it was due to start, the City directors reached agreement with their former manager for a considerable, undisclosed sum of compensation. Hull City was Bob Jackson's last managerial appointment with a Football League club.

Bob Brocklebank
1955-1961

'GENTLEMAN Bob', as he was known in the Midlands, was on West Brom's staff when the Tigers invited him to take over at Boothferry Park in March 1955. He brought with him the experience of a pre-war playing career with Finchley, Aston Villa and Burnley and managerial sojourns at Chesterfield and Birmingham City.

Initially, Brocklebank declined a contract at Hull City. He faced a difficult situation. Confidence was at a low ebb and finances, too, suffered as the great post-war attendance boom evaporated. He released a number of senior players but plans to rebuild around Franklin and Mannion were scuppered in part when the latter was suspended. Relegation overtook the club the following season but the mid-term signings of Doug Clarke and Bill Bradbury pointed to a brighter future.

In the Third Division, the side showed its potential in flashes. The manager's problem was getting the results consistently and his frequent permutations did not go down too well with some of the players. Matters came to a head shortly after the start of the 1958-9 season. Bill Bradbury, Brian Cripsey and Brian Bulless all submitted transfer requests. The manager replied with a public dressing-down: "When the players don the Tigers' jerseys I expect each one to go out on the field and give everything they have got for the club for the full 90 minutes. Is this expecting too much? Mistakes will be forgiven, but lack of effort I will not countenance." The whole situation was a potential disaster but it proved a major turning point. The players could not have responded in a better way than by winning promotion.

Leeds made a bid for Brocklebank's services that Easter. The board responded by adding another five years to his contract, which still had 24 months to run. During the summer, Brocklebank added only Vic Metcalfe to his squad. It was all very well to give the promotion side its chance in the Second Division but a bad start caused irreparable damage and when new faces finally arrived, they were unable to prevent an immediate return to the Third Division.

The old problem of inconsistency further complicated the picture. It was even more in evidence in the lower division. In February 1961 the board threatened a complete clear-out of players if there was no improvement. "I'm not a magician," the unfortunate manager in the middle lamented. "We cannot just wave a wand." Between then and the end of the season, a widening gulf developed between manager and board, culminating in May with Brocklebank's resignation. Just ten days later, he signed a three-year contract to manage Bradford City, where he remained until 1964.

Cliff Britton
1961-1970

CLIFF Britton was in his early 50s when he took the Hull City managership in July

1961. As a player he had been an integral part of Everton's successful side of the 1930s. His precision passing and clear-thinking methods made him a member of one of England's finest half-back lines, along with Stan Cullis and Joe Mercer. Britton progressed into management with Burnley at the end of the war, steering them into the First Division before returning to Goodison in 1948. In 1951 the Toffees slipped into the Second Division but Britton stayed to mastermind their return to the top flight.

In 1956, he and Everton parted again. Britton was disillusioned at being unable to manage the club with what he considered was the necessary freedom to do the job satisfactorily. Preston, then a power in English football, took up his services but in 1961 that club plunged into the Second Division. Cliff Britton was once more penning his resignation.

He came to Boothferry Park with a reputation for being a strict disciplinarian. It was said that his ideal team would have comprised 11 teetotal bachelors. He was fully aware of the difficulties involved in putting the Tigers back on the footballing map. Time, patience and hard work were essential. "We're breeding a race of non-thinking players," he once claimed, "Players who go on making the same mistakes week after week, season after season." Progress was slow. Financial constraints within the club, plus the abolition of the maximum wage limit, hindered player recruitment and led Britton to develop what became a highly-successful youth policy, eventually bringing on the likes of Paddy Greenwood, Malcolm Lord, Don Beardsley and Stuart Pearson.

The board's faith in his methods was such that in January 1963 they extended his contract to a lengthy ten years. Four months later Harold Needler's munificence gave his manager money to spend on team strengthening. It was not easy for Britton, as clubs tried to off-load players at inflated prices. The City boss waited patiently. His thoroughness also included checking character and background as well as form and style. The acquisition of three forwards, Wagstaff, Houghton and Butler, gave the club its most free-scoring attack ever. The side, dubbed 'Britton's bank-busters', raced to the Third Division title in 1966 and, more important, was good enough to more than hold its own in the Second. But for a run of injuries worse than Britton could recall, the Tigers would have been strong challengers for the First Division the following term.

In 1969, Matt Busby's promotion to general manager at Old Trafford made Cliff Britton the League's longest-serving team boss and yet, that November, the Tigers' board decided to offer their manager a similar 'promotion' in the hope that the appointment of a younger man to look after team affairs would carry the club into the top flight. Britton accepted, acting in an advisory capacity to Terry Neill until the end of his contract, when he retired from management.

Terry Neill
1970-1974

THE position of centre-half had long been a source of concern to Cliff Britton. Terry Neill was the ideal man to remedy that deficiency. In February 1970, Arsenal asked a prohibitive £80,000 and Neill himself had been keen to remain a player. After three months of negotiations, the Tigers got their man for £45,000. The eloquent Neill, chairman of the PFA, was impressed, as others before him, with the set-up and potential at Boothferry Park. The promise of an E-type Jaguar car clinched the deal.

Neill joined Arsenal in 1959, as a 17-year-old from Irish club Bangor, and made 240 League appearances for the Gunners, switching with equal efficiency to wing-half. His signing captured the interest of the Hull public and stimulated the players to a promotion bid which failed only in the final games of the 1970-71 season. For Neill the player they became difficult days. Incensed at the treatment given to Chris Chilton in one match, he reacted strongly: "I have been told that you have to kick your way out of the Second Division. It begins to look as if that is true. We don't want to get involved in this way, but if we are not going to be looked after then we will have to look after ourselves." Sadly, the pleas of Neill the manager for his players went largely unheeded, but Neill the player became the subject of close scrutiny from referees. At one stage he was at the FA headquarters appealing against no less than seven bookings and a dismissal. Later signings of Ken Knighton, Bill Baxter and Jimmy McGill bore out Neill's belief that the Tigers needed to blend a touch of steel with their flair.

Neill subsequently took on the added responsibility of Northern Ireland's player-managership. He was capped 59 times, then a record, celebrating his final appearance by scoring the goal which beat England at Wembley in May 1972. The intervening season had fully tested Neill's managerial skills at Boothferry Park, as his club battled against relegation. Calmer waters followed, although mid-table security slowly began to have its effect at the turnstiles.

The signing of Steve Deere in May 1973 brought an end to Terry Neill's playing career. Twelve months later his managerial contract expired. He agreed to remain at Boothferry Park for another season but never put his signature to the deal. Shortly after the start of the new season, Spurs moved in for the Irishman's services as successor to Bill Nicholson and Neill returned to the capital.

In January 1976, he was back at Arsenal, remaining as manager at Highbury until December 1983. Three successive FA Cup Finals between 1978 and 1980, including a 3-2 win over Manchester United in 1979, formed the highlight of his reign at Highbury. Success in the League was elusive and Neill eventually paid the price.

John Kaye
1974-1977

IT was largely due to Terry Neill's persistence that John Kaye joined the Tigers, as a player in November 1971, as a bargain buy at £20,000. Then a few months away from his 32nd birthday, Kaye added much needed backbone to the City defence and was a major factor in avoiding relegation. 'Yorkie' Kaye's wholehearted endeavour and consistency were inspirational to those around him.

The irony was that back in the 1950s, Kaye had turned out for Hull City Juniors but the Goole lad, who began his career as an inside-forward, returned to complete his apprenticeship as a welder in the shipyard. Scunthorpe, who were prepared to let him finish that training, signed him. By May 1963 such career thoughts were long-forgotten as West Brom paid the Iron a sizeable £42,500 for his goalscoring talents. In October 1965, he was back at Boothferry Park, helping the Football League to thrash their League of Ireland counterparts.

A League Cup win climaxed a fine season. Two years later he savoured an FA Cup triumph. By then, though, Kaye had dropped back into the half-back line. Subsequently he fell back still further, although the same 100 per cent commitment characterized his play, no matter what position he filled.

A knee injury sustained at Hillsborough in December 1973 finally ended the veteran's playing days. A cartilage operation failed to repair the damage and, at the start of the following season, Kaye decided to call it a day. The club asked him to help out with coaching and a month later he was taken aback to be offered the managership. He suggested a month's trial and subsequently took the job on a permanent basis. His Yorkshire bluntness could hardly have been in greater contrast to his predecessor. Kaye's teams, too, tended to reflect their manager: solid and hard-working. The 1974-5 campaign saw two records rewritten by Kaye's men. Only ten goals were conceded at home in the League and only 40 goals scored overall. It put the situation firmly into perspective.

Additional attacking flair might have seen the side go places. As it was, the goalscoring problems had their obvious effect on a generation of supporters spoiled by the riches of Wagstaff, Chilton and Co. Nor were Kaye's efforts to recruit new forward power blessed with great success. His contract ended in the summer of 1977, with the side in mid-table in the Second Division. The board gave him an ultimatum. Two months to bring about a marked improvement. Despite an offer to manage West Brom, he opted to remain at Boothferry Park. An hour after the home defeat by Mansfield in October, a fifth game without a win, Kaye was dismissed. Some of the players rated John Kaye as the best manager they had served under. Scunthorpe soon appointed him coach, a position he held until February 1981, when his services were dispensed with as an economy measure.

Bobby Collins
1977-1978

APPOINTED City coach by John Kaye during the summer of 1977, Bobby Collins was elevated to caretaker manager on the Goole man's departure. His success in rallying the players for a morale-boosting victory over high-flying Spurs, only three days after the Mansfield debacle, augured well, and a record of five points out of six saw the little Scot confirmed in office with a two-year contract.

Collins' managerial experience began at Oldham, where he was appointed assistant manager in January 1973. In the summer of 1974 he succeeded Ian Greaves as manager of Huddersfield. The Leeds Road outfit went down to the Fourth Division the following May and in December 1975, Collins quit. He subsequently assisted Leeds as youth coach, returning to the club where his playing career had reached its peak.

As an inside-forward, the 'Little Marshall' helped in the transformation of Leeds into one of the country's top sides. He skippered them at Wembley in 1965, but failed to add an FA Cup-winner's medal to the two Scottish ones he had won with his first senior club, Celtic. Everton paid the Glaswegians £25,000 for his skills in 1958. Collins stayed there for four years before moving to Leeds, completing his playing career at Bury and Morton.

The 46-year-old Scot's early successes at Boothferry Park included a 4-1 win over Cardiff. It was a comfortable enough margin, in a game of numerous errors. Collins was unhappy and publicly criticized his players. It was mid-January before the side won again, picking up only three points from nine games. Not even the recruitment of one-time Leeds coach Sid Owen could halt the slump. Owen's high standards did not meet with overwhelming acceptance. After only four months and ten days in charge, Collins, along with Owen, was dismissed, making him the shortest-reigning manager in the club's history.

He later returned to League soccer as Barnsley's youth coach, taking over as manager at Oakwell in February 1984. He did a sound job and there was some surprise when he was relieved of his responsibilities in June 1985.

Ken Houghton
1978-1979

CLUB youth coach and former 1960s favourite Ken Houghton, whose playing career is discussed elsewhere, had the difficult, if not impossible, task of trying to retrieve the club's failing League position. Despite the respect of players and public, relegation was not to be avoided. As the seniors were slipping into the Third Division, Houghton's success with the Juniors brought the Northern Intermediate League championship to the club for the first time since those 1960s boom days. Amongst Ken's protégés were prospects such as Brian Marwood, Steve McClaren and Garreth Roberts.

Relegation inevitably weakened the manager's hand, with the departure of the cream of his squad. A major bonus was his success in signing a proven goalscorer in Keith Edwards. The side had potential, but manifested it only periodically and inability to bring out that best on a regular basis was ultimately to cost Houghton his position. The investment of a substantial sum in the signings of Trevor Phillips, Paul Moss and Mick Tait, the latter the club's most expensive buy, brought Houghton no nearer to a winning blend.

A poor run culminated in a 7-2 thrashing at Brentford in December 1979. The board, who ironically had given their manager a vote of confidence the previous week, moved to effect their third dismissal in little more than two years. Ken Houghton subsequently joined a local freight forwarding company and continued to turn out regularly for the ex-Tigers side.

Mike Smith
1980-1982

IT WAS either an inspired move, or a desperate gamble, to appoint Welsh team manager Mike Smith as Ken Houghton's successor. Other members of the Welsh set-up, Cyril Lea and Bobby Brown, also moved in at Boothferry Park in a deal reckoned to be worth up to £500,000 over five years if the trio brought success to the club.

Mike Smith, though, for all his achievements from limited resources in the international sphere, was untried in the day-to-day rigours of League club management. A profound technical understanding of the complexities of modern international football was some way removed from the need to revitalize a side struggling to effect the basics successfully.

And even though he won representative honours as an amateur player, Hendon-born Smith had preferred the security of the teaching profession to joining the ranks of paid players.

The new management team officially took over on 1 January 1980 and saw their side, hammered 5-1 at Plymouth, totter into the relegation zone. It was not long before wholesale changes to the playing staff began. The bargain-buy was Burnley's reserve goalkeeper Tony Norman for £30,000, but Smith's spending far outstripped the fees received for outgoing players at a time when the club's finances were in no position to withstand such an outlay.

Amid the comings and goings, consistency on the pitch proved an elusive quality and it was due largely to Keith Edwards' goal-poaching that the drop was avoided. The turnover of players continued during the summer but the result was that the side foundered ignominiously into the Fourth Division for the first time ever. The acquisition of non-League players Billy Whitehurst and Les Mutrie needed the one thing which was not on Mike Smith's side — time to develop their undoubted potential.

As the team embarked upon life in the League's basement, Mike Smith was convinced he had the makings of a useful side, given a good run of results to boost confidence. Initially his hopes appeared ill-founded but, as the year turned, there were signs that at last the manager's methods were beginning to pay off, with two fine performances against Chelsea in the FA Cup and a 5-2 romp against Hartlepool. Then came the inevitable financial crash and in March 1982, Smith was axed by the Receiver, along with Cyril Lea. Bobby Brown remained, on a halved salary, together with Chris Chilton, to prove the sound foundation of the team's improving form. Smith subsequently worked in sports promotions in Nottingham and then took over the Egyptian national side, returning in the autumn of 1988 to work with the Welsh youth side.

Colin Appleton
1982-1984 & 1989-

COLIN Appleton, a long-time friend of new chairman Don Robinson, was an excellent choice to restore the on-field fortunes of the Tigers. As a wing-half he spent over a decade with Leicester City, leading them to two FA Cup Finals and two League Cup Finals. After shorter spells at Charlton and Barrow, he returned to his home-town club, Scarborough, winning a string of non-League honours, first as a player and then as a manager. He was, however, keen to return to League football.

The City chairman's belief that Appleton was the man for Boothferry Park was amply vindicated. He combined the approach of strict discipline with shrewd psychological insight. "I have got to get to know the players personally before I can handle them," he once remarked. There was, too, a refreshing simplicity in his footballing philosophy, of defending as an effective unit and then allowing the players freedom to express themselves in attack. Even if the first half of the theory came to include defending with a sweeper, there was far too much attacking skill from the likes of Marwood, Mutrie, Whitehurst and Flounders to lay the Tigers open to the accusation of being a defensive-minded side.

It soon bore fruit, with the side contending for promotion. For Appleton there was recognition of his efforts in the form of a Divisional Manager of the Month award in January 1983. With negligible cash to spend, Appleton was compelled to look to free-transfer bargains, such as midfield dynamo Billy Askew, and short-term signings such as Billy Woof and former Liverpool legend Emlyn Hughes, to carry the side into the Third Division as runners-up.

The following term, Appleton's successful approach brought the Tigers to within striking distance of the Second Division, only to lose out in the last match. At the end of that encounter, the City manager announced his resignation. Only 24 hours later he took over at Swansea, whose unsuccessful approach the previous December had ruffled relations between the City manager and his chairman. Appleton's stay at Vetch Field lasted less than seven months before the Welsh club dismissed him. In May 1985, he took over as team boss at Exeter but failed to do for the south coast club what he had achieved at Boothferry Park and resigned in December 1987. The following season saw Appleton back in his native Yorkshire, managing Bridlington Town. He was recalled to Boothferry Park in May 1989, a week after his club had beaten the Tigers' Reserves in the East Riding Cup Final.

Brian Horton
1984-1988

BRIAN Horton had been released by Luton at the end of the 1983-4 season in order to find a managerial post after a lengthy, but not yet completed career, as a midfield general, unspectacular yet soundly effective. Fifteen years earlier Port Vale had signed him from his local club, Hednesford Town. In close on six seasons with the Valiants he helped drive them to the brink of promotion from the Third Division. In March 1976, Brighton, in the same division, paid £30,000 for Horton's services. His keen competitiveness led them into the Second Division the following season and almost straight through to the First. Tottenham deprived them of the honour on goal-average but Brighton bounced back the following term to finish runners-up, an experience which stood Horton in good stead at Boothferry Park. He also had the distinction of topping Brighton's goalscorers that season.

In August 1981, a £100,000 deal took the midfielder to Luton, where the same qualities led Town to the Second Division championship that very season. Such a desire for success made a strong impression on Don Robinson, persuading him that Horton was the man to take the Tigers out of the Third Division.

It was not easy to take over a side missing promotion so narrowly. Horton strove to play down the situation. "You can't look back for anything. It all starts from today," he proclaimed. The close-season departure of Brian Marwood left the armchair critics crying out for the signing of a striker. Horton wisely refused to be swayed and his faith in the existing front men was fully justified.

His appointment as player-manager enabled Horton to command his side where it mattered, out on the pitch. He later admitted that the additional responsibilities of management had prevented him from reaching his previous high standards as a player. It was Horton's desire to get his teammates to play a greater percentage of football through midfield, but with the powerful Billy Whitehurst up front, the long ball remained an easy and rewarding option. Nevertheless, the side soon established itself amongst the promotion contenders. Horton did well to keep the ship on course after a barren February and clinch a return to the Second Division. It brought him a personal hat-trick of promotion in his first full seasons at Brighton, Luton and Hull.

Richard Jobson, Frankie Bunn and Bobby Doyle were shrewd buys, each playing influential parts in the club's establishment in the Second Division. Doyle took over the role of midfield general as Horton, who reached the milestone of 600 League appearances in October 1985, began to concentrate on his managerial responsibilities. Doyle's subsequent retirement through injury created a void which his manager searched in vain to fill adequately. It was reflected in the inconsistencies of spells in the higher reaches of the table alternating with slumps down to its lower end.

The start which the team made to the 1987-8 season gave every hope that Horton had at last got the chemistry of the side right, but disappointment followed once more. As he brought in further new faces, the run of poor results cost him his position in April 1988. He became assistant to Mark Lawrenson at Oxford and Lawrenson's resignation, shortly after the start of the 1988-9 season, led to Horton's promotion.

Eddie Gray MBE
1988-1989

AS a player with Leeds United, Eddie Gray's dazzling array of skills made him one of the most incisive attackers of his day. A Glaswegian, he signed professional forms for the Elland Road club in January 1965 and went on to make over 400 League appearances for them. Twice he won League Championship medals; four times he had to settle for second place. Cup successes included the League Cup, FA Cup and European Fairs Cup.

Gray, awarded the MBE for services to football, represented his country at Schoolboy level, but made only a dozen appearances for the senior Scottish side. His contribution would have been much greater but for injury. It spoke volumes for the character of the man that he fought back from some horrific knocks. Towards the end of his career, Gray gained a new lease of life at left-back.

In July 1982, Leeds appointed him player-manager in succession to Allan Clarke. They had been impressed by Gray's work helping to coach the Juniors. He played on for another two seasons before retiring. He built a promising side but failed to put United back in the First Division and, in October 1985, he was sacked after 22 years at the club. Former Leeds colleague David Harvey, in charge at Whitby Town, persuaded Gray to resume his playing career, but in March 1986 further injury brought his playing days to an abrupt end. A brief spell coaching at Middlesbrough gave him a further opening in League football and in December 1986, Rochdale appointed him manager, although Gray was unable to lift the Spotland club out of the lower reaches of the Fourth Division.

Appointed Hull's manager in June 1988, his first signings, striker John Moore and midfielder Lee Warren, had both played under Gray at Rochdale, whilst he sold established first-teamers Peter Skipper and Alex Dyer. Youngsters Mike Smith and Gavin Kelly were introduced to League soccer — Mark Calvert and Paul Mudd made their debuts later — with Neil Buckley and Leigh Jenkinson also given opportunities. Alas, a successful permutation proved elusive, especially in midfield.

Further excursions into the transfer market eventually brought improvement. The big-money deal which took Tony Norman to Sunderland and brought Billy Whitehurst back to Boothferry Park, along with Iain Hesford, was in contrast to the dealings of Gray's immediate predecessors and yet, after a brief revival, he was again facing a decline and again bringing in new faces — Hearts' Malcolm Murray, Notts County's Ian McParland and Leeds' Peter Swan. The latter pair, at £155,000 and £200,000 respectively, were club record signings, but Hull finished the season clinging on to Second Division status and Gray was dismissed.

TIGERS STARS A-Z

ALF ACKERMAN

Alf Ackerman joined the Tigers from Clyde in July 1950, for a sizeable £11,500 fee, as Raich Carter sought to lead the side into the First Division. Two goals on his League debut were an early indication of the ability of the man from Pretoria, who quickly became a firm favourite of the Boothferry Park crowd. The South African's powerful shooting earned him the nickname 'Ack-Ack' Ackerman. When the Tigers demolished Queen's Park Rangers in November 1950, Ackerman's hat-trick was the first by a City player in the Second Division since 1934. There was disappointment on the terraces when he was transferred to Norwich in July 1951, for some £9,500. However, whilst the Canaries were on the brink of the Second Division, the Tigers struggled to stay in it and in October 1953, Ackerman was on his way back to Hull. His return helped to lift the club out of the relegation zone and he cracked in four spectacular goals against Oldham on the Saturday before Christmas. In March 1955, Derby County, in an unsuccessful bid to avoid the Third Division, swooped for Ackerman and teammate Ken Harrison. Alf's impressive form continued at the Baseball Ground and he scored four in a game against Accrington Stanley before a £2,250 move to Carlisle in November 1956 brought about a fruitful partnership with Ivor Broadis. In 1956-7, Ackerman's 35 goals was the best tally in the two Third Divisions. He completed his League career at Millwall, finishing only five goals short of a League double century. Ackerman died in Australia in July 1988.

	LEAGUE		*FA CUP*		*TOTAL*	
	App	*Gls*	*App*	*Gls*	*App*	*Gls*
1950-51	34	21	3	0	37	21
1953-54	29	17	7	2	36	19
1954-55	29	11	1	0	30	11
	92	49	11	2	103	51

In the summer of 1926 the Tigers signed a 20-year-old forward from Tyneside Leaguers Percy Main. Stan Alexander had represented England at Schoolboy level but spent most of his first season at Anlaby Road in the Midland League side, forming a useful right-wing combination with his brother Jack. Occasionally Stan switched to inside-left, a sign of the versatility which characterized his stay with the Tigers. In 1928-9 he finally established himself as a regular first-teamer, making the most of his fleetness of foot. It was in that momentous 1929-30 season that he made his greatest impact in the Tigers' attack. Initially settling in at centre-forward, he was moved to inside-right to accommodate the return of Paddy Mills. The hat-trick which Alexander netted at Plymouth was the spark which ignited the great Cup run and his absence from the semi-finals was a major blow to the side's Wembley aspirations. In the League he was the only City marksman to reach double figures, an illuminating statistic in the Tigers' relegation. He top-scored again in 1931 and was rewarded with a place in the FA party to tour Canada. In November 1931, Alexander was transferred to Bradford City in a deal which brought Jack Hill to Anlaby Road. October 1933 brought a further move, to Millwall, and a reunion with manager Bill McCracken. When the Lions were relegated in 1936, Spurs negotiated Alexander's services but their desire for First Division soccer meant that the Geordie's chances were limited. He joined Accrington in 1938 and, after the war, returned to Hull to help coach City's juniors during the 1950s.

STAN ALEXANDER

	LEAGUE		*FA CUP*		*TOTAL*	
	App	*Gls*	*App*	*Gls*	*App*	*Gls*
1926-27	2	0	0	0	2	0
1927-28	6	2	1	0	7	2
1928-29	16	1	2	0	18	1
1929-30	27	14	6	5	33	19
1930-31	41	24	1	0	42	24
1931-32	6	0	0	0	6	0
	98	41	10	5	108	46

A capable defender, Wally Annables was on the books of the two main clubs either side of the Humber for most of the 1930s. Measured purely in statistical terms, his contribution to League soccer bears little relation to his ability on the field. For most of his senior career Annables had to contend for a first-team place with quality full-backs. A Yorkshire lad, he was signed by Grimsby from Mexborough in April 1932, but he failed to establish himself and in 1936 moved to Anlaby Road, where the Tigers had just been relegatd with the worst defensive record in their history. Annables' skills were at once put to good use and, in contrast to his Blundell Park days, he was an ever-present in his first season in black and amber. In October 1937 matters took a turn for the worse. Annables was injured in a Northern Section Cup match and when fit again found young Dave Parker showing outstanding form alongside Cliff Woodhead. Third-choice full-back yet again, he had a brief trial at centre-forward in the Reserves and spent a season and a half loyally plugging away in the second string. In June 1939, Carlisle moved in for Annables, but hopes of League football were dashed when war was declared after he had made two appearances for the Cumbrians.

WALLY ANNABLES

	LEAGUE		*FA CUP*		*OTHERS*		*TOTAL*	
	App	*Gls*	*App*	*Gls*	*App*	*Gls*	*App*	*Gls*
1936-37	42	1	1	0	1	0	44	1
1937-38	17	0	0	0	2	0	19	0
1938-39	3	0	0	0	0	0	3	0
	62	1	1	0	3	0	66	1

FRANK BANKS

For the greater part of a decade Frank Banks was virtually a fixture in the Tigers' right-back berth. He was a local lad who matured into an outstanding defender and yet it could easily have been so different. Banks' family moved to Southend when he was at an early age. He eventually signed professional forms for Southend United in October 1962, but made only four League appearances for the Roots Hall club. In August 1966, Cliff Britton brought the young half-back to Boothferry Park. For a time Banks found himself on the right wing before being moved to centre-half, where he began to stake a claim for a first-team place, ousting Mick Milner shortly after the start of the 1967-8 season. Three months later he was making the transition to full-back. In 1970, Terry Neill's arrival at Boothferry Park presented Banks with a new challenge. The new manager preferred Roger de Vries and Don Beardsley at full-back. A model professional, Banks fought his way back and, towards the end of the season, showed a new aspect of his play, as a goalscorer, enjoying the modern tactical freedom to push forward down the flanks. On the eve of the 1974-5 season he was struck down with meningitis, but battled back in typical fashion. In March 1976 he returned to Southend, enjoying a couple more seasons of senior soccer before joining United's coaching staff.

	LEAGUE		*FA CUP*		*FL CUP*		*OTHERS*		*TOTAL*	
	App	*Gls*	*App*	*Gls*	*App*	*Gls*	*App*	*Gls*	*App*	*Gls*
1967-68	38/1	0	3	0	1	0	0	0	42/1	0
1968-69	22/1	0	0	0	1	0	0	0	23/1	0
1969-70	34	0	1	0	2	0	0	0	37	0
1970-71	22/2	2	4	0	0	0	0	0	26/2	2
1971-72	38	1	3	0	1	0	0	0	42	1
1972-73	42	1	4	0	2	0	4	0	52	1
1973-74	37	1	2	0	4	1	3	0	46	2
1974-75	33	1	3	0	0	0	0	0	36	1
1975-76	18	0	2	0	3	0	3	0	26	0
	284/4	6	22	0	14	1	10	0	330/4	7

Don Beardsley was an extremely competent full-back whose skills with both feet increased his value to the Tigers defence. He was, though, unfortunate to be at Boothferry Park when the club had strength in depth at full-back. Andy Davidson, Dennis Butler, Frank Banks and Roger de Vries were among his contemporaries and the keen competition is reflected in Beardsley's total of appearances during his 11 years with the Tigers. He joined the club from Eastfield High School, having figured in the Hull Boys side which reached the last eight of the English Schools Shield in 1961-2. In the course of that run he appeared at inside-right and left-half. The following August, Cliff Britton signed him, although it was not until September 1966, at Portsmouth, that he finally made the League side. By 1968-9 he was first-choice left-back and a contender for the Scottish Under-23 squad. In March 1972, with Banks and de Vries first-choice full-backs, Beardsley was loaned to Doncaster. He returned to oust de Vries for much of the following season but in August 1973 was transferred to Grimsby, where he completed his League career. In the serious business of competitive football Beardsley's name never appeared on the score-sheet. His only goal for the club came in one of its most distant games, during the 1973 tour of Guyana.

	LEAGUE		*FA CUP*		*FL CUP*		*OTHERS*		*TOTAL*	
	App	*Gls*	*App*	*Gls*	*App*	*Gls*	*App*	*Gls*	*App*	*Gls*
1966-67	7/1	0	0	0	0	0	0	0	7/1	0
1967-68	3/1	0	0	0	0	0	0	0	3/1	0
1968-69	35	0	1	0	2	0	0	0	38	0
1969-70	26	0	1	0	0	0	0	0	27	0
1970-71	26	0	0	0	1	0	2	0	29	0
1971-72	9	0	0	0	0	0	0	0	9	0
1972-73	22	0	4	0	0	0	3	0	29	0
	128/2	0	6	0	3	0	5	0	142/2	0

DON BEARDSLEY

The man who made more appearances for Hull City than any other outfield player prior to 1939 had no intention of becoming a professional footballer. Matt Bell came to Hull at the end of World War One to join his brother in business. Albert Bell was an amateur goalkeeper, who had occasionally turned out for the Tigers and was assistant trainer for a spell during the 1920s. Matt Bell was soon signed by David Menzies and promoted to the first team with new season only ten days old. His shock of ginger hair was an eye-catching sight but the focus of attention was soon on his sound tackling and clearances. He went on to hold undisputed claim to the left-back berth, eventually taking over captaincy of the side. In an emergency he proved adept as a goalkeeper. With Jock Gibson alongside and Billy Mercer in goal (and later George Maddison) a defensive partnership developed which was as good as any in the Second Division. Bell scored only one goal for the Tigers, a priceless point-clincher in the relegation struggle with Bradford City in 1924. His greatest triumph, however, was in leading the side to the 1930 FA Cup semi-finals. The achievement was the more remarkable in the light of Bell's prophecy on hearing the third-round draw: "I think the Tigers will go a long way in the Cup ties this year." In August 1931, Bell left, with regret, concluding his playing career at Nottingham Forest, whose coaching staff he joined. He subsequently coached in Holland and had to flee the German invasion.

MATT BELL

	LEAGUE		*FA CUP*		*TOTAL*	
	App	*Gls*	*App*	*Gls*	*App*	*Gls*
1919-20	23	0	1	0	24	0
1920-21	25	0	5	0	30	0
1921-22	36	0	2	0	38	0
1922-23	30	0	1	0	31	0
1923-24	41	1	2	0	43	1
1924-25	33	0	3	0	36	0
1925-26	38	0	1	0	39	0
1926-27	40	0	5	0	45	0
1927-28	37	0	1	0	38	0
1928-29	36	0	2	0	38	0
1929-30	29	0	6	0	35	0
1930-31	25	0	1	0	26	0
	393	1	30	0	423	1

TOM BERRY

Tom Berry was signed from Great Harwood in the summer of 1947, after winning county and services representative honours during the war. Although signed as a full-back, he made most of his early League appearances as a wing-half before one of Major Buckley's many experiments converted him to a centre-half, where his 6ft 1in frame was used to best advantage. He was an integral part of the Northern Section championship side the following term, giving accomplished displays at left-back. Berry's composure under pressure was an asset, no matter what position he played in. At one time the great Neil Franklin found himself pushed out to wing-half to allow Berry to retain the pivot's jersey. Berry, like Matt Bell, scored only one League goal for the Tigers. His came against Port Vale, an incredible free-kick from inside his own half, which eluded those who jumped for it, skidded off the frozen surface and past a bemused goalkeeper. After a decade at the club, Berry's chances were restricted by younger talent such as Paul Feasey, but he still performed with reliability, despite impaired vision which was the legacy of an earlier injury. In October 1957 he joined Buxton and soon found himself coaching the Cheshire League side.

	LEAGUE		FA CUP		TOTAL	
	App	Gls	App	Gls	App	Gls
1947-48	32	0	2	0	34	0
1948-49	39	0	7	0	46	0
1949-50	34	0	0	0	34	0
1950-51	30	0	2	0	32	0
1951-52	26	0	2	0	28	0
1952-53	29	0	0	0	29	0
1953-54	35	0	6	0	41	0
1954-55	6	0	1	0	7	0
1955-56	29	1	0	0	29	1
1956-57	12	0	0	0	12	0
1957-58	3	0	0	0	3	0
	275	1	20	0	295	1

A month before the fighting ceased in World War One, City gave an outing to a left-half from Walkden Central. Tommy Bleakley had had a trial with Bolton, so the Tigers moved quickly to sign him on for the resumption of League football. It was the start of an association with the club lasting over a decade. During that period Bleakley formed the mainstay of the Tigers' half-back line, with his unostentatious yet always industrious and highly-effective style. Bleakley played alongside several class centre-halves, forging an especially prominent partnership with Mike Gilhooley and Jock Collier on the other flank. When Gilhooley moved on, Bleakley had a spell in the middle of the line, despite the disadvantage of his 5ft 6in frame. By 1926, Bleakley alone of the trio remained, but it was not until the close of the decade that the likes of Sam Weaver and Bill Gowdy were able to deprive the veteran of a regular place in the side. Bleakley's contribution to the 1930 Cup run was to deputize for Jimmy Walsh in the semi-final replay. Had he played in the first meeting there were sound reasons for believing that the outcome would have been different. At the end of that season Bleakley joined Goole Town, eventually graduating to coaching local sides. Immediately after World War Two he had charge of the Hull Amateurs and at 53 was still fit enough to turn out and prevent his team playing a man short.

TOMMY BLEAKLEY

	LEAGUE		FA CUP		OTHERS		TOTAL	
	App	Gls	App	Gls	App	Gls	App	Gls
1918-19	0	0	0	0	13	0	13	0
1919-20	35	0	0	0	0	0	35	0
1920-21	37	0	5	0	0	0	42	0
1921-22	38	0	2	1	0	0	40	1
1922-23	38	3	1	0	0	0	39	3
1923-24	26	0	2	0	0	0	28	0
1924-25	42	1	5	1	0	0	47	2
1925-26	37	1	1	0	0	0	38	1
1926-27	36	0	1	0	0	0	37	0
1927-28	33	0	1	0	0	0	34	0
1928-29	28	0	2	0	0	0	30	0
1929-30	18	0	1	0	0	0	19	0
	368	5	21	2	13	0	402	7

In October 1921, City manager Harry Lewis paid Cudworth United £100 for their inside-left Ernie Blenkinsop. After a month at Anlaby Road, Blenkinsop was switched to left-back. Such was the origin of one of England's most-capped players of the pre-war period. His positional play was impeccable, as was his timing of a tackle and in constructive clearances there were few who could better his accuracy. Blenkinsop made his League debut at Rotherham over Christmas 1921, in place of the injured Matt Bell, but once Bell was fit again, his young understudy was back in the Reserves. Little more than a year later the City management accepted a £1,000 offer from Sheffield Wednesday and Blenkinsop, who had not even established himself as a regular at Anlaby Road, left for greater things at Hillsborough. In 1926 he helped Wednesday to the Second Division championship. Three years later the Owls won the League and retained the title by a massive ten-point margin. Blenkinsop's defence was the tightest in the division. He made his England debut in April 1928 and went on to a record 26 consecutive appearances for his country. In 1934, Blenkinsop's long association with Wednesday came to an end. He had made close on 400 League appearances for the Owls. Liverpool paid around £5,000 in the hope that he would stiffen the defence of a side struggling in the top flight. He spent a couple of seasons at Cardiff, joining non-League Buxton on the eve of the war, then finding his services in demand as a guest player, particularly with Halifax and the Bradford clubs.

	LEAGUE		*FA CUP*		*TOTAL*	
	App	*Gls*	*App*	*Gls*	*App*	*Gls*
1921-22	3	0	0	0	3	0
1922-23	8	0	0	0	8	0
	11	0	0	0	11	0

ERNIE BLENKINSOP

This England line-up against Scotland in April 1933 includes no less than three former Tigers: Blenkinsop, Starling and Weaver. A fourth, Dally Duncan, was in the Scottish side.

Amongst Hull City goalkeepers Billy Bly has few peers. Not only does he rank as one of the longest-serving players in the club's history, but his performances in the green jersey were of international class. He was selected for the England 'B' team, but was denied the honour due to a broken forearm, one of the many fractures which marred his career and earned him the nickname of 'Brittle-boned Billy'. His courage was limitless, his saves daring and spectacular. During the war Bly kept goal for the British Army side, frequently the only uncapped player in the team but never out of his class. As a lad he did not want to be a goalkeeper, but accepted the promptings of a discerning teacher. He came to Anlaby Road for a trial in August 1937, almost missing his chance due to a late train. Despite his frail appearance, the Walker Celtic 'keeper was signed on. Bly had just made the City first team when the war came, but on the resumption of League football was back in harness and served the club for another 14 seasons. In his penultimate season Bly missed only one match — the nearest he came to being ever-present — as the side won promotion to the Second Division. Ten years earlier he had played just as important a role in winning the Northern Section title and reaching the quarter-final of the FA Cup. The sixth-round defeat by Manchester United was one of Bly's bravest performances. An early knock left him nursing a broken nose. He hardly knew where he was for the rest of the game, but carried on to such good effect that few in the crowd realized his handicap. Bly 'retired' in 1960, but was signed by Weymouth in November 1961, enjoying a final hour of FA Cup glory as the non-Leaguers battled through to the fourth round.

BILLY BLY

	LEAGUE		*FA CUP*		*OTHERS*		*TOTAL*	
	App	*Gls*	*App*	*Gls*	*App*	*Gls*	*App*	*Gls*
1938-39	8	0	0	0	0	0	8	0
1939-40	0	0	-	-	1	0	1	0
1940-41	-	-	-	-	17	0	17	0
1946-47	21	0	4	0	0	0	25	0
1947-48	27	0	2	0	0	0	29	0
1948-49	38	0	7	0	0	0	45	0
1949-50	38	0	4	0	0	0	42	0
1950-51	5	0	0	0	0	0	5	0
1951-52	34	0	0	0	0	0	34	0
1952-53	21	0	0	0	0	0	21	0
1953-54	26	0	6	0	0	0	32	0
1954-55	27	0	1	0	0	0	28	0
1955-56	26	0	2	0	0	0	28	0
1956-57	40	0	3	0	0	0	43	0
1957-58	26	0	4	0	0	0	30	0
1958-59	45	0	1	0	0	0	46	0
1959-60	21	0	1	0	0	0	22	0
	403	0	35	0	18	0	456	0

Below: Bly makes a spectacular save from a shot by Baily of Spurs. Bennett and Duquemin look on.

He was colourful, he was controversial and a great favourite on the terraces and, not least, immensely gifted as a striker. Strangely enough, it was not until Bill Bradbury's £4,000 move from Birmingham to Hull in October 1955 that his career really took off. Joining Coventry from local soccer, Bradbury spent five years at Highfield Road but made only two dozen League appearances. He eventually moved to St Andrew's, where Bob Brocklebank was in charge. Less than a year later they both arrived at Boothferry Park as the Tigers made an unsuccessful bid to stay out of Division Three. Bradbury finished the season as top scorer and struck a memorable hat-trick as Hull beat the mighty Hungarian side Vasas. In the lower division his scoring talents blossomed in partnership with Colin Smith. Bradbury hit 30 goals in the 1958-9 promotion season, a post-war best, even if he had to wait an agonizing 479 minutes before knocking in the goal which overhauled Norman Moore's record of 28 in League and Cup. It was not goals and adulation all the way, though. In the opening weeks of the season the side had struggled. As his teammates were changing for the game against Swindon, Bradbury walked into the manager's office and demanded a transfer. The process was repeated a year later, with the man who had been the hero of Boothferry Park now accusing those same fans of being 'the world's worst'. In February 1960, Bradbury joined Bury in a £5,000 deal. He had scored close on a goal every other game in his spell at Hull. Nine months later he was on the move again, briefly assisting Workington and Southport before joining Wigan Athletic as player-coach.

	LEAGUE		*FA CUP*		*TOTAL*	
	App	*Gls*	*App*	*Gls*	*App*	*Gls*
1955-56	28	9	2	0	30	9
1956-57	37	18	2	1	39	19
1957-58	46	19	6	6	52	25
1958-59	45	30	1	0	46	30
1959-60	22	6	1	0	23	6
	178	82	12	7	190	89

BILL BRADBURY

BILLY BREMNER

In September 1976, Billy Bremner left Leeds United for Hull City. Manager John Kaye's signing was hailed by some as the Tigers' best acquisition since Raich Carter. For over a decade the diminutive redhead had been part of the powerful midfield which had driven Leeds from obscurity to European glory, with Bremner winning the individual accolade of 'Footballer of the Year' in 1970. He was loathe to allow the word 'defeat' a place in his vocabulary as he gave a hundred per cent for his side, whether at club or international level. There were times when his fierce commitment went too far and the wrath of authority descended upon him, but it was a master-stroke on the part of Leeds boss Don Revie to give the little Scot captaincy of the side, for the extra responsibility matured his temperament. He won 54 caps for Scotland. It was hard to believe that Bremner had been rejected by Arsenal and Chelsea, or that he had struggled against homesickness in his early days at Leeds. Bremner gave the same endeavour in the Tigers cause as he had at Leeds. The attendance at Boothferry Park doubled for his debut against Nottingham Forest. Those present saw him display another of his many qualities, the ability to score decisive goals. His free-kick, slotted home with the utmost precision, was the match-winner. The City side as a whole, though, failed to respond to individual example. Twelve months later Kaye was sacked. Bremner was keen to succeed him but the job went to former Leeds teammate Bobby Collins. At the end of the season, Bremner, his contract up, retired. In November 1978, Doncaster gave him an opportunity in management. With limited resources he twice led them out of the Fourth Division. In October 1985 Leeds invited him to take over in succession to Eddie Gray, in the hope of taking United back into the big time, but considerable promise yielded no tangible result and in September 1988, Bremner was dismissed.

	LEAGUE		*FA CUP*		*FL CUP*		*TOTAL*	
	App	*Gls*	*App*	*Gls*	*App*	*Gls*	*App*	*Gls*
1976-77	30	2	2	0	0	0	32	2
1977-78	31	4	1	0	4	1	36	5
	61	6	3	0	4	1	68	7

The second of the brothers from Walbottle, Andy Browell, followed his elder brother George to Anlaby Road in December 1907. Andy — his real name was Anthony — was a centre-half and shared many of his brother's qualities, toughened by working down the local pit from the age of 12. With George Browell, Billy Robinson and Davy Gordon forming a half-back line to be reckoned with, it was quite an upset when Ambrose Langley axed Billy Robinson in November 1908 to give 20-year-old Andy Browell his chance. He grew rapidly in stature and confidence. Three months later Robinson departed. Browell, Browell and Gordon became the driving force which was to take the Tigers so close to Division One in 1910. The following season was barely a month old when the pivot was badly injured against Burnley and out of action for three months. Strangely, it was in the return fixture later that season that brother George was also crocked. In March 1912, Andy Browell, along with Joe Smith, followed younger brother, Tommy, to Everton in a sensational deal which took the Goodison club's spending on three Hull City players to over £3,000 within a couple of months. Browell eventually found it too difficult to make the transition to the top flight. In the summer of 1913 he returned to the North-East, enjoying a lengthy spell with West Stanley. After the war he returned to settle in Hull. He even pulled on the amber and black again, in September 1922, to play in the club's first Yorkshire Midweek League match at the age of 34.

ANDY BROWELL

	LEAGUE		*FA CUP*		*TOTAL*	
	App	*Gls*	*App*	*Gls*	*App*	*Gls*
1908-09	24	1	1	0	25	1
1909-10	38	2	1	0	39	2
1910-11	14	0	4	0	18	0
1911-12	25	2	2	0	27	2
	101	5	8	0	109	5

GEORGE BROWELL

A month into the Tigers' first League campaign, manager Ambrose Langley signed two West Stanley players who were to make a tremendous impact on the fortunes of the club. One of the duo was George Browell. 'Geordie' was thrown straight into the first team and, so readily did he make the transition, that he was rarely missing from the side over the next five seasons. A right-half whose aggressive approach and tireless grafting made the very best of his solid 12½st frame, the eldest of six brothers gave defensive stability to the Tigers' middle line and complemented his partner Davy Gordon's more attacking disposition. City fans took instantly to the Tynesider, affectionately corrupting his name to 'Bovril'. Competitive goals from Geordie were rarities — there were others in the family more adept at that art — but in the relaxed atmosphere of friendly games, especially on tour, the attacking instincts found freer expression. On one occasion he hit the woodwork no less than four times. As 1910 drew to a close, Browell was assisted from the clash with Burnley with a knee injury, which sidelined him for almost three months. The club decided not to re-engage him for the following season. Strong rumours intimated that Browell would try Rugby League with Hull FC, but in November 1911 he was taken on by Grimsby Town, whom he assisted for the remainder of the season.

	LEAGUE		*FA CUP*		*TOTAL*	
	App	*Gls*	*App*	*Gls*	*App*	*Gls*
1905-06	31	1	5	0	36	1
1906-07	38	1	3	0	41	1
1907-08	35	0	3	0	38	0
1908-09	35	0	2	0	37	0
1909-10	34	0	1	0	35	0
1910-11	21	1	0	0	21	1
	194	3	14	0	208	3

Unlike his two elder brothers, Tommy Browell was a forward. Like Andy he began his career with Newburn, a stone's throw down the Tyne from Walbottle. The Tigers gave him a trial in April 1910 and the youngster hammered in four goals against Mexborough and was signed on — for the princely wage of ten shillings (50p) a week. City introduced him to League football on the right wing, before they had actually registered him. Soon he was switched to centre-forward and his precocious talent was unleashed in devastating style with a hat-trick against Stockport. A fortnight later he meted out similar treatment to Barnsley. By the end of 1910, Tommy Browell had bagged 15 goals in a dozen games. Then, mysteriously, the goals dried up and the prodigy did not score again until the end of the season. The following term the youngster continued to accumulate the goals. Inevitably the scouts were watching. Equally inevitably, at the close of 1911, the board succumbed to the tempting offers. Everton paid £1,650, a large fee by the standards of the day. Locally, the sale caused a storm of protest from angered and disillusioned supporters. In 50 games for Everton, Tommy Browell struck an impressive 26 goals. Manchester City paid £1,700 for his talents in October 1913, but although the goals continued to flow, success eluded club and player. City lost to Bolton at Wembley in 1926 and the following term Browell made the short move to Blackpool. One of his final games for the Seasiders was a nostalgic return to Anlaby Road for the 1930 FA Cup encounter. At the season's end he took over as player-coach of Lytham, ending a League career in which he accumulated over 200 goals. He later became a tram driver at the resort.

TOMMY BROWELL

	LEAGUE		*FA CUP*		*TOTAL*	
	App	*Gls*	*App*	*Gls*	*App*	*Gls*
1910-11	32	16	4	0	36	16
1911-12	16	16	0	0	16	16
	48	32	4	0	52	32

WILLIE BUCHAN

	LEAGUE		*FA CUP*		*TOTAL*	
	App	*Gls*	*App*	*Gls*	*App*	*Gls*
1947-48	18	5	0	0	18	5
1948-49	22	7	6	1	28	8
	40	12	6	1	46	13

Willie Buchan was 33 years old when he came to Boothferry Park and in the 'veteran' stage of a distinguished career. The canny inside-forward came to prominence with Celtic in the 1930s. In November 1937, an £8,500 deal took him south to Blackpool. The Seasiders, who could have anticipated Buchan's best years for their outlay, found their plans thwarted by the war. Buchan played only around 50 games for them during those dark years, guesting frequently in other colours. He was recognized with inclusion in the Scottish side against England in 1943. After the war Buchan resumed his First Division career with Blackpool, but in 1947 found himself in the Reserves. What hurt even more was the reduction in wages. A transfer request followed. It was granted in January 1948 and City assistant manager Frank Taylor and coach George Lax were quickly off to Lancashire to set up a City record £5,000 deal. Buchan was the midfield general, the ideal man to bring the best out of those around him, as well as being a telling passer of the ball and incisive dribbler, not forgetting his prowess as a penalty-taker. He struck home two spot-kicks on his debut against Rotherham to turn a fluctuating contest City's way. Willie played a significant part in the 1948-9 Northern Section success, but the arrival of Viggo Jensen and later Don Revie restricted his first-team chances. In November 1949 he left, with Norman Fowler, for Gateshead. Later he managed Coleraine for six months, but on returning to his Grangemouth home, was pressed into service by East Stirling.

In August 1949, with football fever at its peak in Hull, a 15-year-old local lad from Clifton Street School joined those hopeful of emulating the first team's success. Brian Bulless had already represented Hull Boys. His progress was rewarded with a part-time contract in October 1950, going full-time the following February. Bulless worked his way through the ranks to make his League debut on the left wing against Southampton in April 1953. His display was a highlight in a dour struggle, crowned with the winning goal. Keen competition for the left-flank berth eventually led to Bulless moving inside, although his first outing at inside-left was to deputize for the great Wilf Mannion. It marked the start of a phase where Bulless acquired mastery of all left-sided roles. He dropped back to wing-half, linking effectively between defence and attack. Later he held his own at left-back, despite the set-back of a knee injury in his first outing in the position. With typical determination Bulless fought back into the 1959 promotion-winning side. The lean years of the early 1960s were difficult ones. Pulled stomach muscles caused several lengthy absences and a knee injury against Reading on Easter Saturday 1963 marked the beginning of the end. The ligaments failed to stand the strain of a comeback and Bulless was forced to quit. His 326 League appearances were then a club record for a local player.

	LEAGUE		*FA CUP*		*FL CUP*		*TOTAL*	
	App	*Gls*	*App*	*Gls*	*App*	*Gls*	*App*	*Gls*
1952-53	3	1	0	0	-	-	3	1
1953-54	16	1	4	1	-	-	20	2
1954-55	13	2	0	0	-	-	13	2
1955-56	36	4	2	0	-	-	38	4
1956-57	45	9	3	2	-	-	48	11
1957-58	42	7	6	3	-	-	48	10
1958-59	30	2	0	0	-	-	30	2
1959-60	42	0	1	0	-	-	43	0
1960-61	43	2	7	0	2	0	52	2
1961-62	33	2	1	0	3	0	37	2
1962-63	21	0	0	0	2	0	23	0
1963-64	2	0	0	0	0	0	2	0
	326	30	24	6	7	0	357	36

BRIAN BULLESS

EDDIE BURBANKS

Raich Carter's first major signing as Hull City player-manager was his former Sunderland teammate Eddie Burbanks. Burbanks was a youthful 35-year-old when he joined the Tigers and is probably their oldest League debutant. Sunderland had signed him from Denaby United early in 1935. Two years later he and Carter shared in the Rokerites' FA Cup triumph. Further success came to the left winger during the war, as a guest in the Blackpool side which won the League (North) Cup in 1943 and beat Arsenal in a play-off against the Southern winners. Sunderland had narrowly avoided relegation in 1948 and it took a sizeable offer to induce them to part. City tried no less than nine players on the left wing during 1947-8, so it is not difficult to assess the impact of Burbanks at Boothferry Park. His incisive running and ball skills added a new dimension to City's attack. And at their peril opposing defences allowed him a chance to unleash a powerful shot, from either foot. Burbanks continued to display his skills at Boothferry Park until given a free transfer in the summer of 1953. Carter, now Leeds boss, took him to Elland Road for a final couple of seasons of League football.

	LEAGUE		*FA CUP*		*TOTAL*	
	App	*Gls*	*App*	*Gls*	*App*	*Gls*
1948-49	28	9	2	0	30	9
1949-50	24	4	3	1	27	5
1950-51	38	2	3	0	41	2
1951-52	33	4	2	0	35	4
1952-53	20	2	0	0	20	2
	143	21	10	1	153	22

In June 1963, City manager Cliff Britton paid Chelsea £10,000 to bring Dennis Butler to Boothferry Park. It may have seemed a large sum for the club to pay for a full-back, but over the next six and a half seasons the Tigers' boss received fine reward for his investment. Butler had represented Surrey at schoolboy level and in 1958 joined Chelsea's youth set-up, gaining a professional contract in the summer of 1960. In 1961-2 the joy of a first-team place was offset by loss of First Division status. The team bounced straight back, but Butler's contribution was a mere two appearances. It increased his willingness to move to Hull, despite the prospect of playing in the Third Division. He struck up a fine partnership with Andy Davidson, which held together for four seasons, during which the Tigers won the championship and achieved a memorable draw at Stamford Bridge in the FA Cup in March 1966. The stocky, bow-legged back was a sound defender, operating almost exclusively on the left side of the Tigers rearguard. Not until youngsters such as Don Beardsley and Roger de Vries began to make their mark did Cliff Britton feel able to allow Butler to move on to Reading in December 1969. He gave good service to the Elm Park side until hanging up his boots in the summer of 1974.

	LEAGUE		*FA CUP*		*FL CUP*		*TOTAL*	
	App	*Gls*	*App*	*Gls*	*App*	*Gls*	*App*	*Gls*
1963-64	42	0	5	0	2	0	49	0
1964-65	32	0	3	0	2	0	37	0
1965-66	37	0	6	0	2	0	45	0
1966-67	41	0	3	0	1	0	45	0
1967-68	31/1	0	3	0	0	0	34/1	0
1968-69	16/1	0	0	0	0	0	16/1	0
1969-70	16	0	0	0	2	0	18	0
	215/2	0	20	0	9	0	244/2	0

DENNIS BUTLER

In January 1965, Ian Butler became the second of three signings which transformed the Tigers' attack into the most potent in the club's history. The £40,000 fee equalled the record sum paid a few weeks earlier for Ken Wagstaff. Rotherham, striving to make the First Division, resisted all offers for their England Youth international until the winger himself asked for a move. The deal ended a year-long quest by Cliff Britton. Ian — no relation to his contemporary Dennis Butler — was a product of the Millmoor youth policy and made his League debut during the 1960-61 season. His pace and trickery down the left flank were valuable assets to the Tigers. But for that fateful Easter of 1965, Butler would have made an immediate return to the Second Division. The following season brought success in record-breaking style. The extra 12 months allowed the trio of newcomers, Wagstaff, Butler and Ken Houghton, to blend with Chris Chilton and Ray Henderson into an irresistible attacking unit. For seven and a half seasons Ian Butler mesmerized his opponents on that left flank, also contributing a number of vital goals, including the one which clinched the Third Division title in 1966. Sadly, his was a dying art in an age of defensive football and in the summer of 1973 Butler was transferred to York, where he helped take the Minstermen into the Second Division for the first time. He failed by only three goals to complete a League century. His record at Boothferry Park places him in a select quintet who have reached 300 League appearances and scored over 50 goals.

	LEAGUE		*FA CUP*		*FL CUP*		*OTHERS*		*TOTAL*	
	App	*Gls*	*App*	*Gls*	*App*	*Gls*	*App*	*Gls*	*App*	*Gls*
1964-65	20	2	0	0	0	0	0	0	20	2
1965-66	45	13	7	2	2	0	0	0	54	15
1966-67	31	8	3	0	1	0	0	0	35	8
1967-68	34	5	3	0	0	0	0	0	37	5
1968-69	39	10	1	0	2	0	0	0	42	10
1969-70	39	9	1	0	2	0	0	0	42	9
1970-71	36/1	7	4	1	0	0	2	0	42/1	8
1971-72	34/1	8	3	1	0	0	0	0	37/1	9
1972-73	22/3	4	0	0	2	0	1	0	25/3	4
	300/5	66	22	4	9	0	3	0	334/5	70

IAN BUTLER

For many, Raich Carter remains the greatest footballer ever to play for the Tigers. Carter was 34 when he joined the club in March 1948 after a 14-year stay at Sunderland and a spell at Derby which began when he guested for the Rams during the war. Yet there was little indication that he was in the twilight of a great career at Boothferry Park. The silver-haired inside-forward generalled the Tigers superbly to the Northern Section championship in 1949 and still found time to rattle in more goals than any of his colleagues except Norman Moore. It became a part of local folklore that a mule once caught sight of Carter's awesome shooting power and promptly gave up kicking. The following season Carter topped the scoring list as he led Hull in an all-out bid for the First Division. It was quality soccer from the man who had represented his country 21 times through war and peace, to say nothing of winning a League Championship medal with Sunderland in 1936, an FA Cup-winners' medal a year later and Wembley triumph again, this time with Derby, in 1946. The maestro's personal contribution to the Tigers' success in 1949 carried him to runner-up in the Footballer of the Year poll. In November 1950, 19 years after signing professional for Sunderland, he proclaimed: "I am determined to go on playing as long as I can raise a gallop." Three months later his scoring contribution at Southampton brought up 200 goals in peacetime football. Carter the player was still indispensible to the City team. The point was emphasized dramatically in September 1951 when club and town alike were rocked by his resignation as player-manager. Without Raich the side sank down the Second Division like the proverbial stone. So serious did the situation become that the director who suggested that Carter be brought back to fulfil the playing side of his contract and was not entertained by his colleagues, soon found himself with the support of a majority of the board. By December, Raich Carter was back in the side and those around him began to take on a new lease of life. It was a hard struggle to retrieve the situation but, at the end of the season, chairman Harold Needler knew well the club's debt to the inside man: "Without Raich we would have been in the Third Division next season." Carter hung up his boots, until January 1953, when Cork Athletic persuaded him to turn out for the rest of the campaign. The crowds came flocking and Raich's swan-song ended with success in the Irish Cup. A return to management, at Elland Road, ensued. Carter's managerial career is discussed elsewhere in this volume.

	LEAGUE		*FA CUP*		*TOTAL*	
	App	*Gls*	*App*	*Gls*	*App*	*Gls*
1947-48	4	0	0	0	4	0
1948-49	39	14	5	3	44	17
1949-50	39	16	4	0	43	16
1950-51	32	19	3	2	35	21
1951-52	22	8	2	0	24	8
	136	57	14	5	150	62

RAICH CARTER

Chris Chilton, the greatest goalscorer in the history of the club, joined the Tigers groundstaff in the summer of 1959 from local side Bilton. As an inside-forward he progressed rapidly through the junior and reserve sides and in August 1960 was pitched into the battle to regain Second Division status. After only one outing Chilton was switched to centre-forward, a move which brought a remarkable haul of 20 goals that season, including the first of many hat-tricks, against Queen's Park Rangers. The signing of Ken Wagstaff in 1964 marked the start of a unique partnership. Chilton, strong and powerful, found the ideal foil in the trickery of inside-forward Wagstaff. His source of supply was further enriched with the arrival of the Rotherham pair, Houghton and Butler. That season Chilton came within three goals of Bill Bradbury's post-war League best, despite a lean opening to the season which prompted a transfer request. The Third Division championship success coincided with the centre-forward's 100th League goal. In September 1968 came recognition with a place in the FA XI against Guernsey. It was Chilton who spearheaded Terry Neill's assault on the First Division in 1970-71, thrilling the crowds with his fearsome heading power and equally explosive shooting. Further honour followed with an FA tour of Australia. The accolade concluded what was to be his final full season at Boothferry Park. In August 1971 he left for Coventry, for a fee of over £90,000. Sadly, his experience of the top flight was not the happiest. The Tigers dumped his new team out of the FA Cup, with Chilton but a shadow of his former self. A back injury ended his senior career, four goals short of a League double century. After a spell playing and coaching in South Africa, Chilton returned to Hull City in 1978 as youth coach, eventually becoming assistant manager until leaving again in 1985.

CHRIS CHILTON

	LEAGUE		*FA CUP*		*FL CUP*		*OTHERS*		*TOTAL*	
	App	*Gls*	*App*	*Gls*	*App*	*Gls*	*App*	*Gls*	*App*	*Gls*
1960-61	41	19	6	1	2	0	0	0	49	20
1961-62	30	7	2	2	3	4	0	0	35	13
1962-63	43	18	4	2	4	3	0	0	51	23
1963-64	45	22	5	2	2	0	0	0	52	24
1964-65	40	27	3	0	1	0	0	0	44	27
1965-66	45	25	7	3	2	1	0	0	54	29
1966-67	37	17	3	2	1	0	0	0	41	19
1967-68	37	14	3	1	1	0	0	0	41	15
1968-69	22	5	1	1	2	1	0	0	25	7
1969-70	36	18	1	0	2	1	0	0	39	19
1970-71	37	21	4	2	1	0	2	3	44	26
1971-72	2	0	0	0	0	0	0	0	2	0
	415	193	39	16	21	10	2	3	477	222

Chris Chilton signs for Hull City on 21 July 1960.

Bob Brocklebank's attempts to strengthen the Tigers attack to avoid relegation in 1955-6 resulted in three signings within a month: Bill Bradbury, Stan Mortensen and Doug Clarke. Clarke cost the club around £2,000 and proved a real bargain. He joined Bury from Darwen in February 1952, following a spell as an amateur with his home-town club, Bolton. He failed to establish himself at Gigg Lane, but that changed immediately at Boothferry Park, as Clarke and Bradbury played inside-forward to 'Morty'. By the time success came to City in 1958-9, Clarke's role had changed significantly. In November 1957 he was tried on the right wing. With pace enough for the position, Clarke revelled in the extra space on the flank. The switch eventually became a permanent one, even though he had put four goals past Halifax earlier in the season from inside-right. His only previous hat-trick had been for Bury — against the Tigers — in 1955. From the wing Clarke continued to find the net, scoring close on a century in his first-team games. Such became his confidence in the winger's role that Bob Brocklebank even switched him to the left flank on occasion. After almost ten years at Boothferry Park, Clarke moved to Torquay in June 1965, helping United win promotion to the Third Division as well as reaching personal milestones of 100 goals and 500 appearances in the League. At the age of 34, Clarke joined non-League Bath City and continued to play in minor soccer in the South-West until well into his 40s.

DOUG CLARKE

	LEAGUE		*FA CUP*		*FL CUP*		*TOTAL*	
	App	*Gls*	*App*	*Gls*	*App*	*Gls*	*App*	*Gls*
1955-56	26	6	2	1	-	-	28	7
1956-57	40	18	3	2	-	-	43	20
1957-58	46	16	6	2	-	-	52	18
1958-59	45	12	1	0	-	-	46	12
1959-60	34	3	1	0	-	-	35	3
1960-61	39	10	7	1	2	0	48	11
1961-62	46	4	2	0	3	1	51	5
1962-63	41	5	4	0	4	1	49	6
1963-64	35	1	4	0	2	0	41	1
1964-65	16	4	1	0	1	0	18	4
	368	79	31	6	12	2	411	87

JOCK COLLIER

A powerful right-half, Jock Collier joined the Tigers in July 1920 from Inverkeithing United, one of several junior outfits with whom he learned his trade. It was a shrewd signing by David Menzies, for Collier slotted immediately into the City first team. Within months, the half-back line of Collier, Gilhooley and Bleakley had become immortalized for their part in the Cup destruction of 'unbeatable' Burnley. It was no mere one-off, though. In 1922 the trio drove the side to within four points of the First Division. Collier missed the first six games of that campaign. His colleagues picked up only three points in his absence and were bottom of the table before the Scot returned to restore order. Collier continued to be an influential figure until 1925, when Bill McCracken's search for a successful blend saw Collier relegated to the Reserves. In the summer of 1926 he began a two-year spell with Queen's Park Rangers, before returning to Yorkshire as player-coach to York. He helped the Minstermen into the Football League in 1929, leaving the following year to take a pub in York. By 1933 he had been reinstated as manager and remained at the club in managerial and coaching roles until March 1937. Collier died in December 1940, aged 43.

	LEAGUE		*FA CUP*		*TOTAL*	
	App	*Gls*	*App*	*Gls*	*App*	*Gls*
1920-21	38	0	5	0	43	0
1921-22	33	0	2	0	35	0
1922-23	35	0	0	0	35	0
1923-24	26	0	2	0	28	0
1924-25	33	0	5	0	38	0
1925-26	3	0	0	0	3	0
	168	0	14	0	182	0

On his day Les Collinson was the complete wing-half, tackling with power, probing effectively for weaknesses in the opposition and unleashing a ferocious shot. He was one of an increasing number of local products to make good in the 1950s, joining the club in August 1953. Working through the multiplicity of lesser sides, Collinson made his senior bow in the FA Cup tie at Gateshead in 1956, a month before signing professional forms on completion of his National Service in the RAF. Also capable of playing inside-forward, he once found himself tried as leader of the attack. He crashed in a fine goal, but openly preferred the extra freedom of deeper roles. In the early 1960s, as the club sought to rebuild, he was one of the elements of stability in the side. Collinson was still a regular in the line-up which came close to promotion in 1965, but missed out altogether when success did come the following season. He finally left in February 1967, for York, where he reached the milestone of 300 League appearances. After 18 months he stepped down to non-League Goole Town and then assisted a number of other local sides.

LES COLLINSON

	LEAGUE		*FA CUP*		*FL CUP*		*TOTAL*	
	App	*Gls*	*App*	*Gls*	*App*	*Gls*	*App*	*Gls*
1956-57	26	2	3	0	-	-	29	2
1957-58	38	1	6	0	-	-	44	1
1958-59	17	2	1	0	-	-	18	2
1959-60	29	0	1	0	-	-	30	0
1960-61	41	3	5	0	2	0	48	3
1961-62	41	2	2	0	3	1	46	3
1962-63	44	3	3	0	4	1	51	4
1963-64	10	0	2	0	0	0	12	0
1964-65	42	1	3	0	0	0	45	1
1965-66	2	0	0	0	0	0	2	0
1966-67	6/1	0	0	0	0	0	6/1	0
	296/1	14	26	0	9	2	331/1	16

In March 1920 the Tigers filled a blank Saturday with a friendly at South Shields. Having a first outing on the right wing was the diminutive figure of Jackie Crawford, signed that week from Jarrow Town. There was no hesitation in including Crawford for the next League match, against the division's eventual runners-up, Huddersfield, nor in switching the newcomer to the left flank to allow David Mercer to operate on the right. The Tynesider came through the test with flying colours and became an automatic choice for three seasons, delighting the fans with his deft ball control, fine turn of speed and dangerous centres. When Mercer moved on, Crawford reverted to outside-right, sharing in the Cup triumphs of the early 1920s. It was his 38th-minute opening goal which paved the way for the five-goal eclipse of First Division Middlesbrough. These, though, were financially difficult times for the club and, as Crawford's talents began to blossom, his days at Anlaby Road were numbered. A wag in the crowd once shouted to him, "Don't score or you'll be sold." Goals or no, the directors accepted Chelsea's offer of £3,000 in May 1923 and Crawford began a decade-long association with the Pensioners, clocking up close on 300 League appearances for them. In 1930-31, Crawford received overdue international recognition, playing for England against the Scots. By 1934 he had fallen out of favour and moved to Queen's Park Rangers, gaining a new lease of life as a goalscorer. After close on 20 years in League soccer, he retired and helped coach QPR into the Second Division for the first time in 1938.

	LEAGUE		*FA CUP*		*TOTAL*	
	App	*Gls*	*App*	*Gls*	*App*	*Gls*
1919-20	9	1	0	0	9	1
1920-21	34	4	5	2	39	6
1921-22	41	3	2	1	43	4
1922-23	42	1	1	1	43	2
	126	9	8	4	134	13

JACKIE CRAWFORD

It was one of the surprise deals of the summer of 1938 when the Tigers persuaded 29-year-old Arthur Cunliffe to leave Second Division Burnley to play in the Northern Section. The former England international came to prominence a decade earlier with Blackburn, moving to Aston Villa and Middlesbrough before joining the Turf Moor club in April 1937. Cunliffe had established himself as a flying winger and his great asset was a devastating turn of pace which, allied with superb ball control, had made him one of the finest exponents of wing play of his generation. He had made only nine appearances for Burnley in 1937-8 and the critics were writing him off as a spent force. However, City manager Ernie Blackburn was convinced there was still plenty of good football left in the Lancastrian. Events were to prove him right. It was another nine years before Arthur Cunliffe finally called it a day. At Anlaby Road he immediately became the mainspring of the Tigers attack. Not only did his skill create numerous openings, but he also rediscovered the finishing touch which had marked his early days at Blackburn. It was the winger's incisive work which was largely responsible for the magnitude of the Tigers' record victory over Carlisle. At the end of the war Cunliffe was one of many City players given free transfers. Rochdale signed him on for a final season of League soccer, whereupon he became their trainer, a position he later held at Bournemouth.

ARTHUR CUNLIFFE

	LEAGUE		*FA CUP*		*OTHERS*		*TOTAL*	
	App	*Gls*	*App*	*Gls*	*App*	*Gls*	*App*	*Gls*
1938-39	42	20	3	1	1	0	46	21
1939-40	0	0	-	-	13	4	13	4
1940-41	-	-	-	-	16	6	16	6
1944-45	-	-	-	-	2	0	2	0
	42	20	3	1	32	10	77	31

One name stands out on its own at the head of the list of League appearances for Hull City, 90 matches clear of the next contender. Andy Davidson set a record which will take some beating and, including friendly games, he made over 600 first-team appearances for the Tigers. Loyalty and durability went hand in hand with commitment. Davidson's early career was marred after breaking a leg three times and during an FA Cup match against Port Vale in 1957 it was feared that he had suffered a fractured arm. He battled on to the end of a game which went into extra-time and, when only severe bruising was diagnosed, there was no keeping him out of the line-up for the following Saturday. At Swindon in 1958 they had to carry him from the pitch with torn knee ligaments. 'Jock', as he was known, was back to play a valuable part in that season's promotion success. The tide turned in the 1960s and from March 1962 to January 1966, Davidson clocked up 177 consecutive League appearances, then a peacetime record for the Tigers. In April 1965 he overtook George Maddison's aggregate of 430 League appearances. The following term Davidson skippered the side to the Third Division championship. In November 1967 injury caught up with him again at Villa Park. Alas, it was to prove the end of his career. He remained at Boothferry Park in a variety of coaching and scouting roles until December 1979, spending over 30 years on the staff of the club he had joined as a schoolboy in March 1947. Initially homesick for his native Douglas Water, the youngster was persuaded to return to Hull, first making his mark as a wing-half and occasional centre-forward before turning to full-back with equal effectiveness. His rugged tackling and fierce competitiveness made him a respected opponent and an enduring influence on the Tigers' fortunes.

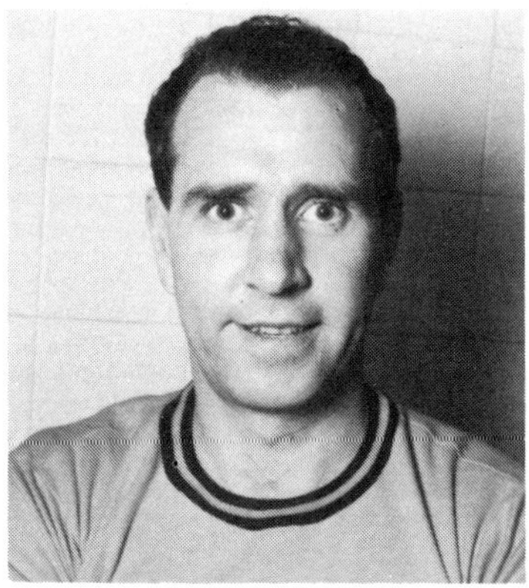

ANDY DAVIDSON

	LEAGUE		*FA CUP*		*FL CUP*		*TOTAL*	
	App	*Gls*	*App*	*Gls*	*App*	*Gls*	*App*	*Gls*
1952-53	11	1	1	0	-	-	12	1
1953-54	0	0	0	0	-	-	0	0
1954-55	2	0	0	0	-	-	2	0
1955-56	42	1	2	0	-	-	44	1
1956-57	41	4	2	0	-	-	43	4
1957-58	46	5	6	1	-	-	52	6
1958-59	26	1	0	0	-	-	26	1
1959-60	42	0	1	0	-	-	43	0
1960-61	46	1	7	0	2	0	55	1
1961-62	43	1	2	0	3	0	48	1
1962-63	46	1	4	0	4	0	54	1
1963-64	46	2	5	0	2	0	53	2
1964-65	46	1	3	0	2	0	51	1
1965-66	45	0	7	0	2	0	54	0
1966-67	29	0	3	0	1	0	33	0
1967-68	9	0	0	0	0	0	9	0
	520	18	43	1	16	0	579	19

But for those seasons when war halted the League programme, the name of Dai Davies might have stood high in the list of most appearances for Hull City. He arrived at Anlaby Road in August 1935 as a 20-year-old, on the recommendation of Jack McQuillan, who had spotted the Welshman — whose first names were David Daniel — playing for Aberaman Athletic, a leading Welsh minor club. Amongst his teammates were Horace Cumner, later to play for Hull, and Bryn Jones, the game's most expensive pre-war player. With a more fashionable club, Davies might well have emulated them in pulling on the Welsh jersey. A side hopelessly out of its depth in the Second Division was no place to develop his potential but, in the three seasons leading up to the war, Davies made his mark as a midfield general, giving unstinting endeavour and scheming constantly to open up opposing defences. As his experience grew, the inside-forward was increasingly prepared to exploit the openings himself. With 17 League and Cup goals in 1938-9 he was third behind Cunliffe and Hubbard amongst City's scorers. The former played outside Davies and the pair formed one of the most powerful wings in the lower divisions. When Hull City resumed after the war, the veteran still had an important part to play in Major Buckley's rebuilding plans, nurturing the Major's young recruits. In November 1947 he went on loan to Scarborough. The following September a permanent deal was struck with Scunthorpe. Before the years finally caught up with him, Davies had a brief spell as player-manager of Barton Town.

	LEAGUE		*FA CUP*		*OTHERS*		*TOTAL*	
	App	*Gls*	*App*	*Gls*	*App*	*Gls*	*App*	*Gls*
1935-36	9	0	0	0	0	0	9	0
1936-37	38	6	0	0	1	0	39	6
1937-38	34	9	3	0	1	0	38	9
1938-39	42	14	3	3	1	0	46	17
1939-40	0	0	-	-	20	4	20	4
1940-41	-	-	-	-	17	3	17	3
1946-47	18	1	2	0	0	0	20	1
	141	30	8	3	40	7	189	40

DAI DAVIES

ROGER DE VRIES

Roger de Vries was one of a number of fine full-backs on the club's books in the 1960s and 1970s. He came to Boothferry Park as an apprentice in August 1966 from Wolfreton School, turning professional at 17. Early in 1968, he tasted senior soccer in friendly matches, although it was not until Terry Neill's arrival that de Vries was given a competitive outing in the Watney Cup. He responded by displaying a remarkable maturity and confidence and kept his place for most of the season. Injuries sidelined him for much of the 1972-3 campaign and in 1975 a new challenge to his tenure of the left-back berth arose from young Peter Daniel. Again, the Willerby lad met the challenge and Daniel was switched to the opposite flank to form an effective partnership with his erstwhile rival. Daniel left for Wolves, but de Vries soldiered on for two more years, making his 300th League appearance in his tenth season, demonstrating the high level of consistency he achieved during that period. Blackburn signed him in June 1980, but he was unable to command a regular place at Ewood Park and concluded his career with a brief spell at Scunthorpe in October 1981.

	LEAGUE		*FA CUP*		*FL CUP*		*OTHERS*		*TOTAL*	
	App	*Gls*	*App*	*Gls*	*App*	*Gls*	*App*	*Gls*	*App*	*Gls*
1970-71	32	0	4	0	1	0	2	0	39	0
1971-72	36/1	0	3	0	1	0	0	0	40/1	0
1972-73	13	0	0	0	2	0	1	0	16	0
1973-74	34/2	0	0	0	3	1	3	0	40/2	1
1974-75	24/1	0	0	0	1	0	0	0	25/1	0
1975-76	38	0	1	0	3	0	3	0	45	0
1976-77	37	0	2	0	1	0	2	0	42	0
1977-78	37	0	0	0	3	0	3	0	43	0
1978-79	29	0	2	0	3	0	0	0	34	0
1979-80	34	0	0	0	0	0	0	0	34	0
	314/4	0	12	0	18	1	14	0	358/4	1

Andy Duncan came to Hull from his local club, Renton Thistle, in May 1930. There were hopes that he would make the transition to League soccer as well as his namesake, Dally Duncan. Andy was an inside-right, thrustful and tenacious, with many of the traits of style which characterized Scottish inside-forward play. The second Duncan, though, took longer to re-adjust. It was the following March before he made the League side, taking his chance well with an impressive four goals in seven games. In March 1932 a knee injury at York brought a premature end to Andy Duncan's season. He bounced back to play a significant part in Hull City winning the Northern Section the following term, but a series of knocks again restricted his participation in the concluding stages. Twelve months later the trip to Bury resulted in yet another early finish to Duncan's season. Despite these set-backs, the side was relying increasingly on his ability as a goalscorer. A hat-trick at Sheffield United in December 1934 meant he had netted close on half his side's goals. Naturally, the big clubs began to dangle the cheque book. In March 1935 an offer of around £6,000 from Spurs proved irresistible. Duncan's arrival at Tottenham failed to save the Londoners from losing their First Division place but he remained at White Hart Lane until the war and continued to assist his club on a fairly regular basis until 1942.

ANDY DUNCAN

	LEAGUE		*FA CUP*		*TOTAL*	
	App	*Gls*	*App*	*Gls*	*App*	*Gls*
1930-31	7	4	0	0	7	4
1931-32	24	2	2	0	26	2
1932-33	28	9	4	0	32	9
1933-34	20	4	3	0	23	4
1934-35	26	12	0	0	26	12
	105	31	9	0	114	31

In the pre-season practice matches in 1928, a stranger from north of the border appeared on the left wing, masquerading under the alias of 'Dunn'. He opened the scoring but, more important, made a deep impression with his wing play. The signature of Douglas Duncan, from Aberdeen Richmond, was obtained as quickly as possible. His talents were to come to maturity the following season in that epic Cup run. It was Duncan whose goal at Home Park checked Plymouth's comeback in the third round. His centre enabled Alexander to clinch the game. The same combination brought the equalizer in the sixth round at Newcastle. And his semi-final strike gave the Tigers a two-goal lead over Arsenal. Wembley, though, was not to be. Disappointment was doubled by relegation but Duncan, unlike some of his teammates, remained at Anlaby Road. In the scarcely ideal arena of the Northern Section he came increasingly to the fore as a goalscorer. Only Alexander accumulated more goals in 1930-31. The following term the Scot led the list. However, as a return to the Second Division was no nearer, Duncan departed for Derby in March 1932. County secured a bargain for the £2,000 fee and in October 1932, Duncan won the first of 14 Scottish caps. In April 1935 his two goals defeated England in front of a 130,000 crowd. A year later Derby were runners-up in the League. The club closed down when war broke out and the winger was a regular guest for Notts County. In 1946, the Rams were 4-1 winners over Charlton in the FA Cup Final and it was Duncan, belying his 35 years, whose shot was turned in by Bert Turner to open the scoring. In October of that year, with 248 League appearances for Derby behind him and 63 goals, Duncan moved to Luton as player-coach. He spent ten years at Kenilworth Road, taking the Hatters into the First Division in 1955. Subsequently he managed Blackburn to the 1960 Cup Final before leaving the game.

DALLY DUNCAN

	LEAGUE		*FA CUP*		*TOTAL*	
	App	*Gls*	*App*	*Gls*	*App*	*Gls*
1928-29	20	3	0	0	20	3
1929-30	24	7	7	2	31	9
1930-31	40	18	1	1	41	19
1931-32	27	19	3	0	30	19
	111	47	11	3	122	50

Denis Durham was one of those who suffered more than his fair share of misfortune during his soccer career. Yet, through it all, he displayed a perseverance and courage which could only inspire those around him. It began even before Durham signed for the Tigers in April 1947. He was invited by Major Buckley for trials in October 1946, having caught the eye with his local club, East Halton United, but appendicitis frustrated those plans. The following season City fans saw his versatility, as left-half, left winger and centre-forward. In the forward line Durham notched a creditable four goals in eight outings, unleashing shots of ferocious power. He began the 1948-9 promotion season at left-half, but lost his place to Alan Mellor in October and failed to win back a regular spot until 1951-2. He then doubled up as a useful left-back. An ever-present the following term, it seemed he had finally arrived. However, in July 1953 he was whisked away to a local hospital with a mystery illness which kept him out until November. Patiently he picked up the pieces, but in the opening match of the 1955-6 season Durham twisted a knee, with neither friend nor foe remotely near. Eventually a cartilage was removed. It was November 1956 before he returned, now settling at left-back due to the departure of Viggo Jensen. Cracked vertebrae followed in April 1957. Then for two seasons the defender was favoured, playing a full part in the 1958-9 promotion run. At 36 his playing days were drawing to a close. He took a part-time job as a salesman, passing on his soccer experience to the Tigers youngsters until released by the club in May 1960.

DENIS DURHAM

	LEAGUE		*FA CUP*		*TOTAL*	
	App	*Gls*	*App*	*Gls*	*App*	*Gls*
1946-47	1	0	0	0	1	0
1947-48	15	4	0	0	15	4
1948-49	15	1	0	0	15	1
1949-50	5	0	0	0	5	0
1950-51	4	0	0	0	4	0
1951-52	30	1	2	0	32	1
1952-53	42	1	2	0	44	1
1953-54	17	0	7	0	24	0
1954-55	34	0	1	0	35	0
1955-56	1	0	0	0	1	0
1956-57	23	0	3	0	26	0
1957-58	41	0	6	0	47	0
1958-59	39	0	1	0	40	0
	267	7	22	0	289	7

Hull City officials, players and staff in 1948-9. Back row (left to right): Craddock, Wright, Taylor, Buchan, Moore, Seddon. Middle row: Hassall, King, Meens, Corbett, Berry, Bly, Durham, Fowler, Bradshaw. Front row: J.Lodge (assistant trainer), Bloomer, Conway, Mr K.Percival (president), H.Carter (player-manager), Mr H.Needler, Greenhalgh, Burbanks, G.Lax (trainer-coach). On ground: Harrison, Mellor.

The early Tigers had been well served at half-back by the Browells, Billy Robinson and Davy Gordon. They set a standard by which subsequent generations were weighed. Tim Wright, Jimmy McIntosh and Patsy O'Connell upheld it well. And from that prolific Lancashire nursery side, St Helens Recs, came Joe Edelston. Signed in March 1913, he made his League debut less than a fortnight later. Such rapid promotion was amply justified. The following season he was first-choice right-half in a City side which at one stage looked 'certainties' for promotion. Four of Edelston's best years were lost to the war, but they did give him opportunities to demonstrate his versatility, at inside-forward, at centre-half and as a more than capable stand-in goalkeeper when Nick Hendry was an absentee. Edelston missed only a dozen games during those difficult seasons and only David Mercer bettered his record. After the war his polished performances brought him to the attention of the selectors, who picked him for the FA side to tour South Africa in the summer of 1920. In June that year, Manchester City paid a substantial sum for his services. However, five months later he was packing his bags again, to move to Fulham. There he remained until his retirement in 1926, joining the club's administrative staff. Later he assisted in the management of Clapton Orient and Brentford, before taking charge at Reading in April 1939. It was at Fulham that his son, Maurice, made his League debut, on his way to international honours and a subsequent career as a top sports commentator.

JOE EDELSTON

	LEAGUE		*FA CUP*		*OTHERS*		*TOTAL*	
	App	*Gls*	*App*	*Gls*	*App*	*Gls*	*App*	*Gls*
1912-13	3	0	0	0	0	0	3	0
1913-14	35	0	2	0	3	0	40	0
1914-15	36	0	5	0	2	0	43	0
1915-16	0	0	0	0	35	1	35	1
1916-17	0	0	0	0	28	0	28	0
1917-18	0	0	0	0	34	0	34	0
1918-19	0	0	0	0	33	0	33	0
1919-20	35	0	1	0	0	0	36	0
	109	0	8	0	135	1	252	1

KEITH EDWARDS

	LEAGUE		*FACUP*		*FLCUP*		*OTHERS*		*TOTAL*	
	App	*Gls*	*App*	*Gls*	*App*	*Gls*	*App*	*Gls*	*App*	*Gls*
1978-79	46	24	2	1	3	0	0	0	51	25
1979-80	41	19	2	0	2	1	0	0	45	20
1980-81	38/2	13	6	4	2	0	3	0	49/2	17
1981-82	5	1	0	0	2	0	1/2	1	8/2	2
1987-88	9	3	0	0	0	0	0	0	9	3
1988-89	44	26	3	3	2	1	1	0	50	30
	183/2	86	13	8	11	2	5/2	1	212/4	97

The arrival of Keith Edwards at Boothferry Park in August 1978 brought a proven goalscorer into the Tigers' ranks. Keith came with three seasons at Sheffield United behind him, having developed from Stockton youth club striker to top-flight player on the fringe of England Under-21 honours. Newcastle United were at one stage prepared to pay £200,000 for his services. Edwards was still only 21 when he came to Hull for a morc modest £60,000. It was not long before City fans were thrilling to his quality finishing skills. Close control, pace and explosive shooting made him the first City player for three seasons to hit double figures in the League. His 24 goals were the best individual performance since 1966. As the club's fortunes declined over the next couple of seasons, the striker's scoring tally diminished, but his contribution in 1979-80 was a decisive factor in keeping the club in the Third Division. The bleak season which followed saw Edwards unsettled and seeking a move. In September 1981 he returned to Bramall Lane, costing the Blades £95,000 according to the terms of the tribunal, but his 35 goals, a career best, helped United win the Fourth Division title. Two seasons later a haul of 33 was a similarly decisive influence on United's elevation to the Second Division. By 1986, Edwards reached the 200 goals mark in League Football. After five seasons at Bramall Lane he was on the move once more, joining Leeds, but at Elland Road he hit a lean spell and headed north to Aberdeen. Here too he found difficulty in settling in and, in March 1988, returned to Boothferry Park. Edwards' 26 goals in 1988-9 was the best haul in the Second Division and a major factor in keeping the Tigers from relegation.

A loyal one-club man, Paul Feasey's association with the Tigers lasted for 17 seasons. He was first spotted by Major Buckley's scouts and played for City's nursery side, Buckley Juniors, in the Doncaster League in 1948-9. Feasey had previously represented York Boys, as a full-back or centre-half and on completion of his training as a bricklayer at York Technical College was able to concentrate on soccer, signing professional forms for City in May 1950. Feasey began to specialize as a centre-half, which did not make for rapid progress with the likes of Neil Franklin, Tom Berry, Frank Seddon and Harold Meens at Boothferry Park. And at 5ft 8in he hardly had the ideal height for the role, but by sheer hard work reached the stage of being able to compete with the best in the air. He later admitted to finding smaller, nippier opponents harder to handle. Feasey eventually made his League debut against Barnsley in 1953, but did not figure in the first team again until December 1955. The signing of big South African Norman Neilson prompted Feasey to revert to full-back, but he was far from happy there. He fought back to hold down the pivot's spot through the 1958-9 promotion season and through the difficult times of the early 1960s before the double challenge of Brian Garvey and Mick Milner finally spelled the end of his domination. In 1966, Feasey was released to join Goole Town, where he also had a period of managerial responsibility. Once his playing days were over, Feasey reverted to the trade for which he had studied.

PAUL FEASEY

	LEAGUE		*FA CUP*		*FL CUP*		*TOTAL*	
	App	*Gls*	*App*	*Gls*	*App*	*Gls*	*App*	*Gls*
1952-53	1	0	0	0	-	-	1	0
1953-54	0	0	0	0	-	-	0	0
1954-55	0	0	0	0	-	-	0	0
1955-56	4	0	0	0	-	-	4	0
1956-57	36	0	3	0	-	-	39	0
1957-58	33	0	5	0	-	-	38	0
1958-59	45	0	1	0	-	-	46	0
1959-60	35	0	1	0	-	-	36	0
1960-61	45	0	7	0	2	0	54	0
1961-62	40	0	2	0	3	0	45	0
1962-63	8	0	1	0	0	0	9	0
1963-64	19	0	5	0	1	0	25	0
1964-65	5	0	0	0	2	0	7	0
	271	0	25	0	8	0	304	0

On leaving the army at the end of World War One, Charlie Flood assisted Plymouth as an amateur, scoring three goals in five games in the season before the Southern League became the Third Division. The Tigers, though, did not wait to see how he fared in the Football League, signing him in August 1920. He occasionally led the attack, but was more at home at inside-forward, forging a fine partnership with Paddy Mills. One five-match spell yielded him six goals, a foretaste of what was to follow. Flood was top scorer in 1921-2 and that marked his most prolific period, for he was equally adept in the traditional inside-forward's role of creating opportunities. In May 1922, his all-too-brief association with City ended with a transfer to Bolton. Early in 1923 he was on the move again, to Nottingham Forest, where he spent three and a half years, his longest spell with one club, all but the last of those years in Division One. In the summer of 1926 he signed for York City, then in the Midland League, and the following year joined Third Division Swindon. They already had two ex-Tigers players in Danny Bew and Sandy Thom. Flood retired in 1928 but continued to play cricket for Hull CC until well after World War Two, as a hard-hitting batsman and reliable wicketkeeper. One of Yorkshire's finest wicketkeepers, Jimmy Binks, benefited from his coaching.

	LEAGUE		*FA CUP*		*TOTAL*	
	App	*Gls*	*App*	*Gls*	*App*	*Gls*
1920-21	14	8	0	0	14	8
1921-22	40	17	2	0	42	17
	54	25	2	0	56	25

CHARLIE FLOOD

ANDY FLOUNDERS

A local striker of considerable promise at schoolboy level, Andy Flounders joined the Tigers from school and worked his way through the junior sides until signing professional in December 1981, at the age of 18. By then Flounders' precocious talent had already earned him a handful of League outings. The first of them came as substitute against Oxford on 4 October 1980. At 16 years and 296 days old, he became the youngest Tiger in League football since the war. As the club struggled to come to terms with Fourth Division football for the first time, the young striker's record as a goalscorer was impressive. Thirteen goals in 23 outings in 1982-3 was the second-highest tally in the side which finished runners-up in the Fourth Division. There was quality as well as quantity, with few better than the strike which clinched three valuable points at Bury in March 1983. In the Third Division, Flounders continued to knock the goals in. As the side returned to the Second Division, 14 was his best haul for the club. By April 1986 that penalty-box sharpness had brought his League tally up to the half-century, but scoring in the Second Division was proving more difficult. In March 1987 he was transferred to Scunthorpe in a £30,000 deal. Back in the Fourth Division the striker hit the goal trail once more. In 1988 he was the Iron's top marksman with 24 goals as United missed promotion in the play-offs.

	LEAGUE		*FACUP*		*FLCUP*		*OTHERS*		*TOTAL*	
	App	*Gls*	*App*	*Gls*	*App*	*Gls*	*App*	*Gls*	*App*	*Gls*
1980-81	3/2	0	0/1	0	0	0	0	0	3/3	0
1981-82	12/1	5	0/1	0	0	0	0	0	12/2	5
1982-83	17/6	13	0	0	1/1	1	0/2	0	18/9	14
1983-84	22/8	9	2	1	0	0	1/2	0	25/10	10
1984-85	34/5	14	3	1	1	1	2	0	40/5	16
1985-86	20/5	10	3	2	1/1	1	1/1	0	25/7	13
1986-87	18/6	3	2/1	0	3	0	2	2	25/7	5
	126/33	54	10/3	4	6/2	3	6/5	22	148/43	63

With 27 England appearances to his credit, Neil Franklin was one of the stars of the immediate post-war period. A centre-half of the highest skill and an unyielding defender, Franklin was further gifted with the ability to organize those around him into a committed and effective unit. He was first associated with Stoke in 1936, but did not make their first team until after the outbreak of war. By the end of the conflict, however, he was an England regular in unofficial internationals and went on to win 27 full caps in peacetime. In the summer of 1949, Franklin refused to re-sign for Stoke. The Tigers were prepared to pay £25-30,000 for the pivot, but with no freedom of contract he had little option but to rejoin the Potters. Twelve months later he departed for Bogota, to coach Santa Fé, which was quite in order even if his club did not like it. However, he was soon playing in Colombian football and returned to find himself in hot water. The FA suspended him for four months, until 31 January 1951. In November the Tigers struck a deal with the Potters and, at the end of his suspension, Franklin signed for a Hull City record £22,500. A long haul back to fitness and form followed, but such was the interest in the international that close on 39,000 watched his debut. The following Saturday the Cup-tied pivot played in the Reserves and visitors Grantham Town found themselves playing before a crowd of 15,042. Sadly, the Tigers did not see the best from Franklin as a series of injuries plagued the defender. In November 1955, Hull agreed to his request for a transfer nearer his Potteries home and the following January he joined Crewe for a £1,250 fee, only raised thanks to a contribution of £500 from their supporters' club. In October 1957 Franklin joined his last League club, Stockport. He played and coached in non-League and in Cyprus, before managing Colchester for four and a half years.

NEIL FRANKLIN

	LEAGUE		*FA CUP*		*TOTAL*	
	App	*Gls*	*App*	*Gls*	*App*	*Gls*
1950-51	14	0	0	0	14	0
1951-52	13	0	0	0	13	0
1952-53	8	0	0	0	8	0
1953-54	15	0	1	0	16	0
1954-55	38	0	0	0	38	0
1955-56	7	0	0	0	7	0
	95	0	1	0	96	0

Brian Garvey was another of the local lads who made good in the 1950s. His association with the club began as a 16-year-old at the start of the 1953-4 season. He broke through into the League side in March 1958, deputizing for Paul Feasey, but his next call was to play at left-half, where he settled to enjoy the Tigers' elevation to the Second Division. In the following ill-fated campaign Garvey's versatility was increasingly recognized, at left-half, centre-half and left-back. As Cliff Britton began to transform the Tigers into a promotion-seeking side, Garvey's participation was increasingly limited. In the summer of 1966 he was allowed to move to Watford after making over 250 first-team appearances for Hull City. At Vicarage Road, Garvey was a regular in the side which won the Third Division in 1969. After one season of Second Division football, Garvey, now 32, joined Fourth Division Colchester, where he completed his League career 11 appearances short of the 500 mark. He took over as player-coach at Bedford Town, later assisting Wolves and Arsenal in a coaching capacity.

BRIAN GARVEY

	LEAGUE		*FA CUP*		*FL CUP*		*TOTAL*	
	App	*Gls*	*App*	*Gls*	*App*	*Gls*	*App*	*Gls*
1957-58	1	0	0	0	-	-	1	0
1958-59	34	1	1	0	-	-	35	1
1959-60	40	0	1	0	-	-	41	0
1960-61	43	0	7	0	2	0	52	0
1961-62	34	0	1	0	2	0	37	0
1962-63	40	0	4	0	4	0	48	0
1963-64	26	2	3	0	0	0	29	2
1964-65	14	0	0	0	1	0	15	0
	232	3	17	0	9	0	258	3

In the summer of 1950, Dundee's signing of Derby's Billy Steel for a Scottish record fee of £23,000 meant they were prepared to allow Syd Gerrie to move to Boothferry Park, for a more modest £11,000 in November. The previous season Gerrie topped the Dens Park scorers with 13 goals in 25 League outings, but after the arrival of Steel he turned out only five times. At 23 he looked a sound investment for a Tigers side setting its sights on the First Division. The burly striker could certainly use his solid 12-stone frame to good effect as a powerful attacking partner for Ackerman and Carter. When Carter departed, the attack struggled, despite Gerrie's attempts to infuse life into it. His personal tally of 24 League goals was a post-war best, but was overshadowed by the spectre of relegation. In the seasons of struggle which followed, Gerrie's goals were invaluable to his side's survival. Injury in the opening match of 1954-5 marked a downturn in his fortunes. He missed three-quarters of the season, put in for a transfer and at one stage might have gone to Shrewsbury but for a dislike of its southerly location. A knee injury forced him to miss an even greater part of 1955-6. The knee gave way again in November 1956 and the following summer Gerrie was forced to quit. He returned to Scotland and, after being in settled employment for a decade, returned to the professional game in January 1968 as manager of Brechin City, whom, for 14 months, he endeavoured to lift from the lower reaches of the Scottish League.

SYD GERRIE

	LEAGUE		*FA CUP*		*TOTAL*	
	App	*Gls*	*App*	*Gls*	*App*	*Gls*
1950-51	23	11	2	1	25	12
1951-52	38	24	2	1	40	25
1952-53	35	13	2	1	37	14
1953-54	23	6	0	0	23	6
1954-55	11	3	0	0	11	3
1955-56	7	1	0	0	7	1
1956-57	9	1	0	0	9	1
	146	59	6	3	152	62

If the Tigers were favoured by having the services of George Maddison in goal, they were doubly favoured during the six seasons when Fred Gibson and Maddison contended for the position. Few clubs can have enjoyed such strength in depth in that position over such a long period. The one brought the best out of the other. Gibson, of course, was not endowed with the same cavalier style as Maddison and yet his qualities were many. He was technically highly competent, his bravery was unquestionable and his agility outstanding for a man of his size. He was 6ft 2in tall and weighed over 13st and was as strong as one would expect of a former miner at Dinnington Colliery. It was from the Dinnington club that Bill McCracken signed Gibson, in August 1926. He had previously assisted two other notable non-League clubs in mining communities, Frickley and Denaby. Gibson had to wait over a year before making his League debut and then had only half a dozen outings while Maddison recovered from injury. By 1929, however, Gibson retained the goalkeeping spot on merit and it was his heroics, particularly against Manchester City and Newcastle, which ensured the Tigers' progress to the Cup semi-finals. Newcastle forward Hughie Gallacher described him after the quarter-final as 'a superman'. Eventually, in November 1932, Gibson left Anlaby Road for Middlesbrough, making over 100 League appearances there. In May 1937 he moved to Bradford City and before the outbreak of war was assisting Midland Leaguers, Boston United.

FRED GIBSON

	LEAGUE		*FA CUP*		*TOTAL*	
	App	*Gls*	*App*	*Gls*	*App*	*Gls*
1927-28	6	0	0	0	6	0
1928-29	8	0	0	0	8	0
1929-30	28	0	7	0	35	0
1930-31	18	0	1	0	19	0
1931-32	34	0	1	0	35	0
1932-33	7	0	0	0	7	0
	101	0	9	0	110	0

Full-back Jock Gibson was one of the integral members of the Tigers' defence of the 1920s and his partnership with Matt Bell one of the highlights of the inter-war period. The understanding between these two was remarkable, especially when it came to working the offside trap. (With Bill McCracken in charge, one could hardly expect his protégés to do otherwise.) Gibson was born in the United States, but settled in Scotland with his family when he was two years old. He was spotted in Scottish junior soccer by Sunderland and signed for them in 1920. He made only four League appearances in two seasons on Wearside but, on moving to Anlaby Road in March 1922, his career soon blossomed. He made his League debut at Bury in August 1922 and had a torrid opening half-hour, later recalling that he never touched the ball once in that spell. By the time McCracken took over the reins, Gibson was first-choice at right-back and it stayed that way until November 1926, when an injury at Darlington kept him out of the side for four months. Prior to that accident, the City defence had conceded only 11 goals in 17 Second Division matches and that after the offside law had been altered to make scoring easier. When the revised law came into operation 12 months earlier, Gibson, Bell and Maddison had played through the first five matches of the season without City letting in a single goal. In the opening months of 1929, as a City promotion bid petered out, the club came under renewed financial pressure. In March, Gibson was transferred to Sheffield United for a sizeable £5,000 fee. He was still playing First Division soccer at the age of 34, but in the summer of 1933 he left Bramall Lane for a final season of League football with Luton before retiring.

JOCK GIBSON

	LEAGUE		*FA CUP*		*TOTAL*	
	App	*Gls*	*App*	*Gls*	*App*	*Gls*
1922-23	30	0	1	0	31	0
1923-24	24	0	2	0	26	0
1924-25	31	0	4	0	35	0
1925-26	35	0	0	0	35	0
1926-27	21	0	0	0	21	0
1927-28	41	0	1	0	42	0
1928-29	28	0	0	0	28	0
	210	0	8	0	218	0

Mike Gilhooley was the central figure in the Tigers' powerful half-back line of the early inter-war period, the outstanding trio of Collier, Gilhooley and Bleakley. The Scot was a club record signing when David Menzies brought him south of the border in July 1920. It was said that the Tigers paid Clydebank up to £2,500 but, whatever the actual sum, it was money well spent, for only on four occasions during his stay at Anlaby Road did a City defence with Gilhooley as its pivot concede more than three goals. The Scot was so powerful in the air that he earned the nickname 'Rubberneck'. Yet there was much more than aerial dominance to the man whom Celtic signed as a professional at the age of 16, for he could shackle the most dangerous of centre-forwards and, with Collier and Bleakley alongside, found a ready outlet for constructive counter-attack. In February 1922, Gilhooley made his debut for Scotland. It was not altogether surprising to find him on the move the following month. Sunderland, as part of a colossal £13,000 spending spree, paid out over £5,000 for the City pivot. By 1925, however, he was back at Anlaby Road, opposing his former team in the colours of Bradford City. A serious knee injury had curtailed his chances in the top flight and in 1927 he moved to Queen's Park Rangers, for what, at 32, was to be his final season of League football.

	LEAGUE		*FA CUP*		*TOTAL*	
	App	*Gls*	*App*	*Gls*	*App*	*Gls*
1920-21	38	0	5	0	43	0
1921-22	27	1	2	0	29	1
	65	1	7	0	72	1

MIKE GILHOOLEY

George Goldsmith arrived at Anlaby Road from Loftus Albion in December 1928 as a promising 23-year-old full-back, who had also assisted Bishop Auckland. Both sides figured in the highly competitive Northern League. Three months after Goldsmith joined the Tigers, Jock Gibson departed for Sheffield United. The move went through partly because Bill McCracken knew that in the Yorkshireman he had an ideal replacement. Goldsmith was fast, strong in the tackle, effective in his clearances and quick to master the mechanics of City's offside game. After Matt Bell's departure he struck up a new partnership with Cliff Woodhead, which endured through the Northern Section championship win and into the Second Division. Goldsmith took a richly-deserved benefit in 1934, the reward for five years' service with one club, but less than two months later found himself transferred to Tottenham. Goldsmith's stay at White Hart Lane lasted only until March 1935. Having played only one League game for Spurs, he was sold to Bolton, heading for the First Division themselves. The defender's return to the top flight proved a better experience than the one he had endured with the Londoners.

	LEAGUE		*FA CUP*		*TOTAL*	
	App	*Gls*	*App*	*Gls*	*App*	*Gls*
1928-29	5	0	2	0	7	0
1929-30	36	0	7	0	43	0
1930-31	37	0	1	0	38	0
1931-32	19	0	1	0	20	0
1932-33	35	0	4	0	39	0
1933-34	40	0	3	0	43	0
	172	0	18	0	190	0

GEORGE GOLDSMITH

Davy Gordon was one of the quality signings made by Ambrose Langley in the summer of 1905. The Scot was signed from Leith Athletic. He was a wing-half, a left-sided player by inclination, but capable of adapting to the other flank when the situation demanded. He came to Hull with a reputation for being a keen tackler and persistent harrier. The truth of that assertion was borne out with remarkable consistency over the next nine seasons. But to sum up Davy Gordon as the ball-winner *par excellence* is to tell only half the story. Once he had the leather, he was equally talented in instigating counter-attacks. His tendency for pushing forward brought him a useful tally of goals. In those early seasons, Langley would move Gordon to inside-left to add power to the attack — and even tried him at centre-forward. In the FA Cup tie at Arsenal in 1908, he retired from the fray nursing a broken collarbone, which kept him out for the rest of the term. Gordon, whose 274 League appearances were a club record, helped the Tigers graduate from League newcomers to challengers for the First Division on several occasions. In the absence of Gordon Wright, he skippered the side which failed so narrowly in 1910. Towards the close of his days at Anlaby Road, he assisted with training, a useful preparation for his return to Leith in 1914 as player-manager. In his first term in charge, Leith finished in a rare three-way tie at the top of the Scottish Second Division. After the war, Gordon had spells in charge of Hibernian, Hartlepools and St Bernard's.

DAVY GORDON

	LEAGUE		*FA CUP*		*OTHERS*		*TOTAL*	
	App	*Gls*	*App*	*Gls*	*App*	*Gls*	*App*	*Gls*
1905-06	37	11	5	0	0	0	42	11
1906-07	37	1	3	0	0	0	40	1
1907-08	23	0	1	0	0	0	24	0
1908-09	36	3	2	0	0	0	38	3
1909-10	36	0	1	0	0	0	37	0
1910-11	32	2	4	0	0	0	36	2
1911-12	30	0	2	0	0	0	32	0
1912-13	29	0	3	0	0	0	32	0
1913-14	14	0	0	0	2	0	16	0
	274	17	21	0	2	0	297	17

'The Ards pocket marvel' was how the *Athletic News* summed up Bill Gowdy, the half-back signed by Bill McCracken in the summer of 1929. Gowdy was short, stocky, a gritty, determined player. Today's comment-ators would praise his high work-rate. Yet, such was the Tigers' strength at wing-half, it was not until the departure of Sam Weaver that he claimed a regular place. When the season ended in relegation, Gowdy battled through a year in the Northern Section. He was rewarded in September 1931 with a place in the Northern Ireland team against Scotland but then, paradoxically, lost his place at club level. Shortly before Christmas, he was transferred to Sheffield Wednesday. The Owls were high in Division One and Gowdy made their League side only once. In 1932-3 he signed for Gateshead but was on the move again that summer, returning home to assist Linfield. The Belfast side were Irish League champions during his two seasons there and he enjoyed a recall to the national side. By December 1935 he was in Hibs' colours before making a surprise return to Yorkshire with Goole Town. Altrincham and Aldershot benefited from his skills and he guested for the Tigers during the war, remaining in Hull after the conflict to achieve further sporting success as a greyhound owner.

	LEAGUE		*FA CUP*		*OTHERS*		*TOTAL*	
	App	*Gls*	*App*	*Gls*	*App*	*Gls*	*App*	*Gls*
1929-30	25	0	7	0	0	0	32	0
1930-31	33	1	1	0	0	0	34	1
1931-32	7	0	0	0	0	0	7	0
1940-41	-	-	-	-	3	0	3	0
	65	1	8	0	3	0	76	1

BILL GOWDY

Jimmy Greenhalgh is best remembered as a highly-effective right-half in the 1949 side which won the Northern Section and reached the Cup quarter-finals. He missed only one match, kept out by an ankle injury, a legacy of the Cup success at Stoke, where his goal clinched victory. Greenhalgh was at the heart of the side's quest for the top flight but, as the promotion bid lost momentum, both Don Revie and Viggo Jensen had a turn at right-half and Greenhalgh found himself tried at centre-forward in the Reserves. Not since his early days at Boothferry Park, under Frank Buckley, had he been switched around like that. The Major had signed the Mancunian from Newton Heath Loco in August 1946 and it was to Lancashire that Greenhalgh returned, joining Bury in November 1950 in a £12,000 deal. The half-back was a regular in the Shakers' line-up until 1954-5, when stepping down to join Lancashire Combination Wigan Athletic. Twelve months later Gillingham brought Greenhalgh back into League soccer but, after one more season, he gave up playing to concentrate on what was to be a lengthy involvement with the coaching and managerial side of the game. He trained Lincoln, but saw them twice relegated and moved to Newcastle to enjoy the Magpies' Second Division championship triumph in 1965. A year later he took over as manager of Darlington, but returned to coaching with Middlesbrough, finally becoming Sunderland's chief scout.

JIMMY GREENHALGH

	LEAGUE		*FA CUP*		*TOTAL*	
	App	*Gls*	*App*	*Gls*	*App*	*Gls*
1946-47	41	1	5	0	46	1
1947-48	27	0	4	0	31	0
1948-49	41	3	7	1	48	4
1949-50	32	1	3	1	35	2
1950-51	7	0	0	0	7	0
	148	5	19	2	167	7

PAUL HAIGH

	LEAGUE		*FA CUP*		*FL CUP*		*OTHERS*		*TOTAL*	
	App	*Gls*	*App*	*Gls*	*App*	*Gls*	*App*	*Gls*	*App*	*Gls*
1974-75	1	0	0	0	0	0	0	0	1	0
1975-76	7	0	0	0	1	0	0	0	8	0
1976-77	42	2	2	0	1	0	3	0	48	2
1977-78	38	1	1	0	4	1	3	0	46	2
1978-79	45	1	2	0	3	1	0	0	50	2
1979-80	28/1	2	2	1	2	0	0	0	32/1	3
1980-81	18	2	0	0	2	0	3	1	23	3
	179/1	8	7	1	13	2	9	1	208/1	12

A great prospect as a youngster, Paul Haigh joined the Tigers as an apprentice on leaving Hessle High School in 1974. He had already assisted Leeds United's nursery side, Pudsey Juniors, and the locally-renowned Schultz Youth Club. His promise was confirmed with a League debut at the end of the 1974-5 season, a couple of weeks before his 17th birthday. Further success was in store with a place in the England Under-21 squad, culminating in June 1977 with a cap as substitute against Norway. Not only was there quality in Haigh's performances, but also versatility. He could link elegantly in midfield, defend effectively at full-back and was even tried as a striker on occasion. But Haigh's preferred position was as a central defender, where he turned in many a commanding display. It was his inclination for this role which led Haigh to seek a move in the summer of 1980. That November, Bob Stokoe, impressed by the Scarborough man's performance against his Carlisle side, had a £100,000 offer accepted. The move to Brunton Park brought a reunion with ex-Tiger Gordon Staniforth and in 1982 the pair helped Carlisle win promotion to the Second Division. Haigh was a regular in the Cumbrians' line-up for six and a half seasons and towards the end of that period his total of League appearances passed the 400 mark. In the summer of 1987 Haigh was released by Carlisle and joined Hartlepool.

BILL HARRIS

In March 1950, Raich Carter paid Llanelli £1,000 for their right winger Bill Harris. There was a clause in the deal which stipulated that the Welsh club would receive an extra £250 if Harris won full international honours. This might have seemed unlikely, for Harris had already had one spell on Swansea's books. The Welshman made his debut on the wing in the closing games of 1949-50, but Carter saw possibilities for the player as a wing-half. He was recalled in his new position the following November and did so well that, three months later, he was reserve for Wales. That extra payment was not such an unrealistic proposition, although it was another three years before Harris won the first of his six caps and, by then, he had left Boothferry Park. It was hardly surprising in the midst of City's struggles in the Second Division that the scouts should be drawn to the Welshman, whose winger's pace and trickery blended with the half-back's ability to spot the vulnerable point in an opposition defence and exploit it with a forward run or defence-splitting pass, not forgetting a thunderbolt of a shot. Harris once crashed one in against Oldham from 35 yards. Rumour flourished and Harris was keen to play in the First Division. In March 1954, Middlesbrough persuaded City to part with him for £15,000, although the signing did not prevent 'Boro dropping into the Second Division. Harris remained at Ayresome Park until March 1965, clocking up 359 League appearances for the Teessiders. On leaving Middlesbrough, he spent 12 difficult months in charge of Bradford City. He returned to the North-East and coached Stockton for a spell.

	LEAGUE		*FA CUP*		*TOTAL*	
	App	*Gls*	*App*	*Gls*	*App*	*Gls*
1949-50	2	0	0	0	2	0
1950-51	22	0	3	0	25	0
1951-52	38	2	2	0	40	2
1952-53	40	2	2	1	42	3
1953-54	29	2	7	0	36	2
	131	6	14	1	145	7

Ken Harrison was one of the promising young players recruited by Major Buckley in his first season at Boothferry Park. Signed from Billingham in April 1947, he made his debut at inside-left towards the close of that protracted campaign. He was switched to the wing and from right to left, with a rapidity which scarcely helped his development. Not until the arrival of Raich Carter did Harrison settle down on the right wing, deriving immense benefit from playing alongside the maestro. He was an ever-present in the 1949 side which carried all before it in the Northern Section and he missed only one League outing in the next two seasons. Harrison was always prepared to strike for goal, netting over 50 times during his eight years at Boothferry Park. One of the most important was at Accrington in September 1948. It clinched the victory which set a new League record of nine successive wins at the start of a season. There were others, too, such as the one which helped dump Manchester United out of the FA Cup in 1952. It was in that competition that Harrison experienced his worst moment as a City player. After three minutes of the tie against Spurs in 1954, he collided with George Robb and was stretchered off with a shattered kneecap. Twelve months later he left, along with Alf Ackerman, for Derby but, after a season with the Rams, joined Goole Town. The signing was part of an ambitious recruiting drive by former Tigers' coach George Lax. That season, Town had their best-ever run in the FA Cup, reaching the third round for the only time in their history, a fine highlight at the conclusion of Harrison's career.

KEN HARRISON

	LEAGUE		*FA CUP*		*TOTAL*	
	App	*Gls*	*App*	*Gls*	*App*	*Gls*
1946-47	2	0	0	0	2	0
1947-48	20	2	2	0	22	2
1948-49	42	12	7	0	49	12
1949-50	41	9	4	1	45	10
1950-51	42	12	3	1	45	13
1951-52	32	5	1	1	33	6
1952-53	17	3	1	0	18	3
1953-54	26	4	6	1	32	5
1954-55	16	0	1	0	17	0
	238	47	25	4	263	51

John Hawley came to prominence in local soccer, playing for the Hull Boys and East Riding representative sides. In April 1970 he signed amateur forms for the Tigers and began to work his way through the ranks, making his League debut in April 1973, playing up front alongside Stuart Pearson. He remained an amateur until August 1976, preferring his father's antiques business until convinced he could make the grade as a professional. A growing confidence and skill made Hawley a forceful striker, although the bare statistical analysis of 22 goals in 114 Second Division outings fails to reflect his performances adequately amidst the paucity of the side's attacking resources at the time. There was never any question about Hawley's commitment. His fearlessness once cost him a punctured lung and three broken ribs in a collision with Bolton goalkeeper Jim McDonagh. Relegation hastened his departure, with an £80,000 move to Elland Road. Hawley adapted well in the top flight and it prompted Sunderland to pay £200,000 for the Withernsea man's skills in October 1979. His next move, to Arsenal in September 1981, brought a reunion with former boss Terry Neill and towards the end of a two-year stay at Highbury, Hawley returned to Boothferry Park on a month's loan, following a similar spell at Orient. Sentimental hopes of a permanent deal did not materialize and he eventually signed for Bradford City. At the age of 30, he was finally a member of a winning side as the Valley Paraders captured the Third Division title. Hawley concluded his career with a season at Scunthorpe.

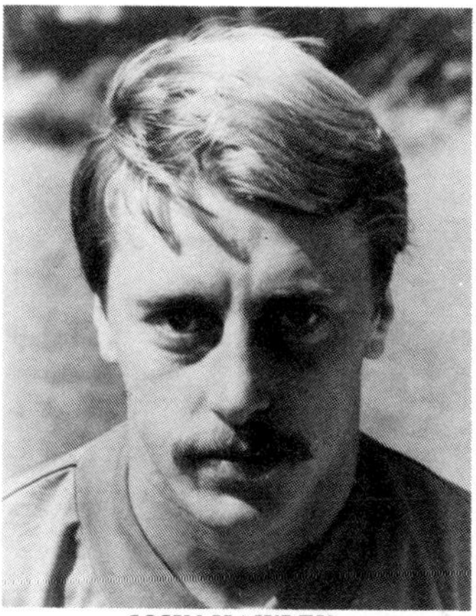

JOHN HAWLEY

	LEAGUE		*FA CUP*		*FL CUP*		*OTHERS*		*TOTAL*	
	App	*Gls*	*App*	*Gls*	*App*	*Gls*	*App*	*Gls*	*App*	*Gls*
1972-73	2	0	0	0	0	0	1	0	3	0
1973-74	17/2	3	0	0	5	0	0	0	22/2	3
1974-75	31	7	0	0	1	0	0	0	32	7
1975-76	17/5	3	3	1	2	1	0	0	22/5	5
1976-77	14/4	5	1	0	1	0	3	0	19/4	5
1977-78	20/2	4	1	0	1/1	1	1/2	0	23/5	5
1982-83	3	1	0	0	0	0	0	0	3	1
	104/13	23	5	1	10/1	2	5/2	0	124/16	26

Ray Henderson was Cliff Britton's first signing for Hull City. A Tynesider, Henderson assisted a number of local outfits before Middlesbrough signed him from North-Eastern League Ashington. It took time for Henderson to adapt to the Second Division, but a record of four goals in seven games in 1960-61 indicated the potential which prompted the Tigers to sign him. Initially used as an inside-left, Henderson was soon demonstrating admirable versatility. Within two seasons he had occupied every position in the City front rank apart from the left wing. Wherever he operated, he always produced the same unstinting effort. Not a prolific scorer, his only hat-trick came on that memorable night in October 1964 when he and Chris Chilton eclipsed Barnsley under the Tigers' new floodlights. Henderson eventually settled to the right-wing berth after the retirement of John McSeveney. Paradoxically, it was a move which brought his best tally of goals, in the 1965-6 Third Division championship win. His role became an increasingly deep-lying one, which did not go down well with a Boothferry Park crowd used to all-out attacking. In the summer of 1967 Henderson obtained his coaching qualification and was persuaded to become assistant to the club's new coach, George Curtis. However, by November, he was pulling on the number-seven shirt again to help the side through a difficult season. In October 1968 he left Boothferry Park to become Reading's player-coach, before taking over as manager of Halifax in August 1971. He was at The Shay for less than 12 months and subsequently held a coaching position at Everton. He was manager of Southport during their penultimate season in the Football League.

RAY HENDERSON

	LEAGUE		*FA CUP*		*FL CUP*		*TOTAL*	
	App	*Gls*	*App*	*Gls*	*App*	*Gls*	*App*	*Gls*
1961-62	28	8	2	1	1	0	31	9
1962-63	31	10	4	2	4	0	39	12
1963-64	43	9	5	2	2	1	50	12
1964-65	25	6	1	0	2	0	28	6
1965-66	38/1	13	7	1	2	0	47/1	14
1966-67	39/1	4	3	0	1	0	43/1	4
1967-68	22/1	4	0/1	0	0	0	22/2	4
	226/3	54	22/1	6	12	1	260/4	61

Nick Hendry had to wait a long time for his chance to capture the Tigers goalkeeping spot. Ambrose Langley signed him from Darlington in April 1910, but it was not until March 1912 that Hendry made his League debut. From the start of the following season, though, he made the position his own, with a run of 97 consecutive Second Division outings. At times his performances were quite brilliant. He was occasionally referred to as the human octopus. After City had knocked West Brom out of the Cup in January 1915 the First Division side's centre-forward, H.G.Bache, said afterwards: "I have never seen finer goalkeeping than Hendry displayed today. He was really uncanny in his exposition and simply refused to be beaten." The war which followed took away four of Hendry's best years. He was employed as a munitions worker in his home town of York and was still able to play for the Tigers. However, on occasion he failed to arrive and half-back Joe Edelston gained quite a reputation as Hendry's stand-in. After the war Hendry continued to be first-choice for half a season, but his place was under threat from Billy Mercer. He spent the 1920-21 season in the Reserves and was then allowed to move, concluding his career back home with York City. By the time the Minstermen rejoined the Midland League, in 1922, Hendry had taken on the additional responsibility of management.

	LEAGUE		*FA CUP*		*OTHERS*		*TOTAL*	
	App	*Gls*	*App*	*Gls*	*App*	*Gls*	*App*	*Gls*
1911-12	2	0	0	0	0	0	2	0
1912-13	38	0	3	0	0	0	41	0
1913-14	38	0	2	0	3	0	43	0
1914-15	37	0	5	0	2	0	44	0
1915-16	0	0	0	0	26	0	26	0
1916-17	0	0	0	0	34	0	34	0
1917-18	0	0	0	0	25	0	25	0
1918-19	0	0	0	0	30	0	30	0
1919-20	25	0	1	0	0	0	26	0
	140	0	11	0	120	0	271	0

When Cliff Britton finally captured the signature of Ken Houghton, it meant the end of a near two-year quest. In January 1965 the signings, within a week, of Houghton and teammate Ian Butler rewarded the manager's patience and persistence. In Houghton he acquired a superb midfield general, the ideal man to harness the skills of Chilton, Wagstaff and Butler into a forward line far above Third Division standard and which would probably have carried the Tigers through to the First Division, given a rearguard of similar effectiveness. Houghton joined Rotherham United in May 1960 from Silverwood Colliery and soon established himself as a regular first-teamer. In four and a half seasons he netted an impressive 56 goals in 148 Second Division games and played in the inaugural League Cup Final. He continued to be a ready scorer at Boothferry Park, with a powerful left foot which rifled in spectacular long-range goals. Some of his goals were key efforts, such as the shot which put Southampton out of the FA Cup in 1966, or the chip which put West Ham out of the same competition in 1973. During the summer of 1973, Houghton moved across to Scunthorpe United. Only six players had scored more goals for the Tigers. After one season at the Old Show Ground, Houghton took over as Scarborough's player-coach, going to Wembley the following May for the FA Trophy Final, along with ex-Tigers Ray Pettit, Ian Davidson and Jeff Barmby. In the close season of 1975 he was replaced by Colin Appleton at Seamer Road, but was soon snapped up as player-coach to Bridlington Town. In 1976, Houghton returned to Boothferry Park as youth coach, eventually taking over as team manager.

KEN HOUGHTON

	LEAGUE		*FA CUP*		*FL CUP*		*OTHERS*		*TOTAL*	
	App	*Gls*	*App*	*Gls*	*App*	*Gls*	*App*	*Gls*	*App*	*Gls*
1964-65	15	5	0	0	0	0	0	0	15	5
1965-66	45	22	7	3	2	2	0	0	54	27
1966-67	20	9	3	2	1	0	0	0	24	11
1967-68	30/1	7	3	0	1	0	0	0	34/1	7
1968-69	22/1	6	1	0	1/1	0	0	0	24/2	6
1969-70	41	16	1	0	2	0	0	0	44	16
1970-71	34/3	7	3/1	2	1	0	2	0	40/4	9
1971-72	19/1	0	0	0	1	0	0	0	20/1	0
1972-73	27/5	7	4	2	1/1	0	3	1	35/6	10
	253/11	79	22/1	9	10/2	2	5	1	290/14	91

The Tigers entered March 1927 in third place in the Second Division. With the intention of adding the final and decisive edge to the team's challenge, the management splashed out a club record fee to sign St Mirren's Jimmy Howieson. There were reports that the fee was as high as £4,000, but a sum of £3,200 is probably nearer the mark. At 26, Howieson had never played in the Football League. Days before signing he had been capped for Scotland against Ireland and, the previous season, had helped St Mirren win the Scottish Cup. Howieson had already gained a reputation as a 'wanderer', having assisted St Johnstone and Dundee United after entering senior soccer with Airdrie in 1921. As an inside-left he was a highly-gifted player with no end of trickery as a dribbler, great vision, a strong shot and a touch of genius in pulling off the unexpected and unorthodox. Genius, though, is seldom without flaw. The Tigers missed out on promotion and never recaptured the momentum the following season. At its end Howieson promptly took himself off to the United States, one of the few British players to make a success of soccer on the other side of the Atlantic between the wars, playing for New Bedford and New York Giants. By the summer of 1929 wanderlust set in again. Howieson returned to Anlaby Road to play an important part in the 1930 Cup run, clearly revelling in the big occasion. Relegation induced him to move again and, despite offers to return to America, he joined Shelbourne. To the Tigers' chagrin there was no transfer agreement with clubs in the Republic of Ireland in those days and they recovered nothing of their large outlay until the 'rolling stone' joined Clyde in September 1932. A brief spell at Alloa and a further stay in Ireland, with Glenavon, concluded the Scot's senior career.

JIMMY HOWIESON

	LEAGUE		*FA CUP*		*TOTAL*	
	App	*Gls*	*App*	*Gls*	*App*	*Gls*
1926-27	12	3	0	0	12	3
1927-28	27	4	1	0	28	4
1929-30	28	5	6	2	34	7
	67	12	7	2	74	14

Scunthorpe's Cliff Hubbard came to the Tigers' attention with his destruction of their Reserve team over Easter 1933. In the two Midland League fixtures, the Iron's attack, spearheaded by the 22-year-old Worsop lad, crashed nine goals past the City defence. The Anlaby Road club signed Hubbard in the course of the summer and the new season was only a week old when the striker was promoted to the first team, deputizing for Andy Duncan. His pace soon prompted a trial on the right wing, the problem position in the Tigers forward line. He demonstrated his versatility still further with a handful of games at centre-forward. In 1934-5, as the side struggled to recover from a bad start, Hubbard found it harder to produce his best amidst such frequent positional switches. Occasionally he even found himself on the left wing. The step down to the Northern Section in 1936 enabled Hubbard to recover his confidence and make his mark as a goal-scorer. He headed the Tigers' marksmen in 1936-7 and hit a personal best of 19 goals two seasons later. Such form persuaded West Ham to lay out £3,000 for his talents. They had little benefit, though, for after a promising start — two goals in three games — football was halted for the war. It was not until 1944-5 that the Hammers had Hubbard in their side again. He also assisted the Tigers as a guest that season. After the war Hubbard returned north, assisting Newark works side, Ransome & Marles, and Goole Town before concluding his playing days with Worksop Town. There he was appointed coach until the illness which brought about his premature demise in 1962.

CLIFF HUBBARD

	LEAGUE		*FA CUP*		*OTHERS*		*TOTAL*	
	App	*Gls*	*App*	*Gls*	*App*	*Gls*	*App*	*Gls*
1933-34	34	3	3	1	0	0	37	4
1934-35	17	4	1	0	0	0	18	4
1935-36	29	4	1	0	0	0	30	4
1936-37	32	15	1	1	1	1	34	17
1937-38	31	11	3	1	1	0	35	12
1938-39	40	19	3	2	0	0	43	21
1944-45	-	-	-	-	6	0	6	0
	183	56	12	5	8	1	203	62

One of the few good things, from the Tigers' angle, which came out of World War One was the stationing near Hull of Northampton Town's Bobby Hughes during the summer of 1917. He was able to guest for City, on the left wing, and spent the season locked in a personal scoring duel with David Mercer. Hughes netted a career best of 25 goals but lost out by a single strike to his colleague. At the end of the war quite a tussle ensued for Hughes's services. He was keen to remain in Hull, but only when the Tigers offered a club record fee, approaching £1,000, did Town agree to part. Hughes was not just a winger with a flare for scoring goals. He had all the attributes of a class outside man — pace, trickery and a telling cross — and could perform equally well on either flank. When the Second Division resumed in 1919, he and Mercer spent a large portion of the season operating together on the right. The following term a recurrence of an old leg injury necessitated surgery. Then, after only a handful of games, the unlucky winger damaged a cartilage. It was over four months before he was back in the side. In the close season of 1922 Hughes left the Tigers for Sheffield United, to be reunited with Mercer, but stayed only briefly in the top flight, moving to Brentford the following summer. Four seasons at Rochdale followed, where Hughes notched a useful 49 goals. He ended his career at Wigan, retiring on a high note as joint leading scorer for 'Boro and became one of an élite group of wingers to score over 100 senior goals.

BOBBY HUGHES

	LEAGUE		*FA CUP*		*OTHERS*		*TOTAL*	
	App	*Gls*	*App*	*Gls*	*App*	*Gls*	*App*	*Gls*
1917-18	0	0	0	0	32	25	32	25
1918-19	0	0	0	0	30	6	30	6
1919-20	27	3	1	0	0	0	28	3
1920-21	12	1	0	0	0	0	12	1
1921-22	27	5	2	0	0	0	29	5
	66	9	3	0	62	31	131	40

VIGGO JENSEN

	LEAGUE		*FA CUP*		*TOTAL*	
	App	*Gls*	*App*	*Gls*	*App*	*Gls*
1948-49	27	14	7	1	34	15
1949-50	36	12	3	0	39	12
1950-51	35	0	3	0	38	0
1951-52	42	1	2	0	44	1
1952-53	42	9	2	1	44	10
1953-54	38	6	7	1	45	7
1954-55	35	4	1	0	36	4
1955-56	35	3	2	0	37	3
1956-57	18	2	0	0	18	2
	308	51	27	3	335	54

Around 9.30am on Monday, 25 October 1948, the SS *Alexandra* docked at Grimsby. Amongst the passengers was a 27-year-old Dane called Viggo Jensen. Jensen was a representative for the Danish fishing industry, but the following day he was at Boothferry Park, signing for the Tigers as an amateur (in those days a two-year residence qualification was necessary for a foreigner to sign professional). Jensen had already accumulated over 250 appearances for his Danish club, Esbjerg EfB, and had represented his country 15 times, as well as playing in the 1948 Olympic Finals in London, where the first tentative negotiations had taken place. Whilst reports of Jensen's versatility had preceded him to Hull, there was mild surprise when he remained at inside-right through his first season with the Tigers. Many had predicted a more defensive role but, with 14 goals in 27 League outings, the Dane decisively vindicated his manager's judgement. The following season he set a new club record by scoring in seven consecutive Second Division games. It was the kind of consistency which was the hallmark of his entire career. Jensen was a superbly fit athlete, with a technique and commitment to match. It marked him out as one of the great players in the Tigers history. Before 1949 was out he had played inside-forward, wing-half, full-back and centre-forward. With advancing years, Jensen eventually settled at left-back, a shining light amidst the growing gloom at Boothferry Park. In September 1956 the 35-year-old played his 300th League game. A couple of months later Jensen was on his way back to Denmark, after, in his words: "eight wonderful years." Back home he was soon involved in coaching his old club and steered them through a lengthy unbeaten run.

There was a night of high nostalgia at Boothferry Park on 8 April 1970. Reminiscences flowed as a galaxy of former Tigers met, together with a near 9,000 crowd, to pay tribute to Jimmy Lodge's half-century of service to Hull City. For the celebrity of the evening it was a rare break from his usual routine as masseur. He first came to Hull in January 1920, one of three triallists from the Tyneside club, Newburn. Terms were offered only to the full-back called 'Barrass' and before the month was out the newcomer had made his League debut. He gave a sound enough performance to hold his place for the rest of the season. At the end of his second term at Anlaby Road came the revelation that 'Barrass' was the alias of Jimmy Lodge. Lodge partnered Matt Bell until the arrival of Jock Gibson. Despite increasingly limited first-team opportunities, Lodge remained at Anlaby Road until the summer of 1924, when he moved to Halifax. After a season at the Shay, the full-back, whose fleetest days, at 30, were behind him, had non-League spells with York City and Nuneaton during 1925-6. However, in August he was back in Hull as assistant trainer to Joe Beck. In that capacity he remained with the club until the war. He was retained after reconstruction, too, as number-two to George Lax, and when coaching began to develop its modern-day tactical complexity, Lodge turned to specialize in the treatment of injuries. Many a Tiger over the years had cause to thank those healing hands for being able to take his place in the side on a match-day.

JIMMY LODGE

	LEAGUE		*FA CUP*		*TOTAL*	
	App	*Gls*	*App*	*Gls*	*App*	*Gls*
1919-20	17	0	0	0	17	0
1920-21	18	0	0	0	18	0
1921-22	27	0	2	0	29	0
1922-23	15	0	0	0	15	0
1923-24	4	0	0	0	4	0
	81	0	2	0	83	0

In 1974 Malcolm Lord was voted the supporters' Player of the Year. It represented a remarkable triumph for a player whose career had been marred by criticism from the terraces, most of it apparently for no better reason than the fact that he played much of his early first-team soccer in the number-seven shirt and seemed to inherit the antagonism his predecessors had suffered for not playing an othodox wing role. Malcolm Lord was a midfield player. By his professional approach he overcame the early handicap and was impressive in his contribution to the side. His work-rate was tremendous and his technique better than sound. His record as a goalscorer culminated in a hat-trick against Burnley in 1977. A Beverley Grammar School product, Lord came to Boothferry Park in August 1964, after success in the English Grammar Schools side, but it was not until 1967 that he finally made the first team. During 1969-70 he seemed to have become 'permanent substitute', missing only eight Second Division games but starting only ten of them. Under Terry Neill, Lord settled into the side and the Driffield lad's development was reflected in his selection as emergency left-back in 1972-3. It led, however, to a serious ankle injury which kept him out for almost three months. In October 1975 came the further blow of an Achilles tendon injury, sustained against Bolton on his 29th birthday. He was out for over a year and battled gamely through a series of set-backs to enjoy a summer in American soccer in 1978 with California Surf. The following March, he fractured a leg against Rotherham and this took a further chunk out of his career. A recurrence of the tendon problem in 1979 finally brought his League career to an end.

MALCOLM LORD

	LEAGUE		*FACUP*		*FLCUP*		*OTHERS*		*TOTAL*	
	App	*Gls*	*App*	*Gls*	*App*	*Gls*	*App*	*Gls*	*App*	*Gls*
1966-67	8	0	0	0	0	0	0	0	8	0
1967-68	3/3	1	0	0	0	0	0	0	3/3	1
1968-69	17/4	3	0	0	0	0	0	0	17/4	3
1969-70	10/11	0	0	0	0	0	0	0	10/11	0
1970-71	31/1	0	4	0	1	0	2	0	38/1	0
1971-72	36/3	2	3	0	1	0	0	0	40/3	2
1972-73	24/1	0	0	0	1	0	1/2	0	26/3	0
1973-74	40	5	2	0	4	0	3	1	49	6
1974-75	36/1	6	3	0	0/1	0	0	0	39/2	6
1975-76	10	1	0	0	1	1	3	0	14	2
1976-77	16/1	3	0	0	0	0	0	0	16/1	3
1977-78	17/1	0	1	0	0	0	2	0	20/1	0
1978-79	23/1	3	1	0	0	0	0	0	24/1	3
	271/27	24	14	0	8/1	1	11/2	1	304/30	26

A strong, powerful centre-forward, Ken McDonald joined the Tigers from Bradford during the close season of 1928, with a reputation as a ready goalscorer for the Park Avenue club. His early days were decidedly itinerant. Born in Wales, he came to prominence in Scotland with Inverness Cachnacuddin. Aberdeen signed him but he returned to Welsh minor soccer before Cardiff gave him another chance. Manchester United moved for him in February 1923, but later that year McDonald left for Bradford and in the Northern Section the goals began to flow. In 1925-6 he scored a club record of 43 goals. In 1928, Bradford won the championship, totalling 101 goals for the third successive season and McDonald's contribution in that period was 112 goals. He then fell into dispute over terms and was transferred to the Tigers. The rich seam of goals continued at Anlaby Road and his new club was soon amongst the Second Division pace-setters. In November, McDonald's scoring exploits reached a peak with a club record five goals in the match against Bristol City. When it seemed his power might carry the Tigers into the First Division, the goals dramatically dried up and the side's challenge collapsed. McDonald recovered briefly at the start of the following season but, in March 1930, was transferred to Halifax. His final League record was a magnificent 175 goals in 214 games.

	LEAGUE		*FA CUP*		*TOTAL*	
	App	*Gls*	*App*	*Gls*	*App*	*Gls*
1928-29	32	23	2	2	34	25
1929-30	9	6	0	0	9	6
	41	29	2	2	43	31

KEN McDONALD

For eight seasons Ian McKechnie delighted Tigers fans with his goalkeeping and showmanship, yet he was on the point of emigrating to Australia when Cliff Britton brought him to Boothferry Park. 'Keckers' began as a left winger with Arsenal before Gunners' boss George Swindin realized the possibilities for the Scot as a goalkeeper. McKechnie managed only 23 appearances at Highbury and, in May 1964, moved to Southend, where he became an ever-present. He denied the Tigers in the Easter fixtures in 1965 and effectively ended their promotion hopes. Then, in the space of 12 months, he fell from favour and was given a free transfer, seemingly unwanted until Britton's approach. At Boothferry Park his huge clearance kicks drew gasps of amazement and his agility belied his burly frame. At times his courage bordered on the foolhardy but there were occasions when he was simply unbeatable. He expressed a liking for oranges and it became a regular occurrence for South Stand fans to inundate him with the fruit as he took up his position. Occasionally, in friendly games McKechnie would take a turn in his old position and proved he had not forgotten the art of goalscoring. Only with the arrival of Jeff Wealands in February 1972 did his place come under threat. In May 1974 the Dunbartonshire man was released. He spent the summer with the Boston Minutemen and should have moved to Mansfield, but Boston's involvement in the NASL play-offs delayed his return and the deal fell through. Shortly after his 33rd birthday he signed for Goole Town. His 255 League appearances were then more than any other City goalkeeper except Maddison and Bly.

IAN McKECHNIE

	LEAGUE		*FA CUP*		*FL CUP*		*OTHERS*		*TOTAL*	
	App	*Gls*	*App*	*Gls*	*App*	*Gls*	*App*	*Gls*	*App*	*Gls*
1966-67	41	0	2	0	0	0	0	0	43	0
1967-68	29	0	3	0	1	0	0	0	33	0
1968-69	42	0	1	0	2	0	0	0	45	0
1969-70	42	0	1	0	2	0	0	0	45	0
1970-71	41	0	4	0	1	0	2	0	48	0
1971-72	38	0	3	0	1	0	0	0	42	0
1972-73	21	0	3	0	0	0	3	0	27	0
1973-74	1	0	0	0	0	0	0	0	1	0
	255	0	17	0	7	0	5	0	284	0

The arrival of William Frederick McNaughton at Anlaby Road from Gateshead in the summer of 1932 was the prelude to one of the most exciting seasons on the old ground. A fee of around £1,000 secured the services of the 26-year-old Londoner, in the face of considerable competition. With Russell Wainscoat alongside, his scoring talents reached heights unsurpassed in the annals of the club. At one time McNaughton's career prospects looked less than promising. After a season with Millwall, he returned to non-League Peterborough. Northampton gave him another chance, but two goals in 11 Southern Section outings in two seasons was not unduly impressive. A move to Gateshead proved the turning point. A tally of 24 goals in his first season on Tyneside was followed by 22 in only 24 games. At Anlaby Road the goals continued to flow. Solo bursts through the middle, searing drives, close range efforts from head or foot from the provision of Sargeant or Forward on the flanks — McNaughton's score mounted in a way City fans had not seen since the halcyon days of Jackie Smith. The McNaughton goal-machine overhauled Smith's best and set a new record of 41. The 39th of them clinched the Northern Section title. Playing in the Second Division for the first time, McNaughton found the going harder and in October 1934 he was transferred to Stockport. Back in the Northern Section, goals came more easily and when his League career ended in 1936, he had netted 137 times in 209 outings, a fine record in the light of his faltering beginning.

	LEAGUE		*FA CUP*		*TOTAL*	
	App	*Gls*	*App*	*Gls*	*App*	*Gls*
1932-33	41	41	4	1	45	42
1933-34	42	15	3	1	45	16
1934-35	2	1	0	0	2	1
	85	57	7	2	92	59

BILL McNAUGHTON

JACK McQUILLAN

Jack McQuillan was one of Ambrose Langley's many early recruits from the North-East. McQuillan, who hailed from Boldon, was spotted playing for Jarrow in the Northern Alliance and signed in October 1906. A week later he made his League debut, as an 18-year-old. Soon he was established as first-choice left-back and it was not until the arrival of Douglas Morgan on the eve of World War One that McQuillan's supremacy came to an end. In 1911 he found his name on the score-sheet in unusual circumstances, in the Cup replay with Bristol Rovers. After 180 minutes neither side had scored. McQuillan had taken a bad knock and was removed to the wing. In extra-time, a long Tommy Nevins clearance found Wally Smith, whose shot the goalkeeper could not hold. In the ensuing scramble the ball broke to the crippled McQuillan and he calmly poked away the winner. In the summer of 1914 the full-back, who had made more appearances for the club than anyone except Davy Gordon, was sold to Leeds City for £100. A month later Europe was at war. McQuillan subsequently reappeared in amber and black as a guest, until incapacitated when a grinding machine blew up near him at work, leaving him with a broken collarbone and head injuries. He later helped the club as a scout, Dai Davies being amongst his discoveries.

	LEAGUE		*FA CUP*		*OTHERS*		*TOTAL*	
	App	*Gls*	*App*	*Gls*	*App*	*Gls*	*App*	*Gls*
1906-07	26	0	3	0	0	0	29	0
1907-08	34	0	3	0	0	0	37	0
1908-09	26	0	2	0	0	0	28	0
1909-10	36	0	1	0	0	0	37	0
1910-11	28	0	4	1	0	0	32	1
1911-12	35	0	2	0	0	0	37	0
1912-13	38	2	3	0	0	0	41	2
1913-14	16	0	0	0	1	0	17	0
1915-16	0	0	0	0	27	2	27	2
1916-17	0	0	0	0	4	0	4	0
	239	2	18	1	32	2	289	5

JOHN McSEVENEY

When joining the Tigers in July 1961, 30-year-old John McSeveney had accumulated the experience of a decade of League football. He had acquired a versatility invaluable at Boothferry Park where financial stringencies limited the size of the playing staff. The Scot joined Sunderland in October 1951 from Hamilton, where he already had three years under his belt. Four seasons later 'Jock' headed south to Cardiff, where he held down a regular place and in 1956-7 was second-highest scorer. Cardiff were relegated from the top flight that year, though, and McSeveney made the short trip to Newport. For four seasons he was an automatic choice and a consistent scorer, passing the half-century before his move to Boothferry Park. He settled in at inside-forward before a mid-season reshuffle pushed him out to the left wing, where his guile made up for the advantage which more youthful legs held over him. The flank role did not deter the Scot from continuing his scoring exploits. In 1962-3 he was the top scorer, his 27 goals bettering Bobby Hughes' tally of 25 from the wing in 1917-18. With the arrival of Ian Butler in January 1965, McSeveney switched to the right flank. At the end of the season he announced his retirement. During his days at Boothferry Park, he had enjoyed a love-hate relationship with the fans and in his last match, Brian Bulless' testimonial, found the ideal way to appease them, with a deliberate own-goal. He coached and scouted for the Tigers until 1971, before managing Barnsley and having a spell on Nottingham Forest's coaching staff.

	LEAGUE		*FA CUP*		*FL CUP*		*TOTAL*	
	App	*Gls*	*App*	*Gls*	*App*	*Gls*	*App*	*Gls*
1961-62	42	14	2	1	3	1	47	16
1962-63	39	22	4	4	4	1	47	27
1963-64	34	9	3	1	2	0	39	10
1964-65	46	15	3	2	1	0	50	17
	161	60	12	8	10	2	183	70

Amongst pre-war Tigers the giant George Maddison was the one to head the list of appearances. In June 1924, Bill McCracken persuaded Spurs manager Peter McWilliam, a former Newcastle teammate, to let the 21-year-old goalkeeper leave White Hart Lane. Maddison, signed from his local side, Birtley, during the 1922-3 season, had established himself in Tottenham's first team and the critics reckoned he would make the England side. At Anlaby Road, Maddison, Gibson and Bell became a legendary trio in the annals of the club, playing McCracken's offside trap to a fine art. After the law was changed, Maddison had to take the responsibility of the missing defender and was often seen rushing beyond the confines of his penalty-area. It was unorthodox, but then much of Maddison's technique defied the textbook. It was a sign of his genius to pick the right moment to produce the unexpected. For almost three years the goalkeeper was an ever-present, until a broken collarbone ended a run of 115 consecutive League outings. Fred Gibson deputized, beginning the rivalry which benefited both men. When Gibson moved, Maddison's position was secure once more. He helped take the club back into the Second Division in 1933 and remained at Anlaby Road until 1938, when injury finally forced his retirement.

GEORGE MADDISON

	LEAGUE		*FA CUP*		*OTHERS*		*TOTAL*	
	App	*Gls*	*App*	*Gls*	*App*	*Gls*	*App*	*Gls*
1924-25	25	0	3	0	0	0	28	0
1925-26	42	0	1	0	0	0	43	0
1926-27	42	0	5	0	0	0	47	0
1927-28	36	0	1	0	0	0	37	0
1928-29	34	0	2	0	0	0	36	0
1929-30	14	0	0	0	0	0	14	0
1930-31	24	0	0	0	0	0	24	0
1931-32	6	0	2	0	0	0	8	0
1932-33	34	0	4	0	0	0	38	0
1933-34	42	0	3	0	0	0	45	0
1934-35	38	0	1	0	0	0	39	0
1935-36	35	0	1	0	0	0	36	0
1936-37	42	0	1	0	1	0	44	0
1937-38	16	0	0	0	1	0	17	0
	430	0	24	0	2	0	456	0

The glittering career of Wilf Mannion appeared to have come to an end in the summer of 1954. His club, Middlesbrough, had been relegated from the First Division and 36-year-old Mannion decided the time had come to retire. He spent close on 18 years at Ayresome Park, signing for the Teessiders from his local club, South Bank St Peter's, in September 1936. Mannion soon became a regular in one of the best sides in the country. He was first selected for England during the war and, in his country's first 'official' international after the conflict, he destroyed the Irish with a hat-trick. He became known as the 'Golden Boy' of English soccer, an inside-forward of exceptional talent. The Tigers found out the hard way in 1948 as Mannion put them out of the FA Cup almost single-handedly. He went on to gain 26 full England caps and in May 1947 scored twice for a Great Britain side which emphasized its mastery over the Rest of Europe to the tune of 6-1. In December 1954 the Tigers persuaded Mannion to make a comeback. A £5,000 fee was on its way to Teesside and the inside-forward made his debut on Boxing Day. A near 40,000 crowd flocked to Boothferry Park, double the average, but the newcomer needed time to recapture his form. Trouble was brewing, though. The League and the FA took exception to his Press involvement during his 'retirement'. Summoned to appear before the League management committee, the player declined and in June 1955 the committee suspended him until he complied. To the Tigers' disappointment, Mannion ducked the challenge and signed up for Poole Town, serving a number of non-League clubs until his final retirement in 1962.

WILF MANNION

	LEAGUE		FA CUP		TOTAL	
	App	Gls	App	Gls	App	Gls
1954-55	16	1	1	0	17	1
	16	1	1	0	17	1

GEORGE MARTIN

In October 1922, City manager Harry Lewis signed inside-forward George Martin from Bo'ness. Hamilton promptly objected, claiming they had only loaned their player to Bo'ness. Lewis was censured for an illegal approach and the club fined £50, but the transfer stood and the stylish Martin struck up a good partnership with Paddy Mills. In 1925, though, the Scot struck a lean spell and was moved out to the right wing to restore his confidence. In January 1927, Hull faced Everton, Dixie Dean and all, in the Cup. At the third meeting the Tigers triumphed. Fittingly, Martin scored the winning goal. His displays in all three games had been inspirational. The impression on Everton led, a year later, to his transfer to Goodison and he played alongside Dean for part of his record-breaking 60-goal season. In 1931, Martin gained a Second Division medal with Everton, but missed out on the League title success the following season and left for a brief spell at Middlesbrough. A lengthy association with Luton followed. There, he netted his 100th League goal. He retired in 1938 to become coach and later manager. Spells in charge of Newcastle and Aston Villa built a sound managerial record.

	LEAGUE		FA CUP		TOTAL	
	App	Gls	App	Gls	App	Gls
1922-23	27	12	0	0	27	12
1923-24	39	9	2	1	41	10
1924-25	35	7	5	0	40	7
1925-26	32	7	1	0	33	7
1926-27	41	12	5	2	46	14
1927-28	30	8	1	0	31	8
	204	55	14	3	218	58

Brian Marwood came to Boothferry Park as an apprentice in June 1976 from Seaham schools football. He was one of a promising squad of juniors assembled by youth coach Ken Houghton. In 1978 they won the Northern Intermediate League for the first time in a decade and Marwood was ever-present, as well as playing in most of the Reserves' matches. He signed professional that February and had an early taste of first-team soccer in the pre-season games later in the year. However, it was Houghton's successor, Mike Smith, who brought Marwood into League football. By 1980-81 he was a regular in the side, although the struggles against relegation were scarcely an ideal training ground for the vital midfield role he was playing. In the Fourth Division his pace was ideal for a wider, more attacking position. He figured among the scorers with increasing regularity and, by 1983, overtook Les Mutrie as top marksman. The following season Marwood showed his colleagues the way to goal. It was to be his last in the Tigers' colours and could scarcely have ended more dramatically. With the side needing a three-goal win at Burnley for promotion, it was Marwood who struck the first after only 75 seconds and added a second after 65 minutes. But the third remained elusive and Marwood, keen to play in the First Division, left for Sheffield Wednesday during the close season for a fee of £115,000. In 1986 he was the Owls' top scorer as fifth place in the First Division was their best in a quarter of a century. In March 1988, Arsenal paid £600,000 for Marwood's skills and in November that year he won his first full England cap.

	LEAGUE		*FA CUP*		*FL CUP*		*OTHERS*		*TOTAL*	
	App	*Gls*	*App*	*Gls*	*App*	*Gls*	*App*	*Gls*	*App*	*Gls*
1979-80	4/2	0	0	0	0	0	0	0	4/2	0
1980-81	31	4	6	0	1	0	2	0	40	4
1981-82	40/2	12	6	1	0/1	0	2	0	48/3	13
1982-83	40	19	2	0	1	0	3	1	46	20
1983-84	39	16	2	0	2	0	5	0	48	16
	154/4	51	16	1	4/1	0	12	1	186/5	53

BRIAN MARWOOD

Harold Meens joined City at the start of 1936-7, as a 16-year-old amateur left-half from minor football in his native Doncaster. As a lad he was fascinated watching Hull City operate their offside trap. Former Rovers' boss David Menzies was in charge at Anlaby Road when he signed. By April 1937, when he became a professional, Meens had switched to centre-half, where he was to make his name. In February 1939 he made his League debut at Darlington and held his place for the rest of the season, returning to the North-East a fortnight later to pit his youthful enthusiasm against the veteran skills of the great Hughie Gallacher at Gateshead. The war delayed the flowering of Meens' talent as a powerful and authoritative defender. Major Buckley saw possibilities for him as a full-back but Raich Carter returned him to the centre-half role and Meens was king-pin in a defence which conceded only 28 goals *en route* to the Northern Section title. The Yorkshireman's opportunities in Division Two were limited by injuries. One of them ended his career and he was released in May 1954. It was a sad ending for a player who had given over a decade of loyal and wholehearted service.

HAROLD MEENS

	LEAGUE		*FA CUP*		*OTHERS*		*TOTAL*	
	App	*Gls*	*App*	*Gls*	*App*	*Gls*	*App*	*Gls*
1938-39	15	0	0	0	1	0	16	0
1939-40	0	0	-	-	24	3	24	3
1940-41	-	-	-	-	24	0	24	0
1946-47	39	0	4	0	0	0	43	0
1947-48	35	0	4	0	0	0	39	0
1948-49	40	0	6	0	0	0	46	0
1949-50	8	0	0	0	0	0	8	0
1950-51	6	0	1	0	0	0	7	0
1951-52	3	0	0	0	0	0	3	0
	146	0	15	0	49	3	210	3

'Six-goal Mercer' was the epithet often used of Tigers forward David Mercer. It referred to that January day in 1919, when he scored all six of his side's goals against Sheffield United in a wartime League match, only for the referee to abandon proceedings ten minutes early on account of appalling conditions. Mercer, at the time, was playing inside-right to Bobby Hughes, although he came to Anlaby Road in January 1914 as a right winger. The Tigers paid Skelmersdale £100 for him and centre-forward Tom Sharrett. The latter soon departed, but Mercer went on to play for England. He made his League debut in April 1914, embarking on a remarkable run of 218 consecutive appearances, right through the difficult war years, until April 1920. In the summer of that year he toured South Africa with the FA side. Perhaps it was not surprising that Sheffield United were prepared to pay over £4,000 for the fleet-footed winger's skills. It made Mercer the most expensive player in the League. Over the next seven and a half seasons, he amassed 223 League appearances for the Blades, sharing in the 1925 Wembley triumph over Cardiff. By 1928, 35-year-old Mercer's League career appeared to be at an end. He joined Midland League Shirebrook, but 12 months later was signed by Torquay for a final season in the Southern Section. The winger settled at the south-coast town and his son, Arthur, made over 60 appearances for the Plainmoor club.

DAVID MERCER

	LEAGUE		*FA CUP*		*OTHERS*		*TOTAL*	
	App	*Gls*	*App*	*Gls*	*App*	*Gls*	*App*	*Gls*
1913-14	2	0	0	0	0	0	2	0
1914-15	38	4	5	0	2	0	45	4
1915-16	0	0	0	0	36	3	36	3
1916-17	0	0	0	0	36	10	36	10
1917-18	0	0	0	0	34	26	34	26
1918-19	0	0	0	0	36	9	36	9
1919-20	41	17	1	0	0	0	42	17
1920-21	10	5	0	0	0	0	10	5
	91	26	6	0	144	48	241	74

BILLY MERCER

	LEAGUE		*FA CUP*		*OTHERS*		*TOTAL*	
	App	*Gls*	*App*	*Gls*	*App*	*Gls*	*App*	*Gls*
1914-15	1	0	0	0	0	0	1	0
1918-19	0	0	0	0	4	0	4	0
1919-20	17	0	0	0	0	0	17	0
1920-21	42	0	5	0	0	0	47	0
1921-22	42	0	2	0	0	0	44	0
1922-23	39	0	1	0	0	0	40	0
1923-24	40	0	2	0	0	0	42	0
1924-25	12	0	0	0	0	0	12	0
	193	0	10	0	4	0	207	0

Billy Mercer, no relation to his contemporary, David, came to Anlaby Road in the summer of 1914, with Nick Hendry established as first-choice goalkeeper. When the war stopped the professional game, Mercer joined the Royal Engineers. His soccer career almost ended, because he was blinded by gas during the fighting and it was amazing that he ever played again. In January 1920, Mercer at last had a chance to claim a first-team place, five and a half years after signing from Prescot Athletic. His soccer career began there, as an outside-left, until, in an emergency, he went in goal and stayed there. He continued to take Prescot's penalties and one season was top scorer with 17 of them. For close on five years, Mercer showed similar efficiency in the Tigers' goal. At one stage he strung together 95 consecutive League appearances. When he was deposed by George Maddison, Mercer promptly submitted a transfer request. Two days later he was on his way to Huddersfield in a £2,000 deal. They were heady years at Leeds Road, with a hat-trick of League titles. Competition for places was extremely keen and Mercer's participation was limited. In 1928 he was on the losing side at Wembley when Blackburn's Roscamp barged ball and goalkeeper into the net in the first minute. Mercer concluded his League career at Blackpool. He was a fine all-round sportsman — once topping Hull Cricket Club's batting averages — and as a leading local billiards player took on the great Joe Davis.

In September 1920 the Tigers gave a trial to a 20-year-old forward from Barton Town. Bert 'Paddy' Mills was to amass more goals for the club than anyone before him. Despite his Lincolnshire upbringing, Mills was born in India. Before his first year with City was out, he was leading the first-team attack. His ceaseless running and harrying soon won him the favour of the Anlaby Road patrons. A productive partnership with Charlie Flood and later George Martin saw Mills come to maturity. His 25 League goals in 1924-5 accounted for half of his side's total. Tempting offers came in for Mills' talents and, in March 1926, Notts County's bid of £3,150 tipped the scales. The deal triggered the resignation of two of the club's directors in protest at their colleagues' method of balancing the books. Mills stayed at Meadow Lane until February 1929. He hit 11 goals in 15 outings that term and First Division Birmingham signed him. The move did not work out and, as 1929 drew to a close, Bill McCracken brought Mills back to Anlaby Road. After relegation and with his 30th birthday behind him, Mills was withdrawn to the half-back line with increasing frequency. Nevertheless he still passed his century of League goals for the club in April 1932. Twelve months later he played in four different positions on the way to the Northern Section title. Released that summer, Mills had a couple of seasons with Scunthorpe before finishing his playing days at Gainsborough.

	LEAGUE		*FA CUP*		*TOTAL*	
	App	*Gls*	*App*	*Gls*	*App*	*Gls*
1920-21	15	4	0	0	15	4
1921-22	24	11	2	1	26	12
1922-23	30	8	1	1	31	9
1923-24	41	11	2	1	43	12
1924-25	36	25	5	4	41	29
1925-26	27	17	1	0	28	17
1929-30	10	2	5	2	15	4
1930-31	30	12	0	0	30	12
1931-32	37	11	3	0	40	11
1932-33	19	0	3	0	22	0
	269	101	22	9	291	110

PADDY MILLS

NORMAN MOORE

Norman Moore joined the Tigers in May 1947 after spending over a decade on Grimsby Town's books. Due largely to the war, he made only a handful of first-team appearances for the Mariners, either as a wing-half or inside-forward. Major Buckley soon tried Moore at centre-forward — with outstanding success. He was top scorer in 1947-8, despite competition for the number-nine shirt from 'Spud' Murphy. Moore repeated the feat the following term, with an impressive 22 goals in 31 games. It was just reward for his exemplary work-rate. His heading ability was outstanding and his many headed goals became affectionately known as 'Norman conquests'. Despite his success as a centre-forward, Moore always retained his preference for the deeper roles of inside-forward and wing-half. In 1949 he returned to Blundell Park in the FA Cup. The man to whom the Mariners had given a free transfer not only opened the scoring but also cracked home the winner with only four minutes remaining. For three months Moore continued to make his mark in the Second Division. It earned him a place in the FA side against Oxford University in November 1949, but by then injuries were affecting his form. By March he had lost his place to Bob Gibson and Blackburn paid £3,500 for the player who had impressed in putting them out of the Cup in 1949. The move failed to rejuvenate Moore and 18 months later he left Ewood Park for Bury. The 1951-2 season was his last in League soccer. Moore joined Goole Town in July 1952 and ended his playing days at Wisbech.

	LEAGUE		*FA CUP*		*TOTAL*	
	App	*Gls*	*App*	*Gls*	*App*	*Gls*
1946-47	3	0	0	0	3	0
1947-48	24	13	1	0	25	13
1948-49	31	22	6	6	37	28
1949-50	23	11	4	1	27	12
	81	46	11	7	92	53

At 34, Stan Mortensen was nearing the end of an illustrious career when he joined the struggling Tigers in November 1955. "I love a fight and there is one for Hull City this season," he replied when asked why he had left Blackpool after 18 years. 'Morty' had enjoyed FA Cup success in that memorable 1953 Cup Final when his hat-trick gave the other Stan — Matthews — a winner's medal. Mortensen had also been on the losing side in 1948 and 1951. As a centre-forward he was fast, powerful and incisive. He totalled 197 goals in 317 League outings with the Seasiders and for England his record was an amazing 24 goals in 25 games, including four on his full international debut in Lisbon. He had earlier played in wartime internationals. In fact he even pulled on the red shirt of Wales in 1943, coming on as a substitute for the injured Ivor Powell. In the season before joining Hull, he was top scorer for Blackpool. He also had two sports shops at the resort and, after the transfer, continued to live and train there. His arrival at Boothferry Park stirred hopes of avoiding the drop. Ultimately it was not to be and Mortensen missed the last crucial month of the season with a thigh injury. As the Tigers struggled in the Northern Section, he found himself out of favour and requested a move. Southport had an offer of £1,500 accepted, a fee some £500 lower than City had paid. Mortensen wound up his career with spells at Bath and Lancaster but, in February 1967, returned to Bloomfield Road as manager. He failed to avert relegation and left in April 1969.

STAN MORTENSEN

	LEAGUE		*FA CUP*		*TOTAL*	
	App	*Gls*	*App*	*Gls*	*App*	*Gls*
1955-56	21	8	2	0	23	8
1956-57	21	10	2	2	23	12
	42	18	4	2	46	20

In December 1980, the Tigers were locked in a three-match FA Cup marathon with Northern League Blyth Spartans. One man who had a considerable influence on the course of the tie was Blyth striker Les Mutrie. Immediately afterwards he signed for the winners in a £30,000 deal. For Mutrie it was a second chance in League football. He made five appearances for Carlisle in 1977-8 but was then released and drifted back into non-League soccer with Blyth. It was not easy for him to re-adjust to the full-time game again, especially in a side falling into the Fourth Division. In the League's basement a promising partnership began to emerge with Billy Whitehurst. In February and March 1982, Mutrie set a club record by scoring in nine consecutive League games and the peak of achievement was the four he grabbed against Hartlepool. The following season the side won promotion, but Mutrie's contribution in terms of goals was reduced, due to a recasting of roles by manager Colin Appleton. The pair became increasingly at odds and in December 1983, Mutrie departed on loan to Doncaster. A permanent move to Colchester followed a month later, bringing a reunion with former City coach Cyril Lea. In August 1984, Mutrie returned to the North-East with Hartlepool but had to give up the game in February 1985 due to ill health.

	LEAGUE		*FA CUP*		*FL CUP*		*OTHERS*		*TOTAL*	
	App	*Gls*	*App*	*Gls*	*App*	*Gls*	*App*	*Gls*	*App*	*Gls*
1980-81	20	5	0	0	0	0	0	0	20	5
1981-82	43	27	6	1	2	0	0	0	51	28
1982-83	40	12	2	0	2	0	3	0	47	12
1983-84	11/1	5	0	0	1/1	0	0	0	12/2	5
	114/1	49	8	1	5/1	0	3	0	130/2	50

LES MUTRIE

Signed from Tyneside junior soccer in September 1968, Gordon Nisbet spent eight years with West Brom before joining the Tigers. He began his career as a goalkeeper and made his League debut in that position. Millions of TV viewers saw his prowess in deputizing for the injured John Osborne. Yet it was at right-back that Nisbet established himself at The Hawthorns, his solid tackling and covering earning him an England Under-23 cap in March 1972. Subsequently he played in midfield and Johnny Giles even tried him as a striker. In four games up front for Albion's Reserves, Nisbet scored three times. John Kaye, well aware of his former colleague's qualities, persuaded him to move to Boothferry Park in September 1976 for a bargain £10,000. For two seasons Nisbet played mainly in midfield for the Tigers but, following relegation in 1978, settled once more at right-back. Cool under pressure, he refused to be beaten and his consistency was remarkable. The Supporters' Club voted him Player of the Year in 1978 and 1979, the only player to win the accolade twice. Between November 1977 and December 1980, Nisbet made 143 consecutive League appearances, a sequence which ended only with a £30,000 transfer to Plymouth. He remained with Argyle until the summer of 1987, clocking up almost 300 League appearances for the Pilgrims and giving the same hundred per cent which had characterized his days at Boothferry Park. At the age of 35 he joined Exeter, but in the course of 1987-8 was forced to quit through injury.

	LEAGUE		*FA CUP*		*FL CUP*		*OTHERS*		*TOTAL*	
	App	*Gls*	*App*	*Gls*	*App*	*Gls*	*App*	*Gls*	*App*	*Gls*
1976-77	37/1	0	2	1	0	0	0	0	39/1	1
1977-78	37/2	0	1	0	4	0	3	0	45/2	0
1978-79	46	1	2	0	3	0	0	0	51	1
1979-80	46	0	2	0	2	0	0	0	50	0
1980-81	24	0	3	0	2	0	3	0	32	0
	190/3	1	10	1	11	0	6	0	217/3	2

GORDON NISBET

TONY NORMAN

Tony Norman proved himself a fitting heir to the rich tradition of Tigers goalkeepers. Ten Hull City 'keepers have, between them, amassed around 2,500 League appearances — around 80 per cent of all the club's League matches since 1905. To Norman came the honour of setting a new club record of 226 consecutive League appearances. He maintained the highest standards at Boothferry Park and his agility and reflexes were, at times, quite uncanny. Welsh international honours came the goalkeeper's way in 1986. The Welsh connection played its part in his move to Hull from Burnley in February 1980. The £30,000 fee may have seemed large for a 22-year-old who had not made a single League appearance, but the man who had such confidence in him was former Welsh team boss Mike Smith. The subsequent trauma of Receivership cast a shadow over Norman's future with the Tigers. He remained, though, to play his part in the club's revival. Hull left the Fourth Division in 1982-3 with the best defence in the competition and, if promotion slipped away the following term, City's 38 goals conceded was a dozen less than champions Oxford. In December 1988, Norman left for Sunderland in a record £400,000 deal.

	LEAGUE		*FA CUP*		*FL CUP*		*OTHERS*		*TOTAL*	
	App	*Gls*	*App*	*Gls*	*App*	*Gls*	*App*	*Gls*	*App*	*Gls*
1979-80	17	0	0	0	0	0	0	0	17	0
1980-81	42	0	6	0	2	0	3	0	53	0
1981-82	36	0	4	0	2	0	3	0	45	0
1982-83	36	0	2	0	1	0	3	0	42	0
1983-84	46	0	2	0	2	0	5	0	55	0
1984-85	46	0	3	0	4	0	2	0	55	0
1985-86	42	0	3	0	4	0	4	0	53	0
1986-87	42	0	3	0	3	0	1	0	49	0
1987-88	44	0	3	0	2	0	0	0	49	0
1988-89	21	0	0	0	2	0	1	0	24	0
	372	0	26	0	22	0	22	0	442	0

Mick O'Brien was a tall, powerful centre-half. During his Anlaby Road days his presence between Tommy Bleakley and Jock Collier created a formidable intermediate line. The Irishman's strengths were well-known to his fellow countryman, Bill McCracken, for they had played together in the Irish side. O'Brien was capped 14 times in all, ten for Ireland and four for the Free State, but his ten-year international career was in marked contrast to his wanderings at club level. He assisted a number of minor sides on Tyneside and had trials in Scotland. Before the first post-war season was out, O'Brien had assisted Brentford, Norwich and South Shields. A two-year stay at Queen's Park Rangers almost amounted to settling down. In March 1922 he moved to Leicester, but in May 1924 was transfer-listed at £2,000. The player appealed to the League who slashed the fee to £750. Hard talking followed before O'Brien agreed to move to Hull. He was already 30 years old but made light of his years, receiving a final international call at 38. Early in 1926, O'Brien joined Brooklyn Wanderers in the United States, tempted by a five-year contract and a weekly wage of £16. By December 1926, though, he was back in Britain, suspended indefinitely on the whim of his coach, who had called the police to escort him from the ground. Hull City agreed a deal with Derby but the League took exception and fined the clubs £100 each. However, the transfer stood, but 18 months later the wanderer continued his travels with spells at Walsall, Norwich and Watford. He tried his hand at management with Queen's Park Rangers, Ipswich and Norwich and also had turns at scout and groundsman, not forgetting times as a farmer and a confectioner. Mick O'Brien died in September 1940, having packed more than a lifetime's experience into his 47 years.

MICK O'BRIEN

	LEAGUE		*FA CUP*		*TOTAL*	
	App	*Gls*	*App*	*Gls*	*App*	*Gls*
1924-25	33	0	5	1	38	1
1925-26	41	0	1	0	42	0
	74	0	6	1	80	1

In May 1965, Stuart Pearson had a trial at Boothferry Park, but for three years he combined soccer with an apprenticeship in the local telephone department. Two years after finally signing professional forms, Pearson broke through into the first team. He was an ideal successor to Chris Chilton, displaying much of Chilton's power and aggression. Pupil subsequently exceeded master in the finer skills and arts and in March 1972, Pearson was included in the England Under-23 squad. In May 1974, Tommy Docherty, once City's assistant manager, paid a Tigers record incoming fee of £200,000 to take the striker to Manchester United. Pearson's 17 goals helped the Reds lift the Second Division title at the first attempt and 12 months later he won the first of 15 full England caps. Pearson was a scorer in United's FA Cup win in 1977. In August 1979, West Ham paid £220,000 for his talents, but in three seasons he made less than three dozen appearances. He did win another FA Cup medal in 1980 but the Londoners released him in 1982. He went on Jimmy Hill's 'rebel' tour of South Africa before an injury, sustained playing in the NASL, forced him to quit. He subsequently played Rugby Union for Sale.

STUART PEARSON

	LEAGUE		*FA CUP*		*FL CUP*		*OTHERS*		*TOTAL*	
	App	*Gls*	*App*	*Gls*	*App*	*Gls*	*App*	*Gls*	*App*	*Gls*
1969-70	1	0	0	0	0	0	0	0	1	0
1970-71	9/3	1	0	0	0	0	0/1	0	9/4	1
1971-72	38	15	2	0	1	0	0	0	41	15
1972-73	37	17	4	0	1	0	3	0	45	17
1973-74	41	11	1	0	5	1	3	0	50	12
	126/3	44	7	0	7	1	6/1	0	146/4	45

DON REVIE

Arsenal, Manchester City and Hull City moved for Don Revie when he wanted away from Leicester, the club he joined in 1944 from minor football in his native Middlesbrough. Hull put a time limit on their £20,000 offer. It forced the issue and, in November 1949, Revie joined a Tigers side pushing strongly for Division One. Alas, Raich Carter and the club's record signing attempted to play the same role. Revie, a fine inside-forward, lost form and was eventually switched to wing-half, where he recovered a measure of confidence. Promotion hopes evaporated, however, and Carter's departure and the subsequent slump prompted a transfer request. In October 1951, Revie joined Manchester City, Hull receiving £13,000 plus full-back Ernie Phillips, valued at £12,000. By 1954-5, Manchester City were one of the country's top sides and Revie was capped for England and voted Footballer of the Year. The innovation which caused much interest and excitement was the so-called 'Revie Plan', using him as a deep-lying centre-forward. In November 1956, Revie joined Sunderland. Two years later he began his great association with Leeds. In March 1961, ex-Tiger Jack Taylor resigned as manager at Elland Road and Revie became player-manager. From the brink of the Third Division, he transformed Leeds into one of the most successful sides in Europe. He was Manager of the Year three times and in 1970 received the OBE. In April 1974 he was appointed England team manager but, without constant involvement with players, was unable to operate as successfully as he had at club level. In July 1977 he resigned sensationally to take a lucrative post in the Middle East. It earned him official disfavour, although there were few not saddened, several years later, by the sight of one of the great names of English football confined to a wheelchair, a victim of motor neurone disease from which he died in May 1989.

	LEAGUE		*FA CUP*		*TOTAL*	
	App	*Gls*	*App*	*Gls*	*App*	*Gls*
1949-50	22	0	3	1	25	1
1950-51	41	8	3	0	44	8
1951-52	13	4	0	0	13	4
	76	12	6	1	82	13

In an age of great change at Boothferry Park over the last decade, one of the unchanging features has been the contribution of Garreth Roberts. The diminutive midfielder has lacked nothing in tenacity and commitment to the Tigers' cause and, for much of the 1980s, has shouldered the extra responsibility of captaincy. In addition to his forceful midfield contribution, Roberts has steadily added to his tally of goals and has over 50 to his credit. Some of them have been struck home with devastating rapidity, such as his equalizer against Birmingham in September 1986, a mere 19 seconds into the second half, or his goal after 52 seconds against Sunderland six months earlier. On the other hand there have been times when Roberts' defensive qualities have qualified him for selection as emergency full-back. He joined the Tigers as an apprentice in the summer of 1977 and 12 months later won a Northern Intermediate League championship medal and signed professional forms on his 18th birthday. Once given a first-team chance, he kept his place in the side, coming to maturity during those difficult days in the Fourth Division. He made an invaluable contribution towards lifting the club back into the Second Division and, in an age when money talks compellingly, Roberts' loyalty to his local club has certainly earned the testimonial awarded to him.

GARRETH ROBERTS

	LEAGUE		*FA CUP*		*FL CUP*		*OTHERS*		*TOTAL*	
	App	*Gls*	*App*	*Gls*	*App*	*Gls*	*App*	*Gls*	*App*	*Gls*
1978-79	18/1	3	0	0	0	0	0	0	18/1	3
1979-80	44	2	2	1	2	1	0	0	48	4
1980-81	20	3	5	0	2	0	2	0	29	3
1981-82	29	6	6	0	1	0	3	0	39	6
1982-83	44	6	2	0	2	0	2	0	50	6
1983-84	37/1	9	2	1	2	0	4/1	4	45/2	14
1984-85	28/1	3	0	0	4	1	0/1	0	32/2	4
1985-86	33	4	3	2	4	0	3	0	43	6
1986-87	34/1	5	1	0	3	0	2	0	40/1	5
1987-88	43/1	3	3	1	2	0	1	1	49/1	5
1988-89	35	3	3	0	2	0	1	0	41	3
	365/5	47	27	5	24	2	18/2	5	434/7	59

In March 1951, Sheffield Wednesday paid Notts County a staggering £34,500 for Jackie Sewell's services. It broke the British record by £5,000. If the inside-forward's arrival at Hillsborough failed to keep the Owls in the top flight, they reaped the benefit the following season as Sewell's attacking skills took Wednesday to the Second Division title. His own contribution was an impressive 23 goals in 35 outings, but equally significant was his partnership with rising star Derek Dooley. Notts County signed Sewell during the war from Cumberland minor soccer and, in 1950, he and Tommy Lawton inspired County to the Southern Section championship. In November 1951, Sewell won the first of six England caps, four months before his record move to Wednesday. The Tigers learned of his skills the hard way, in a 6-0 thrashing at Hillsborough when Sewell scored twice. The City rearguard had no answer to his trickery. His penalty-box opportunism accumulated goals at the rate of one every other game, but in December 1955 he left for Villa Park — and another relegation struggle — for a more modest £17,000. Villa survived until 1959 and in October that year, Sewell, now out of favour, agreed to join Hull City in a £5,000 deal. The 32-year-old was again battling against the drop. He was soon joined by former Wednesday teammate Roy Shiner, but their ageing quality was not enough to transform a City side which was out of its depth. Sewell remained at Boothferry Park until April 1961, when he was attracted by an offer to play and coach in Rhodesia, with City of Lusaka. He later had charge of the Zambian national side.

	LEAGUE		*FA CUP*		*FL CUP*		*TOTAL*	
	App	*Gls*	*App*	*Gls*	*App*	*Gls*	*App*	*Gls*
1959-60	27	3	1	0	-	-	28	3
1960-61	17	5	4	1	1	0	22	6
	44	8	5	1	1	0	50	9

JACKIE SEWELL

In the late 1950s and early 1960s, Ainthorpe High School produced a number of players who made the grade as professional footballers. One was Chris Simpkin, who first joined the Tigers as an amateur in September 1959 to begin the process of development through the club's lower sides. At the beginning of the 1962-3 season, Simpkin had half a dozen League outings at inside-right. It was during the course of the following term that he made the move to wing-half which was to bring the best out of him. By 1965-6 he was an ever-present in the Third Division championship side. Outstanding displays, together with his blond hair, brought favourable comparison with Wolves and England star Ron Flowers. They had much in common — non-stop industry, biting tackling and a penchant for moving up into attack. Simpkin remained a key figure in the Tigers' midfield until the arrival of Ken Knighton and Jimmy McGill. In October 1971 he was transferred to Blackpool for £30,000 but never settled to his best at Bloomfield Road. In fact, for the last four seasons of his career Simpkin became a wanderer, having spells at Scunthorpe, Huddersfield and Hartlepool before stepping out of the League to join Scarborough in May 1978. A brief spell with Hall Road Rangers ended a 20-year playing career. Simpkin remained in Hull, working for a local motor dealer.

	LEAGUE		*FA CUP*		*FL CUP*		*OTHERS*		*TOTAL*	
	App	*Gls*	*App*	*Gls*	*App*	*Gls*	*App*	*Gls*	*App*	*Gls*
1962-63	17	3	0	0	0	0	0	0	17	3
1963-64	21	1	0	0	0	0	0	0	21	1
1964-65	4	0	0	0	0	0	0	0	4	0
1965-66	46	1	6	1	2	1	0	0	54	3
1966-67	36	2	3	0	1	0	0	0	40	2
1967-68	38	3	3	0	1	0	0	0	42	3
1968-69	42	1	1	0	2	0	0	0	45	1
1969-70	40	6	1	0	2	0	0	0	43	6
1970-71	37	2	4	0	1	0	2	0	44	2
1971-72	3/1	0	0	0	0	0	0	0	3/1	0
	284/1	19	18	1	9	1	2	0	313/1	21

CHRIS SIMPKIN

The consistent form of Peter Skipper when he rejoined the Tigers in August 1982 was a major factor in their rise from Fourth to Second Division. It was fitting that the great-hearted defender's header at Walsall in May 1985 should be the goal that clinched the return to Division Two. Skipper scored six goals that season, showing his effectiveness at set-piece moves. In his second spell at Hull he figured as a central defender, apart from the occasional call to act as an emergency goalkeeper. In his early days with local side, Schultz Youth Club, his form in the middle of the back four earned him a trial with City in September 1978. The following February he made his League debut and, almost immediately, was switched to full-back to cover for the injured de Vries. As Hull struggled to stay in the Third Division, 'Skip' found it hard to win a place. In February 1980, Mike Smith loaned him to Doncaster and, at the end of the season, negotiated a permanent deal with Darlington. In two seasons at Feethams, Skipper was seldom missing from the Quakers' defence and his form improved dramatically. He returned to Hull in a £10,000 deal funded partly by the Supporters' Club. Skipper then strung together a run of 149 consecutive League appearances, becoming an indispensable part of the Tigers rearguard until losing his place to Steve Terry shortly after the start of 1988-9. In October he was sold to Oldham for £40,000.

PETER SKIPPER

	LEAGUE		*FA CUP*		*FL CUP*		*OTHERS*		*TOTAL*	
	App	*Gls*	*App*	*Gls*	*App*	*Gls*	*App*	*Gls*	*App*	*Gls*
1978-79	17	2	0	0	0	0	0	0	17	2
1979-80	5/1	0	1	0	0	0	0	0	6/1	0
1982-83	46	4	2	0	2	0	3	0	53	4
1983-84	46	1	2	0	2	1	5	0	55	2
1984-85	46	5	3	1	4	0	2	0	55	6
1985-86	39/1	1	3	0	4	0	3/1	0	49/2	1
1986-87	41	4	3	0	2	0	2	0	48	4
1987-88	43	2	3	0	2	0	1	0	49	2
1988-89	3	0	0	0	0	0	0	0	3	0
	286/2	19	17	1	16	1	16/1	0	335/3	21

Jackie Smith came to Anlaby Road in June 1905 as a raw 19-year-old from Hebburn Argyle and soon hit the headlines with seven goals for the Reserves. A month later the second string beat Denaby 2-0 in the FA Cup after the first team were compelled to play a League match on the same day. Smith grabbed both goals and by the end of the year was a first-team regular, operating mostly at inside-right, but occasionally on the wing or at centre-forward. He scored with growing frequency and by 1908 had raised the club's individual record to 31 goals from 37 Second Division games. His one absence from the side was to play for the Football League against the Scottish League. A strangely muted Smith lost his place the following season, but bounced back to spearhead the Tigers challenge for the First Division in 1909-10, leading the attack for most of the campaign, despite standing only 5ft 7in tall. One commentator summed him up: "A born comedian, he tries to be serious. A little man, he has a big heart and, endowed with any amount of trickery, he prefers to bustle his opponents and glories in charging a six-foot back." Smith bettered his scoring record with 32 goals in 35 outings, including four hat-tricks. With the emergence of Tommy Browell, Smith's days at Anlaby Road ended in November 1910. His last League goal for the side was reckoned as his 100th, although on the basis of the extant evidence it is impossible to reach that total. He left for Sheffield United for around £500 but, four months later, moved to Nottingham Forest. He subsequently assisted Nelson and York City and by April 1915 he was playing full-back for Heckmondwike. Jackie Smith perished in World War One, killed in the fighting in September 1916. He left a widow and five children, the eldest of whom was only eight.

JACKIE SMITH

	LEAGUE		*FA CUP*		*TOTAL*	
	App	*Gls*	*App*	*Gls*	*App*	*Gls*
1905-06	20	5	3	3	23	8
1906-07	34	19	3	0	37	19
1907-08	37	31	3	1	40	32
1908-09	23	10	2	0	25	10
1909-10	35	32	1	0	36	32
1910-11	7	1	0	0	7	1
	156	98	12	4	168	102

Throughout his days at Anlaby Road, Joe Smith was known as 'Stanley' to distinguish him from the other J.Smith (no relation) in the City side. He was signed from West Stanley, hence the name, in September 1905. A strong, powerful front-runner, he was initially assigned the centre-forward berth, but was soon alternating that role with a place on the left wing, where his natural pace was used to good effect. He had won prizes of up to £25 in sprint handicap races. Smith was among the top scorers in the Tigers' first League campaign. Before the following season was over he had completed his set by playing in all five forward positions. Thereafter he settled on the right flank. His performances earned reward with selection as reserve for the Football League against the Scottish League in March 1911. A year later Everton signed him, along with Andy Browell. Smith made only ten First Division appearances in two seasons at Goodison but his career gained a new lease of life with a move to Distillery and two outings for the Irish League. Bury brought him back to England in December 1913 and Smith stayed at Gigg Lane until the war, helping to knock the Tigers out of the FA Cup in 1914. In October 1916 he was back in amber and black as a guest. Then the wrong side of 30 and almost completely bald, Smith could still turn on the style. After the war he returned to West Stanley, helping them to the second round of the FA Cup in 1920 before losing at Tottenham. It was almost full circle, for one of Smith's early Cup ties for the Tigers had been on that same ground.

JOE SMITH

	LEAGUE		*FA CUP*		*OTHERS*		*TOTAL*	
	App	*Gls*	*App*	*Gls*	*App*	*Gls*	*App*	*Gls*
1905-06	30	12	3	4	0	0	33	16
1906-07	29	7	3	0	0	0	32	7
1907-08	38	5	3	0	0	0	41	5
1908-09	37	6	2	0	0	0	39	6
1909-10	33	5	1	0	0	0	34	5
1910-11	30	9	4	2	0	0	34	11
1911-12	16	2	2	0	0	0	18	2
1916-17	0	0	0	0	1	0	1	0
1917-18	0	0	0	0	33	4	33	4
	213	46	18	6	34	4	265	56

MARTIN SPENDIFF

	LEAGUE		*FA CUP*		*TOTAL*	
	App	*Gls*	*App*	*Gls*	*App*	*Gls*
1905-06	38	0	5	0	43	0
1906-07	37	0	3	0	40	0
1907-08	29	0	3	0	32	0
	104	0	11	0	115	0

Martin Spendiff was the first player to keep goal for the Tigers in League football, setting high standards for his successors to maintain. His career began in his home town with North Shields Athletic before Grimsby Town signed him in March 1902. In 1905 he rejected all the Mariners' persuasions to re-sign and opted to move to Anlaby Road for a fee rumoured to be as high as £300. Spendiff was utterly fearless in an age before goalkeepers had the benefit of a distinguishing jersey, let alone the protection they enjoy today. A custodian with the ball in his possession was fair game to be barged into the net or have the ball kicked from his grasp. Yet, for close on three seasons, Spendiff avoided serious injury and missed only six League matches for the Tigers. In those days there was nothing to compel a goalkeeper facing a penalty to stand rooted to his line. Spendiff would prowl to and fro or leap up and down like a tribal warrior about to do battle, often with fitting vocal accompaniment. It came as a shock when the City stalwart demanded a transfer in March 1908. The directors negotiated a move to Bradford City, which was completed the day before the Tigers were to play at Valley Parade. Spendiff spent four years with the West Riding club, although he did not play in their FA Cup-winning side of 1911. He joined Millwall in June 1912 before returning to Blundell Park in the summer of 1913. He assisted the Mariners until 1920, before retiring to run a dairy business in Cleethorpes. He died in October 1943.

Cloaked by the anonymity of the alias 'Smith', Ronnie Starling made his debut in the Tigers Midland League side in April 1926. At 16 he was too young to sign professional, but Bill McCracken was so keen to capture the precocious talent from Washington Colliery that he registered the lad as an amateur and gave him a job as office boy. His judgement was spot-on. In September 1928, Starling made his League debut in the passion of a Humberside derby match and put away the winning goal. Although more at home as an inside-forward, he could, if required, lead the attack quite capably. The return of Jimmy Howieson made life difficult for Starling, whose talent and potential were weighed against the mature skills of the Scot. In the midst of a relegation struggle, a section of the Anlaby Road crowd took to barracking the youngster. Starling sought a move and, in May 1930, returned to his native Newcastle. United paid some £4,000 but were to recoup part of it two years later by allowing Starling to join Sheffield Wednesday. There he soon established himself as a star in one of the country's best sides. He played for England in 1933 and, two years later, captained Wednesday in the FA Cup Final, when his attacking genius eventually tipped an enthralling contest the Owls' way. In January 1937, Aston Villa invested £7,500, seeing Starling as the man to lead them out of the Second Division. During the war he helped Villa win the League (North) Cup in 1944. When League soccer resumed, the veteran made one more appearance for Villa, retiring in the summer of 1948. He coached Nottingham Forest for two seasons before settling in Sheffield.

RONNIE STARLING

	LEAGUE		*FA CUP*		*TOTAL*	
	App	*Gls*	*App*	*Gls*	*App*	*Gls*
1927-28	15	0	0	0	15	0
1928-29	31	8	2	0	33	8
1929-30	32	5	6	1	38	6
	78	13	8	1	86	14

In February 1912, shortly after the departure of City favourite Tommy Browell, it was the Tigers' good fortune to acquire the services of 22-year-old Sammy Stevens from Cradley Heath junior football. The new centre-forward was plunged into Second Division soccer, having to contend not only with the vast difference in playing standards but also a crowd in highly-critical mood. Well before the end of the season he was recovering in the Reserves. Stevens certainly had potential but its realization did not come easily. Perhaps the real turning point came against Leeds City the following season, when he hit four of the Tigers' six goals, realizing the futility of trying to bustle through the middle alone and finding the benefit of opening play out to the wings. The signings of Billy Halligan and 'Kiltie' Cameron did much for Stevens' development. In 1913-14 his 26 goals amounted to nearly half his side's total. The following term his form took him to the brink of England honours when he was reserve for the Football League against the Scots. For most of the war Stevens forged chains in his native Birmingham. His availability for the Tigers was limited and he guested at St Andrew's. When the Second Division resumed, he continued to knock in the goals until, in July 1920, the lure of the cheque book induced City to sell him to Notts County for £1,700. Coventry acquired his skills the following March and during 1921-2 he passed the personal milestone of 100 League goals. The following season was the 33-year-old's last in League football. Despite losing four of his best years to the war, his haul of League goals is the fifth best in the Tigers' history.

SAMMY STEVENS

	LEAGUE		*FA CUP*		*OTHERS*		*TOTAL*	
	App	*Gls*	*App*	*Gls*	*App*	*Gls*	*App*	*Gls*
1911-12	7	1	0	0	0	0	7	1
1912-13	32	15	3	1	0	0	35	16
1913-14	38	26	2	0	3	1	43	27
1914-15	37	24	5	6	2	2	44	32
1915-16	-	-	-	-	10	11	10	11
1916-17	-	-	-	-	9	9	9	9
1918-19	-	-	-	-	11	3	11	3
1919-20	36	18	1	2	0	0	37	20
	150	84	11	9	35	26	196	119

For five seasons Billy Taylor performed competently and effectively on the Tigers' flanks. Like Gordon Wright two decades earlier, he was a provider for his colleagues rather than seeking the limelight as a goalscorer. He was quick and skilful and was equally at home on either wing. Bill McCracken signed Taylor from Aberdare in June 1926, employing him mainly on the left until the arrival of Dally Duncan. Taylor played an important, and often overlooked, part in the 1930 Cup run. It was he who engineered the opening for Stan Alexander's first-minute goal at Plymouth in the third round. The winger's goal at Maine Road dumped Manchester City out of the fifth round after he had set up Paddy Mills' equalizer. He provided Jimmy Howieson with the opportunity to scupper Newcastle in the next round. In the course of that encounter Taylor took a knock to the knee. It kept him out of the line-up for a month, during which Hull lost the semi-final and five out of six League matches. After relegation Taylor remained at Anlaby Road for another season before moving to Norwich for his last term in the League, concluding a career which had begun at West Brom in 1920. A spell at Cardiff followed, but not until joining Aberdare did Taylor enjoy regular first-team football. The winger's performances in the Southern Section impressed City sufficiently to induce them to pay out £500 for his skills.

BILLY TAYLOR

	LEAGUE		*FA CUP*		*TOTAL*	
	App	*Gls*	*App*	*Gls*	*App*	*Gls*
1926-27	42	5	5	0	47	5
1927-28	34	3	1	0	35	3
1928-29	36	3	2	0	38	3
1929-30	23	4	5	1	28	5
1930-31	17	2	0	0	17	2
	152	17	13	1	165	18

Arthur Temple was spotted playing for the Northern Alliance runners-up, Wallsend Park Villa, and was signed up during the close season of 1907. The 20-year-old inside-forward went straight into the first team and did not miss a competitive match for a season and a half. At inside-left he reaped the benefits of playing alongside Gordon Wright and he was also forceful enough to lead the attack to good effect. Temple's first hat-trick for the club, against Leicester Fosse in November 1907, brought him reward from an unusual piece of early sponsorship — an overcoat from a local outfitter. Ability to find the net regularly took the Geordie to the top of the Tigers' scorers in 1908-09, although at the end of that term he was doing sterling work as a makeshift full-back. In 1911-12, Temple shared the scoring honours with Tommy Browell, each reaching the 16-goal mark in the League. A serious knee injury in September 1912 kept the forward out for the whole of his benefit season and his reward for five years' service was the club's maximum sum of £175. Temple spent much of the 1913-14 season in the Reserves, mostly withdrawn to centre-half or full-back. At its conclusion, City allowed him to return north, to Blyth Spartans.

ARTHUR TEMPLE

	LEAGUE		*FA CUP*		*TOTAL*	
	App	*Gls*	*App*	*Gls*	*App*	*Gls*
1907-08	38	18	3	1	41	19
1908-09	36	17	2	1	38	18
1909-10	35	16	1	1	36	17
1910-11	29	10	4	1	33	11
1911-12	32	16	1	0	33	16
1913-14	3	0	0	0	3	0
	173	77	11	4	184	81

The signing of Ken Wagstaff in November 1964 began a transformation of the Tigers attack. The Mansfield Town striker cost £40,000, almost double the club's previous highest outlay. Wagstaff was discovered by Raich Carter and signed for the Stags in May 1960. In four and a half seasons he notched an impressive 96 goals from 181 League outings and in 1963 he was the Fourth Division's top scorer with 34 goals. Two seasons later, his combined total of 35 goals for Mansfield and Hull made him top marksman in the Third Division. Wagstaff was highly gifted and his impudent grin mirrored his footballing brain. His close control carried him through seemingly impossible situations and his turn of speed exploited the long through pass or the self-created opening. Wagstaff and Chilton became a feared partnership. In his first part-season at Boothferry Park, 'Waggy' found the net 23 times in 25 League games. Such form over a full season would have taken him close to McNaughton's club best. The following season Wagstaff overhauled Bradbury's post-war League and Cup record. His total included two remarkable efforts at Chelsea in the FA Cup which brought the Tigers a celebrated draw from a two-goal deficit. In 1971 he joined Chilton on the FA tour of Australia and might well have furthered his international career with a move to a top-flight club. In 1972 he celebrated 150 League goals for the Tigers, but injuries were beginning to take their toll and, in January 1975, cartilage trouble brought a premature end to his testimonial season. The knee never fully mended and he eventually headed for Australia as player-coach to George Cross. The Tigers, meanwhile, struggled to score goals and Wagstaff, rejuvenated by a summer 'Down Under', contemplated a comeback but the League vetoed it on insurance grounds.

KEN WAGSTAFF

	LEAGUE		*FA CUP*		*FL CUP*		*OTHERS*		*TOTAL*	
	App	*Gls*	*App*	*Gls*	*App*	*Gls*	*App*	*Gls*	*App*	*Gls*
1964-65	25	23	2	0	0	0	0	0	27	23
1965-66	46	27	7	3	2	1	0	0	55	31
1966-67	39	21	3	0	1	0	0	0	43	21
1967-68	40	17	3	2	1	1	0	0	44	20
1968-69	39	20	1	0	2	1	0	0	42	21
1969-70	38	18	1	0	2	1	0	0	41	19
1970-71	38	12	4	4	1	0	2	2	45	18
1971-72	32	11	3	3	1	0	0	0	36	14
1972-73	13/3	4	2	1	1	0	1	0	17/3	5
1973-74	32	8	2	0	5	2	3	0	42	10
1974-75	23	10	1	1	1	0	0	0	25	11
1975-76	9/1	2	0	0	2	0	1/1	2	12/2	4
	374/4	173	29	14	19	6	7/1	4	429/5	197

The Hull City squad in 1966-7. Back row (left to right): K.Houghton, K.Wagstaff, C.Chilton, I.McKechnie, M.Milner, C.Simpkin, I.Butler. Front row: R.Henderson, A.Jarvis, A.Davidson, W.Wilkinson, D.Butler.

In October 1931, the Tigers caused a stir when they persuaded Leeds United to part with Russell Wainscoat. True, the 33-year-old former England inside-forward was nearing the end of his playing days, but it was equally undeniable that there was still good football left in him, even amidst the vigour of the Northern Section. Wainscoat joined Barnsley in 1920 from his local side, Maltby Main. In less than four seasons he proved his attacking qualities as a centre-forward by hitting a half-century of League goals. In December 1923, Wainscoat's desire for First Division football was realized by a move to Middlesbrough, who were promptly relegated. In March 1925, Leeds gave him another chance in the top flight. By 1927, United, too, had lost their status but Wainscoat, who toured Canada with the FA side that summer, played a major part in their first-time return to Division One. Playing a deeper role, he exerted a tactical mastery which, allied to his attacking skills, made him the complete inside-forward. In 1931, United were relegated again and Wainscoat fell out of favour. A hat-trick in a Reserve game convinced Hull of his potential to get them out of the Northern Section. The years had broadened his already solid frame, but he retained a deceptive turn of speed and wonderful ball-control. When McNaughton arrived the following summer, Wainscoat found an ideal foil. The centre-forward set a new club scoring record and his provider also enjoyed his most prolific season as a goalscorer. The title success brought Wainscoat's first winner's medal and he stayed to see Hull established in Division Two before retiring.

RUSSELL WAINSCOAT

	LEAGUE		*FA CUP*		*TOTAL*	
	App	*Gls*	*App*	*Gls*	*App*	*Gls*
1931-32	29	16	3	3	32	19
1932-33	34	21	3	5	37	26
1933-34	16	5	0	0	16	5
	79	42	6	8	85	50

For over seven years the lanky 6ft-plus frame of Jeff Wealands was a commanding figure in the Tigers goal. His agility and reflexes were excellent and his technique sound in the best traditions of City goalkeepers. The presence of Ian McKechnie at Boothferry Park meant that Wealands' introduction to Second Division soccer was a gradual one following his £10,000 move from Darlington in February 1972. By 1973-4, though, he ruled supreme and in four seasons missed only three League matches. It was rather different from earlier phases of his career. Two years after his apprenticeship at Wolves he had still not made the first team and in the summer of 1970 left for Feethams. A season elapsed before the chance of Fourth Division soccer finally came. Following the Tigers' relegation in 1978, Wealands remained for one more season. A £30,000 deal took him to Birmingham, who were promoted to the First Division a year later. In March 1983, Wealands was loaned to Manchester United and the move became permanent, but first-team chances at Old Trafford were few and far between. Brief spells at Oldham and Preston followed. A back injury threatened to end his career, but with Altrincham he gained a new lease of life. In May 1986, he helped the Cheshire side win the FA Trophy at Wembley, having earlier that season been part of an FA Cup sensation, when Altrincham won 2-1 at his old club, Birmingham. In 1988, at the age of 36, Wealands was in the spotlight again, turning out for Barrow in the Northern Premier League Cup Final against Goole Town. The match ended with Wealands in the firing line of a penalty decider but he was unable to prevent Town capturing the trophy.

JEFF WEALANDS

	LEAGUE		*FA CUP*		*FL CUP*		*OTHERS*		*TOTAL*	
	App	*Gls*	*App*	*Gls*	*App*	*Gls*	*App*	*Gls*	*App*	*Gls*
1971-72	3	0	0	0	0	0	0	0	3	0
1972-73	21	0	1	0	2	0	1	0	25	0
1973-74	41	0	2	0	5	0	3	0	51	0
1974-75	40	0	3	0	1	0	0	0	44	0
1975-76	42	0	3	0	3	0	2	0	50	0
1976-77	42	0	2	0	1	0	3	0	48	0
1977-78	23	0	0	0	4	0	3	0	30	0
1978-79	28	0	0	0	3	0	0	0	31	0
	240	0	11	0	19	0	12	0	282	0

In April 1928, Hull City signed a 19-year-old half-back from Sutton Town. Sam Weaver cost the Tigers £50, made his League debut early the following season and never looked back. He had all the qualities to make the complete wing-half. He was strong in the tackle and had vision and ability in setting his own attack on the move, having confidence and skill to pursue an opening himself. He could play inside-forward with equal effectiveness, as the Tigers were later to find out to their cost. Weaver's meteoric rise brought the scouts to Anlaby Road. In November 1929, after his 50th League and Cup appearance, the City board capitulated to a £2,500 offer from Newcastle. It was on Tyneside that Weaver began to develop a prodigious throw-in, at times propelling the leather over 35 yards. In 1932, the Derbyshire lad made the first of three appearances for England and helped bring the FA Cup to Tyneside. United were relegated in 1934 and Weaver showed devastating form as he and his colleagues put a dozen goals past the Tigers within the space of three weeks. In August 1936, Weaver moved to Chelsea for a fee of £4,166. He remained at Stamford Bridge until 1945, but during the war guested for Leeds. It brought him into opposition with City again and, at the end of 180 minutes, there were another 12 goals in the Tigers' net. Weaver ended his playing days at Stockport and coached Leeds, Millwall and Mansfield. He also managed the latter for a spell and assisted there as a scout for many years. He was also masseur to Derbyshire CCC.

	LEAGUE		*FA CUP*		*TOTAL*	
	App	*Gls*	*App*	*Gls*	*App*	*Gls*
1928-29	37	4	2	0	39	4
1929-30	11	1	0	0	11	1
	48	5	2	0	50	5

SAM WEAVER

In December 1985 the Tigers accepted a then record fee of £232,000 from Newcastle United for Billy Whitehurst. There was consternation and dismay on the Boothferry Park terraces at the departure of the big striker. The deal indicated the transformation which had taken place during the five years Whitehurst had been with Hull City. Once a bricklayer with Barnsley Council, Whitehurst assisted several non-League clubs, including three games for Bridlington Trinity, before joining Mexborough Town. There he had played in the Midland League representative side. The Tigers invited him for a trial in October 1980 and signed him for around £2,000. He found the transition difficult, but gradually began to prove the doubters wrong. Chris Chilton's coaching turned the raw power of the 13st Yorkshireman into a fearsome target man. His tally of goals began to increase and, by 1984-5, Whitehurst was top scorer for the Tigers. The big clubs began to take note as he rampaged through Second Division defences before speculation ended with the move to Newcastle. In the shadow of great Geordie centre-forwards of the past, Whitehurst found life difficult at St James' Park. In October 1986, Newcastle recouped £175,000 by selling the striker to Oxford and subsequently Whitehurst played for Reading and Sunderland before rejoining the Tigers in December 1988.

	LEAGUE		*FA CUP*		*FL CUP*		*OTHERS*		*TOTAL*	
	App	*Gls*	*App*	*Gls*	*App*	*Gls*	*App*	*Gls*	*App*	*Gls*
1980-81	20/6	1	0	0	0	0	0	0	20/6	1
1981-82	34/2	6	5	2	1/1	0	3	1	43/3	9
1982-83	28/8	3	2	0	2	1	3	1	35/8	5
1983-84	36/1	10	2	1	2	0	5	0	45/1	11
1984-85	40	20	1	0	3	3	2	1	46	24
1985-86	18	7	0	0	3	2	3	3	24	12
1988-89	21	5	3	2	0	0	0	0	24	7
	197/17	52	13	5	11/1	6	16	6	237/18	69

BILLY WHITEHURST

Billy Wilkinson joined the Tigers in August 1961 as an 18-year-old from Stockton. He had an unsuccessful spell at Middlesbrough as an amateur, but after less than a year at Boothferry Park, Wilkinson was signing professional forms for City. He was an inside-forward — perpetual motion from start to finish — and also made his mark as a goalscorer. The arrival of Wagstaff, Houghton and Butler meant that Wilkinson spent most of the 1966 championship season either in the Reserves or sitting patiently on the substitutes' bench. Many players would have wanted to leave, but Wilkinson battled on with characteristic loyalty and determination and became a valuable asset as a utility forward. Only 5ft 8in tall, he could compete with the tallest defenders in the air and would drop back to graft effectively in midfield. Then, as the 1960s closed, Wilkinson took on the role of central defender, again defying his lack of inches. He formed a sound partnership with Terry Neill as the side revived those First Division ambitions. Ankle and knee injuries, which put him out of action for over three months, would have knocked the heart out of lesser men, but not Wilkinson. He was awarded a well-merited testimonial but, before the match took place, Rotherham paid £10,000 for his transfer. Wilkinson spent a season and a half at Millmoor before setting off on a globe-trotting finale to his career, taking in the United States, South Africa and Australia.

BILLY WILKINSON

	LEAGUE		*FA CUP*		*FL CUP*		*OTHERS*		*TOTAL*	
	App	*Gls*	*App*	*Gls*	*App*	*Gls*	*App*	*Gls*	*App*	*Gls*
1962-63	2	1	0	0	0	0	0	0	2	1
1963-64	27	13	5	3	1	0	0	0	33	16
1964-65	23	3	2	2	2	1	0	0	27	6
1965-66	1/3	0	0	0	0	0	0	0	1/3	0
1966-67	19/3	8	0	0	0	0	0	0	19/3	8
1967-68	18/2	2	3	0	1	0	0	0	22/2	2
1968-69	19/2	5	0/1	0	1	1	0	0	20/3	6
1969-70	33/1	1	0	0	1	0	0	0	34/1	1
1970-71	39	0	3	0	1	0	2	0	45	0
1971-72	20/2	1	3	0	1	0	0	0	24/2	1
1972-73	7/2	0	0	0	2	0	0	0	9/2	0
	208/15	34	16/1	5	10	2	2	0	236/16	41

CLIFF WOODHEAD

	LEAGUE		*FA CUP*		*OTHERS*		*TOTAL*	
	App	*Gls*	*App*	*Gls*	*App*	*Gls*	*App*	*Gls*
1930-31	1	0	0	0	0	0	1	0
1931-32	32	0	2	0	0	0	34	0
1932-33	42	0	4	0	0	0	46	0
1933-34	41	0	3	0	0	0	44	0
1934-35	42	0	1	0	0	0	43	0
1935-36	41	0	1	0	0	0	42	0
1936-37	27	0	1	0	1	0	29	0
1937-38	38	0	3	0	1	0	42	0
1938-39	41	0	3	0	1	0	45	0
1939-40	0	0	0	0	23	0	23	0
1940-41	0	0	0	0	26	0	26	0
	305	0	18	0	52	0	375	0

Only a dozen or so players have turned out more times for the Tigers than Cliff Woodhead. That in itself indicates the high standards which this solid Yorkshire full-back set during his decade at Anlaby Road. Against the background of the club's fortunes it becomes an even more outstanding achievement. The turnover of playing staff was rapid at times and a dozen different partners came and went before war halted the League programme in 1939. Woodhead, with George Maddison, formed the point of stability around which successive managers built to try to recapture the club's former standing in the Second Division. It was in May 1930 that Woodhead joined the Tigers from Denaby United, with a brief spell at Southport already behind him. He made his League debut that December, with Matt Bell alongside. Paradoxically, it was not until the master left that the pupil established himself in the side. Woodhead was an ever-present in the 1933 Northern Section championship line-up. There were times when the club received tempting offers, but the removal of Woodhead would have had unthinkable repercussions in the Tigers rearguard. The war halted the club's activities in 1941 and that was probably the only way anyone was going to stop Woodhead pulling on a black and amber shirt. The following season he guested for York and, after the war, had a brief association with Goole Town. Woodhead later returned to Boothferry Park to coach the club's juniors. Under his guidance they won the Northern Intermediate League and Cup double in 1953. Players who benefited from his coaching included Cliff Bursell, Terry Peacock, David Coates, Graham Wilkinson and Johnny Stephens.

Of many fine players at Anlaby Road in the pre-1915 period, one stands out above the rest. Edward Gordon Dundas Wright was an amateur and a player of the highest quality. He was the natural choice to captain the side, despite the drawback of not training with his colleagues during the week. He was an outside-left in the days when a winger received the ball, evaded whatever challenge was offered until reaching the goal-line and then crossed the ball whilst still at top speed. Gordon Wright had few equals in the art of classic flank play. It won him 20 caps for England at amateur level, including a place in the squad which won the 1912 Olympic tournament. Fittingly, he is the only Tiger to win a full England cap and with the famous Corinthians he toured the world. His was the 'sparkling, champagne football' which always ensured an extra thousand or so on the Anlaby Road ground when his availability was certain. The son of an East Riding clergyman, Wright went up to Queen's College, Cambridge. At Christmas 1905 the City directors asked him to assist their side during vacations. Wright agreed and made his debut the following Easter, scoring a spectacular goal almost from the corner-flag. Some observers considered he would have had a rich haul in goals if he had taken the direct route instead of sticking to the textbook. In the summer of 1906, Wright took a teaching post at Hymers College in Hull and was available on a regular basis until admitted to the Royal School of Mines at Kensington in 1909. On completion of his studies in 1913, he took a post as a mining engineer in South Africa and his association with the Tigers came to an end.

GORDON WRIGHT

	LEAGUE		*FA CUP*		*TOTAL*	
	App	*Gls*	*App*	*Gls*	*App*	*Gls*
1905-06	1	1	0	0	1	1
1906-07	26	7	3	0	29	7
1907-08	25	0	3	0	28	0
1908-09	25	1	2	0	27	1
1909-10	16	3	1	0	17	3
1910-11	10	0	4	0	14	0
1911-12	18	2	0	0	18	2
1912-13	31	0	3	0	34	0
	152	14	16	0	168	14

Hull City line-up in July 1975. Back row (left to right): P.Haigh, R.Greenwood, A.Wood, K.Wagstaff, D.Roberts, F.Banks, V.Grimes. Middle row: J.Kaye (manager), R.de Vries, P.Fletcher, J.Wealands, C.Galvin, E.Blackburn, D.Adams, S.Deere, P.Holme (coach). Front row: A.Davidson (assistant manager), M.Lord, P.Daniel, J.Hemmerman, J.McGill, S.Croft, S.Blampey, G.Staniforth, J.Radcliffe (physiotherapist).

Match to Remember 1 — 1 September 1904

Hull City 2 Notts County 2

WITH the visit of Notts County to the Boulevard, professional soccer in Hull became a reality. The Mayor, Alderman Jarman, was there to kick-off, adding civic recognition to the occasion. County had finished a modest 13th in the First Division in 1903-04 but they were still a top-flight club.

So great was interest in the game that the first spectators arrived at the ground almost two hours before the scheduled 5pm start. And the crowd grew steadily, as those for whom Thursday provided a half-day's holiday were joined by those leaving work. By half-time, some 6,000 spectators had brought the City club gate receipts in the region of £80.

After much speculation, County were almost at full strength. The only man not to play in the following Saturday's League match was Albert Iremonger, a young goalkeeper at the beginning of a lengthy career which even included a guest appearance for the Tigers during World War One. The local side had no such selection problems, with only a dozen professionals to choose from.

City were soon on the offensive and after about 15 minutes George Rushton dispossessed Jimmy Montgomery to drive home the first goal. This early success saw the City fans in jubilant mood and they were cheering again as the first half drew to a close. Peter Howe jinked past man after man, only to fire narrowly wide.

Early in the second half, Rushton struck again with a delightful solo effort. This roused the visitors, who put the Hull men under increasing pressure. In a goalmouth mêlée the referee spotted an infringement and awarded County a penalty. Green gave Jimmy Whitehouse no chance with a low, well-struck shot. Then Humphreys had the ball in the net but the Citizens escaped when the referee ruled the effort offside.

In the closing minutes Notts County's superior teamwork again found an opening in the Hull defence. Muir's cross was well controlled by Mainman, who had little difficulty in putting his side back on terms. It was a creditable performance by the newly-assembled Hull City team, auguring well for the future.

Hull City: Whitehouse; Leiper, Jones, Martin, Wolfe, Raisbeck, McKiernan, Rushton, Howe, Spence, Wilkinson.
Notts County: Iremonger; Prescott, Montgomery, Anderson, Mainman, Griffiths, Muir, Humphreys, Green, Reid, Gee.

Referee: J.Plastow (Grimsby) — *Attendance: 6,000*

Group taken prior to the match. Back row (left to right): B.Frost, E.Morison, A.Spring (directors), W.Leach (trainer), F.Levitt (director), Leiper, J.Bielby (director), Whitehouse, J. Ramster (director), Ald W.Jarman JP (mayor), W. Gilyott (chairman), Jones, J.Barraclough (director), Martin, M.Andrews (director), E.Rodgerson (mayor's beadle). Middle row: Dr G.Lilley (vice-chairman), Wolfe, Rushton, Spence, Howe, McKiernan, B.Crompton (secretary). Front row: Raisbeck, Wilkinson.

The squad which began the Tigers' first League campaign in September 1905. Back row (left to right): Martin, Davies, Spence, Spendiff, Langley, Robinson, Gordon. Middle row: W.Leach (trainer), Manning, Simmon, Wilson, Howe, Raisbeck. Front row: Rushton, Thornton, Jack Smith, Lavery.

Match to Remember 2 — 2 September 1905

Hull City 4 Barnsley 1

THE fixture makers favoured Hull City with a home match to start their Football League career, with Yorkshire rivals Barnsley, mid-table the previous season, a crowd-pulling attraction. Spectators rolled up in good numbers but at the appointed hour there was no sign of the opposition. A band, the usual means of pre-match entertainment in those days, had to play on until the West Riding outfit, delayed on the train, eventually arrived. A start was finally made at 3.45pm.

The delay had certainly not affected the City players. With five new faces on show, they stormed into attack and took the lead after only two minutes, George Spence putting the finishing touch to Hull City's first League goal.

The Colliers warmed to their task and struck back with a goal from Bell in the tenth minute. Even exchanges followed, but as the first half drew to a close, the Tigers went ahead again through Davy Gordon, who was emerging as the game's key figure with his powerful display at wing-half.

In the second session the home side's superiority began to tell. 'Soldier' Wilson struck a third and Peter Howe was unfortunate to have an effort disallowed. Ten minutes from the final whistle, Gordon set the seal on a splendid afternoon's work with his side's fourth goal.

Victory became even sweeter when it was learned that the other three clubs new to League fare had all lost.

Hull City: Spendiff; Langley, Jones, Martin, Robinson, Gordon, Rushton, Spence, Wilson, Howe, Raisbeck.
Barnsley: Thorpe; Hay, Stacey, Hellewell, Donagher, Oxspring, Ryall, Beech, Pegg, Bell, Wall.

Referee: F.H.Dennis (Middlesbrough) — *Attendance: 8,000*

Match to Remember 3 — 30 April 1910

Oldham Athletic 3 Hull City 0

AS the final Saturday of the season dawned, it was anyone's guess as to who would fill the two promotion places at the top of the Second Division. Leaders Manchester City needed 'only a point' from their visit to Wolves. Hull City needed 'only a point' from their trip to Oldham. Third-placed Derby needed to beat West Brom and rely on Oldham beating the Tigers, whilst the Latics, in fourth spot, depended on the Rams dropping at least a point, even if they overcame City.

The Anlaby Road men were packed off to Blackpool for special training and the tonic of the sea breezes. They had been promised gold watches and chains if they made the First Division. On the eve of the make-or-break contest, Davy Gordon was asked to predict the outcome: "It is certain to be a tremendously hard game and, with the two sides so nearly on terms of equality, that which gets the most luck may win. It will not be for want of trying if we fail at Oldham. We are all very hopeful, and I will leave it at that."

The previous Saturday, the City side had played like world-beaters to demolish outsiders West Brom 5-1. It appeared that their form had peaked at precisely the right time. What manner of disaster, then, overtook the Tigers on that fateful day? One decisive factor was the absence of Jack McQuillan, who failed to throw off the effects of a knock sustained against the Throstles. Tommy Nevins found himself at left-back, not his preferred flank, and with an unfamiliar partner in late-season signing Dan Gordon. The weak link in City's line-up was quickly spotted by the Latics.

On a rain-saturated pitch, which was not to the Tigers' liking, Broad broke away after 18 minutes and scored. Seven minutes later, in virtually Oldham's second attack, Alf Toward got away to add a second. To City supporters he looked well offside but the goal stood. Here, though, was the bitter irony. Toward had been a Tiger until the close of 1909, unable to command a regular first-team place. His form had improved by leaps and bounds with regular League football at Boundary Park.

After those set-backs the visitors came more into the game, but the lethal finishing of a week ago eluded them and Athletic's two-goal advantage rarely looked under threat. Ten minutes from the finish, Walders added a third.

The news that Derby had only drawn at West Brom brought further jubilation for the vast crowd. The Latics had sneaked ahead of both the Tigers and the Rams on goal-average. Their achievement was all the more remarkable considering that earlier in the season, when Hull City lost their unbeaten record to Manchester City, Oldham were anchored at the foot of the table.

Back in Hull, the City party commiserated at the Station Hotel. Davy Gordon vowed they would be trying even harder the following September.

The end of the season, though, was not entirely the end of the Tigers' hopes. Soon after, Arsenal, who missed relegation by a place, were reported to be in serious financial difficulties. There was talk of the club folding, creating a vacancy in the top flight. City hopes rose once more but the crisis at the Woolwich club was averted and the Tigers remained a Second Division side.

Oldham Athletic: Matthews; Hodson, Cope, Downie, Walders, Wilson, Broad, Fay, Toward, Montgomery, Miller.
Hull City: Roughley; Dan Gordon, Nevins, G.Browell, A.Browell, Davy Gordon, Joe Smith, Temple, Jack Smith, Wally Smith, Neve.

Referee: A.McArthur (Newcastle-upon-Tyne) *Attendance: 29,083*

Hull City 1911-12. Back row (left to right): Townend, Chapman, Robson, Milner, A.Browell, McIntosh, Drewery. Third row: A.Langley (manager), Simmon, McQuillan, Houghton, Roughley, Hendry, Wilkinson, Gordon, W.Leach (trainer). Second row: Joe Smith, W.Wright, Nevins, T.Browell, Temple, Neve, W.Smith. Front row: Pearce, E.Smith, Best, Boland.

Match to Remember 4 — 4 November 1911

Wolverhampton Wanderers 8 Hull City 0

HOW the mighty fell! After victory at Leeds a week earlier, the name of Hull City sat proudly at the head of the Second Division. The identical team set off full of confidence for Wolverhampton, two points behind in third place. There was absolutely no indication of the catastrophe which was to follow.

Billy Halligan put the Wanderers ahead after ten minutes. Then Tim Wright departed to the dressing-room for five minutes with an ankle injury. He returned to battle on gamely. Even when Jack Needham increased his side's advantage before the interval, there was no hint of what was to come in the second half.

After the resumption, Wolves suddenly ran riot. Needham scored the third after 47 minutes. Three minutes later Yule put away a fourth. Then Joe Smith hobbled out of the action with damaged knee ligaments. With his departure went the Tigers' remote hopes of getting back into the match. The ravenous Wolves did as they pleased after that. Needham and Halligan brought up the half dozen before the hour mark. Halligan piled on the agony with a seventh and, two minutes from the end, Yule extended the margin of City's heaviest League defeat to eight. Strangely, both hat-trick scorers were to join the Tigers, Halligan in 1913 and Needham in 1920.

Wolverhampton Wanderers: Boxley; Collins, Garratly, Groves, Hunt, Bishop, Harrison, Hedley, Halligan, Needham, Yule.
Hull City: Roughley; Nevins, McQuillan, W.Wright, A.Browell, Gordon, J.Smith, Chapman, T.Browell, Temple, G.Wright.

Referee: T.Field (Mexborough) — *Attendance: 15,000*

At least the Tigers' programme editor was able to see the brighter side. His comments in the next issue, for the visit of Leicester, included the following gems:
The Wolves Hunt-ed the Tigers to some purpose.
"Yes, our goal-average is equal to 3 to 1," said a visiting official before the match. "Yule Needham," was the reply.
It isn't true that some of the players were heard to remark as late as Wednesday last, "I've 8-0 since Saturday."

Match to Remember 5 19 February 1921

Hull City 3 Burnley 0

AFTER easing past Western League club Bath and surmounting a more difficult obstacle at Southern Section leaders Crystal Palace, the Tigers were drawn at home to 'invincible' Burnley in the third round of the FA Cup. The Turf Moor side had not lost in 26 League and Cup matches.

Their captain, Tom Boyle, unperturbed by the absence of Scottish international right-half George Holley, struck down with pleurisy, commented: "Hull City does not strike me as a difficult proposition. We have the temperament for the stress and strain of present-day football. Our League position is unassailable. We can afford to concentrate on winning the Cup."

Nor did he seem worried that injury would prevent Anderson from leading the attack. His absence was a pity because a fascinating duel had been on the cards between him and Mike Gilhooley. The pair had been teammates at Clydebank.

What followed was the ultimate vindication of a team selection conceived as a desperation measure. Since the departure of David Mercer to Sheffield United, full-back Tommy Brandon had been pushed forward to inside-right. Against Burnley, his finishing was lethal. Not that this was a one-man show, for all the players in black and amber played their parts in an unforgettable 90 minutes.

The Tigers set off at a whirlwind pace. Burnley thought they would never keep it up, but the benefits of special training at Ravenscar told and City never slackened. Seconds before half-time, Tommy Brandon struck a vital blow. Harry Sergeaunt's drive was parried by Dawson and Brandon dived in to head his side in front.

Eighteen minutes later he dealt the Lancastrians a further hammer blow. From all of 30 yards he unleashed a rocket of a shot into the corner of the net.

The large Burnley contingent saw their record crumbling. They were in for another disappointment before the end as Harry Wilson added a third goal after 76 minutes. The Irishman might easily have had another with a little more steadiness in front of goal, but it would have been out of place to criticize after such an outstanding performance.

In the League, Burnley carried on their unbeaten run for another month, 30 games in all. It made the Tigers' win an even greater achievement.

Hull City: W.Mercer; Cheetham, Bell, Collier, Gilhooley, Bleakley, Crawford, Brandon, McKinney, Sergeaunt, Wilson.
Burnley: Dawson; Smelt, Jones, Nesbitt, Boyle, Watson, Mosscrop, Kelly, Freeman, Cross, Weaver.

Referee: A.Kirby (Preston) *Attendance: 26,000*

Bob Coverdale, a key figure in the Tigers' FA Cup victory over Middlesbrough.

Match to Remember 6 — 7 January 1922

Hull City 5 Middlesbrough 0

A YEAR after their eclipse of Burnley, the Tigers took on another top side and there was a sense of expectancy in the days leading up to Middlesbrough's visit to Anlaby Road. Tommy Brandon, scoring hero of the Burnley game, had now lost his place in the side, with Jimmy Lodge occupying the right-back spot and Bob Coverdale, a close-season signing from Sunderland, settling down at inside-right. Indeed, Jackie Crawford was the only forward from the Burnley match to face Middlesbrough. At half-back, though, that great driving force of Collier, Gilhooley and Bleakley survived intact, to be the springboard to stand the form book on its head again.

The Tigers were thoroughly wound up for the big day and soon took the initiative. Mills, Flood and Hughes all came close to breaking the deadlock but, with half-time in sight, 'Boro's defence looked as if it might hold out. With seven minutes left, the City attack swept down on Tim Williamson's goal again and a fine move ended with Crawford giving his side a deserved lead.

The second half began with more City pressure. After 53 minutes Coverdale, the brains of the attack, got on the score-sheet and 'Boro began to crumble. Paddy Mills put away the third after 64 minutes. Such was the Tigers' domination that Tommy Bleakley, supporting his attack, struck the fourth five minutes before the finish. The last word in another famous victory, though, went to Coverdale, who chipped in the fifth after Williamson had parried a shot.

Little had been seen of the Teessiders' own attack. Mick Gilhooley had Scottish international Andy Wilson, 'the most dangerous shot in the three countries', completely subdued. Such a commanding display earned Gilhooley a place in the Scottish side the following month.

Hull City: Mercer; Lodge, Bell, Collier, Gilhooley, Bleakley, Crawford, Coverdale, Mills, Flood, Hughes.
Middlesbrough: Williamson; Marshall, Fox, Davidson, Ellerington, Pender, J.Carr, Birrell, Wilson, Elliott, Urwin.

Referee: J.A.Horsfield (Lincoln) *Attendance: 23,000*

Match to Remember 7 15 February 1930

Manchester City 1 Hull City 2

THE Hull City team had already served notice of their intentions in the 1929-30 FA Cup competition by winning 4-3 at Southern Section leaders Plymouth and disposing of Second Division front-runners Blackpool 3-1. They had been compelled to wait a few days to find out their fifth-round opponents. Swindon Town or Manchester City was to be their destination. The Southern Section side had gained a creditable draw against a team running strongly for the League championship. However, when the clubs replayed at Maine Road, the southerners were thrashed 10-1.

The Hull players preferred to train at home this season, a decided break with tradition, and toned up with 'vapour and sunshine' treatment at the Hull Corporation Electric and Vapour Baths in Epworth Street. On the morning of the match the Tigers' task was made even more difficult. Matt Bell failed a fitness test on his foot, injured at Notts County a fortnight earlier. The Hull manager made a bold choice to fill the left-back spot. Jimmy Howieson moved there with Ronnie Starling occupying the vacant inside-left position. The Scot took on the additional responsibility of captaincy.

Initially it seemed that McCracken's move had misfired. The Tigers' defence began shakily and after a mere three minutes, Bobby Marshall put Ernie Toseland through to score from ten yards out. Visions of Swindon's annihilation crept into the minds of some 58,000 Manchester fans. Perhaps their team had similar ideas, but the Tigers began to warm to their task and the elaborate, perhaps over-elaborate, Manchester attacks came up against an unyielding Hull rearguard. Howieson, the potential weak link, rapidly grew in confidence and when the Mancunians got the better of him, cover was swiftly across. Toseland broke through again, but Fred Gibson brilliantly turned his shot away for a corner.

The Tigers, on the few occasions when they had chance to attack, moved forward with a simplicity and directness which made their opponents' defence look distinctly the poorer of the two. After half an hour, Billy Taylor sped past the challenges of Jimmy McMullan and Billy Felton and drove the ball goalwards, where the leaping Paddy Mills deflected it beyond a helpless goalkeeper.

Manchester City bore down once more on the Tigers' goal and another 15 minutes of wonderful defensive work brought the interval. Matt Bell, who had watched anxiously from the touch-line, said afterwards: "At half-time, when the teams were level, I felt sure that we should not lose."

Inspired by Bill McCracken's words in the dressing-room, the City players kept up the good work after the resumption. With the crack Manchester forwards reduced to nought, a splendid piece of opportunism on the part of Billy Taylor, almost inevitably it seems in retrospect, put the Tigers in front. Stan Alexander got away from McMullan and raced down the right wing. Taylor, with a fine sense of anticipation, had moved in and when Alexander put the ball inside, the winger was there to flash it into the net for the decisive score.

Thereafter the First Division side threw everything into attack. Well before the end they had resorted to 'kick and rush' but the Tigers had not been out-finessed and they were certainly not going to be out-rushed. Even in the last quarter of an hour, with Arthur Childs feeling the effects of a bang in the ribs, the Hull defence just refused to be beaten.

Manchester City: Barber; Ridley, Felton, Barrass, Cowan, McMullan, Toseland, Marshall, Johnson, Tilson, Brook.
Hull City: Gibson; Goldsmith, Howieson, Walsh, Childs, Gowdy, Taylor, Alexander, Mills, Starling, Duncan.

Referee: W.Phipps (West Bromwich) *Attendance: 61,574*

Tigers' goalkeeper Gibson (left) performed wonders. Starling (right) played deep to thwart Newcastle's attack.

Match to Remember 8 — 1 March 1930

Newcastle United 1 Hull City 1

THE sixth-round draw gave the Tigers another away tie and a challenge full of intriguing possibilities, for they had to visit their manager's former club. The pairing brought Sam Weaver in opposition to his former teammates. McCracken was quick to point out that he had not been on the losing side in previous meetings between the pair. United were deep in trouble at the wrong end of the First Division, but Hughie Gallacher had expressly stated that this was going to be his year for a Cup-winners' medal — and scarcely a Tynesider saw reason to disagree with him.

The gates at St James' Park were closed before the start and some of those who made the long journey from Hull were unable to see the thrilling contest. So great was the number inside the ground, including some 6,000 City fans, that in the course of the match the barriers gave way on one corner of the ground.

Those who were inside saw a keen game, with the outcome in doubt to the last. It was a typical Cup-tie. The *Hull Evening News* recorded that 'it was a scrappy contest in which tempers were frayed and free-kicks all too frequent. The spectacular work came from the Magpies, who flashed the ball about at times with remarkable celerity, but without really mastering the opposition.' Jimmy Howieson stuck like the proverbial leech to Hughie Gallacher, who had opted to play inside-right rather than centre-forward. Late in the game Gallacher reverted to centre-forward, but fared no better at the hands of Childs.

Newcastle took the lead after 27 minutes, when Tommy Lang's powerful header from Jimmy Boyd's centre eluded Gibson, but the Tynesiders were given no chance to settle comfortably on their advantage, as the Tigers worried away at their more illustrious opponents with non-stop endeavour. The Tigers' forwards were employing the 'W' formation. That is to say, Howieson and Starling lay deep, forming with Walsh and Gowdy a four-man midfield barrier. The tactic took much of the danger out of United's attacking moves. On the other hand, it left Stan Alexander lacking in support at centre-forward, but it was that 'fleet-footed son of Mercury' whose dashing play eventually brought him the Tigers' equalizer. Dally Duncan swung over a centre and Alexander flung himself bravely between the home backs to head the ball into the net.

For a brief spell the Newcastle defence rocked as the Tigers sought a winner, but by the finish Gibson was performing heroics once more to keep United's forwards at bay, one save from a Gallacher rocket being quite extraordinary. It would have been harsh indeed if City had lost at the death.

Newcastle United: McInroy; J.Richardson, Thomson, Mathison, Harris, Weaver, Boyd, Gallacher, Hutchison, McDonald, Lang.
Hull City: Gibson; Goldsmith, Bell, Walsh, Childs, Gowdy, Taylor, Starling, Alexander, Howieson, Duncan.

Referee: W. Walden (Derby) — *Attendance: 63,486*

Match to Remember 9 — 6 March 1930

Hull City 1 Newcastle United 0

SO great was the interest in the replay that Hull City Council adjourned to allow its members to watch the match. A record crowd of almost 33,000 squeezed into Anlaby Road to witness the resumption of the struggle. With Paddy Mills still unfit, City, for once, were unchanged, but United made several alterations to their side and included their England centre-half, a certain Jack Hill, who had been out of the team since the fourth round.

Fortunes ebbed and flowed in the first half. City, early in the ascendant, concentrating on close-passing movements, could not force the all-important breakthrough. Newcastle, trying to progress by long-passing moves, subjected the home rearguard to intense pressure, but the Tigers' defence was in fine fettle once more. Half-time arrived with neither side having scored.

Then that wizard Jimmy Howieson conjured up one of those inimitable pieces of magic. The words of an eyewitness best tell the story of the sensational restart:

'Following a smart run and kick across by Taylor, Howieson fastened on to the ball. It was here that the Scottish international bluffed the opposition. They fully expected him to whip the ball over to either Duncan on his left or return it to Taylor on the right. However, to the intense jubilation of the home supporters and the chagrin of the visiting defence, he elected to send in a hard left-foot drive, which was delivered with such force and utter unexpectedness that it found the far corner of the net despite McInroy's despairing attempt to save it. The Newcastle custodian got his finger-tips to it, but was powerless to do anything but help the ball on its way. There was a pause, an almost ethereal silence, as the move was entirely unexpected, and the ball was in the back of the net before the huge crowd realized what had happened. Then they let forth a full-blooded Yorkshire roar. It was many moons since such intense enthusiasm had been witnessed at Anlaby Road.'

From that point the game changed and the Tigers were forced on to the defensive. Not only were the visitors desperate for an equalizer, but City's own attacking options also became increasingly limited as both wingers, Taylor and Duncan, felt the effects of strong United challenges. Alexander ploughed a lone furrow, fast and fearless, against Jack Hill. Wave after wave of black and white swept down upon the Tigers' goal and the rest of the game belonged to one man — Fred Gibson. Time after time he was in the right place at the right moment. Hughie Gallacher, as his dream of a Cup-winners' medal began to hang in the balance, tried all his wiles, but Childs, Goldsmith and Bell stuck resolutely to their task and behind them Gibson was there with uncanny anticipation. Hull City had reached their first FA Cup semi-final.

Hull City: Gibson; Goldsmith, Bell, Walsh, Childs, Gowdy, Taylor, Starling, Alexander, Howieson, Duncan.
Newcastle United: McInroy; Maitland, Thomson, McKenzie, Hill, Weaver, Hutchison, J.R.Richardson, Gallacher, McDonald, Lang.

Referee: W. Walden (Derby) — *Attendance: 32,930*

> *Throughout two wars the Press did their best to maintain coverage of the game under difficult circumstances. Occasionally the gremlins would get into the wires. One report credited Tigers' guest George Lamb with this spectacular goal: 'Lamb crossed the ball into the centre and scored with a beautiful header'.*

Match to Remember 10 22 March 1930

Arsenal 2 Hull City 2

THE City players were the only ones to prepare for the 1930 FA Cup semi-finals at home. Arsenal toned up at Harrogate. On the eve of the match, manager McCracken declared: "If our team is fit there is nothing else for it but Wembley for us." The opening proviso was an important one, for several of the City players fought to throw off injuries. Taylor and Duncan had not played since the replay against Newcastle. Others contended with the bumps and bruises of a strenuous month's activity. Taylor was the only one who failed to make the Elland Road game, but with Paddy Mills back in the reckoning, Alexander's removal to the right wing was the simplest rearrangement.

To the surprise of many it was the Tigers, set to play into the wind, who made the early running, as Walsh, Childs and Gowdy kept a tight rein on the Londoners' much-vaunted forward-line, including £10,000 David Jack, the country's most expensive footballer. Behind them Bell and Goldsmith repeatedly worked the offside trap to good effect. Consequently, when City themselves moved forward to attack, they looked a more confident side than Arsenal.

With only 15 minutes gone, the Tigers went into the lead with a quite remarkable goal as the incomparable Jimmy Howieson pulled out another gem from his bag of tricks. The Scot obtained possession just inside the Arsenal half and, noticing that goalkeeper Lewis was well off his line, aimed a huge lob in the direction of the Gunners' goal. The ball hung tantalizingly in the wind and thoroughly deceived Lewis as it descended just below the bar, crossed the line and bounced up into the roof of the net. Howieson was immediately engulfed by his teammates.

From that point on there was only one team in it and, on the half-hour, Howieson

Arsenal goalkeeper Dan Lewis watches the ball flash past his post as the Tigers attack in the semi-final at Leeds Road, Huddersfield. It was one of several near-misses for Hull City but the Gunners eventually pulled back from a two-goal deficit to earn a replay.

played a major part in increasing the Tigers' lead. A masterly interchange between him and Duncan resulted in the latter racing on to the inside man's pass to crash a fierce drive beyond Lewis's despairing dive. Although Eddie Hapgood managed to get a leg to the ball, he could only deflect it on to its original destination, the back of the Arsenal net.

Half-time arrived with the Tigers seemingly set fair for Wembley, but the Londoners came out determined to get back into the game. They altered their tactics, too, making better use of their physical superiority. Speed and weight were made to count. Repeatedly the ball was pushed out to Cliff Bastin and Joe Hulme on the wings, who ran and ran with the speed of hares. David Jack briefly changed places with his centre-forward and the Tigers found much more difficulty in putting the First Division outfit offside. By the time Jack and Lambert switched back, City were feeling the effects of a series of hefty challenges. Bell, Goldsmith, Walsh and Mills were all in the wars.

Eventually, in the 67th minute, Hulme got away down the right and centred for Jack to pull a goal back from close range. Immediately, City moved Walsh, who had a torn muscle, out on to the right wing. Paddy Mills dropped into the half-back line, but he nursed a shoulder injury and was scarcely fitter than Walsh.

Arsenal, growing in confidence all the time, went flat out for an equalizer. The Tigers' depleted forces again defended magnificently and seemed as if they would manage to hold out. They did so until eight minutes from the end. Mills failed to cut off Bastin. The winger had a clear route to goal and from the corner of the penalty-area curled a fierce shot past a helpless Gibson. The luck of the Arsenal had prevailed again.

Arsenal: Lewis; Parker, Hapgood, Baker, Seddon, Jones, Hulme, Jack, Lambert, James, Bastin.
Hull City: Gibson; Goldsmith, Bell, Walsh, Childs, Gowdy, Alexander, Starling, Mills, Howieson, Duncan.

Referee: A.H.Kingscott (Long Eaton) *Attendance: 47,549*

Arsenal's David Jack scores the only goal of the semi-final replay at Villa Park.

Match to Remember 11 — 26 March 1930

Arsenal 1 Hull City 0

THE quest for Wembley moved to Villa Park and outwardly, at any rate, the Tigers remained confident. City's manager, full of Irish witicisms, warned: "Arsenal might like to know that the Tigers have been feeding on blood and raw meat since Saturday and we have had our teeth sharpened for the fray." Matt Bell vowed: "We showed that we could master the Arsenal in the first half at Leeds and tomorrow we shall be out to do the same, only the Tigers will on no account relax their grip this time."

City began the replay without the injured Walsh and Alexander. Into the side came veteran Tommy Bleakley and reserve winger Phil Cartwright. Arsenal surprisingly left out Hulme in favour of Williams.

The Londoners' replacement was soon to the fore in what turned out to be the decisive move of the game, which came after only 11 minutes. James pushed the ball through for Williams to run on to and pull back into the centre where Jack beat Gibson with a low shot. Here, too, was controversy. There were many who thought that the pass from James had run over the dead-ball line before Williams reached it. Bell and Gowdy both felt certain the ball would pass out of play, for neither offered any challenge to Williams. After the match Fred Gibson sportingly confirmed that the goal was in order.

The Tigers struck back spiritedly in search of an equalizer, but the tackling was keen on both sides and good football at a premium. Jimmy Howieson invariably found three men upon him as soon as the ball came his way.

Five minutes after the interval the Tigers suffered another cruel piece of misfortune when the referee sent off Childs after the City centre-half had moved towards James and Jack to attempt to dispossess the Arsenal men. The referee stopped play and ordered Childs to the dressing-room for allegedly kicking at James. The official must have been the only person in the ground to construe the incident in such a way and the crowd viewed the decision in a very poor light and made their feelings known at every suitable opportunity.

The ten men had much the better of the remaining 40 minutes, but with Starling withdrawn to half-back, the forward line lacked effectiveness. Howieson landed an overhead kick on the crossbar. Mills was narrowly off target. A Starling shot almost took Lewis with it into the net but an equalizer just would not come and City were out of the Cup. Dr Pullan felt so strongly about the refereeing of the replay that he resigned the chairmanship in protest.

Arsenal: Lewis; Parker, Hapgood, Baker, Seddon, Jones, Williams, Jack, Lambert, James, Bastin.
Hull City: Gibson; Goldsmith, Bell, Bleakley, Childs, Gowdy, Cartwright, Starling, Mills, Howieson, Duncan.

Referee: A.H.Kingscott (Long Eaton) — *Attendance: 46,200*

Match to Remember 12 — 1 May 1933

Hull City 2 York City 1

FOR most of the season it had been a three-way struggle at the top of the Northern Section, between Chester, Wrexham and Hull City. The Tigers' defeat of Chester had dented the hopes of one rival and victory over Crewe left City needing two points from two games to win promotion for the first time and with it a return to the Second Division.

York were struggling to avoid re-election and the vast crowd which gathered on the Anlaby Road ground doubtless expected City to finish the job in style, but after ten minutes Maddison suffered torn shoulder ligaments. For the next 35 minutes the team seemed as concerned to protect their goalkeeper as to make the all-important score. York, meanwhile, were doing their level best to cause an upset.

The half-time team-talk clearly attempted to dispel the Tigers' caution. After the resumption they began to move on to the offensive in something approaching their customary style. Within ten minutes Fenoughty, back helping his defence, handled the ball and from the resulting penalty, Bill McNaughton gratefully hammered the Tigers into the lead, to the immense relief of every Hull supporter. Only two minutes later the centre-forward worked his way into a shooting position to crack another drive, hard and true, past Fawcett.

News that Stockport were beating Wrexham added to the elation but York refused to permit the hoped-for avalanche. Seven minutes from the end Jenkinson nipped in to get the better of George Maddison, who had soldiered on gallantly in goal. When the final whistle sounded, the crowd surged on to the pitch as the players scampered — not quickly enough — to the dressing-rooms. Cushions from the grandstand seats were flung high into the evening sky. Over 100 of them were never to be seen again.

The last word belonged to chairman Jim Barraclough. When the crowd had finally dispersed, the players and directors moved to Field's Restaurant for a celebration. There Mr Barraclough recalled a piece of advice given to him soon after the club had been relegated. The director of another club had said to him: "You will have to kick your way out of the Third Division." The City chairman looked round at his damaged goalkeeper and at Jack Hill's black eye and quipped, "It seems to me we have been kicked out of the Third Division."

Hull City: Maddison; Goldsmith, Woodhead, Gardner, Hill, Denby, Forward, Longden, McNaughton, Wainscoat, Sargeant.
York City: Fawcett; Wass, T.Maskill, Fox, Spargo, Greener, Jenkinson, Fenoughty, Mitchell, McDonald, Spooner.

Referee: R. W. Blake (Middlesbrough) — *Attendance: 19,233*

The playing staff at the start of the 1932-3 Northern Section championship-winning season. Russell Wainscoat did not train at Anlaby Road, and consequently was not present at the photo-call.

CITY SHOOT ELEVEN GOALS— CLUB'S NEW SCORING RECORD

ALL THE FORWARDS HIT THE TARGET

Successful Shooting Against Carlisle Almost Monotonous

(By "THREE CROWNS")

RESULT: HULL CITY 11, CARLISLE UNITED 1

Match to Remember 13 — 14 January 1939

Hull City 11 Carlisle United 1

THE Tigers ended 1938 with two six-goal defeats within a week, at New Brighton and Bradford City. There was absolutely no indication that they would begin the New Year in record-breaking style.

The side to play Carlisle showed just two changes, one positional, from that beaten so decisively. George Richardson returned, making a belated home League debut almost two months after joining the club, with Cliff Hubbard out on the wing to the exclusion of 'Tolley' Wienand.

A raw afternoon began on a sombre note, with the players, wearing black arm-bands, standing in silence as a mark of respect for the League's president, Mr Charles Sutcliffe, whose death had cast a cloud across the League's Jubilee celebrations.

City had the benefit of an early goal, Bill Dickinson shooting home from close range after six minutes. United struck back and Murphy grazed Jack Ellis's crossbar with a rising shot, but after 20 minutes Arthur Cunliffe centred and Richardson soared to head the second goal. Before United realized, Cunliffe was advancing again, this time cutting in himself and firing in a shot which rolled over the outstretched foot of goalkeeper Knox.

City continued to have the better of it, but Carlisle resisted bravely until two minutes before the break when Charlie Robinson hammered in an unstoppable long-range effort. Before the whistle sounded for half-time, Hunt pulled a goal back for the visitors and the fans wondered what might be in store in the second half.

The answer was barely a minute in coming. Hubbard ran on to Richardson's pass and sent in a low drive to register City's fifth goal. From then on it was almost a 'procession.' Four minutes later the irrepressible Cunliffe outpaced the defence and Dickinson was up to head home off a post. Cunliffe grabbed the next, after the Carlisle 'keeper fumbled a Richardson header. Hubbard made the most of another defensive error and Dai Davies dived to head home a pin-point cross from Cunliffe. Three minutes from the end another centre from the former international was put away by Dickinson, whose hat-trick also brought up double figures.

Then, in the last minute, Davies took the total to 11, Hull City's highest score in the Football League. Once again the provider was the Tigers' outside-left, who, even as the final whistle sounded, was racing goalwards in search of another goal.

Hull City: Ellis; Woodhead, Dowen, Robinson, Blyth, Hardy, Hubbard, Richardson, Dickinson, Davies, Cunliffe.
Carlisle United: Knox; J.Hamilton, Sanderson, Taylor, Howshall, Smith, Embleton, Beresford, Hunt, Murphy, S.Hamilton.

Referee: H.Hartley (Bolton) *Attendance: 5,298*

Match to Remember 14 — 29 January 1949

Grimsby Town 2   Hull City 3

THE Tigers had already made their mark in the FA Cup tournament with the imperious way in which, without Raich Carter, they swept aside Reading in the second-round replay at Elm Park and then proceeded to upstage Second Division Blackburn at Ewood Park. The scene was set for a fourth-round trip to Blundell Park.

Carter was in the side on this occasion and in the cut and thrust of the local derby, he played a key role in opening up the Grimsby defence. Centre-forward Norman Moore, who joined City on a free transfer from the Mariners, also had a decisive influence on the outcome of the game.

After 28 minutes, Viggo Jensen's perfect pass sent Moore racing through the Grimsby defence to score from ten yards out. The home side retaliated and their pressure brought an equalizer eight minutes before the interval, Tommy Briggs heading in Stan Lloyd's cross.

The excitement reached even greater intensity before the first half was over. Carter fired in a power drive from a free-kick with two minutes remaining. From the edge of the area, Ernie Forrest's shot somehow threaded its way through the crowd and past Billy Bly and the Mariners went in on terms.

The sides battled away hammer and tongs in the second half and Bill Cairns felt the effects of a knock. There were three minutes left when Ken Moody dramatically mis-hit a clearance and Moore was on to the ball in a flash to crash home the winner.

In a desperate finale, Jim Whitfield netted but the Tigers heaved a sigh of relief when the referee ruled the effort offside.

Grimsby Town: Chisholm; Moody, Fisher, McKenna, Sibley, Forrest, McStay, Whitfield, Briggs, Cairns, Lloyd.
Hull City: Bly; Taylor, Berry, Greenhalgh, Meens, Mellor, Harrison, Jensen, Moore, Buchan, Carter.

Referee: B.J.Maltby (Nottingham) — *Attendance: 26,505*

Norman Moore challenges Grimsby Town goalkeeper Wilf Chisholm. Viggo Jensen (far left) and Raich Carter (partly hidden) await the outcome.

Match to Remember 15 — 12 February 1949

Stoke City 0 Hull City 2

THE fifth round of the Cup sent the Tigers off to First Division Stoke and they were not in the least bit worried. For the umpteenth time Raich Carter reiterated that his priority was just to play quality soccer and not to worry about the scoreline.

High-class football they certainly produced and Stoke tumbled out of the Cup, beaten by what the critics rated as one of the finest performances of the season, with Carter the controlling figure. 'Fast, scintillating football which bewildered a shaky defence . . .their passing was excellent, their shooting sure and their defensive covering at times brilliant,' wrote Tex Traill. 'Hull had all the method, self-possession and teamcraft, plus the wonderful inspiration of Raich Carter,' said John Martin. 'Carter wandered everywhere,' added W.A.Clarke, 'but always was he in the right place at the right time, scheming, foraging, full of forcefulness.'

At times only England centre-half Neil Franklin prevented Stoke from being overwhelmed. It is true they were handicapped by an injury to Frank Mountford, but it is also true that they were already trailing to a vintage header from Norman Moore after 20 minutes.

City had Jimmy Greenhalgh hobbling, but the difference was that Greenhalgh was in the right place to score the Tigers' second goal a couple of minutes from the end, lobbing the ball over the advancing goalkeeper. The pair raced back after it, Herod fisted it out, but a keen-eyed linesman spotted that the ball was already over the line.

Said Carter after this latest triumph: "This is one of the greatest things that ever happened to me — to have seen the way our lads played football."

Stoke City: Herod; Watkin, Kirton, F.Mountford, Franklin, Sellars, G.Mountford, Bowyer, Steele, Peppitt, Ormston.
Hull City: Bly; Taylor, Berry, Greenhalgh, Meens, Mellor, Harrison, Jensen, Moore, Buchan, Carter.

Referee: W.J.Edwards (Yeovil) — *Attendance: 46,738*

Stoke goalkeeper Dennis Herod almost decapitating Jimmy Greenhalgh as he makes a belated attempt to fist out the half-back's goal-bound lob which clinched the Tigers' place in the quarter-finals.

Jack Taylor (2) and Harold Meens (5) can only watch as Billy Bly dives at the feet of Manchester United's Stan Pearson in a vain attempt to stop the forward scoring the goal which ended the Tigers' giantkilling Cup run.

Match to Remember 16 — 26 February 1949

Hull City 0 Manchester United 1

AFTER three away draws the Tigers pulled out the sixth-round 'plum,' a home tie against FA Cup holders, Manchester United. The Old Trafford club had also finished runners-up in the League and this season were once again among the top half-dozen. The optimists at Boothferry Park began to talk of Wembley. The pessimists were becoming increasingly worried about the club's declared aim of promotion, as the number of games in hand on Rotherham increased to four and the Tigers faced nine fixtures in April.

The day after the side's match at Valley Parade, City's car-park was crammed with thousands queuing for Cup tickets and one side of Boothferry Road had to be closed to traffic. Many went away disappointed and the board contemplated plans to increase the ground capacity still further. A small temporary stand helped push the spiralling attendance record to its all-time high of 55,019. Some were doubly disappointed, as forged tickets began to appear in Hull and Manchester. There were rumours that thousands would be trying to get in, unwittingly, with the wrong tickets. On the day, scrutineers at each turnstile found all but around 50 tickets were genuine.

The game was not a classic like City's previous giantkilling exploits. It developed into a cut and thrust encounter, as both sets of half-backs were quick to the tackle and the pace was never allowed to slacken. United were even fleeter of foot than the Tigers, but City's defence, despite anxious moments, seldom gave the visitors' attack much room to manœuvre. Carter was a forceful figure, but United never allowed him to dictate the exchanges as other sides had to their cost.

For three-quarters of the game the Northern Section side held their illustrious opponents before succumbing to a goal reminiscent of the Arsenal effort which put City out of the semi-final in 1930. The move began in the 72nd minute with City nearly taking the lead, but for Johnny Ball clearing off his own line. The ball came from the full-back, via Ronnie Burke, to Jimmy Delaney in a rapid counter-attack. Delaney pushed the ball past Allan Mellor and produced a phenomenal turn of speed to prevent it running dead. Mellor seemed to think it would and some in the crowd thought it had, but Delaney pulled back for Stan Pearson to turn the ball in as Billy Bly made a courageous effort to beat the inside-right to the ball. Bly had struggled bravely on after an injury in a first-half goalmouth mêlée, which left him with a broken nose, profusely bleeding. The City goalkeeper scarcely knew where he was for most of the game.

Beaten but unbowed, the Tigers were freed to concentrate on the more important matter of promotion.

Hull City: Bly; Taylor, Berry, Greenhalgh, Meens, Mellor, Harrison, Jensen, Moore, Buchan, Carter.
Manchester United: Crompton; Ball, Aston, Cockburn, Chilton, McGlen, Delaney, Pearson, Burke, Rowley, Mitten.

Referee: R.J.Leafe (Nottingham) — *Attendance: 55,019*

Match to Remember 17 — 3 November 1962

Hull City 5 Crook Town 4

THERE have been many gripping contests at Boothferry Park over the years, but few match the Tigers' first round FA Cup tie against the FA Amateur Cup holders, Crook Town. The Northern League side fielded several amateur internationals, including goalkeeper Ray Snowball, who went on to play League football for Darlington.

After Ray Henderson put City in front with 11 minutes gone, their early authority was abruptly jolted when Ken Bowron equalized almost on the half-hour. That shock paled into insignificance in comparison with what followed. Within ten minutes John Cocking and Peter Garbutt cracked in further goals.

Any hopes the Tigers had of re-establishing their initial superiority after the break were shattered inside four minutes when Cocking headed a fourth for Crook. Some teams might have collapsed at that point, but City hung on to a lifeline from the quick-thinking McSeveney, who made the most of a defensive error two minutes later.

That served to remind Crook of their own vulnerability and although it was 20 minutes before another goal came, the challenge of the gallant amateurs was fast ebbing away. Chris Chilton rose superbly to head City's third after 70 minutes. A minute later McSeveney tucked away the equalizer and as the Tigers made the most of a weakness down the Crook left flank, Henderson's winner, with 11 minutes remaining, completed an amazing escape act.

A richly deserved standing ovation greeted the amateurs' efforts and the Tigers progressed with great relief to the second round.

Hull City: Williams; Davidson, Garvey, Sharpe, Feasey, E.McMillan, Clarke, Price, Chilton, Henderson, McSeveney.
Crook Town: Snowball; Gardener, Gale, Storey, Heatherington, Brown, Sparks, Garbutt, Bowron, Cocking, J.McMillan.

Referee: E.Norman (Blackburn) *Attendance: 9,484*

Chris Chilton rose superbly to head the Tigers' third goal against amateurs Crook Town. Chilton's strike brought City back into a game which they had looked like losing in sensational fashion.

George Graham (hidden) heads Chelsea into a two-goal lead at Stamford Bridge.

Match to Remember 18 — 26 March 1966

Chelsea 2 Hull City 2

THE Tigers had caused two upsets in the FA Cup, knocking out Second Division pace-setters Southampton and First Division Nottingham Forest. Chelsea had scraped through the fifth round by the odd goal in five at home to Shrewsbury. When the draw decided the Tigers should follow their Third Division colleagues to visit the side placed fifth in the First Division, they set off for London with distinct grounds for optimism. "We will be going down to Stamford Bridge with hopes of getting through," stated Cliff Britton.

The game was one of two distinct phases. The first belonged to Chelsea, breaking from defence to attack like lightning and switching positions with bewildering fluency. After half an hour of dogged resistance, Bobby Tambling flashed a shot past Maurice Swan from well outside the penalty area. Ten minutes later George Graham rose to head home a corner and the Blues reached the interval in a commanding position, although they were fortunate when John Boyle appeared to clear a Ken Houghton header with his hand.

The home side, in fact, seemed content with their advantage and if there was a slow shift in the territorial balance of play in favour of the Tigers, they did not appear to have the sharpness necessary to outwit a well-organized defence. But as the minutes ticked by, one detected an almost casual manner creeping into the Chelsea play.

A couple of near misses heartened the never-say-die Tigers. With ten minutes to go, Ian Butler fired in a low cross which eluded Peter Bonetti and Ken Wagstaff, hurtling in on to the far post, poked the ball home. The goal was no mere consolation. Chelsea now realized the game was slipping rapidly away from them and that they were struggling to stay in front.

The Tigers threw in everything in an heroic bid for an equalizer. As the final seconds ticked away, Wagstaff broke through, rounded Bonetti and tucked the ball into the empty net. Some 40,000 Chelsea fans stared in disbelief, whilst the 6,000 or so City supporters went delirious with delight.

Chelsea: Bonetti; Kirkup, McCreadie, Hollins, Hinton, Harris, Boyle, Graham, Bridges, Venables, Tambling.
Hull City: Swan; Davidson, D.Butler, Jarvis, Milner, Simpkin, Henderson, Wagstaff, Chilton, Houghton, I.Butler.

Referee: J.K.Taylor (Wolverhampton) — *Attendance: 46,924*

Match to Remember 19 — 31 March 1966

Hull City 1 Chelsea 3

THE Tigers and the Pensioners resumed their quarter-final clash on General Election day, to the consternation of the politicians. It was far from ideal for either club. Chelsea had faced TSV Munich in the second leg of their Fairs Cup quarter-final only two days earlier. City had no time to organize ground tickets for the match which half of Hull wanted to see.

Seat tickets were snapped up in next to no time, despite the rain which fell on the queuing fans. Thousands went away disappointed. But for excellent organization, the big day might have been chaos. A crowd of 45,328 squeezed into the ground. The first of them arrived as early as 7am. Forms for children round the perimeter track enabled an extra few young fans to see the game.

Those who came in anticipation of seeing City 'finish the job' were soon in for a shock. Chelsea were buoyed by their win over Munich, in which Peter Osgood, who missed the first meeting with the Tigers due to tonsillitis, scored the only goal. After just six minutes Osgood had a hand in giving Chelsea the lead at Boothferry Park, flicking on Ron Harris's cross for Bobby Tambling to rifle home. It was 693 minutes since City had conceded a goal in League or Cup on their own pitch.

Chelsea, playing slick soccer, added a second through George Graham, but a quick reply by Chris Simpkin, driving a long-range effort past Bonetti four minutes later, gave City fresh hope. For a spell they threatened an equalizer, but the Pensioners duly reasserted their grip on the Tigers' forwards and on the hour scored the decisive goal. Osgood broke down the right and Tambling's pin-point shot crept between the post and the diving Swan.

There was no way Chelsea were going to ease up a second time. At the close it was the Tigers who looked more tired than their opponents.

Hull City: Swan; Davidson, D.Butler, Jarvis, Milner, Simpkin, Henderson, Wagstaff, Chilton, Houghton, I.Butler.
Chelsea: Bonetti; Kirkup, McCreadie, Hollins, Hinton, Harris, Bridges, Graham, Osgood, Venables, Tambling.

Referee: K.Howley (Middlesbrough) *Attendance: 45,328*

45,328 see Osgood & Co. grind out full 90min. this time

CHELSEA SPEED, CONTROL TOO GOOD FOR TIGERS

Simpkin and Milner City's star men

HULL CITY 1, CHELSEA 3

IN THE END, GREATER CLASS TOLD ITS TALE. That, as simply and succinctly as anything, tells the story of Hull City's exit from the FA Cup at the hands of Chelsea in this sixth-round replay at Boothferry Park last night, when 45,328 exceptionally well-behaved fans paid club record receipts of £12,947—and left with the impression that it will take a very good side to stop the Londoners collecting the trophy, writes BRIAN TAYLOR.

But, though they were outclassed, the Tigers were far from disgraced, for they were in the game with an excellent chance for an hour, the point at which Chelsea wrapped up the match with their third goal.

By coincidence, it was after 60min. at Stamford Bridge that the first meeting turned in City's favour. At Boothferry Park last night it was at the ... that the game swung irrevocably ... they did not

little that got past Milner down ... and Simpkin ...

'WHO ARE YOU?'

WHEN Mr S. T. Kershaw, one of Hull City's directors, arrived at the ground in his car he was almost turned away by police. He was asked, "Who are you?" and, when he had identified himself, policemen

Ken Wagstaff (10) celebrates after putting the Tigers ahead in the 14th minute.

Match to Remember 20 — 6 March 1971

Hull City 2 Stoke City 3

HOME wins over Charlton, Blackpool and Brentford saw the Tigers through to the sixth round of the FA Cup. For the fourth time that season they were favoured with a home tie, against attractive First Division side Stoke.

After only 14 minutes, thousands of Hull supporters thrilled to the sight of Ken Wagstaff weaving through the Stoke defence before planting the ball past England goalkeeper Gordon Banks. Ten minutes later they were wondering who the Tigers would draw in the semi-final as 'Waggy' produced another breathtaking piece of ball skill to put City two goals in front.

Then, with half-time only a minute away, Terry Neill's men paid the penalty for pushing forward over-enthusiastically in search of a third goal. Stoke broke in a swift counter-attack. Terry Conroy rode Wilkinson's challenge and drove the ball past the exposed McKechnie. Instead of rejoicing on the terraces, the half-time interval turned into a period of apprehension.

For 25 minutes the Tigers came under increasing pressure until John Ritchie equalized. There were 11 more minutes of defensive work, as Stoke began to show their class. Then Ritchie again, rising unchallenged, headed the winner, but controversy raged. The move had begun with a throw-in which many City supporters felt should have been awarded to their side.

The Tigers roused themselves in a desperate late effort for an equalizer and Terry Neill powered in a header. With the kind of save which made him a world-class goalkeeper, Banks managed to push the ball out, but Neill and others were convinced that it was over the line. However, the referee decided otherwise and City were denied a semi-final rematch with Arsenal.

Hull City: McKechnie; Banks, de Vries, Wilkinson, Neill, Simpkin, Lord, Houghton, Chilton, Wagstaff, Butler.
Stoke City: Banks; Marsh, Pejic, Skeels, Smith, Bloor, Haslegrave(Mahoney), Bernard, Ritchie, Conroy, Burrows.

Referee: B.J.Homewood (Sunbury-on-Thames) — *Attendance: 41,452*

Match to Remember 21 — 18 February 1989

Hull City 2 Liverpool 3

AFTER six successive away draws in the FA Cup, Hull City scooped the big one — a fifth-round tie at home to Liverpool, the previous season's Finalists and League Champions. Boothferry Park was filled to its much-reduced limit, while a further 5,176 watched on closed-circuit TV at Tranmere Rovers' ground.

After only eight minutes, Kenny Dalglish's men were compelled to reshuffle when defender Gary Gillespie hobbled off with a shin injury. They made light of their loss and, five minutes later, went ahead. John Barnes, in acres of space, met Peter Beardsley's hanging cross to direct a header beyond the despairing dive of Iain Hesford.

Undeterred, Hull battled on and were rewarded after 32 minutes. Gary Ablett, once on loan to the Tigers, slipped, allowing Garreth Roberts to set up Billy Whitehurst and the big striker charged in to drive the ball home. Two minutes before the interval, Liverpool again showed their vulnerability as Keith Edwards pounced to rifle the ball past Bruce Grobbelaar and give his side a 2-1 lead.

Was Boothferry Park about to witness a major upset? The answer was swift and decisive. Seven minutes after the restart, Beardsley's centre was clinically put away by John Aldridge. Seventy seconds later, Beardsley again caused the City rearguard problems with a telling cross. Steve McMahon headed the ball on. Aldridge lunged at it and the Merseysiders were back on course for the quarter-finals.

Driven on by Roberts in midfield, Second Division Hull pressed forward in search of an equalizer. Edwards and Whitehurst had chances in the final fling, but the Anfield men held firm. The Tigers bowed out, but won high praise for their gallant efforts.

Hull City: Hesford; Brown, Jacobs, De Mange, Jobson, Buckley, Payton(Saville), Roberts, Whitehurst, Edwards, Askew.
Liverpool: Grobbelaar; Ablett, Burrows, Nicol, Gillespie(Watson), Molby, Beardsley, Aldridge, Houghton, Barnes, McMahon.

Referee: M.Peck (Kendal) — *Attendance: 20,058*

Andy Payton (centre) takes on John Barnes (left) and Ray Houghton.

Hull City in the Football League 1905 – 1989

		HOME						*AWAY*					
	P	W	D	L	F	A	W	D	L	F	A	Pts	Pos
DIVISION TWO													
1905-06	38	10	5	4	38	21	9	1	9	29	33	44	5th
1906-07	38	11	2	6	41	20	4	5	10	24	37	37	9th
1907-08	38	15	1	3	50	23	6	3	10	23	39	46	8th
1908-09	38	14	2	3	44	15	5	4	10	19	24	44	4th
1909-10	38	13	4	2	52	19	10	3	6	28	27	53	3rd
1910-11	38	8	10	1	38	21	6	6	7	17	18	44	5th
1911-12	38	12	3	4	36	13	5	5	9	18	38	42	7th
1912-13	38	12	2	5	42	19	3	4	12	18	37	36	12th
1913-14	38	9	5	5	29	13	7	4	8	24	24	41	7th
1914-15	38	12	2	5	36	23	7	3	9	29	31	43	7th
1919-20	42	13	4	4	53	23	5	2	14	25	49	42	11th
1920-21	42	7	10	4	24	18	3	10	8	19	35	40	13th
1921-22	42	13	5	3	36	13	6	5	10	15	28	48	5th
1922-23	42	9	8	4	29	22	5	6	10	14	23	42	12th
1923-24	42	8	7	6	32	23	2	10	9	14	28	37	17th
1924-25	42	12	6	3	40	14	3	5	13	10	35	41	10th
1925-26	42	11	4	6	40	19	5	5	11	23	42	41	13th
1926-27	42	13	4	4	43	19	7	3	11	20	33	47	7th
1927-28	42	9	8	4	25	19	3	7	11	16	35	39	14th
1928-29	42	8	8	5	38	24	5	6	10	20	39	40	12th
1929-30	42	11	3	7	30	24	3	4	14	21	54	35	21st
DIVISION THREE NORTH													
1930-31	42	12	7	2	64	20	8	3	10	35	35	50	6th
1931-32	40	14	1	5	52	21	6	4	10	30	32	45	8th
1932-33	42	18	3	0	69	14	8	4	9	31	31	59	1st
DIVISION TWO													
1933-34	42	11	4	6	33	20	2	8	11	19	48	38	15th
1934-35	42	9	6	6	32	22	7	2	12	31	52	40	13th
1935-36	42	4	7	10	33	45	1	3	17	14	66	20	22nd
DIVISION THREE NORTH													
1936-37	42	13	6	2	39	22	4	6	11	29	47	46	5th
1937-38	42	11	8	2	51	19	9	5	7	29	24	53	3rd
1938-39	42	13	5	3	57	25	5	5	11	26	49	46	7th
1946-47	42	9	5	7	25	19	7	3	11	24	34	40	11th
1947-48	42	12	5	4	38	21	6	6	9	21	27	47	5th
1948-49	42	17	1	3	65	14	10	10	1	28	14	65	1st
DIVISION TWO													
1949-50	42	11	8	2	39	25	6	3	12	25	47	45	7th
1950-51	42	12	5	4	47	28	4	6	11	27	42	43	10th
1951-52	42	11	5	5	44	23	2	6	13	16	47	37	18th
1952-53	42	11	6	4	36	19	3	2	16	21	50	36	18th
1953-54	42	14	1	6	47	22	2	5	14	17	44	38	15th
1954-55	42	7	5	9	30	35	5	5	11	14	34	34	19th
1955-56	42	6	4	11	32	45	4	2	15	21	52	26	22nd
DIVISION THREE NORTH													
1956-57	46	14	6	3	45	24	7	4	12	39	45	52	8th
1957-58	46	15	6	2	49	20	4	9	10	29	47	53	5th

		HOME						*AWAY*					
	P	W	D	L	F	A	W	D	L	F	A	Pts	Pos
				DIVISION THREE									
1958-59	46	19	3	1	65	21	7	6	10	25	34	61	2nd
				DIVISION TWO									
1959-60	42	7	6	8	27	30	3	4	14	21	46	30	21st
				DIVISION THREE									
1960-61	46	13	6	4	51	28	4	6	13	22	45	46	11th
1961-62	46	15	2	6	43	20	5	6	12	24	34	48	10th
1962-63	46	12	6	5	40	22	7	4	12	34	47	48	10th
1963-64	46	11	9	3	45	27	5	8	10	28	41	49	8th
1964-65	46	14	6	3	51	25	9	6	8	40	32	58	4th
1965-66	46	19	2	2	64	24	12	5	6	45	38	69	1st
				DIVISION TWO									
1966-67	42	11	5	5	46	25	5	2	14	31	47	39	12th
1967-68	42	6	8	7	25	23	6	5	10	33	50	37	17th
1968-69	42	10	7	4	38	20	3	9	9	21	32	42	11th
1969-70	42	11	6	4	43	28	4	5	12	29	42	41	13th
1970-71	42	11	5	5	31	16	8	8	5	23	25	51	5th
1971-72	42	10	6	5	33	21	4	4	13	16	32	38	12th
1972-73	42	9	7	5	39	22	5	5	11	25	37	40	13th
1973-74	42	9	9	3	25	15	4	8	9	21	32	43	9th
1974-75	42	12	8	1	25	10	3	6	12	15	43	44	8th
1975-76	42	9	5	7	29	23	5	6	10	16	26	39	14th
1976-77	42	9	8	4	31	17	1	9	11	14	36	37	14th
1977-78	42	6	6	9	23	25	2	6	13	11	27	28	22nd
				DIVISION THREE									
1978-79	46	12	9	2	36	14	7	2	14	30	47	49	8th
1979-80	46	11	7	5	29	21	1	9	13	22	48	40	20th
1980-81	46	7	8	8	23	22	1	8	14	17	49	32	24th
				DIVISION FOUR									
1981-82	46	14	3	6	36	23	5	9	9	34	38	69	8th
1982-83	46	14	8	1	48	14	11	7	5	27	20	90	2nd
				DIVISION THREE									
1983-84	46	16	5	2	42	11	7	9	7	29	27	83	4th
1984-85	46	16	4	3	46	20	9	8	6	32	29	87	3rd
				DIVISION TWO									
1985-86	42	11	7	3	39	19	6	6	9	26	36	64	6th
1986-87	42	10	6	5	25	22	3	8	10	16	33	53	14th
1987-88	44	10	8	4	32	22	4	7	11	22	38	57	15th
1988-89	46	7	9	7	31	25	4	5	14	21	43	47	21st

LEAGUE RECORD – DIVISION BY DIVISION

DIVISION TWO

		HOME						*AWAY*				
	P	W	D	L	F	A	W	D	L	F	A	Pts
1905 — 1915	380	116	36	38	406	187	62	38	90	229	308	430
1919 — 1930	462	114	67	50	390	218	47	63	121	197	401	452
1933 — 1936	126	24	17	22	98	87	10	13	40	64	166	98
1949 — 1956	294	72	34	41	275	197	26	29	92	141	316	259
1959-60	42	7	6	8	27	30	3	4	14	21	46	30
1966 — 1978	504	113	80	59	388	245	50	73	129	255	429	479
1985 — 1989	174	38	30	19	127	88	17	26	44	85	150	221
TOTAL	1982	484	270	237	1711	1052	215	246	530	992	1816	1969

DIVISION THREE NORTH

	HOME						AWAY					
	P	W	D	L	F	A	W	D	L	F	A	Pts
1930 — 1933	124	44	11	7	185	55	22	11	29	96	98	154
1936 — 1939	126	37	19	7	147	66	18	16	29	84	120	145
1946 — 1949	126	38	11	14	128	54	23	19	21	73	75	152
1956 — 1958	92	29	12	5	94	44	11	13	22	68	92	105
TOTAL	468	148	53	33	554	219	74	59	101	321	385	556

DIVISION THREE

	HOME						AWAY					
	P	W	D	L	F	A	W	D	L	F	A	Pts
1958-59	46	19	3	1	65	21	7	6	10	25	34	61
1960 — 1966	276	84	31	23	294	146	42	35	61	193	237	318
1978 — 1981	138	30	24	15	88	57	9	19	41	69	144	121
1983 — 1985	92	32	9	5	88	31	16	17	13	61	56	170
TOTAL	552	165	67	44	535	255	74	77	125	348	471	670

DIVISION FOUR

	HOME						AWAY					
	P	W	D	L	F	A	W	D	L	F	A	Pts
1981 — 1983	92	28	11	7	84	37	16	16	14	61	58	159
TOTAL	92	28	11	7	84	37	16	16	14	61	58	159

TOTAL FOR ALL FOOTBALL LEAGUE MATCHES

	HOME						AWAY					
	P	W	D	L	F	A	W	D	L	F	A	Pts
1905 — 1989	3094	825	401	321	2884	1563	379	398	770	1722	2730	3354

ANALYSIS OF ALL FIRST-TEAM MATCHES 1904-1989

Competition	P	W	D	L	For	Agn
Football League	3094	1204	799	1091	4606	4293
FA Cup	226	87	65	74	345	309
World War One Leagues	142	61	25	56	247	262
World War Two Comps.	88	29	10	49	144	232
Football League Cup	67	19	14	34	83	118
Anglo-Scottish Cup	12	2	4	6	8	14
Associate Members Cup	8	5	1	2	15	8
Full Members Cup	8	4	1	3	15	11
Group Cup/League Trophy	6	2	1	3	4	5
West Riding Cup	5	2	1	2	7	6
Watney Cup	5	3	1	1	9	3
Third Division North Cup	4	0	1	3	3	13
Anglo-Italian Tournament	4	2	1	1	4	3
	3669	1420	924	1325	5490	5277
Friendly, charity, tour & abandoned matches	358	205	73	80	935	469
	4027	1625	997	1405	6425	5746

Hull Comet 1899-1900

Hull and District League Division Two

1	Oct	21	(h)	Paull Garrison	W	6-1	Milton 3, Rogerson, Russell, Wright
2		28	(a)	St Mark's	W	5-0	Russell 3, Rogerson, C.Wilkinson
3	Dec	9	(a)	New Holland	W	4-1	Howden 3, W.Hay
4		16	(h)	East Hull	W	2-1	Cockerill, Howden
5		30	(h)	Beverley CI Res	L	0-1	
6	Feb	10	(h)	Dairycoates Res	W	2-0	Howden, W.Hay
7	Mar	3	(a)	Beverley CI Res	W	4-0	W.Hay 2, H.Hay, Robinson
8		17	(a)	Sculcoates Ams	W	4-1	Howden 2, Wright, Opp own-goal
9		24	(a)	East Hull	W	3-1	Howden, W.Hay, Robinson
10		31	(h)	Sculcoates Ams	W	4-1	Robinson 2, Howden, Wright
							Appearances
							Goals

Hull Times Cup

11	Jan	27	(a)	Dairycoates	W	1-0	Howden
12	Feb	24	(a)	Beverley Ch Inst	L	2-6	W.Hay, untraced
							Appearances
							Goals

Other Matches

13	Sep	2	(a)	Corinthians	W	2-0	H.Hay, Robinson
14		23	(a)	Withernsea	D	2-2	Kiddle, Rogerson
15		30	(a)	Wanderers	W	2-0	Wright, Cockerill
16	Oct	7	(a)	Driffield Ch Mut	W	3-2	Untraced 3
17		14	(h)	Kingston Ams Res	W	7-1	Heaton 3, Traynor, Cockerill, untraced 2
18	Nov	18	(a)	Dairycoates	D	2-2	Howden, Wright
19	Dec	2	(a)	Dairycoates	L	1-2	Cockerill
20	Feb	17	(h)	St Mark's	W	6-1	Howden 2, W.Hay 2, H.Hay, Wright
21	Apr	7	(a)	Withernsea	D	1-1	Untraced
22		13	(a)	Withernsea	D	1-1	Untraced
							Appearances
							Goals

Notes:
1. All home matches played on the Newland Park Estate.
2. All opponents were local Hull teams unless stated.
3. Match 16 played as League match but deleted from records on demise of opposition.
4. Matches 18 and 19 were abortive attempts to play the third round Times Cup tie, being abandoned due to fog and bad light respectively.
5. Match 20 scheduled as a League match. The referee failed to appear, so the teams played a friendly. The opposition failed to appear for the rearranged match and Comet claimed the points.
6. Comet awarded points for unplayed League fixtures against Paull Garrison (away), Dairycoates Reserves (away) and New Holland (home).
7. The club received a bye in the first two rounds of the Hull Times Cup.

Levitt F	Wilkinson C	Johnson L	Foggin F	Robinson F	Frost E	Wright A	Cockerill C	Russell W	Milton L	Rogerson H	Dickinson E	Shakespeare A	Wilson L	Hutchinson J	Crompton B	Howden F	Hay W	Sellars E	Hay H	Wilkinson W	Mackay R	White W	Kiddle J	Traynor L	Heaton G	Tyson E	Sanderson E	Kershaw L	
1	2	3	4	5	6	7	8	9	10	11																			1
1	2	3	6	5			7	8		10	4	9	11																2
1	2	5				7	8	11			4			3	6	9	10												3
1	2	3	5	11	4	7	8								6	9	10												4
1	2	3	5	11	4		8								6	9	10												5
	2	3	4		5	7	8			11						9	10	1											6
1	2	5	6	11	4	7								3		9	8		10										7
1	2	5	6	11	4	7	10							3		9	8												8
1	2	5	4	11	6	7	10							3		8	9												9
	2	5	1	11	4	7	10							3	6	8	9												10
8	10	10	9	8	8	8	9	3	1	3	2	1	1	5	4	8	8	1	1										
	1			4		3	1	4	3	2						9	5		1										

1 own-goal

Levitt F	Wilkinson C	Johnson L	Foggin F	Robinson F	Frost E	Wright A	Cockerill C	Russell W	Milton L	Rogerson H	Dickinson E	Shakespeare A	Wilson L	Hutchinson J	Crompton B	Howden F	Hay W	Sellars E	Hay H	Wilkinson W	Mackay R	White W	Kiddle J	Traynor L	Heaton G	Tyson E	Sanderson E	Kershaw L	
	2	5	4		6	7	8							3		9	10	1	11										11
1	2	5		11	4	7	8							3		9	10			6									12
1	2	2	1	1	2	2	2							2		2	2	1	1	1									
																1	1												

1 scorer untraced

Levitt F	Wilkinson C	Johnson L	Foggin F	Robinson F	Frost E	Wright A	Cockerill C	Russell W	Milton L	Rogerson H	Dickinson E	Shakespeare A	Wilson L	Hutchinson J	Crompton B	Howden F	Hay W	Sellars E	Hay H	Wilkinson W	Mackay R	White W	Kiddle J	Traynor L	Heaton G	Tyson E	Sanderson E	Kershaw L	
	3	2	6	10	4	7		1	9										8		5	11							13
1	2	3		10	11	7			9	8				6							5		4						14
1	2	3	4	11	6	7	8		9	10											5								15
																													16
1	2	3	4				7	5	11	10				6										8	9				17
1	2		4	11	6	7	8	9	10					3		5													18
1	2	3		11	6	7	8							4		9	10			5									19
	2	5	4		6	7	8							3		9	10	1	11										20
	2	5	4	11		7										8	9		10							1	3	6	21
																													22
5	8	7	6	6	6	7	5	3	5	3				5		4	3	1	3	1	3	1	1	1	1	1	1	1	
				1		3	3			1						3	2		2				1	1	3				

7 scorers and 22 appearances untraced

Hull Comet fielded ten players in Matches 5 & 6.

1900-01

Hull and District League Division One

1	Nov	10	(a)	Beverley Ch Inst	D	1-1	Ridsdale	
2		24	(h)	Beverley Barracks	W	5-0	Ridsdale 2, Howden 2, Massey	
3	Dec	8	(a)	Withernsea	D	2-2	Untraced 2	
4	Feb	23	(a)	Beverley Barracks	W	3-0	Ridsdale 3	
5	Mar	23	(a)	East Hull	W	2-0	L.Moxley, E.Moxley	
6		30	(h)	East Hull	W	3-2	Ridsdale, E.Moxley, W.Hay	
7	Apr	13	(h)	Withernsea	W	4-1	Blythe 2, Parker, E.Moxley	
8		24	(h)	Beverley Ch Inst	W	2-0	E.Moxley, Bagshaw	
								Appearances
								Goals

Cup ties

9	Dec	15	(a)	Pupil Teachers	W	3-1	Cockerill 2, Massey	TC2
10	Jan	19	(a)	Withernsea	L	0-2		TC3
11	Mar	9	(a)	Beverley Ch Inst	L	1-2	Untraced	BHC1
								Appearances
								Goals

Key to cup competitions: TC Hull Times Cup. BHC Beverley Hospital Cup.

Other matches

12	Sep	8	(a)	Withernsea	D	1-1	Wright	
13		22	(h)	Beverley Ch Inst	L	0-2		
14		29	(h)	Hessle	W	3-2	Traynor, Massey, Robinson	
15	Oct	6	(a)	Patrington	W	4-0	H.Hay 3, Howden	
16		27	(h)	Brunswick Wes	W	3-0	Howden 2, Ridsdale	
17	Dec	1	(h)	Grimsby All Saints	L	1-5	Ridsdale	
18	Jan	12	(a)	Withernsea	L	1-2	Hutchinson	
								Appearances
								Goals

Notes: 1. Home matches played on the Bull Lane Ground except Matches 7 and 8, which were played on Albert United's Cricket Ground, Dairycoates.
2. Match 16 terminated after 60 minutes when the ball burst.
3. Match 18 commenced as Times Cup tie but was abandoned due to bad light.
4. All local matches scheduled for 26 January and 2 February cancelled due to death and funeral of Queen Victoria.
5. The club received a bye in round one of the Hull Times Cup.

Levitt F	Wilkinson C	Massey S	Johnson L	Rogers T	Frost E	Wright A	Howden F	Ridsdale J	Robinson E	Hay H	Wilkinson W	Hay W	Cockerill C	Hutchinson J	Foggin F	McCall R	Moxley L	Moxley E	Bromley E	Parker A	Blythe T	Bagshaw T	Moss C	Crompton B	Richmond F	Gibbs	Traynor L	Collingwood T	Dawson A	Burridge C	
1	2	3	4	5	6	7	8	9	10	11																					1
1	2	3	4	5		7	9	8	11		6	10																			2
1	2	3	4	5	6	7	8	9	11				10																		3
1	2	3	5		6	7	10	9		8		11		4																	4
1		3	4		6			9		11		10			2	5	7	8													5
1		3	5		6			9		11		10		4	2		7	8													6
1	2	3	6					4				8						7	5	9	10	11									7
1	2	3	4	8	6			9				10						7	5			11									8
8	6	8	8	4	6	4	4	8	3	4	1	6	1	2	2	1	2	4	2	1	1	2									
		1					2	7				1					1	4		1	2	1									

2 scorers untraced

Levitt F	Wilkinson C	Massey S	Johnson L	Rogers T	Frost E	Wright A	Howden F	Ridsdale J	Robinson E	Hay H	Wilkinson W	Hay W	Cockerill C	Hutchinson J	Foggin F	McCall R	Moxley L	Moxley E	Bromley E	Parker A	Blythe T	Bagshaw T	Moss C	Crompton B	Richmond F	Gibbs	Traynor L	Collingwood T	Dawson A	Burridge C	
1	2	3	6	5		7		9	11				8		4								10								9
1	2	3	4		6	7		9		8		10												5							10
1	2	4	5		6			9				10					7	8							3	11					11
3	3	3	3	1	2	2		3	1	1		2	1		1		1	1					1	1	1	1					
		1											2																		

1 scorer untraced

Levitt F	Wilkinson C	Massey S	Johnson L	Rogers T	Frost E	Wright A	Howden F	Ridsdale J	Robinson E	Hay H	Wilkinson W	Hay W	Cockerill C	Hutchinson J	Foggin F	McCall R	Moxley L	Moxley E	Bromley E	Parker A	Blythe T	Bagshaw T	Moss C	Crompton B	Richmond F	Gibbs	Traynor L	Collingwood T	Dawson A	Burridge C	
1	2		5		3	7	9		6	11					4												8	10			12
	2	6	5				9	8	3	11		7			4												10		1		13
	2	6	5			7	9	8	4					3													11		1	10	14
1	2	6	3	5		7	9	10	4	11																				8	15
1	2	6		5		7	9	8		11				3	4															10	16
1	2	3	4	5	11	7	9	8	6			10																			17
1	2	3	4	5	6	7		9		8				11													10				18
5	7	6	6	4	3	6	6	6	5	5		2		3	3												4	1	2	3	
		1				1	3	2	1	3				1													1				

Hull Comet fielded ten players in Match 10.

Hull Association FC 1901-02

Cup ties

1	Oct	19	(h)	Brunswick Wes	W 3-0	Paton, Metham, Robinson	TC1
2	Nov	23	(h)	Cosmopolitans	W 1-0	Hobbis	TC2
3	Dec	14	(h)	Scarboro' St Thom	W 5-4	Mackrill 2, W.Hay 2, H.Hay	SERC1
4	Jan	11	(h)	Grimsby Tradesmen	L 0-2		GCC1
5	Feb	1	(h)	Hull Teachers	W 11-0	McDougall 2, H.Hay 2, Barlow 2, W.Hay, Hobbis, Wharton, Robinson, Andrews	BHC2
6		8	(a)	Scarboro'Peasholme	L 1-2	McDougall	SERCSF
7	Mar	8	(n)	Beverley St Mary's	W 5-0	Hobbis 2, McDougall, Barlow, Andrews	BHCSF
8		15	(a)	Withernsea	W 1-0	Andrews	TC3
9	Apr	5	(n)	Hessle	W 4-1	Paton 2, Hobbis 2	TCSF
10		19	(n)	Roslyn	D 1-1	Barlow	BHCF
11		26	(n)	Roslyn	W 6-2	H.Hay 3, W.Hay 2, E.Robson (og)	BHCFR
12		29	(n)	Grimsby West MS	D 1-1*	Paton	TCF
13	May	3	(n)	Grimsby West MS	L 0-8		TCFR

Key to cup competitions: TC Hull Times Cup, SERC Scarborough & East Riding Cup, BHC Beverley Hospital Cup, GCC Grimsby Charity Cup. *After extra time.

Appearances
Goals

Other Matches

14	Sep	7	(a)	Barton St Chad's	W 3-2	Paton 2, Metham
15		14	(h)	Scunthorpe U	D 1-1	Wharton
16		21	(a)	Frodingham U	L 3-6	Wharton, Paton, Andrews
17		28	(h)	Goole T	W 3-2	Wharton 2, W.Hay
18	Oct	5	(a)	Huddersfield	L 0-4	
19		26	(h)	Barton St Chad's	W 2-0	W.Hay 2
20	Nov	2	(a)		W 8-0	H.Hay 4, Wharton 2, Hobbis, Metham
21		16	(h)	Withernsea	W 2-0	Wharton, Metham
22	Dec	7	(h)	Grimsby St John's	L 0-2	
23		21	(a)	Withernsea	W 5-0	McDougall 3, W.Hay, H.Hay
24		25	(h)	Gainsboro' Town	D 0-0	
25		26	(a)	Scunthorpe U	L 1-5	W.Hay
26	Jan	4	(a)	Grimsby West MS	L 1-4	McDougall
27		18	(a)	Grimsby St John's	D 3-3	Wharton 2, Barlow
28	Feb	22	(h)	Roslyn	W 4-1	McDougall 2, Wharton, Robinson
29	Mar	1	(a)	Roslyn	W 5-2	Hobbis 2, Wharton, Robinson, W.Hay
30		29	(a)		L 0-7	

Appearances
Goals

Notes: 1. Home matches played on the Bull Lane Ground.
2. Match 21 ended after 65 minutes when opponents walked off disputing the second goal.
3. Match 7 played on Brunswick Wesleyans' ground, Holderness Road.
4. Match 9 played at Dairycoates.
5. Matches 10 and 11 played at Beverley.
6. Matches 12 and 13 played on the Boulevard.
7. Opponents in Match 20 not known. The game was arranged at the last minute — too late to allow the usual Press coverage — and subsequent comments about the match do not mention the name of the opposition.
8. Opponents in Match 30 not known. They may well have been a minor team from the Sheffield area.

Levitt F	Andrews M	Ridsdale J	Robinson E	Rogers T	Johnson L	Metham R	Hay W	Paton G	Hobbis J	Wharton A	Smith W	Wilkinson C	Hay H	Mackrill H	McDougall D	Barlow E	Hampton C	Reeve A	Massey S	Foggin F	Russell J	Tiplady H	Moody F	Dawson A	Wrightson P	Beacock A	Kiddle J	Brown G	Pearce J	Traynor L	Newton W	Jackson	
1	2	3	4	5	6	7	8	9	10	11																							1
1	3	9	6	5	4	7	8		11	10	2																						2
1	2	8	6		4		7		11	10		3	5	9																			3
1	2	5	6		4		7		11	10		3	8		9																		4
1	2	3	5		4		7		11	10			8		9	6																	5
1	2	3	6		5		7		11	10				8	9	4																	6
1	2	3	5		6		7		11	10			8		9	4																	7
1	2	3					8	9	11				7			4	5	6	10														8
1	2	3	10		5		8	9	11				7			4		6															9
	2	1	6		5		7		11	10			8		9	4			3														10
1	2	3	6		5	9	8		11	10			7			4																	11
1	2	3	6		4	9	8	10	11				7			5																	12
1	2	3	6		4		8	9	11	10			7			5																	13
12	13	13	12	2	12	4	13	5	13	10	1	2	10	2	5	9	1	2	2														
	3		2			1	5	4	6	1			6	2	4	4																	

1 own-goal

Levitt F	Andrews M	Ridsdale J	Robinson E	Rogers T	Johnson L	Metham R	Hay W	Paton G	Hobbis J	Wharton A	Smith W	Wilkinson C	Hay H	Mackrill H	McDougall D	Barlow E	Hampton C	Reeve A	Massey S	Foggin F	Russell J	Tiplady H	Moody F	Dawson A	Wrightson P	Beacock A	Kiddle J	Brown G	Pearce J	Traynor L	Newton W	Jackson	
1				5	4	7		8	10	11		2							3	6	9												14
1				6	5		8	9	10	11		3							4			2	7										15
1	4			5	6	7	8	9	11	10		3										2											16
		9		5		7	8		11	10									3	4				1	2	6							17
1	4	9		5	6	7	8			10							3					2											18
1	2		6	5	4	7	8		11	10									9			3											19
1	2	6		5	4	7			11	8			10						9			3											20
	6	1		5	4	7	8		11	10	2										9	3											21
1	3	9	6	5	4		8		11	10	2								7														22
1	2	8	6		4		7		11	10	3		5		9																		23
1	2		10		5		8		11		4	3	7		9		6																24
1	2		3				7		11	10			8		9		6										4	5					25
1	2	8	6		4		7			10	3				9	5																	26
1	2	3					7		11	10			5		9	4	6				8												27
	2	8	6		4		7			10					9	5		11											1	3			28
1	4		6				7		11	10			8		9										3					2	5		29
1	2		8		5			9		11							4	6	7											3		10	30
14	14	9	9	9	13	7	14	4	13	16	5	4	6		7	3	5	2	7	2	3	6	1	1	2	1	1	1	1	3	1	1	
	1		2			3	6	3	3	11			5		6	1																	

Hull Association FC fielded ten players in Matches 18 and 26.

Hull City 1902-03

East Riding League Division One

1	Oct	11	(h)	Barton St Chad's	W 4-0	Hobbis 2, H.Hay, Ridsdale	
2		18	(a)	Beverley Barracks	W 4-1	Cliffe 2, Ridsdale, Andrews	
3	Nov	1	(h)	St Mark's	W 4-0	Hobbis, W.Hay, Robinson, Cliffe	
4		15	(a)	Withernsea	W 3-1	Hobbis, Machin, W.Hay	
5		22	(h)	Beverley	W 3-0	Hobbis, Ridsdale, W.Hay	
6		29	(h)	Withernsea	W 3-1	W.Hay, Purvis, Andrews	
7	Dec	6	(a)	Brunswick Wes	W 6-0	Massey 2, Cliffe 2, Ridsdale, Traynor	
8		13	(a)	Barton St Chad's	D 0-0		
9	Jan	3	(a)	St Mark's	L 0-2		
10		24	(a)	Beverley	W 3-1	Andrews 2, Reeve	
11	Mar	14	(h)	Brunswick Wes	L 1-2	H.Hay	
12		21	(h)	Beverley Barracks	W 4-0	Hobbis, W.Hay, Robinson, Hebden (og)	
							Appearances
							Goals

Cup ties

13	Oct	25	(a)	Middleton RS	W 14-0	Ridsdale 5, W.Hay 3, Barlow 2, Hobbis, Robinson, Andrews, Traynor	TC
14	Jan	17	(a)	Westbourne	W 7-0	Ridsdale 4, Reeve, W.Hay, Barlow	TC
15		31	(h)	Roslyn	W 4-1	Hobbis 2, Ridsdale, W.Hay	BHC
16	Feb	14	(n)	Whitby	W 4-1	Watts 2, Barnes, Cliffe	SERCS
17	Mar	7	(n)	Beverley Barracks	W 3-2	Watts 3	BHCS
18		12	(a)	Beverley Barracks	W 5-1	W.Hay 2, Ridsdale, Hobbis, Opp own-goal	TC
19		28	(a)	Hessle	W 4-1	Ridsdale, Watts, W.Hay, Andrews	TCS
20	Apr	4	(n)	Sculcoates Ams	W 3-1	Ridsdale 2, Watts	BHC
21		18	(n)	Scarboro' Raincliffe	L 2-3	Mackrill, W.Hay	SERC
22		25	(n)	Grimsby St John's	D 1-1*	Massey	TC
23		28	(n)	Grimsby St John's	W 3-2	Massey, Ridsdale, Watts	TCF

Key to cup competitions: TC Hull Times Cup, BHC Beverley Hospital Cup, SERC Scarborough & East Riding Cup. Appearances
*After extra-time Goals

Other Matches

24	Sep	20	(h)	Grimsby West MS	L 1-3	Unknown	
25		27	(a)	Scarboro'Peasholme	D 3-3	Hobbis, H.Hay, Purvis	
26	Dec	20	(h)	Beverley Barracks	W 4-0	Ridsdale, W.Hay, H.Hay, Barlow	
27		26	(h)	Frodingham U	D 2-2	Bainbridge, W.Hay	
28		27	(h)	Grimsby St John's	W 3-2	Ridsdale, Shaw, Andrews	
29	Feb	21	(h)	Beverley Barracks	W 2-0	Greenfield, Traynor	
30		28	(a)	Grimsby T Res	L 0-8		
31	Apr	11	(a)	Frodingham U	D 0-0		
							Appearances
							Goals

Notes: 1. Home matches played on the Dairycoates Ground.
2. City received a bye in the first round of the Beverley Hospital Cup and the Scarborough & East Riding Cup. In the second round of the latter they had a walk-over against Malton Derwent.
3. Match 6 played on Marlborough RLFC ground in aid of Hull Royal Infirmary Extension Fund.
4. Match 12 played at Beverley.
5. Matches 16 and 21 played on the Athletic Ground, Scarborough.
6. Match 17 played on the ground of Hull & East Riding RUFC.
7. Match 20 played on the Station Ground, Beverley.
8. Matches 22 and 23 played on the Boulevard.
9. Match 26 was a League fixture, but abandoned after 80 minutes due to bad light.
10. Match 29 was a Hull Times Cup tie, abandoned after 33 minutes due to a downpour.
11. Prior to match 24 the visitors were delayed for over an hour on the ferry, due to low tide. Several of the City team, presuming their opponents were not coming, went on to the Boulevard to watch Hull FC. When the Grimbarians finally arrived the home side had to make their numbers up from among the spectators. One of these anonymous replacements scored the Hull team's goal.

This Hull City club disbanded in 1903.

Levitt F	Andrews M	Traynor L	Cliffe E	Barlow E	Robinson E	Purvis J	Hay W	Ridsdale J	Hay H	Hobbis J	Massey S	Machin H	Greenfield H	Smith S	Reeve A	Bainbridge	Johnson L	Barnes F	Watts H	Mackrill H	Wilkinson C	Frost B	Bolton A	Newman S	Shaw W	Kelsey G	Rippon P	Robson F	
1	2	3	4	5	6	7	8	9	10	11																			1
1	2	3	4	5	6	7	8	9	10	11																			2
1	2	3	4	5	6	7	8	9		11	10																		3
1	2	3	4	5	6		8	9	7	11		10																	4
1	2	3	4	5	6	7	8	9	10	11																			5
1	2	3	4	5	6	8	10	9		11			7																6
	2	3	4	5	6	7	8	9	10		11			1															7
1	2		4	5	6	9	8	3	10	11			7																8
1	2		4	5	3		8		7	11	9				6	10													9
1	2	3	4	5			8	9	7	11	6				10														10
1	2		4	5	6			9	8		3		7			11	10												11
1		2	4	5	6		8	9	10	11	3		7																12
11	11	9	12	12	11	7	11	11	10	10	6	1	4	1	2	2	1												
	4	1	5		2	1	5	4	2	6	2	1			1														

1 own-goal

Levitt F	Andrews M	Traynor L	Cliffe E	Barlow E	Robinson E	Purvis J	Hay W	Ridsdale J	Hay H	Hobbis J	Massey S	Machin H	Greenfield H	Smith S	Reeve A	Bainbridge	Johnson L	Barnes F	Watts H	Mackrill H	Wilkinson C	Frost B	Bolton A	Newman S	Shaw W	Kelsey G	Rippon P	Robson F	
1	2	3	4	5	6	7	8	9		11						10													13
1	2	3	4	5	6		8	9	7	11					10														14
	1	2	4	5	3		8	9	10	11	6				7														15
	2	3	4	5	6		7	1		11								8	9	10									16
1	2	3	4	5	6		7	8		11									9	10									17
1		2	4	5	10		7	8	9	11							6				3								18
1	2	3	4	5	10		7	8		11							6		9										19
1	2	3	4	5	10			8	7	11							6		9										20
	3	2	4	5	11		7	1									6	8	9	10									21
	3	2	4	5	7		8	1		11	10						6		9										22
1	3	2	4	5	7		8	11			10						6		9										23
7	10	11	11	11	11	1	10	11	4	9	3				2	1	6	2	7	3	1								
	2	1	1	3	1		9	15		4	2				1			1	8	1									

1 own-goal

Levitt F	Andrews M	Traynor L	Cliffe E	Barlow E	Robinson E	Purvis J	Hay W	Ridsdale J	Hay H	Hobbis J	Massey S	Machin H	Greenfield H	Smith S	Reeve A	Bainbridge	Johnson L	Barnes F	Watts H	Mackrill H	Wilkinson C	Frost B	Bolton A	Newman S	Shaw W	Kelsey G	Rippon P	Robson F	
		2	4		3	7	8		10																				24
1		2	4	5	6	7	9	3	10	11						8													25
	2	3	4	5	6		8	9	7	11	10			1															26
1	2	3			6		8		7		4					10				9		5	11						27
	2				3		8	9	7		4			1	6	10								5	11				28
1	2	3	4	5	6				8	11			7		10				9										29
			4		6		8	1		11			7		9									5		2	3	10	30
	2	3	4	5	10		8	9	7	11				1			6												31
3	5	6	6	4	8	2	7	5	7	5	3		2	3	3	3	1		1	1		1	1	2	1	1	1	1	
	1	1		1		1	2	2	2	1			1			1									1				

5 unknown appearances and 1 unknown goalscorer

1904-05

1	Sep	1	(b)	Notts C	D 2-2	Rushton 2	6,000
2		10	(b)	Everton 'A'	W 2-0	Howe 2	6,000
3		19	(b)	Leicester F	W 2-0	Howe, Spence	4,000
4		24	(b)	Darlington	W 5-1	Rushton 4, Wolfe	4,000
5		29	(b)	Crewe A	D 1-1	Rushton	2,000
6	Oct	1	(a)	Denton	W 2-1	Howe, Williams	3,000
7		8	(b)	Sheffield FC	W 4-1	Rushton 2, Howe, Martin	3,000
8		12	(b)	Middlesbrough Res	D 2-2	A.Smith 2	2,000
9		13	(b)	Derby C	W 3-2	Rushton, A.Smith, Howe	6,500
10		15	(a)	Leeds C	W 2-0	A.Smith, Howe	3,000
11		20	(b)	Lincoln C	W 1-0	Spence	3,000
12		22	(a)	West Hartlepool	W 3-1	Rushton, Martin, Jones	1,500
13		29	(b)	Stockton	D 2-2	Rushton, A.Smith	2,500
14	Nov	3	(b)	Burton U	W 3-1	Spence 2, A.Smith	2,000
15		12	(b)	Bradford C	L 0-2		6,000
16		17	(b)	Port Vale	L 1-2	Wolfe	2,000
17		26	(b)	Grimsby T	W 4-2	Rushton 2, Howe, Wilkinson	4,000
18	Dec	10	(b)	Glossop	W 2-1	A.Smith, Spence	5,000
19		24	(b)	Leeds C	W 3-2	Ridsdale 2, Wilkinson	2,500
20		27	(a)	Preston NE	L 2-3	A.Smith 2	2,000
21		31	(a)	Middlesbrough Res	L 2-3	Rushton 2	300
22	Jan	3	(a)	Darlington	D 3-3	Ford 2, Newton	4,000
23		7	(a)	Scarborough	W 1-0	Newton	1,000
24		14	(b)	Wellingborough	W 3-2	Rushton 2, Howe	2,500
25		28	(b)	Chesterfield	L 1-2	Howe	5,000
26	Feb	2	(b)	Doncaster R	W 3-0	Rushton, A.Smith, Howe	3,000
27		4	(a)	Manchester C Res	L 0-1		5,000
28		11	(a)	Gainsboro' Tr Res	L 1-2	Howe	2,000
29		18	(b)	Liverpool	L 2-6	Rushton, Doig (og)	8,000
30		23	(b)	Army Service Corp	W 5-1	Raisbeck 2, Spence, Wilkinson, A.Smith	2,000
31		25	(a)	Sheffield FC	W 3-1	A.Smith 2, Brooks	1,000
32	Mar	4	(a)	Leeds C	W 5-2	Howe 4, Rushton	2,500
33		18	(d)	Scarborough	W 6-0	Howe 2, A.Smith 2, Spence, Wilkinson	400
34		23	(b)	Prince Wales Huss	W 1-0	Spence	1,500
35		25	(c)	Manchester C	D 0-0		8,000
36	Apr	1	(b)	Coldstream Guards	W 10-3	Spence 4, Howe 3, Wilkinson, Rushton, Thornton	4,000
37		5	(a)	York Garrison	W 7-1	Rushton 3, Spence, Howe, Martin, Wilkinson	1,000
38		8	(b)	Barnsley	W 2-1	Wilkinson, Rushton	7,000
39		15	(b)	Sheffield U	W 3-1	Rushton, Spence, Howe	10,000
40		21	(a)	Grimsby T	L 1-2	Howe	3,000
41		22	(a)	Boston T	W 4-2	A.Smith 2, Martin 2	2,000
42		24	(b)	Preston NE	D 2-2	Spence, Raisbeck	8,000
43		27	(b)	East Riding XI	D 2-2	Howe, Wilkinson	1,500
44		29	(b)	Gainsborough Tr	L 2-3	Rushton 2	3,000

FINAL PLAYING RECORD:

P	W	D	L	F	A
44	26	8	10	115	66

Appearances
Goals

FA Cup

P	Sep	17	(a)	Stockton	D 3-3	Howe, Spence, O.Mackrill	4,000
R		22	(a)	Stockton	L 1-4	Spence	4,000

Appearances
Goals

Notes: An additional pre-season match was played against a local District XI. This was not included in contemporary records, and has not been included here. The details are to be found in the section on 'Other Matches'.
For the FA Cup Preliminary round game on September 17, Hull City gave up ground advantage.

Key to grounds: (a) = away
(b) = Boulevard (Hull RLFC)
(c) = Anlaby Road Cricket Ground
(d) = Dairycoates.

Whitehouse J	Leiper J	Jones T	Martin W	Wolfe F	Raisbeck A	Rushton G	Howe P	Spence G	Wilkinson H	Mackrill O	Andrews M	Williams T	Smith A	Abbot H	Turner J	Horton V	Ford J	Brooks G	Newman S	Newton R	Cook G	Welch C	Thornton W	Davies H	
1	2	3	4	5	6	8	9	10	11																1
1	2	3	4	5	6		9	10	11	7															2
1	2	3		5	6	8	9	10	11	7	4														3
1	2	3	5	10	6	8	9		11	7															4
1		3	4	5	6	8	9		11	7	2	10													5
1		3	4	5	6	8	9	7	11		2	10													6
1		3	4	5	6	7	9	10			2	11	8												7
1		3	4		6	9		10	11		2		8												8
1		3	4	5	6	7	9	10	11				8	2											9
1		3	4	5	11	7	9	10			2		8		6										10
		3	4	9	6	7		10					8	2	5	1									11
		3	9		6	7		10			2		8		5	1	11								12
1		3	4		6	7	9	10			2		8		5		11								13
1		3	4	2	6	7	9	10	11				8		5										14
1		3	4	2	6	7	9	10	11				8		5										15
		3	4	5		7	8	10	11						6	1		2							16
1		3	4	5	6	7	9	10	11				8					2							17
1		3	4	5	6	7	9	10	11				8					2							18
1		3	4	5	6	7		10	11				8					2							19
1		3	4	5	6	7	9	10	11				8					2							20
1		3	4	5		8	9	10	11				7					2	6						21
		3	4	5			9	10					7			1	11	2	6	8					22
1		3	4	5		9		10					7				11	2	6	8					23
		3	4	5	6	8	9	10					7				11				1				24
1		3	4	5		8	9	10					7					6		11		2			25
1		3	4	5	6	8	9	10	11				7					2							26
1		3	4	5	6	8	9	10	11				7					2							27
1		3	4		6	8	9	10	11				7					5				2			28
1		3	4		6	8	9	10	11				7					5				2			29
1			4		11			10	9				8					5					6		30
1		3	4		6	7		8	11				9					2					5		31
		3	4		6	7	8	9	11				10					2			1		5		32
1		3	4		6	7	10	8	11				9					2					5		33
1		2	4		6	7	8	10	11				9										5		34
1		3	4		6	7	8	10	11				9					2					5		35
1		3	4		6	7	10	9	11														8	2	36
1		3	4		6	7	10	9	11				8										5	2	37
1		3	4		6	9	10	8	11														5	2	38
1		3	4			7	10	9	11									6					5	2	39
1			4		6	7	10	9	11				8					3					5	2	40
1			4	5	6	7	10	9	11				8					2						3	41
1			4		6	7	10	9	11				8					2					5	3	42
1			4	3	6	7	10		11				8					2					5		43
1					6	7	10		11				9					3					5		44
38	4	38	42	26	38	41	37	40	35	4	8	3	34	2	7	4	5	24	3	3	2	3	14	7	
		1	5	2	3	29	25	15	8			1	17				2	1		2			1		

1 own-goal

Whitehouse J	Leiper J	Jones T	Martin W	Wolfe F	Raisbeck A	Rushton G	Howe P	Spence G	Wilkinson H	Mackrill O	
1	2	3	4	5	6	8	9	10	11	7	P
1	2	3	4	5	6	8	9	10	11	7	R
2	2	2	2	2	2	2	2	2	2	2	
							1	2		1	

In Match 21 the injured Wilkinson was replaced by an unnamed Middlesbrough player.

McKiernan played number 7 in Match 1; W.Hay played number 8 in Match 2; C.Brown played number 4 in Match 4; B.Frost played number 5 in Match 8; H.Mackrill played number 7 in Match 8; E.Robinson played number 11 in Match 11; L.Johnson played number 4 in Match 12; R.Alexander played number 9 in Match 16; J.Ridsdale played number 9 in Match 19, scoring twice; L.Traynor played number 2 in Match 24; H.Forrester played number 2 in Match 30; W.Cooper played number 3 in Match 30; W.Smith played number 7 in Match 30; F.Robson played number 10 in Match 31; A.Patrick played number 3 in Match 34; W.Hodson played number 5 in Match 36; J.Manning played number 7 in Match 38; A.Glaves played number 8 in Match 39; C.Bouch played number 9 in Match 43; W.Goodin played number 2 in Match 44; M.Carney played number 4 in Match 44; W.Sommerscales played number 8 in Match 44.

1905-06

1	Sep	2	(c)	Barnsley	W	4-1	Gordon 2, Spence, Wilson	8,000
2		9	(a)	Clapton O	W	1-0	Howe	3,000
3		11	(a)	Chelsea	L	1-5	Howe	5,000
4		16	(c)	Burnley	D	1-1	Raisbeck	6,000
5		23	(a)	Leeds C	L	1-3	Wilson	13,645
6		30	(c)	Burton U	D	1-1	Howe	6,000
7	Oct	11	(c)	Chesterfield	W	3-0	Joe Smith, Howe, Raisbeck	3,000
8		14	(c)	Gainsborough T	W	2-0	Wilson, Howe	3,500
9		21	(a)	Bristol C	L	1-2	Joe Smith	7,000
10		28	(b)	Manchester U	L	0-1		12,000
11	Nov	4	(a)	Glossop	L	1-3	Joe Smith	1,000
12		11	(c)	Stockport C	W	3-0	Joe Smith 2, Jack Smith	3,000
13		25	(c)	Bradford C	W	5-2	Joe Smith 2, Gordon, Robinson, Jones	5,000
14	Dec	2	(a)	West Brom A	D	1-1	Gordon	8,000
15		7	(a)	Leicester F	W	2-1	Raisbeck, Manning	3,000
16		16	(c)	Grimsby T	L	0-1		8,000
17		23	(a)	Lincoln C	W	4-1	Joe Smith, Manning, Rushton, Spence	1,500
18		25	(a)	Port Vale	W	3-1	Gordon, Rushton, Jones	4,000
19		26	(a)	Burton U	W	3-0	Gordon 2, Rushton	3,000
20	Jan	6	(b)	Clapton O	W	3-1	Rushton 2, Manning	3,000
21		20	(a)	Burnley	W	3-1	Rushton 2, Gordon	3,000
22		27	(c)	Leeds C	D	0-0		10,000
23	Feb	10	(c)	Chelsea	W	4-3	Joe Smith 2, Gordon, Rushton	7,000
24		17	(a)	Gainsborough T	L	1-3	Raisbeck	4,000
25		24	(c)	Bristol C	L	0-3		8,000
26	Mar	3	(a)	Manchester U	L	0-5		16,000
27		10	(b)	Glossop	L	1-2	Howe	7,000
28		14	(a)	Blackpool	W	2-1	Jack Smith, Howe	2,000
29		17	(a)	Stockport C	L	1-2	Howe	5,000
30		24	(h)	Blackpool	D	2-2	Howe 2	5,000
31		31	(a)	Bradford C	W	2-0	Jack Smith, Hedley	9,000
32	Apr	7	(h)	West Brom A	W	4-0	Joe Smith, Gordon, Raisbeck, Wright	8,000
33		13	(a)	Chesterfield	W	2-1	Gordon, Jack Smith	5,000
34		14	(h)	Leicester F	D	0-0		10,000
35		16	(h)	Port Vale	W	3-2	Howe 2, Browell	7,000
36		17	(a)	Barnsley	L	0-2		5,000
37		21	(a)	Grimsby T	L	0-1		6,000
38		28	(h)	Lincoln C	W	2-1	Jack Smith, Joe Smith	4,000

FINAL LEAGUE POSITION: 5th in Division Two

Appearances
Goals

FA Cup

Q1	Oct	7	(c)	Grimethorpe U	W	8-1	Joe Smith 3, Howe 2, Wilson 2, Robinson	2,000
Q2		28	(a)	Denaby U	W	2-0	Jack Smith 2	3,000
Q3	Nov	22	(c)	Leeds C	D	1-1	Raisbeck	3,000
R		29	(a)	Leeds C	W	2-1	Rushton, Joe Smith	8,000
Q4	Dec	9	(c)	Oldham A	W	2-1	Jack Smith, Howe	4,000
1	Jan	13	(c)	Reading	L	0-1		9,000

Appearances
Goals

Key to grounds: (a) = away
(b) = Boulevard (Hull RLFC)
(c) = Anlaby Road Cricket Ground
(h) = Anlaby Road Football Ground

Note: For the FA Cup first Qualifying round on October 7, Grimethorpe United gave up ground advantage.

Spendiff M	Langley A	Jones T	Martin W	Robinson W	Gordon D	Rushton G	Spence G	Wilson D	Howe P	Raisbeck A	Thornton W	Simmon H	Smith Jack	Browell G	Smith Joe	Manning J	Davies H	Hedley G	Hall E	Hall H	Wright G	Lavery P	Frost W	Goodin W	Cook G	Brooks G	Carney M	
1	2	3	4	5	6	7	8	9	10	11																		1
1	2	3	4	5	6	7	8	9	10	11																		2
1	2	3	4	5	6	7	8	9	10	11																		3
1	2	3	4	5	6	7	8	9	10	11																		4
1	2	3		5	6			9	10	11	4	7	8															5
1	2	3		5	6	7		8	10	11				4	9													6
1	2	3		5	6			8	10	11		7		4	9													7
1	2	3		5	6			8	10	11		7		4	9													8
1	2	3		5	6			8	10	11		7		4	9													9
1	2	3		5	6		8		10	11		7		4	9													10
1	2	3		5	6		8		10	11		7		4	9													11
1	2	3		5	6		8			11			10	4	9	7												12
1		2		5	10	9	8			6				4	11	7	3											13
1		3		5	10	9	8			6				4	11	7	2											14
1		3		5	6		8	10	9	11				4		7	2											15
1		3		5	10	9				6			8	4	11	7	2											16
1		3		5	10	9	8			6				4	11	7	2											17
1		3		5	10	9	8			6				4	11	7	2											18
1	2	3		5	10	9	8			6				4	11	7												19
1		3		5	10	9	8			6				4	11	7	2											20
1		3		5	10	9				6			8	4	11	7	2											21
1		3		5	10	9				6			8	4	11	7	2											22
1		3		5	10	9				6			8	4	11	7	2											23
1		3		5	10					6		9	8	4	11	7	2											24
1		3		5	10					11		6	8	4	9	7	2											25
1		3		5	4		9		10	6			8		11	7	2											26
1		3		5	4		8		10	6			9		11	7	2											27
1							9		10	6			7	4	11		2	3	5	8								28
1					9		8		10	6			7	4	11		2	3	5									29
1				5	9		8		10	6			7	4	11		2	3										30
1				5	6				10	11			8	4	9	7	3	2										31
1				5	10					6			8	4	9	7	3	2			11							32
1				5	6				10	11			8	4	9	7	3	2										33
1				5	6				10	11			8	4	9	7	3	2										34
1				5	9				10	6			8	4		7	3	2				11						35
1					10				9	6		8		2		7		3	5			11	4					36
1				5	10				9	6			8	4	11	7	3	2										37
1				5	10				9	6			8	4	11	7		3						2				38
38	13	27	4	35	37	15	19	10	24	38	1	9	20	31	30	24	23	11	3	1	1	2	1	1				
		2		1	11	8	2	3	12	5			5	1	12	3		1			1							

Spendiff M	Langley A	Jones T	Martin W	Robinson W	Gordon D	Rushton G	Spence G	Wilson D	Howe P	Raisbeck A	Thornton W	Simmon H	Smith Jack	Browell G	Smith Joe	Manning J	Davies H	Hedley G	Hall E	Hall H	Wright G	Lavery P	Frost W	Goodin W	Cook G	Brooks G	Carney M	
1	2	3		5	6			8	10	11		7		4	9													Q1
			4			9					8		10			11	2					7	6		1	3	5	Q2
1	2	3		5	6	9		8		11			10	4		7												Q3
1		2		5	10	9	8			6				4	11	7	3											R
1		3		5	6	9			10	11			8	4		7	2											Q4
1		3		5	10	9	8			6				4	11	7	2											1
5	2	5	1	5	5	5	2	2	2	5	1	1	3	5	3	5	4					1	1		1	1	1	
				1		1		2	3	1			3		4													

1906-07

1	Sep	1	(a)	Wolves	D 1-1	Jack Smith	6,000
2		8	(h)	Clapton O	W 2-0	Jack Smith, Martin (og)	5,000
3		15	(a)	Gainsborough T	D 1-1	Jack Smith	4,000
4		22	(h)	Stockport C	W 3-0	Jack Smith, Joe Smith, Gordon	6,000
5		29	(h)	Chesterfield	W 2-0	Jack Smith, Wright	8,000
6	Oct	6	(a)	Glossop	W 4-2	Pearson 3, Wright	3,000
7		13	(h)	Blackpool	W 3-0	Jack Smith 2, Pearson	8,000
8		20	(a)	Bradford C	L 0-1		16,000
9		27	(h)	West Brom A	L 0-1		10,000
10	Nov	3	(a)	Leicester F	L 0-3		14,000
11		10	(h)	Nottingham F	L 1-2	Jack Smith	8,000
12		17	(a)	Lincoln C	W 1-0	Dagnall	5,000
13		24	(h)	Burton U	W 3-0	Wright 2, Pearson	6,000
14	Dec	1	(a)	Grimsby T	W 3-1	Manning, Pearson, Robinson	7,000
15		8	(h)	Barnsley	W 2-0	Wright, Manning	7,000
16		15	(a)	Burnley	L 2-4	Joe Smith, Rushton	6,000
17		22	(h)	Leeds C	W 2-1	Joe Smith, Rushton	9,000
18		25	(h)	Chelsea	L 0-1		16,000
19		26	(a)	Barnsley	L 2-4	Rushton 2	6,000
20		29	(h)	Wolves	W 5-1	Joe Smith 2, Manning 2, Rushton	9,000
21	Jan	1	(a)	Chesterfield	L 1-3	Jack Smith	4,000
22		5	(a)	Clapton O	L 1-2	Jack Smith	7,000
23		19	(h)	Gainsborough T	L 2-4	Jack Smith, Manning	6,000
24		26	(a)	Stockport C	D 1-1	Jack Smith	6,000
25	Feb	9	(b)	Glossop	W 5-0	Jack Smith 2, Wright 2, Rushton	7,000
26		16	(a)	Blackpool	D 1-1	Jack Smith	2,000
27	Mar	2	(a)	West Brom A	L 0-3		10,000
28		9	(h)	Leicester F	D 1-1	Hedley	7,000
29		14	(h)	Bradford C	L 0-3		5,000
30		16	(a)	Nottingham F	L 1-2	Neve	12,000
31		23	(h)	Lincoln C	L 1-2	Dagnall	6,000
32		29	(a)	Chelsea	L 0-3		60,000
33		30	(a)	Burton U	W 2-1	Jack Smith, Robinson	3,000
34	Apr	1	(h)	Port Vale	W 4-1	Jack Smith 2, Browell, Howe	8,000
35		6	(h)	Grimsby T	W 4-2	Howe 2, Jack Smith, Joe Smith	10,000
36		13	(a)	Port Vale	L 1-2	Neve	2,000
37		20	(h)	Burnley	D 1-1	Manning	7,000
38		27	(a)	Leeds C	D 2-2	Joe Smith, Neve	7,000

FINAL LEAGUE POSITION: 9th in Division Two

Appearances
Goals

FA Cup

1	Jan	12	(a)	Tottenham H	D 0-0		28,000
R		17	(h)	Tottenham H	D 0-0*		21,795
2R		21	(a)	Tottenham H	L 0-1		20,000

*Abandoned in extra-time due to bad light.

Appearances
Goals

Key to grounds: (a) = away
(b) = Boulevard (Hull RLFC)
(h) = Anlaby Road Football Ground

Spendiff M	Hedley G	Davies H	Browell G	Robinson W	Gordon D	Manning J	Smith Jack	Smith Joe	Dagnall W	Raisbeck A	Neve E	Wright G	Pearson F	McQuillan J	Rushton G	Howe P	Hall E	West H	Hall H	Dixon E	Simmon H	Roughley E	
1	2	3	4	5	6	7	8	9	10	11													1
1	2		3	5	4	7	8	9	10	6	11												2
1	2	3	4	5	10	7	8	9		6	11												3
1	2	3	4	5	10	7	8	9		6		11											4
1	2	3	4	5	10	7	8	9		6		11											5
1	2	3	4	5	10	7	8			6		11	9										6
1	2	3	4	5	10	7	8			6		11	9										7
1	2	3	4	5	10	7	8			6		11	9										8
1	2	3	4	5	10	7	8			6		11	9										9
1	2	3	4	5	6	7	8		10			11	9										10
1	2	3	4	5	6	7	8		10			11	9										11
1	2		4	5	6	7	8		10		11		9	3									12
1	2		4	5	6	7	8	9				11	10	3									13
1	2		4	5	6	7	8	9				11	10	3									14
1	2		4	5	6	7	8	9				11	10	3									15
1	2		4	5	6	7		8				11	10	3	9								16
1	2		4	5	6	7		8				11	10	3	9								17
1	2		4	5	6	7		8				11		3	9	10							18
1	2		4		6		7	8				11		3	9	10	5						19
1	2		4		6	7	8	10			11			3	9		5						20
1	2		4		6	7	8	10			11			3	9		5						21
1	2		4	5	6	7	8	10				11		3	9								22
1	2	3	4			7	8	10				11			9		5	6					23
1	2		4	5	6	7	8	10				11		3	9								24
1	2		4	5	6	7	8	10				11		3	9								25
1	2		4	5	6	7	8	10			11			3	9								26
1	2		4	5	6		8	7				11	10	3	9								27
1	2		4	5	6	7	10	8				11		3	9								28
1	2		4	5	6	7	10	9				11		3					8				29
1	2		4	5	6		8	7			11	9		3		10							30
1	2		4		6			7	10		11	9		3			5			8			31
1	2		4	5	6		8	7	10		11			3						9			32
1	2		4	5	6		8		10		11			3						9	7		33
	2		4	5	6		8					11		3	9	10					7	1	34
1	2		4	5	6	7	8	9				11		3		10							35
1	2		4	5	6		8	9			11			3		10					7		36
1	2		4	5	6	7	8	9			11			3		10							37
1	2		4	5	6	7	8	9			11			3		10							38
37	38	11	38	33	37	30	34	29	8	9	13	26	13	26	14	8	5	1	1	3	3	1	
	1		1	2	1	6	19	7	2		3	7	6		6	3							

1 own-goal

Spendiff M	Hedley G	Davies H	Browell G	Robinson W	Gordon D	Manning J	Smith Jack	Smith Joe	Dagnall W	Raisbeck A	Neve E	Wright G	Pearson F	McQuillan J	Rushton G	Howe P	Hall E	West H	Hall H	Dixon E	Simmon H	Roughley E	
1	2		4	5	6	7	8	10				11		3	9								1
1	2		4	5	6	7	8	10				11		3	9								R
1	2		4	5	6	7	8	10				11		3		9							2R
3	3		3	3	3	3	3	3				3		3	2	1							

1907-08

1	Sep	2	(a)	Clapton O	L 0-1		5,000
2		3	(a)	Fulham	W 1-0	Jack Smith	14,000
3		7	(h)	Barnsley	W 2-0	Jack Smith, Shaw	9,000
4		14	(a)	Chesterfield	W 2-1	Shaw, Temple	5,000
5		21	(h)	Burnley	W 3-1	Jack Smith 2, Joe Smith	8,000
6		26	(h)	Chesterfield	W 2-0	Jack Smith, Shaw	5,000
7		28	(a)	Oldham A	L 0-3		18,000
8	Oct	10	(h)	Clapton O	W 5-0	Jack Smith 4, Robinson	4,500
9		12	(a)	Leeds C	L 2-3	Jack Smith 2	14,000
10		19	(h)	Wolves	W 2-0	Temple, Robinson	8,000
11		26	(a)	Gainsborough T	W 2-1	Joe Smith, Temple	4,000
12	Nov	2	(h)	Stockport C	D 0-0		8,000
13		9	(a)	Glossop	L 1-5	Jack Smith	500
14		16	(h)	Leicester F	W 3-2	Temple 3	6,000
15		23	(a)	Blackpool	D 1-1	Jack Smith	2,000
16		30	(h)	Stoke	W 2-1	Jack Smith, Shaw	8,000
17	Dec	7	(a)	West Brom A	L 0-1		15,000
18		14	(h)	Bradford C	L 0-2		10,000
19		21	(h)	Grimsby T	W 4-2	Shaw 2, Temple 2	8,000
20		25	(h)	Lincoln C	W 5-3	Jack Smith 2, Temple 2, Neve	12,000
21		26	(a)	Lincoln C	W 1-0	Temple	6,000
22		28	(a)	Derby C	L 1-4	Jack Smith	12,000
23	Jan	4	(a)	Barnsley	L 2-4	Jack Smith, Martin	4,000
24		18	(a)	Burnley	L 0-5		7,000
25		25	(h)	Oldham A	W 3-2	Jack Smith 2, Robinson	10,000
26	Feb	8	(h)	Leeds C	W 4-1	Shaw 2, Jack Smith, Joe Smith	9,000
27		15	(a)	Wolves	W 2-1	Jack Smith 2	5,000
28		22	(h)	Gainsborough T	L 0-1		5,000
29		29	(a)	Stockport C	W 3-2	Temple 2, Shaw	5,000
30	Mar	7	(h)	Glossop	W 3-2	Jack Smith, Shaw, Temple	8,000
31		14	(a)	Leicester F	L 2-3	Jack Smith, Shaw	12,000
32		21	(h)	Blackpool	W 3-2	Jack Smith 2, Temple	7,000
33		28	(a)	Stoke	D 1-1	Jack Smith	4,000
34	Apr	4	(h)	West Brom A	W 4-2	Temple 2, Jack Smith, Joe Smith	8,000
35		11	(a)	Bradford C	L 1-2	Jack Smith	15,000
36		18	(a)	Grimsby T	D 1-1	Temple	5,000
37		20	(h)	Fulham	L 1-2	Shaw	16,000
38		25	(h)	Derby C	W 4-0	Shaw 2, Joe Smith, Jack Smith	8,000

FINAL LEAGUE POSITION: 8th in Division Two

Appearances
Goals

FA Cup

1	Jan	11	(a)	W Arsenal	D 0-0		15,000
R		16	(h)	W Arsenal	W 4-1	Shaw 2, Temple, Jack Smith	16,000
2	Feb	1	(a)	Aston Villa	L 0-3		35,000

Appearances
Goals

Spendiff M	Hedley G	McQuillan J	Browell G	Robinson W	Gordon D	Smith Joe	Smith Jack	Shaw J	Temple A	Neve E	Martin F	Wright G	Roughley E	Simmon H	Stephenson W	Nevins T	Taylor J	
1	2	3	4	5	6	7	8	9	10	11								1
1	2	3	4	5	6	7	8	9	10	11								2
1	2	3	4	5	6	7	8	9	10	11								3
1	2	3	4	5	6	7	8	9	10	11								4
1	2	3		5	6	7	8	9	10		4	11						5
1	2	3	4	5	6	7	8	9	10			11						6
1	2	3	4	5	6	7	8	9	10			11						7
	2	3	4	5	10	7	8		9			11	1	6				8
	2	3	4	5	6	7	8	9	10			11	1					9
1	2	3	4	5	10	7	8		9			11		6				10
1	2	3	4	5	10	7	8		9			11		6				11
1	2	3		5	10	7	8		9		4	11		6				12
1	2	3		5	10	7	8		9		4	11		6				13
1	2	3	4	5	6	7	8	9	10			11						14
1	2	3	4	5	6	7	8	9	10			11						15
	2	3	4	5	6	7	8	9	10			11	1					16
	2	3	4	5	6	7	8	9	10	11			1					17
1	2	3	4	5	6	7	8	9	10			11						18
1	2	3	4	5	6	7	8	9	10			11						19
1	2	3	4	5	6	7	8	9	10	11								20
1		3	4	5	6	7	8	9	10			11			2			21
1	2	3	4	5	6	7	8	9	10	11								22
1		3	5		6	7	8	9	10		4	11			2			23
			4	5		7	8	9	10	11	6		1		2	3		24
1		3	4	5		7	8	9	10		6	11			2			25
1	2	3	4	5		7	8	9	10		6	11						26
1	2	3	4	5		7	8	9	10		6	11						27
1	2	3	4	5		7	8	9	10		6	11						28
1	2	3	4	5		7		9	10	11	6						8	29
1	2	3	4	5		7	8	9	10		6	11						30
1	2		4	5		7	8	9	10		6	11			3			31
1	2		4	5		7	8	9	10		6	11			3			32
1	2		4	5		7	8	9	10	11	6				3			33
1		3	4	5		7	8	9	10		6	11			2			34
		3	4	5		7	8	9	10		6	11	1		2			35
		3	4	5		7	8	9	10	11	6		1		2			36
		3	4	5		7	8	9	10	11	6		1		2			37
		3	4	5		7	8	9	10	11	6		1		2			38
29	29	34	35	37	23	38	37	33	38	13	19	25	9	5	12	1	1	
				3		5	31	14	18	1	1							

Spendiff M	Hedley G	McQuillan J	Browell G	Robinson W	Gordon D	Smith Joe	Smith Jack	Shaw J	Temple A	Neve E	Martin F	Wright G	
1	2	3	4	5	6	7	8		9		10	11	1
1	2	3	4	5		7	8	9	10		6	11	R
1	2	3	4	5		7	8	9	10		6	11	2
3	3	3	3	3	1	3	3	2	3		3	3	
							1	2	1				

1908-09

1	Sep	1	(a)	Bradford	L	0-1		15,000
2		5	(h)	Clapton O	W	3-2	Shaw 2, Jack Smith	8,000
3		12	(a)	Leeds C	L	0-2		15,000
4		14	(a)	Bolton W	L	0-1		14,000
5		19	(a)	Barnsley	L	1-2	Temple	7,000
6		26	(h)	Tottenham H	W	1-0	Joe Smith	10,000
7	Oct	3	(h)	Bolton W	W	2-0	Temple, Gilberthorpe	10,000
8		10	(a)	Derby C	D	0-0		7,000
9		17	(h)	Blackpool	W	2-0	Jack Smith, Temple	8,000
10		24	(a)	Chesterfield	W	4-0	Joe Smith, Temple, Gilberthorpe, W.Wright	5,000
11		31	(h)	Glossop	D	0-0		8,000
12	Nov	7	(a)	Stockport C	L	1-3	Gilberthorpe	6,000
13		14	(h)	West Brom A	D	2-2	Joe Smith 2	8,000
14		21	(a)	Birmingham	W	2-1	Gilberthorpe, Gordon	15,000
15		28	(h)	Gainsborough T	W	5-1	Shaw 3, Temple 2	7,000
16	Dec	5	(a)	Grimsby T	D	0-0		7,000
17		12	(h)	Fulham	W	2-0	Temple 2	10,000
18		19	(a)	Burnley	L	0-1		7,000
19		25	(h)	Bradford	L	2-3	Jack Smith, Shaw	12,000
20		26	(a)	Wolves	L	0-3		15,000
21	Jan	2	(a)	Clapton O	W	2-1	Jack Smith, Gordon	10,000
22		9	(h)	Leeds C	W	4-1	Joe Smith, Gordon, Temple, G.Wright	8,000
23		23	(h)	Barnsley	W	4-0	Temple, Toward, Jack Smith, A.Browell	8,000
24		30	(a)	Tottenham H	D	0-0		23,000
25	Feb	13	(h)	Derby C	W	4-0	Taylor 2, Temple, Jack Smith	8,000
26		20	(a)	Blackpool	W	3-2	Temple 2, Jack Smith	4,000
27		27	(h)	Chesterfield	W	1-0	Temple	7,000
28	Mar	13	(h)	Stockport C	W	4-1	Temple 2, Joe Smith, Taylor	8,000
29		20	(a)	West Brom A	L	0-1		20,000
30		23	(a)	Glossop	L	1-2	W.Smith	1,500
31		27	(h)	Birmingham	W	4-1	W.Smith 3, Temple	10,000
32	Apr	3	(a)	Gainsborough T	L	0-2		4,000
33		10	(h)	Grimsby T	L	0-1		12,000
34		12	(h)	Wolves	L	0-1		8,000
35		17	(a)	Fulham	W	3-0	Toward 2, Jack Smith	15,000
36		24	(h)	Burnley	W	3-2	Jack Smith, Toward, W.Smith	6,000
37		27	(a)	Oldham A	D	2-2	Toward, W.Smith	3,000
38		29	(h)	Oldham A	W	1-0	Jack Smith	4,000

FINAL LEAGUE POSITION: 4th in Division Two

Appearances
Goals

FA Cup

1	Jan	16	(h)	Chelsea	D	1-1	Temple	18,100
R		20	(a)	Chelsea	L	0-1		25,792

Appearances
Goals

Roughley E	Stephenson W	McQuillan J	Browell G	Robinson W	Gordon D	Smith Joe	Smith Jack	Shaw J	Temple A	Neve E	Nevins T	Morrison J	Gilberthorpe A	Wright G	Taylor J	Wright W	Browell A	Pace A	Storey E	Toward A	Smith W	Martin F	
1	2	3	4	5	6	7	8	9	10	11													1
1	2	3	4	5	6	7	8	9	10	11													2
1	2	3	4	5	6	7	8	9	10	11													3
1	2			5	6	7		9	10	11	3	4	8										4
1	2			5	6	7		9	10		3	4	8	11									5
1	2		6	5		7			9		3	4	10	11	8								6
1	2		4	5	6	7	8		9		3		10	11									7
1	2		4	5	6	7	8		9		3		10	11									8
1	2		4	5	6	7	8		9		3		10	11									9
1	2		4	5	6	8			9		3		10	11		7							10
1	2		4	5	6	8			9		3		10	11		7							11
1	2		4	5	6	7			9	11	3		10		8								12
1	2		4	5	6	7		9	10		3		8	11									13
1	2		4		6	7		9	10	11	3		8				5						14
1	2		4		6	8		9	10	11	3						5	7					15
1		3	4		6	7		9	10	11	2		8				5						16
1		3	4		6	7		9	10		2		8	11			5						17
1		3	4		6	7		9	10	11	2		8				5						18
1		3	4		6	7	8	9	10	11	2						5						19
	2	3	4		6	7	8	9					10	11			5		1				20
	2	3	4		6	7	8					9	10	11			5		1				21
	2	3	4	5	6	7	8		9				10	11					1				22
1	2	3	4		6	7	8		10					11			5			9			23
1	2	3	4		6	7	8		10					11			5			9			24
1	2	3	4		6	7	8		9					11	10		5						25
1	2	3	4		6		8		9					11	10		5	7					26
1	2	3	4		6	7	8		9					11	10		5						27
1	2	3	4		6	7			9					11	8		5				10		28
1	2	3	4		6	7			9					11	8		5				10		29
1	2	3	4		6	7	8		9	11							5				10		30
1	2	3	4		6	7	8		9					11			5				10		31
1	2	3	4		6	7	8		9					11			5				10		32
1		3	4			7	8		9	11	2						5				10	6	33
1		3	4		6	7			9	11	2		10		8		5						34
1		3	4		6	7	8		2					11			5			9	10		35
1		3	4		6	7	8		2					11			5			9	10		36
1		3	4		6	7	8		2					11			5			9	10		37
1		3			6	7	8		2					11		4	5			9	10		38
35	28	26	35	14	36	37	23	13	36	13	18	4	18	25	8	3	24	2	3	6	10	1	
					3	6	10	6	17				4	1	3	1	1			5	6		

1	2	3	4	5	6	7	8		9				10	11									1
1	2	3	4		6	7	8		9				10	11			5						R
2	2	2	2	1	2	2	2		2				2	2			1						
									1														

1909-10

1	Sep	2	(a)	Barnsley	W 2-1	W.Smith, Neve	5,000
2		4	(h)	Leeds C	W 3-1	Jack Smith 3	10,000
3		6	(a)	Burnley	W 1-0	Temple	7,000
4		11	(a)	Wolves	D 2-2	Jack Smith, Joe Smith	10,000
5		18	(h)	Gainsborough T	W 5-1	Jack Smith 2, W.Smith 2, G.Wright	10,000
6		25	(a)	Grimsby T	W 3-2	Jack Smith, W.Smith, A.Browell	8,000
7	Oct	2	(h)	Manchester C	L 1-2	Jack Smith	14,000
8		9	(a)	Leicester F	L 1-3	Temple	12,000
9		11	(h)	Barnsley	W 1-0	Toward	7,000
10		16	(h)	Lincoln C	D 0-0		8,000
11		23	(a)	Clapton O	D 0-0		8,000
12		30	(h)	Blackpool	L 1-2	Jack Smith	8,000
13	Nov	6	(a)	Bradford	W 1-0	Walden	10,000
14		13	(a)	Derby C	L 0-4		10,000
15		20	(h)	Stockport C	D 1-1	Jack Smith	8,000
16		27	(a)	Glossop	L 1-2	Jack Smith	3,000
17	Dec	4	(h)	Birmingham	W 7-0	Temple 3, Jack Smith 2, W.Smith, A.Browell	6,500
18		11	(a)	West Brom A	W 2-0	Temple, G.Wright	6,000
19		18	(h)	Oldham A	W 4-0	Jack Smith 3, Joe Smith	6,000
20		25	(a)	Fulham	L 1-3	Jack Smith	25,000
21		27	(h)	Fulham	W 3-2	W.Smith 2, Temple	16,000
22	Jan	1	(h)	Grimsby T	W 5-1	Temple 2, W.Smith 2, G.Wright	8,000
23		8	(a)	Leeds C	D 1-1	Jack Smith	12,000
24		22	(h)	Wolves	D 2-2	Jack Smith 2	6,000
25	Feb	12	(a)	Manchester C	L 0-3		28,000
26		26	(a)	Lincoln C	W 3-1	Jack Smith, Temple, W.Smith	3,000
27	Mar	5	(h)	Clapton O	W 3-0	W.Smith 3	8,000
28		12	(a)	Blackpool	W 2-1	Temple 2	3,000
29		19	(h)	Bradford	W 2-1	Jack Smith, W.Smith	8,000
30		26	(h)	Derby C	D 0-0		15,000
31		28	(h)	Burnley	W 3-2	Jack Smith, Joe Smith, Temple	10,000
32	Apr	2	(a)	Stockport C	W 5-1	Jack Smith 3, Joe Smith, Temple	5,000
33		9	(h)	Glossop	W 4-2	Temple 2, Jack Smith, W.Smith	6,000
34		14	(h)	Leicester F	W 2-1	Jack Smith, W.Smith	8,000
35		16	(a)	Birmingham	W 2-0	Jack Smith, Neve	5,000
36		20	(a)	Gainsborough T	W 1-0	Neve	2,000
37		23	(h)	West Brom A	W 5-1	Jack Smith 3, Joe Smith, W.Smith	15,000
38		30	(a)	Oldham A	L 0-3		30,000

FINAL LEAGUE POSITION: 3rd in Division Two

Appearances
Goals

FA Cup

1	Jan	15	(a)	Chelsea	L 1-2	Temple	38,000

Appearances
Goals

Roughley E	Stephenson W	McQuillan J	Browell G	Browell A	Gordon Davy	Smith Joe	Smith Jack	Temple A	Smith W	Neve E	Pace A	Nevins T	Wright G	Toward A	Martin F	Musgrave A	Walden G	Wright W	Townend V	Gordon Dan	
1	2	3	4	5	6	7	8	9	10	11											1
1	2	3	4	5	6	7	8	9	10	11											2
1	2	3	4	5	6		8	9	10	11	7										3
1		3	4	5	6	7	8	9	10			2	11								4
1		3	4	5	6	7	8	9	10			2	11								5
1		3	4	5		7	8	6	10			2	11	9							6
1	2	3	4	5		7	8	9	10				11		6						7
1	2	3	4	5	6	7	8	9	10				11								8
1		3	4	5	6	7	8		10	11		2		9							9
1		3	4	5	6	7	8		10			2	11	9							10
1		3	4	5	6	7			10	11		2		9		8					11
1		3	4	5	6	7	8	9	10			2	11								12
1	2	3	4	5	6	7		10	8	11							9				13
1	2	3		5	6			10	8				11				9	4	7		14
1	2	3	4	5	6		9	10	8	11									7		15
1	2		4	5	6		9	8	10	11	7	3									16
1	2	3	4	5	6		9	8	10		7		11								17
1	2	3	4	5	6	7	9	8	10				11								18
1		3	4	5	6	7	9	8	10			2	11								19
1		3	4	5	6	7	9	8	10	11		2									20
1		3	4	5	6	7	9	8	10			2	11								21
1		3	4	5	6	7	9	8	10			2	11								22
1		3		5	6	7	9	8	10			2	11		4						23
1	2	3	4	5	6	7	9	8	10				11								24
1		3	4	5	6	7	9	8	10	11		2									25
1		3	4	5	6	7	9	8	10	11		2									26
1		3	4	5	6	7	9	8	10			2	11								27
1		3	4	5	6	7	9	8	10	11		2									28
1		3	4	5	6	7	9	8	10	11		2									29
1		3	4	5	6	7	9	8	10	11		2									30
1	2	3	4	5	6	7	9	8	10	11											31
1	2	3	4	5	6	7	9	8		11						10					32
1	2	3	4	5	6	7	9	8	10	11											33
1		3	4	5	6	7	9	8	10	11										2	34
1		3	4	5	6	7	9	8	10	11										2	35
1		3		5	6	7	9	8	10	11					4					2	36
1		3		5	6	7	9	8	10	11					4					2	37
1			4	5	6	7	9	8	10	11		3								2	38
38	15	36	34	38	36	33	35	35	37	22	3	20	16	4	4	2	2	1	2	5	
				2		5	32	16	17	3			3	1			1				

Roughley E	Stephenson W	McQuillan J	Browell G	Browell A	Gordon Davy	Smith Joe	Smith Jack	Temple A	Smith W	Neve E	Pace A	Nevins T	Wright G	Toward A	Martin F	Musgrave A	Walden G	Wright W	Townend V	Gordon Dan	
1		3	4	5	6	7	9	8	10			2	11								1
1		1	1	1	1	1	1	1	1			1	1								
								1													

1910-11

1	Sep	3	(h)	West Brom A	D 1-1	Temple	9,000
2		10	(a)	Bolton W	L 1-2	Jack Smith	10,000
3		17	(a)	Fulham	W 1-0	Joe Smith	20,000
4		24	(h)	Bradford C	D 2-2	Joe Smith, Temple	7,000
5	Oct	1	(a)	Burnley	D 0-0		10,500
6		8	(h)	Gainsborough T	W 3-2	Joe Smith, Neve, W.Smith	8,000
7		15	(a)	Leeds C	L 0-1		8,000
8		22	(h)	Stockport C	W 4-1	T.Browell 3, Temple	6,000
9		29	(a)	Derby C	W 3-2	W.Smith, T.Browell, Temple	9,000
10	Nov	5	(h)	Barnsley	W 5-1	T.Browell 3, W.Smith, Davy Gordon	7,000
11		12	(a)	Leicester F	W 2-0	Joe Smith, G Browell	8,000
12		19	(h)	Wolves	D 2-2	T.Browell, W.Smith	9,000
13		26	(a)	Chelsea	L 0-2		30,000
14	Dec	3	(h)	Clapton O	L 1-2	T.Browell	10,000
15		10	(a)	Blackpool	L 0-2		6,000
16		17	(h)	Glossop	W 1-0	W.Smith	3,500
17		24	(a)	Lincoln C	W 4-1	Joe Smith, T.Browell, W.Smith, Temple	5,000
18		26	(h)	Birmingham	W 4-1	T.Browell 2, Temple, Neve	10,500
19		27	(h)	Burnley	W 3-0	T.Browell, Joe Smith, Temple	10,000
20		31	(a)	West Brom A	W 2-0	T.Browell 2	12,000
21	Jan	2	(a)	Huddersfield T	L 0-2		3,000
22		7	(h)	Bolton W	D 1-1	Temple	11,000
23		21	(h)	Fulham	D 0-0		8,000
24		28	(a)	Bradford	L 0-2		10,000
25	Feb	11	(a)	Gainsborough T	D 1-1	W.Smith	2,000
26		18	(h)	Leeds C	D 1-1	W.Smith	6,000
27	Mar	4	(h)	Derby C	W 2-0	Neve, Davy Gordon	5,000
28		11	(a)	Barnsley	W 1-0	W.Smith	5,000
29		18	(h)	Leicester F	D 2-2	Joe Smith 2	7,000
30		25	(a)	Wolves	D 0-0		3,000
31	Apr	1	(h)	Chelsea	D 1-1	Neve	10,000
32		8	(a)	Clapton O	D 1-1	Temple	9,000
33		14	(a)	Birmingham	L 0-1		6,000
34		15	(h)	Blackpool	D 1-1	Temple	8,000
35		17	(h)	Huddersfield T	D 2-2	Houghton, Townend	12,000
36		22	(a)	Glossop	D 0-0		1,000
37		24	(a)	Stockport C	D 1-1	Houghton	2,000
38		29	(h)	Lincoln C	W 2-1	Joe Smith, T.Browell	5,000

FINAL LEAGUE POSITION: 5th in Division Two — Appearances

Note: Match 34 was benefit match for George Browell, Davy Gordon and Joe Smith. — Goals

FA Cup

1	Jan	14	(a)	Bristol R	D 0-0		9,666
R		19	(h)	Bristol R	W 1-0*	McQuillan	13,000
2	Feb	4	(h)	Oldham A	W 1-0	Temple	17,000
3		25	(a)	Newcastle U	L 2-3	Joe Smith 2	46,531

*After extra-time — Appearances

Goals

Roughley E	McIntosh J	McQuillan J	Browell G	Browell A	Gordon David	Smith Jack	Temple A	Smith E	Smith W	Neve E	Browell T	Smith Joe	Musgrave A	Nevins T	Gordon Dan	Houghton J	Wright G	Townend V	Wright W	Martin F	Pearce T	Robson W	Chapman H	
1	2	3	4	5	6	7	8	9	10	11														1
1	2	3	4	5	6	9	8		10	11	7													2
1	2	3	4	5	6	9				11	7	8	10											3
1	2	3	4	5	6	9	8		10	11		7												4
1	4	3		5	6		9		10	11	7	8		2										5
1	5	3	4		6	9			10	11	7	8		2										6
1	5	3	4		6	8	9		10	11		7		2										7
1	5	3	4		6		8		10	11	9	7			2									8
1	5	3	4		6		8		10	11	9	7			2									9
1		3	4		6		8		10		9	7			2	5	11							10
1	5		4		6	9	8		10			7		3	2		11							11
1	5		4		6		8		10	11	9	7		3	2									12
1	5	3	4		6		2		10		9	7	8				11							13
1	5	3	4		6		2	10	8	11	9	7												14
1	5	3	4		6		2	10	8	11	9	7												15
1	5	3	4		6		8		10		9	7		2			11							16
1	5	3	4		6		8		10		9	7		2			11							17
1	5	3	4		6		8		10	11	9	7		2										18
1	6	3	4		10		8			11	9	7		2		5								19
1	4	3			6		8	10			9	7		2		5	11							20
1	4	3			6		8	10		11	9	7		2		5								21
1	4	3			6		8		10		9			2		5	11	7						22
1				5	10		2				9		8	3			11	7	4	6				23
1		3		5	10		9		8					2			11	7	4	6				24
1		3		5			8		10	11	9	7		2					4	6				25
1				5					10	11	9	7	8	2	3				4	6				26
1	6	3		5	10				8	11	9			2					4		7			27
1	6			5	10				8	11	9	7		2					4			3		28
1	6			5			8		10	11	9	7		2					4			3		29
1	5		4		6			10	8		9	7		2			11					3		30
1	4	3		5	6			8	10	11	9			2				7						31
1	6		4				10	9		11		8		2		5		7				3		32
1	6	3		5			8		10	11	9			2				7	4					33
1	5	3	4		6		8		10		9	7		2							11			34
1					6		8		10		9	11		2		5		7	4			3		35
1		3			6				10	11	9	7		2		5			4				8	36
1							8			11	9	7	10	2		5			4	6		3		37
1	5	3			6				10	11	9	7		2					4				8	38
38	30	28	21	14	32	7	29	8	31	26	32	30	5	28	6	9	10	7	12	5	2	6	2	
			1		2	1	10		9	4	16	9				2		1						

Roughley E	McIntosh J	McQuillan J	Browell G	Browell A	Gordon David	Smith Jack	Temple A	Smith E	Smith W	Neve E	Browell T	Smith Joe	Musgrave A	Nevins T	Gordon Dan	Houghton J	Wright G	Townend V	Wright W	Martin F	Pearce T	Robson W	Chapman H	
1	4	3		5	6		8		10		9	7		2			11							1
1	4	3		5	6		8		10		9	7		2			11							R
1		3		5	6		8		10		9	7		2			11		4					2
1		3		5	6		8		10		9	7		2			11		4					3
4	2	4		4	4		4		4		4	4		4			4		2					
		1					1					2												

1911-12

1	Sep	2	(a)	Blackpool	L 2-3	T.Browell 2	7,500
2		9	(h)	Glossop	W 2-0	J.Smith, Temple	8,000
3		16	(h)	Burnley	W 4-1	Temple 3, T.Browell	10,000
4		23	(a)	Barnsley	W 2-1	T.Browell, Temple	9,000
5		30	(h)	Bradford	W 5-1	Temple, Chapman, J.Smith, G.Wright, T.Browell	9,000
6	Oct	7	(a)	Fulham	W 1-0	Temple	12,000
7		14	(h)	Derby C	D 0-0		14,000
8		21	(a)	Stockport C	D 1-1	Temple	4,000
9		25	(a)	Gainsborough T	W 3-0	T.Browell 3	6,000
10		28	(h)	Leeds C	W 1-0	Temple	12,000
11	Nov	4	(a)	Wolves	L 0-8		15,000
12		11	(h)	Leicester F	W 4-1	T.Browell 4	10,000
13		25	(h)	Grimsby T	W 1-0	Chapman	15,000
14	Dec	2	(a)	Nottingham F	D 0-0		10,000
15		9	(h)	Chelsea	W 1-0	T.Browell	13,000
16		16	(a)	Clapton O	L 0-4		11,000
17		23	(h)	Bristol C	W 3-0	T.Browell 2, Temple	8,000
18		25	(h)	Birmingham	W 4-0	Chapman 2, Temple, T.Browell	11,000
19		26	(a)	Birmingham	L 1-5	Temple	12,000
20		30	(h)	Blackpool	W 3-0	A.Browell 2, Temple	9,000
21	Jan	6	(a)	Glossop	D 1-1	Temple	500
22		20	(a)	Burnley	L 1-5	Houghton	10,000
23		27	(h)	Barnsley	D 0-0		10,00
24	Feb	10	(h)	Fulham	L 2-3	Temple, G.Wright	10,00
25		17	(a)	Derby C	W 3-2	Chapman 2, Neve	8,00
26		24	(h)	Stockport C	L 0-2		7,00
27	Mar	2	(a)	Leeds C	D 0-0		10,00
28		9	(h)	Wolves	W 3-0	McDonald, Best, Temple	9,00
29		16	(a)	Leicester F	L 0-3		6,00
30		20	(a)	Bradford	L 1-3	Stevens	2,00
31		23	(h)	Gainsborough T	D 1-1	Fenwick	4,00
32		30	(a)	Grimsby T	L 0-1		6,00
33	Apr	6	(h)	Nottingham F	W 2-1	Chapman, W.Wright	6,50
34		8	(h)	Huddersfield T	L 0-1		7,00
35		9	(a)	Huddersfield T	W 2-0	Best, Shaw	5,00
36		13	(a)	Chelsea	L 0-1		30,00
37		20	(h)	Clapton O	L 0-2		6,00
38		27	(a)	Bristol C	D 0-0		6,00

FINAL LEAGUE POSITION: 7th in Division Two — Appearances

Note: Match 15 was benefit match for Jack McQuillan, Ned Neve and Teddy Roughley. — Goals

FA Cup

1	Jan	13	(a)	Oldham A	D 1-1	Best	12,00
R		16	(h)	Oldham A	L 0-1		13,11

Appearances

Goals

Roughley E	Nevins T	McQuillan J	McIntosh J	Browell A	Gordon D	Smith Joe	Chapman H	Browell T	Temple A	Neve E	Smith E	Wright W	Wright G	Smith W	Best C	Pearce T	Fenwick A	Townend V	Robson W	Houghton J	Hedley T	Stevens S	McDonald W	Hendry N	Shaw F	Fazackerley S	
1	2	3	4	5	6	7	8	9	10	11																	1
1	2	3	4	5	6	7	8		10	11	9																2
1	2	3		5	6	7	8	9	10			4	11														3
1	2	3		5	6	7	8	9	10			4	11														4
1	2	3		5	6	7	8	9	10			4	11														5
1	2	3		5	6	7	8	9	10			4	11														6
1	2	3		5	6	7	8		10			4	11	9													7
1	2	3		5	6	7			10	11		4		9	8												8
1	2	3		5	6	7		9	10			4			8	11											9
1	2	3		5	6	7	8	9	10			4	11														10
1	2	3		5	6	7	8	9	10			4	11														11
1	2	3		5	6		8	9	10			4	11		7												12
1	2	3		5	6		8	9	10			4	11		7												13
1	2	3		5			8	9	10	11		4			7		6										14
1	2	3		5	6		8	9	10	11		4						7									15
1		3			6		8	9		11		4		10	7				2	5							16
1	2	3		5	6		8	9	10			4	11		7												17
1	2	3		5	6		8	9	10	11		4			7												18
1	2	3		5	6			9	10				11	7	8		4										19
1	2	3		5			8		10			4	11	6	9			7									20
1	2	3		5	6		8		10			4	11		9			7									21
1		3		5	6	7				11		4		10	8					2	9						22
1	2	3		5	10	7						4	11	6	8						9						23
1	2	3		5	6	7	8		10			4	11									9					24
1		3		5	6	7	8		10	11		4								2		9					25
1		3		5	6	7	8		10	11		4								2		9					26
1		3	5		6		8		10			4	11							2		9	7				27
1		3	5		6		10		9			4	11		8					2			7				28
1		3	5		6		10			11		4			8					2		9	7				29
1			5		6		10			11		4			8				3	2		9	7				30
	3		5				10					4	11		8		6			2		9	7	1			31
	3						10		9	11		4		5	8		6			2			7	1			32
1		3			6		10		9			4		5	8					2			7		11		33
1		3	5		6				8			4		10	9					2			7		11		34
1		3	5						9			4		10	8		6			2			7		11		35
1		3	5				10		9	11				4	8		6			2			7				36
1		3	5						9	11		4		6	8					2			7			10	37
1		3	6				8		5			4			9					2			7		11	10	38
36	24	35	12	25	30	16	30	16	32	15	1	34	18	13	24	1	6	3	2	16	2	7	12	2	4	2	
				2		2	7	16	16	1		1	2		2		1			1		1	1		1		

Roughley E	Nevins T	McQuillan J	McIntosh J	Browell A	Gordon D	Smith Joe	Chapman H	Browell T	Temple A	Neve E	Smith E	Wright W	Wright G	Smith W	Best C	
1	2	3		5	6	7	8		10	11		4			9	1
1	2	3		5	6	7	8			11		4		10	9	R
2	2	2		2	2	2	2		1	2		2		1	2	
															1	

1912-13

1	Sep	7	(h)	Blackpool	W 4-1	Stevens, Best, Goode, Fazackerley	8,000
2		9	(a)	Burnley	D 0-0		20,000
3		14	(a)	Glossop	W 3-0	Goode 2, Fazackerley	2,000
4		21	(h)	Clapton O	W 2-1	Fazackerley 2	12,000
5		26	(h)	Burnley	D 0-0		8,000
6		28	(a)	Lincoln C	D 1-1	Fazackerley	9,000
7	Oct	5	(h)	Nottingham F	W 2-1	Fazackerley, Best	15,000
8		12	(a)	Bristol C	D 1-1	Fazackerley	17,000
9		19	(h)	Birmingham	L 1-2	Fazackerley	10,000
10		26	(a)	Huddersfield T	L 2-5	Fazackerley, McIntosh	3,000
11	Nov	2	(h)	Leeds C	W 6-2	Stevens 4, McDonald, McIntosh	9,000
12		9	(a)	Grimsby T	L 0-2		8,000
13		16	(h)	Bury	W 2-0	Stevens, Goode	8,000
14		23	(a)	Fulham	L 0-2		17,000
15	Dec	7	(a)	Bradford	L 0-2		10,000
16		14	(h)	Wolves	L 0-1		6,000
17		19	(h)	Barnsley	L 0-1		4,000
18		21	(a)	Leicester F	L 2-3	Fazackerley 2	5,000
19		25	(h)	Stockport C	W 3-2	Fazackerley 2, Goode	8,000
20		26	(a)	Preston NE	L 0-1		15,000
21		28	(a)	Blackpool	W 2-1	Goode 2	3,000
22	Jan	18	(a)	Clapton O	L 1-2	Fazackerley	7,000
23		25	(h)	Lincoln C	W 2-0	Stevens 2	8,000
24	Feb	8	(a)	Nottingham F	L 0-5		10,000
25		15	(h)	Bristol C	W 3-1	Fazackerley, Lyon, McQuillan	6,000
26		22	(a)	Birmingham	L 1-3	Fazackerley	12,000
27	Mar	1	(h)	Huddersfield T	L 1-3	McDonald	6,000
28		8	(a)	Leeds C	L 0-1		16,000
29		15	(h)	Grimsby T	W 5-0	Fazackerley 3, Goode 2	7,000
30		21	(a)	Stockport C	D 3-3	Stevens 2, Goode	7,000
31		22	(a)	Bury	L 0-3		5,000
32		24	(h)	Preston NE	D 2-2	Stevens 2	12,000
33		29	(h)	Fulham	L 0-1		7,000
34	Apr	5	(a)	Barnsley	L 1-2	Stevens	6,000
35		12	(h)	Bradford	W 5-0	Stevens 2, Fenwick 2, McQuillan	5,000
36		17	(h)	Glossop	W 2-0	McDonald, Boyton	5,000
37		19	(a)	Wolves	W 1-0	Fenwick	6,000
38		26	(h)	Leicester F	W 2-1	Fenwick 2	5,000

FINAL LEAGUE POSITION: 12th in Division Two — Appearances

Note: Match 38 was benefit match for Arthur Temple. — Goals

FA Cup

1	Jan	11	(a)	Fulham	W 2-0	Fazackerley, Stevens	10,000
2	Feb	1	(h)	Newcastle U	D 0-0		18,250
R		5	(a)	Newcastle U	L 0-3		32,278

Appearances

Goals

Hendry N	Nevins T	McQuillan J	Wright W	O'Connell P	Gordon D	Best C	Goode H	Stevens S	Fazackerley S	Wright G	Shaw F	McIntosh J	Fenwick A	McDonald W	Houghton J	Boyton J	Lyon S	Potts J	Briggs J	Edelston J	Hewitson R	Pattison J	
1	2	3	4	5	6	7	8	9	10	11													1
1	2	3	4	5	6	7	8	9	10	11													2
1	2	3	4	5	6	7	8	9	10		11												3
1	2	3	4	5	6	7	8	9	10	11													4
1	2	3	4	5	6	7	8	9	10	11													5
1	2	3	4	5		7	8	9	10	11		6											6
1	2	3	4	5		7	8	9	10	11		6											7
1	2	3			6	7	8	9	10	11		5	4										8
1	2	3			6	7	8	9	10	11		5	4										9
1	2	3			6	7	8	9	10	11		5	4										10
1	2	3	4		6	8		9	10	11		5		7									11
1	2	3	4		6		8	9	10		11	5		7									12
1	2	3	4		6		8	9	10	11		5		7									13
1	2	3	4	5	6		8	9	10	11				7									14
1	2	3	4	8	6			9	10	11		5		7									15
1	2	3	4	8	6		10	9		11		5		7									16
1	2	3	4	8			10	9			11	6		7	5								17
1		3	4	5	6		10		9	11				7	2	8							18
1	2	3	4	8	6		11		10			5		7			9						19
1	2	3	4	5			8		10	11		6		7			9						20
1	2	3	4				10		9	11		6		7	5	8							21
1	2	3	4	5	6		10	9	8	11				7									22
1	2	3	4	5	6			9	8	11				7		10							23
1	2	3	4	5	6			9	8		11			7		10							24
1	2	3	4	5	6				8	11				7		10	9						25
1	2	3	4	5	6				8	11				7		10	9						26
1	2	3	4	5	6		9	10	8	11				7									27
1		3	4	5	6			8	9	11				7		10		2					28
1		3	4	5	6		8	10	9	11				7				2					29
1	9	3	4	5	6		8	10			11			7				2					30
1	9	3	4	5	6		8	10		11				7				2					31
1	2	3	4	5	6		9	10		11				7					8				32
1	2	3	5		6		9	10		11				7					8	4			33
1	2	3	4	5	6		8	10		11				7			9						34
1	2	3	4	5			8	10		11		6	9	7									35
1	2	3	4	5				10				6	9	7		8					11		36
1		3		5				10		11		6	9	7		8				4		2	37
1		3		5				10		11		6	9	7		8				4		2	38
38	33	38	33	30	29	11	28	32	27	31	5	18	7	28	3	10	5	4	2	3	1	2	
		2				2	10	15	19			2	5	3		1	1						

Hendry N	Nevins T	McQuillan J	Wright W	O'Connell P	Gordon D	Best C	Goode H	Stevens S	Fazackerley S	Wright G	Shaw F	McIntosh J	Fenwick A	McDonald W	Houghton J	Boyton J	Lyon S	Potts J	Briggs J	Edelston J	Hewitson R	Pattison J	
1	2	3	4	5	6		10	9	8	11				7									1
1	2	3	4	5	6		10	9	8	11				7									2
1	2	3	4	5	6			9	8	11				7		10							R
3	3	3	3	3	3		2	3	3	3				3		1							
								1	1														

1913-14

1	Sep	6	(a)	Blackpool	D 2-2	McCorry, Halligan	7,000
2		13	(h)	Nottingham F	W 1-0	McCorry	8,000
3		20	(a)	W Arsenal	D 0-0		25,000
4		27	(h)	Grimsby T	W 2-1	Lee, McCorry	12,000
5	Oct	4	(a)	Birmingham	D 1-1	Stevens	20,000
6		11	(h)	Bristol C	L 0-1		8,000
7		13	(h)	Lincoln C	D 1-1	Fenwick	11,000
8		18	(a)	Leeds C	W 2-1	Stevens 2	20,000
9		25	(h)	Clapton O	W 2-0	Wright, Stevens	7,000
10	Nov	1	(a)	Glossop	L 1-2	McDonald	500
11		8	(h)	Stockport C	W 3-0	Stevens 3	6,000
12		15	(a)	Bradford	L 0-2		8,000
13		22	(h)	Notts C	W 2-0	Stevens, J.Lyon	10,000
14		29	(a)	Leicester F	W 4-0	Halligan 2, Stevens, J.Lyon	10,000
15	Dec	6	(h)	Wolves	W 7-1	Halligan 4, O'Connell, Stevens, Lee	8,000
16		13	(h)	Fulham	D 1-1	Stevens	10,000
17		20	(a)	Barnsley	W 2-0	Stevens, Lee	4,000
18		25	(a)	Huddersfield T	W 3-0	Stevens, J.Lyon, Halligan	7,000
19		26	(h)	Huddersfield T	W 4-1	Stevens 2, Halligan, J.Lyon	13,000
20		27	(h)	Blackpool	D 0-0		14,000
21	Jan	3	(a)	Nottingham F	W 2-1	Stevens 2	7,000
22		17	(h)	W Arsenal	L 1-2	McCorry	12,000
23		24	(a)	Grimsby T	W 3-1	Stevens 2, Halligan	9,000
24	Feb	7	(h)	Birmingham	D 0-0		12,000
25		14	(a)	Bristol C	L 1-2	Stevens	8,000
26		21	(h)	Leeds C	W 1-0	Stevens	20,000
27		28	(a)	Clapton O	L 0-3		18,000
28	Mar	7	(h)	Glossop	W 3-0	Stevens 2, Cameron	10,000
29		11	(a)	Lincoln C	D 0-0		7,00
30		14	(a)	Stockport C	L 1-2	Halligan	7,000
31		21	(h)	Bradford	L 1-3	Stevens	10,000
32		28	(a)	Notts C	L 1-4	Stevens	25,00
33	Apr	4	(h)	Leicester F	D 0-0		6,00
34		10	(a)	Bury	L 0-2		10,00
35		11	(a)	Wolves	L 0-1		12,00
36		13	(h)	Bury	L 0-1		8,00
37		18	(a)	Fulham	W 1-0	Stevens	8,00
38		25	(h)	Barnsley	L 0-1		5,00

FINAL LEAGUE POSITION: 7th in Division Two — Appearances

Note: Match 33 was benefit match for Tim Wright and Tommy Nevins. — Goals

FA Cup

1	Jan	10	(h)	Bury	D 0-0		12,00
R		14	(a)	Bury	L 1-2	Lee	12,80

Appearances

Goals

Hendry N	Pattison J	Morgan D	Edelston J	O'Connell P	McIntosh J	McDonald W	McCorry H	Halligan W	Stevens S	Byrne A	Nevins T	McQuillan J	Fenwick A	Lee J	Lyon S	Wright W	Lyon J	Gordon D	Temple A	Boyton J	Cameron W	Murray T	Melville D	Mercer D	Potts J	
1	2	3	4	5	6	7	8	9	10	11																1
1			4	5	6	7	8		10	11	2	3	9													2
1			4	5	6	7	8	9	10	11	2	3														3
1			4	5	6	7	8	9	10		2	3		11												4
1			4	5	6	7	10		8		2	3	9	11												5
1			4	5	6	7			8		2	3		11	9	10										6
1	2		4	5	6	7	10		8			3	9	11												7
1	2	3	4	5	6	7			9					11		8	10									8
1	2	3	4	5	6	7			9					11		8	10									9
1	2	3	4	5	6	7			9					11		8	10									10
1	2	3	4		5	7		10	9					11			8	6								11
1	2	3	4		5	7		10	9					11			8	6								12
1	2	3	4		5	7		10	9					11			8	6								13
1	2	3	4		5	7		10	9					11			8	6								14
1	2	3		5	6	7		10	9					11		4	8									15
1	2	3		5	6	7		10	9					11		4	8									16
1	2	3	4	5	6			10	9					11		7	8									17
1	2	3	4	5	6			10	9					11		7	8									18
1	2	3		5	6	7		10	9					11		4	8									19
1	2	3	4	5	6			10	9					11		7	8									20
1	2	3	4	5	6	7		10	9					11			8									21
1			4	5	6	7	8	10	9		2	3		11												22
1	2	3	4	5			10	11	9								7	6	8							23
1	2	3	4	5	6	7	8		9								11			10						24
1		3	4		5	7	8		9			2					11	6			10					25
1	2	3	4	5	6	7		11	9												10	8				26
1	2	3	4	5	6	7		11	9												10	8				27
1			4	5	2	7		10	9			3		11				6			8					28
1			4	5	2	8			9			3				7	11	6			10					29
1			4		2	7		10	9			3						6		11	8		5			30
1			4	5	2	7		10	9			3						6		11	8					31
1	2		4	5	6	7		10	9			3					11				8					32
1	2	3	4			7		10	9							8	11	6					5			33
1	2	3	4					10	9							7	11	6			8		5			34
1	2	3	4					10	9								11	6	5		8		7			35
1	2		4					10	9			3					11	6	5		8		7			36
1	2		4	5				10	9			3	6	11							8			7		37
1			4	5	6			10	9			3		11							8			7	2	38
38	26	23	35	28	32	29	10	28	38	3	6	16	4	22	1	13	23	14	3	3	13	2	5	2	1	
				1		1	4	11	26				1	3		1	4				1					

Hendry N	Pattison J	Morgan D	Edelston J	O'Connell P	McIntosh J	McDonald W	McCorry H	Halligan W	Stevens S	Byrne A	Nevins T	McQuillan J	Fenwick A	Lee J	Lyon S	Wright W	Lyon J	Gordon D	Temple A	Boyton J	Cameron W	Murray T	Melville D	Mercer D	Potts J	
1	2	3	4	5	6	7		10	9					11			8									1
1	2	3	4	5	6	7		10	9					11			8									R
2	2	2	2	2	2	2		2	2					2			2									
														1												

1914-15

1	Sep	3	(h)	Stockport C	W 1-0	Stevens	3,000
2		5	(h)	Blackpool	L 1-3	Stevens	6,000
3		12	(a)	Leeds C	W 3-2	Stevens, Cameron, Lee	8,000
4		19	(h)	Clapton O	L 0-1		6,000
5		26	(a)	Arsenal	L 1-2	Stevens	15,000
6	Oct	3	(h)	Derby C	W 1-0	Halligan	6,000
7		10	(a)	Lincoln C	W 3-0	Cameron 2, Halligan	6,000
8		17	(h)	Birmingham	D 0-0		7,000
9		24	(a)	Grimsby T	D 1-1	Stevens	9,000
10		31	(a)	Huddersfield T	L 0-1		4,000
11	Nov	7	(a)	Bristol C	L 2-5	Stevens 2	8,000
12		14	(h)	Bury	W 3-1	Halligan 2, Stevens	4,000
13		21	(a)	Preston NE	L 1-2	Stevens	10,000
14		28	(h)	Nottingham F	W 3-1	Lee 2, Halligan	6,000
15	Dec	5	(a)	Leicester F	D 1-1	Halligan	4,000
16		12	(h)	Barnsley	W 2-1	Deacey, Stevens	3,000
17		25	(h)	Wolves	W 5-1	Halligan 2, Stevens, Cameron, D.Mercer	8,000
18		26	(a)	Wolves	W 2-1	Lee, Cameron	9,000
19	Jan	1	(a)	Stockport C	L 0-3		4,000
20		2	(a)	Blackpool	W 2-1	D.Mercer, Lee	5,000
21		16	(h)	Leeds C	L 2-6	Halligan, Stevens	5,000
22		23	(a)	Clapton O	W 3-0	Turner 2, Stevens	4,000
23	Feb	6	(a)	Derby C	L 1-4	Turner	5,00
24	Mar	11	(h)	Lincoln C	W 6-1	Stevens 2, Halligan 2, Cameron, Lee	3,000
25		13	(h)	Bristol C	D 1-1	Lee	3,00
26		16	(a)	Glossop	W 5-0	Stevens 2, Halligan 2, Cameron	50
27		20	(a)	Bury	W 1-0	Cameron	2,00
28		24	(a)	Birmingham	D 2-2	Cameron, Halligan	5,00
29		27	(h)	Preston NE	L 0-1		7,00
30	Apr	2	(h)	Arsenal	W 1-0	Stevens	8,00
31		3	(a)	Nottingham F	L 0-1		9,00
32		5	(h)	Fulham	W 2-0	Stevens, D.Mercer	6,00
33		6	(a)	Fulham	L 1-4	Halligan	1,00
34		10	(h)	Leicester F	W 2-1	Stevens, Halligan	5,50
35		15	(h)	Huddersfield T	L 0-4		2,00
36		17	(a)	Barnsley	L 0-1		5,00
37		24	(h)	Glossop	W 2-0	Stevens 2	2,00
38		29	(h)	Grimsby T	W 4-1	Stevens 2, D.Mercer, Halligan	3,00

FINAL LEAGUE POSITION: 7th in Division Two

Appearances
Goals

FA Cup

1	Jan	9	(h)	West Brom A	W 1-0	Stevens	13,00
2		30	(h)	Northampton T	W 2-1	Stevens 2	13,00
3	Feb	20	(a)	Southampton	D 2-2*	Cameron, Lee	15,60
R		27	(h)	Southampton	W 4-0	Stevens 2, Cameron, Lee	11,00
4	Mar	6	(a)	Bolton W	L 2-4	Deacey, Stevens	24,37

*After extra-time

Appearances
Goals

Hendry N	Pattison J	Morgan D	Edelston J	Deacey C	Wright W	Mercer D	Cameron W	Stevens S	Halligan W	Medcalf J	Betts A	Lee J	Middlehurst J	Turner H	Lyon J	Mercer W	Cleland J	
1	2	3	4	5	6	7	8	9	10	11								1
1	2	3	4	5	6	7	8	9	10	11								2
1	2		4	5	6	7	8	9	10		3	11						3
1	2		4	5	6	7	8	9	10		3	11						4
1		6	4	5	10	7	8	9	11		3		2					5
1	2	11	4	5	6	7	8	9	10		3							6
1	2	11	4	5	6	7	8	9	10		3							7
1	2	11	4	5	6	7	8	9	10		3							8
1	2	11	4	5	6	7	8	9	10		3							9
1	2	11	4		6	7	8	9	10		3			5				10
1	2	11	4		6	7	8	9	10		3			5				11
1	2	4		5	6	7	8	9	10		3	11						12
1	2		4	5	6	7	8	9	10		3	11						13
1	2		4	5	6	7	8	9	10		3	11						14
1	2		4	5	6	7	8	9	10		3	11						15
1	2		4	5	6	7	8	9	10		3	11						16
1	2		4	5	6	7	8	9	10		3	11						17
1	2		4	5	6	7	8	9	10		3	11						18
1	2	8	4	5	6	7		9	10		3	11						19
1		2		5	6	7		9	10		3	11		4	8			20
1		3	4	5	6	7	8	9	10		2	11						21
	2	3	4	5	6	7		9	10			11		8		1		22
1	2		4	5	6	7	8	9			3	11		10				23
1		3	4	5	6	7	8	9	10		2	11						24
1		3	4	5	6	7	8	9	10		2	11						25
1		3	4	5	6	7	8	9	10		2	11						26
1		3	4	5	6	7	8		9		2	11		10				27
1		3	4	5	6	7	8	9	10		2	11						28
1		3	4	5	6	7	8	9	10		2	11						29
1		3	4	5	6	7	8	9	10		2	11						30
1		3	4	5	6	7	8	9	10		2	11						31
1		3	4	5	6	7	8	9	10		2	11						32
1		3	4	5	6	7	8	9	10		2	11						33
1		3	4	5	6	7	8	9	10			11	2					34
1		3	4	5	6	7		9	10		2	11					8	35
1		3	4	5	6	7	8	9	10		2	11						36
1		3	4	5	6	7	8	9	10		2	11						37
1		3	4	5	6	7	8	9	10		2	11						38
37	20	29	36	36	38	38	34	37	37	2	34	29	2	6	1	1	1	
				1		4	9	24	17			7		3				

Hendry N	Pattison J	Morgan D	Edelston J	Deacey C	Wright W	Mercer D	Cameron W	Stevens S	Halligan W	Medcalf J	Betts A	Lee J	Middlehurst J	Turner H	Lyon J	Mercer W	Cleland J	
1		2	4	5	6	7	8	9	10		3	11						1
1	2		4	5	6	7	8	9	10		3	11						2
1		3	4	5	6	7	8	9	10		2	11						3
1		3	4	5	6	7	8	9	10		2	11						R
1		3	4	5	6	7	8	9	10		2	11						4
5	1	4	5	5	5	5	5	5	5		5	5						
				1			2	6				2						

1915-16

Midland Section: Principal Competition

1	Sep	4	(a)	Notts C	L 0-2		5,000
2		11	(h)	Derby C	W 4-2	Christmass 2, Bradbury, McQuillan	4,000
3		18	(a)	Sheffield W	W 4-2	Percival 2, Christmass, Lee	5,000
4		25	(h)	Bradford	W 2-0	Christmass, Lee	7,000
5	Oct	2	(a)	Leeds C	L 1-3	Percival	6,000
6		9	(h)	Lincoln C	D 1-1	Wright	4,000
7		16	(h)	Nottingham F	L 1-3	Lee	4,000
8		23	(a)	Barnsley	L 1-4	Bradbury	2,500
9		30	(h)	Leicester F	D 2-2	Stevens, McQuillan	4,000
10	Nov	6	(a)	Sheffield U	L 0-3		5,000
11		13	(h)	Bradford C	D 1-1	Slide	5,000
12		20	(a)	Huddersfield T	L 0-1		2,000
13		27	(h)	Grimsby T	W 4-1	Slide 2, Bradbury 2	3,000
14	Dec	4	(h)	Notts C	W 3-0	Stevens 3	1,000
15		11	(a)	Derby C	L 1-3	Lee	1,000
16		18	(h)	Sheffield W	L 1-3	Mercer	3,000
17		25	(a)	Bradford	W 2-1	Mercer, Slide	10,000
18	Jan	1	(h)	Leeds C	L 0-3		3,000
19		8	(a)	Lincoln C	L 1-4	Edelston	4,500
20		15	(a)	Nottingham F	L 1-4	Saunders	5,000
21		22	(h)	Barnsley	W 1-0	Saunders	3,000
22		29	(a)	Leicester F	L 0-4		3,000
23	Feb	5	(h)	Sheffield U	W 2-0	Stevens, Lee	4,000
24		12	(a)	Bradford C	L 4-8	Stevens 3, Ford	4,000
25		19	(h)	Huddersfield T	W 2-1	Stevens, Mercer	3,000
26		26	(a)	Grimsby T	W 3-2	Lee 3	2,000

FINAL LEAGUE POSITION: 11th in Midland Section Principal Competition

Appearances

Goals

Midland Section: Subsidiary Competition

27	Mar	4	(h)	Sheffield U	W 5-2	Lee 2, Ford, Slide, Simmon	3,000
28		11	(a)	Lincoln C	L 0-7		2,000
29		18	(h)	Grimsby T	L 2-5	Slide, Lee	3,000
30		25	(a)	Sheffield W	W 2-0	Naismith, Lee	6,000
31	Apr	1	(a)	Rotherham C	L 2-4	Slide, Lee	5,000
32		8	(a)	Sheffield U	L 0-2		5,000
33		15	(h)	Lincoln C	W 2-1	Lee 2	3,000
34		22	(a)	Grimsby T	L 0-5		4,000
35		24	(h)	Rotherham C	W 4-1	Stevens 2, Lee, Burton	4,000
36		29	(h)	Sheffield W	W 1-0	Thistleton	3,000

FINAL LEAGUE POSITION: 4th in Midland Section Subsidiary Competition

Appearances

Goals

Hendry N	Betts A	McQuillan J	Edelston J	Deacey C	Sheridan J	Mercer D	Bradbury J	Stevens S	Percival C	Lee J	Bell A	Wright W	Christmass J	Coddington A	Wilson A	Slide R	Pace A	Pattison J	Jacketts G	Voase F	Ainsworth J	Saunders J	Chaplin G	Simmon H	Walters H	Meynell T	McManus T	Ford B	Gordon E	Cameron W	Simpson A	Whitfield N	Hall E	Naismith E	Hobson B	Coverdale R	Hudson T	Wheeldon J	Young R	Burton E	Thistleton M	
1	2	3	4	5	6	7	8	9	10	11																																1
	2	3	4		6	7	8		10	11	1	5	9																													2
1	2	3	4		6	7	8		10	11		5	9																													3
1	2	3	4		6	7	8		10	11		5	9																													4
1	2	3	4	5		7	8		10	11		6	9																													5
1	2	3	4		6	7	8		10	11		5	9																													6
1	2	3	4		6	7	8		10	11		5	9																													7
	2	3	1		6	7	8	9	10	11		5		4																												8
1		3	4		6	7	8	9	10	11		5			2																											9
1		3	4		6	7	8		10	11		5			2	9																										10
1	2	3	4		6	7	10			9		5				8	11																									11
		3	1		6	7	8			9		5				10	11	2	4																							12
1		3	4		6	7	10			9		5				8	11	2																								13
1	3		4		6	7	10	9		11		5				8		2																								14
	3		1		6	7	10	9		11							4	2	5																							15
1		3	4		6	7	10			11		5				9	8	2																								16
	2	3	1		6	7		9	10	11						8		5		4																						17
1	2	3	4		6	7				11		5				8					9	10																				18
1	2	3	4		6	7				11		5				9			8			10																				19
	2	3	1		6	7	8			11			9					5		4		10																				20
1		3	4		6	7				11		5				9						10	2	8																		21
		3	1		6	7				11												9	2	8	4	5	10															22
	3		1		6	7		9		10		5				8							2		4			11														23
	3		1		6	7		9		10						8							2		4			11	5													24
1		3	4		6	7		9		10		5				8							2					11														25
1		3	4		6	7				10		5				9							2					11		8												26
17	17	22	26	2	25	26	17	9	11	26	1	20	7	1	2	14	5	7	3	2	1	5	6	2	3	1	1	4	1	1												
		2	1			3	4	9	3	8		1	4			4						2						1														

Hendry N	Betts A	McQuillan J	Edelston J	Deacey C	Sheridan J	Mercer D	Bradbury J	Stevens S	Percival C	Lee J	Bell A	Wright W	Christmass J	Coddington A	Wilson A	Slide R	Pace A	Pattison J	Jacketts G	Voase F	Ainsworth J	Saunders J	Chaplin G	Simmon H	Walters H	Meynell T	McManus T	Ford B	Gordon E	Cameron W	Simpson A	Whitfield N	Hall E	Naismith E	Hobson B	Coverdale R	Hudson T	Wheeldon J	Young R	Burton E	Thistleton M	
1		3	4		6	7				10		5				9							2	8				11														27
		3	4		6	7				10		5						2			8							11			9						1					28
1		3	4		6	7				10		5				9							2					11				8										29
1		3	4		6	7				10						9							2					11					5	8								30
1		3	4		6	7				10		5				8							2					11			9											31
1			4		6	7				10		2											3					11				8	5					9				32
1			4		6	7				10													2					11				9		8	3	5						33
1	3		5		6	7				10						9				4			2					11						8								34
1						7		9		10									6	4			5					11							2				3	8		35
1			2		6	7				10						9				4			3					11								5					8	36
9	1	5	9		9	10		1		10		5				6		1	1	3	1		9	1				10			2	3	2	3	2	2	1	1	1	1	1	
								2		8						3								1				1						1						1	1	

Hull City fielded ten players in Match 15.

1916-17

Midland Section: Principal Competition

1	Sep	2	(h)	Rotherham C	D 0-0		2,000
2		9	(a)	Huddersfield T	L 1-2	Mercer	3,000
3		16	(h)	Lincoln C	W 2-1	Mercer, Simmon	2,000
4		23	(a)	Sheffield W	L 1-2	Mercer	5,000
5		30	(h)	Bradford	D 1-1	Grimshaw	3,000
6	Oct	7	(a)	Birmingham	L 2-4	Stevens 2	16,000
7		14	(a)	Chesterfield	L 0-5		2,000
8		21	(h)	Nottingham F	W 3-1	W.Wright 2, Stevens	2,500
9		28	(a)	Barnsley	L 2-8	Grimshaw 2	2,000
10	Nov	4	(h)	Leeds C	D 1-1	Grimshaw	3,000
11		11	(a)	Sheffield U	L 1-4	Grimshaw	8,000
12		18	(h)	Bradford C	W 1-0	Higgins	500
13		25	(a)	Leicester F	W 2-0	Grimshaw, Leigh	2,000
14	Dec	2	(h)	Grimsby T	W 2-0	Higgins 2	3,000
15		9	(a)	Rotherham C	D 1-1	Stevens	2,000
16		16	(h)	Huddersfield T	L 0-1		1,500
17		23	(a)	Lincoln C	D 1-1	Stevens	1,500
18		25	(h)	Notts C	W 2-0	Stevens, Sheridan	1,000
19		26	(a)	Notts C	L 1-7	Stevens	6,000
20		30	(h)	Sheffield W	W 1-0	Mercer	2,000
21	Jan	6	(a)	Bradford	L 0-4		2,000
22		13	(h)	Birmingham	L 0-1		2,000
23		20	(h)	Chesterfield	W 3-1	Stevens 2, Leigh	2,000
24		27	(a)	Nottingham F	L 0-3		1,000
25	Feb	3	(h)	Barnsley	L 0-1		1,000
26		10	(a)	Leeds C	D 1-1	W.Wright	3,000
27		17	(h)	Sheffield U	D 1-1	W.Wright	1,500
28		24	(a)	Bradford C	L 1-3	Lee	2,000
29	Mar	3	(h)	Leicester F	W 2-1	Mercer 2	2,000
30		10	(a)	Grimsby T	W 3-2	Osborn 3	2,000

FINAL LEAGUE POSITION: 11th in Midland Section Principal Competition

Appearances
Goals

Midland Section: Subsidiary Competition

31	Mar	17	(a)	Chesterfield	L 1-4	Harvey	1,500
32		31	(a)	Lincoln C	D 2-2	Mercer, Cleland	1,500
33	Apr	6	(a)	Grimsby T	L 1-2	Sheridan	1,500
34		7	(h)	Chesterfield	W 5-1	Cookson 3, Mercer, W.Wright	2,000
35		9	(h)	Grimsby T	D 2-2	D.Brown 2	2,000
36		21	(h)	Lincoln C	W 2-1	Mercer 2	2,000

FINAL LEAGUE POSITION: 9th in Midland Section Subsidiary Competition

Appearances
Goals

Hendry N	Wigglesworth A	Betts A	Jacketts G	Edelston J	Sheridan J	Mercer D	Simmon H	Lee J	Pace A	Ford B	Coverdale R	Wright W	Grimshaw W	Higgins A	Stevens S	Nevin J	Leigh S	Brown D	Thistleton M	Wilde R	McQuillan J	Martin H	Wale L	Cleland J	Osborn F	Cookson S	Isherwood R	Veale W	Halligan W	Hobson B	McCourty W	Deacey C	Smith J	Wright J	Howie D	Hawksworth E	Atkinson W	Fairclough S	McManus T	Haywood	Hawley	
1	2	3	4	5	6	7	8	9	10	11																																1
1	2	3	6	4		7	8				5	10	11															9														2
1	2	3		4	6	7	10			11	5		9	8																												3
1	2	3	5	4	6	7	8			11		10	9																													4
1	2	3		4	6	7						5	11	8	9														10													5
1		3		8	6	7							11		9															2	4	5	10									6
1	2			4		7	8					6	11			5																		3	9	10						7
1	2	3		4	6	7				11		10	8		9	5																										8
1	2	3		4	6	7				10			8																								9	11				9
1	2	3		4	6	7				11		10	8	9		5																										10
1	2		4		6	7				11		10	8			5																							3	9		11
1	2		4		6	7				11	3	10	8	9		5																										12
	2	3	4	1	6	7			10	11			8			5	9																									13
1	2	3			6	7				11		4	8	10		5																									9	14
1	2		5		6	7				11		3	8		9		10																									15
1	2	3	5	4	6	7		11				10	8	9																												16
1	2	3	5	4	6	7			10	11			8		9																											17
1	2	3	4		6	7						5	11		9		8	10																								18
1	2	3	5		6	7				11			8		9		10																									19
1	2	3	4	8	6	7			10	11		5							9																							20
1	2	3	4	5	6	7			10	11									9	8																						21
1	2	3	4	8	6	7			10	11		5									9																					22
1	2	3	4		6	7						5			9		8					11																				23
	2	3	4	8	6	7											9				11																					24
1	2	3	4	8	6	7			10			5			9						11																					25
1	2	3	4	8	6	7						5								10	11																					26
1	2	3	4	10	6	7			8			9										11	5																			27
1	2		4	5	6	7		11	8															9																		28
1	2	3	4	10	6	7						11					8						5		9																	29
1	2	3	4	5	6	7																		8	9	10	11															30
28	29	25	22	23	28	30	5	3	9	16	3	19	18	6	9	7	7	1	2	2	4	2	2	2	2	1	1	1	1	1	1	1	1	1	1	1	1	1	1	1	1	
					1	6	1	1				4	6	3	9		2								3																	

Hendry N	Wigglesworth A	Betts A	Jacketts G	Edelston J	Sheridan J	Mercer D	Simmon H	Lee J	Pace A	Ford B	Coverdale R	Wright W	Grimshaw W	Higgins A	Stevens S	Nevin J	Leigh S	Brown D	Thistleton M	Wilde R	McQuillan J	Martin H	Wale L	Cleland J	Osborn F	Cookson S	Isherwood R	Veale W	Halligan W	Hobson B	McCourty W	Deacey C	Smith J	Wright J	Howie D	Hawksworth E	Atkinson W	Fairclough S	McManus T	Haywood	Hawley	
1	2		5		6	7			4															9			11															31
1	2	3	4	5	6	7	8		11															9		10																32
1	2	3	4	5	6	7	10																			9	11															33
1	2	3	4	5	6	7	8					9														10	11															34
1	2	3	4	5	6	7						8						9								10	11															35
1	2	3	4	5	6	7			10			9												8			11															36
6	6	5	6	5	6	6	3		3			3						1						3		4	5															
					1	4						1						2						1		3																

J.Brown played number 4 in Match 15; H.Crowther played number 4 in Match 19; H.Pepper played number 10 in Match 23; A.Iremonger played number 1 in Match 24; A.Woodland played number 5 in Match 24; E.Cutts played number 10 in Match 24; H.Dick played number 9 in Match 26; J.Pattison played number 3 in Match 28; H.Norton played number 10 in Match 28; J.Matthews played number 3 in Match 31; A.Stables played number 8 in Match 31; A.Harvey played number 10 in Match 31 (1 goal); A.Robinson played number 8 in Match 33.
Played one man short in Match 9.

1917-18

Midland Section: Principal Competition

1	Sep	1	(a)	Birmingham	L 1-2	Hughes	8,00
2		8	(h)	Birmingham	L 1-2	Hughes	2,50
3		15	(a)	Notts C	D 2-2	Mercer 2	3,00
4		22	(h)	Notts C	L 1-2	Hughes	2,00
5		29	(a)	Huddersfield T	L 2-4	Hughes, Smith	2,00
6	Oct	6	(h)	Huddersfield T	W 3-1	Hughes 2, Smith	2,00
7		13	(h)	Sheffield W	D 3-3	Mercer, Hartnell, Osborn	1,50
8		20	(a)	Sheffield W	L 3-4	Wallis 2, Hughes	5,00
9		27	(h)	Bradford C	W 5-1	Mercer 3, Hughes, Wallis	2,00
10	Nov	3	(a)	Bradford C	W 4-2	Hughes 3, Mercer	2,00
11		10	(h)	Rotherham C	W 3-1	Mercer, Hughes, Wright	2,00
12		17	(a)	Rotherham C	W 2-1	Wallis 2	3,00
13		24	(h)	Lincoln C	W 2-0	Mercer, Hughes	1,00
14	Dec	1	(a)	Lincoln C	W 3-1	Mercer 3	2,00
15		8	(h)	Leicester F	W 3-1	Mercer 2, Hughes	2,50
16		15	(a)	Leicester F	L 1-3	Mercer	2,00
17		22	(h)	Nottingham F	W 3-2	Hughes, Jacketts, Deacey	2,00
18		26	(h)	Grimsby T	W 7-1	Hughes 2, Wright 2, Smith 2, Mercer	1,0
19		29	(a)	Nottingham F	L 1-5	Mercer	1,50
20	Jan	5	(h)	Leeds C	L 0-2		3,0
21		12	(a)	Leeds C	W 3-1	Mercer, Wright, Hughes	4,0
22		19	(h)	Sheffield U	L 2-4	Hughes, Wright	3,00
23		26	(a)	Sheffield U	W 1-0	Hughes	12,0
24	Feb	2	(a)	Barnsley	W 3-1	Riley 2, Wallis	2,0
25		9	(h)	Barnsley	W 4-2	Hughes 2, Osborn 2	3,0
26	Mar	2	(h)	Bradford	D 1-1	Mercer	2,0
27		9	(a)	Bradford	W 3-1	Mercer, Hughes, Wright	3,0
28	Apr	13	(a)	Grimsby T	D 0-0		5

FINAL LEAGUE POSITION: 4th in Midland Section Principal Competition — Appearances

Goals

Midland Section: Subsidiary Competition

29	Feb	16	(h)	Gainsborough T	W 4-2	Mercer 3, Hughes	2,0
30		23	(a)	Gainsborough T	W 1-0	Jacketts	2,0
31	Mar	16	(h)	Lincoln C	W 4-2	Hughes, Mercer, Wallis, Osborn	2,0
32		23	(a)	Lincoln C	D 1-1	Mercer	3,0
33		29	(a)	Grimsby T	L 0-2		2,0
34	Apr	1	(h)	Grimsby T	D 2-2	Mercer, Shaw	3,0

FINAL LEAGUE POSITION: 4th in Midland Section Subsidiary Competition — Appearances

Note: Wallis was the assumed name of Harry Walden — Goals

Hendry N	Pattison J	Wigglesworth A	Edelston J	Deacey C	Jacketts G	Mercer D	Goodfellow S	Osborn F	Smith J	Hughes R	Wright W	Cleland J	Betts A	Nevin J	Shaw P	Sheridan J	Hartnell S	Wallis H	Whittingham H	Priestley J	Fearnley E	Elvin R	McManus T	Pace A	Leigh S	Charles F	Riley H	Summers J	Malkinson T	Stevenson T	Milner A	Lee J	Jordan	Brown W	
1	2	3	4	5	6	7	8	9	10	11																									1
1	2	3	4		6	7	9		10	11	5	8																							2
1	4	2	5		6	8	9		7	11		10	3																						3
1	4	2	5		6	8		9	7	11	10		3																						4
1	6	2	4		10	9			7	11			3	5	8																				5
1		2	5		4	8			7	11	10		3			6	9																		6
1		2	4			8		10	7	11	5		3			6	9																		7
1		2	4		6	8			7	11	10		3	5				9																	8
		2	1		4	8			7	11	6		3	5				9	10																9
1		2	5		4	8			7	11			3			6				9	10														10
		2	1		4	8			7	11	5		3			6		9	10																11
1	3	2	5		4	8			7									9				6	10	11											12
1	3	2	4		6	8			7	11	5							9					10												13
	4	2	1		6	8			7	11	5		3					9					10												14
1	4	2	5		6	8			7	11	10		3					9																	15
	6	2	1		4	8			7	11	5		3					9					10												16
1		2	4	5	6	8			7	11	10		3					9																	17
1		2	4	5	6	8			7	11	10		3					9																	18
1		3	2	5	6	8			7	11					10			9							4										19
	4	2	1		6	8			7	11	5		3					9					10												20
1		2	4		6	8			7	11	10		3	5				9																	21
1		2	4		6	8			7	11	9		3	5	10																				22
1		2	5		6	8			7	11	10		3					9								4									23
1	3	2	5		6	7			4	11								9									8	10							24
1		2	5		6	8		9	7	11	10		3											4											25
1		2	4		6	8		10	7	11	5		3					9																	26
	4	2	1		6	8		9	7	11	10		3	5																					27
1	2		5		4	8				11												6							3	7	9	10			28
22	14	27	28	4	27	28	3	6	27	27	20	2	21	6	3	4	2	16	2	1	1	2	5	2	1	1	1	1	1	1	1	1			
				1	1	20		3	4	23	6						1	6									2								

Hendry N	Pattison J	Wigglesworth A	Edelston J	Deacey C	Jacketts G	Mercer D	Goodfellow S	Osborn F	Smith J	Hughes R	Wright W	Cleland J	Betts A	Nevin J	Shaw P	Sheridan J	Hartnell S	Wallis H	Whittingham H	Priestley J	Fearnley E	Elvin R	McManus T	Pace A	Leigh S	Charles F	Riley H	Summers J	Malkinson T	Stevenson T	Milner A	Lee J	Jordan	Brown W	
1		2	5		6	8		10	7	11			3											4									9		29
1			4		5	8		10	7	11			3					9						6										2	30
	6	2	1		4	8		10	7	11	5		3					9																	31
1	6	2	5		4	8		10	7	11			3					9																	32
	4	2	1		5	8		10	7				3		11			9						6											33
	1	2	5		4	8			7	11			3		10			9						6											34
3	4	5	6		6	6		5	6	5	1		6		2			5						4									1	1	
					1	6		1		2					1			1																	

1918-19

Midland Section: Principal Competition

1	Sep	7	(h)	Bradford C	W 2-0	Potter, Lee	4,000
2		14	(a)	Bradford C	L 0-4		3,000
3		21	(h)	Sheffield W	D 0-0		4,000
4		28	(a)	Sheffield W	L 1-3	Lee	6,000
5	Oct	5	(h)	Huddersfield T	W 3-0	Wright, Hughes, Jacketts	3,000
6		12	(a)	Huddersfield T	L 0-1		2,000
7		19	(a)	Notts C	L 0-1		6,000
8		26	(h)	Notts C	D 1-1	Shaw	4,000
9	Nov	2	(a)	Birmingham	L 1-5	Hughes	10,000
10		9	(h)	Birmingham	L 0-3		4,000
11		16	(a)	Rotherham C	D 2-2	Hughes, D.Mercer	2,500
12		23	(h)	Rotherham C	W 4-0	Lee 2, Hughes, D.Mercer	3,000
13		30	(a)	Lincoln C	W 2-0	D.Mercer, Suddes	3,000
14	Dec	7	(h)	Lincoln C	W 5-1	McManus 2, Potter, Lee, D.Mercer	4,000
15		14	(a)	Leeds C	D 0-0		6,000
16		21	(h)	Leeds C	W 2-1	D.Mercer, Stevens	5,000
17		25	(a)	Grimsby T	D 1-1	Newton	3,000
18		26	(h)	Grimsby T	W 2-0	Stevens, Lee	7,500
19		28	(a)	Sheffield U	D 0-0		16,000
20	Jan	11	(h)	Bradford	L 0-2		6,000
21		18	(a)	Bradford	W 1-0	Lee	10,000
22		25	(h)	Coventry C	W 2-0	Lee, Potter	5,000
23	Feb	1	(a)	Coventry C	L 0-3		8,000
24		8	(a)	Barnsley	W 4-3	Lyon 2, Hughes, D.Mercer	3,000
25		15	(h)	Barnsley	L 1-3	Potter	7,000
26		22	(a)	Leicester F	L 2-3	Potter, D.Mercer	7,000
27	Mar	1	(h)	Leicester F	W 5-2	Stevens, Hughes, D.Mercer, Lyon, Deacey	8,000
28		8	(a)	Nottingham F	L 1-2	Wallis	14,000
29		15	(h)	Nottingham F	W 5-0	Lyon 3, Potter, Wright	10,000
30	Apr	18	(h)	Sheffield U	D 1-1	Rentoul	12,000

FINAL LEAGUE POSITION: 7th in Midland Section Principal Competition

Appearances
Goals

Midland Section: Subsidiary Competition

31	Mar	22	(a)	Lincoln C	W 2-1	Wallis 2	4,000
32		29	(h)	Lincoln C	L 1-2	Wallis	8,000
33	Apr	5	(a)	Coventry C	W 3-1	Potter, Lee, Morrall	8,000
34		12	(h)	Coventry C	L 0-1		7,000
35		19	(a)	Grimsby T	W 2-1	Lyon, Wright	7,000
36		26	(h)	Grimsby T	W 3-1	Lee 2, D.Mercer	5,000

FINAL LEAGUE POSITION: 1st in Midland Section Subsidiary Competition

Note: Wallis was the assumed name of Harry Walden

Appearances
Goals

Mercer W	Wigglesworth A	Betts A	Jacketts G	Edelston J	Pattison J	Mercer D	Potter C	Hopkins V	Lee J	Hughes R	Parr J	Pace A	Thorpe T	Peach R	Machin E	Bleakley T	Wright W	Hendry N	Tickle J	Stevens S	Charlesworth A	Suddes F	Shaw P	Smith F	Wootton J	Lindley J	Gillett J	Osborn F	Harrison J	McManus T	Foss F	Newton A	Cutts E	Lyon J	Deacey C	Wallis H	Rentoul R	Little T	Morrall G	Adams P	Brennan T	
1	2	3	4	5	6	7	8	9	10	11																																1
1	2	3	4	5	6	7	8	9	10		11																															2
1	2	3	4	5	6	7	8		10	11		9																														3
	2	3	5	4	6	8			10	11			1	7	9																											4
1	2	3	4	5		7	8		10	11						6	9																									5
	2	3	4	5		7			10	11					9	6		1	8																							6
	2		4	5		7	8		10	11		3				6		1		9																						7
	2		4	5	3	7				11						6		1			8	9	10																			8
	2		4		3	7				11										9				1	5	6	8	10														9
	2	3	4	5		7	8		10	11						6		1		9																						10
	2	3	4	5		7			10	11								1		9			8						6													11
	2	3	4	5	6	8	9		11	7								1					10																			12
	2	3	4	5	6	8	10		11	7								1				9																				13
	2	3	4	5	6	8	10		11	7								1												9												14
	2	3	4	5	6	8	10		11	7								1													9											15
	2	3	4	5	6	8			11	7								1		9												10										16
	2	3	4	5	6	8			11	7								1		9												10										17
	2	3	4	5	6	8			11	7								1		9										10												18
	2	3	4	5	6	8			11	7								1		9													10									19
	2	3	4	5	6	8	10		11	7								1													9											20
	2	3	4	5	6	8	9		11	7								1																10								21
	2	3	4	5	6	8	9		11	7								1																10								22
	2	3	4	5		8	10		11	7						6		1		9																						23
	2	3	4	5		8	9		11	7						6		1																10								24
	2	3	4	5		8	9		11	7						6		1																10								25
	2		4	5	3	7	8			11							6	1		9														10								26
		3	6	4	2	7	8			11								1		9														10	5							27
	2	3	4	5		7				11						6		1				8												10		9						28
	2	3		4		7	8			11							6	1																10	5	9						29
	2	3				8			11	7						6	4	1																10	5		9					30
4	29	26	28	28	19	30	19	2	24	29	1	2	1	1	2	10	4	24	1	11	1	3	3	1	1	1	1	1	1	2	2	2	1	9	3	2	1					
			1			8	6		8	6							2			3		1	1							2		1		6	1	1	1					

Mercer W	Wigglesworth A	Betts A	Jacketts G	Edelston J	Pattison J	Mercer D	Potter C	Hopkins V	Lee J	Hughes R	Parr J	Pace A	Thorpe T	Peach R	Machin E	Bleakley T	Wright W	Hendry N	Tickle J	Stevens S	Charlesworth A	Suddes F	Shaw P	Smith F	Wootton J	Lindley J	Gillett J	Osborn F	Harrison J	McManus T	Foss F	Newton A	Cutts E	Lyon J	Deacey C	Wallis H	Rentoul R	Little T	Morrall G	Adams P	Brennan T	
	2	3				7										6	4	1				11												10	5	9		8				31
	2	3		5		7	8									6	4	1				11												10		9						32
	2	3		4		7	9		11								6	1																8	5				10			33
	2	3		4		7	9			11							6	1																8	5				10			34
	2	3	6	4		7			11							10	8	1																9	5							35
		3	4	2		7			11								6	1																9	5					8	10	36
	5	6	2	5		6	3		3	1						3	6	6				2												6	5	2		1	2	1	1	
						1	1		3								1																	1		3			1			

1919-20

1	Aug	30	(a)	Birmingham	L 1-4	Stevens	20,000
2	Sep	1	(h)	Stoke	W 3-0	Stevens, Lyon, Lee	10,000
3		6	(h)	Birmingham	D 0-0		11,000
4		8	(a)	Stoke	L 1-3	Charlesworth	9,000
5		13	(a)	Leeds C	W 2-1	Stevens, Hughes	12,000
6		20	(h)	Leeds C	D 1-1	Charlesworth	9,000
7		27	(a)	Bury	L 0-2		5,000
8	Oct	4	(h)	Bury	W 4-2	Morrall 2, Lee, D.Mercer	11,000
9		11	(a)	Nottingham F	W 2-0	Morrall, Stevens	9,000
10		13	(h)	Clapton O	W 3-1	Stevens, Lee, D.Mercer	6,000
11		18	(h)	Nottingham F	W 2-0	D.Mercer, Deacey	8,000
12		25	(a)	Grimsby T	L 1-2	Stevens	8,000
13	Nov	1	(h)	Grimsby T	W 4-1	D.Mercer, Charlesworth, Morrall, Lee	12,000
14		8	(a)	Barnsley	W 3-2	Hughes, D.Mercer, Morrall	6,500
15		15	(h)	Barnsley	W 3-1	Stevens, D.Mercer, Wright	8,000
16		22	(h)	Stockport C	W 4-1	D.Mercer 2, Morrall, Lee	8,000
17		29	(a)	Stockport C	L 1-3	Stevens	5,000
18	Dec	6	(h)	Lincoln C	W 5-2	Lee 3, Stevens, D.Mercer	8,000
19		13	(a)	Lincoln C	L 0-2		4,000
20		20	(a)	Wolves	L 2-4	D.Mercer, Hughes	14,000
21		25	(a)	Tottenham H	L 0-4		40,000
22		26	(h)	Tottenham H	L 1-3	Stevens	24,000
23		27	(h)	Wolves	W 10-3	D.Mercer 4, Stevens 3, Morrall 2, Wright	10,000
24	Jan	3	(a)	South Shields	L 1-7	D.Mercer	16,000
25		17	(h)	South Shields	W 3-0	Morrall, Stevens, Frith (og)	7,000
26		24	(a)	Leicester C	L 2-3	Stevens, D.Mercer	15,000
27	Feb	7	(a)	Fulham	L 0-1		18,000
28		12	(h)	Leicester C	W 5-1	Morrall 3, Stevens, Deacey	6,000
29		14	(h)	Fulham	W 2-0	Lee, Stevens	10,000
30		21	(a)	Coventry C	W 1-0	Morrall	18,000
31		28	(h)	Coventry C	L 0-1		7,000
32	Mar	13	(a)	Huddersfield T	L 0-2		8,048
33		18	(h)	Huddersfield T	L 1-4	D.Mercer	12,000
34		20	(h)	Blackpool	L 0-1		11,500
35		27	(a)	Blackpool	L 1-2	Morrall	5,000
36	Apr	2	(a)	Clapton O	D 2-2	Stevens, Morrall	12,000
37		3	(h)	Bristol C	D 0-0		9,000
38		10	(a)	Bristol C	D 2-2	Crawford, Deacey	11,000
39		17	(h)	West Ham U	D 1-1	Morrall	8,500
40		24	(a)	West Ham U	L 1-2	Morrall	20,000
41		26	(h)	Rotherham C	W 1-0	Charlesworth	6,000
42	May	1	(a)	Rotherham C	W 2-1	Charlesworth, Lyon	10,000

FINAL LEAGUE POSITION: 11th in Division Two

Appearances
Goals

FA Cup

1	Jan	14	(a)	Sunderland	L 2-6	Stevens 2	35,586

Note: Barrass was the assumed name of Jimmy Lodge

Appearances
Goals

Hendry N	Wigglesworth A	Betts A	Edelston J	Deacey C	Bleakley T	Mercer D	Potter C	Stevens S	Morrall G	Hughes R	Lee J	Lyon J	Wright W	Charlesworth A	Bell M	Stephenson W	Jacketts G	Mason T	Mercer W	Barrass J	Johnson W	Crawford J	Middlehurst J	Clark W	Needham J	Wadsworth E	
1	2	3	4	5	6	7	8	9	10	11																	1
1	2	3	4	5	6	7		9		11	8	10															2
1	2	3	4	5		7		9		11	8	10	6														3
1	2			5	4	7		10		11	8	6		9	3												4
1			4		5	7		8		11		10		9	3	2	6										5
1			4		5	7		8		11		10		9	3	2	6										6
1		3	4	5	6	8	10	9		7	11					2											7
1	2		4	5	6	8		9	10	7	11				3												8
1		3	4	5	6	8		9	10	7	11				2												9
1		3	4	5	6	8		9	10	7	11				2												10
1		3	4	5	6	8		9	10	7	11				2												11
1		3	4	5	6	8		9	10	7	11				2												12
1		3	4	5	6	8			10	7	11			9	2												13
1		3	4	5		8			10	7	11		6	9	2												14
1		3	4	5		8		9	10	7	11		6		2												15
1			4	5	6	7	8	9	10		11		3		2												16
1			4	5	6	8		9	10	7	11		3		2												17
1		3	4	5		8		9	10		11		6		2			7									18
1		3	4	5		8		9	10	7	11		6		2												19
1		3	4	5		8			10	7	11	9	6		2												20
1	3		4	5		8			10	7	11	9	6		2												21
1		3	4	5	6	8		9		7		10	11		2												22
1			4	5	6	8		9	10	7		3	11		2												23
1			4	5	6	8		9	10		11	3	7		2												24
			4	5	6	8		9	10	7	11					2			1	3							25
			4	5	6	8		9	10	7	11					2			1	3							26
			4	5	6	8		9	10	7	11				3	2			1								27
			4	5	6	8		9	10		11				2				1	3	7						28
			4	5	6	8		9	10		11				2				1	3	7						29
			4	5	6	8		9	10	11						2			1	3	7						30
			4	5	6	8		9	10	11						2			1	3	7						31
				5	6	7	8	9	10				4			2			1	3		11					32
	2			5	6	7		8	10				4	9					1	3		11					33
1				5	6	8	4	9	10											3		7	2	11			34
			5		6	8	4	9	10	7									1	3		11	2				35
		2	4	5	6	7	8	9	10										1	3		11					36
		2	4	5	6			9	10										1	3	7	11			8		37
				5	6	7	4	9	10										1	3		11	2		8		38
				5	6	7	4	9	10										1	3		11	2			8	39
			4		6	7		8	10			5		9		·			1	3		11	2				40
			4	5	6	7			8			11		9					1	3			2		10		41
				5	6	7	4		8			11		9					1	3			2		10		42
25	7	17	35	38	35	41	10	36	35	27	24	13	14	9	23	9	2	1	17	17	5	9	7	1	4	1	
				3		17		18	17	3	9	2	2	5								1					

1 own-goal

1		3	4	5		8		9	10	7	11		6		2												1
1		1	1	1		1		1	1	1	1		1		1												
								2																			

1920-21

1	Aug	28	(a)	West Ham U	D 1-1	Henzell	26,000
2		30	(a)	Birmingham	L 1-5	Charlesworth	25,000
3	Sep	4	(h)	West Ham U	W 2-1	D.Mercer 2	15,000
4		6	(h)	Birmingham	W 1-0	Charlesworth	14,000
5		11	(h)	Bristol C	W 2-0	Flood, D.Mercer	15,000
6		18	(a)	Bristol C	L 1-2	Flood	15,000
7		25	(h)	Barnsley	W 3-0	Crawford, Needham, D.Mercer	15,000
8	Oct	2	(a)	Barnsley	D 0-0		8,000
9		9	(h)	Rotherham C	D 1-1	Crawford	12,000
10		16	(a)	Rotherham C	D 1-1	Wilson	10,000
11		23	(h)	Leeds U	L 0-1		10,000
12		30	(a)	Leeds U	D 1-1	McKinney	20,000
13	Nov	6	(h)	Port Vale	D 1-1	D.Mercer	15,000
14		13	(a)	Port Vale	L 0-4		15,000
15		20	(a)	South Shields	D 0-0		20,000
16		27	(h)	South Shields	L 0-2		9,000
17	Dec	4	(h)	Nottingham F	L 0-3		5,000
18		11	(a)	Nottingham F	L 0-2		10,000
19		18	(h)	Wolves	L 0-1		8,000
20		25	(a)	Clapton O	D 1-1	Crawford	28,000
21		27	(h)	Clapton O	W 3-0	Sergeaunt 3	12,000
22	Jan	1	(a)	Wolves	W 3-1	Sergeaunt 2, Wilson	20,000
23		15	(h)	Coventry C	D 1-1	Crawford	10,000
24		22	(a)	Coventry C	L 2-3	Sergeaunt, McKinney	16,000
25	Feb	3	(h)	Stockport C	D 1-1	Brandon	8,000
26		5	(a)	Stockport C	D 2-2	Sergeaunt, Cheetham	10,000
27		12	(h)	Stoke	D 1-1	McKinney	8,000
28		26	(h)	Sheffield W	D 1-1	Mills	8,000
29	Mar	12	(h)	Notts C	D 1-1	Sergeaunt	8,000
30		19	(a)	Notts C	L 1-4	Mills	15,000
31		21	(a)	Sheffield W	L 0-3		10,000
32		25	(a)	Bury	D 0-0		16,000
33		26	(a)	Blackpool	W 2-1	Flood 2	14,000
34		28	(h)	Bury	D 1-1	Flood	10,000
35	Apr	2	(h)	Blackpool	W 2-1	Flood, Brandon	9,000
36		9	(a)	Leicester C	D 0-0		12,000
37		11	(a)	Stoke	W 3-1	Flood 2, Mills	5,000
38		16	(h)	Leicester C	D 1-1	Mills	9,000
39		23	(a)	Cardiff C	D 0-0		30,000
40		30	(h)	Cardiff C	W 2-0	Hughes, Brandon	10,000
41	May	2	(a)	Fulham	L 0-3		15,000
42		7	(h)	Fulham	D 0 0		8,000

FINAL LEAGUE POSITION: 13th in Division Two — Appearances

Note: Match 13 was benefit match for Nick Hendry. — Goals

FA Cup

1	Jan	8	(h)	Bath C	W 3-0	Wilson, Sergeaunt, Crawford	11,600
2		29	(a)	Crystal P	W 2-0	Wilson, Crawford	21,000
3	Feb	19	(h)	Burnley	W 3-0	Brandon 2, Wilson	26,000
4	Mar	5	(h)	Preston NE	D 0-0		27,000
R		10	(a)	Preston NE	L 0-1		32,853

Appearances

Goals

Mercer W	Brandon T	Barrass J	Collier J	Gilhooley M	Bleakley T	Mercer D	Henzell W	Charlesworth A	Needham J	Crawford J	Mason T	Morrall G	Flood C	Harron J	Wilson H	Hughes R	Deacey C	McKinney D	Wright W	Sergeaunt H	Stoddart G	Bell M	Mills B	Cheetham S	Davies G	Garratt S	McMurray C	Marshall J	Ranby S	Smith I	Ryley H	
1	2	3	4	5	6	7	8	9	10	11																						1
1	2	3	4	5	6	7	8	9	10	11																						2
1	2	3	4	5	6	8		9	10	11	7																					3
1	2	3	4	5	6	7		9	10	11		8																				4
1	2	3	4	5	6	7			10	11		8	9																			5
1	2	3	4	5	6	8			10	7			9	11																		6
1	2	3	4	5	6	8			10	11	7				9																	7
1	2	3	4	5	6	8			10	7					9	11																8
1	2	3	4		6				10	8					9	11	5	7														9
1	2	3	4	5	6					8					9	11		7	10													10
1	2	3	4	5	6				10	7					9	11		8														11
1	2	3	4	5	6			8							9	11		7		10												12
1	2	3	4	5	6	8			10						9	11		7														13
1	2	3	4	5						11					9			7	6	10	8											14
1	2		4	5	6										9	11		7	10		8	3										15
1	2		4	5	6										9	11		7	10		8	3										16
1	2		4	5	6	7			9						10	11					8	3										17
1	2		4	5					10	7					11				6		8	3	9									18
1	2		4	5	6				10	7					11						8	3	9									19
1	8		4	5	6			9		7					11					10		3		2								20
1	8		4	5	6					7					11					10		3	9	2								21
1	8		4	5	6					7					11					10		3	9	2								22
1	8		4	5	6					7					9			11		10		3		2								23
1	8		4	5	6					7					11			9		10		3		2								24
1	8		4	5						7					11			9			10	3		2	6							25
1	8			5						7					11			9		10		3		2		4	6					26
1	8		4							7								9		10		3		2	6		5	11				27
1	8	3	4		6									7	11					10			9	2			5					28
1	8		4	5	6										11			7		10		3	9	2								29
1		3		5	6					7					11			8		10			9	2	4							30
1	9	3	4		5								10		7									2	6				8	11		31
1	8		4	5	6					7			10		11			9				3		2								32
1	8		4	5	6					7			10		11			9				3		2								33
1	8		4	5	6					7			10		11			9				3		2								34
1	8		4	5	6					7			10		11							3	9	2								35
1	8		4	5	6					7			10		11							3	9	2								36
1	8		4	5	6					7			10		11							3	9	2								37
1	8		4	5	6					7			10			11						3	9	2								38
1	8		4	5	6					7			10			11						3	9	2								39
1	8			5	6					7			10			11		11				3	9	2	4							40
1	8			5	6					7			10									3	9	2	4							41
1	8	2	4	5	6					7			10					19				3	9								11	42
42	41	18	38	38	37	10	2	6	14	34	2	2	14	2	30	12	1	3	5	12	7	25	15	22	6	1	3	1	1	1	1	
	3					5	1	2	1	4			8		2	1				8			4	1								

Note: Barrass was the assumed name of Jimmy Lodge.

Mercer W	Brandon T	Barrass J	Collier J	Gilhooley M	Bleakley T	Mercer D	Henzell W	Charlesworth A	Needham J	Crawford J	Mason T	Morrall G	Flood C	Harron J	Wilson H	Hughes R	Deacey C	McKinney D	Wright W	Sergeaunt H	Stoddart G	Bell M	Mills B	Cheetham S	Davies G	Garratt S	McMurray C	Marshall J	Ranby S	Smith I	Ryley H	
1	8		4	5	6					7					11			9		10		3		2								1
1	8		4	5	6					7					11			9		10		3		2								2
1	8		4	5	6					7					11			9		10		3		2								3
1	8		4	5	6					7					11			9		10		3		2								4
1	8		4	5	6					7					11			9		10		3		2								R
5	5		5	5	5					5					5			5		5		5		5								
	2									2					3					1												

1921-22

1	Aug	27	(h)	South Shields	D	1-1	Hughes	14,000
2		29	(a)	Nottingham F	L	2-3	Flood, Crawford	12,000
3	Sep	3	(a)	South Shields	L	0-1		18,000
4		5	(h)	Nottingham F	L	0-1		9,000
5		10	(h)	Fulham	W	2-1	Flood 2	10,000
6		17	(a)	Fulham	L	0-6		18,000
7		24	(h)	Blackpool	W	2-0	Kitchen, Flood	8,000
8	Oct	1	(a)	Blackpool	W	1-0	Flood	10,000
9		8	(h)	Clapton O	W	2-1	Flood, Crawford	10,000
10		15	(a)	Clapton O	W	2-0	Hughes, Coverdale	20,000
11		22	(h)	Bristol C	W	1-0	Gilhooley	6,000
12		29	(a)	Bristol C	L	0-1		12,000
13	Nov	5	(a)	Stoke	D	0-0		12,000
14		12	(h)	Stoke	W	7-1	Mills 4, Flood 2, Coverdale	12,000
15		19	(h)	Leeds U	W	1-0	Flood	12,800
16		26	(a)	Leeds U	W	2-0	Mills 2	20,000
17	Dec	3	(h)	Bradford	W	3-0	Mills 3	14,100
18		10	(a)	Bradford	D	1-1	Coverdale	12,000
19		17	(h)	Notts C	W	2-0	Flood, Hughes	14,000
20		24	(a)	Notts C	L	0-2		14,000
21		26	(h)	Rotherham C	L	0-1		18,000
22		27	(a)	Rotherham C	L	0-2		12,000
23		31	(h)	Crystal P	W	1-0	Flood	10,000
24	Jan	14	(a)	Crystal P	W	2-0	Mills 2	15,000
25		21	(h)	Port Vale	W	2-0	Flood 2	6,000
26	Feb	4	(h)	West Ham U	D	0-0		10,000
27		11	(a)	West Ham U	D	1-1	McKinney	22,000
28		13	(a)	Port Vale	L	0-1		8,000
29		18	(h)	Bury	D	1-1	Hughes	8,000
30		25	(a)	Bury	L	0-4		8,000
31	Mar	4	(h)	Leicester C	W	5-2	McKinney 3, Flood 2	8,000
32		11	(a)	Leicester C	W	1-0	Stansfield	12,000
33		18	(a)	Derby C	D	0-0		10,000
34		25	(h)	Derby C	D	1-1	Crawford	8,000
35	Apr	1	(a)	Coventry C	L	0-2		7,000
36		8	(h)	Coventry C	W	2-0	Flood 2	8,000
37		14	(h)	Sheffield W	D	0-0		12,000
38		15	(a)	Barnsley	L	1-4	McKinney	14,000
39		17	(a)	Sheffield W	D	0-0		10,000
40		22	(h)	Barnsley	L	1-3	McKinney	9,000
41		29	(a)	Wolves	W	2-0	Hughes, McKinney	12,000
42	May	6	(h)	Wolves	W	2-0	McKinney, Eccles	8,000

FINAL LEAGUE POSITION: 5th in Division Two

Note: Match 17 was benefit match for Billy Mercer.

Appearances

Goals

FA Cup

1	Jan	7	(h)	Middlesbrough	W	5-0	Coverdale 2, Mills, Bleakley, Crawford	23,000
2		28	(a)	Nottingham F	L	0-3		28,000

Appearances

Goals

Mercer W	Cheetham S	Bell M	Coverdale R	Gilhooley M	Bleakley T	Crawford J	Brandon T	Flood C	Sergeaunt H	Hughes R	Davies G	Mills B	Kitchen J	Lodge J	Collier J	McKinney D	Blenkinsop E	Stansfield J	McMurray C	Garratt S	Slater H	Scorer R	Eccles T	Doyle D	
1	2	3	4	5	6	7	8	9	10	11															1
1	2	3	4	5	6	7	8	9	10	11															2
1	2	3	4	5		7		8	10	11	6	9													3
1	2	3	4	5		7		8	10	11	6	9													4
1	2	3	4	5		7		10	8	11	6		9												5
1	2		4	5		7		8	10	11	6		9	3											6
1			8	5	6	7	2	10		11			9	3	4										7
1			8	5	6	7	2	10		11		9		3	4										8
1			8	5	6	7	2	10		11		9		3	4										9
1		3	8	5	6	7	2	10		11		9			4										10
1		3	8	5	6	7	2	10		11		9			4										11
1		3	8	5	6	7	2	10		11			9		4										12
1		3	8	5	6	7	2	10		11		9			4										13
1		3	8	5	6	7	2	10		11		9			4										14
1		3	8	5	6	7	2	10		11		9			4										15
1		3	8	5	6	7	2	10		11		9			4										16
1		3	8	5	6	7	2	10		11		9			4										17
1		3	8	5	6	7		10		11		9		2	4										18
1		3	8	5	6	7		10		11		9		2	4										19
1		3	8	5	6	7		10		11		9		2	4										20
1		3	8	5	6	7		10				9		2	4	11									21
1					5	7		10		11	6		9	2	4	8	3								22
1			8	5	6	7		10		11		9		2	4		3								23
1		3	8	5	6	7		10		11		9		2	4										24
1		3	8	5	6	7		10		11		9		2	4										25
1		3	6		5	7		10		11		9		2	4	8									26
1		3	4	5	6	7		10				9		2		8		11							27
1		3	4	5	6	7		10					9	2		8		11							28
1		3	8	5	6	7	2	10		11					4	9									29
1		3	8		6	7	2	9					10		4			11	5						30
1		3	8		6	7		10						2	4	9		11		5					31
1		3	8		6	7		10						2	4	9		11		5					32
1		3	8		6	7		10						2	4	9		11		5					33
1		3	8		6	7		10						2	4	9		11		5					34
1		3	8		6	7		10				9		2	4			11		5					35
1		3	8		6	7		10				9	5	2	4			11							36
1		3	8		6	7		10				9		2	4		5	11							37
1		3	8		6			9	10				5	2		7		11		4					38
1		3	8		6	7		10					5	2	4	9		11							39
1		3	8		6	7		10					5	2	4	9					11				40
1		3			6	7				11		9	10	2	4	8						5			41
1		3			6	7							10	2	4	8						5	9	11	42
42	6	36	39	27	38	41	15	40	7	27	5	24	13	27	33	15	3	12	1	6	1	2	1	1	
			3	1		3		17		5		11	1			8		1					1		

Mercer W	Cheetham S	Bell M	Coverdale R	Gilhooley M	Bleakley T	Crawford J	Brandon T	Flood C	Sergeaunt H	Hughes R	Davies G	Mills B	Kitchen J	Lodge J	Collier J	McKinney D	Blenkinsop E	Stansfield J	McMurray C	Garratt S	Slater H	Scorer R	Eccles T	Doyle D	
1		3	8	5	6	7		10		11		9		2	4										1
1		3	8	5	6	7		10		11		9		2	4										2
2		2	2	2	2	2		2		2		2		2	2										
			2		1	1						1													

1922-23

1	Aug	26	(a)	Bury	L 0-1		12,000
2		28	(h)	Port Vale	W 3-0	Crawford, Kitchen, Bleakley	6,000
3	Sep	2	(h)	Bury	D 2-2	Eccles, Kitchen	10,000
4		4	(a)	Port Vale	L 0-1		10,000
5		9	(a)	Notts C	W 1-0	Kitchen	12,000
6		16	(h)	Notts C	L 0-2		10,000
7		23	(h)	Fulham	W 1-0	Mills	10,000
8		30	(a)	Fulham	D 0-0		20,000
9	Oct	7	(a)	Crystal P	D 1-1	Thom	16,000
10		14	(h)	Crystal P	D 1-1	Bleakley	10,000
11		21	(a)	Rotherham C	W 1-0	Thom	10,000
12		28	(h)	Rotherham C	L 2-3	Martin, McKinney	9,000
13	Nov	4	(a)	Leicester C	W 1-0	Martin	16,000
14		11	(h)	Leicester C	L 1-3	Martin	10,000
15		18	(h)	Sheffield W	D 0-0		7,000
16		25	(a)	Sheffield W	L 0-1		18,000
17	Dec	2	(a)	Barnsley	L 0-1		8,000
18		9	(h)	Barnsley	W 2-1	Martin 2	7,000
19		16	(a)	Blackpool	D 0-0		8,000
20		23	(h)	Blackpool	D 0-0		8,000
21		25	(h)	Southampton	L 1-3	Kitchen	9,000
22		26	(a)	Southampton	L 1-2	Mills	18,000
23		30	(h)	Manchester U	W 2-1	Mills, Wood	10,000
24	Jan	6	(a)	Manchester U	L 2-3	Wood, Thom	15,000
25		20	(a)	Bradford C	L 1-2	Martin	15,000
26		27	(h)	Bradford C	D 0-0		10,000
27	Feb	3	(a)	Clapton O	L 0-2		12,000
28		10	(h)	Clapton O	W 2-1	Mills, Coverdale	8,000
29		17	(a)	Stockport C	D 1-1	Martin	11,000
30		24	(h)	Stockport C	W 1-0	Hall	8,000
31	Mar	3	(a)	Leeds U	D 2-2	Martin, Thom	12,000
32		10	(h)	Leeds U	W 3-1	Martin, Hall, Bleakley	14,000
33		17	(h)	West Ham U	D 1-1	Mills	14,000
34		30	(a)	Derby C	W 2-0	Martin, Hall	14,000
35		31	(h)	South Shields	W 2-0	Mills, Coverdale	11,000
36	Apr	2	(h)	Derby C	W 4-2	Mills, Martin, Thom, Hall	16,000
37		7	(a)	South Shields	D 0-0		4,000
38		9	(a)	West Ham U	L 0-3		18,000
39		14	(h)	Wolves	D 0-0		8,000
40		23	(a)	Wolves	L 0-3		8,000
41		28	(h)	Coventry C	D 1-1	Martin	6,000
42	May	5	(a)	Coventry C	W 1-0	Mills	10,000
FINAL LEAGUE POSITION: 12th in Division Two							Appearances
							Goals

FA Cup

1	Jan	13	(h)	West Ham U	L 2-3	Crawford, Mills	14,000
							Appearances
							Goals

Mercer W	Gibson J	Bell M	Collier J	Bew D	Bleakley T	Crawford J	McKinney D	Eccles T	Kitchen J	Doyle D	Slater H	Briggs A	Mills B	Hall G	Scorer R	Coverdale R	Lodge J	McGee J	Thom A	Martin G	Blenkinsop E	Middlemas J	Garratt S	Wood J	Rumney J	Livingstone A	Loughran J	
1	2	3	4	5	6	7	8	9	10	11																		1
1	2	3	4	5	6	7	8	9	10		11																	2
1	2	3	4	5	6	7	8	9	10		11																	3
	2	3	4	5	6	7	8		10			1	9	11														4
1	2	3	4		6	7	9		10	11					5	8												5
1	2	3	4		6	7	9		10	11					5	8												6
1		3	4		6	7	8		10				9				2	5	11									7
1		3	4		6	7	8		10				9				2	5	11									8
1		3	4		6	7	8		10				9				2	5	11									9
1		3	4		6	7	8		10				9				2	5	11									10
1		3	4	5	6	7	9		10							8	2		11									11
1		3	4	5	6	7	8		10								2		11	9								12
1			4	5		7			10							8	2		11	9	3	6						13
1			4	5		7			10							8	2		11	9	3	6						14
1	2		4			8	7									10		5	11	9	3	6						15
1	2	3	4		6	7							8			10		5	11	9								16
1	2		4		6	7							8			10		5	11	9	3							17
1	2		4		6	7		10					8					5	11	9	3							18
1	2				6	7		10					8					5	11	9	3	4						19
1	2		8		6	7							10					5	11	9	3	4						20
1	2		4		6	7			10				8				3	5	11	9								21
1	2					7		8	10				9		5				11		3	6	4					22
1	2			5	6	7		10					8					3	11			4		9				23
1	2	3		5	6	7		10					8						11			4		9				24
1	2	3	4		6	7							10			8		5	11	9								25
1	2	3		5	6	7							10			8			11			4			9			26
1	2	3			5	7							8			6			11	9		4				10		27
1	2	3	4		5	7	8						10			6			11	9								28
1	2	3	4		5	7							10	8		6			11	9								29
1	2	3	4		5	7				6			10	8					11	9								30
1	2	3	4		5	7							10	8		6			11	9								31
1	2	3	4		5	7							10	8		6			11	9								32
1	2	3	4		5	7	8						10			6			11	9								33
1	2	3	4		5	7							10	8		6			11	9								34
1	2	3	4		5	7							10	8		6			11	9								35
1	2	3	4		5	7				6			10	8					11	9								36
1		3	4		5	7	8							9			2		11	10							6	37
1	2				5	7	8		10							4	3		11	9							6	38
	2		4		5	7	8					1	9			6	3		11	10								39
		3	4		5	7	8					1	9			6	2		11	10								40
1		3	4		5	11	7						9	8		6	2			10								41
1		3	4		5	7	8						9			6	2		11	10								42
39	30	30	35	11	38	42	21	8	17	5	2	3	30	10	3	23	15	13	35	27	8	10	1	2	1	1	2	
					3	1	1	1	4				8	4		2			5	12				2				

Mercer W	Gibson J	Bell M	Collier J	Bew D	Bleakley T	Crawford J	McKinney D	Eccles T	Kitchen J	Doyle D	Slater H	Briggs A	Mills B	Hall G	Scorer R	Coverdale R	Lodge J	McGee J	Thom A	Martin G	Blenkinsop E	Middlemas J	Garratt S	Wood J	Rumney J	Livingstone A	Loughran J	
1	2	3		5	6	7							8			10			11			4		9				1
1	1	1		1	1	1							1			1			1			1		1				
						1							1															

1923-24

1	Aug	25	(h)	Leicester C	D 1-1	Thom	12,500
2		27	(a)	Clapton O	D 0-0		18,000
3	Sep	1	(a)	Leicester C	D 1-1	Smith	23,000
4		3	(h)	Clapton O	D 2-2	Martin, Thomas	10,000
5		8	(h)	Nelson	W 2-1	Rumney 2	9,000
6		15	(a)	Nelson	D 1-1	Walker	12,000
7		22	(h)	Leeds U	L 1-2	Smith	11,500
8		29	(a)	Leeds U	L 2-5	Martin, Duffield (og)	12,000
9	Oct	6	(h)	Derby C	L 0-1		9,000
10		13	(a)	Derby C	L 1-4	Rumney	12,000
11		20	(h)	Stoke	W 2-0	Rumney, Martin	10,000
12		27	(a)	Stoke	L 0-1		11,000
13	Nov	3	(a)	Crystal P	D 0-0		8,000
14		10	(h)	Crystal P	D 2-2	Thom, Feebery (og)	10,000
15		17	(a)	Sheffield W	L 0-1		15,000
16		24	(h)	Sheffield W	D 1-1	Lewis	9,000
17	Dec	8	(h)	Coventry C	W 3-2	Martin 2, Havelock	8,000
18		15	(a)	Bristol C	L 0-1		8,000
19		17	(a)	Coventry C	W 2-0	Martin, Thom	3,000
20		22	(h)	Bristol C	W 5-0	Mills 3, Thom, Richardson	8,000
21		25	(a)	Fulham	D 1-1	Lewis	25,000
22		26	(h)	Fulham	W 4-2	Mills 3, Thomas	14,000
23		29	(a)	Southampton	L 0-2		11,000
24	Jan	5	(h)	Southampton	D 0-0		10,000
25		19	(h)	Stockport C	L 1-2	Martin	8,000
26		26	(a)	Stockport C	L 1-5	Mills	16,000
27	Feb	9	(a)	Oldham A	D 0-0		9,000
28		14	(h)	Oldham A	D 0-0		5,000
29		16	(h)	South Shields	W 1-0	Lewis	8,000
30		23	(a)	South Shields	W 1-0	Havelock	8,000
31	Mar	1	(h)	Bury	L 0-1		8,000
32		8	(a)	Bury	L 0-1		12,000
33		15	(a)	Manchester U	D 1-1	Mills	25,000
34		22	(h)	Manchester U	D 1-1	Mills	8,000
35		29	(a)	Barnsley	D 0-0		3,700
36	Apr	5	(h)	Barnsley	L 1-2	Lewis	8,000
37		12	(a)	Bradford C	L 1-2	Mills	8,000
38		18	(a)	Blackpool	D 0-0		20,000
39		19	(h)	Bradford C	W 2-0	Bell, Lewis	10,000
40		21	(h)	Blackpool	W 2-1	Thomas 2	10,000
41		26	(a)	Port Vale	D 2-2	Martin 2	7,000
42	May	3	(h)	Port Vale	L 1-2	Mills	6,000

FINAL LEAGUE POSITION: 17th in Division Two

Appearances

Goals

FA Cup

1	Jan	12	(h)	Bolton W	D 2-2	Martin, Mills	28,603
R		16	(a)	Bolton W	L 0-4		40,315

Appearances

Goals

Mercer W	Gibson J	Bell M	Collier J	Adey T	Bleakley T	Thomas A	Mills B	Rumney J	Martin G	Thom A	Smith T	Walker W	Johnson W	Loughran J	Lodge J	Hall G	Lewis H	Mordue T	Hamilton T	Richardson G	Havelock H	Hedley R	Briggs A	McGee J	Coverdale R	
1	2	3	4	5	6	7	8	9	10	11																1
1	2	3	4	5		7	6	9	10	11	8															2
1	2	3	4	5		7	6	9	10	11	8															3
1	2	3	4	5		7	6	9	10	11	8															4
1	2	3	4	5		7	6	9	10	11		8														5
1	2	3		5		7	6	9	10	11		8	4													6
1	2	3	4	5		7	9		10	11	8			6												7
1		3	4	5		7	9		10	11	8			6	2											8
1		3	4	5		7	6	9	10	11	8				2											9
1		3		5			6	9	10	11	8		4		2	7										10
1	2	3		5		11	6	9	8				4			7	10									11
1	2	3		5		11	6	9	8				4				10	7								12
1		3		5			6	9	8	11			4		2		10	7								13
1	2	3		5			6	9	8	11			4				10	7								14
1	2	3	4	5			9		8	11			6				10		7							15
1	2	3	4	5			9		8	11			6				10		7							16
1	2	3	4		5		6		8	11							10			7	9					17
1	2	3			5		6		8	11			4				10			7	9					18
1	2	3	4		5		9		8	11			6				10			7						19
1	2	3	4		5		9		8	11			6				10			7						20
1	2	3	4		5	7	9		8	11			6				10									21
1		3	4		5	7	9		8	11			6				10					2				22
1		3	4		5	7	9		8	11			6				10					2				23
1	2	3	4		5		9		8	11			6				10			7						24
	2	3	4		5	7	9		8	11			6				10						1			25
	2	3	4		5	7	9		10	11			6				8						1			26
1		3			6	11			9			8	4				10			7		2		5		27
1		3			6	11	7		9			8	4				10					2		5		28
1		3			6	11	7				8		4				10				9	2		5		29
1	2	3			6	11	7					8	4				10				9			5		30
1	2	3			6	7	8			11			4				10				9			5		31
1	2	3			6	7	9		10	11			4				8							5		32
1			4		5	11	8		10				6					7			9	2		3		33
1		3			6	11	9		8				4				10	7				2		5		34
1		3			6	11	9		8				4				10	7				2		5		35
1		3			6	7	9		8				4				10					2		5	11	36
1	2	3	4			7	9		8	11			6				10							5		37
1		3	4		5	7	9		8	11			6				10							2		38
1		3	4		5	7	9		8	11			6				10							2		39
1		3	4		5	7	9		8	11			6				10							2		40
1		3	4		5	7	9		8	11			6				10							2		41
1		3	4		5	7	9		8	11			6				10							2		42
40	24	41	26	16	26	32	41	12	39	32	8	5	33	2	4	2	31	6	2	6	6	9	2	16	1	
		1				4	11	4	9	4	2	1					5			1	2					

2 own-goals

Mercer W	Gibson J	Bell M	Collier J	Adey T	Bleakley T	Thomas A	Mills B	Rumney J	Martin G	Thom A	Smith T	Walker W	Johnson W	Loughran J	Lodge J	Hall G	Lewis H	Mordue T	Hamilton T	Richardson G	Havelock H	Hedley R	Briggs A	McGee J	Coverdale R	
1	2	3	4		5		9		8	11			6				10			7						1
1	2	3	4		5		9		8	11			6				10			7						R
2	2	2	2		2		2		2	2			2				2			2						
							1		1																	

1924-25

1	Aug	30	(a)	Derby C	L 0-4		15,000
2	Sep	1	(h)	Bradford C	D 0-0		13,000
3		6	(h)	Blackpool	D 1-1	Mills	12,000
4		8	(a)	Bradford C	L 1-4	Mills	8,000
5		13	(a)	Crystal P	L 0-1		12,000
6		20	(a)	Portsmouth	L 0-2		25,000
7		27	(h)	Fulham	W 3-0	Mills, Hamilton, Thom	9,000
8	Oct	4	(a)	Wolves	L 1-2	Mills	20,000
9		11	(h)	Barnsley	W 5-2	Mills 2, Haworth 2, Thom	12,000
10		18	(a)	Middlesbrough	W 1-0	Mills	18,000
11		25	(h)	Southampton	D 1-1	Haworth	10,000
12	Nov	1	(a)	Chelsea	L 0-1		10,000
13		8	(h)	Stockport C	W 3-0	Mills, Haworth, Hamilton	8,000
14		15	(a)	Manchester U	L 0-2		30,000
15		22	(h)	Leicester C	W 2-1	Mills 2	11,000
16		29	(a)	Stoke	L 0-2		7,000
17	Dec	6	(h)	Coventry C	W 4-1	Mills 2, Martin, Thom	9,000
18		13	(a)	Oldham A	L 0-1		3,000
19		20	(h)	Sheffield W	W 4-2	Mills 3, Martin	10,000
20		25	(a)	Clapton O	D 0-0		26,000
21		26	(h)	Clapton O	W 2-1	Haworth, Martin	14,000
22		27	(h)	Derby C	D 1-1	Mills	12,000
23	Jan	3	(a)	Blackpool	D 0-0		7,000
24		17	(h)	Crystal P	W 5-0	Martin 2, Hamilton 2, Mills	12,000
25		24	(h)	Portsmouth	W 5-0	Mills 2, Martin 2, Hamilton	8,000
26	Feb	7	(h)	Wolves	L 0-1		12,000
27		9	(a)	Fulham	L 0-4		7,000
28		14	(a)	Barnsley	W 2-1	Mills, Haworth	6,000
29		28	(a)	Southampton	D 2-2	Hamilton, Mills	7,000
30	Mar	7	(h)	Chelsea	W 1-0	Mills	10,000
31		14	(a)	Stockport C	W 2-0	Mills, Haworth	7,000
32		19	(h)	Middlesbrough	D 0-0		5,000
33		21	(h)	Manchester U	L 0-1		8,000
34		28	(a)	Leicester C	L 0-1		23,000
35	Apr	1	(a)	South Shields	L 0-2		9,000
36		4	(h)	Stoke	D 0-0		6,000
37		10	(a)	Port Vale	D 1-1	Mills	15,000
38		11	(a)	Coventry C	D 0-0		14,000
39		13	(h)	Port Vale	W 2-1	Mills, Bleakley	4,000
40		18	(h)	Oldham A	W 1-0	Hamilton	5,000
41		25	(a)	Sheffield W	L 0-5		10,000
42	May	2	(h)	South Shields	L 0-1		5,000

FINAL LEAGUE POSITION: 10th in Division Two — Appearances

Note: Match 17 was benefit match for Tommy Bleakley; Match 26 was benefit match for Matt Bell. — Goals

FA Cup

1	Jan	10	(h)	Wolves	D 1-1	Mills	22,000
R		15	(a)	Wolves	W 1-0*	Mills	24,447
2		31	(h)	Crystal P	W 3-2	Mills 2, Bleakley	22,500
3	Feb	21	(h)	Leicester C	D 1-1	O'Brien	27,000
R		26	(a)	Leicester C	L 1-3	Hamilton	19,864

*After extra-time — Appearances

Goals

Mercer W	McGee J	Bell M	Collier J	Bleakley T	Johnson W	Keen J	Martin G	Owen G	Lewis H	Thom A	Mills B	Gibson J	Jordan A	Hamilton S	O'Brien M	Thomas A	Haworth R	Goulden J	Maddison G	Richardson G	Iremonger J	Robson C	Bown H	Mitchell R	Wilkinson T	
1	2	3	4	5	6	7	8	9	10	11																1
1	2	3	4	5	6	7	8	9	10	11																2
1	2	3	4	5	6	7	9		10	11	8															3
1	2	3	4	5	6	7	8		10	11	9															4
1	5	3		6		7	10			11	9	2	4	8												5
1		3		6						11	9	2	4	8	5	7	10									6
1	3		4	6						11	9	2		8	5	7	10									7
1	3		4	6						11	9	2		8	5		10	7								8
1		3	4	6						11	9	2		8	5		10	7								9
1		3	4	6		7				11	9	2		8	5		10									10
1		3	4	6		7				11	9	2		8	5		10									11
1		3	4	6			7			11	9	2		8	5		10									12
		3	4	6			7			11	9	2		8	5		10		1							13
		3	4	6			7			11	9	2		8	5		10		1							14
		3	4	6			8			11	9	2			5		10		1	7						15
		3	4	6			8			11	9	2			5		10		1	7						16
		3	4	6			8			11	9	2			5		10		1	7						17
		3	4	6			8			11	9	2			5		10		1	7						18
		3	4	6			8			11	9	2			5		10			7	1					19
	3			6	4		8		10		9	2			5				1	7		11				20
	2	3		6	4		8			11	9				5		10		1	7						21
		3	4	6			8			11	9	2			5		10		1	7						22
		3	4	6			8			11	9	2			5		10		1	7						23
	3		4	6			10			11	9	2		8	5					7			1			24
	3		4	6			10			11	9	2		8	5					7			1			25
	2	3	4	6			10			11	9			8	5					7			1			26
	2	3	4	6			8			11	9				5		10			7			1			27
	3		4	6			10				9	2		8		7	11		1					5		28
		3	4	6			10			11	9	2		8		7			1					5		29
		3	4	6		7	10				9	2		8	5		11		1							30
		3	4	6		7	10				9	2		8	5		11		1							31
		3	4	6		7	10				9	2		8	5		11		1							32
		3	4	6		7	10				9	2		8	5		11		1							33
		3	4	6		7	9					2		8	5		11		1						10	34
		3	4	6		11	9					2		8	5		10		1	7						35
		3		6		11	9					2		8	5		10		1	7				4		36
		3		6			10				9	2		8	5		11		1	7				4		37
		3		6		11	9					2		8	5		10		1	7				4		38
	2	3		6			10				9			8	5		11		1	7				4		39
	3		4	6	2		10			11	9			8					1	7				5		40
	3		4	6	2	7	10			11	9			8					1					5		41
	3			6	2	7				11	9		8		5		10		1					4		42
12	18	33	33	42	9	17	35	2	5	30	36	31	3	27	33	4	30	2	25	19	1	1	4	9	1	
				1			7			3	25			7			7									

Mercer W	McGee J	Bell M	Collier J	Bleakley T	Johnson W	Keen J	Martin G	Owen G	Lewis H	Thom A	Mills B	Gibson J	Jordan A	Hamilton S	O'Brien M	Thomas A	Haworth R	Goulden J	Maddison G	Richardson G	Iremonger J	Robson C	Bown H	Mitchell R	Wilkinson T	
		3	4	6			8			11	9	2			5		10		1	7						1
	3	1	4	6			10			11	9	2		8	5					7						R
	2	3	4	6			10			11	9			8	5					7			1			2
	3		4	6			10			11	9	2		8	5	7			1							3
	3		4	6			10			11	9	2		8	5	7			1							R
	4	3	5	5			5			5	5	4		4	5	2	1		3	3			1			
				1							4			1	1											

1925-26

1	Aug	29	(h)	Derby C	D 0-0		11,209
2		31	(a)	Southampton	W 2-0	Mills, Richardson	9,433
3	Sep	5	(a)	Bradford C	W 1-0	Swan	15,078
4		7	(h)	Southampton	W 4-0	Mills 2, Lee 2	9,921
5		12	(h)	Port Vale	W 3-0	Mills 2, Lee	12,523
6		19	(a)	Barnsley	L 1-2	Thom	3,314
7		26	(h)	Clapton O	W 2-0	Swan, Mitchell	9,695
8	Oct	3	(a)	Chelsea	L 0-4		47,428
9		10	(h)	South Shields	L 1-3	Mills	10,092
10		12	(h)	Nottingham F	W 4-1	Haworth, Cowan, Horne, Thom	4,839
11		17	(a)	Preston NE	L 0-4		17,542
12		24	(h)	Middlesbrough	L 1-2	Wilkinson	10,358
13		31	(a)	Stockport C	W 1-0	Mills	7,445
14	Nov	7	(h)	Fulham	W 1-0	Mills	6,992
15		14	(a)	Swansea T	L 0-2		15,947
16		21	(h)	Sheffield W	L 0-1		8,623
17		28	(a)	Stoke C	L 1-3	Thom	7,204
18	Dec	5	(h)	Oldham A	L 1-2	Thom	7,747
19		12	(a)	Portsmouth	D 2-2	Thom, Mills	15,520
20		19	(h)	Wolves	W 3-1	Mills 2, Whitworth	6,018
21		25	(a)	Darlington	W 2-1	Thom, Whitworth	9,249
22		26	(h)	Darlington	D 1-1	Mills	17,422
23	Jan	2	(a)	Derby C	L 1-3	Whitworth	12,881
24		16	(h)	Bradford C	W 5-0	Mills 2, Martin 2, Whitworth	6,836
25		23	(a)	Port Vale	L 1-3	Bleakley	7,579
26		30	(h)	Barnsley	D 2-2	Cowan, Whitworth	8,478
27	Feb	6	(a)	Clapton O	D 0-0		14,710
28		13	(h)	Chelsea	L 0-1		9,464
29		27	(h)	Preston NE	D 1-1	Martin	8,953
30	Mar	3	(a)	South Shields	W 3-1	Martin, Mills, Whitworth	5,770
31		6	(a)	Middlesbrough	D 3-3	Mills 2, Whitworth	8,843
32		13	(h)	Stockport C	W 4-0	Whitworth, Martin, Jones, Keers	6,522
33		20	(a)	Fulham	D 1-1	Whitworth	14,602
34	Apr	2	(a)	Blackpool	D 2-2	Whitworth, Wilkinson	13,676
35		3	(a)	Sheffield W	L 0-2		29,075
36		5	(h)	Blackpool	L 1-2	Horne	7,365
37		10	(h)	Stoke C	W 1-0	Martin	4,211
38		17	(a)	Oldham A	L 1-2	Whitworth	5,626
39		21	(a)	Nottingham F	L 0-4		4,706
40		24	(h)	Portsmouth	W 1-0	Swan	4,559
41		26	(h)	Swansea T	W 4-2	Haworth 2, Whitworth, Martin	4,146
42	May	1	(a)	Wolves	L 1-3	Whitworth	9,283

FINAL LEAGUE POSITION: 13th in Division Two — Appearances

Notes: Match 24 was benefit match for Jock Collier; Match 32 was benefit match for Paddy Mills. — Goals

FA Cup

3	Jan	9	(h)	Aston Villa	L 0-3	26,000

Appearances

Goals

Maddison G	Gibson J	Bell M	Johnson W	O'Brien M	Bleakley T	Richardson G	Swan C	Mills B	Martin G	Thom A	Lee J	Mitchell R	Horne A	Cowan W	Haworth R	Wilkinson T	Collier J	Whitworth G	Jordan A	McGee J	Campbell J	Jones E	Keers J	Murray J	Wilson G	
1	2	3	4	5	6	7	8	9	10	11																1
1	2	3	4	5	6	7	8	9		11	10															2
1	2	3		5	6	7	8	9		11	10	4														3
1	2	3		5	6	7	8	9		11	10	4														4
1	2	3		5	6	7	8	9		11	10	4														5
1	2	3		5	6	7	8	9		11	10	4														6
1	2	3		5	6	7	8	9		11	10	4														7
1	2	3		5	6	7	8	9		11	10	4														8
1	2	3		5	6			9	8	11	10	4	7													9
1	2	3		5	6				8	11		4	7	9	10											10
1	2	3		5	6		8		9	11		4	7		10											11
1	2	3		5	6		8		10	11		4	7			9										12
1	2	3		5	6			9	10	11		8	7				4									13
1	2	3		5	6			9	10	11		8	7				4									14
1	2	3		5	6	7		9		11		4	8		10											15
1	2	3	4	5	6	7		9	10	11								8								16
1	2	3	4	5	6	7		9	10	11								8								17
1	2	3		5				9	10	11	6		7					8	4							18
1	2	3		5				9		11			7		10		4	8	6							19
1	2	3		5	6			9		11			7		10			8	4							20
1	2	3		5	6	7		10	8	11								9	4							21
1	2	3		5	6	7		10	8	11								9	4							22
1	2	3		5	6	7		10	8	11		4						9								23
1		3		5	6			10	8	11	4		7					9		2						24
1		3		5	6			10	8	11	4		7					9		2						25
1	2	3		5	6				10	11	4		7	9				8								26
1	2	3		5	6				10	11			7	9				8			4					27
1	2	3			6	7		10	8	11		5		9							4					28
1	2	3		5	6			8	7	11	10							9			4					29
1	2	3		5	6			10	7									9			4	8	11			30
1	2	3		5	6			10	7									9			4	8	11			31
1		3		5	6			10	7									9		2	4	8	11			32
1		3		5	6		8		7									9		2	4	10	11			33
1		3		5			4		7		6					10		9		2		8	11			34
1		3		5	4				7		6					10		9		2		8	11			35
1		3		5			4		10		6		7					9		2		8	11			36
1	2	3		5	6				8			4	7									9	11	10		37
1	2	3		5	6				8	11		4	7					9						10		38
1	2			5	6				8	11	10	4	7					9		3						39
1	2			5	6		4		8	11			7					9		3				10		40
1	2			5	6		4		8	11			7		10			9		3						41
1	2			5			4		8	11	10		7					9	6						3	42
42	35	38	4	41	37	15	16	27	32	34	18	18	21	4	6	3	3	25	6	10	7	8	8	3	1	
					1	1	3	17	7	6	3	1	2	2	3	2		13				1	1			

Maddison G	Gibson J	Bell M	Johnson W	O'Brien M	Bleakley T	Richardson G	Swan C	Mills B	Martin G	Thom A	Lee J	Mitchell R	Horne A	Cowan W	Haworth R	Wilkinson T	Collier J	Whitworth G	Jordan A	McGee J	Campbell J	Jones E	Keers J	Murray J	Wilson G	
1		3		5	6	7		8	11	10	4							9		2						3
1		1		1	1	1		1	1	1	1							1		1						

1926-27

1	Aug	28	(h)	Wolves	W 1-0	Whitworth	8,321
2		30	(h)	South Shields	W 2-0	Whitworth, McLaughlin	7,002
3	Sep	4	(a)	Notts C	L 0-1		9,629
4		11	(h)	Clapton O	W 4-0	Lee 2, Whitworth 2	8,235
5		15	(a)	Reading	W 1-0	Evans (og)	12,078
6		18	(a)	Middlesbrough	L 0-2		11,618
7		20	(h)	Reading	D 1-1	Martin	6,744
8		25	(h)	Port Vale	D 0-0		7,793
9	Oct	2	(a)	Southampton	W 1-0	Swan	10,890
10		9	(h)	Bradford C	W 4-0	Whitworth 3, Swan	6,549
11		16	(a)	Grimsby T	W 1-0	Whitworth	16,023
12		23	(h)	Blackpool	W 3-0	Swan 2, McLaughlin	11,363
13		30	(a)	Swansea T	L 0-1		20,772
14	Nov	6	(h)	Nottingham F	L 1-2	Lee	7,256
15		13	(a)	Barnsley	W 2-1	Martin, Dixon	4,159
16		20	(h)	Manchester C	W 3-2	Cowan, Scott, Taylor	11,582
17		27	(a)	Darlington	W 3-1	Cowan 3	9,267
18	Dec	4	(h)	Portsmouth	W 2-1	Whitworth, Taylor	13,501
19		11	(a)	Oldham A	D 1-1	Cowan	14,800
20		18	(h)	Fulham	W 2-0	Whitworth, Cowan	11,109
21		25	(a)	Chelsea	L 0-1		34,306
22		27	(h)	Chelsea	L 0-1		23,440
23	Jan	1	(a)	South Shields	L 1-3	Guyan	9,549
24		15	(a)	Wolves	L 2-5	Whitworth, Taylor	16,793
25		22	(h)	Notts C	W 2-0	Whitworth 2	8,891
26	Feb	5	(h)	Middlesbrough	D 3-3	Guyan 2, Wyper	24,110
27		12	(a)	Port Vale	D 0-0		10,654
28		23	(a)	Clapton O	W 2-1	Martin, Taylor	4,428
29		26	(a)	Bradford C	W 2-1	Guyan 2	15,181
30	Mar	5	(h)	Grimsby T	L 2-3	Guyan 2	22,274
31		12	(a)	Blackpool	L 0-4		9,195
32		14	(h)	Southampton	D 0-0		6,912
33		19	(h)	Swansea T	W 2-1	Martin, Taylor	13,143
34		26	(a)	Nottingham F	L 1-3	Martin	10,007
35	Apr	2	(h)	Barnsley	W 5-1	Howieson 2, Martin 2, Whitworth	8,671
36		9	(a)	Manchester C	D 2-2	Whitworth, Martin	21,508
37		15	(a)	Preston NE	L 0-1		17,192
38		16	(h)	Darlington	W 2-1	Howieson, Whitworth	10,298
39		18	(h)	Preston NE	W 3-1	Martin 3	12,281
40		23	(a)	Portsmouth	L 0-2		17,049
41		30	(h)	Oldham A	L 1-2	Martin	7,267
42	May	7	(a)	Fulham	L 1-3	Sullivan	8,910

FINAL LEAGUE POSITION: 7th in Division Two

Appearances
Goals

FA Cup

3	Jan	8	(h)	West Brom A	W 2-1	Cowan, Scott	18,000
4		29	(h)	Everton	D 1-1	Martin	22,000
R	Feb	2	(a)	Everton	D 2-2*	Guyan, Scott	45,000
2R		7	(n+)	Everton	W 3-2*	Whitworth, Guyan, Martin	16,800
5		19	(a)	Wolves	L 0-1		48,948

*After extra-time. +Played at Villa Park, Birmingham.

Appearances
Goals

Maddison G	Gibson J	Bell M	Swan C	Dixon S	Bleakley T	Taylor W	Martin G	Whitworth G	McLaughlin G	Brayson J	McGee J	Horne A	Lee P	Wilson G	Hart J	Campbell J	Sullivan N	Scott H	Cowan W	Guyan G	Wyper T	Lloyd C	Morris J	Howieson J	Alexander S	
1	2	3	4	5	6	7	8	9	10	11																1
1	2	3	4	5	6	7	8	9	10	11																2
1	2	3	4	5	6	7	8	9	10	11																3
1	2	3	4		6	11	8	9			5	7	10													4
1	2	3	4	5	6	11	8	9				7	10													5
1	2	3	4	5	6	11	8	9				7	10													6
1	2		4	5	6	11	7	9					10	3	8											7
1			4	5	6	11	7	9			2		10	3	8											8
1		3	8	5	6	11	7	9	10		2					4										9
1	2	3	8	5	6	11	7	9	10							4										10
1	2	3	8	5	6	11	7	9	10							4										11
1	2	3	8	5	6	11	7	9	10								4									12
1	2	3	8	5	6	11	7	9	10								4									13
1	2	3	8	5	6	11	7	9					10				4									14
1	2	3	4	5	6	11	7	10										8	9							15
1	2	3	4	5	6	11	7	10										8	9							16
1	2	3	4	5	6	11	7	10										8	9							17
1		3	4	5	6	11	7	10			2							8	9							18
1		3	4	5	6	11	7	10			2							8	9							19
1		3	4	5	6	11	7	10			2							8	9							20
1		3	4	5	6	11	7	10			2							8		9						21
1		3	4	5	6	11	7	10			2							8		9						22
1		3		5	6	11	7	10			2						4	8		9						23
1		3		5		11	7	10			2					6	4	8	9							24
1		3	4	5	6	11	10	9			2	7						8								25
1		3	4	5		11	10				2						6	8		9	7					26
1		3	8	5		11					2		6				4	10		9	7					27
1		3	4	5		11	8	10									6			9	7	2				28
1		3	4	5		11	8										6	10		9	7	2				29
1		3	4			11	8										6			9	7	2	5	10		30
1		3			5	11	4										6	8		9	7	2		10		31
1		2	4		5	11	8							3			6			9	7			10		32
1		3	4		5	11	8										6			9	7	2		10		33
1		2	4		5	11	8							3			6			9	7			10		34
1		3	4		5	11	9	8									6				7	2		10		35
1	2	3	4		5	11	9	8									6				7			10		36
1	2	3	4		5	11	9	8									6				7			10		37
1	2	3	4		5	11	9	8									6				7			10		38
1	2	3	4		5	11	9	8									6				7			10		39
1	2	3	4		5	11	9	8									6				7			10		40
1		3	4		5	11	9										6				7	2		10	8	41
1	2	3	4		5	11	9	10									6				7				8	42
42	21	40	39	28	36	42	41	33	8	3	13	4	7	4	2	4	22	15	7	12	17	7	1	12	2	
			4	1		5	12	16	2				3				1	1	6	7	1			3		

1 own-goal

Maddison G	Gibson J	Bell M	Swan C	Dixon S	Bleakley T	Taylor W	Martin G	Whitworth G	McLaughlin G	Brayson J	McGee J	Horne A	Lee P	Wilson G	Hart J	Campbell J	Sullivan N	Scott H	Cowan W	Guyan G	Wyper T	Lloyd C	Morris J	Howieson J	Alexander S	
1		3		5	6	11	7	10			2						4	8	9							3
1		3	4	5		11	10	9			2	7					6	8								4
1		3	4	5		11	7		10		2						6	8		9						R
1		3	4	5		11	7	10			2						6	8		9						2R
1		3	4	5		11	7	10			2						6	8		9						5
5		5	4	5	1	5	5	4	1		5	1					5	5	1	3						
							2	1										2	1	2						

1927-28

1	Aug	27	(a)	Barnsley	D 1-1	Guyan	10,830
2		29	(a)	Preston NE	L 2-4	Scott 2	21,811
3	Sep	3	(h)	Wolves	W 2-0	Scott, Taylor	11,050
4		5	(h)	Preston NE	D 0-0		8,915
5		10	(a)	Port Vale	W 2-1	Scott 2	12,169
6		17	(h)	South Shields	W 1-0	Martin	10,252
7		24	(a)	Leeds U	L 0-2		21,943
8	Oct	1	(h)	Nottingham F	W 2-0	Martin 2	8,274
9		8	(a)	Manchester C	L 1-2	Scott	42,038
10		15	(h)	Grimsby T	L 0-1		18,862
11		22	(a)	Chelsea	L 0-2		15,153
12		29	(h)	Blackpool	D 2-2	Nelson, Howieson	9,067
13	Nov	5	(a)	Reading	L 0-3		9,935
14		12	(h)	Clapton O	D 2-2	Martin 2	6,682
15		19	(a)	West Brom A	D 1-1	Sullivan	8,857
16		26	(h)	Southampton	W 1-0	Keeping (og)	8,081
17	Dec	3	(a)	Stoke C	L 1-3	Howieson	9,638
18		10	(h)	Bristol C	D 1-1	Martin	6,716
19		17	(a)	Notts C	D 1-1	Taylor	8,758
20		24	(h)	Oldham A	D 2-2	Nelson, Alexander	6,662
21		27	(h)	Fulham	W 3-2	Nelson 3	14,050
22		31	(h)	Barnsley	W 2-1	Alexander, Scott	9,569
23	Jan	7	(a)	Wolves	D 1-1	Nelson	12,106
24		21	(h)	Port Vale	W 1-0	Nelson	7,106
25	Feb	4	(h)	Leeds U	W 3-1	Martin 2, Wyper	12,520
26		11	(a)	Nottingham F	D 1-1	Swan	6,617
27		22	(a)	South Shields	L 0-1		4,322
28		25	(a)	Grimsby T	D 1-1	Guyan	15,986
29	Mar	3	(h)	Chelsea	L 0-2		12,679
30		10	(a)	Blackpool	L 1-2	Sullivan	9,988
31		17	(h)	Reading	L 0-1		6,493
32		24	(a)	Clapton O	D 0-0		8,869
33		26	(a)	Fulham	W 2-0	Nelson, Taylor	7,023
34		31	(h)	West Brom A	D 1-1	Howieson	7,964
35	Apr	6	(h)	Swansea T	L 0-2		8,877
36		7	(a)	Southampton	L 0-2		11,955
37		9	(a)	Swansea T	L 0-2		15,732
38		14	(h)	Stoke C	W 1-0	Howieson	4,848
39		16	(h)	Manchester C	D 0-0		6,088
40		21	(a)	Bristol C	W 1-0	Whitworth	10,198
41		28	(h)	Notts C	D 1-1	Whitworth	5,284
42	May	5	(a)	Oldham A	L 0-5		4,936

FINAL LEAGUE POSITION: 14th in Division Two

Appearances
Goals

FA Cup

3	Jan	14	(h)	Leicester C	L 0-1		23,141

Appearances
Goals

Maddison G	Gibson J	Bell M	Mooney P	Dixon S	Sullivan N	Wyper T	Scott H	Guyan G	Martin G	Taylor W	Wilson G	Starling R	Whitworth G	Bleakley T	Howieson J	Swan C	Nelson A	Crozier J	Watson J	Gibson F	Alexander S	Barraclough W	
1	2	3	4	5	6	7	8	9	10	11													1
1	2	3	4	5	6	7	8	9	10	11													2
1	2		4	5	6	7	8	9	10	11	3												3
1	2	3	4	5	6	7	8		10	11		9											4
1	2	3	4	5	6	7	8		10	11			9										5
1	2	3	4	5	6	7	8		10	11			9										6
1	2	3	4	5	6		8	9	7	11			10										7
1	2	3	4	5		7	8		9	11				6	10								8
1	2	3	4	5		7	8		9	11				6	10								9
1	2	3		5		7	8		9	11				6	10	4							10
1		2	4	5	6				8		3				10	7	9	11					11
1	2	3	4	5	6				8						10	7	9	11					12
1	2	3		5	4				8	11			9	6	10	7							13
1	2	3		8	4				9	11				6	10	7			5				14
1	2	3		8	4				9	11				6	10	7			5				15
1	2	3		8		7			9	11				6	10	4			5				16
	2	3				7			9	11		8		6	10	4			5	1			17
	2	3		8		7			9	11				6	10	4			5	1			18
	2	3		4					7	11				6	10		9		5	1	8		19
	2	3		4					7	11				6	10		9		5	1	8		20
	2	3		4					7	11				6	10		9		5	1	8		21
	2	3		4			8		7	11				6			9		5	1	10		22
1	2	3		4			8		7	11				6			9		5		10		23
1	2	3		4					7			10		6			9		5		8	11	24
1	2	3		5	4	7			10					6		8	9					11	25
1	2	3		5	4	7			10					6		8	9					11	26
1	2	3		5	4	7			10					6		8	9					11	27
1	2	3		5	4	7	8	9	10					6								11	28
1	2	3		5	4	7	8	9	10	11				6									29
1	2	3		5	4				8	11				6	10	7	9						30
1	2	3		5	4			9		11		8		6	10	7							31
1	2	3		5	4	7				11		8		6	10		9						32
1	2	3		5	4	7				11		8		6	10		9						33
1	2	3		5	4	7				11		8		6	10		9						34
1	2	3		5	4	7				11		8		6	10		9						35
1	2	3		5	4	7				11		8		6	10		9						36
1	2	3			4	7				11		8	9	6	10				5				37
1	2	3			4							8		6	10	7	9		5			11	38
1	2			5	4					7	3	8	9	6	10							11	39
1	2			5	4					7	3	8	9	6	10							11	40
1	2			5	4					7	3	8	9	6	10			11					41
1	2			5	4					7	3	8	9	6	10							11	42
36	41	37	11	39	30	23	14	7	30	34	6	15	9	33	27	15	18	3	13	6	6	9	
					2	1	7	2	8	3			2		4	1	8				2		

1 own goal

Maddison G	Gibson J	Bell M	Mooney P	Dixon S	Sullivan N	Wyper T	Scott H	Guyan G	Martin G	Taylor W	Wilson G	Starling R	Whitworth G	Bleakley T	Howieson J	Swan C	Nelson A	Crozier J	Watson J	Gibson F	Alexander S	Barraclough W	
1	2	3		4					7	11				6	10		9		5		8		3
1	1	1		1					1	1				1	1		1		1		1		

1928-29

1	Aug	25	(h)	Southampton	D 2-2	McDonald, Childs	11,232
2		27	(h)	Oldham A	W 1-0	Smith	7,468
3	Sep	1	(a)	Wolves	W 4-2	McDonald 3, Childs	18,230
4		3	(a)	Oldham A	W 1-0	McDonald	10,121
5		8	(h)	Notts C	D 1-1	McDonald	14,790
6		12	(a)	Middlesbrough	D 1-1	McDonald	15,998
7		15	(a)	Millwall	D 0-0		23,357
8		22	(h)	Port Vale	W 2-0	McDonald, Walsh	11,728
9		29	(a)	Grimsby T	W 1-0	Starling	17,048
10	Oct	6	(a)	Tottenham H	L 1-4	McDonald	28,737
11		13	(h)	Reading	W 3-0	Walsh 2, McDonald	12,657
12		20	(h)	Stoke C	L 1-3	Starling	11,919
13		27	(a)	Clapton O	W 2-0	McDonald, Walsh	9,496
14	Nov	3	(h)	West Brom A	W 4-1	McDonald, Walsh, Starling, Duncan	11,301
15		10	(a)	Bradford	L 1-5	Walsh	17,877
16		17	(h)	Bristol C	W 5-1	McDonald 5	8,545
17		24	(a)	Barnsley	D 2-2	McDonald 2	4,693
18	Dec	1	(h)	Chelsea	D 2-2	McDonald, Walsh	16,925
19		8	(a)	Blackpool	L 1-2	Duncan	9,033
20		15	(h)	Swansea T	D 1-1	Walsh	10,702
21		22	(a)	Nottingham F	L 1-3	Starling	6,758
22		25	(h)	Preston NE	W 5-1	McDonald 2, Alexander, Taylor, Smith	17,254
23		26	(a)	Preston NE	L 0-1		26,706
24		29	(a)	Southampton	L 2-3	Weaver, Dixon	18,384
25	Jan	5	(h)	Wolves	L 1-3	Childs	8,232
26		19	(a)	Notts C	L 0-6		13,271
27	Feb	2	(a)	Port Vale	L 1-4	Walsh	6,065
28		9	(h)	Grimsby T	L 2-3	Starling, Weaver	10,453
29		23	(a)	Reading	L 0-3		7,502
30	Mar	2	(a)	Stoke C	D 1-1	Taylor	10,925
31		9	(h)	Clapton O	D 0-0		7,916
32		16	(a)	West Brom A	L 0-2		7,952
33		23	(h)	Bradford	W 1-0	Taylor	6,980
34		30	(a)	Bristol C	D 0-0		15,426
35	Apr	1	(h)	Middlesbrough	D 1-1	Wilson	19,740
36		6	(h)	Barnsley	D 0-0		6,977
37		13	(a)	Chelsea	D 0-0		9,654
38		15	(h)	Tottenham H	D 1-1	Weaver	4,139
39		20	(h)	Blackpool	L 1-3	Weaver	4,945
40		22	(h)	Millwall	W 4-0	Starling 3, Duncan	3,164
41		27	(a)	Swansea T	W 1-0	McDonald	11,242
42	May	4	(h)	Nottingham F	L 0-1		4,294

FINAL LEAGUE POSITION: 12th in Division Two

Appearances
Goals

FA Cup

3	Jan	12	(h)	Bradford	D 1-1	McDonald	23,000
R		16	(a)	Bradford	L 1-3	McDonald	21,072

Appearances
Goals

Maddison G	Gibson J	Bell M	Dixon S	Childs A	Sullivan N	Taylor W	Walsh J	McDonald K	Smith S	Prince A	Wilson G	Weaver S	Bleakley T	Duncan D	Swan C	Starling R	Hedley F	Gibson F	Alexander S	Murray J	Goldsmith G	Nelson A	Watson J	Turner A	Rodgers A	Vickers J	
1	2	3	4	5	6	7	8	9	10	11																	1
1	2		4	5	6	7	8	9	10	11	3																2
1	2			5		7	8	9	10	11	3	4	6														3
1	2			5		7	8	9	10		3	4	6	11													4
1	2	3		5		7	8	9	10	11		4	6														5
1	2	3		5		7	8	9	10	11		4	6														6
1	2	3		5		11	8	9	10			4	6		7												7
1	2	3		5		7	8	9	10			4	6	11													8
1	2	3		5		7	8	9				4	6	11		10											9
1	2	3		5		7	8	9				4	6	11		10											10
1	2	3		5		7	8	9				4	6			10	11										11
1	2	3		5		7	8	9				4	6			10	11										12
1	2	3	4	5		7	8	9				6		11		10											13
1	2	3	4	5		7	8	9				6		11		10											14
1	2	3	4	5		7	8	9				6		11		10											15
	2	3	5		4		8	9				6		11		10		1	7								16
	2	3	5		4		8	9				6		11		10		1	7								17
	2	3	5		4		8	9				6		11		10		1	7								18
1	2	3	5		4		8	9				6		11		10			7								19
1	2	3	5		4		8	9				6		11		10			7								20
1	2	3	5		4			9				6		11		8			7	10							21
1	2	3	4	5		11		9	10			6				8			7								22
1	2	3	5			11		9	10			6	4			8			7								23
1		3	8	5	4	11		9				10	6		7						2						24
1		3		5	4	11		9				10	6		8				7		2						25
1		3	8	5		11			10			4	6						7		2	9					26
1	2	3				11	10	9				4	6			8			7				5				27
1	2	3				11	10	9				4	6			8			7				5				28
1	2	3				11	10	9				6	4			8			7				5				29
1	2		5		4	11	10				3		6			8			7			9					30
1	2		5		4	7	10				3		6			8						9		11			31
1		2	5		4	7	8	9			3		6			10								11			32
1		2	4			7	9				3	10	6	11		8							5				33
1		2	4			7	9				3	10	6	11		8							5				34
1		2	4			7	9				3	10	6	11		8							5				35
1			4			7	9				3	10	6	11		8					2		5				36
1		2	4			7	8				3	10	6	11		9							5				37
		2	4			7	8				3	10	6			9		1					5	11			38
		2	4	5		7	8				3	10	6	11		9		1									39
		2	5			7		9	10		3	4	6	11		8		1									40
		2	5			11		9	10			6				8		1	7						3	4	41
		3		5		11		9	10			6				8		1	7		2					4	42
34	28	36	27	21	13	36	33	32	14	5	14	37	28	20	3	31	2	8	16	1	5	3	9	3	1	2	
			1	3		3	9	23	2		1	4		3		8			1								

Maddison G	Gibson J	Bell M	Dixon S	Childs A	Sullivan N	Taylor W	Walsh J	McDonald K	Smith S	Prince A	Wilson G	Weaver S	Bleakley T	Duncan D	Swan C	Starling R	Hedley F	Gibson F	Alexander S	Murray J	Goldsmith G	Nelson A	Watson J	Turner A	Rodgers A	Vickers J	
1		3	4	5		11		9				10	6			8			7		2						3
1		3	4	5		11		9				10	6			8			7		2						R
2		2	2	2		2		2				2	2			2			2		2						
								2																			

1929-30

1	Aug	31	(h)	Swansea T	W 1-0	McDonald	10,06
2	Sep	2	(a)	Southampton	D 2-2	Starling, Turner	11,38
3		7	(a)	Cardiff C	W 1-0	McDonald	12,66
4		14	(h)	Preston NE	W 2-0	McDonald, Weaver	10,23
5		16	(h)	Southampton	W 2-0	McDonald, Howieson	7,11
6		21	(a)	Bristol C	L 0-4		13,1
7		23	(a)	Wolves	L 2-4	McDonald, Howieson	9,14
8		28	(h)	Notts C	D 0-0		8,68
9	Oct	5	(a)	Reading	D 1-1	Alexander	15,31
10		12	(h)	Charlton A	L 0-2		9,32
11		19	(h)	Millwall	W 3-2	Alexander 2, Starling	6,40
12		26	(a)	Oldham A	L 1-3	Childs	13,56
13	Nov	2	(h)	Nottingham F	L 1-2	Alexander	6,18
14		9	(a)	Chelsea	L 0-3		23,4
15		16	(h)	Bury	L 1-3	Alexander	4,86
16		23	(a)	Blackpool	W 2-1	Duncan 2	10,3
17		30	(h)	Barnsley	W 2-0	Duncan, Childs	5,7
18	Dec	7	(a)	Bradford	L 2-4	Starling, Taylor	6,9
19		14	(h)	West Brom A	W 3-2	Alexander 2, Taylor	4,9
20		21	(a)	Tottenham H	D 2-2	Duncan, Taylor	9,1
21		25	(h)	Stoke C	W 3-0	Starling, Duncan, Howieson	10,6
22		26	(a)	Stoke C	L 1-3	Alexander	17,8
23		28	(a)	Swansea T	L 0-2		4,5
24	Jan	4	(h)	Cardiff C	D 2-2	Alexander, Taylor	11,6
25		18	(a)	Preston NE	W 2-1	McDonald, Kerr (og)	13,3
26	Feb	1	(a)	Notts C	L 1-4	Duncan	11,7
27		8	(h)	Reading	W 4-2	Alexander 2, Howieson, Childs	7,5
28		22	(a)	Millwall	D 0-0		17,5
29	Mar	8	(a)	Nottingham F	L 1-2	Howieson	11,3
30		15	(h)	Chelsea	L 1-3	Starling	4,8
31		17	(a)	Charlton A	L 0-4		5,9
32		29	(h)	Blackpool	L 0-3		10,1
33		31	(h)	Oldham A	W 1-0	Murray	5,4
34	Apr	5	(a)	Barnsley	L 0-3		6,2
35		12	(h)	Bradford	L 0-2		5,5
36		18	(h)	Bradford C	D 0-0		8,9
37		19	(a)	West Brom A	L 1-7	Mills	6,9
38		21	(a)	Bradford C	L 1-2	Duncan	14,2
39		23	(a)	Bury	L 1-2	Dixon	4,6
40		26	(h)	Tottenham H	W 2-0	Mills, Alexander	6,
41	May	1	(h)	Bristol C	L 0-1		10,
42		3	(h)	Wolves	W 2-0	Alexander 2	8,

FINAL LEAGUE POSITION: 21st in Division Two — Relegated | Appearance
Note: Match 32 was benefit match for Matt Bell, Tommy Bleakley and George Maddison. | Goals

FA Cup

3	Jan	11	(a)	Plymouth A	W 4-3	Alexander 3, Duncan	28,
4		25	(h)	Blackpool	W 3-1	Alexander, Starling, Mills	23,
5	Feb	15	(a)	Manchester C	W 2-1	Taylor, Mills	61,
6	Mar	1	(a)	Newcastle U	D 1-1	Alexander	63,
R		6	(h)	Newcastle U	W 1-0	Howieson	32,
SF		22	(n*)	Arsenal	D 2-2	Howieson, Duncan	47,
R		26	(n†)	Arsenal	L 0-1		46,

*Played at Elland Road, Leeds. †Played at Villa Park, Birmingham. | Appearance
Goals

Maddison G	Goldsmith G	Bell M	Bleakley T	Childs A	Weaver S	Cartwright P	Starling R	McDonald K	Howieson J	Turner A	Gibson F	Walsh J	Gowdy W	Rodgers A	Taylor W	Watson J	Alexander S	Duncan D	Bradford B	Dixon S	March H	Mills B	Fawcett R	Wilson G	Williams E	Murray J	Surrey T	Flannigan T	
1	2	3	4	5	6	7	8	9	10	11																			1
1	2	3	4	5	6	7	8	9	10	11																			2
	2	3	4	5	6	7		9	10	11	1	8																	3
	2	3	4	5	6	7	8	9	10	11	1																		4
	2	3	6	5	4	7	8	9	10	11	1																		5
	2	3	6	5		7	8	9	10	11	1		4																6
	2		6	5				9	10	11	1	8	4	3	7														7
1	2		6	5		7			10	11		8		3		4	9												8
1	2		6	5		7			10			8		3		4	9	11											9
1	2		6	5		7			10			8		3		4	9	11											10
1	2	3		5	6	7	8		10						11	4	9												11
1	3		6	5	10	7	8					2			11	4	9												12
1	2		6	5	4	7	8		10						11		9		3										13
1	2	3		5	10		8	9					6		11	4	7												14
1	2	3			6	7	8								11	4	9			5	10								15
	2	3		5	4		8		10		1	6			7		9	11											16
	2			5			8		10		1	4	6	3	7		9	11											17
	2	3		5			8		10		1	4	6		7		9	11											18
	2	3		5			8		10		1	4	6		7		9	11											19
	2	3		5			8		10		1	4	6		7		9	11											20
	2	3		5			8		10		1	4	6		7		9	11											21
	2	3		5			8		10		1	4	6		7		9	11											22
	2	3		5			8				1	4	6		7		9	11			10								23
1	2	3		5					10			4	6		7		8	11				9							24
	2	3					10	9			1	4	6		7	5	8	11											25
	2	3		5			10				1	4	6		7		8	11				9							26
	2			5					10		1	4	6	3	7		8	11				9							27
	2						8				1	4	6	3	7	5	9	11			10								28
	2		6				8		10	11	1	4		3		5	9						7						29
	2	3		5			8		10	11	1	4	6				9						7						30
				5			10				1		6	2		4	8						7	3	9	11			31
		3	6	5		7	8		10		1			2		4		11									9		32
		3	6	5		7	9		10		1			2		4										11		8	33
		3		5		7	8				1		6	2		4					9					11		10	34
	2	3	5				8				1		6		7	4		11			10	9							35
	2	3				7			10		1	4	6			5		11			8	9							36
	2	3				7	8				1	4	6			5		11			10	9							37
		2	4			7	8				1		6			5		11			10	9		3					38
		3	4			7	8			10	1			2		5		11		9						6			39
1	2								10				6	3	7	5	8	11		4		9							40
1	2	3							10				6		7	5	8	11		4		9							41
1	2						10						6	3	7	5	8	11		4		9							42
14	36	29	18	30	11	20	32	9	28	11	28	23	25	15	23	22	27	24	1	5	8	10	3	2	1	4	1	2	
				3	1		5	6	5	1					4		14	7		1		2				1			

1 own goal

Maddison G	Goldsmith G	Bell M	Bleakley T	Childs A	Weaver S	Cartwright P	Starling R	McDonald K	Howieson J	Turner A	Gibson F	Walsh J	Gowdy W	Rodgers A	Taylor W	Watson J	Alexander S	Duncan D	Bradford B	Dixon S	March H	Mills B	Fawcett R	Wilson G	Williams E	Murray J	Surrey T	Flannigan T	
	2	3		5					10		1	4	6		7		8	11				9							3
	2	3		5			10				1	4	6		7		8	11				9							4
	2			5			10		3		1	4	6		7		8	11				9							5
	2	3		5			8		10		1	4	6		7		9	11											6
	2	3		5			8		10		1	4	6		7		9	11											R
	2	3		5			8		10		1	4	6				7	11				9							SF
	2	3	4	5		7	8		10		1		6					11				9							R
	7	6	1	7		1	6		6		7	6	7		5		6	7				5							
							1		2						1		5	2				2							

1930-31

1	Aug	30	(a)	Stockport C	L 2-3	Mills, Gowdy	12,09
2	Sep	2	(a)	Nelson	W 2-0	Alexander, Fairhurst (og)	5,12
3		6	(h)	Gateshead	W 4-0	Mills 2, D.Duncan, Weldon	8,64
4		10	(a)	Darlington	W 4-2	Mills, Weldon, D.Duncan, Childs	5,34
5		13	(a)	Doncaster R	W 2-0	Mills, D.Duncan	6,23
6		15	(h)	Darlington	D 1-1	Taylor	7,42
7		20	(h)	Chesterfield	W 3-1	Alexander, Weldon, Taylor	7,93
8		27	(h)	Lincoln C	L 1-3	Childs	12,63
9	Oct	4	(a)	Hartlepools U	W 3-1	Alexander 3	6,99
10		11	(h)	Wigan B	D 0-0		9,33
11		18	(a)	Barrow	L 0-3		5,59
12		25	(h)	Rotherham U	D 2-2	Alexander, D.Duncan	5,80
13	Nov	1	(a)	Accrington S	W 3-1	Longden, Alexander, Turner	2,73
14		8	(h)	Rochdale	W 3-1	Alexander 2, Barber (og)	7,7
15		15	(a)	Crewe A	W 4-3	Alexander 3, Davin	4,94
16		22	(h)	Wrexham	L 2-3	D.Duncan 2	8,2
17	Dec	6	(h)	Carlisle U	D 1-1	Longden	6,1
18		13	(a)	Tranmere R	L 0-4		5,69
19		20	(h)	Southport	W 5-1	Alexander 2, D.Duncan 2, Longden	5,6
20		25	(a)	Halifax T	D 1-1	Raleigh	7,49
21		26	(h)	Halifax T	W 10-0	Raleigh 5, Longden 2, D.Duncan 2, Alexander	4,0
22		27	(h)	Stockport C	D 1-1	Raleigh	9,5
23	Jan	3	(a)	Gateshead	L 0-1		7,4
24		17	(h)	Doncaster R	W 8-2	Raleigh 3, Longden 2, Alexander 2, D.Duncan	5,5
25		24	(a)	Chesterfield	W 4-0	D.Duncan, Raleigh, Alexander, Weldon	7,7
26		31	(a)	Lincoln C	L 0-3		9,7
27	Feb	14	(a)	Wigan B	L 1-3	Raleigh	4,9
28		21	(h)	Barrow	D 1-1	Speed	6,0
29	Mar	7	(h)	Accrington S	D 1-1	D.Duncan	2,8
30		14	(a)	Rochdale	L 0-1		3,4
31		18	(a)	York C	L 2-3	Alexander, Speed	3,5
32		21	(h)	Crewe A	W 5-1	Raleigh 2, Alexander 2, Sharpe (og)	4,3
33		28	(a)	Wrexham	L 0-2		4,7
34	Apr	3	(a)	New Brighton	D 1-1	D.Duncan	4,5
35		4	(h)	Tranmere R	W 1-0	Mills	7,5
36		6	(h)	New Brighton	W 3-0	A.Duncan 2, Alexander	5,8
37		11	(a)	Carlisle U	W 5-1	Mills 3, D.Duncan 2	4,5
38		18	(h)	York C	W 3-1	Mills, Weldon, A.Duncan	4,4
39		20	(h)	Hartlepools U	W 5-0	Mills 2, Weldon, Alexander, A.Duncan	3,2
40		25	(a)	Southport	L 0-1		2,8
41		27	(a)	Rotherham U	D 1-1	Raleigh	2,7
42	May	2	(h)	Nelson	W 4-0	D.Duncan 2, Speed, Alexander	4,5

FINAL LEAGUE POSITION: 6th in Division Three North

Appearances
Goals

FA Cup

3	Jan	10	(h)	Blackpool	L 1-2	D.Duncan	17,0

Appearances
Goals

Maddison G	Goldsmith G	Bell M	Walsh J	Childs A	Gowdy W	Taylor W	Alexander S	Mills B	Weldon A	Duncan D	Rodgers A	Murray J	Harris A	Watson J	Raleigh S	Turner A	Cooke A	Longden E	Davin M	Gibson F	Fawcett R	Woodhead C	Speed F	Jobson J	Wright F	Wilson G	Duncan A	
1	2	3	4	5	6	7	8	9	10	11																		1
1	2		4	5	6	7	8	9	10	11	3																	2
1	2	3	4	5	6	7	8	9	10	11																		3
1		3	4	5		7	8	9	10	11	2	6																4
1	2	3	4	5	6	7	8	9		11		10																5
1	2	3	4	5	6	7	8	9		11		10																6
1	2	3	4	5	6	7	8	9	10	11																		7
1	2	3	4	5	6		8	9	10	11			7															8
1	2	3		5			9	6	10	11			7	4	8													9
1	2	3		5			9	6	10	11			7	4	8													10
1	2	3		5	6		9		10	11			7	4	8													11
1	2		8	5	4		9		10	11	3		7			6												12
1	2	3			4	7	9			11		6				10	5	8										13
1	2	3			4	7	9	6		11							5	10	8									14
1	2	3			4	7	9	6		11							5	10	8									15
1	2	3			4		9	6	7	11							5	10	8									16
	2	3			4		9	6		11							5	10	8	1	7							17
	2	3	4	5			7	6	9	11								10	8	1								18
		3	4	5			7	6	10	11					9			8		1		2						19
	2	3	4	5			7	6	10	11					9			8		1								20
	2		4	5	6		7		10	11	3				9			8		1								21
	2		4	5	6		7			11	3				9			8	10	1								22
	2		4	5	6	7			10	11	3				9			8		1								23
		3	4	5			7		10	11	2	6			9			8		1								24
	2	3		5	4		7		10	11		6			9			8		1								25
	2	3		5	4	7	9		10	11		6						8		1								26
1	2			5	4	11	7	6	10		3				9				8									27
1	2	3		5	4	7	8	6	10														9	11				28
1	2	3			4		8	6	10	11							5						9	7				29
1	2	3			4		8		10	11		6					5				7		9					30
1	2	3			4		8	6		11						10	5				7		9					31
1					4		7	6	8	11					9	10	5								2	3		32
1			4		6		7		10	11	3				9		5								2		8	33
1	2		6		4		7	10		11	3				9		5										8	34
	2		6		4	7	8	9		11	3	10					5			1								35
	2		4			7	9	6	10	11	3						5			1							8	36
	2		6		4	7	8	9	10	11	3						5			1								37
	2		6		4		7	9	10	11	3						5			1							8	38
	2		6		4		7	9	10	11	3						5			1							8	39
	2		6		4		7	9	10	11	3						5			1							8	40
	2		6				7			11	3				9	10	5		4	1							8	41
	2		6		4		7	8	10	11	3						5			1			9				'	42
24	37	25	26	23	33	17	41	30	31	40	18	9	5	3	15	5	19	14	8	18	3	1	5	2	2	1	7	
				2	1	2	24	12	6	18					15	1		7	1				3				4	

3 own-goals

Maddison G	Goldsmith G	Bell M	Walsh J	Childs A	Gowdy W	Taylor W	Alexander S	Mills B	Weldon A	Duncan D	Rodgers A	Murray J	Harris A	Watson J	Raleigh S	Turner A	Cooke A	Longden E	Davin M	Gibson F	Fawcett R	Woodhead C	Speed F	Jobson J	Wright F	Wilson G	Duncan A	
	2	3	4	5	6		7		10	11					9			8		1								3
	1	1	1	1	1		1		1	1					1			1		1								
										1																		

1931-32

1	Aug	29	(h)	Halifax T	W 1-0	Raleigh	8,50
2	Sep	5	(a)	Walsall	W 4-1	D.Duncan 2, Raleigh, Barley	3,65
3		7	(h)	Darlington	W 4-1	Raleigh 2, D.Duncan, Munnings	5,36
4		12	(h)	Gateshead	L 0-1		9,49
5		16	(a)	Darlington	L 1-2	D.Duncan	3,72
6		19	(a)	New Brighton	W 2-1	D.Duncan 2	3,02
7		26	(h)	Barrow	W 3-0	D.Duncan 2, Raleigh	6,99
8	Oct	3	(a)	Stockport C	L 0-2		4,81
9		10	(a)	Lincoln C	L 0-1		9,49
10		17	(h)	Rotherham U	L 0-1		6,64
11		24	(a)	Tranmere R	D 2-2	Speed 2	5,41
12		31	(h)	York C	L 2-3	Speed 2	7,15
13	Nov	7	(a)	Southport	L 0-1		4,85
14		14	(h)	Doncaster R	W 4-1	Wainscoat 2, Speed, D.Duncan	5,17
15		21	(a)	Rochdale	W 6-3	D.Duncan 2, Wainscoat, A.Duncan, Speed, Munnings	4,59
16	Dec	5	(a)	Carlisle U	W 1-0	Speed	4,67
17		19	(a)	Accrington S	D 1-1	Wainscoat	3,67
18		25	(h)	Hartlepools U	W 3-1	Wainscoat 2, Speed	13,06
19		26	(a)	Hartlepools U	W 3-2	D.Duncan 2, Wainscoat	5,89
20	Jan	2	(a)	Halifax T	D 2-2	Wainscoat, Munnings	4,16
21		14	(h)	Crewe A	L 2-4	Speed, Wainscoat	5,23
22		16	(h)	Walsall	W 3-0	Mills 3	6,28
23		23	(a)	Gateshead	L 1-2	Mills	4,49
24		30	(h)	New Brighton	W 4-1	Wainscoat, Mills, Hill, D.Duncan	5,91
25	Feb	6	(a)	Barrow	W 2-0	D.Duncan, Raleigh	7,25
26		13	(h)	Stockport C	D 4-4	Wainscoat 3, D.Duncan	6,14
27		20	(h)	Lincoln C	W 4-1	D.Duncan 2, A.Duncan, Wainscoat	13,60
28		27	(a)	Rotherham U	L 0-2		4,03
29	Mar	5	(h)	Tranmere R	W 3-0	Mills 2, D.Duncan	7,45
30		12	(a)	York C	D 0-0		5,01
31		19	(h)	Southport	W 1-0	Allen	6,20
32		25	(a)	Chester	L 0-2		13,64
33		26	(a)	Doncaster R	L 1-2	Mills	4,63
34		28	(h)	Chester	L 0-2		7,91
35	Apr	2	(h)	Rochdale	W 4-1	Mills 2, Munnings 2	3,61
36		9	(a)	Crewe A	L 3-4	Wainscoat, Speed, Shelton	4,53
37		16	(h)	Carlisle U	W 2-0	Munnings, Downes	2,39
38		23	(a)	Wrexham	L 1-2	Brown (og)	2,47
39		30	(h)	Accrington S	W 3-0	Wainscoat, Munnings, Downes	3,53
40	May	7	(h)	Wrexham	W 5-0	Speed 2, Downes, Barley, Mills	3,19

FINAL LEAGUE POSITION: 8th in Division Three North

Appearances
Goals

FA Cup

1	Nov	28	(h)	Mansfield T	W 4-1	Wainscoat 2, Speed, Munnings	10,00
2	Dec	12	(a)	New Brighton	W 4-0	Speed 2, Wainscoat, Munnings	5,00
3	Jan	9	(a)	Stoke C	L 0-3		22,18

Appearances
Goals

Gibson F	Goldsmith G	Rodgers A	Newton W	Wrack C	Gowdy W	Barley H	Alexander S	Raleigh S	Duncan A	Duncan D	Woodhead C	Cooke A	Mills B	Munnings E	Havelock H	Diamond J	Thompson J	Speed F	Wainscoat R	Maddison G	Hill J	Turner R	Downes P	Allen M	Shelton T	
1	2	3	4	5	6	7	8	9	10	11																1
1		2			4	7		9	8	10	3	5	6	11												2
1		3				7		9	8	10	2	5	6	11	4											3
1		3				7		9	8	10	2	5	6	11	4											4
1		3			4	7		9	8	11	2	5	6		10											5
1	4	3				7	8	9		10	2	5	6	11												6
1		3			4	7		10		11	2	5	6	8		9										7
1		3	4		8	7		9		10	2	5	6	11												8
1		3	4		6	7	8			11	2	5	10				9									9
1		3	4		6	7	8	9		11	2	5	10													10
1		3	4					8	10	11	2	5	6	7				9								11
1		3	4			7		8			2	5	6	11				9	10							12
1		3	4				7		8	11	2	5	6					9	10							13
1		3	4	5			7		8	11	2		6					9	10							14
		3	4						8	11	2		6	7				9	10	1	5					15
		3	4						8	11	2		6	7				9	10	1	5					16
	2	3	4			7			8	11			6					9	10	1	5					17
	2	3	4						8	11			6	7				9	10	1	5					18
	2	3	4						8	11			6	7				9	10	1	5					19
	2	3	4						8	11			6	7				9	10	1	5					20
1	2	3	4						8	11			6	7				9	10		5					21
1		3							8	11	2	4	9	7				6	10		5					22
1		3						7	8		2	4	9	11				6	10		5					23
1		3	4						8	11	2		9	7				6	10		5					24
1		3						9	8	11	2			7				6	10		5	4				25
1		3						9	8	11	2		4	7				6	10		5					26
1		3	4						8	11	2		9	7				6	10		5					27
1		3	4						8	11	2		9	7				6	10		5					28
1	2		4						8	11	3		9	7				6	10		5					29
1	2		4						8		3		9	7				6	10		5		11			30
1	2		4								3		9	7				6	10		5		11	8		31
1	2		4								3		9	7				6	10		5		11	8		32
1	2							9			3		4	7				6	10		5		11	8		33
1	2		4	5				9			3		7					6	10				11	8		34
1	2										3	4	9	7				6	10		5		11	8		35
1	2										3	4		7				6	10		5		11	8	9	36
1	2	3											4	7				6	10		5		11	8	9	37
1	2	3											4	7				6	10		5		11	8	9	38
1	2										3		4	7				6	10		5		11	8	9	39
1	2		4			7					3		6					10	9		5		11	8		40
34	19	30	24	3	7	13	6	16	24	27	32	16	37	31	3	1	1	30	29	6	25	1	11	10	4	
						2		6	2	19			11	7				12	16		1		3	1	1	

1 own-goal

Gibson F	Goldsmith G	Rodgers A	Newton W	Wrack C	Gowdy W	Barley H	Alexander S	Raleigh S	Duncan A	Duncan D	Woodhead C	Cooke A	Mills B	Munnings E	Havelock H	Diamond J	Thompson J	Speed F	Wainscoat R	Maddison G	Hill J	Turner R	Downes P	Allen M	Shelton T	
		3	4	5					8	11	2		6	7				9	10	1						1
		3	4						8	11	2		6	7				9	10	1	5					2
1	2	3	4					8		11			6	7				9	10		5					3
1	1	3	3	1				1	2	3	2		3	3				3	3	2	2					
														2				3	3							

1932-33

1	Aug	27	(a)	Walsall	L 0-1		7,067
2		29	(h)	Wrexham	W 4-1	Duncan 2, Wainscoat, Sargeant	7,467
3	Sep	3	(h)	Gateshead	D 1-1	Wainscoat	10,204
4		7	(a)	Wrexham	L 1-3	McNaughton	7,034
5		10	(a)	Stockport C	W 5-3	Wainscoat 2, McNaughton, Forward, Gardner	7,009
6		17	(h)	Darlington	W 3-1	Wainscoat 2, McNaughton	8,147
7		24	(a)	Doncaster R	D 1-1	Sargeant	5,882
8	Oct	1	(h)	Southport	W 4-0	McNaughton 3, Sargeant	6,061
9		8	(h)	Barnsley	W 5-1	McNaughton 4, Sargeant	7,857
10		15	(a)	Hartlepools U	W 1-0	Sargeant	4,55
11		22	(a)	Mansfield T	L 1-2	McNaughton	8,43
12		29	(h)	Rotherham U	W 4-2	McNaughton, Wainscoat, Forward, Duncan	7,99
13	Nov	5	(a)	Accrington S	W 2-1	Duncan, Sargeant	4,47
14		12	(h)	New Brighton	W 5-0	Wainscoat 3, McNaughton 2	6,79
15		19	(a)	Chester	D 1-1	Wainscoat	10,06
16	Dec	3	(a)	Carlisle U	D 1-1	McNaughton	4,07
17		17	(a)	Crewe A	D 1-1	Jordan	4,94
18		24	(h)	Rochdale	D 1-1	Wainscoat	10,88
19		26	(h)	Halifax T	W 3-1	Sargeant 2, McNaughton	15,19
20		27	(a)	Halifax T	W 3-1	McNaughton 2, Longden	9,31
21		31	(h)	Walsall	D 0-0		9,80
22	Jan	7	(a)	Gateshead	W 3-2	McNaughton 2, Sargeant	7,72
23		19	(h)	Barrow	W 3-0	Duncan, Forward, Sargeant	4,63
24		21	(h)	Stockport C	W 3-0	McNaughton 2, Duncan	8,88
25	Feb	1	(a)	Darlington	L 2-3	McNaughton, Fielden (og)	2,21
26		4	(h)	Doncaster R	W 6-1	Duncan 3, McNaughton 2, Sargeant	7,98
27		11	(a)	Southport	W 1-0	McNaughton	4,74
28		18	(a)	Barnsley	L 0-1		7,36
29		25	(h)	Hartlepools U	W 3-0	McNaughton 2, Wainscoat	5,32
30	Mar	4	(h)	Mansfield T	W 4-1	McNaughton 3, Wainscoat	8,63
31		11	(a)	Rotherham U	L 2-3	Longden, Bullock	6,86
32		18	(h)	Accrington S	W 4-2	Wainscoat 2, McNaughton, Bullock	9,70
33		25	(a)	New Brighton	L 0-1		4,37
34	Apr	1	(h)	Chester	W 2-0	Wainscoat, Forward	20,24
35		8	(a)	Barrow	W 2-0	McNaughton, Wainscoat	5,14
36		14	(a)	Tranmere R	L 0-2		11,01
37		15	(h)	Carlisle U	W 6-1	Sargeant 2, McNaughton, Forward, Wainscoat, Gomm (og)	12,02
38		17	(h)	Tranmere R	W 3-0	McNaughton 2, Wainscoat	16,1
39		22	(a)	York C	W 2-1	Wainscoat, Forward	8,67
40		29	(h)	Crewe A	W 3-0	McNaughton, Longden, Hill	8,83
41	May	1	(h)	York C	W 2-1	McNaughton 2	19,2
42		6	(a)	Rochdale	L 2-3	McNaughton 2	4,38

FINAL LEAGUE POSITION: 1st in Division Three North Promoted

Appearances
Goals

FA Cup

1	Nov	26	(a)	Stalybridge	W 8-2	Wainscoat 4, McNaughton, Forward, Sargeant, Hill	6,6
2	Dec	10	(a)	Carlisle U	D 1-1	Sargeant	10,3
R		15	(h)	Carlisle U	W 2-1*	Wainscoat, Forward	12,0
3	Jan	14	(h)	Sunderland	L 0-2		22,5

*After extra-time

Appearances
Goals

Gibson F	Woodhead C	Rodgers A	Mills B	Hill J	Speed F	Stott G	Duncan A	McNaughton W	Wainscoat R	Sargeant C	Bell W	Gardner T	Forward F	Maddison G	Goldsmith G	Denby S	Jordan D	Longden E	Allen M	Bullock A	Ainsworth E	
1	2	3	4	5	6	7	8	9	10	11												1
1	2	3	4	5	6	7	8	9	10	11												2
1	2	3	4	5	6	7	8	9	10	11												3
1	3		6	5		7		9	10	11	2	4	8									4
1	3		6	5			8	9	10	11	2	4	7									5
1	3		6	5			8	9	10	11	2	4	7									6
1	3		6	5	8			9	10	11	2	4	7									7
	3			5			8	9	10	11		4	7	1	2	6						8
	3			5			8	9	10	11		4	7	1	2	6						9
	3			5			8	9	10	11		4	7	1	2	6						10
	3			5	6		8	9	10	11		4	7	1	2							11
	3			5	6		8	9	10	11		4	7	1	2							12
	3			5	6		8	9	10	11		4	7	1	2							13
	3			5			8	9	10	11		4	7	1	2	6						14
	3			5			8	9	10	11		4	7	1	2	6						15
	3			5	10		8	9		11		4	7	1	2	6						16
	3		6	5			8		10	11		4	7	1	2		9					17
	3			5				9	10	11		4	7	1	2	6		8				18
	3			5				9		11		4	7	1	2	6		8	10			19
	3		6	5				9	10	11		4	7	1	2			8				20
	3		6	5				9	10	11		4	7	1	2			8				21
	3		10				8	9		11		4	7	1	2	6		5				22
	3		10				8	9		11		4	7	1	2	6		5				23
	3		10				8	9		11		4	7	1	2	6		5				24
	3						8	9	10	11		4	7	1	2	6		5				25
	3			5			8	9		11		4	7	1	2	6		10				26
	3			5			8	9		11		4	7	1	2	6		10				27
	3			5			8	9	10	11		4	7	1	2			6				28
	3			5			8	9	10	11		4	7	1	2			6				29
	3			5			8	9	10			4	7	1	2			6		11		30
	3			5			8	9	10			4	7	1	2			6		11		31
	3			5			8	9	10			4	7	1	2			6		11		32
	3			5			8	9	10	11		4	7	1	2			6				33
	3		4	5				9	10	11		8	7	1	2	6						34
	3		4		5			9	10	11		8	7	1	2	6						35
	3		8		5			9	10	11		4	7	1	2	6						36
	3		8	5				9	10	11		4	7	1	2	6						37
	3		8	5				9	10	11		4	7	1	2	6						38
	3		8	5				9	10	11		4	7	1	2	6						39
	3			5				9	10	11		4	7	1	2	6		8				40
	3			5				9	10	11		4	7	1	2	6		8				41
	3			5			8	9		11		4	7		2	6		10			1	42
7	42	3	19	36	10	4	28	41	34	39	4	39	39	34	35	23	1	19	1	3	1	
				1			9	41	21	13		1	6				1	3		2		

2 own-goals

Gibson F	Woodhead C	Rodgers A	Mills B	Hill J	Speed F	Stott G	Duncan A	McNaughton W	Wainscoat R	Sargeant C	Bell W	Gardner T	Forward F	Maddison G	Goldsmith G	Denby S	Jordan D	Longden E	Allen M	Bullock A	Ainsworth E	
	3			5			8	9	10	11		4	7	1	2	6						1
	3		6	5			8	9	10	11		4	7	1	2							2
	3		6	5			8	9	10	11		4	7	1	2							R
	3		10				8	9		11		4	7	1	2	6		5				3
	4		3	3			4	4	3	4		4	4	4	4	2		1				
				1				1	5	2			2									

1933-34

1	Aug	26	(h)	Notts C	L 0-1		13,4
2		30	(a)	Bradford C	W 2-1	McNaughton, Wainscoat	14,5
3	Sep	2	(a)	Swansea T	D 1-1	McNaughton	9,7
4		9	(h)	Millwall	W 3-2	McNaughton, Wainscoat, Sargeant	11,6
5		11	(h)	Bradford C	D 2-2	McNaughton, Denby	11,3
6		16	(a)	Lincoln C	L 1-2	McNaughton	8,8
7		23	(h)	Bury	W 3-1	McNaughton 2, Duncan	11,2
8		30	(a)	Brentford	D 2-2	Duncan, Sargeant	14,5
9	Oct	7	(a)	Fulham	D 1-1	McNaughton	22,8
10		14	(h)	Southampton	W 1-0	McNaughton	11,7
11		21	(h)	Bolton W	W 1-0	Wainscoat	16,1
12		28	(a)	Manchester U	L 1-4	Gardner	16,2
13	Nov	4	(h)	Plymouth A	W 5-4	Wainscoat, Duncan, Longden, Denby, T.Black (og)	12,2
14		11	(a)	West Ham U	L 1-2	Hubbard	19,3
15		18	(h)	Nottingham F	D 2-2	McNaughton, Wainscoat	8,1
16		25	(a)	Grimsby T	L 1-4	McNaughton	16,6
17	Dec	2	(h)	Bradford	L 1-2	McNaughton	9,0
18		9	(a)	Preston NE	L 0-5		8,8
19		16	(h)	Oldham A	W 2-0	Sargeant, MacKenzie	8,4
20		23	(a)	Burnley	L 1-3	Duncan	10,2
21		25	(a)	Blackpool	D 0-0		24,6
22		26	(h)	Blackpool	W 3-0	MacKenzie 2, Denby	15,0
23		30	(a)	Notts C	D 0-0		9,2
24	Jan	6	(h)	Swansea T	D 0-0		9,3
25		20	(a)	Millwall	L 0-2		13,5
26	Feb	3	(a)	Bury	L 1-3	Melville	7,2
27		8	(h)	Lincoln C	W 2-0	McNaughton, MacKenzie	6,4
28		10	(h)	Brentford	L 0-1		10,5
29		17	(h)	Fulham	D 0-0		7,9
30		24	(a)	Southampton	D 1-1	Jordan	7,9
31	Mar	7	(a)	Bolton W	D 3-3	Jordan 2, Hubbard	5,1
32		10	(h)	Manchester U	W 4-1	McNaughton 2, Jordan, Bullock	5,7
33		17	(a)	Plymouth A	D 1-1	Jordan	6,0
34		24	(h)	West Ham U	W 2-0	Jordan 2	7,8
35		30	(a)	Port Vale	L 0-3		10,5
36		31	(a)	Nottingham F	W 1-0	Jordan	10,1
37	Apr	2	(h)	Port Vale	W 2-1	Jordan, Hubbard	13,3
38		7	(h)	Grimsby T	L 0-1		20,0
39		14	(a)	Bradford	L 1-3	Jordan	8,4
40		21	(h)	Preston NE	L 0-1		8,2
41		28	(a)	Oldham A	L 0-7		2,9
42	May	5	(h)	Burnley	L 0-1		3,7
	FINAL LEAGUE POSITION: 15th in Division Two						Appearances
							Goals

FA Cup

3	Jan	13	(h)	Brentford	W 1-0	Hubbard	18,
4		27	(h)	Manchester C	D 2-2	Hill, Dale (og)	25,
R		31	(a)	Manchester C	L 1-4	McNaughton	40,
							Appearances
							Goals

Maddison G	Goldsmith G	Woodhead C	Gardner T	Hill J	Denby S	Mitchell A	Duncan A	McNaughton W	Wainscoat R	Sargeant C	Hubbard C	Longden E	Atkinson A	MacKenzie G	Shelton T	McAinsh J	Bullock A	Melville J	Jordan D	Quantick J	Speed F	Allen M	Lloyd E	Burdett T	Lawrence R	Dodds L	
1	2	3	4	5	6	7	8	9	10	11																	1
1	2	3	4	5	6	7	8	9	10	11																	2
1	2	3	4	5	6	7		9	10	11	8																3
1	2	3	4	5	6	7		9	10	11		8															4
1	2	3	4	5	6	7		9	10	11		8															5
1	2	3	4	5	6	7	8	9	10	11																	6
1	2	3	4	5	6	7	10	9		11	8																7
1	2	3	4	5	6		10	9		11	8		7														8
1	2	3	4	5	6		10	9		11	8		7														9
1	2	3	4	5	6		8	9	10	11	7																10
1	2	3	4	5	6		8	9	10	11	7																11
1	2	3	4	5	6		8	9	10	11	7																12
1	2	3		5	6		8	9	10		7	4		11													13
1	2	3		5	6			9	10	11	8	4	7														14
1	2	3	4		6			9	10		8	5	7	11													15
1	2	3	4	5	6	7		9	10		8			11													16
1	2	3	4	5	6		8	9	10					11	7												17
1	2	3	8	5	6		10	9		11	7	4															18
1	2	3	4	5	6		10	8		9				11		7											19
1	2	3	4	5	6		10	8		9						7	11										20
1	2	3	4	5	6		10	8			9					7	11										21
1	2	3	4	5	6		10	8			9			11		7											22
1	2	3	4	5			10	8			9					7	11	6									23
1	2	3	4	5	6		10	8		11	9					7											24
1	2	3	4	5	6		8	9		11	7	10															25
1	2	3	4		6		8	9		11	7	10						5									26
1	2	3	4	5	6			9	10		7	8		11													27
1	2	3	4	5	6			9	10		7	8		11													28
1	2	3	4	5	6			8			9	10		11		7											29
1	2	3		4	6			8		11	7	10						5	9								30
1	2	3		4	6			8		11	7	10						5	9								31
1	2	3		4	6			8			7	10					11	5	9								32
1	2	3		4	6			8			7	10					11	5	9								33
1	2	3		4	6			8			7	10					11	5	9								34
1	2	3		4	6			8			7	10					11	5	9								35
1		3			6			8			7	10					11	5	9	2	4						36
1	2	3			6			8			7	10					11	5	9		4						37
1	2	3						8			7	10					11	5	9		6	4					38
1	2				6			10			7						11	5	9			4	3	8			39
1	2	3			6			8			7	10	9				11	5				4					40
1		3						9			7	10					11	5		2	6	4		8			41
1	2	3			6			10			7	8					11		9						5	4	42
42	40	41	27	33	39	8	20	42	16	21	34	23	5	9	1	7	14	14	11	2	4	4	1	2	1	1	
			1		3		4	15	5	3	3	1		4			1	1	10								

1 own-goal

Maddison G	Goldsmith G	Woodhead C	Gardner T	Hill J	Denby S	Mitchell A	Duncan A	McNaughton W	Wainscoat R	Sargeant C	Hubbard C	Longden E	Atkinson A	MacKenzie G	Shelton T	McAinsh J	Bullock A	Melville J	Jordan D	Quantick J	Speed F	Allen M	Lloyd E	Burdett T	Lawrence R	Dodds L	
1	2	3	4	5	10		8	9			7			11				6									3
1	2	3	4	5			8	9		11	7	10						6									4
1	2	3	4	5	6		8	9		11	7	10															R
3	3	3	3	3	2		3	3		2	3	2		1				2									
				1				1			1																

1 own-goal

1934-35

1	Aug	29	(a)	Plymouth A	L 4-6	Duncan 3, Dodds	17,2
2	Sep	1	(a)	Blackpool	L 1-2	Jordan	18,4
3		8	(h)	Bury	L 0-1		12,7
4		10	(h)	Plymouth A	D 1-1	Jordan	7,5
5		15	(a)	Southampton	L 0-3		6,2
6		17	(h)	West Ham U	W 4-0	Duncan 2, Wright, Dodds	5,3
7		22	(a)	Nottingham F	L 1-2	Dodds	7,6
8		29	(h)	Brentford	W 2-1	Jordan 2	7,7
9	Oct	6	(a)	Fulham	L 0-4		20,4
10		13	(h)	Bradford	W 2-0	McNaughton, Hutchison	10,2
11		20	(h)	Bolton W	L 0-2		12,7
12		27	(a)	Oldham A	L 0-5		5,7
13	Nov	3	(h)	Burnley	L 1-3	Hutchison	5,8
14		10	(a)	Swansea T	L 1-2	Duncan	7,7
15		17	(h)	Manchester U	W 3-2	Wright 2, Duncan	6,4
16		24	(a)	Port Vale	W 2-1	Duncan, Hubbard	6,0
17	Dec	1	(h)	Barnsley	D 1-1	Charlton	10,3
18		8	(a)	Sheffield U	W 4-3	Duncan 3, Hutchison	12,2
19		15	(h)	Bradford C	W 1-0	Wright	8,8
20		22	(a)	Notts C	D 1-1	Acquroff	5,6
21		25	(a)	Newcastle U	L 2-6	Duncan, Longden	26,9
22		26	(h)	Newcastle U	D 1-1	Hutchison	21,
23		29	(a)	West Ham U	W 2-1	Wright, Hutchison	25,3
24	Jan	5	(h)	Blackpool	D 2-2	Acquroff, Wright	10,6
25		19	(a)	Bury	W 1-0	Acquroff	7,
26		31	(h)	Southampton	D 0-0		5,
27	Feb	2	(h)	Nottingham F	W 5-0	Wright 2, Hubbard, Acquroff, Hutchison	6,5
28		9	(a)	Brentford	L 1-2	Hutchison	14,
29		16	(h)	Fulham	L 1-2	Hubbard	5,
30		23	(a)	Bradford	W 2-1	Acquroff, Thorley	6,
31	Mar	6	(a)	Bolton W	W 2-1	Acquroff, Wright	13,
32		9	(h)	Oldham A	D 1-1	Hutchison	5,
33		19	(a)	Burnley	W 3-1	Acquroff 2, Thorley	4,
34		23	(h)	Swansea T	L 0-1		4,
35		30	(a)	Manchester U	L 0-3		15,
36	Apr	6	(h)	Port Vale	W 1-0	Pinkerton	3,
37		13	(a)	Barnsley	D 2-2	Wright, Dodds	9,
38		19	(a)	Norwich C	L 0-3		11,
39		20	(h)	Sheffield U	L 0-3		6,
40		22	(h)	Norwich C	W 1-0	Hubbard	5,
41		27	(a)	Bradford C	L 2-3	Mackie, Acquroff	3,
42	May	4	(h)	Notts C	W 5-1	Thorley 2, Acquroff, Mackie, Wright	2,
	FINAL LEAGUE POSITION: 13th in Division Two						Appearances
							Goals

FA Cup

3	Jan	12	(h)	Newcastle U	L 1-5	Charlton	23,
							Appearances
							Goals

Maddison G	Woodhead C	Thomson R	Helsby T	Tabram W	Higgins W	Hutchison D	Duncan A	Jordan D	Moore J	Dodds L	Quantick J	Wright D	Bullock A	Miller A	Hubbard C	Longden E	Farquharson H	McNaughton W	Denby S	Charlton W	Acquroff J	Thorley E	Sims S	Mackie J	Pinkerton H	Lawrence R	Foster T	Burdett T	Spivey R	
1	2	3	4	5	6	7	8	9	10	11																				1
1	2	3	4	5	6	7	8	9	10	11																				2
1	2	3	4	5	6	7	8	9	10	11																				3
1	2		4	5	6	7	8	9	10	11	3																			4
1	2		4	5	6	7	8	9			3	10	11																	5
1	3		4	5		7	8	9		11	2	10		6																6
1	3		4	5		9	8			11	2	10		6	7															7
1	3			5		7	8	9		11	2	10		6		4														8
	3			5		7	8	9		11	2	10		6		4	1													9
	3		6	5		7	8			11	2	10				4	1	9												10
	3		6	5			8			11	2	10			7	4	1	9												11
	3		6	5		8		9	10	11	2				7	4	1													12
1	2	3		5		7	10	9		11					8	4			6											13
1	3		6	5		7	8			11	2	10			9	4														14
1	3		4	5		7	8			11	2	10							6	9										15
1	3		4	5		7	8				2	10			11				6	9										16
1	3			5		7	8				2					4			6	10	9	11								17
1	3		6	5		7	8				2	10				4					9	11								18
1	3		6	5		7	8				2	10				4					9	11								19
1	3		6	5		7	8			11	2	10				4					9									20
1	3		6	5		7	8			11	2	10				4					9									21
1	3		6	5		7				11	2	10			8	4					9									22
1	3		6	5		7					2	10			8	4					9		11							23
1	3		6	5		7					2	10			8	4					9	11								24
1	3			5		7					2	10			8	4			6		9		11							25
1	3			5		7					2	10			8	4			6		9		11							26
1	3			5		11	8				2	10			7	4			6		9									27
1	3			5		9	8				2	10			7	4			6			11								28
1	3			5		10	8				2				7	4			6		9	11								29
1	3			5			8				2	10			7	4			6		9	11								30
1	3			5		7	8				2	10				4			6		9	11								31
1	3			5		7	8				2	10				4			6		9	11								32
1	3			5		7					2	10				4			6		9	11		8						33
1	3			5		7					2	10				4			6		9	11		8						34
1	3			5		7					2				8	4			6		9	11			10					35
1	3					7					2					4			6		9	11		8	10	5				36
1	3			5		9				11	2	10				4			6		7			8						37
1	3			5		9				11	2	10				4			6		7			8						38
1	3		8			7					2	10				6					9	11				5	4			39
1	3										2	10			7	4			6		9	11					5	8		40
1	3			5		7					2	10				4			6		9	11		8						41
1	3		4								2	10							6		9	11		8		5			7	42
38	42	4	22	38	5	38	26	10	5	19	38	32	1	4	17	32	4	2	21	3	25	17	3	7	2	3	2	1	1	
						8	12	4		4		11			4	1		1		1	10	4		2	1					

Maddison G	Woodhead C	Thomson R	Helsby T	Tabram W	Higgins W	Hutchison D	Duncan A	Jordan D	Moore J	Dodds L	Quantick J	Wright D	Bullock A	Miller A	Hubbard C	Longden E	Farquharson H	McNaughton W	Denby S	Charlton W	Acquroff J	Thorley E	Sims S	Mackie J	Pinkerton H	Lawrence R	Foster T	Burdett T	Spivey R	
1	3		6	5		7					2	10			8	4				9		11								3
1	1		1	1		1					1	1			1	1				1		1								
																				1										

1935-36

1	Aug	31	(h)	Fulham	D 1-1	Cameron	11,657
2	Sep	2	(a)	Tottenham H	L 1-3	Acquroff	25,603
3		7	(a)	Burnley	L 0-2		10,082
4		9	(h)	Tottenham H	W 1-0	Acquroff	9,616
5		14	(h)	Charlton A	L 2-4	Holmes, Oakes (og)	7,550
6		18	(a)	Manchester U	L 0-2		15,739
7		21	(a)	Bury	L 1-3	Cameron	7,244
8		28	(a)	Barnsley	L 1-5	Cameron	9,718
9	Oct	5	(h)	Plymouth A	W 2-1	Acquroff, Martin	4,990
10		12	(a)	Bradford C	D 1-1	Cameron	6,844
11		19	(h)	Doncaster R	L 2-3	Acquroff, Sharp	7,213
12		26	(a)	Blackpool	L 1-4	Cameron	10,624
13	Nov	2	(h)	Nottingham F	W 2-1	Acquroff, Cameron	5,526
14		9	(a)	Norwich C	L 0-3		11,906
15		16	(h)	Southampton	D 2-2	Sharp, Holmes	7,315
16		23	(a)	West Ham U	L 1-4	Cameron	21,114
17		30	(h)	Bradford	D 1-1	Sharp	5,557
18	Dec	7	(a)	Leicester C	D 2-2	Cameron, Cassidy	8,561
19		14	(h)	Swansea T	W 3-2	Hubbard, Acquroff, Sharp	4,863
20		21	(a)	Sheffield U	L 0-7		10,413
21		26	(h)	Port Vale	L 1-2	Cameron	5,359
22		28	(a)	Fulham	L 0-3		13,082
23	Jan	4	(h)	Burnley	L 1-2	Hubbard	5,811
24		18	(a)	Charlton A	L 1-4	Acquroff	14,222
25	Feb	1	(h)	Barnsley	L 1-3	Kitchen	4,804
26		8	(a)	Plymouth A	W 1-0	Acquroff	12,604
27		15	(h)	Bury	L 2-3	Hubbard, Lawrance	4,982
28		20	(h)	Bradford C	L 2-5	Acquroff, Spivey	3,750
29		22	(a)	Doncaster R	L 1-6	Nicol	10,309
30		29	(h)	Leicester C	D 3-3	Nicol, Acquroff, Cameron	2,284
31	Mar	2	(a)	Port Vale	L 0-4		2,669
32		7	(a)	Southampton	L 0-1		5,476
33		14	(h)	Norwich C	D 0-0		3,759
34		21	(a)	Nottingham F	D 0-0		6,233
35		28	(h)	West Ham U	L 2-3	Cameron, Spivey	5,038
36	Apr	4	(a)	Bradford	L 1-2	Spivey	4,746
37		10	(a)	Newcastle U	L 1-4	Hubbard	16,928
38		11	(h)	Blackpool	L 0-3		4,309
39		13	(h)	Newcastle U	L 2-3	Acquroff, Thorley	5,638
40		18	(a)	Swansea T	L 1-6	Acquroff	6,264
41		30	(h)	Sheffield U	D 2-2	Cameron, Spivey	5,411
42	May	2	(h)	Manchester U	D 1-1	Acquroff	4,540

FINAL LEAGUE POSITION: 22nd in Division Two — Relegated

Appearances
Goals

FA Cup

3	Jan	11	(a)	West Brom A	L 0-2		27,50[illegible]

Appearances
Goals

Maddison G	Dunne L	Woodhead C	Dreyer G	Tabram W	Yorke R	Hubbard C	Mackie J	Holmes M	Cameron K	Thorley E	Denby S	Davies D	Acquroff J	Farquharson H	Neish J	Lawrence R	Spivey R	Quantick J	Ainsworth E	Martin J	McPheat J	Jordan D	Sharp A	Don R	Campbell A	Cassidy J	Kitchen N	Foster T	Nicol J	Bennett R	Dimbleby S	
1	2	3	4	5	6	7	8	9	10	11																						1
1	2	3	4	5		7	10	11			6	8	9																			2
1	2	3	4	5		7	10	11			6	8	9																			3
1	2	3	4	5		7	10	11			6	8	9																			4
	2	3	4	5				11	10		6	8	9	1	7																	5
		3		5	6		8		10	11			9	1		4	7	2														6
		3		5	6		8		10	11			9			4	7	2	1													7
1		3		5	6		8	10	7				9			4		2		11												8
1		3		4				9	7		6		10			5		2		11	8											9
1		3		4					7		6		10			5		2		11	8	9										10
1		3		4					10		6		9			5		2		11	7		8									11
1		3							7	11	6		9			5		2			8		10	4								12
1		3							7	11	6		9			5		2			8		10	4								13
1		3		4					7	11	6		9			5		2			8		10									14
1		3		4				9	7	11			10			5		2					8		6							15
1		3		5					7	11			9			4		2			8		10		6							16
1		3				7			11		4		9			5		2					8		6	10						17
1		3				7			11		6		9			5		2					8	4		10						18
1		3				7			11		6		9			5		2					8	4		10						19
1		3				7			11		4		9			5		2					8		6	10						20
1	2	3				7			8	11	4		9			5									6	10						21
1		3			2	7			8	11	4		9			5									6	10						22
1		3		5	2	7			10	11			9								8			4	6							23
1	2	3		5		7				11	4		10									9	8		6							24
1	2	3		5		8							9			6	11	4					10				7					25
1		3		6		8							9			5	11	2					10				7	4				26
1		3		6		8							9			5	11	2					10				7	4				27
1		3		6		7							10			5	11	2							4			8	9			28
		3		6		7							10			5	11	2			8			4					9	1		29
		3		5		8			7	11			10			4		2										6	9	1		30
1		3		5		8			7	11			10			4		2										6	9			31
1		3		5		8			7				10			4	11	2											9		6	32
1		3		5		8			7				10			4	11	2											9		6	33
1		3		5		8			7				9			4	11	2					10								6	34
1		3		5		8			7				9			4	11	2					10								6	35
1		3		5					7			8	9			4	11	2					10								6	36
1		3			4	8			7				9			5	11	2					10								6	37
1		3		5	4	8						10	9				11	2									7				6	38
1				5	3	8				11	4	10	9				7	2							6							39
		3		5		8				11	4	10	9	1			7	2							6							40
		3		5		7			10		6	8	9				11	2						4						1		41
1		3		5		7			10	11	6		9					2						4		8						42
35	8	41	5	33	9	29	7	8	30	17	21	9	41	3	1	30	17	33	1	4	9	2	18	8	11	7	4	5	6	3	7	
						4		2	12	1			13			1	4			1			4			1	1		2			

1 own-goal

Maddison G	Dunne L	Woodhead C	Dreyer G	Tabram W	Yorke R	Hubbard C	Mackie J	Holmes M	Cameron K	Thorley E	Denby S	Davies D	Acquroff J	Farquharson H	Neish J	Lawrence R	Spivey R	Quantick J	Ainsworth E	Martin J	McPheat J	Jordan D	Sharp A	Don R	Campbell A	Cassidy J	Kitchen N	Foster T	Nicol J	Bennett R	Dimbleby S	
1		3		5		7				11	6		10					2				9	8					4				3
1		1		1		1				1	1		1					1				1	1					1				

1936-37

1	Aug	29	(a)	Port Vale	W	3-1	Mayson 2, Spivey	9,207
2		31	(h)	Rotherham U	W	2-1	Davies, Holmes	9,267
3	Sep	5	(h)	Oldham A	W	2-0	Holmes, Mayson	8,710
4		7	(a)	Rotherham U	D	0-0		5,277
5		12	(a)	Accrington S	W	1-0	Holmes	3,136
6		19	(h)	Lincoln C	D	1-1	Hubbard	10,462
7		26	(a)	New Brighton	D	1-1	Hubbard	4,319
8	Oct	3	(h)	Halifax T	D	0-0		9,642
9		10	(h)	Gateshead	W	3-2	Hubbard, Mayson, Treanor	8,080
10		17	(a)	Mansfield T	L	2-5	Edwards, Davies	9,776
11		24	(h)	Crewe A	W	2-0	Acquroff 2	6,468
12		31	(a)	Chester	L	1-3	Mayson	10,235
13	Nov	7	(h)	Rochdale	D	1-1	Holmes	6,963
14		14	(a)	Barrow	W	3-2	Best, Wilkinson, Mayson	5,323
15		21	(h)	York C	W	1-0	Holmes	7,039
16	Dec	5	(h)	Hartlepools U	W	1-0	Wilkinson	5,676
17		12	(a)	Tranmere R	L	1-2	Best	4,338
18		19	(h)	Tranmere R	W	5-2	Best 4, Bell	4,855
19		25	(h)	Wrexham	W	1-0	Davies	9,448
20		26	(h)	Port Vale	D	1-1	Bell	14,928
21	Jan	1	(a)	Darlington	D	2-2	Mayson 2	6,297
22		2	(a)	Oldham A	L	1-3	Hubbard	7,505
23		9	(h)	Accrington S	L	0-3		6,165
24		16	(a)	Southport	W	4-1	Best 2, Davies, Hubbard	5,717
25		21	(a)	Carlisle U	D	1-1	Hubbard	2,678
26		23	(a)	Lincoln C	L	0-5		5,098
27		30	(h)	New Brighton	W	4-1	Hubbard 2, Tabram 2	2,928
28	Feb	6	(a)	Halifax T	L	0-1		8,251
29		13	(a)	Gateshead	L	3-6	Hubbard, Best, Holmes	2,332
30		20	(h)	Mansfield T	W	3-0	Holmes 2, Best	4,249
31		27	(a)	Crewe A	L	1-2	Tabram	2,549
32	Mar	6	(h)	Chester	D	1-1	Bell	7,966
33		13	(a)	Rochdale	L	0-4		3,952
34		20	(h)	Barrow	W	3-2	Hubbard, Davies, Quantick	4,637
35		26	(a)	Stockport C	L	1-3	Foster	13,580
36		27	(a)	York C	D	1-1	Hubbard	6,975
37		29	(h)	Stockport C	L	0-1		11,230
38	Apr	3	(h)	Carlisle U	D	1-1	Davies	4,355
39		10	(a)	Hartlepools U	D	2-2	Best, Hubbard	4,93[illegible]
40		17	(h)	Southport	W	3-2	Tabram 2, Hubbard	2,00[illegible]
41		19	(a)	Wrexham	L	1-2	Baldry	2,10[illegible]
42	May	1	(h)	Darlington	W	4-3	Hubbard 2, Baldry, Annables	2,20[illegible]

FINAL LEAGUE POSITION: 5th in Division Three North

Appearances
Goals

FA Cup

1	Nov	28	(a)	York C	L	2-5	Mayson, Hubbard	7,70[illegible]

Appearances
Goals

Maddison G	Annables W	Woodhead C	Don R	Tabram W	Dimbleby S	Mayson J	Edwards E	Acquroff J	Davies D	Spivey R	Holmes M	Llewellyn G	Hubbard C	Denby S	Treanor J	Foster T	Wilkinson J	Quantick J	Best J	Bell E	Baldry G	Cassidy J	
1	2	3	4	5	6	7	8	9	10	11													1
1	2	3	4	5	6	7	8	9	10		11												2
1	2	3	4	5	6	7	8		10	11	9												3
1	2	3		5	6		8		10	11	9	4	7										4
1	2	3	4	5		11	8		10		9	6	7										5
1	2	3	4	5		11	8		10		9		7	6									6
1	2	3	4	5		7	8		10		9		11		6								7
1	2	3	4			7	8	9	10				11		6	5							8
1	2	3	4			7	8		10				9		6	5	11						9
1	3		4	5		7	10		8				9		6		11	2					10
1	3		4		5	7		9	10				8		6		11	2					11
1	3		4		5	7			8		10				6		11	2	9				12
1	2	3	4		5	7					10		8		6		11		9				13
1	2	3		5		7					10		8	4	6		11		9				14
1	2	3		5		7					10		8	4	6		11		9				15
1	2	3		5							10		7	4	6		11		9	8			16
1	2	3		5	6	7			10						4		11		9	8			17
1	2	3		5	6	7			10						4		11		9	8			18
1	2	3		5	6	7			10						4		11		9	8			19
1	2	3		5	6	7			10						4		11		9	8			20
1	2	3		5	6	7			10						4		11		9	8			21
1	2	3		5		7			10				8	6	4		11		9				22
1	2	3		5	6				10				7		4		11		9	8			23
1	2	3		8		7			10				9	4	6	5			11				24
1	2	3		8					10				9	4	6	5			11		7		25
1	2	3		8		7			10				9	4	6	5			11				26
1	2	3		8					10		9		7	4	6	5			11				27
1	2	3		8					10		9		7	4	6	5			11				28
1	2	3	4						8		9		7		6	5			11			10	29
1	3								10		9	4	7	6		5		2	11	8			30
1	3	2		8					10		9		7	4	6	5			11				31
1	3			5					10		9		7	4	6			2	11	8			32
1	3			5					10				7	4	6		11	2	9	8			33
1	3			5					10		9		7	4	6			2	11	8			34
1	3			5					10		9		7		6	4		2	11	8			35
1	3			8					10		9		7	4	6	5		2	11				36
1	3			5					10		9		7		6	4		2	11	8			37
1	3			5		7			10			6				4	11	2	9	8			38
1	3			8					10				9	4	6	5		2	11		7		39
1	3			8					10				9	4	6	5		2	11		7		40
1	3			8					10				9	4	6	5		2	11		7		41
1	3			8					10				9	4	6	5		2	11		7		42
42	42	27	13	35	13	23	10	4	38	3	21	4	32	20	34	18	17	15	31	14	5	1	
	1			5		8	1	2	6	1	8		15		1	1	2	1	11	3	2		

Maddison G	Annables W	Woodhead C	Don R	Tabram W	Dimbleby S	Mayson J	Edwards E	Acquroff J	Davies D	Spivey R	Holmes M	Llewellyn G	Hubbard C	Denby S	Treanor J	Foster T	Wilkinson J	Quantick J	Best J	Bell E	Baldry G	Cassidy J	
1	2	3		5		7					10		8	4	6		11		9				1
1	1	1		1		1					1		1	1	1		1		1				
						1							1										

1937-38

1	Aug	28	(h)	Wrexham	W 3-2	Fryer 2, MacNeill	8,668
2		30	(a)	Barrow	L 0-1		5,761
3	Sep	4	(a)	Hartlepools U	D 2-2	MacNeill, Pears	8,173
4		6	(h)	Barrow	W 4-0	MacNeill 3, Fryer	6,742
5		11	(h)	Lincoln C	D 1-1	Fryer	10,615
6		15	(a)	Crewe A	W 1-0	MacNeill	3,810
7		18	(a)	Halifax T	L 0-1		6,142
8		25	(a)	New Brighton	D 0-0		5,792
9	Oct	2	(h)	Gateshead	W 3-1	Fryer 2, Davies	11,082
10		9	(a)	Oldham A	D 1-1	MacNeill	10,007
11		16	(h)	Carlisle U	W 2-1	MacNeill, Fryer	10,837
12		23	(a)	Accrington S	W 2-0	MacNeill, Davies	3,198
13		30	(h)	Chester	D 2-2	MacNeill, Hubbard	11,383
14	Nov	6	(a)	Rotherham U	D 2-2	Hubbard, Fryer	5,371
15		13	(h)	Rochdale	W 4-1	MacNeill 2, Fryer 2	8,848
16		20	(a)	Doncaster R	L 1-2	MacNeill	13,868
17	Dec	4	(a)	Bradford C	W 2-1	MacNeill, Davies	3,877
18		18	(a)	Tranmere R	L 1-3	Hubbard	7,455
19		25	(a)	Darlington	W 3-1	MacNeill, Fryer, Davies	6,070
20		27	(h)	Darlington	W 4-0	Fryer 2, Pears 2	16,783
21	Jan	1	(a)	Wrexham	W 1-0	MacNeill	8,363
22		13	(h)	Southport	W 10-1	Pears 3, Davies 2, Hubbard 2, MacNeill 2, Fryer	5,816
23		15	(h)	Hartlepools U	W 4-0	Pears 2, MacNeill, Hubbard	8,607
24		22	(a)	Lincoln C	L 1-2	Hubbard	9,107
25		29	(h)	Halifax T	L 0-1		7,588
26	Feb	5	(h)	New Brighton	D 1-1	Hubbard	9,337
27		12	(a)	Gateshead	L 2-3	MacNeill, Fryer	10,307
28		19	(h)	Oldham A	W 4-1	Fryer 2, Hubbard, Milligan (og)	9,951
29		26	(a)	Carlisle U	W 1-0	MacNeill	7,525
30	Mar	5	(h)	Accrington S	D 0-0		10,343
31		12	(a)	Chester	W 3-1	MacNeill, Fryer, Cumner	6,864
32		19	(h)	Rotherham U	D 1-1	Bell	15,687
33		26	(a)	Rochdale	D 0-0		5,761
34	Apr	2	(h)	Doncaster R	W 2-1	Davies 2	15,069
35		9	(a)	Southport	L 1-2	Fryer	5,581
36		15	(a)	Port Vale	W 4-2	Davies, Hubbard, Fryer, Cumner	10,984
37		16	(h)	Bradford C	D 2-2	MacNeill, Cumner	14,159
38		18	(h)	Port Vale	D 0-0		13,564
39		23	(a)	York C	W 1-0	Fryer	9,494
40		25	(h)	York C	W 3-1	Fryer 2, Hubbard	15,41[illegible]
41		30	(h)	Tranmere R	L 0-1		21,75[illegible]
42	May	7	(h)	Crewe A	D 1-1	Cumner	4,41[illegible]

FINAL LEAGUE POSITION: 3rd in Division Three North

Note: Match 42 was benefit match for George Maddison.

Appearances

Goals

FA Cup

1	Nov	27	(h)	Scunthorpe U	W 4-0	MacNeill 2, Pears 2	6,00[illegible]
2	Dec	11	(a)	Exeter C	W 2-1	Hubbard, Fryer	9,00[illegible]
3	Jan	8	(a)	Huddersfield T	L 1-3	Pears	25,44[illegible]

Appearances

Goals

Maddison G	Annables W	Woodhead C	Robinson C	Blyth J	Treanor J	Mackay W	Fryer J	MacNeill J	Davies D	Pears J	Hardy J	Goodall E	Hubbard C	Parker D	Lawrence M	Bell E	Cumner H	
1	2	3	4	5	6	7	8	9	10	11								1
1	2	3	4	5	6	7	8	9	10	11								2
1	2	3	4	5		7	8	9	10	11	6							3
1	2	3	4	5		7	8	9	10	11	6							4
1	2	3	4	5		7	8	9	10	11	6							5
1	2	3	4	5		7	8	9	10	11	6							6
1	2	3	4	5		7	8	9	10	11	6							7
1	2	3	4	5		7	8	9	10	11	6							8
1	2	3	4	5		7	8	9	10	11	6							9
1	2	3	4	5		7	8	9	10	11	6							10
1	2	3	4	5		7	8	9	10	11	6							11
	2	3	4	5			8	9	10	11	6	1	7					12
1		2	4	5			8	9	10	11	6		7	3				13
1		2	4	5			8	9	10	11	6		7	3				14
1		2	4	5			8	9	10	11	6		7	3				15
		2	4	5			8	9	10	11	6	1	7	3				16
		2	4	5			8	9	10	11	6	1	7	3				17
	10	2	4	5			8	9		11		1	7	3	6			18
		2	4	5			8	9	10	11	6	1	7	3				19
		2	4	5			8	9	10	11	6	1	7	3				20
		2	4	5			8	9	10	11	6	1	7	3				21
		2		5			8	9	10	11	6	1	7	3	4			22
		2		5			8	9		11	6	1	7	3	4	10		23
		2		5			8	9	10	11	6	1	7	3	4			24
1		2		5			8	9	10	11	6		7	3	4			25
1		2		5			8	9	10	11	6		7	3	4			26
		2		5			8	9	10	11	6	1	7	3	4			27
		2		5			8	9	10	11	6	1	7	3	4			28
		2		5			8	9	10	11	6	1	7	3	4			29
		2		5			8	9		11	6	1	7	3	4	10		30
		2	4	5			8	9				1	7	3	6	10	11	31
		2	4	5			8	9				1	7	3	6	10	11	32
		2	4	5		7	8		10			1	9	3	6		11	33
	2		4	5			8		7			1	9	3	6	10	11	34
	2		4	5			8		7			1	9	3	6	10	11	35
	2			5			8	9	10		6	1	7	3	4		11	36
	2		4	5				9	10		6	1	7	3		8	11	37
		2		5				9	10		6	1	7	3	4	8	11	38
		2		5	4		8	9			6	1	7	3	10		11	39
		2		5	4		8	9			6	1	7	3	10		11	40
		2		5	4		8	9			6	1	7	3	10		11	41
		2		5			8	9	10		6	1	7	3	4		11	42
16	17	38	27	42	5	12	40	39	34	30	34	26	31	30	21	8	12	
							23	23	9	8			11			1	4	

1 own-goal

Maddison G	Annables W	Woodhead C	Robinson C	Blyth J	Treanor J	Mackay W	Fryer J	MacNeill J	Davies D	Pears J	Hardy J	Goodall E	Hubbard C	Parker D	Lawrence M	Bell E	Cumner H	
		2	4	5			8	9	10	11	6	1	7	3				1
		2	4	5			8	9	10	11	6	1	7	3				2
		2	4	5			8	9	10	11	6	1	7	3				3
		3	3	3			3	3	3	3	3	3	3	3				
							1	2		3				1				

1938-39

1	Aug	27	(a)	Chester	D 1-1	Cunliffe	8,98
2		29	(h)	Oldham A	L 0-2		7,67
3	Sep	3	(h)	Bradford C	W 3-2	Hubbard 2, Huxford	4,75
4		5	(a)	Barrow	L 1-3	Cunliffe	4,79
5		10	(a)	Carlisle U	W 2-1	Cunliffe 2	7,23
6		12	(h)	Barrow	W 4-0	Robinson 2, MacNeill, Davies	5,19
7		17	(a)	Lincoln C	W 3-0	Hubbard 2, Cunliffe	5,98
8		24	(h)	Stockport C	D 4-4	Davies 2, Hubbard, Reid (og)	8,65
9	Oct	1	(a)	Accrington S	D 1-1	MacNeill	3,79
10		8	(h)	Barnsley	L 0-1		10,38
11		15	(h)	Darlington	W 3-2	Cunliffe, Davies, Salvidge	7,61
12		22	(a)	Hartlepools U	D 3-3	Cunliffe, MacNeill, Davies	6,18
13		29	(h)	Gateshead	W 1-0	Hubbard	9,98
14	Nov	5	(a)	Wrexham	L 2-4	Hubbard, MacNeill	5,33
15		12	(h)	York C	W 2-0	Cunliffe 2	8,15
16		19	(a)	Rochdale	L 0-4		6,61
17	Dec	3	(a)	Doncaster R	L 0-1		13,69
18		17	(a)	Crewe A	W 1-0	Hubbard	4,23
19		24	(h)	Chester	W 3-0	Cunliffe, Wienand, Davies	5,91
20		26	(h)	New Brighton	W 3-0	Hubbard 2, Robinson	8,05
21		27	(a)	New Brighton	L 1-6	Cunliffe	5,96
22		31	(a)	Bradford C	L 2-6	Hubbard 2	8,88
23	Jan	14	(h)	Carlisle U	W 11-1	Dickinson 3, Cunliffe 2, Hubbard 2, Davies 2, Robinson, Richardson	5,2
24		21	(h)	Lincoln C	W 4-2	Davies 2, Dickinson, Hubbard	4,9
25		28	(a)	Stockport C	D 2-2	Hubbard, Richardson	7,6
26	Feb	4	(h)	Accrington S	W 6-1	Cunliffe 3, Richardson, Hubbard, Dickinson	5,5
27		11	(a)	Barnsley	L 1-5	Cunliffe	16,8
28		18	(a)	Darlington	W 1-0	Wienand	4,3
29		25	(h)	Hartlepools U	W 4-1	Richardson 3, Wienand	4,5
30	Mar	4	(a)	Gateshead	D 2-2	Davies 2	4,9
31		9	(h)	Rotherham U	L 0-2		4,0
32		11	(h)	Wrexham	D 1-1	Davies	4,1
33		18	(a)	York C	L 0-1		5,0
34		25	(h)	Rochdale	D 3-3	Richardson 2, Hubbard	3,9
35	Apr	1	(a)	Rotherham U	W 2-0	Richardson 2	5,4
36		7	(h)	Halifax T	D 1-1	Davies	10,6
37		8	(h)	Doncaster R	D 0-0		8,1
38		10	(a)	Halifax T	L 0-1		4,2
39		15	(a)	Southport	L 0-4		3,8
40		17	(h)	Southport	W 2-1	Cunliffe 2	2,3
41		22	(h)	Crewe A	W 2-1	Cunliffe, Hubbard	2,9
42		29	(a)	Oldham A	L 1-4	Lawrence	3,4

FINAL LEAGUE POSITION: 7th in Division Three North

Appearances
Goals

FA Cup

1	Nov	26	(h)	Rotherham U	W 4-1	Hubbard 2, Cunliffe, Davies	8,0
2	Dec	10	(a)	Chester	D 2-2	Davies 2	9,9
R		15	(h)	Chester	L 0-1		9,0

Appearances
Goals

Ellis J	Dowen J	Woodhead C	Hardy J	Blyth J	Robinson C	Hubbard C	White W	Huxford H	Davies D	Cunliffe A	Lawrence M	Dickinson W	Treanor J	MacNeill J	Sherwood C	Salvidge G	Wienand G	Darling B	Richardson G	Meens H	Stokes A	Annables W	Bly W	
1	2	3	4	5	6	7	8	9	10	11														1
1	2	3		5	6	7	8	9	10	11	4													2
1	3	2		5	4	7		9	10	11	6	8												3
1	3	2		5	4	7			10	11		8	6	9										4
1	3	2		5	4	8			10	11			6	9	7									5
1	3	2		5	4	8		7	10	11			6	9										6
1	3	2	6	5	4	8			10	11				9	7									7
1	3	2	6	5	4	8			10	11				9	7									8
1	3	2	6	5	4	8			10	11				9	7									9
1	3	2	6	5	4	8			10	11				9		7								10
1	3	2	6	5	4	8			10	11				9		7								11
1	3	2	6	5	4	8			10	11				9			7							12
1	3	2	6	5	4	8			10	11				9			7							13
1	3	2	6	5	4	8			10	11				9			7							14
1	3	2	6	5	4	8		9	10	11							7							15
	3	2		5	4	8		9	10	11	6						7	1						16
	3	2	6		4	7			10	11			5	9				1	8					17
1	3	2	6	5	4	8			10	11				9			7							18
1	3	2	6	5	4	8			10	11		9					7							19
1	3	2	6	5	4	8			10	11		9					7							20
1	3	2	6	5	4	8			10	11		9					7							21
1	3	2	6	5	4	8			10	11		9					7							22
1	3	2	6	5	4	7			10	11		9							8					23
1	3	2	6	5	4	7			10	11		9							8					24
1	3	2	6	5	4	7			10	11		9							8					25
1	3	2	6	5	4	7			10	11		9							8					26
1	3	2	6	5	4	7			10	11		9							8					27
1	3	2		6	4				10	11		9					7		8	5				28
1	3	2		6	4				10	11		9					7		8	5				29
1	3	2		6	4	9			10	11							7		8	5				30
1		2		6	4	9			10	11							7		8	5	3			31
1		2	6		4	7			10	11		9							8	5		3		32
1		2	6		4	7			10	11		9							8	5		3		33
1	3	2	6		4	7			10	11		9							8	5				34
	3	2	6		4	8			10	11						7			9	5			1	35
	3	2	6		4	8			10	11						7			9	5			1	36
	3	2	6		4	7			10	11		9							8	5			1	37
	3	2	6		4	7			10	11		9							8	5			1	38
	3	2	6		4	8		9	10	11							7			5			1	39
	3		6		4	7		9	10	11									8	5		2	1	40
	3	2	6		4	9		7	10	11									8	5			1	41
	3	2				9		7	10	11	6		4						8	5			1	42
32	39	41	31	30	41	40	2	10	42	42	4	18	5	13	4	4	15	2	20	15	1	3	8	
					4	19		1	14	20	1	5		4		1	3		10					

1 own-goal

Ellis J	Dowen J	Woodhead C	Hardy J	Blyth J	Robinson C	Hubbard C	White W	Huxford H	Davies D	Cunliffe A	Lawrence M	Dickinson W	Treanor J	MacNeill J	Sherwood C	Salvidge G	Wienand G	Darling B	Richardson G	Meens H	Stokes A	Annables W	Bly W	
	3	2	6	5	4	8		7	10	11				9				1						1
1	3	2	6	5	4	7			10	11				9					8					2
1	3	2	6	5	4	7			10	11				9					8					R
2	3	3	3	3	3	3		1	3	3				3				1	2					
						2			3	1														

1939-40

Third Division North

1	Aug	26	(h)	Lincoln C	D 2-2	Lowe, Davies	8,696
2	Sep	2	(a)	Southport	D 1-1	Lowe	3,711

Competition abandoned upon outbreak of war — Appearances / Goals

North East Regional League

3	Oct	21	(a)	Darlington	L 0-2		3,778
4		28	(h)	Hartlepools U	L 2-3	Prescott 2	3,000
5	Nov	4	(h)	Leeds U	L 0-3		3,000
6		11	(a)	York C	L 1-3	Woods	3,000
7		18	(h)	Huddersfield T	L 1-5	Meens	5,000
8		25	(a)	Bradford	L 1-2	E.Richardson	1,259
9	Dec	2	(h)	Middlesbrough	W 3-0	Anderson, Prescott, Meens	3,000
10		9	(a)	Newcastle U	L 0-3		2,500
11	Jan	6	(h)	Halifax T	W 2-0	Prescott, Anderson	1,500
12	Feb	24	(a)	Hartlepools U	L 2-3	Prescott 2	1,200
13	Mar	9	(a)	Bradford C	L 0-4		1,887
14		16	(a)	Huddersfield T	L 0-1		2,961
15		23	(h)	Bradford	W 4-1	Prescott 2, Anderson 2	5,000
16		25	(h)	York C	W 4-1	Prescott 4	5,000
17		30	(a)	Middlesbrough	W 3-2	Cunliffe, Prescott, Anderson	1,500
18	Apr	6	(h)	Newcastle U	W 3-1	Davies 2, Prescott	6,000
19	May	18	(a)	Halifax T	W 1-0	Prescott	500
20		25	(h)	Bradford C	W 3-0	Dawson, Cunliffe, Meens	2,000
21	Jun	1	(a)	Leeds U	L 1-3	Anderson	500
22		8	(h)	Darlington	D 4-4	Anderson 3, Davies	1,000

FINAL LEAGUE POSITION: 7th in North East Regional League — Appearances / Goals

Football League War Cup

P	Apr	13	(h)	Lincoln C	W 1-0	Davies	6,000
1		20	(a)	York C	D 1-1	Prescott	4,000
		27	(h)	York C	W 1-0	Cunliffe	6,000
2	May	4	(a)	Huddersfield T	D 1-1	Cunliffe	6,000
		11	(h)	Huddersfield T	L 0-1		6,500

Appearances
Goals

Curnow J	Woodhead C	Watson A	Robinson C	Meens H	Smith T	Quigley D	Richardson G	Lowe R	Davies D	Cunliffe A	Gilmore P	Richardson E	Prescott J	Spivey R	Robinson J	Crawford E	Woods C	Anderson N	Young H	Clubley R	Stephenson E	Dyer R	Bly W	Riches W	Dawson D	Reeve E	
1	2	3	4	5	6	7	8	9	10	11																	1
1	2	3		5	6	7	8	9	10	11	4																2
2	2	2	1	2	2	2	2	2	2	2	1																
								2	1																		

Curnow J	Woodhead C	Watson A	Robinson C	Meens H	Smith T	Quigley D	Richardson G	Lowe R	Davies D	Cunliffe A	Gilmore P	Richardson E	Prescott J	Spivey R	Robinson J	Crawford E	Woods C	Anderson N	Young H	Clubley R	Stephenson E	Dyer R	Bly W	Riches W	Dawson D	Reeve E	
1	2	3	8	5	6				10		4	7	9	11													3
1	2	3		5	6				8		4	11	9		7	10											4
1	2	3	4	5	6							11	9		7		8	10									5
1		3		5	6						4		9		7		8	10	2	11							6
1	2	3		5	6						4	11			7		8	9			10						7
1	2	3		5	6						4	7	9				10	11				8					8
1	2	3	8	5	6						4	11	9		7			10									9
1	2	3		5	6				8		4	11	9		7			10									10
1	2	3		5	6				8		4	11	9		7			10									11
	2	3			6				8	11	5	7	9		4			10					1				12
1	2	3		5	6				8	11	4		9		7			10									13
1	2	3		5	6				8	11	4		9		7			10									14
1	2	3		5	6				8	11	4		9		7			10									15
1	2	3		5	6				8	11	4		9	7				10									16
1	2	3		5					8	11	4		9		7			10						6			17
1	2	3		5	6				8	11	4		9		7			10									18
1		3		5	2				8	11	4		9		7			10						6			19
1	2	3		5	6				10	11	4				7			9							8		20
1	2	3		5	6				10		4			11	7			9							8		21
1	2	3		5	6				10		4				7			9							8	11	22
19	18	20	3	19	19				15	9	19	9	16	3	17	1	4	18	1	1	1	1	1	2	3	1	
				3					3	2		1	15				1	9							1		

Curnow J	Woodhead C	Watson A	Robinson C	Meens H	Smith T	Quigley D	Richardson G	Lowe R	Davies D	Cunliffe A	Gilmore P	Richardson E	Prescott J	Spivey R	Robinson J	Crawford E	Woods C	Anderson N	Young H	Clubley R	Stephenson E	Dyer R	Bly W	Riches W	Dawson D	Reeve E	
1	2	3		5	6				8	11	4		9		7			10									P
1	2	3		5	6				8	11	4		9		7			10									1
1	2	3		5	6				8	11	4		9		7			10									
1	2	3		5	6				8	11	4		9		7			10									2
1	2	3		5	6				8		4		9	11	7			10									
5	5	5		5	5				5	4	5		5	1	5			5									
									1	2			1														

1940-41

North Regional League

1	Aug	31	(h)	Halifax T	W 4-2	Anderson 2, Davies, Dawson	1,50
2	Sep	7	(a)	Bradford C	W 5-4	Burdett 2, Cunliffe, Dawson, I.Powell (og)	1,43
3		14	(a)	York C	L 1-4	Burdett	2,00
4		21	(h)	Bradford	W 2-1	Burdett, Cunliffe	2,00
5		28	(h)	York C	L 1-3	Cunliffe	1,50
6	Oct	5	(h)	Rotherham U	L 0-2		1,50
7		12	(a)	Doncaster R	L 2-4	Burdett, Knott	2,41
8		19	(h)	Newcastle U	W 2-1	Anderson, Barraclough	3,00
9		26	(h)	Bradford C	W 5-2	Anderson 3, Knott 2	2,00
10	Nov	2	(a)	Lincoln C	D 1-1	Cunliffe	1,23
11		9	(a)	Halifax T	L 0-3		1,00
12		16	(h)	Doncaster R	W 5-4	Knott 3, Anderson, Davies	1,50
13		23	(a)	Leeds U	L 2-3	Cunliffe, Anderson	3,00
14		30	(h)	Lincoln C	L 1-2	Knott	1,00
15	Dec	7	(a)	Newcastle U	L 1-3	Knott	3,00
16		14	(h)	Barnsley	L 1-2	Knott	50
17		21	(a)	Barnsley	L 0-5		1,59
18		25	(a)	Grimsby T	D 1-1	Knott	4,50
19	Jan	18	(h)	Leeds U	W 4-1	Knott 2, Spivey, Barraclough	1,50
20		25	(a)	York C	D 3-3	Anderson 2, Knott	2,00
21	Mar	22	(h)	Grimsby T	L 2-8	Spivey, Bratley	1,00
22		29	(a)	Grimsby T	W 1-0	Anderson	1,1
23	Apr	5	(h)	Middlesbrough	L 0-8		2,0

FINAL LEAGUE POSITION: 33rd in North Regional League (from 36 clubs)

Appearances
Goals

Football League War Cup

1	Feb	15	(h)	Lincoln C	W 4-1	Knott 4	2,0
		22	(a)	Lincoln C	L 2-3	Knott, Cunliffe	1,5
2	Mar	1	(h)	Sheffield U	W 1-0	Knott	4,0
		8	(a)	Sheffield U	L 1-3*	Davies	1,6

*After extra-time

Appearances
Goals

Matches 1-23 inclusive were in the North Regional League, positions of which were decided on goal average alone as clubs did not play the same number of games. No reference was made to games played home and away and no points were awarded.

1941-1944

No matches played during this period

Curnow J	Gowdy W	Woodhead C	Robinson J	Meens H	Herdman H	Dawson D	Davies D	Burdett T	Anderson N	Cunliffe A	Ross A	Heelbeck L	Lucas W	Rogers W	Cottam A	Bly W	Knott H	Neary J	Bradley G	Barraclough W	Bratley G	Spivey R	Sullivan M	Reeve E	McCurdie J	Raynor G	Green R	Twells D	Bratton W	French J	Porteous J	Selby W	Sherwood G	Wilson D	Hewick A	Butcher R	Pritchard T		
1	2	3	4	5	6	7	8	9	10	11																												1
1		3	4	5		7	8	9		11	2	6	10																										2
1		3	4	5		7	8	9		11	2		10	6																									3
1	6	3	4	5		7	8	9		11			10		2																								4
	6	3	7	5			8	9		11	2		10		4	1																							5
		3	4	5			7	9	8	11	2	6	10			1																							6
		3	4	5		7		9		11	2	6	10			1	8																						7
		3	4			7	10		9		2					1	8	5	6	11																			8
		3	4	5			10		9	7	2					1	8		6	11																			9
		3	4	5			10		9	7	2					1	8		6	11																			10
		3	4	6			10		9	7	2					1	8	5		11																			11
		3	4	5			10		9	7	2					1	8		6	11																			12
		3	4	5			10		9	7	2					1	8			11	6																		13
		3	4	5			7		9		2					1	8		6	11	10																		14
		3	4	5					9		2					1	8		6			7	10	11															15
		3	4	5					9		2					1	8		6	11		10			7														16
		3	4	5					9	10	2					1	8			11		6				7													17
		3							9							1	8		4	11	6	10					2	5	7										18
		3	4	5					9	7							1	8		6	11	2	10																	19
		3	4	5			7		9							1	8		6	11	2	10																	20
		3							9		2									11	6	10						5		1	4	7	8						21
				5					7										2	11	6	10											8	1	3	4	9		22
		3		5					7								9			11	6	10						2					8	1		4			23
4	3	22	19	20	1	6	14	7	18	14	16	3	6	1	2	16	15	2	11	15	8	9	1	1	1	1	1	3	1	1	1	1	3	2	1	2	1		
						2	2	5	11	5							13			2	1	2																	

1 own-goal

		3	4	5			10			7						1	9			11	6	8						2											1
1		3	4	5						7							9			11	6	10						2					8						
1		3	4	5			10										9			11	6	7						2					8						2
1		3	4	5			7										9			11	6	10						2					8						
3		4	4	4			3			2						1	4			4	4	4						4					3						
							1			1							6																						

1944-45

Football League North: First Championship

1	Aug	26	(h)	Doncaster R	L 1-8	Sargent	6,980
2	Sep	2	(a)	Doncaster R	L 1-2	Glaister	7,000
3		9	(a)	Halifax T	D 1-1	H.Johnson	5,000
4		16	(h)	Halifax T	W 2-0	Sargent, Talbot	7,500
5		23	(h)	York C	W 1-0	Montgomery	5,000
6		30	(a)	York C	L 0-1		4,000
7	Oct	7	(a)	Leeds U	L 2-5	Glaister, Montgomery	8,000
8		14	(h)	Leeds U	D 0-0		5,000
9		21	(h)	Darlington	W 3-2	Montgomery 2, Glaister	5,000
10		28	(a)	Darlington	L 1-7	Glaister	7,883
11	Nov	4	(a)	Newcastle U	L 0-7		8,000
12		11	(h)	Newcastle U	L 3-6	J.Smith, Spencer, Finch	2,000
13		18	(h)	Gateshead	L 1-3	Glaister	5,000
14		25	(a)	Gateshead	L 2-5	Finch, Dixon	3,000
15	Dec	2	(h)	Grimsby T	W 4-3	McDowell 2, Knott, Flinton	4,000
16		9	(a)	Grimsby T	D 0-0		3,604
17		16	(h)	Bradford	L 0-4		3,000
18		23	(a)	Bradford	L 1-6	Beeson	6,562

FINAL LEAGUE POSITION: 49th in Football League — North (First Championship). Note: Home matches played on the Boulevard except for 11 November which was played at Bootham Crescent, York (Hull RLFC were at home in Yorkshire Cup). Appearances Goals

Football League War Cup: North (Qualifying Competition)

19	Dec	25	(a)	York C	L 1-5	Brailsford	2,043
20		30	(h)	York C	W 6-1	McDowell 2, Talbot 2, Flinton, Bell	4,300
21	Jan	6	(h)	Bradford C	L 1-3	Flinton	4,000
22		13	(a)	Bradford C	L 1-2	Bell	4,000
23		27	(a)	Bradford	L 1-2	Glaister	4,791
24	Feb	3	(a)	Leeds U	L 1-6	Bell	8,000
25		10	(h)	Leeds U	D 1-1	Butterworth (og)	4,000
26		17	(h)	Barnsley	W 3-0	Howe 2, Armeson	4,000
27		24	(a)	Barnsley	L 0-3		7,567
28	Mar	10	(h)	Bradford	L 0-2		4,000

FINAL LEAGUE POSITION: 51st in Football League War Cup — North (Qualifying Competition) Appearances Goals

Football League North: Second Championship

29	Mar	3	(h)	Grimsby T	W 3-1	Howe 3	5,000
30		17	(a)	Grimsby T	L 0-4		3,000
31		24	(h)	Lincoln C	L 1-4	Vaughan	4,000
32	Apr	2	(h)	Bradford C	W 3-1	Knot 3	5,000
33		7	(a)	Lincoln C	L 2-4	Knott 2	3,055
34		14	(a)	Leeds U	L 2-6	Harris, Sykes	2,000
35		21	(h)	Rotherham U	L 2-8	Bell, Rothery	3,000
36		28	(a)	Rotherham U	W 2-1	K.Smith, Eatherington	3,098

FINAL LEAGUE POSITION: 56th in Football League — North (Second Championship) Appearances Goals

Matches 1-18 inclusive were played in the Football League — North (First Championship) which comprised 54 clubs.
Matches 19-28 inclusive were in the Football League War Cup — North (Qualifying Competition), the early stages of which were played on a 'mini-league' basis. The top 32 clubs went into a knock-out competition but Hull City were amongst the non-qualifiers, having finished 51st out of the 60 competing clubs. All Cup matches counted towards the Football League — North (Second Championship).
Matches 19-36 inclusive were in the Football League — North (Second Championship) which comprised 60 clubs.

1945-46

No matches played during this season

Wilkinson N	Kingwell L	Prescott J	Archer J	Neary J	Harris J	Sargent F	Talbot L	Miller D	Bell E	Glaister G	Curnow J	Beeson G	Montgomery S	Beardshaw C	Hubbard C	Richardson G	Singleton E	Hewick A	Sherwood G	Dickinson P	White L	Stone J	Harvey G	Finch R	Brewer C	Thomas R	Stokes E	McDowell C	Johnson J	Symons J	Knott H	Flinton W	Collier T	Hollis H	Armeson L	Huxford H	Howe L	Vaughan E	Walker FA	Whitchurch S	Adams C	Rothery H	Match
1	2	3	4	5	6	7	8	9	10	11																																	1
		3			6			10		11	1	2	4	5	7	8	9																											2
					6				7		1	2	4	5		8		3	9																									3
					6	7	8	9	11	10	1	2	5	4				3																									4
			4		6			10	8	11	1	2	9	5				3		7																								5
		2	4		6			10		11	1			5		8		3			7	9																						6
		3	4		6			10	7	11	1		9	5									8																						7
					6					11	1		4	5						2			3	10																						8
			4		6			10	8	11	1	2	9	5									3																						9
					6			10	8	11	1	2	5								7				4																					10
	5				6			8		11	1	2											3		4																					11
					6				7	11	1	2	4											3	10		5																				12
					6			10	8	11	1	2	9	5	7													4	3																	13
					6								2												11	4			9																	14
					6				7							10				2						5		9	4	3	8	11												15
					6				7						9	8										5	3		4	2		11												16
					6		8			11		2			7	10											5		9	4				1	3										17
					6		8					2			7	10											5		9	4				1											18
1	2	4	5	1	18	2	4	10	11	13	12	12	10	9	5	7	1	4	1	3	2	2	4	3	3	6	2	4	4	2	1	2	2	1										
						2	1			5		1	4											2				2				1	1											

Wilkinson N	Kingwell L	Prescott J	Archer J	Neary J	Harris J	Sargent F	Talbot L	Miller D	Bell E	Glaister G	Curnow J	Beeson G	Montgomery S	Beardshaw C	Hubbard C	Richardson G	Singleton E	Hewick A	Sherwood G	Dickinson P	White L	Stone J	Harvey G	Finch R	Brewer C	Thomas R	Stokes E	McDowell C	Johnson J	Symons J	Knott H	Flinton W	Collier T	Hollis H	Armeson L	Huxford H	Howe L	Vaughan E	Walker FA	Whitchurch S	Adams C	Rothery H	Match
							8		7			2								11			3									10	1	5									19
					6		8		7			2		5														3	9	4			10	1											20
					6		8		7	10		2		5									3			9						11	1											21
					4				7	11	1			5	9												3			2		8												22
									7	11	1	2		5																8	3		10		4	6								23
					10				9	11	1	2																		4	3		8		5	6								24
					4						11	1	2										8							5	3					6	7	9						25
					4			10	7		1	2																3		5			11			6		8						26
					4			10	7		1					9												3						11		2	6		8	5					27
					4			10	7		1	2										9										3		11			6			5					28
					8		3	3	9	5	7	8		4	1	1				1		2	2			1	4	1	5	5		9	3	4	6	1	3	2						
							2		3	1																			2				2			1		2						

1 own-goal

Wilkinson N	Kingwell L	Prescott J	Archer J	Neary J	Harris J	Sargent F	Talbot L	Miller D	Bell E	Glaister G	Curnow J	Beeson G	Montgomery S	Beardshaw C	Hubbard C	Richardson G	Singleton E	Hewick A	Sherwood G	Dickinson P	White L	Stone J	Harvey G	Finch R	Brewer C	Thomas R	Stokes E	McDowell C	Johnson J	Symons J	Knott H	Flinton W	Collier T	Hollis H	Armeson L	Huxford H	Howe L	Vaughan E	Walker FA	Whitchurch S	Adams C	Rothery H	Match
					4			10	7		1																				3		11			6		8	5		2			29
					6			10													7	8								3				4		9		5		2	1		30
					6			10	7		1			5													3					11				9	8	4		2			31
					6				7																			3				9	11		2			8	5	10		1		32
					6				7		1																					3	8			2			10	5				4	33
					6				7		1																3			2		11					9	5	10			4	34
					6				7																						2		11					9	5	10		1	8	35
					6						1					4						8				5	3													2				36
					8			3	6		5			1		1					1	2				1	4			5	2	5		3	1	2	6	7	3	4	3	3	
					1				1																						5						3	1				1	

.Johnson played number 10 in Match 3, scoring once; G.Brown played number 11 in Match 3; G.Shephard played number 2 in Match 7; J.Landles ayed number 7 in Match 8; S.Read played number 8 in Match 8; T.Ward played number 9 in Match 8; A.Drummond played number 7 in Match J.Dowen played number 3 in Match 10; A.Bunting played number 9 in Match 10; G.Lamb played number 7 in Matches 11 and 14; E.Gobey ayed number 9 in Match 11; C.Hope played number 10 in Match 11; J.Smith played number 8 in Match 12, scoring once; E.Spencer played number in Match 12, scoring once; B.Bircham played number 1 in Match 14; D.Harnby played number 3 in Match 14; J.Dixon played number 8 in Match , scoring once; B.Rhodes played number 10 in Match 14; D.Richardson played number 5 in Match 14 and number 6 in Match 22; J.Jones played mber 1 in Match 15; R.Moore played number 1 in Match 16; J.Dowling played number 10 in Match 16; W.Riches played number 3 in Match ; A.Cunliffe played number 11 in Matches 18 and 20; S.Clark played number 4 in Match 19; H.Gilmore played number 6 in Match 19 and number in Match 32; T.Brailsford played number 9 in Match 19, scoring once; A.Galloway played number 4 in Match 21; J.Downie played number 10 Match 22; S.Greaves played number 9 in Match 23; K.Johnson played number 7 in Match 24; E.Vaux played number 10 in Match 25 and number in Match 26; F.Walker played number 8 in Match 28; A.Meese played number 9 in Match 29; D.Waters played number 11 in Match 30; E.Crofts ayed number 9 in Matches 33 and 36; H.Eatherington played number 11 in Matches 33 and 36, scoring once; H.Sykes played number 8 in Match , scoring once; W.Skidmore played number 3 in Match 35; J.Robinson played number 4 in Match 35; K.Smith played number 7 in Match 36, oring once; J.Hutchinson played number 10 in Match 36.

1946-47

1	Aug	31	(h)	Lincoln C	D 0-0		25,586
2	Sep	2	(h)	Crewe A	D 2-2	Crawshaw, Sheen	24,828
3		7	(a)	Southport	L 1-3	Crawshaw	5,607
4		9	(a)	Crewe A	L 0-2		6,996
5		14	(h)	Rotherham U	L 0-2		22,187
6		16	(h)	Gateshead	L 1-2	Lester	17,770
7		21	(a)	Chester	L 1-5	Knott	7,766
8		28	(h)	York C	D 2-2	McGorrighan, Wright	22,249
9	Oct	5	(a)	Tranmere R	W 3-1	Lester 3	8,588
10		12	(h)	Darlington	W 2-1	Lester, Chadwick	22,296
11		19	(h)	Halifax T	W 3-0	Chadwick 2, Lester	23,289
12		26	(a)	New Brighton	W 5-1	Watson 2, Lester 2, Hassall	5,005
13	Nov	2	(h)	Rochdale	L 0-1		22,616
14		9	(a)	Doncaster R	L 1-4	Chadwick	17,820
15		16	(h)	Wrexham	W 1-0	Lester	19,081
16		23	(a)	Stockport C	L 0-2		8,586
17	Dec	7	(a)	Bradford C	D 1-1	Lester	6,453
18		21	(a)	Accrington S	D 0-0		2,672
19		25	(a)	Hartlepools U	D 0-0		8,130
20		26	(h)	Hartlepools U	D 1-1	Chadwick	30,064
21		28	(a)	Lincoln C	W 3-0	Lester 2, Davidson	10,996
22	Jan	1	(a)	Gateshead	L 0-1		5,277
23		4	(h)	Southport	W 4-0	Lester, Peach, Chadwick, Hassall	18,800
24		18	(a)	Rotherham U	L 0-2		16,971
25	Feb	1	(a)	York C	L 0-3		7,099
26		15	(a)	Darlington	W 2-0	Lester 2	6,310
27	Mar	6	(h)	Chester	W 1-0	R.Brown	10,367
28		8	(a)	Rochdale	L 2-5	Peach, Mills	6,565
29		15	(h)	Doncaster R	L 0-1		29,579
30		22	(a)	Wrexham	W 1-0	R.Brown	9,394
31		29	(h)	Stockport C	L 0-3		17,209
32	Apr	4	(a)	Carlisle U	W 2-0	Davidson, Greenhalgh	11,704
33		5	(a)	Oldham A	W 2-1	Davidson 2	9,561
34		7	(h)	Carlisle U	W 2-0	Davies, R Brown	21,854
35		12	(h)	Bradford C	L 0-2		21,289
36		19	(a)	Barrow	L 0-1		7,400
37		26	(h)	Accrington S	W 3-0	Thompson 3	13,023
38	May	10	(h)	Tranmere R	W 1-0	Bell	15,562
39		17	(a)	Halifax T	L 0-2		4,888
40		24	(h)	Oldham A	L 0-1		14,954
41		31	(h)	Barrow	W 1-0	Chadwick	10,725
42	Jun	7	(h)	New Brighton	D 1-1	Thompson	9,802

FINAL LEAGUE POSITION: 11th in Division Three North

Appearances
Goals

FA Cup

1	Nov	30	(h)	New Brighton	D 0-0		21,895
R	Dec	4	(a)	New Brighton	W 2-1*	Lester, Chadwick	7,688
2		14	(a)	Darlington	W 2-1	Lester, Peach	8,077
3	Jan	11	(a)	Blackburn R	D 1-1	Cook	23,500
R		16	(h)	Blackburn R	L 0-3		30,501

*After extra-time

Appearances
Goals

By W	Meens H	Watson H	Greenhalgh J	Brown H	Sheen J	Bell E	Smith D	Knott H	McGorrighan F	Koffman J	Montgomery S	Crawshaw C	Jones G	Fowler N	Cook P	Hassall W	Davies D	Lester B	Smith A	Brownsword J	Chadwick C	Wright G	Hannaby C	Mills J	Peach J	Davidson D	Elliott H	Carter J	Atkinson T	Brown R	Thompson D	Major J	Harrison K	Atkinson P	Moore N	Durham D	Jones J	Johnson S	Robertson L	Alberry E	Teasdale T	Reagan M	
	2	3	4	5	6	7	8	9	10	11																																	1
	2	3	6	5	10			7		9	4	8	11																														2
	3	2	10	5	6		8		7	11	4	9																															3
	5	2		6		7	8	9	10		4			3	11																												4
	5	3	2	6	10		7	9	8		4		11																														5
	5	3	2	6	10						4					7	8	9	11																									6
	5		4				8	9	10	11				2			6			3	7																							7
	5	2	4				7		8									6	9		3	11	10																						8
	5	2	4				7		10									6	9		3	11	8																						9
	5	2	4	6			7		10									8	9		3	11		1																						10
	5	2	4				7		10									8	9		3	11		1	6																					11
	5	2	4														11	10	9		3	7	8	1	6																					12
	5	2	4														11	8	9		3	7	10	1	6																					13
	5	2	4						10							11	8	9		3	7		1	6																					14
	3	2	4	5			8		10									9		11	7		1	6																					15
	3	2	4	5			8		10									9		11	7		1	6																					16
	3	2	4	5				7	10									9			11			6	8																				17
	3	2	4	5					10								7	9			11			6	8																				18
	3	2	4	5					8								7	9			11			6	10																				19
	3	2	4	5					8									9			11			6	10	7																			20
	3	2	4	5									11					9						6	10	7	8																		21
	3	2	4	5					10			11					9						6	8	7																			22
	3	2	4	5					10						7		9			11			6	8																				23
		2	4	5					10				3	9						11			6		7	8	1																	24
		2	4	5			9		8				3							11			6	10	7		1																	25
	3	2	4	5														9						6	8	7	10	1	11																26
	3	2	4	5												11		8						6	10	7		1		9															27
	3		4	5										2		11		8						6	10	7		1		9															28
		2	4				5							3			8				7			6	10	11				9															29
	3	2	4			8											11		5						6	10	7				9															30
	3	2	4				5											11								6	10	7	8			9															31
	3	2	4	5									11					9						6	10	7				8															32
	5	2	4									11	3				9			8			6	10	7																				33
	5	2	4										3			8				11		1	6	10	7				9															34
	5	2	4										3			8	9			11		1	6	10	7																			35
	5	2	4									11	3			8	9					1	6		7					10												36
	5	2	4			10	7						3			8						1	6							9	11											37
	5		4			8								2		3							1	6		7					9	11	10										38
	5		4											3		2	8	9					1	6		7			11				10										39
	5		4											3		2	8																9	11		1	7	6	10						40
	5		4														3					7			6											1	8			2	10	9	11		41
	5		4														3					7			6								9			1	8			2	10			11	42
	39	35	41	22	5	5	15	6	20	4	5	2	7	14	2	14	18	26	1	10	23	4	13	31	18	18	4	5	2	7	5	3	2	3	3	1	1	2	2	1	1	1	
		2	1		1	1		1	1			2				2	1	15			7	1		1	2	4				3	4											

By W	Meens H	Watson H	Greenhalgh J	Brown H	Sheen J	Bell E	Smith D	Knott H	McGorrighan F	Koffman J	Montgomery S	Crawshaw C	Jones G	Fowler N	Cook P	Hassall W	Davies D	Lester B	Smith A	Brownsword J	Chadwick C	Wright G	Hannaby C	Mills J	Peach J	Davidson D	Elliott H	Carter J	Atkinson T	Brown R	Thompson D	Major J	Harrison K	Atkinson P	Moore N	Durham D	Jones J	Johnson S	Robertson L	Alberry E	Teasdale T	Reagan M	
	3	2	4	5					8										9		11	7			6	10																					1
	3	2	4	5				7	10									9			11			6	8																				R
	3	2	4	5					10								7	9			11			6	8																				2
	3	2	4	5					10						9	7					11			6	8																				3
		2	4	5					10				3	9	11	8								6		7		1																	R
	4	5	5	5				1	5				1	2	2	2	3		1	4			5	4	1		1																
															1			2				1				1																		

1947-48

1	Aug	23	(a)	Lincoln C	W 3-2	Thompson 2, Gallacher	11,116
2		28	(h)	Rochdale	D 0-0		25,525
3		30	(h)	Accrington S	W 4-2	Gallacher 2, Thompson 2	23,356
4	Sep	2	(a)	Rochdale	L 0-1		9,027
5		6	(a)	Rotherham U	D 0-0		15,205
6		11	(h)	Halifax T	L 1-2	Moore	21,642
7		13	(a)	Stockport C	D 0-0		9,712
8		15	(a)	Halifax T	W 2-0	Moore, Robertson	8,565
9		20	(h)	Bradford C	W 2-1	Moore, Robertson	22,810
10		27	(a)	Barrow	W 2-0	Moore, Richardson	9,182
11	Oct	4	(h)	Wrexham	D 1-1	Richardson	32,188
12		11	(h)	Hartlepools U	W 5-0	Moore 3, Richardson, Tootill (og)	25,414
13		18	(a)	Gateshead	W 1-0	Moore	7,684
14		25	(h)	Darlington	L 0-3		26,240
15	Nov	1	(a)	Tranmere R	L 1-2	Moore	9,630
16		8	(h)	Oldham A	W 1-0	Moore	20,551
17		15	(a)	York C	D 2-2	Lester 2	14,125
18		22	(h)	Mansfield T	D 1-1	Richardson	20,677
19	Dec	20	(h)	Lincoln C	L 0-1		20,923
20		25	(a)	Southport	W 2-1	Richardson, Murphy	8,223
21		26	(h)	Southport	W 1-0	Murphy	25,769
22	Jan	3	(a)	Accrington S	W 4-2	Murphy 2, Moore, Reagan	7,363
23		17	(h)	Rotherham U	W 5-3	Murphy 2, Buchan 2, Mellor	29,821
24		24	(a)	Carlisle U	D 0-0		17,339
25		31	(h)	Stockport C	W 1-0	Harrison	27,410
26	Feb	7	(a)	Bradford C	L 0-2		12,543
27		14	(h)	Barrow	D 0-0		25,103
28		21	(a)	Wrexham	L 0-1		9,522
29		28	(a)	Hartlepools U	L 1-3	Murphy	8,303
30	Mar	6	(h)	Gateshead	L 2-3	Murphy, Bloomer	17,737
31		13	(a)	Darlington	L 0-2		6,063
32		17	(a)	Chester	L 1-4	Harrison	6,087
33		20	(h)	Tranmere R	W 3-0	Conway 2, Murphy	13,558
34		26	(a)	New Brighton	L 0-1		7,591
35		27	(a)	Oldham A	D 0-0		16,061
36		29	(h)	New Brighton	W 3-0	Buchan, Mellor, Hassall	21,860
37	Apr	3	(h)	York C	D 1-1	Durham	32,466
38		10	(a)	Mansfield T	D 1-1	Buchan	11,098
39		17	(h)	Chester	W 2-1	Moore 2	24,138
40		22	(h)	Crewe A	W 2-1	Buchan, Durham	22,096
41		24	(a)	Crewe A	L 1-3	Conway	6,182
42	May	1	(h)	Carlisle U	W 3-1	Durham 2, Bloomer	25,123

FINAL LEAGUE POSITION: 5th in Division Three North

Appearances
Goals

FA Cup

1	Nov	29	(h)	Southport	D 1-1*	Gallacher	20,000
R	Dec	6	(a)	Southport	W 3-2	Richardson, Reagan, McGorrighan	11,000
2		13	(h)	Cheltenham T	W 4-2	Richardson 3, Reagan	21,000
3	Jan	10	(h)	Middlesbrough	L 1-3	Murphy	40,179

*After extra-time

Appearances
Goals

Bly W	Johnson S	Taylor J	Greenhalgh J	Meens H	Mills J	Davidson D	Gallacher C	Thompson D	Peach J	Cook P	Reagan M	Robertson L	Hassall W	Berry T	Richardson G	Moore N	Mellor A	Fowler N	Daley A	Atkinson P	Bloxham A	Hannaby C	Harrison K	McGorrighan F	Lester B	Murphy G	Wright J	Corbett A	Buchan W	Durham D	Bloomer J	Conway A	Carter H	King G	
1	2	3	4	5	6	7	8	9	10	11																									1
1	2	3	4	5	6		8	9		11	7	10																							2
1		3	4	5	6	11	8	9			7	10	2																						3
1		3	4	5	6		8	9		11	7	10	2																						4
1		3	4	5	11	7						8	2	6	10	9																			5
1			4	5	6		11				7	8	2	3	10	9																			6
1				5	6	11	8				7		2	4	10	9	3																		7
1				5	6		8					7	3	4	10	9		2	11																8
1			7	5	6		11					8	3	4	10	9		2																	9
1	11			5	6		8				7		3		10	9	4	2																	10
1	11			5	6		8				7		3		10	9	4	2																	11
				5			8				7		3	6	10	9	4	2	11	1															12
				5			8				7		3	6	10	9	4	2	11	1															13
				5			8						3	6	10	9	4	2	11	1	7														14
			4	5			8						3	6	10	9		2			7	1	11												15
		3	4	5							7		2	6		9					11	1	8	10											16
		3	4	5							7		2	6							11	1	8	10	9										17
		3	4	5							7		2	6	10	9					11	1	8												18
1		3	4	5			8						2				6				7		11	10		9									19
1			4	3									2		10	8	6				11		7			9	5								20
1		3	4				8						2	5	10		6				11		7			9									21
1		3	4	5							7		2		10	8	6						11			9									22
		3	4	5							7		2				6				11		10			9		1	8						23
				3							7		2	5		4					11		10			9		1	8	6					24
				3							7		2	5		4					11		10			9		1	8	6					25
				3							7		2	5		4					11		10			9		1	8	6					26
							10						3	5	9	4		2	11				7					1	8	6					27
													3	5			4	2	11		8		7			9		1	10	6					28
1													3	5			4	2			11			10		9			8	6	7				29
	3		6				11						2	5		4					10					9		1	8		7				30
	3												2	5			4		11		10			6		9		1	8		7				31
1	3												2	5		10					11		7	4		9			8	6					32
1		3	4	5										6			10	2			11		7			9						8			33
1		3	4	5										6			10	2			11		7			9						8			34
1		3	4	5									7	6			10	2					11						8	9					35
1		3	4	5									7	6			10	2					11						8	9					36
1		3	4	5									7	6				2					11						10	9			8		37
1		3	4	5									7	6		8		2			11								10	9					38
1		3	4	5										6		9		2			7								10	11			8		39
1		3	4	5										6		9		2			7								10	11			8		40
1	3		4	5										6				2			7								10	11		8		9	41
1			4	5										3			6	2											10	11	7		8	9	42
27	8	20	27	35	11	4	18	4	1	3	17	7	34	32	16	24	19	21	7	3	23	4	20	6	1	15	1	8	18	15	4	3	4	2	
							3	4			1	2	1		5	13	2						2		2	9			5	4	2	3			

1 own-goal

Bly W	Johnson S	Taylor J	Greenhalgh J	Meens H	Mills J	Davidson D	Gallacher C	Thompson D	Peach J	Cook P	Reagan M	Robertson L	Hassall W	Berry T	Richardson G	Moore N	Mellor A	Fowler N	Daley A	Atkinson P	Bloxham A	Hannaby C	Harrison K	McGorrighan F	Lester B	Murphy G	Wright J	Corbett A	Buchan W	Durham D	Bloomer J	Conway A	Carter H	King G	
		3	4	5			10				7		2	6							11	1	8		9										1
1		3	4	5			8				7		2		9		6				11			10											R
1	2		4	5			8				7		3	6	9						11			10											2
		3	4	5							7		2		10	9	6					1	11			8									3
2	1	3	4	4			3				4		4	2	3	1	2				3	2	2	2	1	1									
							1				2				4									1		1									

1948-49

1	Aug	21	(a)	Tranmere R	W 2-1	Moore, Harrison	10,107
2		26	(h)	Oldham A	W 6-0	Moore 2, Carter 2, Harrison, Greenhalgh	32,679
3		28	(h)	Mansfield T	W 4-0	Moore 2, Buchan, Harrison	34,075
4	Sep	4	(a)	Barrow	W 2-1	Burbanks, Conway	12,759
5		9	(h)	Accrington S	W 3-1	Carter, Conway, Durham	33,512
6		11	(h)	Wrexham	W 3-0	Moore 2, Buchan	32,075
7		18	(a)	Halifax T	W 4-2	Burbanks, Moore, Greenhalgh, Harrison	18,563
8		25	(h)	Bradford C	W 2-0	Carter, Burbanks	36,207
9		28	(a)	Accrington S	W 2-1	Harrison, Burbanks	13,162
10	Oct	2	(a)	Doncaster R	D 0-0		37,099
11		9	(a)	Hartlepools U	W 2-0	Moore, Burbanks	17,118
12		16	(h)	Darlington	L 0-1		43,801
13		23	(a)	Rochdale	D 1-1	Harrison	14,967
14		30	(h)	New Brighton	W 4-1	Moore, Carter, Burbanks, Jensen	31,039
15	Nov	6	(a)	Chester	W 2-0	Carter, Jensen	13,509
16		13	(h)	Southport	W 5-1	Burbanks 2, Moore, Carter, Jensen	25,215
17		20	(a)	Crewe A	D 0-0		11,138
18	Dec	4	(a)	Stockport C	D 0-0		15,049
19		25	(h)	Rotherham U	W 3-2	Buchan 2, Bloxham	49,655
20		27	(a)	Rotherham U	D 0-0		22,159
21	Jan	1	(a)	Mansfield T	D 1-1	Buchan	11,735
22		15	(h)	Barrow	W 3-0	Price 2, Carter	26,881
23		22	(a)	Wrexham	W 2-0	Price, Greenhalgh	18,551
24	Feb	5	(h)	Halifax T	W 6-0	Jensen 3, Buchan 2, Mellor	37,114
25		19	(a)	Bradford C	L 2-4	Jensen, Harrison	27,083
26	Mar	5	(h)	Hartlepools U	W 2-0	Carter, Price	35,357
27		12	(a)	Darlington	W 1-0	Shepherd	17,978
28		19	(h)	Rochdale	D 1-1	Price	36,509
29		23	(h)	Carlisle U	W 3-0	Moore, Carter, Simpson (og)	36,864
30		26	(a)	New Brighton	D 0-0		8,650
31		30	(h)	Tranmere R	W 2-0	Harrison 2	33,008
32	Apr	2	(h)	Chester	W 3-2	Moore 2, Jensen	36,167
33		6	(h)	York C	L 2-3	Carter, Moore	40,002
34		9	(a)	Southport	D 0-0		10,010
35		15	(h)	Gateshead	W 2-0	Harrison, Jensen	43,795
36		16	(h)	Crewe A	W 5-0	Moore 2, Jensen 2, Burbanks	38,089
37		18	(a)	Gateshead	W 2-0	Moore, Harrison	17,538
38		23	(a)	York C	W 3-1	Carter, Moore, Jensen	21,010
39		26	(a)	Oldham A	D 1-1	Harrison	34,968
40		30	(h)	Stockport C	W 6-1	Moore 3, Carter 2, Jensen	38,192
41	May	4	(h)	Doncaster R	L 0-1		46,725
42		7	(a)	Carlisle U	D 1-1	Jensen	15,519

FINAL LEAGUE POSITION: 1st in Division Three North — Promoted

Appearances
Goals

FA Cup

1	Nov	27	(h)	Accrington S	W 3-1	Carter 2, Jensen	21,926
2	Dec	11	(h)	Reading	D 0-0*		29,692
R		18	(a)	Reading	W 2-1	Moore 2	21,920
3	Jan	8	(a)	Blackburn R	W 2-1*	Moore, Buchan	33,200
4		29	(a)	Grimsby T	W 3-2	Moore 2, Carter	26,505
5	Feb	12	(a)	Stoke C	W 2-0	Moore, Greenhalgh	46,738
6		26	(h)	Manchester U	L 0-1		55,019

*After extra-time

Appearances
Goals

Bly W	Fowler N	Berry T	Greenhalgh J	Meens H	Durham D	Harrison K	Carter H	Moore N	Buchan W	Burbanks E	Conway A	Taylor J	Mellor A	King G	Jensen V	Bloxham A	Price W	White K	Robinson J	Shepherd E	Wright J	
1	2	3	4	5	6	7	8	9	10	11												1
1	2	3	4	5	6	7	8	9		11	10											2
1	2	3	4	5	6	7	8	9	10	11												3
1	2	3	4	5	6	7	8	9		11	10											4
1	2	3	4	5	6	7	8	9		11	10											5
1	2	3	4	5	6	7	8	9	10	11												6
1	2	3	4	5	6	7	8	9	10	11												7
1	2	3	4	5	6	7	8	9	10	11												8
1	2	3	4	5	6	7	8	9	10	11												9
1		3	4	5		7	8		10	11		2	6	9								10
1		3	4	5		7	8	9	10	11		2	6									11
1		3	4	5		7	8	9	10	11		2	6									12
1		3	4	5		7	8	9	10	11		2	6									13
1		3	4	5		7	10	9		11		2	6		8							14
1		3	4	5		7	10	9		11		2	6		8							15
1		3	4	5		7	10	9		11		2	6		8							16
1		3	4	5		7	10	9		11		2	6		8							17
1		3	4	5		7	10	9		11		2	6		8							18
1		3	4	5		7	9		10			2	6		8	11						19
1	2		4	5		7	9		10			3	6		8	11						20
1		3	4	5		7		9	10			2	6		8	11						21
1		3	4	5		7	11		10			2	6		8		9					22
1		3	4	5		7	11		10			2	6		8		9					23
1	2	3	4	5		7	11		10				6		8		9					24
1		3		5		7	11		10			2	6		8		9	4				25
		3	4	5		7	10		8			2	6			11	9		1			26
		3	4	5		7	10					2	6		8		9		1	11		27
		3	4	5		7	10					2	6		8		9		1	11		28
1		3	4	5		7	10	9		11		2	6		8							29
1		3	4	5		7	10	9		11		2	6		8							30
1	2		4	5		7	8	9	10	11		3	6									31
1	2		4	5		7		9	10	11		3	6		8							32
	2	5	4			7	10	9		11		3	6		8				1			33
1		5	4		6	7	8		10			3			2		9			11		34
1		3	4	5	6	7	10	9		11		2			8							35
1		3	4	5	6	7	10	9		11		2			8							36
1		3	4	5	6	7	10	9		11		2			8							37
1		3	4	5	6	7	10	9		11		2			8							38
1		3	4	5	6	7	10	9		11		2			8							39
1		3	4	5		7	10	9				2	6		8					11		40
1		3	4	5		7	10	9				2	6		8					11		41
1		3	4	5		7		9	10			2	6		8					11		42
38	14	39	41	40	15	42	39	31	22	28	3	32	27	1	27	4	8	1	4	6		
			3		1	12	14	22	7	9	2		1		14	1	5			1		

1 own goal

Bly W	Fowler N	Berry T	Greenhalgh J	Meens H	Durham D	Harrison K	Carter H	Moore N	Buchan W	Burbanks E	Conway A	Taylor J	Mellor A	King G	Jensen V	Bloxham A	Price W	White K	Robinson J	Shepherd E	Wright J	
1		3	4	5		7	10	9		11		2	6		8							1
1		3	4	5		7	10		8	11		2	6		9							2
1		3	4			7		9	10			2	6		8	11					5	R
1		3	4	5		7		9	10			2	6		8	11						3
1		3	4	5		7	11	9	10			2	6		8							4
1		3	4	5		7	11	9	10			2	6		8							5
1		3	4	5		7	11	9	10			2	6		8							6
7		7	7	6		7	5	6	6	2		7	7		7	2					1	
			1				3	6	1						1							

1949-50

1	Aug	20	(h)	Bury	W	3-2	Moore, Carter, Burbanks	42,666
2		22	(a)	Blackburn R	L	2-4	Jensen, Harrison	30,982
3		27	(a)	Leicester C	W	2-1	Carter, Burbanks	37,659
4	Sep	1	(h)	Blackburn R	W	3-1	Moore 2, Harrison	43,812
5		3	(h)	Bradford	D	3-3	Carter 2, Moore	41,624
6		5	(a)	Cardiff C	L	0-2		40,254
7		10	(a)	Chesterfield	W	1-0	Carter	22,868
8		17	(h)	Plymouth A	W	4-2	Moore 2, Jensen, Carter	38,296
9		24	(a)	Sheffield W	L	2-6	Jensen 2	52,40
10	Oct	1	(h)	Grimsby T	D	2-2	Carter, Jensen	46,28
11		8	(a)	Queen's Park R	W	4-1	Carter 2, Jensen, Harrison	28,72
12		15	(h)	Preston NE	W	4-2	Moore 2, Burbanks, Jensen	46,17
13		22	(a)	Swansea T	W	2-1	Burbanks, Jensen	22,27
14		29	(h)	Leeds U	W	1-0	Jensen	47,63
15	Nov	5	(a)	Southampton	L	0-5		23,27
16		12	(h)	Coventry C	W	2-1	Carter 2	40,17
17		19	(a)	Luton T	W	3-0	Carter, Harrison, Mellor	22,26
18		26	(h)	Barnsley	W	2-0	Shepherd, Carter	31,52
19	Dec	3	(a)	West Ham U	L	1-2	Harrison	29,42
20		10	(h)	Sheffield U	L	0-4		28,85
21		17	(a)	Bury	D	0-0		17,51
22		24	(h)	Leicester C	W	4-0	Moore 2, Harrison 2	35,20
23		26	(a)	Brentford	L	1-3	Carter	33,79
24		27	(h)	Brentford	W	2-0	Jensen, Shepherd	48,44
25		31	(a)	Bradford	L	1-5	R.Gibson	27,02
26	Jan	14	(h)	Chesterfield	W	1-0	Harrison	37,89
27		21	(a)	Plymouth A	W	3-1	Moore, Jensen, Greenhalgh	29,53
28	Feb	4	(h)	Sheffield W	D	1-1	Jensen	50,10
29		18	(a)	Grimsby T	L	0-1		26,47
30		25	(h)	Queen's Park R	D	1-1	Carter	24,58
31	Mar	4	(a)	Preston NE	L	2-4	Harrison, R.Gibson	27,74
32		11	(h)	Swansea T	D	0-0		32,87
33		18	(a)	Leeds U	L	0-3		49,46
34		25	(h)	Southampton	L	1-2	R.Gibson	31,93
35	Apr	1	(a)	Barnsley	D	1-1	R.Gibson	22,04
36		7	(a)	Tottenham H	D	0-0		66,88
37		8	(h)	West Ham U	D	2-2	R.Gibson, Bloxham	31,04
38		10	(h)	Tottenham H	W	1-0	Smith	38,34
39		15	(a)	Coventry C	L	0-2		25,5
40		22	(h)	Luton T	D	1-1	Carter	28,2
41		29	(a)	Sheffield U	L	0-5		29,6
42	May	6	(h)	Cardiff C	D	1-1	Lee	18,2

FINAL LEAGUE POSITION: 7th in Division Two

Appearances
Goals

FA Cup

3	Jan	7	(a)	Southport	D	0-0		15,6
R		12	(h)	Southport	W	5-0	Moore, Revie, Harrison, Burbanks, Greenhalgh	28,0
4		28	(a)	Stockport C	D	0-0		26,6
R	Feb	2	(h)	Stockport C	L	0-2		24,5

Appearances
Goals

Bly W	Taylor J	Berry T	Greenhalgh J	Bowler G	Mellor A	Harrison K	Jensen V	Moore N	Carter H	Burbanks E	Fowler N	Hassall W	Seddon F	Meens H	Revie D	Shepherd E	Gibson R	Bloxham A	Robinson J	Smith F	Gibson A	Durham D	Neal J	Lee J	Harris W	
1	2	3	4	5	6	7	8	9	10	11																1
1	2	3	4	5	6	7	8	9	10	11																2
1	2	3	4	5	6	7	8	9	10	11																3
1		3	4	5	6	7	8	9	10	11	2															4
1		3	4	5	6	7	8	9	10	11	2															5
1			4	5	6	7	8	9	10	11	2	3														6
1	3		4	5	6	7	8	9	10	11		2														7
1		3	4	5	6	7	8	9	10	11		2														8
1	2	3	4	5	6	7	8	9	10	11																9
1	2	3	4		6	7	8	9	10	11			5													10
1		3	4	2	6	7	8	9	10	11			5													11
1		3	4	2	6	7	8	9	10	11			5													12
1		3	4	2	6	7	8	9	10	11				5												13
1		3	4	2	6	7	8	9	10	11				5												14
1		3	4	2	6	7	8	9	10	11				5												15
1		3	4	2	6	7	9		10	11				5	8											16
1		3	4		6	7	2	9	10					5	8	11										17
1		3	4	5	6	7	2	9	10						8	11										18
1		3	4	5	6	7	2	9	10						8	11										19
1		3	4	5	6	7	2		10						8	11	9									20
1	2	3		5	6	7	4		10						8		9	11								21
1	2	3		5	6	7	4	9	10	11					8											22
1	2			5	6	7	4	9	10	11				3	8											23
1	3		4		6	7	8		10			2		5		11	9									24
1	2	3	4		6	7	8		10					5		11	9									25
1		3	4	5	6	7	10	9				2			8	11										26
1	3		4	5	6	7	10	9	11			2			8											27
1	3	2	4	5	6	7	10		9	11					8											28
1	3	2	4	5	6	7	10		9	11					8											29
	3	2		5	6	7	4	9	10	11					8				1							30
	3	2		5	6	7	4		10	11							9		1	8						31
	3	2	4	5	6		8		10							11	9		1	7						32
	3		4	5	6	7	10		9						8	11			1		2					33
1		3	4	5	6	7	8		10	11							9				2					34
1		3		5	6	7			10						4		9	11		8	2					35
1		3		5		7			10	11					4		9			8	2	6				36
1		3		5		7			10						4		9	11		8	2	6				37
1	2	3		5		7			10						4		9	11		8		6				38
1		3	10	5		7									4		9	11		8	2	6				39
1			6	5		11			10						4			7		8	2		3	9		40
1	3			5		11	6		10						4					8	2			9	7	41
1		3	4	5		11	10								8						2	6		9	7	42
38	20	34	32	38	35	41	36	23	39	24	3	6	3	8	22	9	12	6	4	9	9	5	1	3	2	
			1		1	9	12	11	16	4						2	5	1		1				1		

Bly W	Taylor J	Berry T	Greenhalgh J	Bowler G	Mellor A	Harrison K	Jensen V	Moore N	Carter H	Burbanks E	Fowler N	Hassall W	Seddon F	Meens H	Revie D	
1	3			5	6	7	4	9	10	11		2			8	3
1	3		4	5	6	7		9	10	11		2			8	R
1	3		4	5	6	7	10	9	11			2			8	4
1	3		4	5	6	7	8	9	10	11		2				R
4	4		3	4	4	4	3	4	4	3		4			3	
			1			1		1		1					1	

1950-51

1	Aug	19	(a)	West Ham U	D 3-3	Ackerman 2, Carter	30,0
2		24	(h)	Barnsley	D 3-3	Carter 2, Ackerman	40,8
3		26	(h)	Swansea T	W 2-1	Carter, Revie	34,2
4		30	(a)	Barnsley	L 2-4	Carter, Ackerman	24,5
5	Sep	2	(h)	Grimsby T	W 2-1	Carter 2	38,3
6		6	(a)	Luton T	W 2-1	Ackerman 2	14,9
7		9	(h)	Doncaster R	L 1-2	Carter	40,2
8		16	(h)	Brentford	W 3-0	Carter 2, Revie	31,9
9		23	(a)	Blackburn R	D 2-2	Carter, Harrison	28,9
10		30	(h)	Southampton	W 4-1	Ackerman 2, Harrison 2	22,7
11	Oct	7	(h)	Leicester C	L 1-3	Ackerman	33,6
12		14	(a)	Chesterfield	D 0-0		17,4
13		21	(h)	Coventry C	L 0-2		33,2
14		28	(a)	Manchester C	D 0-0		45,8
15	Nov	4	(h)	Birmingham C	W 3-2	Harrison 2, Carter	32,0
16		11	(a)	Cardiff C	L 1-2	Ackerman	25,0
17		18	(h)	Queen's Park R	W 5-1	Ackerman 3, Carter, Gerrie	33,8
18		25	(a)	Bury	W 2-0	Gerrie, Harrison	15,3
19	Dec	2	(h)	Preston NE	D 0-0		37,2
20		9	(a)	Notts C	D 2-2	Gerrie, Ackerman	32,
21		16	(h)	West Ham U	L 1-2	Burbanks	20,6
22		23	(a)	Swansea T	L 0-1		16,
23		25	(a)	Sheffield U	L 1-3	Ackerman	34,
24		26	(h)	Sheffield U	D 1-1	Revie	37,
25		30	(a)	Grimsby T	D 1-1	Carter	20,
26	Jan	13	(a)	Doncaster R	W 4-2	Carter, Ackerman, Gerrie, Revie	30,
27		20	(a)	Brentford	L 1-2	Revie	20,
28	Feb	3	(h)	Blackburn R	D 2-2	Gerrie, Ackerman	38,
29		17	(a)	Southampton	W 3-2	Carter, Gerrie, Harrison	23,
30		24	(a)	Leicester C	L 0-4		35,
31	Mar	3	(h)	Chesterfield	W 2-1	Ackerman, Burbanks	30,
32		10	(a)	Coventry C	L 1-4	Revie	22,
33		17	(h)	Manchester C	D 3-3	Carter 2, Harrison	26
34		23	(h)	Leeds U	W 2-0	Harrison, Carter	46,
35		24	(a)	Birmingham C	L 1-2	Harrison	27,
36		26	(a)	Leeds U	L 0-3		27
37		31	(h)	Cardiff C	W 2-0	Ackerman, Gerrie	20,
38	Apr	7	(a)	Queen's Park R	L 1-3	Ackerman	14
39		14	(h)	Bury	W 4-0	Gerrie 2, Harrison, Revie	25
40		21	(a)	Preston NE	L 0-1		37
41		28	(h)	Notts C	W 1-0	Gerrie	24
42	May	5	(h)	Luton T	W 5-3	Ackerman, Revie, Gerrie, Harrison, Shanks (og)	17

FINAL LEAGUE POSITION: 10th in Division Two

Appearances
Goals

FA Cup

3	Jan	6	(h)	Everton	W 2-0	Carter, Gerrie	36
4		27	(h)	Rotherham U	W 2-0	Carter, Harrison	50
5	Feb	10	(a)	Bristol R	L 0-3		30

Appearances
Goals

Bly W	Gibson A	Berry T	Jensen V	Meens H	Mellor A	Harrison K	Revie D	Ackerman A	Carter H	Burbanks E	Robinson J	Greenhalgh J	Durham D	Tarrant E	Smith F	Hassall W	Inwood G	Varney J	Harris W	Gerrie S	Franklin N	Savage J	Gaynor L	
1	2	3	4	5	6	7	8	9	10	11														1
1	2	3	4	5	6	7	8	9	10	11														2
1	2	3	4	5	6	7	8	9	10	11														3
1	2	3	4	5	6	7	8	9	10	11														4
	2	3		5		7	8	9	10	11	1	4	6											5
	2	5	3			7	8	9	10	11	1	4	6											6
	2	5	3			7	8	9	1C	11	1	4	6											7
	2	5	3			7	8	9	10	11	1	4	6											8
	2	5	3			7	8	9	10	11	1	4		6										9
	2	5	3			7	8	9	10	11	1	4		6										10
	2	5	3		4	7	8	9	10	11	1			6										11
1			3	5	6	7	4	9	10	11					8	2								12
		5	3		6	9	4		10	7	1				8	2	11							13
		5			6	7	8	9	10		1					2	11	3	4					14
		5			6	7	8	9	10	11	1					2		3	4					15
		5				7	4	9	10	11	1					2		3	6	8				16
		5	3			7	4	9	10	11	1					2			6	8				17
		5	3			7	8	9		11	1	4				2			6	10				18
		5	3			7	4	9		11	1				10	2			6	8				19
		5	3			7	4	9		11	1				10	2			6	8				20
		5	3		6	7	8	9		11	1					2			4	10				21
		5	3		6	7	8	9		11	1					2			4	10				22
		5	3		6	7	10	9			1				8	2	11		4					23
		5			6	7	10			11	1				8	2		3	4	9				24
		5				7	4		10	11	1				8	2		3	6	9				25
		5	3			7	4	9	8	11	1					2			6	10				26
		5	3			7	4	9	8	11	1					2			6	10				27
			3			7	4	9	8	11	1					2			6	10	5			28
			3			7	4	9	8	11	1					2			6	10	5			29
			3			7	4	9	8	11						2			6	10	5	1		30
		3				7	4	9	8	11						2			6		5	1	10	31
		3	4			7	8	9		11						2			6		5	1	10	32
		3	4			7	8		10	11						2			6	9	5	1		33
			4			7	8		10	11	1					2		3	6	9	5			34
	3		4			7	8		10	11	1					2			6	9	5			35
			4		6	7	8	9		11	1				10	2		3			5			36
			4		6	7	8	11	10		1					2		3		9	5			37
			4		6	7	8	11	10		1					2		3		9	5			38
			3		6	7	8		10	11	1			4		2				9	5			39
			3		6	7		8	10	11	1			4		2				9	5			40
		5	3		6	7	8		10	11	1			4		2				9				41
			3		6	7	10	8		11	1			4		2				9	5			42
5	12	30	35	6	20	42	41	34	32	38	33	7	4	7	8	31	3	9	22	23	14	4	2	
						12	8	21	19	2										11				

1 own-goal

Bly W	Gibson A	Berry T	Jensen V	Meens H	Mellor A	Harrison K	Revie D	Ackerman A	Carter H	Burbanks E	Robinson J	Greenhalgh J	Durham D	Tarrant E	Smith F	Hassall W	Inwood G	Varney J	Harris W	Gerrie S	Franklin N	Savage J	Gaynor L	
		5	3			7	4	9	8	11	1					2			6	10				3
		5	3			7	4	9	8	11	1					2			6	10				4
			10	5		7	4	9	8	11	1					2		3	6					5
		2	3	1		3	3	3	3	3	3					3		1	3	2				
						1			2											1				

1951-52

1	Aug	18	(h)	Barnsley	D 0-0		37,05
2		20	(a)	Queen's Park R	D 1-1	Duthie	15,80
3		25	(a)	Sheffield U	L 1-4	Duthie	34,4
4		30	(h)	Queen's Park R	W 4-1	Gerrie 3, Revie	19,66
5	Sep	1	(h)	West Ham U	D 1-1	Moore	33,44
6		6	(a)	Notts C	L 0-4		38,20
7		8	(a)	Coventry C	W 4-1	Moore, Harrison, Gerrie, Revie	25,3
8		15	(h)	Swansea T	W 5-2	Gerrie 3, Revie 2	27,94
9		20	(h)	Notts C	L 1-3	Gerrie	35,4
10		22	(a)	Bury	L 1-3	Moore	16,86
11		29	(h)	Luton T	L 1-2	Harris	29,64
12	Oct	6	(a)	Southampton	D 1-1	Gerrie	22,8
13		13	(h)	Sheffield W	L 0-1		34,0
14		20	(a)	Leeds U	L 0-2		24,65
15		27	(h)	Rotherham U	D 3-3	Gerrie, Harrison, Nicklas	31,3
16	Nov	3	(a)	Cardiff C	L 0-1		23,4
17		10	(h)	Birmingham C	L 0-1		27,4
18		17	(a)	Leicester C	L 0-1		25,0
19		24	(h)	Nottingham F	L 1-4	Jensen	24,9
20	Dec	1	(a)	Brentford	L 1-2	Robson	26,0
21		8	(h)	Doncaster R	W 2-0	Burbanks, Gerrie	28,5
22		15	(a)	Barnsley	D 2-2	Carter, Gerrie	12,8
23		22	(h)	Sheffield U	W 2-1	Gerrie 2	26,9
24		25	(a)	Blackburn R	L 0-1		34,0
25		26	(h)	Blackburn R	W 3-0	Gerrie, Todd, Harrison	36,6
26		29	(a)	West Ham U	L 0-2		19,6
27	Jan	5	(h)	Coventry C	W 5-0	Gerrie 2, Moore, Carter, Burbanks	25,6
28		19	(a)	Swansea T	L 0-3		17,0
29		26	(h)	Bury	W 5-0	Gerrie 4, Todd	26,7
30	Feb	9	(a)	Luton T	D 1-1	Carter	16,5
31		16	(h)	Southampton	D 0-0		26,4
32	Mar	1	(a)	Sheffield W	L 0-6		41,8
33		8	(h)	Leeds U	W 3-2	Carter 2, Gerrie	28,7
34		15	(a)	Rotherham U	D 1-1	Burbanks	19,0
35		22	(h)	Cardiff C	D 0-0		27,0
36		29	(a)	Birmingham C	D 2-2	Carter, Harris	14,6
37	Apr	5	(h)	Leicester C	W 3-1	Carter, Harrison, Gerrie	24,3
38		11	(a)	Everton	L 0-5		42,9
39		12	(a)	Nottingham F	L 0-4		26,2
40		14	(h)	Everton	W 1-0	Gerrie	30,2
41		19	(h)	Brentford	W 4-1	Burbanks, Harrison, Duthie, Durham	30,8
42		26	(a)	Doncaster R	W 1-0	Carter	24,4

FINAL LEAGUE POSITION: 18th in Division Two

Appearances
Goals

FA Cup

3	Jan	12	(a)	Manchester U	W 2-0	Harrison, Gerrie	43,5
4	Feb	2	(a)	Blackburn R	L 0-2		45,3

Appearances
Goals

Bly W	Hassall W	Jensen V	Harris W	Franklin N	Mellor A	Harrison K	Revie D	Duthie J	Carter H	Burbanks E	Durham D	Gerrie S	Moore A	Tarrant E	Fagan F	Meens H	Todd P	Linaker J	Berry T	Porteous T	Nicklas C	Phillips E	Robson L	Robinson J	Murray T	
1	2	3	4	5	6	7	8	9	10	11																1
1	2	3	4	5		7	8	9		11	6	10														2
1	2	3	4	5		7	8	9		11	6	10														3
1	2	3	4	5			8	9		11	6	10	7													4
1	2	3	4	5			8	9		11	6	10	7													5
1	2	3	4	5			8	9		11	6	10	7													6
1	2	3	4	5		10	8			11		9	7	6												7
1	2	3	4	5		10	8			11		9	7	6												8
1	2	3	4	5		10	8			11		9	7	6												9
1		3	4	5	6	10	8					9	7	2	11											10
1	2	3	4		6	10	8					9	7	5	11											11
1	2	4	6			7	8				3	9			11	5	10									12
1	2	4	6			7	8			11	3	9				5	10									13
1	2	4	6			11		8			3	9				5	10	7								14
1	2	4				11					3	8					10	7	5	6	9					15
1	2	4								11	3	8					10	7	5	6	9					16
1		8	4								3	9			11		10	7	5	6		2				17
1	2	4	8			11					3	9	7				10		5	6						18
1		4				11					3	9	7				8		5	6		2	10			19
1	3	4				11							7	6			8		5		9	2	10			20
1	2	3	4			7			8	11		9		6			10		5							21
1	2	3	4			7			8	11		9		6			10		5							22
1	2	3	4			7			8	11		9		6			10		5							23
1	2	3	4			7				11		9		6			8		5				10			24
1		3	4			7			8	11	6	9		2			10		5							25
1	2	3	4						8	11	6	9	7				10		5							26
1	2	3	4						8	11	6	9	7				10		5							27
	2	3	4			7			8	11	6	9					10		5					1		28
	2	3	4			7			8	11	6	9					10		5					1		29
	2	3	4						8	11	6	9					10	7	5					1		30
	2	3	4			7			8	11	6	9					10		5					1		31
	2	3	4			7			8	11	6	9					10		5					1		32
1	2	3	4			7			10	11	6	8							5		9					33
1	2	3	4						10	11	6	8			7				5		9					34
1	2	3	4						10	11	6	8			7				5		9					35
1	2	4	8			7			10	11	6	9							5			3				36
1	2	4	8	5		7			10	11	6	9										3				37
1	2	4	8	5		7			10	11	6	9										3				38
1		3	6	4		7		9	8	11							10		5			2				39
	2	3	4			7			10	11	6	9							5					1	8	40
	2	3	4			7		9	10	11	6								5					1	8	41
	2	3	4			7			10	11	6	9							5					1	8	42
34	37	42	38	13	3	32	13	9	22	33	30	38	13	11	6	3	22	5	26	5	16	7	3	8	3	
		1	2			5	4	3	8	4	1	24	4				2				1		1			

Bly W	Hassall W	Jensen V	Harris W	Franklin N	Mellor A	Harrison K	Revie D	Duthie J	Carter H	Burbanks E	Durham D	Gerrie S	Moore A	Tarrant E	Fagan F	Meens H	Todd P	Linaker J	Berry T	Porteous T	Nicklas C	Phillips E	Robson L	Robinson J	Murray T	
	2	3	4			7			8	11	6	9					10		5					1		3
	2	3	4						8	11	6	9					10	7	5					1		4
	2	2	2			1			2	2	2	2					2	1	2					2		
						1						1														

1952-53

1	Aug	23	(a)	Everton	W 2-0	Jensen 2	43,03
2		25	(h)	West Ham U	W 1-0	Gerrie	35,96
3		30	(h)	Brentford	D 2-2	Jensen 2	35,99
4	Sep	1	(a)	West Ham U	D 0-0		19,72
5		6	(a)	Doncaster R	L 1-3	Jensen	21,15
6		8	(a)	Blackburn R	L 0-2		21,14
7		13	(h)	Swansea T	D 1-1	Harris	29,08
8		15	(h)	Blackburn R	W 3-0	K.Harrison 2, Davidson	24,84
9		20	(a)	Huddersfield T	D 1-1	Gerrie	34,41
10		27	(h)	Sheffield U	W 4-0	Gerrie, Tarrant, Linaker, Burbanks	32,06
11	Oct	4	(a)	Barnsley	L 1-5	Jensen	12,34
12		11	(h)	Fulham	W 3-1	Jensen, Gerrie, Burbanks	30,16
13		18	(a)	Rotherham U	L 1-2	Jensen	19,92
14		25	(h)	Plymouth A	L 0-1		31,77
15	Nov	1	(a)	Leeds U	L 1-3	Todd	25,53
16		8	(h)	Luton T	L 0-2		22,48
17		15	(a)	Birmingham C	L 3-4	Bursell 2, Durham	17,52
18		22	(h)	Bury	L 0-2		22,56
19		29	(a)	Southampton	L 1-5	Horton	8,86
20	Dec	6	(h)	Notts C	W 6-0	Horton 3, Murray, K.Harrison, Fagan	18,33
21		13	(a)	Leicester C	L 0-5		16,46
22		20	(h)	Everton	W 1-0	Murray	15,70
23		26	(a)	Nottingham F	L 1-4	Jensen	25,36
24		27	(h)	Nottingham F	W 3-1	Gerrie 2, Horton	22,83
25	Jan	3	(a)	Brentford	L 0-1		16,03
26		17	(h)	Doncaster R	D 1-1	Horton	28,48
27		24	(a)	Swansea T	L 0-3		18,32
28	Feb	7	(h)	Huddersfield T	L 0-2		26,08
29		21	(h)	Barnsley	D 2-2	Linaker 2	25,01
30		28	(a)	Fulham	L 1-2	Horton	24,99
31	Mar	7	(h)	Rotherham U	W 3-2	Gerrie, Murray, Selkirk (og)	25,21
32		14	(a)	Plymouth A	W 2-1	Murray, Horton	19,75
33		21	(h)	Leeds U	W 1-0	Harris	25,38
34		28	(a)	Luton T	L 2-3	Horton, Gerrie	13,74
35	Apr	3	(a)	Lincoln C	L 1-2	Gerrie	18,44
36		4	(h)	Birmingham C	W 2-0	Horton, Murray	23,48
37		6	(h)	Lincoln C	D 1-1	Gerrie	26,86
38		11	(a)	Bury	L 1-2	Gerrie	11,8
39		16	(h)	Leicester C	D 1-1	Gerrie	16,6
40		18	(h)	Southampton	W 1-0	Bulless	25,3
41		25	(a)	Notts C	L 0-2		11,6
42		29	(a)	Sheffield U	W 2-0	Gerrie, Furniss (og)	28,1

FINAL LEAGUE POSITION: 18th in Division Two

Appearances
Goals

FA Cup

3	Jan	10	(h)	Charlton A	W 3-1	Horton, Jensen, Harris	37,5
4		31	(h)	Gateshead	L 1-2	Gerrie	37,0

Appearances
Goals

Robinson J	Hassall W	Berry T	Harris W	Franklin N	Durham D	Linaker J	Murray T	Gerrie S	Jensen V	Burbanks E	Harrison F	Davidson A	Fagan P	Harrison K	Tarrant E	Bly W	Horton K	Duthie J	Todd P	Phillips E	Neal J	Bursell C	Porteous T	Cripsey B	Stephens J	Feasey P	Bulless B	
1	2	3	4	5	6	7	8	9	10	11																		1
1	2	3	4	5	6	7	8	9	10	11																		2
1	2	3	4	5	6	7	8	9	10	11																		3
1	2	3	4	5	6	7	8	9	10	11																		4
1	2	3	4	5	6	7	8	9	10	11																		5
1	2	3	4		6			8	10		5	9	7	11														6
1	2	3	4		6	7		8	10		5	9		11														7
1	2	3	4	5	6	7		8	10			9		11														8
1	2	3	4	5	6	7		8	10			9		11														9
1	2	3	4	5	6	7		8	10	11					9													10
1	2	3	4		6	7		8	10	11	5				9													11
	2	3	4		6	7		8	10	11	5				9	1												12
	2	3	4		6	7			10	11	5				9	1	8											13
	2		4		6	7		10	3	11	5				9	1	8											14
	2		4		6		7	9	3	11						1	8	5	10									15
	2		4		6		7		3	11				9		1	8	5	10									16
		5	4		6				9					7		1	11		10	2	3	8						17
		5	4		6				9	11	3			7		1			10	2		8						18
	3		4		6				9	11		5		7		1	8		10	2								19
1					6		10	9	3			5	11	7			8			2			4					20
1					6		10	9	3			5	11	7			8			2			4					21
1		5	4		6		10	9	3				11	7			8			2								22
1		5	4		6	7	10	9	3	11							8			2								23
1		3	4		6	7		9	10	11		5					8			2								24
1		3	4		6			9	10			5		7			8			2				11				25
1	2		4		6	7		9	10			5					8			3				11				26
1	2		4		6		7	9	10			5					8			3				11				27
1		5	4		6	7	8		3								9			2				11	10			28
			4		6	7			3						9	1	8			2				11	10	5		29
		5	4		6	7		9	3						10	1	8			2				11				30
		5	4		6	7	10	9	3							1	8			2				11				31
			4		6		10	9	3				7			1	8	5		2				11				32
			4		6		10	9	3				7			1	8	5		2				11				33
			4		6		10	9	3				7			1	8	5		2				11				34
		3	4		6		10	9	8	11			7			1		5		2								35
			4		6		10	9	3	11				7		1	8	5		2								36
1		5	4		6		10	9	3								8			2				11	7			37
		5	4		6		10	9	3	11				7		1	8			2								38
		5	4		6		10	9	3	11				7		1	8			2								39
		5	4		6	7	10	9	3							1	8			2							11	40
		5	4		6		10	9	3					7		1	8			2							11	41
		5	4		6			10	3					7		1	8	9		2							11	42
21	19	29	40	8	42	21	24	35	42	20	7	11	8	17	7	21	28	8	5	26	1	2	2	11	3	1	3	
			2		1	3	5	13	9	2		1	1	3	1		10		1			2					1	

2 own-goals

Robinson J	Hassall W	Berry T	Harris W	Franklin N	Durham D	Linaker J	Murray T	Gerrie S	Jensen V	Burbanks E	Harrison F	Davidson A	Fagan P	Harrison K	Tarrant E	Bly W	Horton K	Duthie J	Todd P	Phillips E	Neal J	Bursell C	Porteous T	Cripsey B	Stephens J	Feasey P	Bulless B	
1	2		4		6			9	10			5		7			8			3				11				3
1			4		6		7	9	3		5						8		10	2				11				4
2	1		2		2		1	2	2		1	1		1			2		1	2				2				
			1					1	1								1											

1953-54

1	Aug	19	(a)	Birmingham C	L 0-2		23,846
2		22	(a)	Oldham A	D 0-0		22,934
3		24	(h)	Everton	L 1-3	Jensen	26,511
4		29	(h)	Bury	W 3-0	Gerrie 2, Wilkinson	16,295
5	Sep	2	(a)	Everton	L 0-2		35,126
6		5	(a)	Doncaster R	L 1-4	Jensen	21,226
7		7	(h)	Nottingham F	W 3-0	Wilkinson 2, Jensen	17,288
8		12	(h)	Blackburn R	L 0-2		23,564
9		16	(a)	Nottingham F	L 0-2		13,573
10		19	(a)	Derby C	L 0-2		19,175
11		26	(h)	Brentford	W 2-0	Murray, Fagan	19,501
12	Oct	3	(a)	Bristol R	L 2-4	Tarrant, K.Harrison	25,244
13		10	(a)	Luton T	L 1-3	Porteous	14,754
14		17	(h)	Plymouth A	W 2-0	Ackerman, Jensen	24,653
15		24	(a)	Swansea T	L 0-1		18,925
16		31	(h)	Rotherham U	W 1-0	Ackerman	24,831
17	Nov	7	(a)	Leicester C	W 3-1	Crosbie 2, Jensen	28,726
18		14	(h)	Stoke C	L 1-2	Harris	26,581
19		21	(a)	Fulham	L 1-5	Ackerman	21,716
20		28	(h)	West Ham U	W 2-1	Horton, K.Harrison	21,620
21	Dec	5	(a)	Leeds U	D 0-0		21,070
22		12	(h)	Birmingham C	W 3-0	Crosbie, K.Harrison, Green (og)	19,752
23		19	(h)	Oldham A	W 8-0	Ackerman 4, Crosbie 2, Horton, Harris	18,245
24		26	(h)	Lincoln C	W 3-0	Ackerman 2, Cripsey	26,47
25		28	(a)	Lincoln C	L 0-3		16,91
26	Jan	16	(h)	Doncaster R	W 3-1	Horton 2, Ackerman	23,82
27		23	(a)	Blackburn R	L 1-3	Ackerman	24,19
28	Feb	6	(h)	Derby C	W 3-0	Horton, Crosbie, K.Harrison	23,36
29		13	(a)	Brentford	D 2-2	Ackerman, Bulless	11,52
30		27	(h)	Luton T	L 1-2	Crosbie	21,55
31	Mar	6	(a)	Plymouth A	D 2-2	Crosbie, Ackerman	18,21
32		13	(h)	Swansea T	W 4-3	Crosbie 2, Ackerman, Cripsey	16,61
33		20	(a)	Rotherham U	L 2-3	Ackerman, Atkinson	13,03
34		27	(h)	Fulham	W 2-1	Crosbie, Cripsey	16,94
35	Apr	3	(a)	West Ham U	L 0-1		13,46
36		7	(a)	Bury	L 0-3		8,52
37		10	(h)	Leicester C	L 0-3		19,08
38		12	(h)	Bristol R	W 4-1	Gerrie 3, Jensen	11,54
39		16	(h)	Notts C	L 0-2		24,03
40		17	(a)	Stoke C	W 1-0	Gerrie	17,37
41		19	(a)	Notts C	D 1-1	Ackerman	13,02
42		24	(h)	Leeds U	D 1-1	Ackerman	18,61
	FINAL LEAGUE POSITION: 15th in Division Two						Appearances
							Goals

FA Cup

3	Jan	9	(a)	Brentford	D 0-0		15,18
R		14	(h)	Brentford	D 2-2*	Horton, Crosbie	20,12
2R		18	(n†)	Brentford	W 5-2	Horton 2, Crosbie 2, Ackerman	10,17
4		30	(a)	Blackburn R	D 2-2	Crosbie, K.Harrison	33,23
R	Feb	4	(h)	Blackburn R	W 2-1	Ackerman, Bulless	23,43
5		20	(h)	Tottenham H	D 1-1	Jensen	46,8
R		24	(a)	Tottenham H	L 0-2		52,9
	*After extra-time. †Played at the Belle Vue Ground, Doncaster.						Appearances
							Goals

Bly W	Phillips E	Jensen V	Harris W	Berry T	Porteous T	Fagan P	Horton K	Gerrie S	Atkinson C	Cripsey B	Franklin N	Harrison K	Neal J	Wilkinson N	Bulless B	Harrison F	Tarrant E	Forgan T	Murray T	Crosbie R	Ackerman A	Durham D	Stephens J	Teece D	
1	2	3	4	5	6	7	8	9	10	11															1
1	2	3	4	5	6	7	8	9	10	11															2
1	2	3	4	6			8	9	10	11	5	7													3
1	2	6	4	5				8	10			7	3	9	11										4
1	2	6	4	5		11		8	10			7	3	9											5
1		10	4	5				8				7	3	9	11	2	6								6
1		6	4	5			10	8				7	3	9	11	2									7
1		6	4	5			10	8				7	3	9	11	2									8
	2	6	4			11	10	8				7	3	9		5		1							9
		6	4			11					5	7	3	9		2	10	1	8						10
		6	4			11		9			5	7	3			2	10	1	8						11
		6	4			11					5	7	3	9		2	10	1	8						12
		6		5	4	11		9				7	3			2	10	1	8						13
1		6	4	5				8				7	3		11	2				9	10				14
1		6	4	5				8				7	3		11	2				9	10				15
1		6	4	5		11		8				7	3			2				9	10				16
1		6	4	5		11		8				7	3			2				9	10				17
1		6	4	5		11		8				7	3			2				9	10				18
1		6	4	5		11		8				7	3			2				9	10				19
1		3	4	5			8			11		7				2				9	10	6			20
1		3	4	5			8			11		7				2				9	10	6			21
1		3	4	5			8			11		7				2				9	10	6			22
1		3	4	5			8			11		7				2				9	10	6			23
1		3	4	5			8			11		7				2				9	10	6			24
1	3		4	5			8			11						2			7	9	10	6			25
1		3	4	5			8			11		7				2				9	10	6			26
1		3	4	5			8	9				7			11	2					10	6			27
1			4	5			8					7	3		11	2				9	10	6			28
1		3	4	5			8					7			11	2				9	10	6			29
1	7	3	4	5			8				6				11	2				9	10				30
1		3		5	6		8				4				11	2				9	10		7		31
	2	3		5			8		7	11	4							1		9	10	6			32
		3		5	6		8		7	11	4					2		1		9	10				33
		3		5	6		8		7	11	4					2		1		9	10				34
				5			8		7	11	4		3			2		1		9	10	6			35
					4		8		7	11	5		3			2		1		9	10	6			36
		3		5			8		7	11	4					2				9	10	6		1	37
		3			6		4	10	7		5				11	2				8	9			1	38
		3		5	6			10	7		4				11	2				8	9			1	39
		3					4	8	7		5				11	2				9	10	6		1	40
		3		5			4	8	7						11	2				9	10	6		1	41
		3		5			4	8	7						11	2				9	10	6		1	42
26	9	38	29	35	9	12	28	23	16	16	15	26	19	8	16	36	5	10	5	28	29	17	1	6	
		6	2		1	1	5	6	1	3		4		3	1		1		1	11	17				

1 own-goal

Bly W	Phillips E	Jensen V	Harris W	Berry T	Porteous T	Fagan P	Horton K	Gerrie S	Atkinson C	Cripsey B	Franklin N	Harrison K	Neal J	Wilkinson N	Bulless B	Harrison F	Tarrant E	Forgan T	Murray T	Crosbie R	Ackerman A	Durham D	Stephens J	Teece D	
1		3	4	5			8			11		7				2				9	10	6			3
1		3	4	5			8			11		7				2				9	10	6			R
1		3	4	5			8			11		7				2				9	10	6			2R
		3	4	5			8					7			11	2		1		9	10	6			4
1		3	4	5			8					7			11	2				9	10	6			R
1		3	4	5			8					7			11	2				9	10	6			5
1	7	3	4				8				5				11	2				9	10	6			R
6	1	7	7	6			7			3	1	6			4	7		1		7	7	7			
		1					3					1			1					4	2				

1954-55

1	Aug	21	(h)	Leeds U	L 0-2		32,071
2		25	(a)	Lincoln C	W 1-0	Ackerman	13,827
3		28	(a)	Nottingham F	W 1-0	Thomas (og)	18,805
4		30	(h)	Lincoln C	W 4-0	Downie 2, Ackerman, Crosbie	21,818
5	Sep	4	(h)	Ipswich T	W 4-2	Crosbie 4	28,091
6		6	(a)	West Ham U	D 1-1	Crosbie	17,615
7		11	(a)	Birmingham C	D 0-0		23,846
8		13	(h)	West Ham U	L 0-1		25,851
9		18	(h)	Middlesbrough	W 1-0	Brown (og)	26,485
10		25	(a)	Stoke C	D 0-0		27,201
11	Oct	2	(h)	Rotherham U	L 1-2	Jensen	31,814
12		9	(a)	Plymouth A	W 2-1	Ackerman, Crosbie	21,466
13		16	(h)	Port Vale	W 2-1	Ackerman, Dryburgh	23,892
14		23	(a)	Swansea T	L 0-1		18,067
15		30	(h)	Notts C	W 5-2	Ackerman 2, Downie, Crosbie, Deans (og)	22,995
16	Nov	6	(a)	Liverpool	L 1-2	Downie	32,595
17		13	(h)	Bristol R	L 0-1		19,023
18		20	(a)	Blackburn R	L 0-4		26,873
19		27	(h)	Fulham	D 0-0		17,869
20	Dec	4	(a)	Doncaster R	D 2-2	Horton, Dryburgh	8,372
21		11	(h)	Derby C	D 1-1	Ackerman	16,472
22		18	(a)	Leeds U	L 0-3		23,991
23		25	(a)	Luton T	D 1-1	Downie	15,853
24		27	(h)	Luton T	L 0-4		39,890
25	Jan	1	(h)	Nottingham F	L 2-3	Mannion, Jensen	18,997
26	Feb	5	(a)	Middlesbrough	W 2-1	Ackerman, Dryburgh	32,619
27		12	(h)	Stoke C	D 1-1	Ackerman	10,192
28		19	(a)	Rotherham U	L 0-2		11,447
29		26	(h)	Plymouth A	L 0-2		14,896
30	Mar	5	(a)	Port Vale	L 0-3		16,658
31		12	(h)	Swansea T	W 4-3	Crosbie 2, Ackerman 2	12,700
32		19	(a)	Notts C	L 1-3	Bulless	15,103
33		26	(h)	Liverpool	D 2-2	Jensen 2	6,771
34	Apr	2	(a)	Bristol R	L 0-1		17,044
35		8	(a)	Bury	L 1-4	Crosbie	11,38
36		9	(h)	Blackburn R	L 1-4	Gerrie	17,34
37		11	(h)	Bury	W 1-0	Gerrie	13,70
38		16	(a)	Fulham	W 1-0	Gerrie	13,25
39		18	(a)	Ipswich T	L 0-2		11,93
40		23	(h)	Doncaster R	D 1-1	Bulless	12,27
41		25	(h)	Birmingham C	L 0-3		12,84
42		30	(a)	Derby C	L 0-3		7,76

FINAL LEAGUE POSITION: 19th in Division Two

Appearances
Goals

FA Cup

3	Jan	8	(h)	Birmingham C	L 0-2		25,92

Appearances
Goals

Bly W	Harrison F	Jensen V	Downie J	Franklin N	Durham D	Atkinson C	Gerrie S	Crosbie R	Ackerman A	Dryburgh T	Porteous T	Harrison K	Teece D	Bulless B	Horton K	Berry T	Smith R	Tulloch R	Cripsey B	Neal J	Davidson A	Whitnall B	Mannion W	Dennison R	Head M	Capewell R	Patterson G	
1	2	3	4	5	6	7	8	9	10	11																		1
1	2	3	8	5	6	7		9	10	11	4																	2
1	2	3	8	5	6			9	10	11	4	7																3
1	2	3	8	5	6			9	10	11	4	7																4
1	2	3	8	5	6			9	10	11	4	7																5
	2	3	8	5	6			9	10	11	4	7	1															6
	2	3	8	5	6			9	10		4	7	1	11														7
	2	3	8	5	6			9	10		4	7	1	11														8
	2	3	8	5	6			9	10			7	1	11	4													9
1	2	3	8	5	6			9	10			7		11	4													10
1	2	3	8	5	6			9	10	11		7			4													11
1	2	3	8	5	6			9	10	11		7			4													12
1	2	3		5	6			9	10	11	4	7			8													13
1	2	3		5	6			9	10	11	4	7			8													14
1	2	3	10	5	6			7	9	11	4				8													15
1		3	10	5	6			7	9	11	4				8	2												16
1		3	10	5	6			9	11		4				8	2	7											17
	2	3		5	6			9	11		4	7	1					8	10									18
	2	3	10	5	6				9	11	4	7	1		8													19
	2		6	5				10	9	11	4	7	1		8					3								20
	2			5	6	7	8	9	10				1		4				11	3								21
	2			5	6	7		8	10				1		4				11	3	9							22
		10	8	5	6	7		9	11				1		4					3		2						23
			8	5	6	7		9	11				1		4					3		2	10					24
		3	8	5	6	7		9		11	4		1										10	2				25
1		3	4	5		7			9	11	6				8								10	2				26
1		3	4	5		7	8		9	11	6												10	2				27
1		3	4			7	8		9	11	6					5							10	2				28
1		3	4			8			9	11	6					5							10	2	7			29
1		3	4	5				9		11	6								10				8	2	7			30
1		3		5				9	10		6	7		11				4					8	2				31
1		3		5				9			6			11	8			4					10	2	7			32
1		3	4	5	6		9	8		11							7			2			10					33
1				5	6	8		9			4			11			7		10	3				2				34
				5	6			9			4		1	11			7		10	3			8	2				35
				5	6		9	8			4		1	11			7			3			10	2				36
		3	7	5	6		9				4				8				11				10	2		1		37
1		3			6		9			11	4				8	5	7				2		10					38
1		3			6		9	7		11	4			10	8	5								2				39
1		3		5	6		9	7			4			10					11				8	2				40
1		3		5	6	8	9				4			10					11					2			7	41
1		3		5	6	9					4			10					11				8	2			7	42
27	20	35	27	38	34	14	11	33	29	23	32	16	14	13	20	6	6	3	10	9	2	2	16	16	3	1	2	
		4	5				3	11	11	3				2	1								1					

3 own-goals

1		3	8		6				9	11		7			4	5							8	2				3
1		1	1		1				1	1		1			1	1							1	1				

1955-56

1	Aug	20	(h)	Leicester C	L 2-4	Gerrie, Jensen	20,431
2		24	(a)	Lincoln C	L 0-2		13,391
3		27	(a)	Liverpool	L 0-3		38,928
4		29	(h)	Lincoln C	W 2-1	Bulless 2	14,810
5	Sep	3	(h)	Plymouth A	L 0-1		17,815
6		5	(a)	Leeds U	L 0-1		17,524
7		10	(a)	Stoke C	L 1-4	Bulless	19,965
8		17	(h)	Bristol R	L 1-2	Patterson	14,014
9		24	(a)	Doncaster R	L 0-3		12,629
10	Oct	1	(h)	Sheffield W	D 2-2	Bulless, Cripsey	16,748
11		8	(a)	Fulham	L 0-5		21,207
12		15	(h)	Bury	L 2-3	Bradbury, Duncan	14,042
13		22	(a)	Swansea T	L 1-4	Duncan	16,648
14		29	(h)	Middlesbrough	D 2-2	Atkinson, Davidson	14,013
15	Nov	5	(a)	Bristol C	L 2-5	Cripsey, Jensen	22,776
16		12	(h)	West Ham U	W 3-1	Bradbury, Mortensen, Clarke	24,050
17		19	(a)	Port Vale	W 1-0	Mortensen	17,778
18		26	(h)	Rotherham U	L 0-3		22,830
19	Dec	3	(a)	Barnsley	L 1-2	Mortensen	14,050
20		10	(h)	Notts C	W 2-0	Bradbury, Stephens	12,842
21		17	(a)	Leicester C	W 2-1	Bradbury, Mortensen	27,013
22		24	(h)	Liverpool	L 1-2	Bradbury	19,537
23		26	(a)	Nottingham F	L 1-2	Mortensen	15,740
24		27	(h)	Nottingham F	L 0-3		21,407
25		31	(a)	Plymouth A	D 1-1	Martin	20,930
26	Jan	21	(a)	Bristol R	L 2-4	Clarke 2	23,801
27	Feb	11	(a)	Sheffield W	L 1-4	Mortensen	18,845
28		18	(h)	Port Vale	W 2-1	Bradbury, Berry	6,884
29		25	(a)	Bury	L 2-3	Mortensen, Stephens	10,859
30	Mar	3	(h)	Swansea T	L 1-4	Mortensen	12,943
31		10	(a)	Notts C	W 2-0	Clarke, Neal	12,707
32		17	(h)	Bristol C	L 1-3	Jensen	11,174
33		24	(a)	West Ham U	D 1-1	Smith	12,718
34		30	(a)	Blackburn R	L 0-2		25,327
35		31	(h)	Fulham	D 2-2	Bradbury 2	12,683
36	Apr	2	(h)	Blackburn R	L 0-3		14,135
37		7	(a)	Rotherham U	W 2-0	Fraser 2	9,619
38		10	(h)	Doncaster R	D 1-1	Fraser	8,155
39		14	(h)	Barnsley	W 4-1	Clarke, Bradbury, Smith, Betts (og)	8,931
40		21	(a)	Middlesbrough	L 1-5	Fraser	11,190
41		28	(h)	Leeds U	L 1-4	Martin	31,123
42	May	1	(h)	Stoke C	W 3-2	Fraser 2, Clarke	5,232

FINAL LEAGUE POSITION: 22nd in Division Two — Relegated

Appearances
Goals

FA Cup

3	Jan	7	(a)	Aston Villa	D 1-1	Clarke	32,865
R		12	(h)	Aston Villa	L 1-2	Atkinson	15,685

Appearances
Goals

Bly W	Davidson A	Jensen V	Martin T	Berry T	Durham D	Major J	Smith R	Gerrie S	Bulless B	Cripsey B	Porteous T	Teece D	Neal J	Atkinson C	Kirman H	Peacock T	Franklin N	Duncan J	Patterson G	Bradbury W	Fisher B	Dennison R	Clarke D	Mortensen S	Stephens J	Feasey P	Harrison F	Fraser D	
1	2	3	4	5	6	7	8	9	10	11																			1
1	2	3	4	5		7	8	9	10	11	6																		2
	2		4	5		7	10	9		11	6	1	3	8															3
	2		4	5		7			10	11		1	3	8	6	9													4
	2		4	5		7		9	10	11		1	3	8	6														5
	2		4			7			10	11	6	1	3				5	8	9										6
1	2	8	4	5		7			10	11	6		3			9													7
1	2	8	4	5		7			10	11	6		3						9										8
1	4	3	8	5				9	10	11	6		2						7										9
1	4	3	8	5			7		10	11	6		2						9										10
1	4	3	8	5			7		10	11	6		2	9															11
	5	3	4						10	11	6	1	2	7				9		8									12
	6	3	4				7		10	11			2				5	9		8	1								13
	6	3	4				7		11				2	8			5	9		10	1								14
	6	3	4				7			11							5	9	10	8	1	2							15
1	6	3	4	2									11				5	7		10			8	9					16
1	6	3	4							11			2				5	7		10			8	9					17
1	6	3	4							11			2				5	7		10			8	9					18
1	6	3	4	5		7				11			2							10			8	9					19
1	4	3		5					6	11			2							10			8	9	7				20
1	4	3		5					6	11			2							10			8	9	7				21
1	4	3		5					6	11			2							10			8	9	7				22
1	4	3	8	5					6	11			2							10				9	7				23
1	4	3	8	5					6	11			2										10	9	7				24
1	4	3	7						11		6		2					9		8			10			5			25
1	4	3							6	11	5		2	7						10			8	9					26
1	4			5					6	11			3							10			8	9	7		2		27
1	4			5				9	6		3									10		2	8	7	11				28
1	4	3		5				11	6											10		2	8	9	7				29
1	4	3	6						11		5		2							8			10	9	7				30
1	4	3							6	11			2							8			10	9	7	5			31
1	4	3					7		6	11			2							8			10	9		5			32
1	4	3		5			7		6	11			2					8					10	9					33
1	4	3		5			7		6	11			2					8					10	9					34
	4	3		5			7		6	11										8	1		10	9			2		35
	4			5			7		6	11			3							8	1		10	9			2		36
	4	3		5			7		6											8	1		10	9			2	11	37
	4	3		5			7		6									9		8	1		10				2	11	38
	4	3		5			7		6											9	1		10		8		2	11	39
	4	3					7		6											9	1		10		8	5	2	11	40
	4	3	8	5					6											9	1		10		7		2	11	41
	4	3	8	5					6											9	1		10		7		2	11	42
26	42	35	25	29	1	9	17	7	36	30	13	5	30	7	2	2	7	12	5	28	11	3	26	21	14	4	9	6	
	1	3	2	1			2	1	4	2			1	1				2	1	9			6	8	2			6	

1 own-goal

Bly W	Davidson A	Jensen V	Martin T	Berry T	Durham D	Major J	Smith R	Gerrie S	Bulless B	Cripsey B	Porteous T	Teece D	Neal J	Atkinson C	Kirman H	Peacock T	Franklin N	Duncan J	Patterson G	Bradbury W	Fisher B	Dennison R	Clarke D	Mortensen S	Stephens J	Feasey P	Harrison F	Fraser D	
1	4	3							6	11	5		2	7						10			8	9					3
1	4	3							6	11	5		2	7						10			8	9					R
2	2	2							2	2	2		2	2						2			2	2					
														1									1						

1956-57

1	Aug	18	(a)	Halifax T	L 0-1		8,402
2		20	(h)	Tranmere R	W 4-1	Mortensen 2, Bradbury, Jensen	12,222
3		25	(h)	Rochdale	W 2-0	Bradbury, Clarke	13,089
4		28	(a)	Tranmere R	W 4-2	Bradbury 3, Clarke	5,894
5	Sep	1	(a)	Scunthorpe U	D 1-1	Bradbury	11,004
6		3	(h)	Workington	L 0-2		14,491
7		8	(h)	Crewe A	W 2-0	Bradbury, Jensen	12,947
8		12	(a)	Workington	L 3-4	Mortensen 3	8,484
9		15	(a)	Derby C	L 0-1		20,124
10		17	(a)	Bradford	L 1-4	Stephens	7,102
11		22	(h)	Wrexham	L 1-2	Duncan	10,667
12		24	(h)	Bradford	W 2-0	Mortensen, Stephens	8,349
13		29	(a)	Gateshead	L 0-2		5,535
14	Oct	6	(a)	York C	L 1-2	Clarke	10,763
15		13	(h)	Oldham A	W 2-1	Clarke, Gerrie	9,400
16		20	(a)	Stockport C	W 2-1	Clarke, Bulless	9,272
17		27	(h)	Southport	W 2-1	Mortensen 2	10,443
18	Nov	3	(a)	Chesterfield	L 1-3	Clarke	10,610
19		10	(h)	Chester	W 2-0	Bradbury, Stephens	8,571
20		24	(h)	Bradford C	W 1-0	Currie (og)	11,825
21	Dec	1	(a)	Mansfield T	L 1-2	Stephens	8,809
22		15	(h)	Halifax T	W 3-1	Mortensen, Cripsey, Davidson	9,837
23		25	(a)	Darlington	D 1-1	Clarke	5,546
24		26	(h)	Darlington	D 1-1	Mortensen	9,872
25		29	(h)	Scunthorpe U	D 2-2	Bulless, Cripsey	12,873
26	Jan	1	(a)	Hartlepools U	D 3-3	Stephens, Cripsey, Davidson	9,768
27		12	(a)	Crewe A	W 3-2	Bradbury 2, Edwards (og)	4,285
28		19	(h)	Derby C	D 3-3	Clarke 2, Bulless	14,543
29		26	(a)	Barrow	W 2-1	Stephens, Bradbury	7,728
30	Feb	2	(a)	Wrexham	L 2-5	Clarke 2	11,841
31		9	(h)	Gateshead	D 1-1	Bradbury	11,689
32		16	(h)	York C	D 1-1	Bradbury	15,697
33		23	(a)	Oldham A	W 3-1	Stephens 2, Clarke	2,500
34	Mar	2	(h)	Stockport C	W 5-3	Bradbury 2, Clarke 2, Stephens	12,222
35		5	(a)	Rochdale	L 3-4	Bradbury, Bulless, Collinson	4,296
36		9	(a)	Southport	L 0-1		4,439
37		16	(h)	Chesterfield	W 3-2	Bradbury 2, Collinson	11,660
38		18	(h)	Barrow	W 3-0	Bulless 3	11,728
39		23	(a)	Chester	D 1-1	Cripsey	6,272
40		30	(h)	Hartlepool	W 2-0	Bulless, Clarke	13,310
41	Apr	6	(a)	Bradford C	L 1-2	Clarke	9,434
42		9	(a)	Carlisle U	W 3-1	Cripsey, Bulless, Stephens	6,297
43		13	(h)	Mansfield T	L 1-2	Stephens	10,550
44		19	(h)	Accrington S	W 2-1	Cripsey, Clarke	18,304
45		22	(a)	Accrington S	W 3-0	Davidson 2, Clarke	11,400
46		27	(h)	Carlisle U	D 0-0		13,010

FINAL LEAGUE POSITION: 8th in Division Three North

Appearances
Goals

FA Cup

1	Nov	17	(h)	Gateshead	W 4-0	Mortensen 2, Bradbury, Cripsey	12,26[illegible]
2	Dec	8	(h)	York C	W 2-1	Bulless 2	24,15[illegible]
3	Jan	5	(h)	Bristol R	L 3-4	Clarke 2, Stephens	22,75[illegible]

Appearances
Goals

Bly W	Harrison F	Jensen V	Davidson A	Berry T	Bulless B	Stephens J	Bradbury W	Mortensen S	Gerrie S	Cripsey B	Clarke D	Martin T	Fraser D	Rintanen M	Dennison R	Smales K	Duncan J	Feasey P	Major J	Coates D	Fisher B	Durham D	Collinson L	Smith C	Neilson N	
1	2	3	4	5	6	7	8	9	10	11																1
1	2	3	4	5	6	7	8	9		11	10															2
1	2	3	4	5	6	7	9		10	11	8															3
1	2	3	4	5	6	7	9		10	11	8															4
1	2	3	4	5	6	7	9	10		11	8															5
1	2	3	4	5	6	7	9		10	11	8															6
1	2	3	6	5	10	7	8	9		11		4														7
1	2	3	6	5	10	7	8	9				4	11													8
1	2	3	4	5	6	7	8	9			10		11													9
			4	5	6	11	7				10	8		1	2	3	9									10
	2	3	4		6	11	9							1			10	5	7	8						11
	2	3	4		6	11	7	9						1			10	5		8						12
	2	3	4		6	11	10	9									7	5		8	1					13
	2	3	4		6	7		9	10	11	8							5			1					14
	2	3			6	7		9	10	11	8	4		1				5								15
1	2	3	4		6	7		9	10	11	8							5								16
1	2	3	4		6	7		9	10	11	8							5								17
1	2	3	4		6	7		9	10	11	8							5								18
1	2	3	4			7	10	9		11	8							5				6				19
1	2				6	7	10	9		11	8							5				3	4			20
1	2				6	7	10	9		11	8							5				3	4			21
1	2		6		10	7		9		11	8							5				3	4			22
1	2		6		10	7		9		11	8							5				3	4			23
1	2		6		10	7		9		11	8							5				3	4			24
1	2		6		10	7		9		11	8							5				3	4			25
1	2		6		10	7	9			11	8							5				3	4			26
1	2		4		6	7	10	9		11	8							5				3				27
1			6		10	7	9			11	8				2			5				3	4			28
1	2		6		10	7	9			11	8							5				3	4			29
1	2		6		11	7	10				8							5				3	4	9		30
1	2		6		11	7	10				8							5				3	4	9		31
1	2		6		10	7	9			11	8							5				3	4			32
1	2		6		10	7	9			11	8							5				3	4			33
1	2		6		10	7	9			11	8							5				3	4			34
1	2		6		10	7	9			11	8							5				3	4			35
1	2		6		10	7	9			11	8							5				3	4			36
1	2		6		10	7	9			11	8							5				3	4			37
1	2		6		10	7	9			11	8							5				3	4			38
1	2		6		10	7	9			11	8							5				3	4			39
1	2		6		10	7	9			11	8							5				3	4			40
1	2		6		10	7	9			11	8							5				3	4			41
1	2		3		10	7	9			11	8	6						5					4			42
1	2				10	7	9			11	8	6						3					4		5	43
1	2			5	10	7	9			11	8	6						3					4			44
1	2		6	5	10	7	9			11	8							3					4			45
1			6		10	7	9			11	8				2			3					4		5	46
40	43	18	41	12	45	46	37	21	9	38	40	7	2	4	3	1	4	36	1	3	2	23	26	2	2	
		2	4		9	11	18	10	1	6	18						1						2			

2 own-goals

Bly W	Harrison F	Jensen V	Davidson A	Berry T	Bulless B	Stephens J	Bradbury W	Mortensen S	Gerrie S	Cripsey B	Clarke D	Martin T	Fraser D	Rintanen M	Dennison R	Smales K	Duncan J	Feasey P	Major J	Coates D	Fisher B	Durham D	Collinson L	Smith C	Neilson N	
1	2				6	7	10	9		11	8							5				3	4			1
1	2		6		10	7		9		11	8							5				3	4			2
1	2		6		10	7	9			11	8							5				3	4			3
3	3		2		3	3	2	2		3	3							3				3	3			
					2	1	1	2		1	2															

1957-58

1	Aug	24	(h)	York C	L 0-1		17,671
2		26	(h)	Barrow	D 1-1	Dennison	11,684
3		31	(a)	Stockport C	L 0-1		13,091
4	Sep	2	(a)	Barrow	D 0-0		8,681
5		7	(h)	Halifax T	W 5-2	Clarke 4, Bradbury	11,593
6		9	(h)	Workington	W 3-2	Stephens 2, Bradbury	11,433
7		14	(a)	Rochdale	L 1-2	Bradbury	7,612
8		18	(a)	Workington	L 2-3	Stephens, Davidson	6,734
9		21	(h)	Crewe A	W 1-0	Cripsey	10,966
10		23	(a)	Mansfield T	W 3-1	Davidson 2, Stephens	6,860
11		28	(a)	Wrexham	L 0-6		8,755
12		30	(h)	Mansfield T	D 1-1	Clarke	7,878
13	Oct	5	(h)	Scunthorpe U	W 2-0	Bradbury, Stephens	12,009
14		12	(a)	Carlisle U	W 1-0	Clarke	11,178
15		19	(h)	Bury	W 2-1	Stephens 2	15,236
16		26	(a)	Accrington S	L 0-3		7,107
17	Nov	2	(h)	Chester	W 3-0	Bradbury, Cripsey, Clarke	11,732
18		9	(a)	Chesterfield	D 0-0		7,922
19		23	(a)	Hartlepools U	L 1-5	Bradbury	8,754
20		30	(h)	Bradford	D 3-3	Collinson, Bradbury, Perry (og)	11,042
21	Dec	14	(h)	Southport	W 3-2	Clarke, Bradbury, Davidson	9,148
22		21	(a)	York C	L 1-3	Clarke	7,031
23		25	(h)	Gateshead	D 1-1	Fraser	8,950
24		26	(a)	Gateshead	L 1-3	Smith	5,148
25		28	(h)	Stockport C	W 1-0	Bradbury	11,719
26	Jan	11	(a)	Halifax T	D 2-2	Bradbury, Bulless	5,858
27		18	(h)	Rochdale	W 2-1	Cripsey, Clarke	8,991
28	Feb	1	(a)	Crewe A	W 2-1	Cripsey, Clarke	4,370
29		8	(h)	Wrexham	W 2-0	Bradbury, Clarke	8,241
30		20	(a)	Scunthorpe U	L 0-2		11,408
31		22	(h)	Hartlepools U	D 1-1	Bulless	11,926
32	Mar	1	(a)	Bury	D 1-1	Coates	10,250
33		10	(h)	Darlington	W 2-1	Bradbury, Cripsey	6,519
34		15	(a)	Chester	D 1-1	Bradbury	5,721
35		17	(h)	Tranmere R	D 0-0		8,950
36		22	(h)	Carlisle U	W 4-0	Smith 2, Bulless, Davidson	9,917
37		25	(h)	Accrington S	W 1-0	Smith	9,382
38		29	(a)	Tranmere R	D 4-4	Bradbury, Clarke, Smith, Cripsey	8,459
39	Apr	5	(h)	Oldham A	W 9-0	Bradbury 3, Smith 3, Clarke, Bulless, Cripsey	11,007
40		7	(h)	Bradford C	L 1-3	Cripsey	16,763
41		8	(a)	Bradford C	L 0-1		13,789
42		12	(a)	Bradford	D 4-4	Smith 2, Clarke, Bulless	5,910
43		15	(a)	Oldham A	D 1-1	Bulless	6,894
44		19	(h)	Chesterfield	W 1-0	Bulless	9,625
45		23	(a)	Darlington	D 2-2	Bradbury, Smith	4,056
46		26	(a)	Southport	W 2-1	Bradbury, Clarke	1,862

FINAL LEAGUE POSITION: 5th in Division Three North

Appearances
Goals

FA Cup

1	Nov	16	(h)	Crewe A	W 2-1	Bradbury, Clarke	10,773
2	Dec	7	(a)	Port Vale	D 2-2	Bradbury, Davidson	14,338
R		9	(h)	Port Vale	W 4-3*	Bradbury 2, Bulless, Cleary (og)	17,403
3	Jan	4	(h)	Barnsley	D 1-1	Bradbury	21,868
R		8	(a)	Barnsley	W 2-0	Clarke, Bulless	20,890
4		29	(a)	Sheffield W	L 3-4	Bradbury, Bulless, Stephens	51,834

*After extra-time

Appearances
Goals

Bly W	Feasey P	Durham D	Collinson L	Neilson N	Davidson A	Dennison R	Clarke D	Bradbury W	Bulless B	Cripsey B	Bennion J	Round L	Stephens J	Berry T	Cubie N	Coates D	Bentley K	Harrison F	Smith C	Fraser D	Fisher B	Bridges B	Garvey B	
1	2	3	4	5	6	7	8	9	10	11														1
1	2	3	4	5	6	7	8	9	11		10													2
	2	3		5	6		8	9	10	11	4	1	7											3
	2	3		5	6		8	9	10	11	4	1	7											4
	3		6	5	2		8	9	10	11	4	1	7											5
	2	3	4	5	6		8	9	11		10	1	7											6
	2	3	4	5	6		8	9	11		10	1	7											7
	2	3	4		6		8	9	10	11		1	7	5										8
	2	3	4		9		8	10	6	11		1	7	5										9
			4	3	9		8	10	6	11		1	7	5	2									10
	5		4	3	9		8	10	6	11		1	7		2									11
1	3		4	5	2		8	9	10	11	6		7											12
1		3	4	5	2		8	9	10	11	6		7											13
1		3	4	5	2		8	9	10	11	6		7											14
		3	4	5	2		8	9	10	11	6	1	7											15
		3	4	5	2		8	9	10	11	6	1	7											16
		3	4	5	2		8	9	10	11	6	1	7											17
		3	4	5	2		8	9	10	11	6	1	7											18
1		3	4	5	2		8	9	10	11	6		7											19
1		3	9	5	2		7	10	6		4		11			8								20
	2	3	4	5	6		8	9	11			1	7				10							21
	5	3			4		8	9	11		6	1	7				10	2						22
	3			5	6		7	8				1			4		10	2	9	11				23
		3		5	6		7	8				1			4		10	2	9	11				24
	5	3	4		6		8	9					7					2		11	1	10		25
		2	4	5	6		8	9	10	11			7					3			1			26
		3	4	5	6		8	9	10	11			7					2			1			27
1	5	3	4		6		8	9	10	11			7					2						28
1	5	3	4		6		8	9		11			7			10		2						29
1	5	3			6		7	9	10	11	4					8		2						30
1	5	3			6		8	9	11		4		7			10		2						31
1		3			6		8	9	11		4		7			10		2					5	32
1	5	3	4		6		8	9	10	11			7					2						33
1	5	3	4		6		8	9	10	11			7					2						34
1	5	3	4		6		8	9	10	11			7					2						35
1	5	3	4		6		7	8	10	11								2	9					36
1	5	3	4		6		7	8	10	11								2	9					37
1	5	3	4		6		7	8	10	11								2	9					38
1	5	3	4		6		7	8	10	11								2	9					39
1	5	3	4		6		7	8	10	11								2	9					40
1	5	3	4		6		7	8	10	11								2	9					41
1	5	3	4		6		7	8	10	11								2	9					42
1	5	3	4		6		7	8	10	11								2	9					43
1	5	3	4		6		7	8	10	11								2	9					44
1	5	3	4		6		7	8	10	11								2	9					45
1	5	3	4		6		7	8	10	11								2	9					46
26	33	41	38	23	46	2	46	46	42	35	19	17	30	3	4	5	4	25	13	3	3	1	1	
			1		5	1	16	19	7	8			7			1			11	1				

1 own-goal

Bly W	Feasey P	Durham D	Collinson L	Neilson N	Davidson A	Dennison R	Clarke D	Bradbury W	Bulless B	Cripsey B	Bennion J	Round L	Stephens J	Berry T	Cubie N	Coates D	Bentley K	Harrison F	Smith C	Fraser D	Fisher B	Bridges B	Garvey B	
1		3	4	5	2		8	9	10	11	6		7											1
1	2	3	4	5	6		8	9	11				7				10							2
1	2	3	4	5	6		8	9	11				7				10							R
	5	3	4		6		8	9	10	11			7					2			1			3
	5	3	4		6		8	9	10	11			7					2			1			R
1	5	3	4		6		8	9	10	11			7					2						4
4	5	6	6	3	6		6	6	6	4	1		6				2	3			2			
					1		2	6	3				1											

1 own-goal

1958-59

No	Month	Day	Venue	Opponents	Result	Score	Scorers	Attendance
1	Aug	23	(h)	Plymouth A	D	1-1	Smith	14,318
2		27	(a)	Swindon T	L	0-2		14,355
3		30	(a)	Bradford C	L	1-2	Bradbury	12,165
4	Sep	1	(h)	Swindon T	D	0-0		12,035
5		6	(h)	Wrexham	W	1-0	Smith	10,898
6		11	(a)	Notts C	D	1-1	Bowering	8,584
7		13	(a)	Southampton	L	1-6	Bradbury	14,461
8		15	(h)	Notts C	W	5-0	Smith 2, Bradbury, Collinson, Clarke	8,521
9		20	(h)	Accrington S	W	4-2	Bradbury 2, Clarke, Coates	11,858
10		22	(h)	Brentford	W	3-1	Coates, Smith, Clarke	14,172
11		27	(a)	Halifax T	W	2-1	Bradbury, Collinson	7,730
12		30	(a)	Brentford	D	1-1	Clarke	12,441
13	Oct	4	(h)	Newport C	L	2-3	Bradbury, Smith	14,753
14		6	(h)	Chesterfield	W	3-1	Bowering 2, Bradbury	12,305
15		11	(a)	Stockport C	L	1-2	Bradbury	9,521
16		18	(h)	Reading	W	2-0	Bowering, Coates	13,955
17		25	(a)	Colchester U	W	3-1	Bradbury, Smith, Coates	9,277
18	Nov	1	(h)	Bournemouth	W	5-3	Smith 3, Bowering, Coates	14,400
19		8	(a)	Norwich C	W	1-0	Smith	15,929
20		22	(a)	Rochdale	W	1-0	Bradbury	5,562
21		29	(h)	Queen's Park R	W	1-0	Smith	11,705
22	Dec	6	(a)	Bournemouth	L	0-1		9,869
23		13	(h)	Doncaster R	W	5-1	Bradbury 2, Clarke 2, Smith	10,411
24		20	(a)	Plymouth A	D	1-1	Smith	20,238
25		26	(h)	Mansfield T	W	5-2	Bradbury 3, Smith, Clarke	20,836
26		27	(a)	Mansfield T	D	1-1	Coates	7,916
27	Jan	1	(a)	Chesterfield	L	1-2	Bradbury	10,374
28		3	(h)	Bradford C	W	4-0	Bradbury 3, Coates	14,168
29		10	(h)	Southend U	W	3-2	Bradbury, Smith, Coates	12,908
30		24	(a)	Bury	L	1-2	Smith	7,932
31		31	(h)	Southampton	W	3-0	Bradbury 2, Clarke	14,441
32	Feb	7	(a)	Accrington S	W	1-0	Lord (og)	6,610
33		14	(h)	Halifax T	W	4-0	Smith 2, Bradbury, Bulless	13,233
34		21	(a)	Newport C	W	3-1	Bradbury, Smith, Garvey	6,988
35		28	(h)	Stockport C	W	3-1	Bradbury 2, Clarke	16,177
36	Mar	14	(h)	Colchester U	W	3-0	Smith 2, Davidson	16,468
37		27	(a)	Tranmere R	L	0-1		15,956
38		28	(h)	Norwich C	D	3-3	Clarke 2, Smith	24,156
39		30	(h)	Tranmere R	W	1-0	Bradbury	19,090
40	Apr	4	(a)	Southend U	D	1-1	Coates	12,279
41		11	(h)	Rochdale	W	2-1	Bowering, Clarke	13,377
42		15	(a)	Reading	L	0-2		13,548
43		18	(a)	Queen's Park R	D	1-1	Smith	9,325
44		23	(a)	Doncaster R	W	2-0	Bradbury, Smith	8,881
45		25	(h)	Bury	W	2-0	Bradbury, Bulless	16,447
46		29	(a)	Wrexham	L	1-5	Smith	7,677
	FINAL LEAGUE POSITION: 2nd in Division Three — Promoted							Appearances
								Goals

FA Cup

No	Month	Day	Venue	Opponents	Result	Score	Scorers	Attendance
1	Nov	15	(h)	Stockport C	L	0-1		17,441
								Appearances
								Goals

Bly W	Harrison F	Durham D	Bennion J	Feasey P	Davidson A	Clarke D	Bradbury W	Smith C	Bulless B	Metcalfe V	Cripsey B	Garvey B	Duncan J	Morris C	Coates D	Bowering M	Collinson L	Lord B	Wilkinson G	Milner M	
1	2	3	4	5	6	7	8	9	10	11											1
1	2	3	4	5	6	7	8	9	10		11										2
1	2	3	4	5		7	8	9	10		11	6									3
1	2	3		5			8		6				7	9	10	11	4				4
1	2	3		5		8		9	6				7		10	11	4				5
1	2	3		5		8	10		6		11				9	7	4				6
1	2	3		5		8	10		6		11				9	7	4				7
1	2	3		5		7	8	9	6		11				10		4				8
1	2	3		5		7	8	9	6						10	11	4				9
1	2	3		5		7	8	9	6						10	11	4				10
1	2	3		5		7	8	9	6						10	11	4				11
1	2	3		5		7	8	9	6						10	11	4				12
1	2	3		5		7	8	9	6						10	11	4				13
			4	5		7	8	9	3			6			10	11		1	2		14
1		3	4	5		7	8	9				6			10	11			2		15
1	2	3	4	5		7	8	9				6			10	11					16
1	2	3		5		7	8	9				6			10	11	4				17
1	2	3		5		7	8	9				6			10	11	4				18
1	2	3		5		7	8	9				6			10	11	4				19
1	2	3		5		7	8	9				6			10	11	4				20
1	2	3		5		7	8	9				6			10	11	4				21
1	2	3		5		7	8	9				6			10	11	4				22
1	2	3		5	4	7	8	9				6			10	11					23
1	2	3		5	4	7	8	9				6			10	11					24
1	2	3		5	4	7	8	9				6			10	11					25
1	2	3		5	4	7	8	9				6			10	11					26
1	2	3		5	4	7	8	9				6			10	11					27
1	2			5	4	7	8	9	3			6			10	11					28
1	2			5	4	7	8	9	3			6			10	11					29
1	2			5	4	7	8	9	3			6			10	11					30
1	2	3		5	4	7	8		11			6	9		10						31
1	2	3		5	4	7	8		11			6	9		10						32
1	2	3		5	4	7	8	9	11			6			10						33
1	2	3		5	4	7	8	9				6			10	11					34
1	2	3		5	4	7	8	9	11			6			10						35
1	2			5	4	7	8	9	3			6			10	11					36
1	2			5	4	7	8	9	3			6			10	11					37
1	2			5	4	7	8	9	3			6			10	11					38
1	2	3			4	7	10		11			6	9				8			5	39
1	2	3		5	4	7	8	9				6			10	11					40
1	2	3		5	4	7	8	9				6			10	11					41
1	2	3		5	4	7	8	9	10			6				11					42
1	2	3		5	4	7	8	9	11			6			10						43
1	2	3		5	4	7	8	9	11			6			10						44
1	2	3		5	4	7	8	9	11			6			10						45
1	2	3		5	4	7	8	9	11			6			10						46
45	44	39	6	45	26	45	45	40	30	1	5	34	5	1	41	33	17	1	2	1	
					1	12	30	26	2			1			9	6	2				

1 own-goal

1	2	3		5		7	8	9				6			10	11	4				1
1	1	1		1		1	1	1				1			1	1	1				

1959-60

1	Aug	22	(h)	Plymouth A	W	3-1	Metcalfe 2, Robertson (og)	17,319
2		24	(a)	Sheffield U	L	0-6		16,532
3		29	(a)	Liverpool	L	3-5	Coates 2, Metcalfe	35,520
4		31	(h)	Sheffield U	L	0-2		23,168
5	Sep	5	(h)	Charlton A	L	0-4		17,387
6		9	(a)	Middlesbrough	L	0-4		28,368
7		12	(a)	Bristol C	W	1-0	Coates	16,427
8		14	(h)	Middlesbrough	D	3-3	Bradbury 2, Bowering	22,024
9		19	(h)	Scunthorpe U	L	0-2		18,459
10		26	(a)	Rotherham U	L	0-1		11,646
11	Oct	3	(h)	Cardiff C	D	0-0		14,933
12		10	(h)	Lincoln C	L	0-5		17,170
13		17	(a)	Leyton O	L	1-3	Bradbury	13,002
14		24	(h)	Huddersfield T	D	1-1	Gubbins	15,864
15		31	(a)	Ipswich T	L	0-2		12,738
16	Nov	7	(h)	Bristol R	W	3-1	Shiner 2, Bradbury	16,972
17		14	(a)	Swansea T	D	0-0		11,886
18		21	(h)	Brighton & HA	W	3-1	Gubbins, Shiner, Bradbury	17,107
19		28	(a)	Stoke C	L	1-3	Sewell	12,481
20	Dec	5	(h)	Portsmouth	L	1-3	Gubbins	14,675
21		12	(a)	Sunderland	W	3-1	King 2, Shiner	17,695
22		19	(a)	Plymouth A	L	2-3	Sewell, Shiner	8,546
23		26	(h)	Aston Villa	L	0-1		29,399
24		28	(a)	Aston Villa	D	1-1	Bradbury	33,386
25	Jan	2	(h)	Liverpool	L	0-1		18,681
26		16	(a)	Charlton A	L	2-3	Clarke, Bennion	11,032
27		23	(h)	Bristol C	D	1-1	Clarke	12,605
28	Feb	6	(a)	Scunthorpe U	L	0-3		10,885
29		13	(h)	Rotherham U	W	1-0	Smith	10,171
30		20	(a)	Cardiff C	L	2-3	Gubbins, Smith	21,580
31		27	(a)	Lincoln C	L	0-3		10,043
32	Mar	5	(h)	Leyton O	L	1-2	Gubbins	10,580
33		12	(a)	Huddersfield T	L	0-1		12,167
34		17	(h)	Stoke C	W	4-0	Morris 2, Shiner, McCue (og)	11,750
35		26	(a)	Bristol R	L	0-1		12,236
36	Apr	2	(h)	Swansea T	W	3-1	Shiner, King, Clarke	8,691
37		9	(a)	Brighton & HA	D	1-1	King	14,318
38		15	(h)	Derby C	D	1-1	King	13,062
39		16	(h)	Sunderland	D	0-0		9,744
40		18	(a)	Derby C	W	3-1	King, Sewell, Shiner	11,197
41		23	(a)	Portsmouth	D	1-1	Morris	12,205
42		30	(h)	Ipswich T	W	2-0	King, Crickmore	5,719

FINAL LEAGUE POSITION: 21st in Division Two — Relegated

Appearances
Goals

FA Cup

3	Jan	9	(a)	Fulham	L	0-5		22,157

Appearances
Goals

Bly W	Harrison F	Bulless B	Davidson A	Feasey P	Garvey B	Clarke D	Bradbury W	Smith C	Coates D	Metcalfe V	Fisher B	Duncan J	Collinson L	Bowering M	Morris C	Crickmore C	Bennion J	Sewell J	Brown M	Gubbins R	Shiner R	Lord B	King D	Stocks J	Wilkinson G	
1	2	3	4	5	6	7	8	9	10	11																1
1	2	3	4	5	6	7	8	9	10	11																2
	2	3	4	5	6	7	8		10	11	1	9														3
	2	3	4	5	6	7	8		10	11	1	9														4
	2	3	4	5	6	7		9	10		1		8	11												5
	2	3	4	5	6				10		1	7	8	11	9											6
	2	3	4	5	6		10		9		1		8	7		11										7
		3	2	5	6		10	9	8		1		4	7		11										8
		3	2	5	6		10	9	8		1		4	7		11										9
1	2	3	9	5	6	7	10		8				4	11												10
1	2	3	6	5		7	9		10				8	11			4									11
1	2	3	6	5		7	8	9					4	11				10								12
1	2	10	3	5	6	9	8							7		11	4									13
1		3	4	5	6	7		9				11						8	2	10						14
1		3	4	5	6	7	9			11								8	2	10						15
1		3	2	5	6	7	11										4	8		10	9					16
1		3	2	5	6	7	11										4	8		10	9					17
1		3	2	5	6	7	11										4	8		10	9					18
		3	2	5	6	7	11										4	8		10	9	1				19
		3	2	5	6	7	11										4	8		10	9	1				20
1		3	2	4	5	7							6	11				8			9		10			21
1		3	2	4	5	7							6					8		11	9		10			22
1		3	2	4	5	7	11						6					8		10	9					23
1		3	2	4	5	7	11						6					8		10	9					24
1		3	2	4	5	7	11						6					8		10	9					25
1		3	2		5	7							6	11			4	8		10	9					26
1		3	2		5	7							6	11			4	8		10	9					27
	2	11	3		5	7	10										4	8			9	1		6		28
	2	3	6		5	11	8	9			1		4		7					10						29
	2	3	6		5	11		9	8		1		4		7					10						30
	2	3	6		5	11		9	8		1	7	4							10						31
		6	2		5	11					1		4		7			8		10	9				3	32
1		6	2	5	3	11							4		7			8		10	9					33
1		6	2	5	3	11							4		7			8		10	9					34
1		6	2	5	3	11							4		7			8		10	9					35
		6	2	5	3	7					1		4			11		8			9		10			36
		6	2	5	3	7					1		4			11		8		9			10			37
		6	2	5	3	7					1		4			11		8		9			10			38
		6	2	5	3						1		4		7	11		8			9		10			39
		6	2	5	3						1		4		7	11		8			9		10			40
		6	2	5	3						1		4		7	11		8			9		10			41
		6	2	5	3						1		4		7	11		8			9		10			42
21	15	42	42	35	40	34	22	10	13	5	18	5	29	12	11	11	10	27	2	22	22	3	9	1	1	
						3	6	2	3	3				1	3	1	1	3		5	8		7			

2 own-goals

1		3	2	4	5	7	11						6					8		10	9					3
1		1	1	1	1	1	1						1					1		1	1					

1960-61

1	Aug	20	(a)	Colchester U	L 0-4		6,731
2		22	(h)	Newport C	W 5-1	Collinson 2, Chilton, Clarke, Morris	9,811
3		27	(h)	Grimsby T	L 2-3	McMillan, Clarke	14,252
4		29	(a)	Newport C	L 1-3	Clarke	7,347
5	Sep	3	(a)	Southend U	L 1-3	Chilton	8,434
6		5	(h)	Bournemouth	W 2-0	Chilton, King	8,496
7		10	(a)	Reading	W 4-2	Clarke 2, McMillan, Chilton	7,043
8		12	(a)	Bournemouth	D 2-2	Price 2	5,315
9		17	(h)	Coventry C	D 1-1	Chilton	10,374
10		19	(h)	Barnsley	W 2-0	Price, McMillan	10,527
11		24	(a)	Bristol C	W 2-1	Price, Gubbins	14,899
12		28	(a)	Barnsley	L 0-1		4,840
13	Oct	1	(h)	Queen's Park R	W 3-1	Chilton 3	9,333
14		3	(h)	Notts C	W 3-1	Chilton, Price, Gubbins	12,199
15		8	(h)	Bury	L 0-1		13,164
16		15	(a)	Walsall	L 0-1		10,125
17		22	(h)	Shrewsbury T	W 3-1	Chilton 2, Sewell	9,095
18		29	(a)	Halifax T	L 0-3		6,734
19	Nov	12	(a)	Watford	D 2-2	Price 2	13,746
20		19	(h)	Brentford	W 3-0	Chilton, Price, Bulless	7,798
21	Dec	3	(h)	Torquay U	L 2-3	Crickmore, Stocks	6,175
22		10	(a)	Port Vale	L 1-4	Chilton	9,006
23		17	(h)	Colchester U	D 1-1	Sewell	6,047
24		26	(a)	Bradford C	D 0-0		11,450
25		27	(h)	Bradford C	W 3-0	Gubbins, Price, Sewell	13,947
26		31	(a)	Grimsby T	L 0-2		12,712
27	Jan	14	(h)	Southend U	L 0-1		9,744
28		28	(h)	Tranmere R	W 4-2	Price 2, Gubbins, Sewell	3,950
29	Feb	4	(a)	Coventry C	L 0-4		11,160
30		13	(h)	Bristol C	D 3-3	Chilton, Clarke, Gubbins	7,077
31		18	(a)	Queen's Park R	L 1-2	King	12,210
32		25	(a)	Torquay U	W 2-1	Crickmore, Price	4,587
33	Mar	4	(h)	Walsall	W 2-1	Sewell, Clarke	7,118
34		11	(a)	Shrewsbury T	D 0-0		8,698
35		18	(h)	Halifax T	W 4-2	Chilton 2, Price, Clarke	4,997
36		24	(a)	Tranmere R	L 0-1		12,260
37		31	(a)	Chesterfield	W 2-1	Chilton 2	12,079
38	Apr	1	(h)	Watford	W 3-2	Crickmore, Collinson, Holah	7,267
39		3	(h)	Chesterfield	D 2-2	Clarke 2	7,162
40		8	(a)	Brentford	D 2-2	Price, Bulless	6,390
41		12	(a)	Swindon T	D 1-1	Crickmore	10,877
42		15	(h)	Swindon T	D 0-0		5,514
43		20	(h)	Reading	W 1-0	Davidson	5,498
44		22	(a)	Bury	L 0-3		10,907
45		27	(a)	Notts C	L 1-2	King	4,941
46		29	(h)	Port Vale	D 2-2	King, Chilton	4,439

FINAL LEAGUE POSITION: 11th in Division Three

Appearances
Goals

FA Cup

1	Nov	5	(h)	Sutton T	W 3-0	Sewell, Price, Gubbins	8,482
2		26	(a)	Darlington	D 1-1	Price	8,613
R		28	(h)	Darlington	D 1-1*	Chilton	18,125
2R	Dec	5	(n†)	Darlington	D 1-1	Price	9,801
3R		12	(n‡)	Darlington	D 0-0*		5,313
4R		15	(n§)	Darlington	W 3-0	Clarke, Gubbins, King	19,366
3	Jan	7	(h)	Bolton W	L 0-1		18,771

*After extra-time. †Played at Elland Road, Leeds (abandoned after 90 minutes). ‡Played at the Belle Vue Ground, Doncaster. §Played at Ayresome Park, Middlesbrough.

Appearances
Goals

FL Cup

1	Oct	10	(h)	Bolton W	D 0-0		11,980
R		19	(a)	Bolton W	L 1-5	Gubbins	10,781

Appearances
Goals

Fisher B	Davidson A	Garvey B	McMillan E	Feasey P	Collinson L	Morris C	Chilton C	Nicholson P	King D	Crickmore C	Bulless B	Sewell J	Clarke D	Lord B	Gubbins R	Price D	Milner M	Stocks J	Holah E	
1	2	3	4	5	6	7	8	9	10	11										1
1	2	3	10	5	4	7	9				6	8	11							2
1	2	3	10	5	4	7	9				6	8	11							3
	2	3	8	5	4		9				6	7	11	1	10					4
1	2	3	10	5	4	7	9				6	8	11							5
1	2	3	8	5	4		9		10		6		7		11					6
1	2	3	8	5	4		9		10		6		7		11					7
1	2	3		5	4		9		10		6		7		11	8				8
1	2	3	10	5	4		9				6		7		11	8				9
1	2	3	10	5	4		9				6		7		11	8				10
1	2	3	10		4		9				6		7		11	8	5			11
1	2	3	10	5	4		9				6		7		11	8				12
1	2	3	10	5	4		9				6		7		11	8				13
1	2	3	10	5	4		9				6		7		11	8				14
1	2	3	10	5	4		9				6		7		11	8				15
1	2	3		5	4	7	9		10		6				11	8				16
1	2	3		5	4		9				6	8	7		11	10				17
1	2	3		5	4		9				6	8	7		11	10				18
1	2	3	10	5	4		9				6		7		11	8				19
1	2	3	10	5	4		9				6		7		11	8				20
1	2	3		5	4		9		10	11			7			8		6		21
1	2	3	10	5	4		9				6		7			8		11		22
1	2	3	4	5					11		6	10	7		9	8				23
1	2	3	4	5					11		6	10	7		9	8				24
1	2	3	4	5					11		6	10	7		9	8				25
1	2	3	4	5			7		11		6	10			9	8				26
1	2	3	4	5	6						11	10	8		9	7				27
1	2	3	6	5	4		9					10	7		11	8				28
1	2	3		5	4		9				11	10	7			8		6		29
1	2	3		5	4		9			11	6		7		10	8				30
1	2	3	10	5	4		9		7	11	6					8				31
1	2	3	10	5	4		9			11	6		7			8				32
1	2	3	10	5			9			11	6	8	7					4		33
1	2	3	10	5	4		9			11	6	8	7							34
1	2	3		5	4		9			11	6	8	7			10				35
1	2		6	5	4		9			11	3	8	7			10				36
1	2	3	4	5	8		9			11	6		7			10				37
1	2		4	5	8					11	3		7			10		6	9	38
1	2		4	5	8		9			11	3		7			10		6		39
1	2	3	4	5	8		9			11	6		7			10				40
1	2	3	4	5	8		9			11	6		7			10				41
1	2	3	4	5	8		9			11	6		7			10				42
1	2	3	10	5	4		8			11	6					7	9			43
1	2	3	10	5	4		8			11	6					7	9			44
1	2	3	7	5	4		9		8	11	6							10		45
1	2	3		5	4		9		8	11	6		7					10		46
45	46	43	37	45	41	5	41	1	13	19	43	17	39	1	23	35	3	8	1	
	1		3		3	1	19		4	4	2	5	10		5	14		1	1	

Fisher B	Davidson A	Garvey B	McMillan E	Feasey P	Collinson L	Morris C	Chilton C	Nicholson P	King D	Crickmore C	Bulless B	Sewell J	Clarke D	Lord B	Gubbins R	Price D	Milner M	Stocks J	Holah E	
1	2	3		5	4		9				6	8	7		11	10				1
1	2	3	10	5	4		9				6		7		11	8				2
1	2	3	10	5	4		9				6		7		11	8				R
1	2	3	10	5	4		9				6		7			8		11		2R
1	2	3	10	5	4		9				6	8	11			7				3R
1	2	3	4	5					11		6	10	7		11	8				4R
1	2	3	4	5			9				6	10	7		11	8				3
7	7	7	6	7	5		6		1		7	4	7		5	7		1		
							1		1			1	1		2	3				

Fisher B	Davidson A	Garvey B	McMillan E	Feasey P	Collinson L	Morris C	Chilton C	Nicholson P	King D	Crickmore C	Bulless B	Sewell J	Clarke D	Lord B	Gubbins R	Price D	Milner M	Stocks J	Holah E	
1	2	3		5	4		9		10		6		7		11	8				1
1	2	3		5	4		9				6	8	7		11	10				R
2	2	2		2	2		2		1		2	1	2		2	2				
															1					

1961-62

1	Aug	19	(a)	Peterborough U	L 2-3	Chilton, Crickmore	14,730
2		21	(a)	Port Vale	L 0-4		11,480
3		26	(h)	Northampton T	W 1-0	Chilton	8,027
4		31	(h)	Port Vale	W 3-1	Chilton, Clarke, Crickmore	8,095
5	Sep	2	(a)	Lincoln C	W 3-0	Chilton, Crickmore, Henderson	6,495
6		6	(a)	Bournemouth	D 1-1	Crickmore	8,370
7		9	(h)	Torquay U	W 4-0	McSeveney 2, Henderson 2	9,535
8		16	(a)	Swindon T	D 1-1	Crickmore	9,325
9		21	(h)	Watford	W 1-0	Chilton	14,376
10		23	(h)	Halifax T	L 1-2	Bulless	13,611
11		26	(a)	Watford	D 1-1	McSeveney	12,406
12		30	(a)	Queen's Park R	D 1-1	McSeveney	10,076
13	Oct	7	(a)	Bristol C	D 1-1	Connor (og)	10,088
14		11	(a)	Portsmouth	L 1-2	Bulless	14,107
15		14	(h)	Bradford	L 0-1		12,096
16		28	(h)	Shrewsbury T	W 3-1	McSeveney, Henderson, Crickmore	6,229
17	Nov	11	(h)	Reading	L 0-1		6,952
18		18	(a)	Newport C	W 2-0	Crickmore, Henderson	5,089
19	Dec	2	(a)	Grimsby T	L 0-1		6,871
20		9	(h)	Coventry C	W 3-1	Henderson, McSeveney, Clarke	3,817
21		16	(h)	Peterborough U	D 1-1	Crickmore	6,674
22		23	(a)	Northampton T	L 0-2		10,203
23		26	(h)	Crystal P	L 2-4	Price 2	7,559
24	Jan	6	(h)	Portsmouth	L 0-1		6,454
25		13	(h)	Lincoln C	W 1-0	Price	4,634
26		20	(a)	Torquay U	L 2-4	Clarke, Smith (og)	3,176
27		27	(h)	Southend U	D 0-0		4,517
28	Feb	3	(h)	Swindon T	L 0-1		3,729
29		10	(a)	Halifax T	L 1-2	King	4,124
30		16	(h)	Queen's Park R	W 3-1	King, Price, McSeveney	3,237
31		24	(h)	Bristol C	W 3-2	Price, McSeveney, Henderson	3,876
32	Mar	3	(a)	Bradford	L 0-1		7,736
33		10	(h)	Notts C	W 2-1	McSeveney, Henderson	3,911
34		17	(a)	Shrewsbury T	L 0-2		4,722
35		21	(a)	Crystal P	W 2-1	Chilton, McSeveney	7,041
36		24	(h)	Brentford	W 3-0	McSeveney, Price, Clarke	3,849
37		30	(a)	Reading	D 1-1	Collinson	7,210
38	Apr	3	(a)	Notts C	L 0-3		3,688
39		7	(h)	Newport C	W 4-0	King 3, Chilton	3,235
40		12	(h)	Bournemouth	W 2-1	Collinson, King	5,289
41		14	(a)	Southend U	L 1-2	Price	5,354
42		20	(h)	Barnsley	W 4-0	Price 3, Davidson	6,296
43		21	(h)	Grimsby T	W 2-1	McSeveney, King	12,404
44		23	(a)	Barnsley	L 0-1		4,781
45		28	(a)	Coventry C	W 2-0	Price 2	7,589
46	May	3	(a)	Brentford	W 2-0	McSeveney 2	3,583

FINAL LEAGUE POSITION: 10th in Division Three

Appearances
Goals

FA Cup

1	Nov	4	(h)	Rhyl	W 5-0	Chilton 2, McSeveney, Henderson, McMillan	7,451
2		25	(h)	Bradford C	L 0-2		10,124

Appearances
Goals

League Cup

1	Sep	11	(h)	Bradford	W 4-2	Chilton 2, Crickmore, Atkinson (og)	10,401
2	Oct	3	(a)	Bury	W 4-3	Chilton 2, Collinson, Clarke	8,204
3	Nov	15	(a)	Sunderland	L 1-2	McSeveney	15,969

Appearances
Goals

Fisher B	Davidson A	Garvey B	Collinson L	Feasey P	Bulless B	Clarke D	Price D	Chilton C	King D	Crickmore C	Henderson R	McSeveney J	McMillan E	Green L	Milner M	Shaw A	
1	2	3	4	5	6	7	8	9	10	11							1
1	2	3	4	5	6	7	8	9		11	10						2
1	2	3	4	5	6	7	8	9		11	10						3
1	2	3	4	5	6	7		9		11	10	8					4
1	2	3	4	5		7		9		11	10	8	6				5
1	2	3	4	5		7		9		11	10	8	6				6
1	2	3	4	5		7		9		11	10	8	6				7
1	2	3	4	5	10	7		9		11		8	6				8
1	2	3	4	5	10	7		9		11		8	6				9
1	2	3	4	5	10	7		9		11		8	6				10
1	2	3	4	5	10	7		9		11		8	6				11
1	2	3	4	5	10	7		9		11		8	6				12
1	2	3	4	5	10	7		9		11	8		6				13
1	2	3	4	5	10	7		9		11		8	6				14
1	2	3	4	5	10	7		9		11		8	6				15
1	2	3	4	5	10	7				11	9	8	6				16
1	2	3	4	5		7		9		11	10	8	6				17
1	2		4	5	3	7		9		11	10	8	6				18
1	2		4	5	3	7		9		11	10	8	6				19
1	2		4	5	3	7	8			11	9	10	6				20
1	2		4	5	3	7	8			11	9	10	6				21
1	2		4	5	3	7	8			11	9	10	6				22
	2		4		3	7	8			11	9	10	6	1	5		23
	2	3		5	6	7	8	9			10	11	4	1			24
	2	3		5	6	7	8	9			10	11	4	1			25
	2	3		5	6	7	8	9			10	11	4	1			26
1	2	3		5	6	7	8				9	10	4			11	27
1	2	3		5	6	7	8		9			10	4			11	28
1		2	4	5	3	7	8		9		10	11	6				29
1		2	4	5	3	7	8		9		10	11	6				30
1		2	4	5	3	7	8		9		10	11	6				31
1	2		4	5	3	7	8		9		10	11	6				32
1	2	3	4	5		7	8		9		10	11	6				33
1	2		4	5	3	7	8		9		10	11	6				34
1	2		4	5	3	7	8	9	10			11	6				35
1	2		4	5	3	7	8	9	10			11	6				36
1	2		4	5	3	7	8	9	10			11	6				37
1	2		4	5	3	7	8	9	10			11	6				38
1	2	3	4	5		7	8	9	10			11	6				39
1	2	3	4	5		7	8	9	10			11	6				40
1	2	3	4	5		7	8	9	10			11	6				41
1	2	3	4			7	8	9	10			11	6		5		42
1	2	3	4			7	8	9	10			11	6		5		43
1	2	3	4			7	8		9		10	11	6		5		44
1	2	3	4			7	8		10		9	11	6		5		45
1	2	3	4			7	8		10		9	11	6		5		46
42	43	34	41	40	33	46	30	30	20	23	28	42	42	4	6	2	
	1		2		2	4	12	7	7	8	8	14					

2 own-goals

Fisher B	Davidson A	Garvey B	Collinson L	Feasey P	Bulless B	Clarke D	Price D	Chilton C	King D	Crickmore C	Henderson R	McSeveney J	McMillan E	Green L	Milner M	Shaw A	
1	2	3	4	5		7		9		11	10	8	6				1
1	2		4	5	3	7		9		11	10	8	6				2
2	2	1	2	2	1	2		2		2	2	2	2				
								2			1	1	1				

Fisher B	Davidson A	Garvey B	Collinson L	Feasey P	Bulless B	Clarke D	Price D	Chilton C	King D	Crickmore C	Henderson R	McSeveney J	McMillan E	Green L	Milner M	Shaw A	
1	2	3	4	5	10	7		9		11		8	6				1
1	2	3	4	5	10	7		9		11		8	6				2
1	2		4	5	3	7		9		11	10	8	6				3
3	3	2	3	3	3	3		3		3	1	3	3				
			1			1		4		1		1					

1 own-goal

1962-63

1	Aug	18	(h)	Bristol R	W 3-0	McSeveney 2, King	8,261
2		23	(h)	Wrexham	L 1-3	Chilton	8,535
3		25	(a)	Brighton & HA	L 1-2	Bertolini (og)	16,051
4		29	(a)	Wrexham	L 0-2		11,347
5		31	(h)	Carlisle U	W 3-1	Chilton, McSeveney, Davidson	8,325
6	Sep	3	(a)	Millwall	L 1-5	Chilton	19,619
7		8	(a)	Swindon T	L 0-2		10,144
8		13	(h)	Millwall	W 4-1	Chilton 3, Henderson	7,100
9		15	(h)	Peterborough U	W 3-2	Henderson 2, McSeveney	8,158
10		20	(h)	Crystal P	D 0-0		9,718
11		22	(a)	Barnsley	W 2-1	Chilton, Henderson	6,848
12		29	(h)	Northampton T	W 2-0	Chilton, McSeveney	9,536
13	Oct	6	(h)	Colchester U	D 2-2	Clarke 2	9,360
14		13	(a)	Notts C	D 1-1	McSeveney	9,595
15		20	(h)	Bournemouth	D 1-1	McSeveney	8,702
16		22	(a)	Queen's Park R	L 1-4	Henderson	18,281
17		27	(a)	Coventry C	D 2-2	Chilton, McSeveney	11,821
18	Nov	10	(a)	Watford	L 2-4	McSeveney 2	7,518
19		17	(h)	Bristol C	W 4-0	Chilton 3, McSeveney	7,367
20	Dec	1	(h)	Port Vale	L 0-1		7,259
21		8	(a)	Shrewsbury T	W 4-1	Chilton 2, Henderson, Cummins	6,976
22		15	(a)	Bristol R	W 5-2	Henderson, Chilton, McSeveney, Clarke, Collinson	5,989
23		22	(h)	Brighton & HA	W 2-1	McSeveney, King	8,050
24		26	(a)	Southend U	W 1-0	King	9,783
25		29	(h)	Southend U	L 1-2	King	9,577
26	Mar	4	(a)	Colchester U	W 3-2	McSeveney 2, Henderson	4,143
27		9	(a)	Bournemouth	L 0-3		6,613
28		13	(h)	Bradford	W 1-0	McSeveney	7,635
29		20	(a)	Reading	D 2-2	McSeveney, King	7,167
30		23	(a)	Bradford	L 1-3	Chilton	7,529
31		25	(a)	Peterborough U	W 3-1	McSeveney 2, Chilton	10,193
32		30	(h)	Watford	W 1-0	McSeveney	5,462
33	Apr	6	(a)	Bristol C	L 1-3	McSeveney	8,794
34		12	(h)	Halifax T	W 2-0	King, Wilkinson	9,831
35		13	(h)	Reading	L 0-1		5,978
36		15	(a)	Halifax T	W 2-0	Simpkin, Shaw	3,633
37		20	(a)	Port Vale	L 0-1		4,673
38		25	(h)	Queen's Park R	W 4-1	Henderson, Clarke, Simpkin, Taylor (og)	5,894
39		27	(h)	Shrewsbury T	D 2-2	Chilton, Collinson	5,607
40	May	1	(a)	Crystal P	D 1-1	Henderson	11,210
41		4	(h)	Barnsley	L 0-2		4,923
42		7	(h)	Coventry C	W 2-0	Cummins, Collinson	5,255
43		11	(a)	Carlisle U	L 1-2	Simpkin	2,519
44		18	(h)	Swindon T	D 1-1	McSeveney	4,361
45		20	(h)	Notts C	D 1-1	Clarke	4,145
46		24	(a)	Northampton T	L 0-3		12,110

FINAL LEAGUE POSITION: 10th in Division Three

Appearances
Goals

FA Cup

1	Nov	3	(h)	Crook Town	W 5-4	McSeveney 2, Henderson 2, Chilton	9,484
2		24	(h)	Workington	W 2-0	McSeveney 2	8,686
3	Feb	11	(a)	Leyton O	D 1-1	Chilton	9,752
R		19	(h)	Leyton O	L 0-2*		14,214

*After extra-time

Appearances
Goals

League Cup

2	Sep	24	(h)	Middlesbrough	D 2-2	Chilton, Collinson	10,640
R	Oct	8	(a)	Middlesbrough	D 1-1*	Clarke	15,612
2R		10	(h)	Middlesbrough	W 3-0*	Chilton, Price, McSeveney	11,964
3		17	(h)	Fulham	L 1-2	Chilton	20,308

*After extra-time

Appearances
Goals

Fisher B	Davidson A	Bulless B	Collinson L	Milner M	McMillan E	Clarke D	Simpkin C	Chilton C	King D	McSeveney J	Granger M	Feasey P	Garvey B	Taylor A	Sharpe L	Williams M	Price D	Henderson R	Shaw A	Cummins G	Wilkinson W	
1	2	3	4	5	6	7	8	9	10	11												1
1	2	3	4	5	6	7	8	9	10	11												2
1	2	3	4	5	6	7	8	9	10	11												3
	2	3	4	5	6	7	8	9	10	11	1											4
1	2	3	4	5	6	7	8	9	10	11												5
1	2	3	4		6	7	8	9	10	11		5										6
	2	11	4		6			9		10	1	5	3	7	8							7
	2	3	4		6	7		9		11			5			1	8	10				8
	2	3	4		6	7		9		11			5			1	8	10				9
	2	3	4		6	7		9		11			5			1	8	10				10
	2	3	4		6	7		9		11			5			1	8	10				11
	2	3	4		6	7		9		11			5			1	8	10				12
	2	3	4		6	7		9		11			5			1	8	10				13
	2		4		6	7		9		11			5		3	1	8	10				14
	2		4		6	7		9		11			5		3	1	8	10				15
	2		4		6	7			9				5		3	1	8	10	11			16
	2		4		6	7		9		11		5	3			1	8	10				17
	2		4		6	7		9	8	11			5		3	1		10				18
	2		4		6	7		9		11			5		3	1		8		10		19
	2		4		6	7		9	10	11			5		3	1		8				20
	2		4		6	7		9		11			5		3	1		8		10		21
	2		4		6	7		9	10	11			5		3	1		8				22
	2		4		6	7		9	10	11			5		3	1		8				23
	2		4		6	7		9	10	11			5		3	1		8				24
	2		4		6	7			9	11			5		3	1	8	10				25
	2		4		6			9	8	11			5		3	1		7		10		26
	2		4		6			9	8	11			5		3	1		7		10		27
	2	3	4		6	7			9	11			5			1		8		10		28
	2	3	4		6	7		9	10	11			5			1		8				29
	2	3	4		6	7		9	10	11			5			1		8				30
	2	3	4		6	7		9	8	11			5			1				10		31
	2	3	4		6	7		9	8	11			5			1				10		32
	2	3	4		6	7		9	8	11			5			1				10		33
	2	3	4		6			9	10				5			1		7		11	8	34
	2	3	4		6			9	10				5			1		7		11	8	35
	2		4		6	7	10	9					5		3	1		8	11			36
	2		4		6	7	10	9					5		3	1		8	11			37
	2		4		6	7	10	9		11			5		3	1		8				38
	2		4		6	7	10	9		11			5		3	1		8				39
	2		4		6	7	10	9					5		3	1		8	11			40
	2		4		6	7	10	9					5		3	1		8	11			41
	2		4		6	7	8	9		11		5	3			1				10		42
	2		4		6	7	8	9		11		5	3			1				10		43
	2				6	7	8	9		11		5	3		4	1				10		44
	2				6	7	8	9		11		5	3		4	1				10		45
	2		4		6	7	8	9		11		5	3			1				10		46
5	46	21	44	5	46	41	17	43	23	39	2	8	40	1	22	39	11	31	5	15	2	
	1		3			5	3	18	6	22								10	1	2	1	

2 own-goals

Fisher B	Davidson A	Bulless B	Collinson L	Milner M	McMillan E	Clarke D	Simpkin C	Chilton C	King D	McSeveney J	Granger M	Feasey P	Garvey B	Taylor A	Sharpe L	Williams M	Price D	Henderson R	Shaw A	Cummins G	Wilkinson W	
	2				6	7		9		11		5	3		4	1	8	10				1
	2		4		6	7		9		11			5		3	1		8		10		2
	2		4		6	7		9		11			5		3	1		8		10		3
	2		4		6	7		9		11			5		3	1		8		10		R
	4		3		4	4		4		4		1	4		4	4	1	4		3		
								2		4								2				

Fisher B	Davidson A	Bulless B	Collinson L	Milner M	McMillan E	Clarke D	Simpkin C	Chilton C	King D	McSeveney J	Granger M	Feasey P	Garvey B	Taylor A	Sharpe L	Williams M	Price D	Henderson R	Shaw A	Cummins G	Wilkinson W	
	2	3	4		6	7		9		11			5			1	8	10				2
	2	3	4		6	7		9		11			5			1	8	10				R
	2		4		6	7		9		11			5		3	1	8	10				2R
	2		4		6	7		9		11			5		3	1	8	10				3
	4	2	4		4	4		4		4			4		2	4	4	4				
			1			1		3		1							1					

1963-64

1	Aug	24	(a)	Watford	D 3-3	McSeveney 2, Chilton	9,251
2		28	(h)	Peterborough U	D 0-0		18,433
3		31	(h)	Colchester U	D 0-0		11,844
4	Sep	7	(a)	Millwall	W 1-0	Henderson	10,240
5		9	(a)	Peterborough U	L 1-5	Henderson	12,859
6		14	(h)	Barnsley	D 2-2	Chilton, Sharpe	8,920
7		16	(a)	Southend U	D 1-1	Chilton	11,764
8		21	(h)	Coventry C	W 2-1	McSeveney, Simpkin	12,315
9		28	(a)	Bournemouth	L 0-1		11,175
10	Oct	2	(h)	Southend U	W 1-0	Clarke	10,706
11		5	(h)	Wrexham	W 4-2	Chilton 4	8,510
12		8	(a)	Bristol R	L 0-4		10,681
13		12	(a)	Reading	L 0-2		8,214
14		19	(h)	Shrewsbury T	W 4-2	Chilton 2, Wilkinson 2	7,057
15		21	(a)	Queen's Park R	W 2-0	McSeveney, Malcolm (og)	9,836
16		26	(a)	Bristol C	L 0-1		10,568
17		30	(h)	Queen's Park R	W 3-0	Chilton, Henderson, Wilkinson	7,932
18	Nov	2	(h)	Port Vale	W 4-1	Chilton 2, Wilkinson 2	8,460
19		23	(a)	Crystal P	D 2-2	Wilkinson, Sharpe	16,929
20		30	(h)	Walsall	W 3-1	Wilkinson 3	7,578
21	Dec	14	(h)	Watford	D 2-2	Chilton, Garvey	8,011
22		21	(a)	Colchester U	D 1-1	Wilkinson	3,609
23		26	(h)	Mansfield T	W 3-1	Chilton, Henderson, Wilkinson	14,132
24		28	(a)	Mansfield T	L 0-2		7,790
25	Jan	11	(h)	Millwall	D 0-0		10,014
26		17	(a)	Barnsley	D 2-2	Henderson 2	8,193
27		25	(a)	Notts C	W 1-0	Chilton	9,065
28	Feb	1	(a)	Coventry C	D 2-2	Chilton, Davidson	23,476
29		8	(h)	Bournemouth	L 3-4	Rafferty 2, McSeveney	11,511
30		15	(a)	Wrexham	L 1-3	Rafferty	5,552
31		22	(h)	Reading	D 1-1	Chilton	7,561
32		26	(h)	Bristol R	L 0-2		3,907
33		29	(a)	Luton T	L 1-2	Henderson	5,267
34	Mar	7	(h)	Bristol C	D 4-4	Wilkinson, Davidson, Garvey, Low (og)	4,726
35		11	(h)	Crewe A	W 2-1	Chilton, Rafferty	3,931
36		21	(h)	Luton T	W 2-0	Henderson, Rafferty	3,576
37		27	(h)	Oldham A	L 0-1		8,696
38		28	(a)	Crewe A	W 4-1	McSeveney 2, Henderson, Sharpe	3,335
39		30	(a)	Oldham A	D 1-1	Chilton	7,878
40	Apr	4	(h)	Crystal P	D 1-1	McSeveney	6,602
41		11	(a)	Walsall	D 1-1	Rafferty	5,093
42		13	(a)	Port Vale	L 0-1		6,090
43		18	(h)	Brentford	D 0-0		6,798
44		22	(h)	Notts C	W 4-1	Chilton 3, McSeveney	5,106
45		25	(a)	Shrewsbury T	L 1-5	Sharpe	3,125
46		28	(a)	Brentford	W 3-1	Corner 2, Wilkinson	6,818

FINAL LEAGUE POSITION: 8th in Division Three

Appearances
Goals

FA Cup

1	Nov	16	(h)	Crewe A	D 2-2	Chilton, Shaw	10,013
R		20	(a)	Crewe A	W 3-0	Wilkinson 2, Henderson	7,955
2	Dec	7	(a)	Wrexham	W 2-0	Chilton, Henderson	8,323
3	Jan	4	(h)	Everton	D 1-1	Wilkinson	36,478
R		7	(a)	Everton	L 1-2	McSeveney	56,613

Appearances
Goals

League Cup

2	Sep	25	(h)	Exeter C	W 1-0	Henderson	9,313
3	Oct	16	(h)	Manchester C	L 0-3		13,880

Appearances
Goals

Williams M	Davidson A	Butler D	Collinson L	Garvey B	McMillan E	Clarke D	Rafferty R	Chilton C	Simpkin C	McSeveney J	Sharpe L	Henderson R	Swan M	Milner M	Cummins G	Bulless B	Wilkinson W	Feasey P	Shaw A	Summers G	Brown M	Corner N	
1	2	3	4	5	6	7	8	9	10	11													1
1	2	3	4	5	6	7	8	9	10	11													2
1	2	3		5	6	7	8	9	10	11	4												3
1	2	3		5	6	7		9	10	11	4	8											4
1	2	3		5	6	7		9	10	11	4	8											5
1	2	3		5	6	7		9	10	11	4	8											6
	2	3			6	7		9	10	11	4	8	1	5									7
	2	3			6	7		9	10	11	4	8	1	5									8
	2	3			6	7		9		11	4	8	1	5	10								9
	2	3			6	7		9			4	8	1	5	10	11							10
	2	3			6	7		9	10		4	8	1	5		11							11
	2	3			6	7		9		11	4	8	1	5	10								12
	2	3			6	7		9		11	4	10	1	5			8						13
	2	3		4	6	7		9		11		10	1				8	5					14
	2	3		4	6	7		9		11		10	1				8	5					15
	2	3		4	6	7		9		11		10	1				8	5					16
	2	3		4		7		9			6	10	1				8	5	11				17
	2	3		4		7		9			6	10	1				8	5	11				18
	2	3		4				9		7	6	10	1				8	5	11				19
	2	3		4		7		9			6	10	1				8	5	11				20
	2	3		4				9		7	6	10	1				8	5	11				21
1	2	3	4			7		9			6	10					8	5	11				22
1	2	3	4			7		9			6	10					8	5	11				23
1	2	3	4		6	7		9				10					8	5	11				24
1	2	3	4		6	7		9		11		10					8	5					25
1	2	3	4		6	7		9				10			11		8	5					26
1	2	3	4		6	7		9				10			11		8	5					27
1	2	3	4		6	7		9		11		10					8	5					28
1	2	3	4		6	7	8	9		11		10						5					29
	2			3	6	7	8	9		11	4	10	1					5					30
	2	3			6	7	11	9			4	10	1				8	5					31
	2	3			6	7	11	9			4	10	1				8	5					32
	2	3					9	7	6	11	4	10	1	5			8						33
	2	3		4			9	7	6	11		10	1	5			8						34
	2	3		4			9	7	6	11		10	1	5			8						35
	2	3		4			9	7	6	11		10	1	5			8						36
	2	3		4			9	7	6	11		10	1	5			8						37
	2	3		6		7		9		11	4	10	1	5			8						38
	2	3		6		7		9		11	4	8	1	5	10								39
	2	3		4		7		9	6	11	8	10	1	5									40
	2	3		4			7	9	6	11	8	10	1	5									41
	2	3		4			7	9	6	11	8	10	1	5									42
	2	3		4		7		9	8	11		10	1	5						6			43
	2			3				9	4	11	7	10	1	5			8			6			44
	3							9	4	11	7	10	1	5			8			6	2		45
	2					7			4	11	3	10	1	5			8			6		9	46
14	46	42	10	26	25	35	14	45	21	34	30	43	32	21	6	2	27	19	8	4	1	1	
	2			2		1	6	22	1	9	4	9					13					2	

2 own-goals

Williams M	Davidson A	Butler D	Collinson L	Garvey B	McMillan E	Clarke D	Rafferty R	Chilton C	Simpkin C	McSeveney J	Sharpe L	Henderson R	Swan M	Milner M	Cummins G	Bulless B	Wilkinson W	Feasey P	Shaw A	Summers G	Brown M	Corner N	
	2	3		4		7		9			6	10	1				8	5	11				1
	2	3		4				9		7	6	10	1				8	5	11				R
	2	3		4		7		9			6	10	1				8	5	11				2
1	2	3	4		6	7		9		11		10					8	5					3
1	2	3	4		6	7		9		11		10					8	5					R
2	5	5	2	3	2	4		5		3	3	5	3				5	5	3				
								2		1		2					3		1				

Williams M	Davidson A	Butler D	Collinson L	Garvey B	McMillan E	Clarke D	Rafferty R	Chilton C	Simpkin C	McSeveney J	Sharpe L	Henderson R	Swan M	Milner M	Cummins G	Bulless B	Wilkinson W	Feasey P	Shaw A	Summers G	Brown M	Corner N	
	2	3			6	7		9		11	4	8	1	5	10								2
	2	3			6	7		9		11	4	10	1				8	5					3
	2	2			2	2		2		2	2	2	2	1	1		1	1					
												1											

1964-65

1	Aug	22	(a)	Watford	L	1-2	Clarke	9,586
2		26	(h)	Walsall	W	2-0	Clarke, McSeveney	10,605
3		29	(h)	Workington	D	2-2	McSeveney, Davidson	8,725
4	Sep	5	(a)	Colchester U	W	2-1	Wilkinson 2	3,310
5		9	(h)	Scunthorpe U	L	1-2	McSeveney	8,754
6		12	(a)	Gillingham	L	0-1		11,144
7		15	(a)	Scunthorpe U	D	1-1	Wilkinson	7,525
8		19	(h)	Bristol C	W	3-2	McSeveney 2, Corner	7,485
9		25	(a)	Queen's Park R	L	1-2	Corner	6,639
10		30	(a)	Barnsley	D	1-1	Clarke	6,940
11	Oct	3	(h)	Shrewsbury T	L	1-2	McSeveney	6,731
12		7	(h)	Barnsley	W	7-0	Chilton 4, Henderson 3	7,830
13		9	(h)	Carlisle U	W	1-0	Chilton	10,931
14		12	(h)	Reading	W	1-0	McSeveney	12,107
15		17	(a)	Luton T	W	3-1	Chilton 2, Young	6,020
16		21	(a)	Reading	D	3-3	Chilton 2, Henderson	8,582
17		24	(h)	Mansfield T	D	1-1	McSeveney	8,482
18		27	(a)	Brentford	W	3-1	Chilton 3	12,745
19		31	(a)	Grimsby T	L	0-3		9,650
20	Nov	7	(h)	Peterborough U	L	0-2		8,054
21		21	(h)	Exeter C	W	3-1	Wagstaff, Chilton, Collinson	11,786
22		28	(a)	Oldham A	L	1-2	Wagstaff	8,516
23	Dec	12	(h)	Watford	D	1-1	Wagstaff	6,165
24		19	(a)	Workington	W	3-1	Chilton 2, McSeveney	3,851
25		26	(a)	Port Vale	W	3-0	Chilton, Wagstaff, Clarke	6,099
26		28	(h)	Port Vale	W	4-0	Wagstaff 3, Henderson	12,468
27	Jan	2	(h)	Colchester U	W	5-1	Wagstaff 2, Chilton, Henderson, McSeveney	16,928
28		9	(a)	Bournemouth	W	3-2	Chilton 2, Wagstaff	7,515
29		16	(h)	Gillingham	D	1-1	Wagstaff	24,426
30		23	(a)	Bristol C	W	2-1	Wagstaff 2	14,131
31		30	(h)	Bristol R	W	3-2	Chilton, McSeveney, Wagstaff	28,399
32	Feb	6	(h)	Queen's Park R	W	3-1	Houghton, Chilton, McSeveney	23,574
33		13	(a)	Shrewsbury T	W	4-0	Chilton, McSeveney, I.Butler, Summers	7,652
34		20	(a)	Carlisle U	D	0-0		17,174
35		27	(h)	Luton T	W	3-1	Houghton, Wagstaff, Chilton	22,986
36	Mar	6	(a)	Bristol R	D	1-1	Chilton	19,905
37		13	(h)	Grimsby T	D	3-3	Wagstaff 2, McSeveney	26,564
38		20	(a)	Peterborough U	L	1-2	Wagstaff	9,136
39		27	(h)	Bournemouth	W	2-1	Houghton 2	18,530
40	Apr	3	(a)	Exeter C	W	2-0	McSeveney, Wagstaff	6,571
41		6	(a)	Walsall	D	3-3	Wagstaff, Chilton, I Butler	12,097
42		10	(h)	Oldham A	W	2-1	Chilton, Wagstaff	19,032
43		16	(a)	Southend U	L	1-2	Chilton	11,023
44		17	(a)	Mansfield T	L	1-2	Wagstaff	19,500
45		19	(h)	Southend U	D	0-0		20,984
46		24	(h)	Brentford	W	2-1	Houghton, Wagstaff	14,924

FINAL LEAGUE POSITION: 4th in Division Three

Appearances
Goals

FA Cup

1	Nov	14	(a)	Kidderminster H	W	4-1	Wilkinson 2, McSeveney, Heath	6,619
2	Dec	5	(h)	Lincoln C	D	1-1	Summers	10,167
R		9	(a)	Lincoln C	L	1-3	McSeveney	8,383

Appearances
Goals

League Cup

2	Sep	22	(h)	Southend U	D	0-0		4,012
R		28	(a)	Southend U	L	1-3	Wilkinson	5,089

Appearances
Goals

Swan M	Davidson A	Butler D	Simpkin C	Milner M	Summers G	Clarke D	Wilkinson W	Henderson R	Heath T	McSeveney J	Collinson L	Chilton C	Garvey B	Sharpe L	Feasey P	Corner N	Rafferty R	Young R	Williams M	Wagstaff K	Butler I	Houghton K	McMillan E	
1	2	3	4	5	6	7	8	9	10	11														1
1	2	3		5	6	7	8	10		11	4	9												2
1	2	3		5	6	7	8		10	11	4	9												3
1	2			5	6	7	8		10	11	4	9	3											4
1	2	3		5	6	7	8		10	11	4	9												5
1	2	3		5	6	7	8		10	11	4	9												6
1	2	3				7	8	10		11	4			6	5	9								7
1	2	3			6	7	8	10		11	4				5	9								8
1	2				6	7	8	10		11			4	3	5	9								9
1	2	3		5	6	7	8	10		11	4						9							10
1	2	3		5	6	7	8	10		11	4						9							11
1	2			5	6		8	10		11	4	9	3					7						12
1	2			5	6		8	10		11	4	9	3					7						13
1	2			5	6		8	10		11	4	9	3					7						14
1	2			5	6		8	10		11	4	9	3					7						15
1	2			5	6		8	10		11	4	9	3					7						16
1	2			5	6		8	10		11	4	9	3					7						17
1	2			5	6		8	10		11	4	9	3					7						18
1	2			5	6		8	10		11	4	9	3					7						19
	2			5	6	7	8	10		11	4	9	3						1					20
1	2	3		5	6		7		10	11	4	9								8				21
1	2	3		5	6		7		10	11	4	9								8				22
	2	3		5	6	7		10		11	4	9							1	8				23
	2	3		5	6	7		10		11	4	9							1	8				24
	2	3		5	6	7		10		11	4	9							1	8				25
	2			5	6	7		10		11	4	9	3						1	8				26
	2	3		5	6			10		7	4	9							1	8	11			27
	2	3		5	6					7	4	9							1	8	11	10		28
	2	3		5	6					7	4	9							1	8	11	10		29
	2	3		5	6					7	4	9							1	8	11	10		30
	2	3		5	6					7	4	9							1	8	11	10		31
	2	3		5	6					7	4	9							1	8	11	10		32
	2	3		5	6			10		7	4	9							1	8	11			33
	2	3		5	6			10		7	4	9							1	8	11			34
	2	3		5	6					7	4	9							1	8	11	10		35
	2	3		5	6		8			7	4	9							1		11	10		36
	2	3		5	6					7	4	9							1	8	11	10		37
	2	3		5	6					7	4	9							1	8	11	10		38
	2	3		5	6					7	4	9							1	8	11	10		39
	2	3		5	6					7	4	9							1	8	11	10		40
	2	3	6	5				10		7	4	9							1	8	11			41
	2	3		5	6			10		7	4	9							1	8	11			42
	2			5	6					7	4	9	3						1	8	11	10		43
	2				6					7	4	9	3		5				1	8	11	10		44
	2	3	4		6					7		9			5				1	8	11	10		45
	2	3	4	5	6					7		9							1	8	11	10		46
21	46	32	4	41	44	16	23	25	7	46	42	40	14	2	5	3	2	8	25	25	20	15		
	1				1	4	3	6		15	1	27				2		1		23	2	5		

Swan M	Davidson A	Butler D	Simpkin C	Milner M	Summers G	Clarke D	Wilkinson W	Henderson R	Heath T	McSeveney J	Collinson L	Chilton C	Garvey B	Sharpe L	Feasey P	Corner N	Rafferty R	Young R	Williams M	Wagstaff K	Butler I	Houghton K	McMillan E	
1	2	3		5	6		8		10	11	4	9						7						1
1	2	3		5	6		7		10	11	4	9								8				2
1	2	3		5	6	7		10		11	4	9								8				R
3	3	3		3	3	1	2	1	2	3	3	3						1		2				
					1		2		1	2														

Swan M	Davidson A	Butler D	Simpkin C	Milner M	Summers G	Clarke D	Wilkinson W	Henderson R	Heath T	McSeveney J	Collinson L	Chilton C	Garvey B	Sharpe L	Feasey P	Corner N	Rafferty R	Young R	Williams M	Wagstaff K	Butler I	Houghton K	McMillan E	
1	2	3				7	8	10		11				4	5	9							6	2
1	2	3			6		7	10				8	4	11	5	9								R
2	2	2			1	1	2	2		1		1	1	2	2	2							1	
							1																	

1965-66

1	Aug	21	(h)	Scunthorpe U	W 3-2	Wagstaff 2, Houghton	18,829
2		24	(a)	Watford	D 1-1	Chilton	10,648
3		28	(a)	Brighton & HA	W 2-1	Wagstaff, Henderson	16,560
4	Sep	1	(h)	Swindon T	W 1-0	Wagstaff	23,163
5		4	(h)	Queen's Park R	L 1-3	Chilton	20,478
6		11	(a)	Mansfield T	W 2-1	Chilton, Houghton	14,081
7		18	(h)	York C	L 1-4	I.Butler	20,554
8		25	(h)	Reading	D 3-3	Houghton 2, Chilton	14,686
9	Oct	2	(a)	Exeter C	W 4-1	Houghton 2, Chilton, Wagstaff	7,125
10		6	(h)	Oldham A	W 5-1	Chilton 3, Houghton, Wagstaff	17,028
11		9	(a)	Swansea T	L 2-4	Henderson, I.Butler	7,949
12		13	(a)	Oldham A	D 2-2	Houghton 2	5,883
13		16	(h)	Walsall	W 3-2	Chilton, Henderson, Wagstaff	15,931
14		22	(a)	Workington	L 0-3		5,482
15		30	(h)	Bournemouth	W 3-0	Chilton, Henderson, Wagstaff	12,440
16	Nov	6	(a)	Southend U	W 2-0	Henderson, Bradbury (og)	8,088
17		20	(a)	Shrewsbury T	D 2-2	Wagstaff, I.Butler	5,316
18		24	(h)	Watford	W 3-1	Houghton 2, Chilton	15,511
19		27	(h)	Grimsby T	D 1-1	Wagstaff	20,681
20	Dec	11	(h)	Bristol R	W 6-1	Houghton 2, Henderson, I.Butler, Simpkin, Davis (og)	16,349
21		17	(a)	Walsall	W 4-2	I.Butler 3, Chilton	8,617
22		27	(h)	Millwall	W 1-0	Gilchrist (og)	40,231
23		28	(a)	Millwall	L 0-3		17,184
24	Jan	1	(h)	Swansea T	W 4-1	Wagstaff 2, Henderson, Chilton	22,700
25		8	(a)	Swindon T	L 1-3	Houghton	15,875
26		15	(h)	Workington	W 6-0	I.Butler 2, Wagstaff, Houghton, Jarvis, Brown (og)	14,704
27		29	(a)	Scunthorpe U	W 4-2	Henderson 2, Houghton, Chilton	15,570
28	Feb	5	(h)	Brighton & HA	W 1-0	Wagstaff	25,374
29		19	(a)	Queen's Park R	D 3-3	Chilton, Houghton, Wagstaff	12,327
30		23	(a)	Gillingham	W 3-0	Chilton, Houghton, Wagstaff	10,527
31		26	(h)	Mansfield T	W 4-0	Wagstaff 2, Henderson, Houghton	28,214
32	Mar	9	(h)	Gillingham	W 1-0	Wagstaff	30,122
33		12	(a)	York C	W 2-1	Wagstaff, I.Butler	19,420
34		18	(a)	Reading	W 1-0	I.Butler	14,196
35	Apr	8	(a)	Oxford U	W 2-0	Houghton, Wagstaff	14,359
36		9	(a)	Brentford	W 4-2	Wagstaff 4	9,919
37		11	(h)	Oxford U	W 2-1	Chilton, Wagstaff	31,992
38		16	(h)	Shrewsbury T	W 2-1	Chilton, Jarvis	24,333
39		20	(h)	Exeter C	W 6-1	Chilton 3, Henderson 2, Houghton	28,055
40		23	(a)	Grimsby T	L 0-1		18,018
41		25	(a)	Peterborough U	L 1-4	Chilton	9,547
42		30	(h)	Brentford	W 4-1	Chilton, Henderson, Jarvis, Crisp (og)	25,039
43	May	6	(a)	Bristol R	W 2-1	Chilton, Wagstaff	9,234
44		10	(a)	Bournemouth	D 1-1	I.Butler	7,861
45		17	(h)	Peterborough U	W 2-1	Houghton, Chilton	28,255
46		20	(h)	Southend U	W 1-0	I.Butler	30,371

FINAL LEAGUE POSITION: 1st in Division Three — Promoted

Appearances
Sub Appearances
Goals

FA Cup

1	Nov	13	(a)	Bradford	W 3-2	Houghton, Chilton, I.Butler	11,487
2	Dec	8	(a)	Gateshead	W 4-0	Henderson, Wagstaff, Houghton, I.Butler	5,935
3	Jan	22	(h)	Southampton	W 1-0	Houghton	28,851
4	Feb	12	(h)	Nottingham F	W 2-0	Heath 2	38,055
5	Mar	5	(h)	Southport	W 2-0	Chilton 2	38,871
6		26	(a)	Chelsea	D 2-2	Wagstaff 2	46,924
R		31	(h)	Chelsea	L 1-3	Simpkin	45,328

Appearances
Goals

League Cup

1	Sep	22	(h)	Derby C	D 2-2	Houghton 2	15,601
R		29	(a)	Derby C	L 3-4	Chilton, Wagstaff, Simpkin	9,645

Appearances
Goals

Williams M	Davidson A	Butler D	Simpkin C	Milner M	Summers G	Wilkinson W	Wagstaff K	Chilton C	Houghton K	Heath T	Butler I	Henderson R	Sharpe L	Swan M	Collinson L	Jarvis A	Greenwood P	Brown M	
1	2	3	4	5	6	7	8	9	10	11									1
1	2	3	4	5	6		8	9	10	7	11								2
1	2	3*	4	5	6		8	9	10	7	11	12							3
1	2		4	5	6		8	9	10	7	11		3						4
	2		4	5	6		8	9	10	7	11		3	1					5
	2	3	6	5			8	9	10	7	11			1	4				6
1	2	3	6	5			8	9	10	7	11				4				7
1	2	3	4	5	6		8	9	10		11	7							8
1	2	3	4	5	6		8	9	10		11	7							9
1	2	3	4	5	6		8	9	10		11	7							10
1	2	3	4	5	6		8	9	10		11	7							11
1	2	3	4	5	6		8	9	10		11	7							12
	2	3	4	5	6		8	9	10		11	7		1					13
	2	3	6	5			8	9	10		11	7		1		4			14
	2*	3	6	5		12	8	9	10		11	7		1		4			15
	2	3	6	5			8	9	10		11	7		1		4			16
	2	3	6	5			8	9	10		11	7		1		4			17
	2	3	6	5			8	9	10	12	11	7*		1		4			18
	2	3	6	5			8	9	10		11	7		1		4			19
	2	3	6	5			8	9	10		11	7		1		4			20
	2	3	6	5			8	9	10		11	7		1		4			21
	2		6	5			8	9	10		11	7	3	1		4			22
	2		6	5			8	9	10		11	7	3	1		4			23
	2	3	6	5			8	9	10		11	7		1		4			24
		3	6	5			8	9	10		11	7		1		4	2		25
	2	3	6	5			8	9	10		11	7		1		4			26
	2	3	6	5			8	9	10		11	7		1		4			27
	2	3	6	5			8	9	10		11	7		1		4			28
	2*	3	6	5			8	9	10	12	11	7		1		4			29
	2	3	6	5			8	9	10		11	7		1		4			30
	2	3	6	5		12	8	9	10*		11	7		1		4			31
	2	3	6	5			8	9	10		11	7		1		4			32
	2	3	6	5			8	9	10		11	7		1		4			33
	2	3	6	5			8	9		10	11	7		1		4			34
	2		6	5			8	9	10		11	7		1		4		3	35
	2		6	5			8	9	10		11	7		1		4		3	36
	2		6	5			8	9	10		11	7		1		4		3	37
	2	3	6	5			8	9	10		11	7		1		4			38
	2	3	6	5			8	9	10		11	7		1		4			39
	2	3	6	5			8		9	10	11	7		1		4			40
	2	3	6	5			8	9	10		11	7		1		4			41
	2	3	6	5			8	9	10		11	7		1		4			42
	2	3*	6	5		12	8	9	10	7	11			1		4			43
	2	3*	6	5			8	9	10	12	11	7		1		4			44
	2		6	5			8	9	10		11	7		1		4		3	45
	2		6	5			8	9	10		11	7		1		4		3	46
10	45	37	46	46	11	1	46	45	45	10	45	38	4	36	2	33	1	5	
						3				3		1							
			1				27	25	22		13	13				3			

5 own-goals

Williams M	Davidson A	Butler D	Simpkin C	Milner M	Summers G	Wilkinson W	Wagstaff K	Chilton C	Houghton K	Heath T	Butler I	Henderson R	Sharpe L	Swan M	Collinson L	Jarvis A	Greenwood P	Brown M	
	2	3	6	5			8	9	10		11	7		1		4			1
	2	3	6	5			8	9	10		11	7		1		4			2
	2	3	6	5			8	9	10		11	7		1		4			3
	2			5			8	9	6	10	11	7		1		4		3	4
	2	3	6	5			8	9	10		11	7		1		4			5
	2	3	6	5			8	9	10		11	7		1		4			6
	2	3	6	5			8	9	10		11	7		1		4			R
	7	6	6	7			7	7	7	1	7	7		7		7		1	
			1				3	3	3	2	2	1							

Williams M	Davidson A	Butler D	Simpkin C	Milner M	Summers G	Wilkinson W	Wagstaff K	Chilton C	Houghton K	Heath T	Butler I	Henderson R	Sharpe L	Swan M	Collinson L	Jarvis A	Greenwood P	Brown M	
1	2	3	4	5	6		8	9	10		11	7							1
1	2	3	4	5	6		8	9	10		11	7							R
2	2	2	2	2	2		2	2	2		2	2							
			1				1	1	2										

1966-67

1	Aug	20	(a)	Coventry C	L 0-1		27,933
2		27	(h)	Bury	W 2-0	Wagstaff 2	20,438
3		31	(a)	Norwich C	W 2-0	Wagstaff, Houghton	14,215
4	Sep	3	(a)	Preston NE	L 2-4	Chilton, Houghton	14,959
5		7	(a)	Portsmouth	W 1-0	Chilton	15,710
6		10	(h)	Rotherham U	W 1-0	Houghton	25,209
7		17	(a)	Millwall	L 1-2	Houghton	14,340
8		20	(h)	Norwich C	W 5-0	Chilton 2, Wagstaff, Houghton, I.Butler	24,871
9		23	(h)	Northampton T	W 6-1	Wagstaff 2, Chilton 2, I.Butler, Henderson	29,122
10		28	(h)	Portsmouth	W 2-0	Houghton, Wagstaff	35,929
11	Oct	1	(a)	Plymouth A	L 1-3	Wagstaff	15,776
12		8	(a)	Cardiff C	W 4-2	Wagstaff 4	9,407
13		15	(h)	Wolves	W 3-1	Chilton, Henderson, I.Butler	32,522
14		22	(a)	Ipswich T	L 4-5	Wagstaff 2, Houghton, Henderson	20,024
15		29	(h)	Bristol C	L 0-2		26,630
16	Nov	5	(a)	Carlisle U	L 0-2		14,157
17		12	(h)	Blackburn R	L 2-3	Houghton, Wagstaff	22,887
18		19	(a)	Bolton W	L 1-2	Henderson	14,950
19		26	(h)	Charlton A	D 2-2	Chilton, Heath	20,383
20	Dec	3	(a)	Derby C	W 3-2	Wilkinson 2, Wagstaff	18,793
21		10	(h)	Crystal P	W 6-1	Chilton 3, Wagstaff, I.Butler, Wilkinson	21,818
22		17	(h)	Coventry C	D 2-2	I.Butler 2	25,577
23		26	(h)	Huddersfield T	W 2-0	Chilton, Wagstaff	35,630
24		27	(a)	Huddersfield T	L 0-1		32,268
25		31	(a)	Bury	L 2-3	Chilton, Wagstaff	7,652
26	Jan	7	(h)	Preston NE	D 2-2	Wilkinson, Jarvis	22,047
27		14	(a)	Rotherham U	D 1-1	Chilton	17,684
28		21	(h)	Millwall	W 2-0	Simpkin, Jarvis	27,189
29	Feb	4	(a)	Northampton T	D 2-2	Houghton, Young	12,396
30		11	(h)	Plymouth A	W 4-2	Wagstaff, Wilkinson, Chilton, Jarvis	24,702
31		25	(h)	Cardiff C	W 1-0	Wilkinson	23,629
32	Mar	4	(a)	Bristol C	L 1-2	Chilton	23,496
33		18	(h)	Ipswich T	D 1-1	Jarvis	22,775
34		25	(a)	Wolves	L 0-4		30,991
35		27	(a)	Birmingham C	L 1-2	Wilkinson	17,066
36		28	(h)	Birmingham C	L 0-2		23,122
37	Apr	1	(h)	Carlisle U	L 1-2	Chilton	19,029
38		8	(a)	Blackburn R	L 1-4	I.Butler	11,622
39		15	(h)	Bolton W	D 1-1	Simpkin	16,480
40		23	(a)	Charlton A	W 3-1	Wilkinson, Lill, Wagstaff	12,285
41		27	(h)	Derby C	L 1-3	Saxton (og)	19,345
42	May	6	(a)	Crystal P	L 1-4	I.Butler	12,329

FINAL LEAGUE POSITION: 12th in Division Two

Appearances
Sub Appearance
Goals

FA Cup

3	Jan	28	(h)	Portsmouth	D 1-1	Houghton	29,381
R	Feb	1	(a)	Portsmouth	D 2-2*	Houghton, Chilton	33,107
2R		6	(n†)	Portsmouth	L 1-3	Chilton	18,448

*After extra-time. †Played at Highfield Road, Coventry.

Appearances
Sub Appearance
Goals

League Cup

1	Aug	24	(a)	Lincoln C	L 0-1		6,238

Appearances
Sub Appearance
Goals

McKechnie I	Davidson A	Butler D	Jarvis A	Milner M	Simpkin C	Henderson R	Wagstaff K	Chilton C	Houghton K	Butler I	Heath T	Collinson L	Young R	Wilkinson W	Beardsley D	Pettit R	Davidson I	Swan M	Greenwood P	Corner N	Lord M	Lill D	Lees N	
1	2	3	4	5	6	7	8	9	10	11														1
1	2	3	4	5		7	8	9	6	11	10													2
1	2	3	4	5	6*	7	8	9	10	1'	12													3
1	2	3	4	5		7	8	9*	6		10		11	12										4
1		3	4	5		7	8	9	10			6	11		2									5
1		3	4	5		7	8	9	10	11		6			2									6
1			4	5	3	7	8	9	10	11		6			2									7
1	2	3	4	5	6	7	8	9	10	11														8
1	2	3	4	5	6	7	8	9	10	11														9
1	2	3	4	5	6	7	8	9	10	11														10
1	2	3	4	5	6	7	8	9	10	11														11
1	2	3	4	5	6	7	8	9	10				11*	12										12
1	2	3	4	5	6	7	8	9	10	11														13
1	2	3		5	6*	7	8	9	10	11	12	4												14
1	2	3	4			7	8	9	10	11		6				5								15
1		3	4	5*		7	8	9	10			6	11		2		12							16
1		3	4		6	7	8	9	10	11					2	5								17
1		3	4		6	7	8	9	10	11					2	5								18
1		3	4	5	6	7	8	9		11	10				2									19
1	2	3	4	5	6	7	8	9		11				10										20
1	2	3	4*	5	6	7	8	9		11				10	12									21
	2	3	4	5	6	7	8	9		11				10				1						22
1	2	3	4	5	6	7	8	9		11				10										23
1	2	3	4	5	6	7	8	9		11				10										24
1	2	3		5	6	7	8*	9		11		12		10					4					25
1	2	3	4	5	6	7		9		11	10			8										26
1	2	3	4	5	6	7	8	9		11				10										27
1	2	3	4	5	6	7	8	9		11				10										28
1	2	3	4	5*	6	7	8	9	10				11	12										29
1	2	3	4	5	6*	7	8	9		11				10					12					30
1		3	4	5	6	7	8	9		11				10					2					31
1	2	3	4	5	6	7	8	9					11	10										32
1		3	4	5	6	7	8	9		11				10					2					33
1	2	3	10	5	6	7	8	9					11						4					34
1		3	4		6	7		9					11	10					2	5	8			35
1	2	3			6		8	9			11			10		5			4		7			36
1	2	3		5	6	7	8	9		11									4		10			37
1	2	3	4	5	6	12	8			11				9					7*		10			38
1	2	3	4		6	7				11				8		5					10	9		39
1		3	4		6	7	8							10		5			2		11	9		40
1		3	4		6	7	8		10							5			2		11	9		41
1		2	4		6		8			11				10		5*			12		7	9	3	42
41	29	41	38	33	36	39	39	37	20	31	5	6	8	19	7	8		1	10	1	8	4	1	
						1					2	1		3	1		1		2					
			4		2	4	21	17	9	8	1		1	8								1		

1 own-goal

McKechnie I	Davidson A	Butler D	Jarvis A	Milner M	Simpkin C	Henderson R	Wagstaff K	Chilton C	Houghton K	Butler I	Heath T	Collinson L	Young R	Wilkinson W	Beardsley D	Pettit R	Davidson I	Swan M	Greenwood P	Corner N	Lord M	Lill D	Lees N	
1	2	3	4	5	6	7	8	9	10	11														3
1	2	3	4	5	6	7	8	9	10	11														R
	2	3	4		6	7	8	9	10	11								1		5				2R
2	3	3	3	2	3	3	3	3	3	3								1		1				
								2	2															

McKechnie I	Davidson A	Butler D	Jarvis A	Milner M	Simpkin C	Henderson R	Wagstaff K	Chilton C	Houghton K	Butler I	Heath T	Collinson L	Young R	Wilkinson W	Beardsley D	Pettit R	Davidson I	Swan M	Greenwood P	Corner N	Lord M	Lill D	Lees N	
	2	3	4	5	6	7	8	9	10	11	12							1*						1
	1	1	1	1	1	1	1	1	1	1								1						
											1													

1967-68

1	Aug	19	(h)	Carlisle U	W 1-0	Simpkin	19,123
2		23	(a)	Bolton W	L 1-6	Houghton	9,653
3		26	(a)	Blackburn R	L 0-2		16,240
4		30	(h)	Bolton W	L 1-2	Simpkin	15,776
5	Sep	2	(h)	Blackpool	L 0-1		16,958
6		4	(a)	Birmingham C	L 2-6	Chilton, Wagstaff	25,931
7		9	(a)	Millwall	D 1-1	Wagstaff	11,897
8		16	(h)	Crystal P	D 1-1	I.Butler	15,993
9		23	(h)	Middlesbrough	L 0-2		17,727
10		30	(a)	Bristol C	D 3-3	Houghton 2, Chilton	11,630
11	Oct	7	(a)	Preston NE	L 2-3	Wagstaff, Chilton	14,318
12		14	(h)	Queen's Park R	W 2-0	Houghton, Wagstaff	14,240
13		21	(a)	Plymouth A	W 5-2	Houghton, Chilton, Wagstaff, Simpkin, Young	8,577
14		27	(h)	Cardiff C	L 1-2	Wagstaff	18,579
15	Nov	4	(a)	Portsmouth	L 0-3		17,606
16		11	(h)	Norwich C	L 0-2		14,720
17		18	(a)	Aston Villa	W 3-2	Wagstaff, Chilton, Greenwood	19,675
18		25	(h)	Derby C	W 3-0	Wilkinson 2, Chilton	14,767
19	Dec	2	(a)	Rotherham U	W 3-1	Chilton 2, Henderson	15,578
20		9	(h)	Charlton A	D 1-1	Wagstaff	13,697
21		16	(a)	Carlisle U	D 1-1	Wagstaff	9,063
22		22	(h)	Blackburn R	D 1-1	I.Butler	18,662
23		26	(a)	Huddersfield T	L 0-2		19,739
24		30	(h)	Huddersfield T	D 1-1	I.Butler	17,656
25	Jan	6	(a)	Blackpool	L 1-3	Chilton	13,227
26		13	(h)	Millwall	D 1-1	Wagstaff	13,669
27		20	(a)	Crystal P	W 1-0	Chilton	15,43
28	Feb	3	(a)	Middlesbrough	L 1-2	Young	16,028
29		10	(h)	Bristol C	W 4-2	Wagstaff 3, I.Butler	12,596
30		24	(h)	Preston NE	D 1-1	Chilton	14,082
31	Mar	9	(a)	Queen's Park R	D 1-1	Chilton	17,70
32		16	(h)	Plymouth A	L 0-2		11,948
33		22	(a)	Cardiff C	W 3-2	Henderson 2, Wagstaff	11,97
34		30	(h)	Portsmouth	D 1-1	Wagstaff	11,490
35	Apr	6	(a)	Norwich C	D 2-2	Wagstaff, Chilton	14,05
36		13	(h)	Aston Villa	W 3-0	Houghton, Wagstaff, Chilton	15,96
37		15	(h)	Ipswich T	D 1-1	Houghton	19,55
38		16	(a)	Ipswich T	L 0-2		24,61
39		20	(a)	Derby C	W 2-1	I.Butler, Lord	15,71
40		25	(h)	Rotherham U	W 2-1	Henderson, I.Davidson	20,59
41	May	4	(a)	Charlton A	L 1-5	Young	10,35
42		11	(h)	Birmingham C	L 0-1		10,34

FINAL LEAGUE POSITION: 17th in Division Two

Appearances
Sub Appearan
Goals

FA Cup

3	Jan	27	(a)	Middlesbrough	D 1-1	Chilton	28,50
R		31	(h)	Middlesbrough	D 2-2*	Wagstaff 2	33,91
2R	Feb	7	(n†)	Middlesbrough	L 0-1		16,52

*After extra-time. †Played at Bootham Crescent, York.

Appearances
Sub Appearar
Goals

League Cup

2	Sep	12	(a)	Queen's Park R	L 1-2	Wagstaff	16,60

Appearances
Sub Appeara
Goals

Swan M	Davidson A	Butler D	Jarvis A	Milner M	Simpkin C	Heath T	Wagstaff K	Lill D	Houghton K	Butler I	McKechnie I	Chilton C	Greenwood P	Beardsley D	Banks F	Young R	Lord M	Wilkinson W	Lees N	Davidson I	Pettit R	Wilson T	Henderson R	
1	2	3	4	5	6	7	8	9	10	11														1
	2	3	4	5	6	7	8		10	11	1	9												2
1			4	5		7	8	9	10				2	3	6	11								3
1		3		5	4	7	8	9	10	11			2		6									4
1		3	4		6		8		10	11		9	2		5		7							5
1		3	4		6		8		10	11		9	2	7	5									6
	2*	3	4		6		8		10		1	9	7		5	11		12						7
			4		6	7*	8		10	11	1		2		5	12		9	3					8
1		12	4				8		10			9	2		5	11		7	3*	6				9
1		2	4		6		8		10	11		9				7		12	3*		5			10
1	2	3			6		8			11		9	7		5			10			4			11
1	2	3			6		8		10	11		9	4		5	12		7*						12
1	2	3			6		8		10	11		9	4		5	7								13
1	2	3			6		8		10	11		9	4		5	7								14
1		3			6		8			11*		9	7	2	5		12	10			4			15
1	2	3*					8		10			9	6	12	4			11				5	7	16
	2*	3			6		8		10		1	9	4		12			11				5	7	17
		3			6	12	8		10*		1	9	2		4			11				5	7	18
		3			6		8			11	1	9	4		2			10				5	7	19
		3			6		8			11	1	9	4		2			10				5	7	20
		3			6		8			11	1	9	4		2			10				5	7	21
		3			6		8			11	1	9	4		2			10				5	7	22
		3			6		8		12	11	1	9*	4		2			10				5	7	23
		3			6		8			11	1	9	4		2			10				5	7	24
		3			6		8			11	1	9	4		2			10				5	7	25
		3			6		8		7	11	1	9	4		2			10				5		26
		3			6		8		7	11	1	9	4		2			10				5		27
		3			6				8		1		4		2	11		9		10		5	7	28
		3			6		8		7*	11	1	9	4		2					10		5	12	29
		3			6		8			11	1	9	4		2						10	5	7	30
		3					8		6	11	1	9	4		2		10					5	7	31
		3			6		8			11	1	9	4		2		10					5	7	32
		3	10		6		8			11	1	9	4		2							5	7	33
			4		6		8		10	11	1	9	3		2							5	7	34
			4		6		8		10	11	1	9	3		2							5	7	35
			4		6		8		10	11	1	9	3		2							5	7	36
			4		6		8		10	11	1	9	3		2							5	7	37
			4		6*		8		10	11	1	9	3		2		12					5	7	38
			4		6		8*		10	11	1	9	3		2		12					5	7	39
			4		6				10	11	1	9	3		2					8		5	7	40
			6		10		8		3		1	9	4		2	11				7		5		41
		3	6		10		8		7	11	1	9	4		2							5		42
13	9	31	19	4	38	5	40	3	30	34	29	37	39	3	38	8	3	18	3	5	4	27	22	
		1				1			1					1	1	2	3	2					1	
					3		17		7	5		14	1			3	1	2		1			4	

Swan M	Davidson A	Butler D	Jarvis A	Milner M	Simpkin C	Heath T	Wagstaff K	Lill D	Houghton K	Butler I	McKechnie I	Chilton C	Greenwood P	Beardsley D	Banks F	Young R	Lord M	Wilkinson W	Lees N	Davidson I	Pettit R	Wilson T	Henderson R	
		3			6		8		7	11	1	9	4		2			10				5		3
		3			6		8		7	11	1	9	4		2			10				5		R
		3			6		8		7	11	1	9	4		2			10*				5	12	2R
		3			3		3		3	3	3	3	3		3			3				3		
																							1	
							2					1												

Swan M	Davidson A	Butler D	Jarvis A	Milner M	Simpkin C	Heath T	Wagstaff K	Lill D	Houghton K	Butler I	McKechnie I	Chilton C	Greenwood P	Beardsley D	Banks F	Young R	Lord M	Wilkinson W	Lees N	Davidson I	Pettit R	Wilson T	Henderson R	
			4		6		8		10		1	9	7		5	11		3	2					2
			1		1		1		1		1	1	1		1	1		1	1					
							1																	

1968-69

1	Aug	10	(a)	Blackpool	L 0-2		17,364
2		17	(h)	Blackburn R	L 1-3	Chilton	13,345
3		21	(a)	Fulham	D 0-0		15,072
4		24	(a)	Oxford U	D 1-1	Wagstaff	9,637
5		28	(a)	Derby C	D 2-2	Wagstaff, Jarvis	24,650
6		31	(h)	Middlesbrough	W 3-0	Wagstaff, Simpkin, Jarvis	16,838
7	Sep	7	(h)	Bristol C	D 1-1	Chilton	12,309
8		14	(a)	Aston Villa	D 1-1	I.Butler	17,688
9		18	(h)	Sheffield U	D 1-1	I.Butler	17,480
10		21	(h)	Bolton W	W 1-0	Wagstaff	13,487
11		28	(a)	Millwall	W 3-2	Houghton 3	13,493
12	Oct	5	(a)	Norwich C	W 2-1	Houghton, I.Butler	17,985
13		9	(h)	Derby C	W 1-0	I.Butler	24,307
14		12	(h)	Huddersfield T	W 3-0	Houghton 2, Wagstaff	21,344
15		19	(a)	Preston NE	L 0-1		13,864
16		26	(h)	Cardiff C	D 3-3	Wagstaff 3	17,027
17	Nov	4	(a)	Carlisle U	L 0-1		9,374
18		8	(h)	Bury	W 3-0	Wagstaff 2, Wilson	13,531
19		16	(a)	Charlton A	D 1-1	Wagstaff	10,232
20		23	(h)	Portsmouth	D 2-2	Wagstaff, Lord	14,257
21		30	(a)	Birmingham C	L 2-5	I.Butler, Greenwood	21,352
22	Dec	7	(h)	Crystal P	W 2-0	Chilton, I.Butler	13,785
23		14	(a)	Huddersfield T	W 3-0	Chilton 2, Lill	12,418
24		20	(h)	Preston NE	D 1-1	Wagstaff	15,976
25		26	(h)	Norwich C	L 0-1		20,312
26		28	(a)	Cardiff C	L 0-3		24,815
27	Jan	11	(h)	Carlisle U	L 1-2	I.Butler	12,389
28		18	(a)	Bury	D 0-0		5,659
29	Feb	1	(h)	Charlton A	W 5-2	I.Butler 2, Wagstaff, Wilkinson, Greenwood	11,475
30		8	(a)	Portsmouth	L 0-1		13,960
31		22	(a)	Crystal P	L 0-2		14,172
32	Mar	1	(h)	Blackpool	D 2-2	Lord, I.Butler	10,89
33		8	(a)	Blackburn R	D 1-1	Wagstaff	9,018
34		14	(h)	Oxford U	D 0-0		8,905
35		22	(a)	Middlesbrough	L 3-5	Wilkinson 2, Jarvis	18,33
36		29	(a)	Bristol C	D 1-1	Jarvis	13,10
37	Apr	5	(h)	Millwall	W 2-0	Wilkinson, Jarvis	10,78
38		7	(h)	Fulham	W 4-0	Wagstaff 3, Lord	10,85
39		8	(a)	Sheffield U	D 1-1	Wagstaff	12,56
40		12	(a)	Bolton W	L 0-1		5,10
41		15	(h)	Birmingham C	L 1-2	Wagstaff	8,70
42		19	(h)	Aston Villa	W 1-0	Wilkinson	10,53

FINAL LEAGUE POSITION: 11th in Division Two

Appearances
Sub Appearar
Goals

FA Cup

3	Jan	4	(h)	Wolves	L 1-3	Chilton	27,52

Appearances
Sub Appearar
Goals

League Cup

1	Aug	14	(a)	Halifax T	W 3-0	Wagstaff, Wilkinson, Chilton	4,49
2	Sep	4	(a)	Brentford	L 0-3		11,48

Appearances
Sub Appeara
Goals

McKechnie I	Beardsley D	Butler D	Greenwood P	Simpkin C	Jarvis A	Wilkinson W	Wagstaff K	Chilton C	Houghton K	Butler I	Pettit R	Lill D	Banks F	Wilson T	Lord M	O'Riley P	Barker G	
1	2	3	4	5	6	7	8	9	10	11								1
1	3		2	5	4	7*	8	9	10	11	6	12						2
1	3		12	6	7			9	10	11	4		2*	5	8			3
1	3			6	7		8		10	11	4		2	5	12	9*		4
1	3		6	10	7		8	9		11	4		2	5				5
1	3		6	10	7		8	9		11	4		2	5				6
1	3		6	10	7*		8	9	12	11	4		2	5				7
1	3		7	6			8	9	10	11	4		2	5				8
1	3		7*	6		12	8	9	10	11	4		2	5				9
1	3	2	7	6			8	9	10	11	4			5				10
1	3		7	6			8	9	10	11	4		2	5				11
1	3		7	6	12		8	9	10	11	4		2	5*				12
1	3	2	5	6	4		8	9	10	11					7			13
1	3	2*	5	6	7		8	9	10	11	4				12			14
1	3		2	6	4		8	9	10	11	5				7			15
1	3		2	6	4		8	9	10	11	5				7			16
1			3	6	7		8	9*	10	11	4		2	5	12			17
1	3		2	6	7		8	9	10	11	4			5				18
1	3		2	6	7		8	9	10*	11	4		12	5				19
1	3		6	10	7		8			11	4		2	5	9			20
1	3		6	10*	7		8			11	4	9	2	5		12		21
1	3	2		6	7		8	9		11	4	10		5				22
1	3		2	6	7		8	9		11	4	10		5				23
1	3		2	6	7		8	9		11	4	10		5				24
1	3		2	6	7	10	8	9		11	4			5				25
1	3		2	6	7	10	8			11	4	9*		5	12			26
1	3		2	6	7	12	9		10*	11	4			5	8			27
1	3		7	6		8			10		4		2	5	11	9		28
1	3		7	6		9	8		10	11	4		2	5				29
1	3	2	7	6	12	9	8		10*	11	4			5				30
1	3	2	7*	6	12	9	8			11	4			5	10			31
1	3	2*	7	6	12	9	10			11	4			5	8			32
1	3	2	7	6		9	10				4	8		5	11			33
1	3	2	7	6		9	10			11	4			5	8			34
1	3		7	6	4	9	10		8	11	5		2					35
1	3	12	7*	6	4	9	10			11	5		2		8			36
1		3		6	7	9	10			11	4		2		8		5	37
1		3		6	7	9	10			11	4		2		8		5	38
1		3		6	7	9	10			11	4		2		8		5	39
1		3		6	7	9			10	11*	4	12	2		8		5	40
1		3		6	7	9	10				4	8	2		11		5	41
1		3		6	7	9	10			11	4	8	2				5	42
42	35	16	33	42	30	19	39	22	22	39	40	8	22	28	17	2	6	
		1	1		4	2			1			2	1		4	1		
			2	1	5	5	20	5	6	10		1		1	3			

McKechnie I	Beardsley D	Butler D	Greenwood P	Simpkin C	Jarvis A	Wilkinson W	Wagstaff K	Chilton C	Houghton K	Butler I	Pettit R	Lill D	Banks F	Wilson T	Lord M	O'Riley P	Barker G	
1	3		2	6	7	12	8	9*	10	11	4			5				3
1	1		1	1	1		1	1	1	1	1			1				
						1												
								1										

McKechnie I	Beardsley D	Butler D	Greenwood P	Simpkin C	Jarvis A	Wilkinson W	Wagstaff K	Chilton C	Houghton K	Butler I	Pettit R	Lill D	Banks F	Wilson T	Lord M	O'Riley P	Barker G	
1	3		2	5	4	7	8	9	10	11	6							1
1	3		6	10	7		8	9	12	11	4		2*	5				2
2	2		2	2	2	1	2	2	1	2	2		1	1				
									1									
						1	1	1										

1969-70

1	Aug	9	(a)	Queen's Park R	L 0-3		15,781
2		13	(h)	Norwich C	W 1-0	Houghton	11,791
3		16	(h)	Bristol C	W 2-0	Chilton, Blampey	10,170
4		20	(a)	Norwich C	L 1-2	I.Butler	18,158
5		23	(a)	Blackburn R	L 1-2	I.Butler	11,627
6		27	(h)	Birmingham C	D 0-0		12,242
7		29	(h)	Blackpool	W 1-0	Simpkin	9,701
8	Sep	6	(a)	Carlisle U	L 1-2	I.Butler	10,049
9		13	(h)	Bolton W	W 4-2	Chilton 2, Wagstaff, I.Butler	10,646
10		17	(a)	Portsmouth	W 4-1	Wagstaff, Chilton, Houghton, Hand (og)	14,786
11		20	(a)	Aston Villa	L 2-3	Houghton, Chilton	23,666
12		27	(h)	Charlton A	D 1-1	Simpkin	10,771
13	Oct	4	(a)	Sheffield U	L 0-3		16,246
14		7	(a)	Bristol C	L 1-3	Chilton	18,132
15		11	(h)	Oxford U	W 3-1	Wilkinson, Simpkin, Barker	8,176
16		18	(a)	Swindon T	L 0-1		19,013
17		25	(h)	Huddersfield T	L 2-3	Houghton, I.Butler	11,375
18	Nov	1	(a)	Cardiff C	L 0-6		20,419
19		8	(h)	Preston NE	W 3-1	Chilton 2, Wagstaff	7,474
20		15	(a)	Middlesbrough	L 0-1		14,235
21		22	(h)	Watford	D 1-1	Chilton	9,146
22	Dec	13	(a)	Bolton W	L 1-2	Chilton	7,059
23		17	(a)	Leicester C	D 2-2	Chilton, Wagstaff	16,059
24		20	(h)	Carlisle U	L 2-4	Houghton, Wagstaff	9,295
25		26	(h)	Blackburn R	W 3-0	Houghton, Chilton, I.Butler	11,486
26	Jan	17	(a)	Charlton A	W 4-1	Chilton, Wagstaff, Simpkin, I.Butler	10,677
27		24	(h)	Millwall	W 2-1	Wagstaff, Houghton	11,286
28		31	(h)	Sheffield U	L 2-3	Wagstaff 2	15,551
29	Feb	7	(a)	Oxford U	D 0-0		9,177
30		14	(h)	Queen's Park R	L 1-2	Chilton	12,698
31		21	(a)	Preston NE	D 3-3	Chilton, Wagstaff, Simpkin	10,038
32		28	(h)	Swindon T	D 1-1	Chilton	10,855
33	Mar	6	(a)	Watford	D 1-1	Houghton	15,470
34		10	(h)	Aston Villa	W 3-1	Wagstaff 2, Houghton	9,688
35		14	(h)	Leicester C	W 4-1	Chilton, Wagstaff, Simpkin, Nish (og)	11,536
36		18	(a)	Blackpool	W 1-0	Wagstaff	15,724
37		21	(a)	Millwall	L 1-2	Houghton	10,350
38		28	(h)	Middlesbrough	W 3-2	Wagstaff 2, Chilton	17,434
39		30	(a)	Huddersfield T	D 2-2	Houghton, I.Butler	26,046
40		31	(h)	Cardiff C	D 1-1	I.Butler	13,038
41	Apr	4	(a)	Birmingham C	W 4-2	Houghton 3, Wagstaff	13,530
42		15	(h)	Portsmouth	D 3-3	Houghton 2, Wagstaff	11,468

FINAL LEAGUE POSITION: 13th in Division Two

Appearances
Sub Appearance
Goals

FA Cup

3	Jan	3	(h)	Manchester C	L 0-1		30,271

Appearances
Sub Appearance
Goals

League Cup

2	Sep	3	(h)	Norwich C	W 1-0	Wagstaff	10,824
3		24	(a)	Derby C	L 1-3	Chilton	31,603

Appearances
Sub Appearanc
Goals

McKechnie I	Banks F	Butler D	Pettit R	Barker G	Simpkin C	Jarvis A	Wagstaff K	Wilkinson W	Houghton K	Butler I	Lord M	Blampey S	Chilton C	Lill D	Greenwood P	Beardsley D	Wilson T	McCunnell B	Pearson S	
1	2	3	4	5	6	7*	8	9	10	11	12									1
1	2	3	4*	5	6		8		10	11	12	7	9							2
1	2*	3		5	6	4	8	12	10	11		7	9							3
1	2	3	4	5	6	12	8		10	11		7*	9							4
1	2	3	4	5	6	7	8		10	11			9							5
1	2	3	4	5	6		8		10		11	7	9							6
1	2	3	4	5	6		8		10		11	7	9							7
1	2	3	4	5	6		8	9	10	11		7								8
1	2	3	4*	5	6		8	7	10	11	12		9							9
1	2	3		5	6		8	4	10	11	7		9							10
1	2	3		5	6		8	4	10	11	7		9							11
1	2	3*	4	5	6	12			10	11		7	9	8						12
1	2	3	4	5	6			7	10*	11	8		9		12					13
1	2	3	4	5	6			7	10	11	8		9*		12					14
1	2		4	5	6		9*	7	10	11	8				12	3				15
1	2		4	5	6			9	10	11	8				7	3				16
1			4*	5	6		10	7	8	11	12		9		2	3				17
1	2		12	5	6		10*	4		11	8		9		7	3				18
1	2	3		5	6		10	4	8	11	12		9*		7					19
1	2	3		5	6		10	4	8	11			9		7					20
1	2			5	6*		10	4	8	11	12		9		7	3				21
1	2					6	10	4	8	11			9		7	3	5			22
1	2			12		6	10	4*	8	11			9		7	3	5			23
1	2			5	10	4	8		11				9*		7	3	6	12		24
1	2				6		10	4	8	11	12		9*		7	3	5			25
1	2				6	7	10	5	8	11			9		4	3				26
1	2				6	7	10	5	8	11			9		4	3				27
1	2				6	7	10	5	8	11			9		4	3				28
1	2				6	7	10	5	8	11			9		4	3				29
1	2				6	7	10	5	8*	11	12		9		4	3				30
1	2				6	7	10		8	11			9		4	3	5			31
1	2				6	7	10	5	8	11			9		4	3				32
1	2				6	7	10	5	8*	11	12		9		4	3				33
1	2				6	7	10	5	8	11			9		4	3				34
1	2*				6	7	10	5	8	11	12		9		4	3				35
1			4		6	7	10	5	8	11	12		9*		2	3				36
1			4		6	7	10	5	8	11	9				2	3				37
1			4		6	7	10	5	8	11			9		2	3				38
1			4		6	7	10	5	8	11			9		2	3				39
1			4		6	7	10	5	8	11			9		2	3				40
1			4		6	7	10	5	8	11			9		2	3				41
1			4		6	7	10	5	8	11					2	3			9	42
42	34	16	21	22	40	23	38	33	41	39	10	7	36	1	27	26	5		1	
			1	1		2		1			11				3			1		
				1	6		18	1	16	9		1	18							

2 own-goals

McKechnie I	Banks F	Butler D	Pettit R	Barker G	Simpkin C	Jarvis A	Wagstaff K	Wilkinson W	Houghton K	Butler I	Lord M	Blampey S	Chilton C	Lill D	Greenwood P	Beardsley D	Wilson T	McCunnell B	Pearson S	
1	2				6	7	10		8	11			9		4	3	5			3
1	1				1	1	1		1	1			1		1	1	1			

McKechnie I	Banks F	Butler D	Pettit R	Barker G	Simpkin C	Jarvis A	Wagstaff K	Wilkinson W	Houghton K	Butler I	Lord M	Blampey S	Chilton C	Lill D	Greenwood P	Beardsley D	Wilson T	McCunnell B	Pearson S	
1	2	3	4	5	6		8		10	11		7	9							2
1	2	3	4	5	6	12	8*	7	10	11			9							3
2	2	2	2	2	2		2	1	2	2		1	2							
						1														
							1						1							

1970-71

1	Aug	15	(a)	Swindon T	D	1-1	Butler	16,446
2		22	(h)	Middlesbrough	W	1-0	Simpkin	20,929
3		29	(a)	Watford	W	2-1	Chilton, Wagstaff	17,034
4	Sep	1	(a)	Carlisle U	L	0-2		8,847
5		5	(h)	Bolton W	W	1-0	Chilton	16,290
6		12	(a)	Bristol C	D	3-3	Chilton 2, Butler	12,978
7		19	(h)	Millwall	W	2-0	Wagstaff, Pearson	15,593
8		26	(a)	Norwich C	W	2-0	Houghton, Wagstaff	16,258
9	Oct	3	(h)	Birmingham C	L	0-1		17,582
10		7	(a)	Sunderland	W	1-0	Chilton	18,741
11		10	(a)	Orient	W	1-0	Chilton	9,445
12		16	(h)	Swindon T	W	2-0	Chilton, Wagstaff	20,958
13		21	(h)	Charlton A	W	2-0	Chilton, Houghton	17,528
14		24	(h)	Sheffield U	D	1-1	Wagstaff	25,340
15		31	(a)	Cardiff C	L	1-5	Barker	21,837
16	Nov	7	(h)	Luton T	L	0-2		18,343
17		14	(a)	Oxford U	W	3-0	Chilton, Wagstaff, Houghton	8,850
18		21	(h)	Queen's Park R	D	1-1	Chilton	15,606
19		28	(a)	Portsmouth	D	2-2	Chilton, Butler	13,360
20	Dec	5	(h)	Leicester C	W	3-0	Chilton, Houghton, Butler	21,210
21		12	(a)	Blackburn R	W	1-0	Chilton	7,490
22		19	(a)	Middlesbrough	L	0-1		17,957
23		26	(h)	Sheffield W	D	4-4	Chilton 2, Wagstaff, Houghton	24,399
24	Jan	9	(h)	Sunderland	W	4-0	Chilton 3, Wagstaff	20,532
25		16	(a)	Charlton A	W	1-0	Chilton	9,656
26		30	(h)	Portsmouth	L	0-1		19,958
27	Feb	6	(a)	Leicester C	D	0-0		31,076
28		20	(a)	Queen's Park R	D	1-1	Wagstaff	13,418
29		23	(h)	Blackburn R	D	0-0		23,976
30		27	(h)	Cardiff C	D	1-1	Carver (og)	25,091
31	Mar	9	(a)	Sheffield U	W	2-1	Simpkin, Wagstaff	40,277
32		13	(h)	Oxford U	L	0-1		26,772
33		20	(a)	Luton T	L	1-3	Houghton	19,566
34		27	(a)	Bolton W	D	0-0		8,759
35	Apr	3	(h)	Watford	W	1-0	Butler	17,199
36		10	(a)	Sheffield W	D	1-1	Banks	21,787
37		12	(h)	Bristol C	W	1-0	Banks	22,178
38		13	(a)	Birmingham C	D	0-0		33,109
39		17	(h)	Orient	W	5-2	Chilton 2, Wagstaff 2, Butler	19,320
40		24	(a)	Millwall	L	0-4		10,740
41		28	(h)	Carlisle U	L	1-2	Butler	14,36[illegible]
42	May	1	(h)	Norwich C	W	1-0	Houghton	11,301

FINAL LEAGUE POSITION: 5th in Division Two

Appearances
Sub Appearan[illegible]
Goals

FA Cup

3	Jan	2	(h)	Charlton A	W	3-0	Wagstaff, Houghton, Butler	19,92[illegible]
4		23	(h)	Blackpool	W	2-0	Wagstaff, Chilton	34,75[illegible]
5	Feb	13	(h)	Brentford	W	2-1	Houghton, Chilton	29,70[illegible]
6	Mar	6	(h)	Stoke C	L	2-3	Wagstaff 2	41,45[illegible]

Appearances
Sub Appearan[illegible]
Goals

League Cup

2	Sep	9	(a)	West Ham U	L	0-1		19,26[illegible]

Appearances
Sub Appearar[illegible]
Goals

McKechnie I	Beardsley D	de Vries R	Wilkinson W	Neill T	Simpkin C	Lord M	Houghton K	Pearson S	Wagstaff K	Butler I	Jarvis A	Chilton C	Greenwood P	Lees N	Pettit R	Banks F	Barker G	Holbrook S	Baxter W	Knighton K	Walters P	
1	2	3	4	5	6*	7	8	9	10	11	12											1
1	2	3	4	5	6	7	8		10	11		9										2
1	2	3	4	5	6	7	8		10		11	9										3
1	2	3	4	5	6	7	8		10	11		9										4
1	2	3	4	5	6	7	8		10	11*	12	9										5
1	2	3*	4	5	6	7		12	10	11		9	8									6
1	2	3	4	5	6	7		9	10	11	8											7
1	2	3	4	5	6	7	8		10	11		9										8
1	2	3	4*	5	6	7	8		10	11		9		12								9
1	2	3	4	5	6	7	8		10	11		9										10
1	2	3	4	5	6	7	8		10	11		9										11
1	2	3	4	5	6	7	8	12	10	11		9*										12
1	2	3	4		6		8	12	10	11*	7	9			5							13
1	2	3	4	5	6		8	11	10		7	9*				12						14
1	2	3	4	5	6		8	9	10	12	7						11*					15
1	2*	3	4	5	6		8		10	11		9				12		7				16
1		3	4	5	6		8		10	11		9	7			2						17
1		3	4*	5	6		8		10	11		9	7			2		12				18
1	3		4	5	6	10	8			11		9	7			2						19
1		3	4	5	6	8	10			11		9	7			2						20
1		3	4	5	6	8	10			11		9	7			2						21
1		3	4	5	6	11	8		10			9	7			2						22
1		3	4		6	7	8*		10	11		9	12		5	2						23
1		3	5		6	7	8		10	11		9	4			2						24
1		3	4	5	6	8	10			11		9	7			2						25
1		3*	4	5	6	8	12		10	11		9	7			2						26
1		3	4	5	6	7	8		10	11		9				2						27
1		3	4	5		7	8*		10	11	12	9	6			2						28
1		3		5	6	7	8		10	11	12	9	4*			2						29
1		3	4	5	6	7		8	10	11	12	9*				2						30
1		3	4	5	6	7			10	11		9							2	8		31
1		3*	4	5	6	7	12		10	11		9							2	8		32
1	3		4	5	6	9	7		10	11									2	8		33
1	3		4	5	6	7	11		10			9							2	8		34
1	3			5	6		7	9	10	11					4	2				8		35
1	3		4	5	6		7		10	11		9	12			2				8*		36
1	3		4	5		8	6		10	11		9				2				7		37
1		3	4	5	6	11			10			9	12			2			8	7*		38
1	3				6		12	8	10	11		9	4		5*	2				7		39
1	3		4				6	8	10	11		9				2			5	7		40
1	3		5			12	7	8*	10	11		9	4			2				6		41
	3		5			8	7		10	11		9	4			2				6	1	42
41	26	32	39	35	37	31	34	9	38	36	5	37	15		4	22	1	1	6	12	1	
						1	3	3		1	5		3	1		2		1				
					2		7	1	12	7		21				2	1					

1 own-goal

McKechnie I	Beardsley D	de Vries R	Wilkinson W	Neill T	Simpkin C	Lord M	Houghton K	Pearson S	Wagstaff K	Butler I	Jarvis A	Chilton C	Greenwood P	Lees N	Pettit R	Banks F	Barker G	Holbrook S	Baxter W	Knighton K	Walters P	
1		3		5	6	7	8		10	11		9	4			2						3
1		3	4	5	6	8	12		10	11		9	7			2*						4
1		3	4	5	6*	7	8		10	11		9	12			2						5
1		3	4	5	6	7	8		10	11		9				2						6
4		4	3	4	4	4	3		4	4		4	2			4						
							1						1									
							2		4	1		2										

McKechnie I	Beardsley D	de Vries R	Wilkinson W	Neill T	Simpkin C	Lord M	Houghton K	Pearson S	Wagstaff K	Butler I	Jarvis A	Chilton C	Greenwood P	Lees N	Pettit R	Banks F	Barker G	Holbrook S	Baxter W	Knighton K	Walters P	
1	2	3	4	5	6	7	8*		10		11	9	12									2
1	1	1	1	1	1	1	1		1		1	1										
													1									

1971-72

1	Aug	14	(a)	Charlton A	L 0-1		9,332
2		21	(h)	Oxford U	W 1-0	Butler	14,304
3		28	(a)	Cardiff C	D 1-1	Pearson	17,110
4	Sep	1	(h)	Birmingham C	W 1-0	Pearson	16,746
5		4	(h)	Blackpool	W 1-0	Pearson	18,288
6		11	(a)	Bristol C	L 0-4		16,659
7		18	(h)	Portsmouth	L 1-3	Pearson	14,363
8		25	(a)	Carlisle U	L 1-2	Wagstaff	9,879
9		29	(h)	Swindon T	W 2-0	Pearson, Lord	10,788
10	Oct	2	(h)	Luton T	D 0-0		13,904
11		9	(a)	Fulham	L 0-1		8,352
12		16	(h)	Charlton A	L 2-3	Clarke (og), Went (og)	9,933
13		20	(a)	Watford	W 2-1	Wagstaff, Butler	7,983
14		23	(h)	Burnley	L 1-2	Pearson	15,469
15		30	(a)	Preston NE	L 1-3	Lord	14,413
16	Nov	6	(h)	Norwich C	L 1-2	Knighton	11,878
17		13	(a)	Orient	L 0-1		6,614
18		20	(a)	Queen's Park R	L 1-2	Neill	12,627
19		27	(h)	Millwall	D 0-0		12,505
20	Dec	4	(a)	Sheffield W	L 1-2	Pearson	20,223
21		11	(h)	Middlesbrough	W 4-3	Kaye 2, Pearson, Banks	13,532
22		18	(a)	Blackpool	D 1-1	McGill	9,349
23		27	(h)	Sunderland	L 2-3	Pearson, Knighton	26,091
24	Jan	1	(a)	Portsmouth	D 0-0		8,665
25		8	(h)	Cardiff C	D 0-0		12,678
26		22	(a)	Swindon T	L 1-2	Wagstaff	11,796
27		29	(h)	Watford	W 4-0	Butler 2, Wagstaff, Pearson	10,546
28	Feb	12	(a)	Burnley	W 2-0	Wagstaff, Butler	11,751
29		19	(h)	Preston NE	W 3-2	Wagstaff 2, Wilkinson	14,313
30	Mar	4	(h)	Orient	D 1-1	Butler	12,845
31		11	(h)	Fulham	W 4-0	Pearson 2, Wagstaff 2	11,112
32		15	(a)	Norwich C	L 0-2		30,432
33		18	(a)	Oxford U	D 2-2	Butler, Pearson	7,910
34		25	(h)	Bristol C	D 1-1	Wagstaff	11,700
35	Apr	1	(a)	Sunderland	W 1-0	Wagstaff	17,621
36		3	(h)	Carlisle U	W 2-0	Pearson, Butler	16,403
37		4	(a)	Luton T	W 1-0	Knighton	9,763
38		8	(h)	Queen's Park R	D 1-1	Neill	12,830
39		15	(a)	Millwall	L 1-2	Pearson	15,494
40		22	(h)	Sheffield W	W 1-0	O'Riley	13,177
41		25	(a)	Birmingham C	L 0-2		40,749
42		29	(a)	Middlesbrough	L 0-3		9,539

FINAL LEAGUE POSITION: 12th in Division Two

Appearances
Sub Appearances
Goals

FA Cup

3	Jan	15	(a)	Norwich C	W 3-0	Wagstaff, Butler, McGill	22,044
4	Feb	5	(a)	Coventry C	W 1-0	Wagstaff	24,632
5		26	(a)	Stoke C	L 1-4	Wagstaff	34,558

Appearances
Sub Appearances
Goals

League Cup

2	Sep	7	(a)	Liverpool	L 0-3		31,612

Appearances
Sub Appearances
Goals

McKechnie I	Beardsley D	de Vries R	Wilkinson W	Neill T	Knighton K	Lord M	Houghton K	Chilton C	Wagstaff K	Butler I	Blampey S	Pettit R	O'Riley P	Greenwood P	Pearson S	Banks F	Simpkin C	Greenwood R	Holbrook S	Walters P	Green M	McGill J	Kaye J	Baxter W	Wealands J	
1	2	3	4	5	6	7	8	9	10	11																1
1	2	3		5	6	7		9	10	11	8	4*	12													2
1	2	3	5		6	7			10		8		11	4	9											3
1		3	5		6	7			10		8		11	4	9	2										4
1		3	4	5	6	7			10		8*		11	12	9	2										5
1		3	4		6	7	8		10				11*	5	9	2	12									6
1		3	4	5	6	12			10	11				7	9	2*	8									7
1	3		7	5	6	11	8		10*	12			2	4	9											8
1	3			5	6	7	10			11				4	9*	2	8	12								9
1	3			5	6*	7	10			11			9	4		2	8	12								10
1	3	12		5	6	7	8			11			10*	4	9	2										11
1	3			5	6	7	8		10	11				4	9	2										12
1		3		5	6	7	8		10	11*				4	9	2		12								13
1		3		5	6	11	8		10					4	9	2		12	7							14
		3		5	6	11	8		10					12	9	2*				1	4	7				15
1		3		5	6		8		10	11					9	2					4	7				16
1		3*		5	6	10	8			11				12	9	2					4	7				17
1	3			5		10	8			11	12			6	9	2					7*	4				18
1		3		5		7	8		10	11					9	2						6	4			19
1		3			7		8*		10	11	12				9	2					5	6	4			20
1		3			6	12	8		10	11*					9	2					5	7	4			21
1		3			6		8		10	11			12		9	2					5	7*	4			22
1		3			6	12	8		10	11					9	2					5	7	4*			23
1		3	4		6	8			10	11					9	2					5	7				24
1		3	4	5	6	8	12		10	11					9	2						7*				25
1		3	4	5	6	8			10	11					9	2						7				26
1		3	4	5	6	8			10	11					9	2						7*		12		27
1		3	4*	5		8			10	11			12		9	2						7		6		28
1		3	4	5		8			10	11					9	2						7		6		29
1		3		5		8	4		10*	11			12		9	2						7		6		30
		3	4	5		8			10	11					9	2						7		6	1	31
		3	4	5		8			10	11*					9	2						7	12	6	1	32
		3	4	5		8			10	11					9	2						7		6	1	33
1		3		5	6	8			10	11*					9	2		12				7	4			34
1		3		5		8			10	11					9	2						7	4	6		35
1		3	12	5		8			10	11					9	2						7*	4	6		36
1		3	4	5	7	8			10	11			9			2								6		37
1		3	12	5	7	8							10		9	2		11*				4		6		38
1		3		5		8				11			10		9	2						7	4	6		39
1		3	4	5		7				11			10		9	2							8	6		40
1		3	7	5		8				11			10		9	2							4	6		41
1		3	4*		8	7				11			10		9	2		12					6	5		42
38	9	36	20	33	29	36	19	2	32	34	4	1	13	12	38	38	3	1	1	1	9	24	12	14	3	
		1	2			3	1			1	2		4	3			1	6					1	1		
			1	2	3	2			11	8			1		15	1						1	2			

2 own-goals

McKechnie I	Beardsley D	de Vries R	Wilkinson W	Neill T	Knighton K	Lord M	Houghton K	Chilton C	Wagstaff K	Butler I	Blampey S	Pettit R	O'Riley P	Greenwood P	Pearson S	Banks F	Simpkin C	Greenwood R	Holbrook S	Walters P	Green M	McGill J	Kaye J	Baxter W	Wealands J	
1		3	4	5	6	8			10	11					9	2						7				3
1		3	4	5		8			10	11					9	2						7		6		4
1		3	4	5		8			10	11			12			2						7	9	6*		5
3		3	3	3	1	3			3	3					2	3						3	1	2		
													1													
									3	1												1				

McKechnie I	Beardsley D	de Vries R	Wilkinson W	Neill T	Knighton K	Lord M	Houghton K	Chilton C	Wagstaff K	Butler I	Blampey S	Pettit R	O'Riley P	Greenwood P	Pearson S	Banks F	Simpkin C	Greenwood R	Holbrook S	Walters P	Green M	McGill J	Kaye J	Baxter W	Wealands J	
1		3	4		6	7	8		10				11	5	9	2										2
1		1	1		1	1	1		1				1	1	1	1										

1972-73

1	Aug	12	(a)	Millwall	L 0-2		13,2
2		19	(h)	Nottingham F	D 0-0		11,1
3		26	(a)	Sheffield W	L 2-4	Pearson 2	19,8
4		29	(h)	Bristol C	W 2-0	Pearson, Holme	8,8
5	Sep	2	(h)	Orient	W 2-0	Knighton, Harris (og)	7,9
6		9	(a)	Preston NE	L 0-1		8,1
7		16	(h)	Burnley	D 1-1	Holme	8,9
8		20	(a)	Fulham	L 0-2		7,6
9		23	(a)	Middlesbrough	L 0-1		9,1
10		26	(h)	Queen's Park R	W 4-1	Pearson, Wagstaff, Houghton, Holme	8,2
11		30	(h)	Swindon T	W 3-2	Butler, Neill, Holme	9,1
12	Oct	7	(a)	Brighton & HA	D 1-1	Holme	14,3
13		14	(h)	Portsmouth	W 5-1	Pearson 4, Holme	9,5
14		21	(a)	Luton T	W 2-1	Houghton 2	11,5
15		27	(h)	Oxford U	L 0-1		13,4
16	Nov	4	(a)	Queen's Park R	D 1-1	Pearson	13,6
17		11	(h)	Fulham	D 2-2	Pearson, Butler	9,4
18		18	(a)	Sunderland	D 1-1	Butler	11,1
19		25	(h)	Blackpool	L 1-2	Butler	8,9
20	Dec	2	(a)	Aston Villa	L 0-2		21,2
21		9	(h)	Carlisle U	D 1-1	Knighton	7,0
22		16	(h)	Cardiff C	D 1-1	Kaye	5,8
23		23	(a)	Huddersfield T	W 3-1	Houghton, Wagstaff, Greenwood	6,8
24		26	(h)	Middlesbrough	W 3-1	Wagstaff, Knighton, Kaye	13,5
25	Jan	6	(h)	Sheffield W	D 1-1	Wagstaff	11,5
26		20	(a)	Orient	D 0-0		3,8
27		27	(h)	Preston NE	W 6-2	Pearson 2, Houghton, Knighton, McGill, Neill	9,1
28	Feb	10	(a)	Burnley	L 1-4	Pearson	13,7
29		17	(h)	Millwall	L 0-2		9,8
30	Mar	2	(h)	Brighton & HA	W 2-0	Pearson 2	7,7
31		10	(a)	Portsmouth	D 2-2	Holme, Kaye	8,1
32		13	(a)	Nottingham F	W 2-1	Holme 2	7,7
33		23	(a)	Oxford U	L 2-5	Holme, Kaye	6,7
34		31	(a)	Blackpool	L 3-4	Houghton, Pearson, Wood (og)	5,6
35	Apr	7	(h)	Aston Villa	L 1-2	Banks	8,0
36		10	(h)	Luton T	W 4-0	Houghton, Knighton, Kaye, Holme	5,2
37		14	(a)	Carlisle U	W 1-0	Knighton	5,8
38		21	(h)	Sunderland	L 0-2		12,6
39		23	(h)	Huddersfield T	D 0-0		7,4
40		24	(a)	Swindon T	L 1-2	Kaye	8,4
41		28	(a)	Bristol C	L 1-2	Pearson	11,0
42	May	9	(a)	Cardiff C	W 2-0	Greenwood 2	6,2

FINAL LEAGUE POSITION: 13th in Division Two

Appearances
Sub Appeara
Goals

FA Cup

3	Jan	13	(a)	Stockport C	D 0-0		8,2
R		23	(h)	Stockport C	W 2-0*	Wagstaff, Houghton	13,5
4	Feb	3	(h)	West Ham U	W 1-0	Houghton	32,2
5		24	(a)	Coventry C	L 0-3		31,6

*After extra-time

Appearances
Sub Appeara
Goals

League Cup

2	Sep	5	(h)	Fulham	W 1-0	Knighton	6,3
3	Oct	3	(h)	Norwich C	L 1-2	Holme	11,5

Appearances
Sub Appeara
Goals

McKechnie I	Banks F	de Vries R	Kaye J	Neill T	Knighton K	McGill J	Lord M	O'Riley P	Holme P	Wilkinson W	Pearson S	Butler I	Houghton K	Wealands J	Beardsley D	Greenwood R	Wagstaff K	Blampey S	Green M	Hawley J	Croft S	
1	2	3	4	5	6	7	8	9	10	11												1
1	2	3	5		6	8	7*		10	4	9	11	12									2
1	2	3	5		6	8	7		10	4	9	11										3
	2	3	5		6	8*	7		10	4	9	11	12	1								4
	2	3	5		6*	8	7		10	4	9	11	12	1								5
	2*		5	10	6	8	7	9		4			12	1	3	11						6
	2		4	5	6	8	7		9				10	1	3	11						7
	2		4	5	6	8	7		9		10			1	3	11*	12					8
	2	3	4*	5		6	7				9	11	8	1			10	12				9
	2	3	4	5		6	7		12		9	11	8	1			10*					10
	2	3	4	5		6*	7		12		9	11	8	1			10					11
	2		4	5	3	6			10	7	9*	11	8	1			12					12
	2	3	4	5*	6	7			10	12	9	11	8	1								13
	2		4*	5	6	7			10	12	9	11	8	1	3							14
	2		4	5	6	7			10		9*	11	8	1	3	12						15
	2		4	5	6	7			10		9	11	8	1	3							16
	2		4	5	6	7			10		9	11	8	1	3							17
	2		4		6	7	8		10		9	11		1	3			5				18
	2		4		6	7	8*		10		9	11	12	1	3			5				19
	2		4	5	6	7			10		9	11	8	1	3							20
	2		4	5	6	7					9	11	8	1	3		10					21
	2	3	4	5	6	7	11*		12		9		8	1			10					22
1	2		4	5	6	7	3		12		9		8			11	10*					23
1	2		4	5	6	7	3*		12		9					11	10	8				24
1	2		4		6	7					9		8		3	11	10		5			25
1	2		4	5	6	7					9		8		3	11	10					26
1	2		4	5	6*	7			10		9	12	8		3	11						27
	2		4	5	6	7			10		9		8	1	3	11						28
	2		4	5	6	7			10		9	12	8	1	3	11*						29
1	2		4	5	6	7			12		9	11			3	8	10*					30
1	2		4	5	6	7			10		9*		8		3	11		12				31
1	2		4	5	6	7			10		9	11	8		3							32
1	2		4	5	6	7	8*		10		9	11			3			12				33
1	2		4	5	6	7			10		9	11	8*		3			12				34
1	2		4	5	6	7	12		10			11*	8		3	9						35
1	2		4	5	6	7	3		10*		9	12	8			11						36
1	2		4	5	6*	7	3		10		9		8			11		12				37
1	2		4	5	6	7	3				9		8			11				10		38
1	2		4	5	6	7	3				9		8			11	12			10*		39
1	2	3	4	5	12	7	8	9								11	10	6*				40
1	2	3	4	5	6	7	8				9					11	10					41
1	2	3		4	6	7	8				9					11	10				5	42
21	42	13	41	35	38	42	24	3	26	7	37	22	27	21	22	20	13	4	1	2	1	
					1		1		6	2		3	5			1	3	5				
	1		6	2	6	1			11		17	4	7			3	4					

2 own-goals

McKechnie I	Banks F	de Vries R	Kaye J	Neill T	Knighton K	McGill J	Lord M	O'Riley P	Holme P	Wilkinson W	Pearson S	Butler I	Houghton K	Wealands J	Beardsley D	Greenwood R	Wagstaff K	Blampey S	Green M	Hawley J	Croft S	
1	2		4	5	6	7			12		9		8		3	11	10*					3
1	2		4	5	6	7			12		9		8		3	11*	10					R
1	2		4	5	6	7			10		9		8		3	11						4
	2		4	5	6	7			10		9		8*	1	3	11		12				5
3	4		4	4	4	4			2		4		4	1	4	4	2					
									2									1				
													2				1					

McKechnie I	Banks F	de Vries R	Kaye J	Neill T	Knighton K	McGill J	Lord M	O'Riley P	Holme P	Wilkinson W	Pearson S	Butler I	Houghton K	Wealands J	Beardsley D	Greenwood R	Wagstaff K	Blampey S	Green M	Hawley J	Croft S	
	2	3*	5		6	8	7	9		4		11	12	1		10						2
	2	3		5	6	7			12	4	9	11	8	1			10*					3
	2	2	1	1	2	2	1	1		2	1	2	1	2		1	1					
									1				1									
					1				1													

1973-74

1	Aug	25	(h)	Oxford U	D 0-0		7,721
2	Sep	1	(a)	Bolton W	L 0-1		13,065
3		8	(h)	Preston NE	W 1-0	Pearson	7,009
4		11	(h)	Nottingham F	D 0-0		8,134
5		15	(a)	Millwall	L 0-3		7,537
6		18	(a)	Bristol C	L 1-3	Pearson	10,711
7		22	(h)	West Brom A	D 0-0		7,089
8		29	(a)	Cardiff C	W 3-1	Lord 2, Wagstaff	10,522
9	Oct	2	(h)	Bristol C	W 2-1	Wagstaff, Greenwood	7,235
10		6	(h)	Orient	D 1-1	Pearson	7,454
11		13	(a)	Middlesbrough	L 0-1		22,135
12		20	(h)	Portsmouth	W 4-1	Wagstaff 2, Greenwood, Hawley	6,874
13		23	(a)	Nottingham F	D 0-0		10,392
14		27	(a)	Luton T	D 2-2	Lord, Greenwood	11,408
15	Nov	3	(h)	Sunderland	W 2-0	Hawley, Pearson	17,409
16		10	(a)	Carlisle U	L 0-4		6,563
17		17	(a)	Aston Villa	D 1-1	Burnett	23,773
18		24	(h)	Blackpool	W 1-0	Banks	9,004
19	Dec	1	(a)	Fulham	D 0-0		5,636
20		8	(h)	Crystal P	W 3-0	Wagstaff, Greenwood, Deere	7,996
21		15	(a)	Notts C	L 2-3	Wagstaff, Kaye	8,574
22		22	(h)	Cardiff C	D 1-1	Greenwood	6,826
23		26	(a)	Sheffield W	D 1-1	Greenwood	15,373
24		29	(a)	Preston NE	L 0-2		10,052
25	Jan	1	(h)	Bolton W	D 0-0		12,210
26		12	(h)	Millwall	D 1-1	Lord	5,659
27		19	(a)	Oxford U	D 1-1	Burnett	6,336
28		26	(a)	Swindon T	D 1-1	Greenwood	4,605
29	Feb	2	(h)	Notts C	W 1-0	Wagstaff	6,384
30		16	(h)	Middlesbrough	L 1-3	Pearson	15,287
31		23	(a)	Orient	D 1-1	Pearson	9,830
32	Mar	2	(h)	Sheffield W	W 2-1	Pearson, Greenwood	8,193
33		9	(h)	Luton T	L 1-3	O'Riley	7,027
34		16	(a)	Portsmouth	L 1-3	Pearson	9,838
35		19	(a)	West Brom A	W 3-2	Pearson, Wagstaff, Greenwood	13,712
36		23	(h)	Carlisle U	D 1-1	Grimes	6,137
37		30	(a)	Sunderland	L 0-1		20,418
38	Apr	6	(a)	Blackpool	W 2-1	Pearson, Hemmerman	8,159
39		13	(h)	Aston Villa	D 1-1	Grimes	7,810
40		15	(h)	Swindon T	L 0-1		5,348
41		20	(a)	Crystal P	W 2-0	Greenwood, Hawley	21,909
42		27	(h)	Fulham	W 2-0	Pearson, Lord	5,731

FINAL LEAGUE POSITION: 9th in Division Two

Appearances
Sub Appearances
Goals

FA Cup

3	Jan	5	(a)	Bristol C	D 1-1	Galvin	8,968
R		8	(h)	Bristol C	L 0-1		5,340

Appearances
Sub Appearances
Goals

League Cup

2	Oct	8	(a)	Leicester C	D 3-3	Wagstaff, Galvin, Whitworth (og)	9,777
R		31	(h)	Leicester C	W 3-2	Pearson, Greenwood, de Vries	16,003
3	Nov	6	(h)	Stockport C	W 4-1	Holme 2, Wagstaff, Banks	13,753
4		27	(h)	Liverpool	D 0-0		19,748
R	Dec	4	(a)	Liverpool	L 1-3	Lindsay (og)	17,120

Appearances
Sub Appearance
Goals

Wealands J	Banks F	de Vries R	Kaye J	Deere S	Galvin C	McGill J	Lord M	Pearson S	Wagstaff K	Greenwood R	Blampey S	O'Riley P	Holme P	Hemmerman J	Hawley J	Burnett D	Grimes V	McKechnie I	Staniforth G	
1	2	3	4	5	6*	7	8	9	10	11	12									1
1	2	3	4	5		7	8	9	10*	11	6	12								2
1	2	3	4	5		7	8	9		11	6		10							3
1	2	3	4	5		7	8	9		11	6		10							4
1	2	3*	4	5		7	8	9	10	11	6			12						5
1	2	3	4	5		7	8	9	10	11	6									6
1	2	3	4	5		7	8		10	11	6			9						7
1	2	3	4	5		7	8	9	10	11	6									8
1	2	3	4	5		7	8	9	10*	11	6				12					9
1	2	3	4	5	12	7		9	10	11	6				8*					10
1	2	3	4*	5	8			9	10	11	6	12			7					11
1	2	3		5	6*		8	9	10	11	4	12			7					12
1	2	3		5	6		8	9	10	11	4				7					13
1	2	3		5	6		8	9	10	11	4				7					14
1	2	3		5	6		8	9	10	11	4				7					15
1	2	3		5	6	12	8	9	10	11					7*	4				16
1	2	3	4	5	11		8	9	10	7						6				17
1	2	3	4	5	11		8	9	10	7						6				18
1	2		4	5	11	3	8	9	10	7						6				19
1	2		4	5	6	3	8	9	10	11*			12			7				20
1	2	12	4	5	6*	3	8	9	10	11						7				21
1	2	3	4	5		6	8	9	10	11						7				22
1	2	3	4*	5		6	8	9	10	11			12			7				23
1	2	3*		5	4	6	8	9	10	11		12				7				24
1	2			5	4	3	8	9	10	11			7			6				25
1	2			5		3	8	9		11	4		10		7	6				26
1	2	12		5		3	8	9	10	11*	4				7	6				27
1	2	3		5		4	8	9	10	11					7	6				28
1	2*	3		5		4	8	9	10	11			12		7	6				29
1		3		5		2	8	9	10	11	6				7	4				30
1		3		5		2	8	9		11	6	10			7	4				31
1		3		5		2*	8	9	10	11	6	12			7	4				32
1		3		5		2	8	9		11*	6	12		10	7	4				33
1		3		5		2	8	9		11	6			10		4	7			34
1	2	3		5		6	8	9	10	11						4	7			35
1	2	3		5		6	8	9	10	11						4	7			36
1	2	3		5		6	8	9*	10	11	12					4	7			37
1	2	3		5		6	8	9		11				10		4	7			38
1	2	3		5			8	9		11	6			10		4	7			39
	2	3		5			8	9		11				10*	12	4	6	1	7	40
1	2			5		3	8	9		11	6				10	4	7			41
1	2			5		3	8	9		11	6				10	4	7			42
41	37	34	18	42	14	32	40	41	32	42	24	1	3	6	17	27	9	1	1	
		2			1	1					2	6	3	1	2					
	1		1	1			5	11	8	10		1		1	3	2	2			

Wealands J	Banks F	de Vries R	Kaye J	Deere S	Galvin C	McGill J	Lord M	Pearson S	Wagstaff K	Greenwood R	Blampey S	O'Riley P	Holme P	Hemmerman J	Hawley J	Burnett D	Grimes V	McKechnie I	Staniforth G	
1	2			5	4	3	8	9	10	11			7			6				3
1	2			5	4	3	8		10	11			7	9		6				R
2	2			2	2	2	2	1	2	2			2	1		2				
					1															

Wealands J	Banks F	de Vries R	Kaye J	Deere S	Galvin C	McGill J	Lord M	Pearson S	Wagstaff K	Greenwood R	Blampey S	O'Riley P	Holme P	Hemmerman J	Hawley J	Burnett D	Grimes V	McKechnie I	Staniforth G	
1	2		4	5	8	3		9	10	11	6				7					2
1	2	3		5	6		8	9	10	11	4				7					R
1	2	3		5	6	4	8	9*	10			12	11		7					3
1	2		4	5	6	3	8	9	10	11					7					4
1		3	4	5	6	2	8	9	10	11					7					R
5	4	3	3	5	5	4	4	5	5	4	2		1		5					
												1								
	1	1			1			1	2	1			2							

2 own-goals

1974-75

1	Aug	17	(a)	Southampton	D 3-3	Wagstaff 2, Grimes	16,730
2		20	(h)	Aston Villa	D 1-1	Wagstaff	8,712
3		24	(h)	West Brom A	W 1-0	Wagstaff	7,864
4		28	(a)	Aston Villa	L 0-6		18,973
5		31	(a)	Bristol R	L 0-2		11,191
6	Sep	7	(h)	Norwich C	D 0-0		5,436
7		14	(a)	Nottingham F	L 0-4		9,427
8		18	(a)	West Brom A	D 2-2	Hawley 2	9,973
9		21	(h)	Oldham A	D 1-1	Greenwood	6,659
10		24	(h)	Millwall	D 1-1	Wagstaff	5,997
11		28	(a)	Cardiff C	W 2-1	Greenwood, Deere	5,648
12	Oct	5	(a)	Blackpool	W 2-1	Greenwood, Galvin	8,406
13		12	(h)	Bolton W	W 2-0	Wagstaff 2	7,353
14		19	(a)	Sheffield W	L 1-2	Lord	11,643
15		26	(h)	Sunderland	W 3-1	Wagstaff, Hawley, Banks	15,010
16	Nov	2	(a)	Notts C	L 0-5		9,032
17		9	(h)	Fulham	W 2-1	Lord, Staniforth	7,571
18		16	(a)	Portsmouth	D 1-1	Wood	9,045
19		23	(h)	Manchester U	W 2-0	Wagstaff, Lord	23,287
20		30	(h)	Bristol C	W 1-0	Lord	9,612
21	Dec	7	(a)	Oxford U	L 1-3	Lord	6,751
22		14	(h)	Southampton	D 1-1	Hawley	9,004
23		21	(a)	Orient	D 0-0		4,678
24		26	(h)	Nottingham F	L 1-3	Wagstaff	12,278
25		28	(a)	York C	L 0-3		10,857
26	Jan	11	(h)	Oxford U	W 1-0	Galvin	7,175
27		18	(a)	Bristol C	L 0-2		10,423
28	Feb	1	(a)	Fulham	D 1-1	Wood	5,739
29		8	(h)	Notts C	W 1-0	Greenwood	6,700
30		15	(a)	Manchester U	L 0-2		44,712
31		22	(h)	Portsmouth	D 0-0		6,919
32	Mar	1	(h)	Bristol R	W 2-0	Wood, Hawley	6,223
33		8	(a)	Millwall	L 0-2		6,918
34		15	(h)	Cardiff C	D 1-1	Lord	5,248
35		22	(a)	Norwich C	L 0-1		20,724
36		28	(a)	Oldham A	W 1-0	Greenwood	11,987
37		29	(h)	Orient	D 0-0		5,203
38		31	(h)	York C	W 2-0	Hawley, Croft	10,095
39	Apr	5	(a)	Sunderland	L 0-1		29,838
40		12	(h)	Blackpool	W 1-0	Hawley	6,027
41		19	(a)	Bolton W	D 1-1	Wood	8,522
42		26	(h)	Sheffield W	W 1-0	Fletcher	7,652

FINAL LEAGUE POSITION: 8th in Division Two

Appearances
Sub Appearances
Goals

FA Cup

3	Jan	4	(a)	Fulham	D 1-1	Wagstaff	8,897
R		7	(h)	Fulham	D 2-2*	Fletcher, Croft	11,850
2R		13	(n†)	Fulham	L 0-1		4,929

*After extra-time. †Played at Filbert Street, Leicester.

Appearances
Sub Appearances
Goals

League Cup

2	Sep	11	(h)	Burnley	L 1-2	Fletcher	7,544

Appearances
Sub Appearances
Goals

Wealands J	Blampey S	de Vries R	Burnett D	Deere S	Lord M	Grimes V	Hawley J	Hemmerman J	Wagstaff K	Greenwood R	McGill J	Fletcher P	Galvin C	Croft S	Daniel P	Banks F	Staniforth G	Wood A	Roberts D	Blackburn E	Stewart D	Haigh P	
1	2	3	4	5	6	7	8	9	10*	11	12												1
1	2	3	4	5	6	7	8	9	10	11													2
1	2	3	4	5	6	7	8	9	10	11*		12											3
1	2	3	4	5	6	7		9	10		8*	11	12										4
1	2	3	4	5	6	7		9*	10			11	8	12									5
1	2	3	4	5		7			10	11	8	9	6										6
1	2*	3	4	5	12	7	8		10	11	6	9											7
1		3	6	5	8	7	9		10	11	4*			12	2								8
1		3	4*	5	8	7	9		10	11			6	12	2								9
1		3	6	5	8	7	9		10	11			4			2							10
1		3	6	5	8	7	9		10	11			4			2							11
1	12	3	6	5	8	7*	9		10	11			4			2							12
1	12	3	6	5	8		9		10	11	7*		4			2							13
1		3	6	5	8		9		10	11	7		4			2							14
1	11	3	6	5	8		9		10		7		4			2							15
1	11	3	6	5	8		9	12	10		7*		4			2							16
1	6	3			8		9		10		7	12	4	5		2	11*						17
1	6	3			8		11		10		7		4	5		2		9					18
1	6	3			8		11		10		7		4	5		2		9					19
1	6	3			8		11		10	12	7		4*	5		2		9					20
1	6	3			8		10	12		11	7		4	5		2		9*					21
1	6	3				8	9		10	11	7		4	5		2							22
1	6	3				8	10			11	7		4	5		2		9					23
1	6	3			8*	12	11		10		7		4	5		2		9					24
1	8		6			7	11		10		3		4	5		2		9					25
1			6		8	10		12		11	7*	9	4	5	3	2							26
1			6	5	8	10				11	7		4		3	2		9					27
1	6			5	8	10				11	7		4		3	2		9					28
1	6			5	8	10				11	7		4		3	2		9					29
1	10			5	8					11	7		4		3	2		9	6				30
1	10			5	8			9		11	7	12	4		3	2*			6				31
1				5	8		10			11	7		4		3	2		9	6				32
1				5	8		10	12		11	7		4*		3	2		9	6				33
				12	8		10			11	7		4*	5	3	2		9	6	1			34
1		12			8	4		10*		11	7			5	3	2		9	6				35
1					8	4	10			11	7			5	3	2		9	6				36
1					8	4	10			11	7			5	3	2		9	6				37
1						4	10			11	7		8	5	3	2		9	6				38
1					8		10			11	7		4	5	3	2		9	6				39
1					8		10				7		4	5	3	2		9	6		11		40
1					8	12	10			11	7*		4	5	3	2		9	6				41
					8	7				11		10	4		3	2	12	9	5*	1		6	42
40	22	24	19	23	36	24	31	7	23	31	33	6	33	18	19	33	1	22	13	2	1	1	
	2	1		1	1	2		4		1	1	3	1	3			1						
				1	6	1	7		10	5		1	2	1		1	1	4					

Wealands J	Blampey S	de Vries R	Burnett D	Deere S	Lord M	Grimes V	Hawley J	Hemmerman J	Wagstaff K	Greenwood R	McGill J	Fletcher P	Galvin C	Croft S	Daniel P	Banks F	Staniforth G	Wood A	Roberts D	Blackburn E	Stewart D	Haigh P	
1			6	12	8	7			10*	11			4	5	3	2		9					3
1			6	12	8	7		10		11		9	4*	5	3	2							R
1			6	5	8	10				11	7*	12	4		3	2		9					2R
3			3	1	3	3		1	1	3	1	1	3	2	3	3		2					
				2								1											
									1			1		1									

Wealands J	Blampey S	de Vries R	Burnett D	Deere S	Lord M	Grimes V	Hawley J	Hemmerman J	Wagstaff K	Greenwood R	McGill J	Fletcher P	Galvin C	Croft S	Daniel P	Banks F	Staniforth G	Wood A	Roberts D	Blackburn E	Stewart D	Haigh P	
1	2	3	4	5	12	7*	8		10	11	6	9											2
1	1	1	1	1		1	1		1	1	1	1											
					1																		
												1											

1975-76

1	Aug	16	(a)	Luton T	L 0-2		10,389
2		19	(h)	Blackpool	W 1-0	Galvin	5,364
3		23	(h)	Bristol C	W 3-1	Greenwood 2, Fletcher	5,076
4		30	(a)	Oldham A	L 0-1		6,365
5	Sep	6	(h)	Orient	W 1-0	Wood	5,194
6		13	(a)	Nottingham F	W 2-1	Greenwood, Galvin	12,191
7		20	(h)	Fulham	L 1-2	Grimes	8,471
8		23	(h)	Notts C	L 0-2		8,068
9		26	(a)	Charlton A	L 0-1		10,319
10	Oct	4	(h)	Southampton	D 0-0		6,342
11		11	(h)	Bristol R	D 0-0		5,642
12		18	(a)	Portsmouth	D 1-1	Grimes	8,155
13		25	(h)	Bolton W	D 2-2	Wagstaff, Lord	7,369
14	Nov	1	(a)	Oxford U	W 3-2	Wagstaff, Galvin, Grimes	4,931
15		4	(a)	Blackburn R	L 0-1		8,816
16		8	(h)	Chelsea	L 1-2	Grimes	9,097
17		15	(a)	West Brom A	L 0-2		14,398
18		22	(h)	Portsmouth	W 1-0	Galvin	4,549
19		29	(h)	Plymouth A	W 4-0	Greenwood 2, Wood, Grimes	5,098
20	Dec	6	(a)	York C	W 2-1	Fletcher, Greenwood	7,037
21		13	(a)	Bristol C	L 0-3		10,361
22		20	(h)	Luton T	L 1-2	Wood	5,449
23		26	(a)	Sunderland	L 1-3	Hawley	35,210
24		27	(h)	Carlisle U	L 2-3	Hawley, Wood	7,056
25	Jan	10	(h)	Nottingham F	W 1-0	Wood	6,465
26		17	(a)	Orient	L 0-1		3,876
27		31	(a)	Blackpool	D 2-2	Wood, Fletcher	4,966
28	Feb	6	(h)	Blackburn R	L 0-1		6,205
29		18	(a)	Chelsea	D 0-0		10,254
30		21	(h)	West Brom A	W 2-1	Fletcher, Lyall	6,496
31		24	(a)	Notts C	W 2-1	Hawley, Sunley	15,293
32		28	(a)	Bolton W	L 0-1		22,592
33	Mar	6	(h)	Oxford U	W 2-0	Daniel, C.Clarke (og)	4,820
34		13	(a)	Bristol R	W 1-0	Sunley	6,230
35		20	(a)	Plymouth A	D 1-1	McIntosh	10,631
36		27	(h)	York C	D 1-1	Daniel	6,306
37	Apr	3	(h)	Charlton A	D 2-2	Hemmerman, Sunley	4,656
38		10	(a)	Fulham	D 1-1	Hemmerman	5,624
39		16	(h)	Oldham A	W 3-0	Hemmerman, Sunley, Lyall	5,906
40		17	(h)	Sunderland	L 1-4	Croft	21,296
41		20	(a)	Carlisle U	D 0-0		8,185
42		24	(a)	Southampton	L 0-1		18,272

FINAL LEAGUE POSITION: 14th in Division Two

Appearances
Sub Appearance
Goals

FA Cup

3	Jan	3	(h)	Plymouth A	D 1-1	Grimes	6,515
R		6	(a)	Plymouth A	W 4-1	Wood 2, Hawley, Sutton (og)	20,208
4	Feb	2	(a)	Sunderland	L 0-1		32,320

Appearances
Sub Appearance
Goals

League Cup

2	Sep	9	(h)	Preston NE	W 4-2	Greenwood 2, Wood, Lord	5,095
3	Oct	7	(h)	Sheffield U	W 2-0	Greenwood, Hawley	9,536
4	Nov	11	(a)	Doncaster R	L 1-2	Wood	20,476

Appearances
Sub Appearance
Goals

Wealands J	Banks F	de Vries R	Galvin C	Croft S	Roberts D	Grimes V	Lord M	Wood A	Wagstaff K	Greenwood R	Fletcher P	McGill J	Hawley J	Daniel P	Stewart D	Haigh P	Gibson D	Lyall G	Staniforth G	Sunley D	Hemmerman J	McIntosh J	Dobson I	Deere S	
1	2	3	4	5	6	7	8	9	10	11															1
1	2	3	4	5	6	7	8	9	10	11															2
1	2	3	4	5*	6	7	8	9		11	10	12													3
1	2	3	4	5	6	7	8	9		11	10														4
1	2*	3	4	5	6	7	8	9		11	10	12													5
1	2	3	4	5	6	7	8	9		11	10*	12													6
1	2	3	4	5	6	7	8*	9		11	10	12													7
1	2	3	4	5	6	7*		9		11	10	8	12												8
1	2	3	4	5	6			9		11		8	10	7											9
1	2	3	4	5	6			9	12	11		8*	10	7											10
1	2	3	12	5	6			9	10	11		8	7		4*										11
1	2	3	4	5	6	7	9		10	11		8													12
1	2	3	4	5	6	7	9		10	11		8													13
1	2	3	4	5	6	7	8*	12	10	11			9												14
1	2	3	4	5	6*	7		12	10	11		8	9												15
1	2	3	4	5		7			10	11					9	6	8								16
1		3	4	5		7		9		11		8	10	2		6									17
1		3	4			7		5	10	11			9	2		6	8								18
1		3	4	5	6	7		9		11	10		12	2			8*								19
1		3	4	5	6	7		9		11*	10		12	2			8								20
1	3		4	5	6	7		9		11	10		12	2			8*								21
1		3*		5		7		9		11	8		4	2		6	12	10							22
1				5	6	7		9		11		8	4	2		3		10							23
1				5	6	8		9		11		2	4			3		10	7						24
1	3		10	5	6	7		9			12		4	2				8	11*						25
1		3		5	6	7		9			12		4	2			10	8	11*						26
1		3	4	5	6			9			10*			2	11			8		7	12				27
1		3	4	5	6			9			10		12	2				8*	11	7					28
1		3	4	5	6	7		9			10			2				8		11					29
1		3	4	5	6	7		9			10			2				8		11					30
1		3	4	5	6	7		9					10	2				8		11					31
1		3	4	5	6	7		9			8*		10	2						11	12				32
1		3	4	5	6	7		9*			12		10	2				8		11					33
1		3	4	5	6	11					10			2				8		9		7			34
1		3	4	5	6	11					10*			2				8		9	12	7			35
1		3	4	5	6	11					10		9	2				8			12	7*			36
1		3	4	5	6	11					12		10*	2				8		9	7				37
1		3	4	6		11					12			2				8		9*	10	7	5		38
1		3	4*	6		11					12			2				8		9	10	7	5		39
1		3	4	6		11					12			2				8		9	10	7*	5		40
1		3	5	6	4	11					10			2				8		9	7				41
1		3	5	6		11					10			2		4		8		9	7				42
42	18	38	37	41	34	37	10	28	9	24	20	10	17	27	3	7	6	20	4	15	6	6	3		
			1					2	1		7	4	5				1				4				
			4	1		5	1	6	2	6	4		3	2				2		4	3	1			

1 own-goal

Wealands J	Banks F	de Vries R	Galvin C	Croft S	Roberts D	Grimes V	Lord M	Wood A	Wagstaff K	Greenwood R	Fletcher P	McGill J	Hawley J	Daniel P	Stewart D	Haigh P	Gibson D	Lyall G	Staniforth G	Sunley D	Hemmerman J	McIntosh J	Dobson I	Deere S	
1	2		10	5	6	7		9		11		3	4					8							3
1	3		10	5	6	7		9		11			4	2				8							R
1		3	7	5	6			9			10		4	2	11*			8						12	4
3	2	1	3	3	3	2		3		2	1	1	3	2	1			3							
																								1	
						1		2					1												

1 own-goal

Wealands J	Banks F	de Vries R	Galvin C	Croft S	Roberts D	Grimes V	Lord M	Wood A	Wagstaff K	Greenwood R	Fletcher P	McGill J	Hawley J	Daniel P	Stewart D	Haigh P	Gibson D	Lyall G	Staniforth G	Sunley D	Hemmerman J	McIntosh J	Dobson I	Deere S	
1	2	3	4	5	6	7	8	9		11	10														2
1	2	3		5	6			9	10	11		8	7		4										3
1	2	3	4	5		7		9	10	11		12	8*			6									4
3	3	3	2	3	2	2	1	3	2	3	1	1	2		1	1									
												1													
							1	2		3			1												

1976-77

1	Aug	21	(a)	Hereford U	L 0-1		7,323
2		24	(h)	Luton T	W 3-1	Sunley, Hemmerman, Daniel	5,499
3		28	(h)	Southampton	W 4-0	Sunley, Stewart, Lyall, Hawley	7,774
4	Sep	4	(a)	Carlisle U	D 1-1	Hawley	7,530
5		11	(a)	Bolton W	L 1-5	Stewart	13,396
6		17	(h)	Sheffield U	D 1-1	Croft	10,494
7		25	(a)	Burnley	D 0-0		10,320
8	Oct	2	(h)	Nottingham F	W 1-0	Bremner	16,096
9		9	(a)	Charlton A	L 1-3	Galvin	10,345
10		16	(h)	Wolves	W 2-0	Hawley 2	12,015
11		23	(a)	Fulham	D 0-0		18,671
12	Nov	6	(h)	Blackpool	D 2-2	Daniel, Haigh	9,541
13		13	(a)	Blackburn R	L 0-1		8,807
14		20	(h)	Plymouth A	W 3-1	Hemmerman, Hawley, Staniforth	8,161
15		27	(a)	Bristol R	L 0-3		6,426
16	Dec	11	(a)	Cardiff C	D 1-1	Daniel	8,270
17		18	(h)	Chelsea	D 1-1	Hemmerman	11,774
18		27	(a)	Notts C	D 1-1	Hemmerman	10,634
19		28	(h)	Oldham A	L 0-1		11,149
20	Jan	1	(a)	Blackpool	D 0-0		12,508
21		22	(h)	Hereford U	D 1-1	Sunley	7,819
22		24	(a)	Luton T	L 1-2	Lyall	8,455
23	Feb	5	(a)	Southampton	D 2-2	Sunley 2	20,353
24		12	(h)	Carlisle U	W 3-1	Sunley, Hickton, MacDonald (og)	6,524
25		15	(h)	Millwall	D 0-0		6,642
26		19	(h)	Bolton W	D 2-2	Lyall, Daniel	9,913
27		26	(a)	Sheffield U	D 1-1	Hemmerman	14,174
28	Mar	5	(h)	Burnley	W 4-1	Lord 3, Grimes	6,636
29		12	(a)	Nottingham F	L 0-2		15,116
30		19	(h)	Charlton A	D 0-0		5,575
31		26	(a)	Wolves	L 1-2	Hemmerman	19,598
32	Apr	2	(h)	Fulham	W 1-0	Daniel	6,158
33		8	(h)	Notts C	L 0-1		7,225
34		9	(a)	Oldham A	L 0-3		7,522
35		12	(h)	Blackburn R	W 1-0	Keeley (og)	4,800
36		16	(a)	Plymouth A	W 2-1	Dobson 2	8,694
37		19	(h)	Orient	D 1-1	Bremner	4,494
38		23	(h)	Bristol R	L 0-1		4,599
39		30	(a)	Millwall	L 1-2	Moore (og)	5,462
40	May	7	(h)	Cardiff C	L 1-2	Daniel	3,511
41		14	(a)	Chelsea	L 0-4		43,718
42		17	(a)	Orient	D 1-1	Haigh	8,397

FINAL LEAGUE POSITION: 14th in Division Two

Appearances
Sub Appearances
Goals

FA Cup

3	Jan	8	(h)	Port Vale	D 1-1	Nisbet	9,694
R		10	(a)	Port Vale	L 1-3*	Hemmerman	10,668

*After extra-time

Appearances
Sub Appearances
Goals

League Cup

2	Aug	31	(a)	Orient	L 0-1		3,578

Appearances
Sub Appearances
Goals

Wealands J	Daniel P	de Vries R	Croft S	Haigh P	Roberts D	Grimes V	Lyall G	Wood A	Sunley D	Stewart D	Hemmerman J	Hawley J	Gibson D	Galvin C	Nisbet G	Bremner W	Staniforth G	Lord M	McIntosh J	Dobson I	Hickton J	McDonald R	McGifford G	
1	2	3	4	5	6	7*	8	9	10	11	12													1
1	2	3	6	4			8		9	11	10	5	7											2
1	2	3	6	4			8		9	11	10	5	7*	12										3
1	2	3	6	4			8		9		10	5	7	11										4
1	2	3	6	4			8		9	11	10	5*		12	7									5
1	2	3	6	4			8		9*	11	10	5	7		12									6
1	2	3	6	4			8		9	11*	10	5	12		7									7
1	2	3	5	6			8*		9	11	10	12			7	4								8
1	2	3	5	6					9*		10	8		11	7	4	12							9
1	2	3	5	6			8		12		10*	9		11	7	4								10
1	2	3	5	6			8		12		10	9*		11	7	4								11
1	2	3	5	6			8				10	9*		11	7	4	12							12
1	2	3	5	6			8		12		10			11	7	4	9*							13
1	2	3	5	6							10	9		11*	7	4	12	8						14
1	2	3	5	6			8				10	9		11*	7	4	12							15
1	2	3	5	6					9		10*	12			7	4		8	11					16
1	2	3	5	6					9		10	11			7	4		8						17
1	2	3	5	6			8		9		10*	12			7	4			11					18
1	2	3	5	6			8		9		10	12			7	4*			11					19
1	2	3	4	6			8		9		12	10	11*		7					5				20
1	2	3	5	6			8		9	11					7	4					10			21
1	2	3	5	6			8		9						7	4			11		10			22
1	2	3	5	6			8		9		12				7	4			11		10*			23
1	2	3	5	6			8		9		12				7	4			11		10*			24
1	2	3	5	6			8		9		12				7	4			11		10*			25
1	2	3	5	6			8*		9						7	4		12	11		10			26
1	2	3	5	6					9*		10				7	4		8	11	12				27
1	2	3	5	6		12			9						7	4		8	11			10*		28
1	2		5	4		7			9		10		12		6			8*	11	3				29
1	2	3	5	6		8			9		10				7	4			11					30
1	2	3	5	6		8			9		10				7	4			11					31
1	2	3	5	6		8			9		10		11		7	4								32
1	2	3	5	6		11*			9	12	10				7	4		8						33
1		3		6					9	12	10				7	4		8*	11	5			2	34
1	2	3		6					9*	11	10		12		7	4		8		5				35
1	2		5	6					9	11			7		3	4		8		10				36
1	5			3	6				9	11			7		2	4		8		10				37
1	5			3	6				9	11			7		2	4		8		10				38
1	2	3	5	10	6				9					11	7	4*		8		12				39
1	2	3	5	4*	6				9				12	11	7			8				10		40
1	2	3	5	4	6				9					11	7			8				10		41
1	3		5	4	6				9*				7	11	2			8		12		10		42
42	41	37	38	42	7	6	22	1	36	12	26	14	10	12	37	30	1	16	14	7	6	4	1	
						1			3	2	5	4	4	2	1		4	1		3				
	6		1	2		1	3		6	2	6	5		1		2	1	3		2	1			

3 own-goals

Wealands J	Daniel P	de Vries R	Croft S	Haigh P	Roberts D	Grimes V	Lyall G	Wood A	Sunley D	Stewart D	Hemmerman J	Hawley J	Gibson D	Galvin C	Nisbet G	Bremner W	Staniforth G	Lord M	McIntosh J	Dobson I	Hickton J	McDonald R	McGifford G	
1	2	3	5	6			8		9	11		10*			7	4			12					3
1	2	3	6	11			8		9		10				7	4				5				R
2	2	2	2	2			2		2	1	1	1			2	2				1				
																			1					
											1				1									

Wealands J	Daniel P	de Vries R	Croft S	Haigh P	Roberts D	Grimes V	Lyall G	Wood A	Sunley D	Stewart D	Hemmerman J	Hawley J	Gibson D	Galvin C	Nisbet G	Bremner W	Staniforth G	Lord M	McIntosh J	Dobson I	Hickton J	McDonald R	McGifford G	
1	2	3	6	4			8		9	11*	10	5	7	12										2
1	1	1	1	1			1		1	1	1	1	1											
														1										

1977-78

1	Aug	20	(h)	Sunderland	W 3-0	Roberts 2, Bannister	16,189
2		23	(a)	Sheffield U	L 0-2		13,945
3		27	(a)	Crystal P	W 1-0	Hawley	14,618
4	Sep	3	(h)	Bolton W	D 0-0		10,106
5		10	(a)	Brighton & HA	L 1-2	Sunley	20,733
6		17	(h)	Stoke C	D 0-0		9,126
7		24	(a)	Southampton	L 0-1		18,503
8	Oct	1	(h)	Mansfield T	L 0-2		6,263
9		4	(h)	Tottenham H	W 2-0	Warboys 2	10,966
10		8	(a)	Millwall	D 1-1	Stewart	6,506
11		15	(h)	Blackpool	W 2-0	Bannister, Stewart	6,800
12		22	(a)	Burnley	D 1-1	Bremner	8,592
13		29	(h)	Blackburn R	L 0-1		7,932
14	Nov	5	(a)	Luton T	D 1-1	Bannister	8,936
15		12	(h)	Cardiff C	W 4-1	Stewart 2, Warboys, Dobson	5,228
16		19	(a)	Fulham	L 0-2		6,161
17		26	(h)	Charlton A	L 0-2		5,699
18	Dec	3	(a)	Bristol R	D 1-1	Roberts	5,351
19		10	(h)	Orient	D 2-2	Daniel, Dobson	4,279
20		17	(a)	Cardiff C	D 0-0		5,663
21		26	(h)	Oldham A	L 0-1		7,270
22		27	(a)	Notts C	L 1-2	Haigh	9,486
23		31	(h)	Sheffield U	L 2-3	Dobson, Bannister	8,134
24	Jan	2	(a)	Sunderland	L 0-2		29,396
25		14	(h)	Crystal P	W 1-0	Bremner	5,617
26		21	(a)	Bolton W	L 0-1		20,244
27	Feb	4	(h)	Brighton & HA	D 1-1	Hoult	4,543
28		25	(a)	Mansfield T	L 0-1		7,379
29	Mar	4	(h)	Millwall	W 3-2	Warboys 3	5,095
30		8	(a)	Stoke C	L 0-1		13,890
31		11	(a)	Blackpool	L 0-3		6,220
32		18	(h)	Burnley	L 1-3	Hawley	5,936
33		24	(a)	Blackburn R	D 1-1	Hawley	11,561
34		25	(h)	Notts C	D 1-1	Bremner	5,392
35		27	(a)	Oldham A	L 1-2	Bremner	6,614
36	Apr	1	(h)	Luton T	D 1-1	Roberts	4,054
37		8	(a)	Charlton A	W 1-0	Hawley	7,.014
38		11	(h)	Southampton	L 0-3		7,299
39		15	(h)	Fulham	L 0-1		3,961
40		22	(a)	Orient	L 1-2	Warboys	5,776
41		26	(a)	Tottenham H	L 0-1		36,913
42		29	(h)	Bristol R	L 0-1		3,645

FINAL LEAGUE POSITION: 22nd in Division Two — Relegated

Appearances
Sub Appearances
Goals

FA Cup

3	Jan	7	(h)	Leicester C	L 0-1		12,374

Appearances
Sub Appearances
Goals

League Cup

2	Aug	31	(a)	Southport	D 2-2	Haigh, Bannister	3,864
R	Sep	14	(h)	Southport	W 1-0	Bannister	4,846
3	Oct	25	(h)	Oldham A	W 2-0	Bannister, Bremner	6,923
4	Nov	29	(a)	Arsenal	L 1-5	Hawley	25,922

Appearances
Sub Appearances
Goals

Wealands J	Daniel P	de Vries R	Haigh P	Croft S	Roberts D	Nisbet G	Lord M	Hawley J	Bannister B	Stewart D	Galvin C	Bremner W	Sunley D	Grimes V	Warboys A	Dobson I	Hawker D	Blackburn E	Hoult A	Gibson D	Hood D	McDonald R	
1	2*	3	4	5	6	7	8	9	10	11	12												1
1		3	7	5	6	2	8	9		11*	10	4	12										2
1		3	7	5	6	2	8	9	10		11	4											3
1		3	7	5	6	2		9*		11	8	4	10	12									4
1		3	7	5	6	2	8*			11	4		10	12	9								5
1		3	7	5	6	2			10	11	8	4			9								6
1		3	7	5	6*				10		8	4	12	11	9	2							7
1		3	7		6	2	8		10		11*	4	12		9	5							8
1		3	7		6	2			10	11	4			8	9	5							9
1		3	7		6	2	12		10	11	4*			8	9	5							10
1		3	6			2			10	11	7	4	9	8		5							11
1	3		6			2			10	11	7	4		8	9	5							12
1	2	3	6			7			10		11	4		8	9	5							13
1	2	3	6						10	11	7	4		8	9	5							14
1	2	3	8		6				10	11	7	4			9	5							15
1	2	3	8	5	6	12			10	11*	7	4			9								16
1	3		8		6	2			10*	11		4	12	7	9	5							17
1	2	3	8		6	7			10	11		4			9	5							18
1	2	3	8*		6	7		12	10	11		4			9	5							19
1	2	3			6	7	8		10	11		4	9			5							20
1	2	3	8		6	7	4		12	11			10*		9	5							21
1	2	3	8		6	7	4	10	11		12				9*	5							22
1		3	8		6	2		9	10	11	4					5	7						23
		3	8		6*	2		9	10	11	4		12			5	7	1					24
	2	3		6		7	8	9	10	11		4				5		1					25
	2	3				6	8	9			11	4				5	7	1	10				26
	2	3	6			7	8	9	12		11*	4				5		1	10				27
	2	3	6			7		12		11		4			9	5		1	10*	8			28
	2	3	7			6	11	10				4			9	5		1		8			29
	2	3	7			6	11*	10				4	12		9	5		1		8			30
	2	3*	8		6	7		10			11	4	12		9	5		1					31
	2	3	11	5	6	7		10			8	4			9			1					32
	2	3	11	5	6	7*	8	10				4	12		9			1					33
	2	3	11		6	12	8	10				4	7*		9	5		1					34
		3	11	5	6	7	8	10				4			9	2		1					35
	3		7	5	6	2	8	10		11		4			9			1					36
			8	5	6	3		7	10	11		4			9	2		1					37
	2		8	5	6	3		7*	10	11		4			9	12		1					38
		3	8	5	6	2				11		4	10*		9		12	1			7		39
		3	8	5	6	4			10	11					9	2		1			7		40
	2	3	8	5	6	4			10	11					9			1			7		41
	2	3		5	6	4			10	11*					12		8	1			7	9	42
23	26	37	38	19	32	37	17	20	26	28	21	31	7	8	30	28	4	19	3	3	4	1	
						2	1	2	2		2		8	2	1	1	1						
	1		1		4			4	4	4		4	1		7	3			1				

Wealands J	Daniel P	de Vries R	Haigh P	Croft S	Roberts D	Nisbet G	Lord M	Hawley J	Bannister B	Stewart D	Galvin C	Bremner W	Sunley D	Grimes V	Warboys A	Dobson I	Hawker D	Blackburn E	Hoult A	Gibson D	Hood D	McDonald R	
	3		6			2	8	9*	12	11		4	10			5	7	1					3
	1		1			1	1	1		1		1	1			1	1	1					
									1														

Wealands J	Daniel P	de Vries R	Haigh P	Croft S	Roberts D	Nisbet G	Lord M	Hawley J	Bannister B	Stewart D	Galvin C	Bremner W	Sunley D	Grimes V	Warboys A	Dobson I	Hawker D	Blackburn E	Hoult A	Gibson D	Hood D	McDonald R	
1		3	7	5	6	2		9	10*	8	11	4	12										2
1		3	7	5	6	2			10	11	8	4	9										R
1	3		6			2			10	11	7	4	9	8		5							3
1		3	8		6	2		12	10		11	4*	9	7		5							4
4	1	3	4	2	3	4		1	4	3	4	4	3	2		2							
								1					1										
			1					1	3			1											

1978-79

1	Aug	19	(h)	Carlisle U	D 1-1	Horswill	5,062
2		26	(a)	Tranmere R	W 3-1	Edwards, Bannister, Lord	1,948
3	Sep	2	(h)	Chester	W 3-0	Edwards 3	5,325
4		5	(a)	Rotherham U	W 2-0	Bannister, Horswill	6,389
5		9	(a)	Brentford	L 0-1		6,528
6		12	(h)	Walsall	W 4-1	Edwards 2, Bannister, Lord	6,784
7		16	(h)	Chesterfield	D 1-1	Bannister	7,705
8		23	(a)	Exeter C	L 1-3	Edwards	3,733
9		26	(a)	Shrewsbury T	L 0-1		3,777
10		30	(h)	Oxford U	L 0-1		5,263
11	Oct	7	(h)	Peterborough U	D 1-1	Lord	4,531
12		14	(a)	Gillingham	L 0-2		5,460
13		21	(h)	Swansea C	D 2-2	Warboys, Haigh	6,152
14		23	(a)	Southend U	L 0-3		6,894
15		28	(a)	Bury	D 1-1	Bannister	4,088
16	Nov	4	(h)	Watford	W 4-0	Bannister 2, Edwards, Nisbet	7,739
17		11	(a)	Chester	L 1-2	Edwards	4,467
18		18	(h)	Tranmere R	W 2-1	Edwards, Horswill	4,350
19	Dec	9	(a)	Swindon T	L 0-2		5,872
20		26	(h)	Mansfield T	W 3-0	Edwards 2, Bannister	4,706
21	Jan	6	(a)	Walsall	W 2-1	Galvin 2	4,061
22	Feb	3	(h)	Shrewsbury T	D 1-1	Bannister	5,129
23		10	(a)	Oxford U	L 0-1		3,694
24		20	(a)	Blackpool	L 1-3	Warboys	3,636
25		24	(h)	Gillingham	L 0-1		4,345
26	Mar	2	(a)	Swansea C	L 3-5	Bannister 2, Horswill	8,919
27		6	(h)	Brentford	W 1-0	Edwards	3,418
28		10	(h)	Bury	W 4-1	Edwards, Bannister, Farley, Skipper	3,940
29		13	(h)	Colchester U	W 1-0	Stewart	4,201
30		24	(h)	Rotherham U	W 1-0	Hawker	4,717
31		27	(a)	Carlisle U	D 2-2	Edwards, Roberts	6,234
32		31	(h)	Lincoln C	D 0-0		4,103
33	Apr	4	(a)	Chesterfield	W 2-1	Edwards, Galvin	3,003
34		7	(a)	Plymouth A	W 4-3	Edwards 2, Bannister, Skipper	5,816
35		13	(h)	Sheffield W	D 1-1	Galvin	10,336
36		14	(a)	Mansfield T	W 2-0	Edwards, Bannister	5,138
37		16	(h)	Blackpool	D 0-0		6,000
38		21	(a)	Colchester U	L 1-2	Edwards	2,762
39		24	(h)	Southend U	W 2-0	Edwards, McDonald	3,960
40		28	(h)	Swindon T	D 1-1	Bannister	4,980
41	May	1	(h)	Plymouth A	W 2-1	Edwards, Horswill	3,646
42		5	(a)	Lincoln C	L 2-4	Roberts, Horswill	2,532
43		7	(h)	Exeter C	W 1-0	Edwards	4,079
44		11	(a)	Peterborough U	L 0-3		1,875
45		14	(a)	Watford	L 0-4		26,347
46		19	(a)	Sheffield W	W 3-2	Edwards, Roberts, McDonald	9,098

FINAL LEAGUE POSITION: 8th in Division Three

Appearances
Sub Appearanc
Goals

FA Cup

1	Nov	25	(h)	Stafford R	W 2-1	Edwards, Sargeant (og)	5,411
2	Dec	16	(a)	Carlisle U	L 0-3		5,335

Appearances
Sub Appearanc
Goals

League Cup

1	Aug	12	(h)	Peterborough U	L 0-1		4,165
		15	(a)	Peterborough U	W 2-1	Bannister, Haigh	4,387
R		22	(h)	Peterborough U	L 0-1		4,990

Appearances
Sub Appearanc
Goals

Wealands J	Nisbet G	de Vries R	Croft S	Dobson I	Haigh P	Hood D	Horswill M	Edwards K	Bannister B	Farley J	Warboys A	Lord M	Hawker D	McDonald R	Galvin C	Stewart D	Blackburn E	Skipper P	Roberts G	Norrie C	
1	2	3	4	5	6	7*	8	9	10	11	12										1
1	2	3	4	5	6	7	8*	9	10	11		12									2
1	2	3	4	5*	6	7		9	10	11	12	8									3
1	2	3	4		6	7	5	9	10	11		8									4
1	2	3			6	7	5	9	10	11	4	8									5
1	2	3			6	7	5	9	10	11		8		4							6
1	2	3	4		6	7	5	9	10	11			8								7
1	2	3	4		6	7*	5	9	10	11	12	8									8
1	2	3	4		6		5	9	10		7	8			11						9
1	2	3	4		6	7	5	9	10*	11	12	8									10
1	2	3	4		6	7*	5	9	10	11		8			12						11
1	2	3		5	6		4	9	10	11		8			7						12
1	2	3		5	6		4	9	10	11	7*	8			12						13
1	2	3		5	6		4	9	10	11		8			7*	12					14
1	2	3		5	6	7		9	10	11		8			4						15
1	2	3		5	6		4	9	10	11	7	8									16
1	2	3		5	6		4	9	10	11	7	8									17
	2	3		5	6		4	9	10	11	7	8					1				18
	2	3	4	5	6		10	9	12	11	7	8*					1				19
	2	3	4		6		5	9	10	11		8*			7	12	1				20
	2	3	4	5	6			9	10	11		8			7		1				21
	2	3		5	6			9	10		7	8	4		11		1				22
	2	3		5	6			9	10		7	8	4		11		1				23
	2	3		5	6		10*	9	12	11	7	8	4				1				24
	2	3		5	6		10	9	12	11	7		4		8*		1				25
	2	3		5	6		8	9	10		7		11				1	4			26
	2	3		5	6		8	9	10	11	7						1	4			27
	2	3			6		8	9	10	11	7*		4				1	5	12		28
	2		5		6		8	9	10				4			11	1	3	7		29
	2		5		6			9	10			8	4		12	11*	1	3	7		30
	2		5		6		8	9	10			11*	4		12		1	3	7		31
	2		5		6		8*	9	10				4		11	12	1	3	7		32
	2		5		6		8	9	10				4		11		1	3	7		33
	2		5		6	12	8	9	10				4		11*		1	3	7		34
	2		5		6		8	9*	10				4	12	11		1	3	7		35
1	2		5		6		8	9	10				4		11			3	7		36
1	2		5		6		8	9	10				4		11			3	7		37
1	2		5		6		8	9	10	11			4					3	7		38
1	2		5*		6		8	9	10	11			4	12				3	7		39
1	2				6	12	8	9	10	11			4	5				3*	7		40
1	2			12		6	8	9	10	11			4*	5				3	7		41
1	2			3	6		8	9	10	11			4	5					7		42
1	2			5	6	4	8	9	10	11*				3					7	12	43
1	2		3	5	6	4	8	9	10					11					7		44
1	2			12	6		8	9	10	11			7*	5				4	3		45
1	2	3*		5	6	12	8	9	10	11				4					7		46
28	46	29	24	22	45	14	40	46	43	32	14	23	22	8	15	2	18	17	18		
				2		3			3		4	1		2	4	3			1	1	
	1				1		6	24	15	1	2	3	1	2	4	1		2	3		

Wealands J	Nisbet G	de Vries R	Croft S	Dobson I	Haigh P	Hood D	Horswill M	Edwards K	Bannister B	Farley J	Warboys A	Lord M	Hawker D	McDonald R	Galvin C	Stewart D	Blackburn E	Skipper P	Roberts G	Norrie C	
	2	3			6	5	4	9	10	11	7	8*	12				1				1
	2	3	4		6	8	5	9	10	11					7		1				2
	2	2	1		2	2	2	2	2	2	1	1			1		2				
													1								
								1													

1 own-goal

Wealands J	Nisbet G	de Vries R	Croft S	Dobson I	Haigh P	Hood D	Horswill M	Edwards K	Bannister B	Farley J	Warboys A	Lord M	Hawker D	McDonald R	Galvin C	Stewart D	Blackburn E	Skipper P	Roberts G	Norrie C	
1	2	3	4	5	6	7*	8	9	10	11			12								1
1	2	3	4	5	6	7	8	9	10	11											
1	2	3	4	5	6	7	8	9	10	11											R
3	3	3	3	3	3	3	3	3	3	3											
													1								
					1				1												

1979-80

1	Aug	18	(h)	Colchester U	L 0-2		4,463
2		21	(a)	Sheffield W	D 0-0		14,562
3		25	(h)	Oxford U	D 2-2	Phillips, G.Roberts	4,029
4	Sep	1	(a)	Mansfield T	D 1-1	Haigh	4,320
5		8	(h)	Sheffield U	W 3-1	Edwards, Farley, Moss	9,556
6		15	(a)	Bury	W 1-0	Edwards	3,422
7		18	(a)	Chesterfield	D 1-1	Edwards	5,034
8		22	(h)	Gillingham	D 0-0		6,142
9		29	(a)	Millwall	L 2-3	Phillips, Tait	6,001
10	Oct	2	(h)	Chesterfield	W 2-1	Moss, Tait	5,971
11		6	(a)	Swindon T	D 0-0		7,672
12		9	(h)	Sheffield W	D 1-1	Dobson	10,306
13		13	(h)	Carlisle U	W 2-0	Phillips, Farley	5,838
14		20	(a)	Chester	L 1-2	Tait	3,391
15		23	(a)	Rotherham U	L 1-2	Edwards	5,916
16		27	(h)	Exeter C	D 2-2	Croft, Dobson	5,196
17	Nov	2	(a)	Colchester U	D 1-1	Moss	4,466
18		6	(h)	Rotherham U	D 1-1	Edwards	5,899
19		10	(a)	Reading	L 0-3		6,909
20		17	(h)	Barnsley	L 0-2		8,327
21	Dec	1	(h)	Wimbledon	D 1-1	Hawker	3,750
22		8	(a)	Brentford	L 2-7	Bannister, Farley	6,793
23		21	(h)	Blackburn R	L 0-1		3,720
24		26	(a)	Blackpool	D 2-2	Edwards 2	4,535
25		29	(a)	Oxford U	L 0-3		3,888
26	Jan	5	(a)	Plymouth A	L 1-5	Norrie	6,341
27		12	(h)	Mansfield T	W 3-1	Edwards 2, Moss	4,243
28		19	(a)	Sheffield U	D 1-1	Norrie	14,960
29		25	(a)	Southend U	L 0-3		3,920
30	Feb	16	(h)	Millwall	W 1-0	Edwards	5,013
31		23	(a)	Carlisle U	L 2-3	Edwards, G.Roberts	4,263
32	Mar	1	(h)	Chester	W 1-0	Farley	5,771
33		4	(a)	Gillingham	L 0-1		4,161
34		8	(a)	Exeter C	D 2-2	Edwards 2	3,771
35		14	(h)	Swindon T	W 1-0	Moss	5,346
36		22	(h)	Reading	L 0-1		4,293
37		25	(h)	Grimsby T	D 2-2	Edwards 2	14,176
38	Apr	4	(a)	Blackburn R	L 0-1		14,571
39		5	(h)	Blackpool	W 3-1	Edwards 2, Moss	5,425
40		7	(a)	Grimsby T	D 1-1	Deacy	18,360
41		12	(h)	Plymouth A	W 1-0	Norrie	5,369
42		19	(a)	Wimbledon	L 2 3	Norrie, D.Roberts	2,046
43		22	(a)	Barnsley	L 1-3	Cooper (og)	11,016
44		26	(h)	Brentford	W 2-1	Edwards, Haigh	5,382
45	May	3	(h)	Southend U	W 1-0	Edwards	3,297
46		5	(h)	Bury	L 0-1		6,158

FINAL LEAGUE POSITION: 20th in Division Three

Appearances
Sub Appearances
Goals

FA Cup

1	Nov	24	(a)	Carlisle U	D 3-3	Haigh, Tait, G.Roberts	4,970
R		28	(h)	Carlisle U	L 0-2		6,657

Appearances
Sub Appearances
Goals

League Cup

1	Aug	11	(a)	Sheffield W	D 1-1	Edwards	9,134
		14	(h)	Sheffield W	L 1-2	G.Roberts	7,059

Appearances
Sub Appearances
Goals

Blackburn E	Nisbet G	McDonald R	Hawker D	Croft S	Haigh P	Roberts G	Horswill M	Edwards K	Bannister B	Phillips T	Skipper P	de Vries R	Dobson I	Farley J	Hood D	Tait M	Moss P	Norrie C	Marwood B	Norman A	Roberts D	Deacy N	Richards S	Bennyworth I	McClaren S	
1	2	3	4*	5	6	7	8	9	10	11	12															1
1	2	3			6	7	8		10	11		4	5	9												2
1	2	3			6	7	8		10	11		4	5	9												3
1	2	10	4	6	8	7		9*		11		3	5		12											4
1	2			4		7		9		10		3	5	11		6	8									5
1	2	12		4		7		9*		10		3	5	11		6	8									6
1	2			4	7			9		10		3	5	11		6	8									7
1	2	12		4		7		9*		10		3	5	11		6	8									8
1	2			4		7		9		10		3	5	11		6	8									9
1	2	12		4		7		9		10*		3	5	11		6	8									10
1	2			4		7		9		10		3	5	11		6	8									11
1	2			4		7		9		10		3	5	11		6	8									12
1	2			4		7			9	10		3	5	11		6	8									13
1	2			4		7			9	10		3	5	11		6	8									14
1	2			4	12	7*		9		10		3	5	11		6	8									15
1	2	12		4	7			9		10		3	5	11*		6	8									16
1	2		11	4		7		9		10		3	5			6	8									17
1	2		12	4*		7		9		10		3	5	11		6	8									18
1	2	12			4	7		9		10*		3	5	11		6	8									19
1	6		11		3	7		9			4		5		2	10	8									20
1	2		6		4	7		9	10			3	5	11			8									21
1	2		6	5	4	7		9	10					11	3		8									22
1	2		6	4		7		9		10	5	3					8	11								23
1	2			4	3	7		9		11	5	6					8	10								24
1	2			4	8	7		9		11	3	6	5					10								25
1	2			4	6	7		9			11	3	5	12			8*	10								26
1	2	12		4	6	7		9				3	5				11	10*	8							27
1	2			4	6	7		9				3	5				11	10	8							28
1	2			4	6	7		9				3	5			12	11*	10	8							29
	2			4	6	7	3	9	10					11		8				1	5					30
	2			4	6	7		9	10			3		11		8				1	5					31
	2			4	6	7	3	9						11		8				1	5	10				32
	2			4	6*	7	3	9	12					11		8				1	5	10				33
	2			4	6*	7	3	9						11		8			12	1		10	5			34
	2				6	7	3	9					5	11		8	4			1		10				35
	2			4		7		9				3		11		8	6			1	5	10				36
	2				4	7		9				3		11		8	6			1	5	10				37
	2			4		7		9				3		11		8	6			1	5	10				38
	2			4	5	7		9				3				8	6	12	11*	1		10				39
	2			4		7		9				3				8	6	11		1	5	10				40
	2			4		7		9				3*				8	6	11	12	1	5	10				41
	2			4		7	12	9*				3				8	6	11		1	5	10				42
	2			4	3	7	8		10*							12	6	11		1	5	9				43
	2			4	3	7	8	9								12	6	11*		1	5	10				44
	2			4	3	7	8	9								12	6	11*		1	5	10				45
	2			4	3	7	8	9									12	11		1		10		5	6*	46
29	46	4	7	39	28	44	12	41	10	22	5	34	26	27	2	29	35	14	4	17	13	15	1	1	1	
		6	1		1		1		1		1			1	1	4	1	1	2							
			1	1	2	2		19	1	3			2	4		3	6	4			1	1				

1 own-goal

Blackburn E	Nisbet G	McDonald R	Hawker D	Croft S	Haigh P	Roberts G	Horswill M	Edwards K	Bannister B	Phillips T	Skipper P	de Vries R	Dobson I	Farley J	Hood D	Tait M	Moss P	
1	6		11		3	7		9			4*		5	12	2	10	8	1
1	6		4		3	7		9	10				5	11	2		8	R
2	2		2		2	2		2	1		1		2	1	2	1	2	
														1				
					1	1										1		

Blackburn E	Nisbet G	McDonald R	Hawker D	Croft S	Haigh P	Roberts G	Horswill M	Edwards K	Bannister B	Phillips T	Skipper P	de Vries R	Dobson I	
1	2	3	4		6	7	8	9	10	11			5	1
1	2	3	4		6	7	8	9	10	11			5	
2	2	2	2		2	2	2	2	2	2			2	
						1		1						

1980-81

1	Aug	16	(a)	Millwall	D 1-1	Edwards	3,831
2		19	(h)	Barnsley	L 1-2	McCarthy (og)	6,978
3		23	(h)	Exeter C	D 3-3	Edwards, Moss, Deacy	3,559
4		29	(a)	Fulham	D 0-0		4,585
5	Sep	6	(h)	Walsall	L 0-1		4,211
6		13	(a)	Blackpool	D 2-2	Haigh 2	6,138
7		16	(a)	Burnley	L 0-2		4,933
8		20	(h)	Portsmouth	W 2-1	Edwards, Swann	4,613
9		27	(a)	Brentford	D 2-2	Edwards, Swann	6,305
10		30	(h)	Burnley	D 0-0		5,497
11	Oct	4	(h)	Oxford U	L 0-1		4,211
12		8	(a)	Chester	L 1-4	Edwards	2,141
13		11	(a)	Chesterfield	L 0-1		7,546
14		18	(h)	Charlton A	L 0-2		3,551
15		21	(h)	Carlisle U	L 0-1		3,603
16		25	(a)	Gillingham	L 0-2		4,100
17		28	(a)	Colchester U	L 0-2		2,239
18	Nov	1	(h)	Plymouth A	W 1-0	Deacy	3,367
19		4	(h)	Chester	D 0-0		3,335
20		8	(a)	Newport C	L 0-4		5,496
21		11	(a)	Barnsley	L 0-5		11,628
22		15	(h)	Millwall	W 3-1	Edwards, Marwood, G.Roberts	3,210
23		29	(a)	Swindon T	L 1-3	Marwood	5,518
24	Dec	6	(h)	Reading	W 2-0	Edwards, G.Roberts	3,130
25		20	(a)	Sheffield U	L 1-3	Edwards	10,720
26		26	(h)	Rotherham U	L 1-2	Edwards	8,618
27		27	(a)	Huddersfield T	L 0-5		13,240
28	Jan	10	(a)	Charlton A	L 2-3	Edwards, J.Roberts	6,493
29		31	(a)	Exeter C	W 3-1	Mutrie, Marwood, McClaren	5,022
30	Feb	7	(h)	Blackpool	W 2-1	Edwards, Whitehurst	5,315
31		14	(a)	Walsall	D 1-1	G.Roberts	3,914
32		21	(h)	Brentford	D 0-0		4,535
33		28	(a)	Portsmouth	L 1-2	Mutrie	13,505
34	Mar	7	(a)	Oxford U	D 1-1	D.Roberts	3,165
35		14	(h)	Chesterfield	D 0-0		5,488
36		17	(h)	Colchester U	L 0-1		3,586
37		21	(a)	Carlisle U	L 0-2		4,103
38		28	(h)	Gillingham	D 2-2	Mutrie, Richards	3,309
39	Apr	4	(a)	Plymouth A	D 0-0		4,668
40		7	(h)	Fulham	L 0-1		3,152
41		14	(h)	Swindon T	D 0-0		2,789
42		18	(h)	Huddersfield T	W 2-1	Deacy, Marwood	6,328
43		20	(a)	Rotherham U	D 1-1	Edwards	11,602
44		25	(h)	Sheffield U	D 1-1	Deacy	4,895
45	May	2	(a)	Reading	L 0-2		3,399
46		7	(h)	Newport C	W 3-1	Mutrie 2, Edwards	2,059

FINAL LEAGUE POSITION: 24th in Division Three — Relegated

Appearances
Sub Appearanc
Goals

FA Cup

1	Nov	22	(h)	Halifax T	W 2-1	Edwards 2	4,024
2	Dec	13	(h)	Blyth Spartans	D 1-1	Edwards	6,050
R		16	(a)	Blyth Spartans	D 2-2*	Edwards, Norrie	5,870
2R		22	(n†)	Blyth Spartans	W 2-1*	Norrie, Croft	5,914
3	Jan	3	(h)	Doncaster R	W 1-0	Deacy	10,709
4		24	(a)	Tottenham H	L 0-2		37,432

*After extra-time. †Played at Elland Road, Leeds.

Appearances
Sub Appearanc
Goals

League Cup

1	Aug	9	(a)	Lincoln C	L 0-5		3,538
		12	(h)	Lincoln C	L 0-2		2,933

Appearances
Sub Appearanc
Goals

Norman A	Nisbet G	Horswill M	Booth D	Roberts J	Haigh P	Norrie C	Roberts G	Edwards K	Moss P	Deacy N	Kilgallon M	Swann G	McClaren S	Roberts D	McNeil R	Croft S	Kynman D	Flounders A	Richards S	Marwood B	Whitehurst W	Hoolickin S	Ferguson B	Mutrie L	Davies J	Eccleston S	McDonald R	
1	2	3	4	5	6	7	8	9	10	11																		1
1	2	3	4	5	6	7*	8	9	10	11	12																	2
1	2	3	4	5	6	7	8	9*	10	11		12																3
1	2	3	4	5	6			9	10	11		8	7*	12														4
1	2	3	4	5	6			9	10	11		8		7														5
1	8	3	4	5	6			9	10	11*		7		12	2													6
1	7	3	4	5	11			9	10*	12		8		6	2													7
1	7	3	4	5	11			9	10			8		6	2													8
1	7	3	4	5	6			9	10	11		8			2													9
1	7	3*	4	5	6			9	10	11		8		12	2													10
1	2		4	5	10			9	7	8*					3	6	11	12										11
1	2		4	5	10			9	7	8					3*	6	11	12										12
1	2		4	5	3	12	7	9*		11								10	6	8								13
1	2		4	5	3	10			9*	11						6		8	12	7								14
1	2		4	5	3*			9	10	12		11						8	6	7								15
1	2		4	5	3	12				11		8					10*		6	7	9							16
1	2			5	3	12		9	8	11		4		6						7	10*							17
1	2			5	3			9	8	11		4		6						7	10							18
1	2			5				9	8	11*		4	12	6	3					7	10							19
1	2			5			4	12	8	11			9	6	3					7	10*							20
1	2		10	5			4	9		11			8*	6	3					7	12							21
1	2			5			4	9		11			10	6	3					7	8							22
1	2		12	5*		11	4	9					8	6	3					7	10							23
1	3						5	9		11			8	6		4				7	10	2						24
1				6			5	9		11*			8		3	4			12	7	10	2						25
1				6			5	9		11			8			4				7		2	3	10				26
1			7*			12	6	9		11			8			4			5			2	3	10				27
1				5				9		11			6						4	7	10	2	3	8				28
1			3				5	9		11			8	6					4	7		2		10				29
			3				5	9		11*			8	6					4	7	12	2		10	1			30
			3				5	9		11			8	6					4	7	12	2		10*	1			31
			3				5	9*		11			8	6					4	7	12	2		10	1			32
			3				5	9		11			8	6					4	7		2		10	1			33
1			3				5	9		11			8*	6					4	7		2	12	10				34
1*			3			12	5	9		11				6					4		7	2	8	10				35
1			3			12	5	9		11				6*					4		7	2	8	10				36
1			3			9				11			6						4	7*	12	2	8	10		5		37
1			3					9		11			8*						4	7	12	2	6	10		5		38
1			3							11		8							6	7	9	2	4	10		5		39
1			3							11*		12	8						4	7	9	2	6	10		5		40
1			3			12				11		8		5					4	7	9*	2	6	10				41
1			3					12		11		8*							4	7	9	2	6	10		5		42
1		6	3			10*		9		11		12							4	7	8	2				5		43
1		6	3					9		11									4	7	8	2		10		5		44
1			3					9				6							4	7	10	2	8	11		5		45
1		6	3					9				8			2				4	7	11			10		5		46
42	24	13	36	26	18	7	20	38	18	40		17	19	20	14	7	3	3	23	31	20	22	12	20	4	9		
			1			7		2		2	1	3	1	3				2	2		6		1					
				1	2		3	13	1	4		2	1	1					1	4	1			5				

1 own-goal

Norman A	Nisbet G	Horswill M	Booth D	Roberts J	Haigh P	Norrie C	Roberts G	Edwards K	Moss P	Deacy N	Kilgallon M	Swann G	McClaren S	Roberts D	McNeil R	Croft S	Kynman D	Flounders A	Richards S	Marwood B	Whitehurst W	Hoolickin S	Ferguson B	Mutrie L	Davies J	Eccleston S	McDonald R	
1	2	3		5		8	4	9		11*			10	6				12		7								1
1	2					10	5	9		11			8		3	4			6	7								2
1	2					10	5	9		11			8		3	4			6	7								R
1			2	6		10	5	9	12	11			8		3	4				7*								2R
1						10	6	9		11			8			4			5	7		2	3					3
1			5	6		10		9		11			8		3				4	7		2						4
6	3	1	2	3		6	5	6		6			6	1	4	4			4	6		2	1					
									1									1										
						2		4		1						1												

Norman A	Nisbet G	Horswill M	Booth D	Roberts J	Haigh P	Norrie C	Roberts G	Edwards K	Moss P	Deacy N	Kilgallon M	Swann G	McClaren S	Roberts D	McNeil R	Croft S	Kynman D	Flounders A	Richards S	Marwood B	Whitehurst W	Hoolickin S	Ferguson B	Mutrie L	Davies J	Eccleston S	McDonald R	
1	2		4*	5	3	10	8	9	11				12						6	7								1
1	2	3	4	5	6	7	8	9	10*				12														11	
2	2	1	2	2	2	2	2	2	2										1	1							1	
													2															

1981-82

1	Aug	29	(a)	Torquay U	L 1-2	Mutrie	2,651
2	Sep	5	(h)	Bradford C	W 2-1	Mutrie, Ferguson	3,916
3		12	(a)	Northampton T	D 1-1	Mutrie	1,938
4		19	(h)	Sheffield U	W 2-1	Edwards, Booth	7,219
5		22	(h)	Peterborough U	D 1-1	Ferguson	3,712
6		26	(a)	Blackpool	L 1-3	Mutrie	4,838
7		30	(a)	Hartlepool U	L 2-3	Mutrie, Whitehurst	2,654
8	Oct	3	(h)	Tranmere R	L 1-2	Whitehurst	3,087
9		10	(a)	Mansfield T	D 3-3	Mutrie, Marwood, Deacy	3,464
10		17	(h)	Wigan A	L 0-2		3,600
11		20	(a)	Scunthorpe U	D 4-4	Marwood 2, G.Roberts, Richards	3,575
12		24	(h)	Aldershot	L 1-2	Mutrie	2,999
13		31	(a)	Port Vale	L 1-2	Mutrie	2,591
14	Nov	3	(h)	York C	W 2-0	Marwood, G.Roberts	3,340
15		7	(h)	Colchester U	L 2-3	G.Roberts, Mutrie	3,040
16		14	(a)	Hereford U	D 2-2	Whitehurst 2	2,652
17		28	(a)	Bury	W 2-0	McClaren, G.Roberts	4,508
18	Dec	5	(h)	Crewe A	W 1-0	Mutrie	3,184
19	Jan	9	(a)	Bradford C	D 1-1	G.Roberts	5,183
20		23	(h)	Torquay U	W 1-0	Flounders	3,003
21		30	(a)	Sheffield U	D 0-0		12,612
22	Feb	6	(h)	Northampton T	L 0-1		3,341
23		10	(a)	Peterborough U	L 0-3		3,161
24		13	(a)	Tranmere R	D 2-2	Mutrie 2	1,735
25		20	(h)	Hartlepool U	W 5-2	Mutrie 4, Lowe (og)	2,825
26		27	(h)	Mansfield T	W 2-0	Mutrie, Flounders	4,958
27	Mar	2	(h)	Halifax T	W 2-0	Mutrie, Davis	6,952
28		6	(a)	Wigan A	L 1-2	Mutrie	6,008
29		9	(h)	Scunthorpe U	W 2-0	Mutrie, McClaren	6,121
30		12	(a)	Aldershot	W 3-0	Mutrie 2, Marwood	2,059
31		16	(a)	York C	W 3-1	Mutrie, Marwood, Whitehurst	4,771
32		20	(h)	Port Vale	W 3-1	Mutrie, Deacy, Booth	5,506
33		23	(a)	Darlington	L 1-2	Flounders	2,651
34		26	(a)	Colchester U	L 0-2		2,193
35	Apr	3	(h)	Hereford U	W 2-1	Flounders 2	3,713
36		6	(a)	Rochdale	W 1-0	Mutrie	1,738
37		10	(h)	Darlington	L 1-3	McClaren	4,589
38		12	(a)	Stockport C	W 2-1	Mutrie, McClaren	2,450
39		17	(a)	Crewe A	D 1-1	Marwood	1,592
40		20	(h)	Stockport C	D 0-0		3,526
41		24	(h)	Bury	W 3-2	Whitehurst, Mutrie, G.Roberts	3,602
42	May	1	(a)	Bournemouth	L 0-1		8,055
43		4	(h)	Blackpool	W 1-0	Marwood	3,206
44		8	(h)	Rochdale	W 2-1	Marwood 2	3,012
45		11	(h)	Bournemouth	D 0-0		3,387
46		14	(a)	Halifax T	D 2-2	Marwood 2	2,293

FINAL LEAGUE POSITION: 8th in Division Four

Appearances
Sub Appearance
Goals

FA Cup

1	Nov	21	(a)	Rochdale	D 2-2	Whitehurst, McClaren	2,722
R		24	(h)	Rochdale	D 2-2*	Whitehurst, Swann	4,063
2R		30	(n†)	Rochdale	W 1-0*	McClaren	3,268
2	Jan	4	(h)	Hartlepool U	W 2-0	Marwood, Mutrie	4,975
3		18	(a)	Chelsea	D 0-0		14,899
R		21	(h)	Chelsea	L 0-2		13,238

*After extra-time. †Played at Elland Road, Leeds.

Appearances
Sub Appearance
Goals

League Cup

1	Sep	2	(a)	Lincoln C	L 0-3		3,498
		15	(h)	Lincoln C	D 1-1	Ferguson	2,702

Appearances
Sub Appearance
Goals

Norman A	McNeil R	Booth D	Richards S	Eccleston S	Horswill M	Roberts G	Edwards K	Whitehurst W	Mutrie L	Ferguson B	Deacy N	Hoolickin S	Marwood B	McClaren S	Roberts D	Swann G	Davies J	Kynman D	Norrie C	Parkinson K	Flounders A	Thompson N	Davis I	
1	2	3	4	5	6	7	8	9	10*	11	12													1
1		3	4	5		6	8	12	10*	11	9	2	7											2
1		3	4	5			8		10	11	9	2	7	6										3
1		3	4	5		6	8	9	10	11		2	12	7*										4
1		3	4	5		6	8	9	10	11		2		7										5
1		3	4	5	6	8*		9	10	11	12	2		7										6
1		3		5	6			9	10	11	8	2		7	4									7
1		3		5	6			9	10	11*	8	2	12	7	4									8
1		3	4*		6			9	10		8	2	11	7	5	12								9
1		3	4		6	8		9	10		11*	2	7	12	5									10
	2		4	5	3	6		9	10				7	8			1	11						11
	2		4	5	3	6		9*	10		12		7	8			1	11						12
	2*		4	5	3	8		9	10		12		7	6			1	11						13
	2	11	4	5	3	6		9	10				7	8			1							14
	2	11	4	5	3*	6		9	10		12		7	8			1							15
1	2	3				6		9	10		5		7	8	4	11								16
1	2	3				6		9	10		5		7*	8	4	11				12				17
1	2	3				6		9	10		5		7	8	4	11								18
1	2	3				6			10		5		7	8	4	11			9					19
	2	3				6			10	8	5		7		4	11	1				9			20
	2	3				6		9	10	8	5		7*		4	11	1				12			21
	2*	3				6		9		8	5		7	12	4	11	1				10			22
1	2	3*			12	6		9	10		5		7	8	4	11								23
1	2*				5	6		9	10		11		7	8	4	12						3		24
1					5	6		9	10		11		7	8	4	2						3		25
1					5	6*			10	12	11		7	8	4	2					9	3		26
1				12	5				10		11		7	8	4*	2					9	3	6	27
1			4		5			9	10		11		7	8		2						3	6	28
1		3			5*			9	10		11		7	8	4	2						12	6	29
1		3						9	10		11		7	8	4	2						5	6	30
1		3						9	10		11		7	8	4	2						5	6	31
1		3	12					9	10		11		7	8	4	2*						5	6	32
1		3	2					9			11		7	8	4						10	5	6	33
1		3	2*					9		12	11		7	8	4						10	5	6	34
1	2	3	11						10				7	8	4						9	5	6	35
1	2	3	11						10	12			7	8*	4						9	5	6	36
1	2	3	11					12	10				7	8	4						9	5	6*	37
1	2	3	11						10				7	8	4						9	5	6	38
1	2		11			3		9	10				7	8	4							5	6	39
1	2*	3	11			6		9	10				7	8	4							5	12	40
1		3	11			6		9	10				7	8	4							5	2	41
1		3	11			6			10				7		4			8			9	5	2	42
1		3	11						10	6			7		4			8			9	5	2	43
1		3	11			5		9	10				7		4	2		8				12	6*	44
		3	11			5		9	10				7		4	2*	1	8				6	12	45
		3	11			5		9	10				7		4		1	8				6	2	46
36	21	37	28	13	17	29	5	34	43	12	25	9	40	35	34	18	10	8	1		12	21	18	
			1	1	1			2		3	5		2	2		2				1	1	2	2	
		2	1			6	1	6	27	2	2		12	4							5		1	

1 own-goal

Norman A	McNeil R	Booth D	Richards S	Eccleston S	Horswill M	Roberts G	Edwards K	Whitehurst W	Mutrie L	Ferguson B	Deacy N	Hoolickin S	Marwood B	McClaren S	Roberts D	Swann G	Davies J	Kynman D	Norrie C	Parkinson K	Flounders A	Thompson N	Davis I	
1	2	3				6		9	10		5		7	8	4	11								1
1	2	3				6		9	10*		5		7	8	4	11			12					R
1	2	3				6		9	10		5		7	8	4	11								2R
1	2	3				6			10		5		7	8	4	11			9					2
	2	3				6		9	10	8	5		7		4	11	1							3
	2	3				6		9*	10	8	5		7		4	11	1				12			R
4	6	6				6		5	6	2	6		6	4	6	6	2		1					
																			1		1			
								2	1				1	2		1								

Norman A	McNeil R	Booth D	Richards S	Eccleston S	Horswill M	Roberts G	Edwards K	Whitehurst W	Mutrie L	Ferguson B	Deacy N	Hoolickin S	Marwood B	McClaren S	Roberts D	Swann G	Davies J	Kynman D	Norrie C	Parkinson K	Flounders A	Thompson N	Davis I	
1	2	3	4	5	6*	7	8	12	10	11	9													1
1		3	4	5	6		8	9	10	11		2	12	7*										
2	1	2	2	2	2	1	2	1	2	2	1	1		1										
								1					1											
										1														

1982-83

1	Aug	28	(a)	Bristol C	L	1-2	Flounders	4,853
2	Sep	4	(h)	Wimbledon	D	1-1	Flounders	3,674
3		7	(h)	York C	W	4-0	Mutrie 2, McClaren, Flounders	3,769
4		10	(a)	Stockport C	D	1-1	Marwood	2,252
5		18	(h)	Hartlepool U	D	1-1	G.Roberts	3,913
6		25	(a)	Aldershot	W	2-1	McClaren, G.Roberts	2,345
7		28	(a)	Colchester U	D	0-0		3,071
8	Oct	2	(h)	Swindon T	D	0-0		3,,786
9		9	(h)	Torquay U	W	4-1	Mutrie 2, D.Roberts, Skipper	3,909
10		15	(a)	Scunthorpe U	W	1-0	Mutrie	7,483
11		20	(a)	Hereford U	L	0-2		2,320
12		23	(h)	Northampton T	W	4-0	Marwood 2, Whitehurst, Flounders	4,317
13		30	(a)	Tranmere R	W	1-0	McClaren	1,568
14	Nov	2	(h)	Bury	W	2-1	Marwood, Skipper	6,101
15		6	(h)	Peterborough U	W	4-1	Marwood 2, Woof, Slack (og)	5,535
16		13	(a)	Port Vale	L	0-1		5,298
17		27	(h)	Chester	W	2-0	Marwood, McClaren	4,606
18	Dec	4	(a)	Blackpool	D	1-1	Mutrie	3,395
19		11	(h)	Colchester U	W	3-0	Flounders 2, Hawley	4,323
20		17	(a)	Crewe A	W	3-0	Marwood 2, Mutrie	1,404
21		27	(h)	Halifax T	D	1-1	Skipper	9,692
22		28	(a)	Darlington	W	2-1	Marwood, Askew	2,519
23	Jan	1	(h)	Rochdale	W	2-1	Marwood, G.Roberts	9,059
24		3	(a)	Mansfield T	L	1-3	Marwood	4,517
25		8	(a)	Wimbledon	W	2-1	Whitehurst, D.Roberts	2,766
26		15	(h)	Bristol C	W	1-0	Mutrie	6,835
27		22	(a)	Hartlepool U	D	0-0		2,295
28		29	(h)	Stockport C	W	7-0	Flounders 3, Mutrie, G.Roberts, Skipper, Askew	5,901
29	Feb	5	(h)	Aldershot	D	2-2	Mutrie, Flounders	6,633
30		15	(h)	Hereford U	W	2-0	Whitehurst, Woof	6,533
31		19	(a)	Torquay U	D	0-0		2,817
32		26	(h)	Scunthorpe U	D	1-1	Marwood	11,933
33	Mar	1	(a)	Bury	W	3-2	Flounders, G.Roberts, Askew	4,239
34		5	(a)	Northampton	W	2-1	Flounders, Askew	2,879
35		12	(h)	Tranmere R	L	0-1		7,198
36		19	(a)	Peterborough U	D	1-1	Mutrie	3,805
37		26	(h)	Port Vale	W	1-0	Marwood	14,410
38	Apr	2	(h)	Darlington	D	0-0		7,459
39		4	(a)	Halifax T	W	2-1	Marwood, Woof	5,011
40		9	(h)	Blackpool	W	3-1	Marwood 2, Bardsley (og)	6,972
41		16	(a)	Swindon T	W	1-0	Marwood	3,937
42		19	(a)	York C	L	0-1		9,909
43		23	(h)	Crewe A	W	1-0	Askew	7,041
44		30	(a)	Chester	D	0-0		2,450
45	May	2	(h)	Mansfield T	D	2-2	Flounders, Askew	7,875
46		14	(a)	Rochdale	W	3-1	Marwood, Mutrie, G.Roberts	2,730

FINAL LEAGUE POSITION: 2nd in Division Four — Promoted

Appearances
Sub Appearan
Goals

FA Cup

1	Nov	20	(h)	Sheffield U	D	1-1	Kenworthy (og)	9,152
R		23	(a)	Sheffield U	L	0-2		12,232

Appearances
Sub Appearan
Goals

League Cup

1	Aug	31	(a)	Sheffield U	L	1-3	Whitehurst	12,23
	Sep	14	(h)	Sheffield U	W	1-0	Flounders	7,11

Appearances
Sub Appearan
Goals

Norman A	Swann G	Thompson N	Richards S	Skipper P	Booth D	Marwood B	Askew W	Whitehurst W	Mutrie L	Roberts G	Flounders A	McNeil R	Roberts D	McClaren S	Davies J	Woof W	Davis I	Hawley J	Hughes E	
1	2	3	4	5	6	7	8*	9	10	11	12									1
1		3		5	6	7		12	10	11	9*	2	4	8						2
1				5	6	7	3	9	10	11	12	2	4	8*						3
1				5	6	7	3	9	10	11		2	4	8						4
				5	6		3	9	10	11	7	2	4	8	1					5
1				5	6	7	3	9		11	10	2	4	8						6
1				5	6	7	3	9		11	10	2	4	8						7
1				5	6	7	3	9	10	11		2	4	8						8
1				5	6	7	3	9	10	11		2	4	8						9
1				5	6	7	3	9	10	11		2	4	8						10
1	6			5		7	3	9	10*	11	12	2	4	8						11
1	6		4	5		7	3	9		11	10*	2		8		12				12
1	3		4	5		7			10	11		2		8		9	6			13
1				5	3	7	6*	12	10	11		2	4	8		9				14
1				5	3	7		12	10*	11		2	4	8		9	6			15
1	6			5	3	7		9	10	11		2	4	8						16
				5	6	7	3	9	10	11		2	4	8	1					17
	12			5	6	7	3		10	11		2	4	8*	1			9		18
1				5	6	7	3			11	9	2	4	8				10		19
1	2			5	6	7	3		10	11	9		4	8						20
1	2			5	6		3		10	11	9		4	8				7		21
1	2			5	6	7	3	9	10	11			4				8			22
1	2			5	6	7	3	9	10	11			4	8						23
	2			5	6	7	3	9*	10	11	12		4	8	1					24
	2			5	6	7	3*	9	10	11		12	4	8	1					25
	2			5	6	7	3	9*	10	11		12	4	8	1					26
	8	3		5	6	7			10	11	9	2	4		1					27
1				5	6	7	3		10*	11	9	2	4			12	8			28
1				5	6	7	3		10	11	9	2	4	8						29
1	7			5	6		3	9	10		12	2	4	8		11*				30
1				5	6		3	9	10			2	4	8		11	7			31
1				5	6	7	3	9*	10	11		2	4	8			12			32
1				5	6		3		10	11	9	2	4	8			7			33
1	6			5			3	12	10	11	9	2	4	8*			7			34
1				5	6	7	3	12	10	11	9*	2	4	8						35
1	12			5	6	7	3	8	10	11	9*	2	4							36
1				5	6	7	3	9	10	11		2	4						8	37
1		3		5	6	7		9	10	11			4	8					2	38
1	6	3		5		7			10	11			4	8		9			2	39
1	6			5		7	3	12	10*	11			4	8		9			2	40
1	6	3		5		7		10		11	12		4	8		9*			2	41
1	6	3		5		7		10		11		12	4	8		9			2*	42
1	3			5		7	6	12	10	11	9*		4	8					2	43
	3	6		5		7		9	10	11			4	8	1				2	44
	3			5		7	6	12	10*	11	9		4	8	1				2	45
	3			5		7	6	9	10	11		2	4	8	1					46
36	23	8	3	46	34	40	36	28	40	44	17	30	43	40	10	9	7	3	9	
	2							8			6	3				2	1			
				4		19	6	3	12	6	13		2	4		3		1		

2 own-goals

1	6			5	3	7		9	10	11		2	4	8						1
1				5	6	7	3	9	10	11		2	4	8						R
2	1			2	2	2	1	2	2	2		2	2	2						

1 own-goal

1	2			5	6	7		9	10	11	12	3	4	8*						1
				5	6		3	9	10	11	7	2	4	8	1					
1	1			2	2	1	1	2	2	2	1	2	2	2	1					
											1									
								1			1									

1983-84

1	Aug	27	(h)	Burnley	W 4-1	Whitehurst 2, Massey 2	8,394
2	Sep	3	(a)	Gillingham	W 2-1	Marwood, Mutrie	2,919
3		7	(a)	Bradford C	D 0-0		3,510
4		10	(h)	Millwall	W 5-0	Mutrie 2, Marwood, G.Roberts, McNeil	6,357
5		17	(a)	Preston NE	D 0-0		6,661
6		24	(h)	Lincoln C	W 2-0	Whitehurst 2	7,523
7		27	(h)	Wimbledon	W 1-0	Whitehurst	8,133
8	Oct	1	(a)	Wigan A	D 1-1	Flounders	4,858
9		8	(h)	Sheffield U	W 4-1	Marwood 2, McClaren, Mutrie	14,775
10		15	(a)	Brentford	D 1-1	Mutrie	4,258
11		18	(a)	Bolton W	D 0-0		6,397
12		22	(h)	Plymouth A	L 1-2	McClaren	7,707
13		29	(a)	Oxford U	D 1-1	Marwood	8,064
14	Nov	1	(h)	Walsall	D 2-2	Marwood, Askew	7,573
15		5	(a)	Bournemouth	W 3-2	Whitehurst, Marwood, Hollifield	4,644
16		12	(h)	Newport C	D 0-0		7,235
17		26	(h)	Orient	W 2-1	Whitehurst 2	6,557
18	Dec	3	(a)	Exeter C	L 1-2	McNeil	3,099
19		17	(a)	Bristol R	W 3-1	G.Roberts 2, Marwood	5,653
20		26	(h)	Scunthorpe U	W 1-0	Massey	15,461
21		27	(a)	Rotherham U	W 1-0	Skipper	6,298
22		31	(h)	Port Vale	W 1-0	G.Roberts	8,736
23	Jan	2	(a)	Southend U	D 2-2	Flounders 2	3,014
24		28	(a)	Millwall	L 0-1		3,996
25	Feb	4	(h)	Wigan A	W 1-0	Marwood	6,341
26		11	(a)	Lincoln C	W 3-1	Swann 2, Marwood	5,370
27		25	(a)	Plymouth A	L 0-2		10,023
28		28	(h)	Oxford U	L 0-1		11,192
29	Mar	3	(h)	Bolton W	D 1-1	D.Roberts	6,569
30		6	(h)	Bournemouth	W 3-1	Flounders, Taylor, McNeil	6,897
31		10	(a)	Newport C	D 1-1	G.Roberts	2,813
32		17	(a)	Sheffield U	D 2-2	Marwood, McClaren	15,374
33		24	(h)	Brentford	W 2-0	Marwood, D.Roberts	5,572
34		27	(a)	Walsall	L 1-2	Flounders	6,851
35		31	(h)	Bradford C	W 1-0	G.Roberts	6,943
36	Apr	7	(a)	Wimbledon	W 4-1	Flounders, G.Roberts, Marwood, McEwan	4,495
37		10	(h)	Preston NE	W 3-0	Flounders, Taylor, G.Roberts	6,834
38		14	(h)	Exeter C	W 1-0	Taylor	6,889
39		17	(h)	Gillingham	D 0-0		7,779
40		21	(a)	Scunthorpe U	L 0-2		8,286
41		23	(h)	Rotherham U	W 5-0	Flounders 2, Whitehurst, Marwood, Johnson (og)	7,712
42		28	(a)	Orient	L 1-3	Whitehurst	3,020
43	Mah	5	(h)	Southend U	W 2-1	Massey, G.Roberts	5,900
44		7	(a)	Port Vale	L 0-1		3,958
45		12	(h)	Bristol R	D 0-0		9,857
46		15	(a)	Burnley	W 2-0	Marwood 2	8,051

FINAL LEAGUE POSITION: 4th in Division Three

Appearances
Sub Appearanc
Goals

FA Cup

1	Nov	19	(a)	Penrith	W 2-0	Whitehurst, G.Roberts	1,828
2	Dec	10	(a)	Rotherham U	L 1-2	Flounders	6,885

Appearances
Sub Appearanc
Goals

League Cup

1	Aug	30	(h)	Lincoln C	D 0-0		6,396
	Sep	14	(a)	Lincoln C	L 1-3*	Skipper	4,630

*After extra-time

Appearances
Sub Appearanc
Goals

Norman A	McNeil R	Wassell K	Roberts D	Skipper P	Booth D	Marwood B	McClaren S	Whitehurst W	Massey S	Roberts G	Mutrie L	Hollifield M	Askew W	Swann G	Flounders A	Gill G	Saville A	Taylor A	McEwan S	Cockin N	
1	2	3	4	5	6*	7	8	9	10	11	12										1
1	2		4	5		7		9	10	11	8	3	6								2
1	2		4	5		7		9		11	10	3	6	8							3
1	2		4	5		7		9*	12	11	10	3	6	8							4
1	2		4	5		7		9		11	10*	3	6	8	12						5
1	2		4	5		7	12	9		11*	10	3	6	8							6
1	2		4	5		7	8	9			10	3	6	11							7
1	2		4	5		7	8	9				3	6	11	10						8
1	2		4	5		7	8	9			10	3	6	11							9
1	2		4	5		7	8	9			10	3*	6	11	12						10
1	2		4	5		7	8				10	3	6	11	9						11
1	2		4	5		7	8	9			10	3	6	11*	12						12
1	2		4	5		7	8	9		12		3	6	11	10*						13
1	2		4	5		7	8	9		11		3	6		10						14
1	2		4	5		7	8	9		11		3	12	6*	10						15
1	2		4	5	6	7	8	9		11	10	3									16
1	2		4	5	6	7	12	9	10	11		3	8*								17
1	2		4	5	6	7	8	9	10	11				3							18
1	2			5	6	7	8	9		11		3		4	10						19
1	2			5	6		8	9	10	11		3		4	7						20
1	2			5	6		8	9	10*	11		3		4	7	12					21
1	2			5	6	7	8			11		3		4	9		10				22
1	2			5	6	7	8		10	11		3		4	9						23
1	2			5	6	7	12	9	4*	11			8	3	10						24
1	2			5	6	7	8	9		11		3		4				10			25
1	2			5	6	7	8	9				3	11	4				10			26
1	2			5	6	7	8	9		11		3		4				10			27
1	2			5	6	7	8	9		11		3		4	12			10*			28
1	2		4	5		7	8	9		11			6	3	10						29
1	2		4	5			8	9		11			6	3	10			7			30
1	2		4	5		7			10*	11			6	3	9			12	8		31
1	2		4	5		7	9		12	11			6*	3				10	8		32
1	2		4	5		7	8	9*		11			12	3				10	6		33
1	2		4	5		7	8			11			12	3	9			10*	6		34
1	2			5		7	8			11		4	10	3	9				6		35
1	2		12	5		7*	8			11		3	10	6	9				4		36
1	2			5			8			11		3	10	6	9			7	4		37
1	2			5			8	12		11		3	10	6	9			7*	4		38
1	2		11	5			8	9				3*	10	6	12			7	4		39
1	2			5		7	8*	11		9		3	12	6	10				4		40
1	2		3	5		7		9		11			10	6	8				4		41
1	2		3	5		7*	12	9		11			10	6	8				4		42
1	2			5		7	8	9	10	11			6	3					4		43
1	2		4	5		7	8	9	10*	11				3	12				6		44
1	2			5			8	9		11		4	10*	3	12			7	6		45
1	2			5		7	8	9		11		4		3	12			10*	6		46
46	46	1	28	46	14	39	36	36	11	37	11	33	29	41	22		1	13	16		
			1				4	1	2	1	1		4		8	1		1			
	3		2	1		16	3	10	4	9	5	1	1	2	9			3	1		

1 own-goal

Norman A	McNeil R	Wassell K	Roberts D	Skipper P	Booth D	Marwood B	McClaren S	Whitehurst W	Massey S	Roberts G	Mutrie L	Hollifield M	Askew W	Swann G	Flounders A	Gill G	Saville A	Taylor A	McEwan S	Cockin N	
1	2		4	5	6	7		9		11		3	8		10						1
1	2			5	3	7	8	9		11		6	4		10						2
2	2		1	2	2	2	1	2		2		2	2		2						
								1		1					1						

Norman A	McNeil R	Wassell K	Roberts D	Skipper P	Booth D	Marwood B	McClaren S	Whitehurst W	Massey S	Roberts G	Mutrie L	Hollifield M	Askew W	Swann G	Flounders A	Gill G	Saville A	Taylor A	McEwan S	Cockin N	
1	2		4	5		7		9	10	11	12	3		8*						6	1
1	2		4	5		7		9	12	11	10	3	6	8*							
2	2		2	2		2		2	1	2	1	2	1	2						1	
									1		1										
				1																	

1984-85

1	Aug	25	(a)	Lincoln C	D 0-0		4,139
2	Sep	1	(h)	Bournemouth	W 3-0	Whitehurst, Massey, Ring	4,828
3		8	(a)	Bolton W	D 0-0		5,403
4		15	(h)	Preston NE	L 1-2	McEwan	5,742
5		18	(h)	Gillingham	W 2-0	Askew 2	5,240
6		22	(a)	Burnley	D 1-1	McEwan	5,526
7		29	(h)	Reading	D 0-0		5,366
8	Oct	3	(a)	Bradford C	L 0-2		4,446
9		6	(a)	Plymouth A	W 1-0	Flounders	5,505
10		13	(h)	Doncaster R	W 3-2	Flounders, McEwan, Skipper	7,071
11		20	(a)	Derby C	L 1-3	Skipper	13,422
12		23	(h)	Swansea C	W 4-1	Whitehurst 2, Skipper, G.Roberts	5,306
13		27	(a)	Bristol R	D 1-1	Whitehurst	5,438
14	Nov	3	(h)	Rotherham U	D 0-0		6,137
15		6	(h)	Cambridge U	W 2-1	Flounders, McClaren	5,472
16		10	(a)	Orient	W 5-4	Flounders 2, Askew, Massey, McEwan	2,365
17		24	(h)	Newport C	W 2-0	Whitehurst, McClaren	4,809
18	Dec	1	(a)	Wigan A	D 1-1	Askew	3,743
19		15	(h)	Walsall	W 1-0	Whitehurst	6,075
20		18	(a)	Millwall	D 2-2	Swann, Smith (og)	5,001
21		22	(h)	Brentford	W 4-0	Whitehurst 2, McClaren, Askew	6,354
22		29	(a)	York C	W 2-1	Flounders, Askew	9,565
23	Jan	1	(h)	Bristol C	W 2-1	Whitehurst, McEwan	9,753
24		12	(a)	Bournemouth	D 1-1	Flounders	4,454
25	Feb	2	(a)	Reading	L 2-4	Skipper, Hicks (og)	4,612
26		9	(h)	Burnley	W 2-0	Whitehurst, Massey	6,478
27		16	(h)	Bradford C	L 0-2		14,752
28		23	(a)	Rotherham U	D 1-1	Whitehurst	7,068
29		26	(a)	Gillingham	L 0-1		6,051
30	Mar	2	(h)	Bristol R	W 2-0	Whitehurst, Flounders	6,380
31		5	(a)	Swansea C	W 2-0	McClaren, Williams	4,104
32		9	(h)	Derby C	W 3-2	Whitehurst 2, Flounders	9,782
33		16	(a)	Doncaster R	W 2-1	Flounders, Williams	5,942
34		19	(h)	Lincoln C	W 1-0	Williams	7,029
35		23	(h)	Plymouth A	D 2-2	Flounders, G.Roberts	6,947
36		30	(a)	Cambridge U	W 3-1	Whitehurst, Saville, McEwan	2,137
37	Apr	2	(h)	Bolton W	D 2-2	Whitehurst, McEwan	7,863
38		6	(h)	Millwall	W 2-1	Flounders, McEwan	10,426
39		8	(a)	Bristol C	L 0-2		11,964
40		13	(h)	Orient	W 5-1	Whitehurst 3, Flounders, McEwan	7,434
41		20	(a)	Newport C	W 1-0	Swann	1,885
42		23	(a)	Preston NE	W 4-1	Flounders, Massey, G.Roberts, McEwan	4,635
43		27	(h)	Wigan A	W 3-1	Whitehurst, McEwan, Massey	8,620
44	May	4	(a)	Walsall	W 1-0	Skipper	4,809
45		6	(h)	York C	L 0-2		15,795
46		11	(a)	Brentford	L 1-2	Swann	4,309

FINAL LEAGUE POSITION: 3rd in Division Three — Promoted

Appearances
Sub Appearances
Goals

FA Cup

1	Nov	17	(h)	Bolton W	W 2-1	Massey, Flounders	6,424
2	Dec	8	(a)	Tranmere R	W 3-0	Ring, McClaren, Skipper	4,269
3	Jan	5	(a)	Brighton & HA	L 0-1		11,681

Appearances
Sub Appearances
Goals

League Cup

1	Aug	29	(a)	Lincoln C	W 2-0	Whitehurst, McEwan	3,465
	Sep	4	(h)	Lincoln C	W 4-1	Whitehurst, Massey, Ring, Strodder (og)	4,042
2		25	(a)	Southampton	L 2-3	D.Roberts, G.Roberts	11,824
	Oct	9	(h)	Southampton	D 2-2	Whitehurst, Flounders	14,613

Appearances
Sub Appearances
Goals

Norman A	Roberts D	Pearson L	Horton B	Skipper P	McEwan S	Massey S	McClaren S	Whitehurst W	Askew W	Roberts G	Ring M	Booth D	Flounders A	Swann G	McNeil R	Williams N	Brentano S	Hollifield M	Jobson R	Saville A	
1	2	3	4	5	6	7	8	9	10	11											1
1	2	3		5	6	7	4	9	10*	11	8	12									2
1	2	3	11	5	6	7	4	9	10		8										3
1	2	3		5	6	7	4	9	10	11	8*		12								4
1	2	3	8	5	6	7	4	9*	10	11	12										5
1	2	3	8	5	6	7	4		10	11	9*		12								6
1	2	3	8	5	6	7*	4		10	11	9		12								7
1	2	3	8	5	6		4	9	10	11			7								8
1	2	3	8	5	6		4	9	10	11			7								9
1	2	3		5	6		4	9	10	11			7	8							10
1	2	3	4	5	6			9	10		11		7	8							11
1		3	4	5	6			9	10	11			7	8	2						12
1		3	4	5	6	11		9	10				7	8	2						13
1			4	5	6		8	9	10	11			7	3	2						14
1			4	5	6	11	8	9	10				7	3	2						15
1		12	4	5	6	11	8	9	10				7	3*	2						16
1		3	4	5	6	11	8	9	10				7		2						17
1		3	4	5	6	11	8	9	10				7*	12	2						18
1		3	4	5	6	11*	8	9	10		7				2	12					19
1		3		5	6		8	9	10		11		7	4	2						20
1		3		5	6		8	9	10		11*		7	4	2	12					21
1		3		5	6		8	9	10		11*		7	4	2	12					22
1		3		5	6		8	9*	10		11		7	4	2	12					23
1		3		5	6	9	8		10*		11		7	4	2	12					24
1		3	4	5	6*	12	8	9	10				7			11	2				25
1			4	5		12	8	9	10		11		7		2			3	6		26
1			4*	5		11	8	9	10	12			7		2			3	6		27
1			4	5		7	8	9	10	11				2				3	6		28
1				5		7*	8	9	10	11			12	2		4		3	6		29
1				5		12	8	9	10	11			7*	2	6	4		3			30
1				5			8	9	10	11			7	2	6	4		3			31
1				5			8	9	10	11			7	2	6	4*		3	12		32
1				5			8		10	11			7	6	2	4		3		9	33
1				5		12	8*	9	10	11			7	6	2	4		3			34
1				5	6	12	8	9	10	11			7	2		4*		3			35
1				5	6			9	10	11				8	2	4		3		7	36
1				5	6		8	9	10				12	11	2	4		3		7*	37
1		3		5	6		8	9	10	11			7	2		4					38
1		3		5	6		8	9	10				7	2		4*			11	12	39
1		3		5	6	4	8	9	10	11	12		7*	2							40
1		3	4	5	6	9			10	11			7	8	2						41
1		3	4	5	6	9			10	11			7	8	2						42
1		3		5	6	4	8	9	10	11			7	2							43
1		3		5	6	4	8	9	10	11			7	2							44
1		3*		5	6	4	8	9	10	11			7	2					12		45
1				5	6	12	8	9	10	11			7	4			2*		3		46
46	11	30	22	46	37	23	40	40	46	28	13		34	31	24	12	2	12	6	3	
		1				6				1	2	1	5	1		5			2	1	
				5	11	5	4	20	6	3	1		14	3		3				1	

2 own-goals

1		3	4	5	6	11	8	9	10		12		7*		2						1
1		3	4	5	6	11	8		10		9		7		2						2
1		3		5	6		8		10		11		7	4	2	9					3
3		3	2	3	3	2	3	1	3		2		3	1	3	1					
											1										
				1		1	1				1		1								

1	2	3		5	6	7	8	9	10	11		4									1
1	2	3		5	6	7	4	9	10	11	8										
1	2	3	8	5	6	7	4		10	11	9*			12							2
1	2	3	8*	5	6		4	9	10	11	12		7								
4	4	4	2	4	4	3	4	3	4	4	2	1	1								
											1			1							
	1				1	1		3		1	1		1								

1 own-goal

1985-86

1	Aug	17	(h)	Portsmouth	D	2-2	Whitehurst, Bunn	8,221
2		24	(a)	Leeds U	D	1-1	Jobson	16,731
3		26	(h)	Blackburn R	D	2-2	Bunn, Rathbone (og)	7,288
4		31	(a)	Oldham A	L	1-3	Whitehurst	4,500
5	Sep	7	(h)	Middlesbrough	D	0-0		7,710
6		14	(a)	Bradford C	L	2-4	Swann, McEwan	4,930
7		17	(h)	Millwall	W	3-0	Bunn 2, McEwan	6,021
8		21	(h)	Carlisle U	W	4-0	Whitehurst, Roberts, Swann, Doyle	6,117
9		28	(a)	Norwich C	L	0-2		11,945
10	Oct	1	(a)	Crystal P	W	2-0	Bunn, McEwan	5,226
11		5	(h)	Stoke C	L	0-2		6,890
12		12	(a)	Sunderland	D	1-1	Whitehurst	16,613
13		19	(h)	Huddersfield T	W	3-1	Whitehurst 2, Williams	8,128
14		26	(a)	Shrewsbury T	D	0-0		3,587
15	Nov	2	(a)	Sheffield U	L	1-3	Skipper	13,272
16		9	(h)	Fulham	W	5-0	McEwan 2, Whitehurst, Roberts, Bunn	5,344
17		16	(a)	Charlton A	W	2-1	Bunn 2	4,140
18		23	(h)	Wimbledon	D	1-1	McEwan	6,576
19		30	(a)	Brighton & HA	L	1-3	Saville	8,496
20	Dec	7	(h)	Crystal P	L	1-2	Bunn	6,058
21		14	(a)	Portsmouth	D	1-1	McEwan	13,371
22		22	(h)	Leeds U	W	2-1	Bunn, Jobson	11,852
23		26	(h)	Grimsby T	W	2-0	Askew, Jobson	12,824
24		28	(a)	Millwall	L	0-5		3,783
25	Jan	1	(a)	Barnsley	W	4-1	Ring, Doyle, McEwan, Jobson	8,363
26		11	(h)	Bradford C	W	1-0	Jobson	9,333
27		18	(h)	Oldham A	W	4-2	Flounders 2, Jobson 2	6,909
28	Feb	1	(a)	Blackburn R	D	2-2	Bunn, McEwan	5,414
29		25	(a)	Huddersfield T	L	1-2	Roberts	4,518
30	Mar	4	(h)	Shrewsbury T	W	4-3	Flounders 3, Bunn	6,253
31		8	(a)	Stoke C	W	1-0	McEwan	9,112
32		11	(a)	Carlisle U	L	1-2	Flounders	3,248
33		15	(h)	Sunderland	D	1-1	Roberts	9,295
34		22	(a)	Middlesbrough	W	2-1	Flounders, Bunn	6,227
35		29	(h)	Barnsley	L	0-1		7,903
36	Apr	1	(a)	Grimsby T	W	1-0	Flounders	9,121
37		5	(h)	Sheffield U	D	0-0		9,645
38		12	(a)	Fulham	D	1-1	Bunn	2,799
39		19	(h)	Charlton A	D	1-1	Askew	7,139
40		26	(a)	Wimbledon	L	1-3	Flounders	5,171
41		29	(h)	Norwich C	W	1-0	Williams	6,146
42	May	2	(h)	Brighton & HA	W	2-0	Williams, Flounders	5,459

FINAL LEAGUE POSITION: 6th in Division Two

Appearances
Sub Appearanc
Goals

FA Cup

3	Jan	4	(h)	Plymouth A	D	2-2	Flounders 2	6,776
R		7	(a)	Plymouth A	W	1-0	Roberts	13,940
4		25	(h)	Brighton & HA	L	2-3	Roberts, McEwan	12,228

Appearances
Sub Appearanc
Goals

League Cup

1	Aug	20	(a)	Halifax T	D	1-1	Flounders	820
	Sep	3	(h)	Halifax T	W	3-0	Bunn 2, Whitehurst	3,299
2		24	(a)	Queen's Park R	L	0-3		7,021
	Oct	8	(h)	Queen's Park R	L	1-5	Whitehurst	4,287

Appearances
Sub Appearanc
Goals

Norman A	Jobson R	Pearson L	Swann G	Skipper P	McEwan S	Williams N	Bunn F	Whitehurst W	Askew W	Roberts G	Flounders A	Doyle R	Ring M	Horton B	Brentano S	Saville A	Parker G	Heard P	Brown N	
1	2	3	4	5	6	7	8	9	10	11										1
1	2	3	4	5	6	7	8	9	10	11										2
1	2	3	4	5	6	7	8	9	10	11										3
1	2	3	7	5	6		8	9	10*	11	12	4								4
1	2	3	7*	5	6		8	9	10	11		4	12							5
1	2	3	12	5	6		8	9	10*	11		4	7							6
1	2	3	7	5	6		8	9		11		4		10						7
1	2	3	7	5	6		8	9		11		4		10						8
1	2	3	7*	5	6		8	9		11		4		10	12					9
1	2	3	7	5	6		8	9			11	4		10						10
1	2	3*	7	5	6		8	9		11	12	4		10						11
1	2		3		6	7	8*	9	10	11		4		5		12				12
1	5		3		6	7	8	9	10	11		4			2					13
1	5		3	12	6	7	8	9	10	11*		4			2					14
1	2		3	5	6	7	8	9	10*	11	12	4								15
1	2		3	5	6	7	8	9	10	11*		4				12				16
1	2		3	5	6	7	8	9	10			4			11					17
1			3	5	6	7	8	9	10	11		4			2					18
1	2			5	6	7	8		10		11*	4	12		3	9				19
1	2			5	6	7*	8		10	11		4	12		3	9				20
1	2		3	5	6	7*	8		10	11	12	4				9				21
1	2		3	5	6	7	8		10	11		4	12			9*				22
1	2		3	5	6	7	8		10	11		4	9							23
1	2		3	5	6	7*	8		10		12	4	9		11					24
1	2		3	5	6		8		10		9	4	7	11						25
1	2		3	5	6		8		10	11	9	4		7						26
1	2		3	5	6		8		10	11	9	4		7						27
1	2*		3	5	6		8		10	11	9	4	12	7						28
1		2	3	5	6		8		10	11	9	4					7			29
1		3	2	5	6		8		10	11	9	4				12	7*			30
1		3	2	5	6		8		10	11	9	4					7			31
1		3	2	5	6		8		10	11	9	4					7			32
1	2	3		5	6		8		10	11	9	4					7			33
1	2*	3	12	5	6		8		10	11	9	4					7			34
1		3*	2	5	6		8		10	11	9	4					7	12		35
1	2		3	5	6		8			11	9	4					7	10		36
1	2		3	5	6		8		12	11	9	4					7*	10		37
1	2		3	5	6		8			11	9*	4					7	10	12	38
1	2		3	5	6		8		11		9	4					7	10		39
1	2		3	5	6	12	8		11*		9	4					7	10		40
1	2	11	3	5	6	7	8				9*	4				12		10		41
1	2	11	3*	5	6	7	8				9	4				12		10		42
42	36	20	37	39	42	18	42	18	32	33	20	39	4	10	7	4	12	7		
			2	1		1			1		5		5		1	5		1	1	
	7		2	1	10	3	14	7	2	4	10	2	1			1				

1 own-goal

Norman A	Jobson R	Pearson L	Swann G	Skipper P	McEwan S	Williams N	Bunn F	Whitehurst W	Askew W	Roberts G	Flounders A	Doyle R	Ring M	Horton B	Brentano S	Saville A	Parker G	Heard P	Brown N	
1	2		3	5	6		8		10	11	9	4	7							3
1	2		3	5	6		8		10	11	9	4		7						R
1	2		3	5	6		8		10	11	9	4		7						4
3	3		3	3	3		3		3	3	3	3	1	2						
					1					2	2									

Norman A	Jobson R	Pearson L	Swann G	Skipper P	McEwan S	Williams N	Bunn F	Whitehurst W	Askew W	Roberts G	Flounders A	Doyle R	Ring M	Horton B	Brentano S	Saville A	Parker G	Heard P	Brown N	
1	2	3	4	5	6	7	8		10	11	9									1
1	2	3	7	5	6		8	9	10*	11		4	12							
1	2	3	7	5	6		8*	9		11	12	4		10						2
1	2		3	5	6	7	8	9	10	11		4								
4	4	3	4	4	4	2	4	3	3	4	1	3		1						
											1		1							
							2	2			1									

1986-87

1	Aug	23	(h)	West Brom A	W 2-0	Flounders, Roberts	8,658
2		26	(a)	Millwall	W 1-0	Bunn	4,300
3		30	(a)	Oldham A	D 0-0		5,104
4	Sep	2	(h)	Portsmouth	L 0-2		7,706
5		6	(h)	Plymouth A	L 0-3		6,451
6		13	(a)	Sunderland	L 0-1		12,911
7		20	(h)	Birmingham C	W 3-2	Roberts 2, Skipper	6,851
8		27	(a)	Leeds U	L 0-3		13,542
9	Oct	4	(h)	Ipswich T	W 2-1	Saville 2	6,872
10		11	(a)	Derby C	D 1-1	Pratley (og)	12,353
11		18	(h)	Reading	L 0-2		5,705
12		25	(a)	Huddersfield T	W 3-1	Saville, Flounders, Skipper	5,406
13	Nov	1	(a)	Brighton & HA	L 1-2	Jobson	7,318
14		8	(h)	Stoke C	L 0-4		5,252
15		15	(a)	Blackburn R	W 2-0	Saville, Corkain	4,149
16		22	(h)	Bradford C	W 2-1	McEwan, Skipper	6,423
17		29	(a)	Shrewsbury T	L 0-3		2,869
18	Dec	6	(h)	Grimsby T	D 1-1	McEwan	7,217
19		13	(a)	Crystal P	L 1-5	Roberts	4,839
20		26	(a)	Sheffield U	L 2-4	Flounders, Jobson	11,296
21		27	(h)	Blackburn R	D 0-0		5,789
22	Jan	1	(h)	Barnsley	L 3-4	Bunn, Roberts, McEwan	4,879
23		3	(a)	Plymouth A	L 0-4		12,064
24		24	(a)	West Brom A	D 1-1	Jobson	6,707
25	Feb	7	(h)	Oldham A	W 1-0	Saville	5,651
26		14	(a)	Portsmouth	L 0-1		11,098
27		28	(a)	Birmingham C	D 0-0		6,858
28	Mar	3	(h)	Sunderland	W 1-0	Saville	5,713
29		7	(h)	Huddersfield T	D 0-0		5,872
30		14	(a)	Reading	L 0-1		5,493
31		21	(h)	Derby C	D 1-1	Saville	9,684
32		28	(a)	Ipswich T	D 0-0		10,340
33	Apr	4	(a)	Stoke C	D 1-1	Bunn	8,146
34		8	(h)	Leeds U	D 0-0		9,351
35		14	(h)	Millwall	W 2-1	Bunn, Jobson	5,327
36		18	(a)	Barnsley	D 1-1	Skipper	5,607
37		20	(h)	Sheffield U	D 0-0		8,765
38		25	(a)	Bradford C	L 0-2		10,390
39		28	(h)	Brighton & HA	W 1-0	Jobson	5,219
40	May	2	(h)	Shrewsbury T	W 3-0	Dyer 2, Heard	5,114
41		5	(a)	Grimsby T	D 2-2	Saville 2	6,757
42		9	(h)	Crystal P	W 3-0	Dyer 2, Williams	7,656

FINAL LEAGUE POSITION: 14th in Division Two

Appearances
Sub Appearances
Goals

FA Cup

3	Jan	31	(a)	Shrewsbury T	W 2-1	Bunn, Saville	4,130
4	Feb	3	(a)	Swansea T	W 1-0	Jobson	8,853
5		21	(a)	Wigan A	L 0-3		11,453

Appearances
Sub Appearances
Goals

League Cup

2	Sep	23	(h)	Grimsby T	W 1-0	Saville	5,115
	Oct	7	(a)	Grimsby T	D 1-1	McEwan	6,192
3		28	(a)	Shrewsbury T	L 0-1		3,077

Appearances
Sub Appearances
Goals

Norman A	Jobson R	Swann G	Heard P	Skipper P	McEwan S	Parker G	Bunn F	Flounders A	Daniel R	Roberts G	Williams N	Askew W	Saville A	Ablett G	Horton B	Pearson L	Curran E	Corkain S	Buckley N	Brentano S	Palmer C	Dyer A	Doyle R	Payton A	
1	2	3	4	5	6	7	8	9	10*	11	12														1
1	2	3	4	5	6*	7	8	9	10	11	12														2
1	2	3	4	5*		7	8	9		11	6	10	12												3
1	2	3	4	5		7	8	9*		11	6	10	12												4
1	2	3	4	5		7	8	9		11	6	10*	12												5
1	2	6	4	5		7	8			11	12	10*	9	3											6
1	2	6	4	5		7	8			11			9	3	10										7
1	2	6	4	5		7		9*		11	12		8	3	10										8
1			4	5	6	7		9		11	2		8	3	10										9
1		10	4	5	6	7*		12		11	2		8	3			9								10
1	4		3*	5	6			9		11	2	12	8			10	7								11
1	4		3	5	6	12		8		11	2	10	9				7*								12
1	4		3		6	5	12	9		11	2	10	8				7*								13
1	2		3	5*	6	4	8	12		11	7	10	9												14
1	2			5	6	4		9		11	7		8			3		10							15
1	2			5	6	4	12	9		11	7		8			3*		10							16
1	2		3	5	6	4	12	9		11	7		8*					10							17
1	2		3	5	6	4	8	9		11					7			10							18
1	2		3	5	6	4	8	9		11					7			10							19
1	2		3	5	6	4*	8	12		11	7	10	9												20
1	2			5	6	4	8	9	10*	11	7		12			3									21
1	2			5	6	4	8	9	10	11	7		12			3*									22
1	10		3	5		4	8	9		11	2		12		7*				6						23
1	4		9	5	6		8	12		11	7	10*				3				2					24
1	4		6	5			8	12		11*	7	10	9			3				2					25
1	4			5		6	8	12			7	10*	9			3					2	11			26
1	4		3	5		6					7	10	9								2	11	8		27
1	4		3	5		7	8					10	9								2	11	6		28
1	4		3	5		7	8*			12		10	9								2	11	6		29
1	4		3	5		7*	12			11		10	9								2	8	6		30
1	4		3	5		6	8			11		10	9								2	7			31
1	4		3	5		6	8			11		10	9								2	7			32
1	4		3	5		6*	8			11		10	9								2	7		12	33
1	4		3	5		6	8			11		10	9								2	7			34
1	4		3	5		6	8			11		10	9								2	7			35
1	4		3	5		6	8			11		10	9								2	7			36
1	4		3	5		6	8*			11	12	10	9								2	7			37
1	4*		3	5		6	8		10	11	12		9								2	7			38
1	4		3	5		6	8		11		7	10									2	9			39
1	4		3	5		6*	8		11		7	10									2	9		12	40
1	4		3	5		6*	8		11		7	10	12								2	9			41
1	4		3	5			6		11		7	10	8								2	9			42
42	40	9	37	41	17	37	31	18	9	34	24	26	28	5	6	8	4	5	1	2	17	17	4		
						1	4	6		1	6	1	7											2	
	5		1	4	3		4	3		5	1		9					1				4			

1 own-goal

Norman A	Jobson R	Swann G	Heard P	Skipper P	McEwan S	Parker G	Bunn F	Flounders A	Daniel R	Roberts G	Williams N	Askew W	Saville A	Ablett G	Horton B	Pearson L	Curran E	Corkain S	Buckley N	Brentano S	Palmer C	Dyer A	Doyle R	Payton A	
1	4		6	5			8	9			7	10	11			3				2					3
1	4		6	5			8	9			7	10	11			3				2					4
1	4			5		6		12		11	7	10*	9			3					2	8			5
3	3		2	3		1	2	2		1	3	3	3			3				2	1	1			
								1																	
	1						1						1												

Norman A	Jobson R	Swann G	Heard P	Skipper P	McEwan S	Parker G	Bunn F	Flounders A	Daniel R	Roberts G	Williams N	Askew W	Saville A	Ablett G	Horton B	Pearson L	Curran E	Corkain S	Buckley N	Brentano S	Palmer C	Dyer A	Doyle R	Payton A	
1	2	6	4	5		7		9		11	3		8		10										2
1		10	4	5	6	7		9		11	2		8			3									
1	4		3		6	5	12	9		11	2	10	8				7*								3
3	2	2	3	2	2	3		3		3	3	1	3		1	1	1								
							1																		
					1								1												

1987-88

1	Aug	15	(h)	Blackburn R	D 2-2	Bunn, Skipper	6,462
2		18	(a)	Stoke C	D 1-1	Parker	9,139
3		22	(a)	Crystal P	D 2-2	Parker, Bunn	6,688
4		29	(h)	Aston Villa	W 2-1	Heard, Dyer	8,315
5		31	(a)	Swindon T	D 0-0		9,600
6	Sep	5	(h)	Bournemouth	W 2-1	Dyer, Askew	5,807
7		12	(a)	Leeds U	W 2-0	Dyer, Parker	18,205
8		15	(h)	Shrewsbury T	D 1-1	Roberts	7,949
9		19	(h)	Oldham A	W 1-0	Skipper	7,183
10		29	(h)	Manchester C	W 3-1	Bunn 2, Parker	9,650
11	Oct	3	(a)	Sheffield U	L 1-2	Bunn	10,446
12		10	(h)	Ipswich T	W 1-0	Thompson	6,962
13		17	(a)	Barnsley	W 3-1	Saville, Heard, Askew	7,310
14		20	(a)	Huddersfield T	W 2-0	Thompson, Parker	8,033
15		24	(h)	Leicester C	D 2-2	Roberts, Williams	8,826
16		31	(a)	Plymouth A	L 1-3	Saville	8,550
17	Nov	3	(h)	Bradford C	D 0-0		15,443
18		7	(h)	Birmingham C	W 2-0	Williams, Overson (og)	7,909
19		14	(a)	Middlesbrough	L 0-1		15,709
20		21	(h)	West Brom A	W 1-0	Askew	7,654
21		28	(a)	Millwall	L 0-2		6,743
22	Dec	5	(h)	Reading	D 2-2	Dyer, Parker	5,797
23		12	(a)	Shrewsbury T	D 2-2	Roberts, Saville	2,588
24		19	(h)	Crystal P	W 2-1	Parker, Dyer	6,780
25		28	(a)	Oldham A	W 2-1	Heard, Dyer	8,080
26	Jan	1	(a)	Aston Villa	L 0-5		19,236
27		3	(h)	Leeds U	W 3-1	Payton, Jobson, Dyer	14,694
28		16	(a)	Blackburn R	L 1-2	Jobson	9,692
29	Feb	6	(a)	Bournemouth	L 2-6	Payton, Dyer	5,901
30		13	(h)	Stoke C	D 0-0		6,424
31		27	(h)	Sheffield U	L 1-2	Saville	8,832
32	Mar	2	(a)	Manchester C	L 0-2		16,040
33		5	(h)	Barnsley	L 1-2	Saville	7,662
34		12	(a)	Ipswich T	L 0-2		9,728
35		19	(h)	Plymouth A	D 1-1	Parker	5,172
36		26	(a)	Leicester C	L 1-2	Edwards	10,353
37	Apr	2	(a)	Birmingham C	D 1-1	Heard	7,059
38		4	(h)	Middlesbrough	D 0-0		10,758
39		9	(a)	Bradford C	L 0-2		13,659
40		12	(h)	Swindon T	L 1-4	Jenkinson	4,58
41		23	(h)	Huddersfield T	W 4-0	Edwards 2, Daniel, Saville	5,22
42		30	(a)	West Brom A	D 1-1	Daniel	8,004
43	May	2	(h)	Millwall	L 0-1		10,81
44		7	(a)	Reading	D 0-0		6,71

FINAL LEAGUE POSITION: 15th in Division Two

Appearances
Sub Appearan
Goals

FA Cup

3	Jan	9	(a)	Watford	D 1-1	Roberts	12,76
R		12	(h)	Watford	D 2-2*	Williams, Dyer	13,68
2R		18	(a)	Watford	L 0-1		15,26

*After extra-time

Appearances
Sub Appearar
Goals

League Cup

2	Sep	23	(a)	Manchester U	L 0-5		25,04
	Oct	7	(h)	Manchester U	L 0-1		13,58

Appearances
Sub Appeara
Goals

Norman A	Palmer C	Heard P	Jobson R	Skipper P	McEwan S	Parker G	Bunn F	Dyer A	Askew W	Roberts G	Saville A	Daniel R	Williams N	Payton A	Thompson L	Jenkinson L	Owen G	Brown N	De Mange K	Barnes P	Jacobs W	Edwards K	Hotte T	
1	2	3	4	5	6	7	8	9	10	11														1
1	2	3	4	5		6	8		10	7	9	11												2
1	2	3	4	5		6	8		10	7	9	11												3
1	2	3	4	5		6	8	9	10	7		11												4
1	2	3	4	5		6	8	9	10	7		11												5
1	2	3	4	5		6	8	9	10	7	12	11*												6
1	2	3	4	5		6	8	9	10	7		11												7
1	2	3	4	5		6	8*	9	10	7	12	11												8
1	2	3	4	5		6	8	9*	10	7	12	11†	14											9
1	2	3	4	5†		6	8		10	7	9	11*	12	14										10
1	2	3	4	5		6	8		10	7	9		11											11
1	2	3	4	5		6			10	7	9		11		8									12
1	2	3	4	5		6			10	7	9		11		8									13
1	2	3	4	5		6		12	10	7	9		11		8*									14
1	2	3	4	5		6	12	8	10	7	9*		11											15
1	2	3	4	5		6	12		10	7	9		11		8*									16
1	2	3	4	5		6	8	9	10	7			11											17
1	2	3	4	5		6	8	9	10	7			11											18
1	2		4	5		6	8	9	10	7		3	11*	12										19
1	2		4	5		6	8	9	10	7		3	11											20
1	2		4	5		6	8	9	10	7	12	3	11*											21
1	2		4	5		6		9	10	7	8*	3	11	12										22
1	2		4	5		6		9	10	7	8	3	11											23
1	2		4	5		6		9	10	7	8*	3	12				11							24
1	2	10	4	5		6		9		7		3	8				11							25
1	2	11	4	5		6		9	10	7	8†	3*	12	14										26
1	2	3	4	5		12		9	10	7			6	8*			11							27
1	2	3	4	5		6*		9	10	7		12	11	8										28
1	2†	3	4	5		6		9	10*	7	12		11	8				14						29
1	2	3	4	5		6		9	10	7	12		11*	8										30
1	2	3	4	5		6†		9	10*	7	8	14		12		11								31
1		3	4	5		6		9		7	8	10	11					2						32
1		3	4	5		6		9		7	8			12				2	10*	11				33
1			4	5				9†		7	8	3	2	12	14			6*	10	11				34
1		3	4	5		6		9*		7	8		2	12					10	11				35
1	2		4	5						7	8	12		6*					10	11	3	9		36
1	2	6	4	5						7	8*			12					10	11	3	9		37
1	2	6	4	5						7				8					10	11	3	9		38
1	2*	6†	4							7	12			8		14		5	10	11	3	9		39
1			4	5						12	14			8	10†	11		2*	6	7	3	9		40
1		3	4	5						7	8	10		6*	12			2		11†		9	14	41
1		3	4	5						7	8	10		6*				2		11		9	12	42
1		3	4	5						7	8	10		6†				2	12	11*		9	14	43
1		3	4	5						7	8	10		12				2			11	9*	6	44
44	35	35	44	43	1	33	16	27	30	43	24	23	21	11	5	2	3	9	8	11	6	9	1	
						1	2	1		1	8	3	4	10	2	1		1	1				3	
		4	2	2		8	5	8	3	3	6	2	2	2	2	1						3		

1 own-goal

Norman A	Palmer C	Heard P	Jobson R	Skipper P	McEwan S	Parker G	Bunn F	Dyer A	Askew W	Roberts G	Saville A	Daniel R	Williams N	Payton A	Thompson L	Jenkinson L	Owen G	Brown N	De Mange K	Barnes P	Jacobs W	Edwards K	Hotte T	
1	2	3	4	5		6		9	10	7			11	8										3
1	2	3	4	5		6		9	10	7			11	8										R
1		3	4	5		6		9	10†	7	12	14	11	8*				2						2R
3	2	3	3	3		3		3	3	3			3	3				1						
											1	1												
								1		1			1											

Norman A	Palmer C	Heard P	Jobson R	Skipper P	McEwan S	Parker G	Bunn F	Dyer A	Askew W	Roberts G	Saville A	Daniel R	Williams N	Payton A	Thompson L	Jenkinson L	Owen G	Brown N	De Mange K	Barnes P	Jacobs W	Edwards K	Hotte T	
1	2	3	4	5		6	8		10	7	9	11*	12											2
1	2	3	4	5		6			10	7	9*		11†	12	8	14								
2	2	2	2	2		2	1		2	2	2	1	1		1									
													1	1		1								

1988-89

1	Aug	27	(h)	Manchester C	W 1-0	Edwards	11,653
2		29	(a)	Oxford U	L 0-1		5,772
3	Sep	3	(a)	Plymouth A	L 0-2		8,202
4		10	(h)	Barnsley	D 0-0		5,654
5		17	(a)	Portsmouth	W 3-1	Edwards 2, Dyer	11,599
6		20	(h)	Blackburn R	L 1-3	Edwards	6,681
7		24	(a)	Oldham A	D 2-2	Terry, Milligan (og)	6,319
8	Oct	1	(h)	Walsall	D 0-0		4,845
9		4	(h)	Leicester C	D 2-2	Edwards, De Mange	5,079
10		8	(a)	Shrewsbury T	W 3-1	Edwards 2, Roberts	3,287
11		15	(h)	Sunderland	D 0-0		8,261
12		22	(a)	Crystal P	L 1-3	Dyer	8,464
13		25	(h)	Chelsea	W 3-0	Edwards 2, Smith	6,953
14		29	(a)	Leeds U	L 1-2	Palmer	17,536
15	Nov	5	(h)	Swindon T	W 1-0	Moore	5,192
16		13	(a)	Stoke C	L 0-4		10,505
17		19	(h)	Birmingham C	D 1-1	Edwards	5,134
18		26	(a)	Watford	L 0-2		10,404
19		29	(a)	Bournemouth	L 1-5	Payton	5,420
20	Dec	3	(h)	Brighton & HA	W 5-2	Payton 2, Daniel, Saville, Gatting (og)	5,686
21		10	(a)	West Brom A	L 0-2		10,094
22		26	(h)	Bradford C	D 1-1	Payton	8,791
23		31	(h)	Ipswich T	D 1-1	Whitehurst	7,800
24	Jan	2	(a)	Barnsley	W 2-0	Edwards 2	9,879
25		14	(h)	Bournemouth	W 4-0	Edwards 3, Whitehurst	5,690
26		21	(a)	Manchester C	L 1-4	Edwards	20,485
27	Feb	4	(a)	Leicester C	W 2-0	Edwards 2	9,996
28		11	(h)	Shrewsbury T	W 3-0	Edwards 2, Whitehurst	11,472
29		25	(a)	Sunderland	L 0-2		14,719
30		28	(a)	Chelsea	L 1-2	Roberts	11,407
31	Mar	4	(h)	Stoke C	L 1-4	Whitehurst	5,915
32		11	(a)	Swindon T	L 0-1		7,090
33		14	(h)	Leeds U	L 1-2	Roberts	8,887
34		18	(a)	Blackburn R	L 0-4		5,864
35		25	(h)	Plymouth A	W 3-0	Edwards 2, Jobson	5,851
36		27	(a)	Bradford C	D 1-1	Edwards	11,802
37	Apr	1	(h)	Portsmouth	D 1-1	Edwards	5,325
38		4	(h)	Oxford U	L 1-2	Swan	6,260
39		8	(a)	Ipswich T	D 1-1	Whitehurst	10,191
40		11	(h)	Crystal P	L 0-1		5,050
41		15	(a)	Walsall	D 1-1	Edwards	3,935
42		22	(h)	Oldham A	D 1-1	McParland	6,748
43		29	(h)	Watford	L 0-3		5,225
44	May	1	(a)	Brighton & HA	D 1-1	Edwards	6,750
45		6	(a)	Birmingham C	L 0-1		4,686
46		13	(h)	West Brom A	L 0-1		5,217

FINAL LEAGUE POSITION: 21st in Division Two

Appearances
Sub Appearan[illegible]
Goals

FA Cup

3	Jan	7	(a)	Cardiff C	W 2-1	Brown, Edwards	7,128
4		28	(a)	Bradford C	W 2-1	Whitehurst, Edwards	13,748
5	Feb	18	(h)	Liverpool	L 2-3	Whitehurst, Edwards	20,058

Appearances
Sub Appearan[illegible]
Goals

League Cup

2	Sep	28	(h)	Arsenal	L 1-2	Edwards	11,450
	Oct	12	(a)	Arsenal	L 0-3		17,885

Appearances
Sub Appearan[illegible]
Goals

Norman A	Jobson R	Jacobs W	Warren L	Skipper P	Terry S	Dyer A	Roberts G	Moore J	Edwards K	Saville A	Palmer C	Payton A	Daniel R	De Mange K	Thompson L	Kelly G	Smith M	Askew W	Hotte T	Jenkinson L	Buckley N	Hesford I	Whitehurst W	Brown N	Calvert M	Murray M	Swan P	McParland I	Bell D	Mudd P	
1	2	3	4*	5	6	7	8	9	10	11	12																				1
1	2	3	4	5	6	7	8	9	10	11																					2
1	2	3	4	5	6	7	8	9	10	11*		12																			3
1	5	3	4*		6	7	8	9	10		2		11	12																	4
1	5	3*	4		6	7	8†		10	12	2	9	11	14																	5
1	5		4		6	7	8	12	10		2†	9	11*	14	3																6
	5		4		6	7	8		10		2	9		12	3*	1	11														7
1	5	3†	4		6	11	8	12	10		2	9*		14	7																8
1	5		4		6	11	8	9	10	12	2†		3	14				7*													9
1	5		2		6	11	8	9	10	7			3	4																	10
1	5	3	2		6	11	8	9	10			12	7*	4†			14														11
1	5	3	4		6	11			10	9	2		7				8*		12												12
1	5	3*	4		6	11			10	9	2		7	12			8														13
1	5	3	4		6	11			10	9†	2	14	7	12			8*														14
1	5	3	4		6	11	7	9	10		2			8																	15
1	5	3	4		6		7*	9	10		2	12		8						11											16
1	5		4†		6		7	9*	10	12	2	11	3	8						14											17
1	5		4		6		7	12	10	9*	2	11	3	8																	18
1	5		4		6		7	9*	10	12		11	3	8							2										19
1	5		4		6		8		10	9	2	7	3							11											20
1	5		4		6		8		10	9	2	7	3				12			11*											21
1	5		4				8			9	2	7	3	10			11				6										22
	5		4				8			12	2	7	3	10			11*				6	1	9								23
	5	3	14				8		10	12		7†	11*	4							6	1	9	2							24
	5	3					8		10			7		4				11			6	1	9	2							25
	5	3					8		10			7		4				11			6	1	9	2							26
	5	3					8		10			7		4				11			6	1	9	2							27
	5	3					8		10			7		4				11			6	1	9	2							28
	5	3					8		10			7		4*			12	11			6	1	9	2							29
	5	3					8		10				7	4				11			6	1	9	2							30
	5	3					8		10				11	4				7			6	1	9	2							31
	4	3			5		8		10	9		12						7			6†	1		2	11*	14					32
	5	3			4		8		10*	6		12						7		11		1	9			2					33
	4	3	6		5		8		10*	9		12		14			7			11†		1				2					34
	5	3			6		8*		10			12								14		1	9			2†	4	7	11		35
	5	3			6				10						8							1	9	2			4	7	11		36
	5	3			6				10						8*					12		1	9	2			4	7	11		37
	5	3			6				10									8		12		1	9	2			4	7	11*		38
	5	3			6				10						12		11	8				1	9	2			4*	7			39
	5	3	4		6		11		10*			12						8				1	9			2		7			40
	5	3	6				8		10					12	11							1	9			2	4	7*			41
	5	3	6†				8		10					12				11*		14		1	9			2	4	7			42
	2	3							10				6	12				11			5	1	9		8*		4	7			43
	2	3			5				10			12	6	11		1							9*		8		4	7			44
	2				5				10			9	6	11		1									8		4	7		3	45
	2				5				10				3	12			7†	6		11		1	9		8*	14	4				46
21	46	33	27	3	33	15	35	11	44	14	17	18	23	19	6	3	9	16		6	13	22	21	13	5	6	11	11	4	1	
			1					3		6	1	10		13	1		3		1	5						2					
	1				1	2	3	1	26	1	1	4	1	1			1						5				1	1			

2 own-goals

Norman A	Jobson R	Jacobs W	Warren L	Skipper P	Terry S	Dyer A	Roberts G	Moore J	Edwards K	Saville A	Palmer C	Payton A	Daniel R	De Mange K	Thompson L	Kelly G	Smith M	Askew W	Hotte T	Jenkinson L	Buckley N	Hesford I	Whitehurst W	Brown N	Calvert M	Murray M	Swan P	McParland I	Bell D	Mudd P	
	5	3					8		10			7		4				11			6	1	9	2							3
	5	3					8		10			7		4				11			6	1	9	2							4
	5	3					8		10	12		7*		4				11			6	1	9	2							5
	3	3					3		3			3		3				3			3	3	3	3							
										1																					
									3														2	1							

Norman A	Jobson R	Jacobs W	Warren L	Skipper P	Terry S	Dyer A	Roberts G	Moore J	Edwards K	Saville A	Palmer C	Payton A	Daniel R	De Mange K	Thompson L	Kelly G	Smith M	Askew W	Hotte T	Jenkinson L	Buckley N	Hesford I	Whitehurst W	Brown N	Calvert M	Murray M	Swan P	McParland I	Bell D	Mudd P	
1	5		4		6	11	8	12	10		2	9			3		7*														2
1	5	3	2		6	11	8	9*	10	7		12		4																	
2	2	1	2		2	2	2	1	2	1	1	1		1	1		1														
								1				1																			
									1																						

Other Competitions

Detailed here is the Tigers' match-by-match record in a variety of minor competitions through the years. Pre-season tournaments played abroad are not included here on account of uncertainty as to their status, but are listed among the 'Other Matches' section.

West Riding Cup

1913-14
Round 2
Oct 2 v Leeds City (h) 1-1
Stevens
Hendry; Nevins, McQuillan, Edelston, McIntosh, Gordon, McDonald, Stevens, Halligan, McCorry, Lee.
Att: 4,000
Replay
Oct 8 v Leeds City (a) 3-2
S.Lyon 3
Hendry; Nevins, Morgan, Edelston, O'Connell, Gordon, McDonald, Stevens, S.Lyon, Wright, Lee.
Att: 2,000
Semi-final
Oct 22 v Bradford City (a) 0-1
Hendry; Pattison, Morgan, Edelston, O'Connell, McIntosh, McDonald, Wright, Stevens, McCorry, Lee.
Att: 5,000

1914-15
Semi-final
Oct 15 v Huddersfield Town (h) 3-1
Stevens 2, Morgan
Hendry; Pattison, Betts, Edelston, Deacey, Wright, D.Mercer, Cameron, Stevens, Halligan, Morgan.
Att: 3,000
Final
Nov 11 v Leeds City (a) 0-1
Hendry; Pattison, Betts, Edelston, Wright, Morgan, D.Mercer, Cameron, Stevens, Halligan, Lee.
Att: 850

Third Division North Cup

1936-37
Round 1
Sep 16 v York City (a) 2-3
Hubbard, Edwards
Maddison; Annables, Woodhead, Yorke, Tabram, Llewellyn, Hubbard, Edwards, Acquroff, Davies, Mayson.
Att: 7,022

1937-38
Round 1
Oct 21 v Hartlepools United (h) 1-1
Fryer
Maddison; Annables, Woodhead, Robinson, Blyth, Hardy, Mackay, Fryer, MacNeill, Davies, Pears.
Att: 4,000
Replay
Oct 27 v Hartlepools United (a) 0-3
Goodall; Annables, Parker, Treanor, Foster, Hardy, Mackay, Bell, MacNeill, Hubbard, Pears.
Att: 1,600

1938-39
Round 2
Feb 22 v Bradford City (a) 0-6
Ellis; Woodhead, Dowen, Lawrence, Meens, Blyth, Clubley, Richardson, Dickinson, Davies, Cunliffe.
Att: 1,678

Watney Cup

1970-71
Round 1
Aug 1 v Peterborough United (a) 4-0
Chilton 2, Wagstaff 2
McKechnie; Beardsley, de Vries, Wilkinson, Neill, Simpkin, Lord, Houghton, Chilton, Wagstaff, Butler.
Att: 9,353
Semi-final
Aug 5 v Manchester United (h) 1-1 (aet)
Chilton
McKechnie; Banks, de Vries, Wilkinson, Neill, Simpkin, Lord, Houghton, Chilton(Pearson), Wagstaff, Butler.
Att: 34,007
Manchester United won 4-3 on penalties — the first competitive match in England to be decided in such a manner.

1974-74
Round 1
Aug 11 v Mansfield Town (a) 3-0
Galvin, McGill, Greenwood
Wealands; Banks, de Vries, Kaye, Deere, Galvin, McGill, Lord, Pearson, Wagstaff, Greenwood.
Att: 6,340
Semi-final
Aug 14 v Bristol Rovers (a) 1-0
Lord
Wealands; Banks, de Vries, Kaye, Deere, Galvin, McGill, Lord, Pearson, Wagstaff, Greenwood.
Att: 12,693
Final
Aug 18 v Stoke City (a) 0-2
Wealands; Banks, de Vries, Kaye, Deere, Galvin, McGill, Lord, Pearson, Wagstaff(Hemmerman), Greenwood.
Att: 18,914

Anglo-Italian Tournament

1972-73
Group 1
Feb 21 v Lazio (h) 2-1
Knighton, Greenwood
Wealands; Banks, Beardsley, Kaye, Neill, Knighton, McGill, Houghton, Pearson, Holme, Greenwood.
Att: 7,325
Group 1
Mar 21 v Fiorentina (a) 0-1
McKechnie; Banks, Beardsley, Kaye, Neill, Knighton, McGill, Houghton(Lord), Pearson, Holme(Blampey), Butler.
Att: 4,980
Group 1
Apr 4 v Verona (h) 2-1
Knighton, Houghton
McKechnie; Banks, Beardsley, Neill, Croft, Knighton, McGill(Lord), Houghton, Pearson, Holme(Hemmerman), Greenwood.
Att: 3,965
Group 1
May 2 v Bari (a) 0-0
McKechnie; Banks, de Vries, Kaye, Neill, Knighton, McGill, Lord, Hawley, Wagstaff, Greenwood.
Att: 10,000
City failed to qualify for the semi-finals.

Anglo-Scottish Cup

1975-76
Group 2
Aug 2 v Leicester City (h) 1-1
Fletcher
Wealands; Banks, de Vries, Grimes, Deere, Roberts, McGill, Lord, Wood, Fletcher, Greenwood.
Att: 3,524
Group 2
Aug 6 v West Bromwich Albion (h) 1-2
Wagstaff
Blackburn; Banks, de Vries, McGill, Deere, Roberts(Wagstaff), Grimes, Lord, Wood, Fletcher, Greenwood.
Att: 3,054
Group 2
Aug 9 v Mansfield Town (a) 1-2
Wagstaff
Wealands; Banks, de Vries, McGill, Deere, Croft, Galvin, Lord, Fletcher, Wagstaff, Greenwood.
5,757

1976-77
Group D
Aug 7 v Middlesbrough (a) 0-2
Wealands; McGifford, Daniel, Croft, Galvin(McIntosh), Haigh, Gibson, Lyall, Wood, Hawley, Sunley.
Att: 6,812

Group D
Aug 10 v Newcastle United (h) 0-0
Wealands; Daniel, de Vries, Croft, Galvin, Haigh, Gibson, Lyall, Wood, Hawley(Stewart), Sunley.
Att: 4,715
Group D
Aug 14 v Sheffield United (h) 1-0
Lyall
Wealands; Daniel, de Vries, Roberts, Galvin, Haigh, Gibson, Lyall, Wood, Hawley, Sunley.
Att: 3,610

1977-78
Group D
Aug 6 v Notts County (a) 0-1
Wealands; Daniel, de Vries, Grimes, Dobson(Hawley), Haigh, Nisbet, Lord, Sunley, Bannister, Stewart.
Att: 4,020
Group D
Aug 9 v Sheffield U (h) 0-2
Wealands; Daniel, de Vries, Grimes(Hawley), Dobson, Haigh, Nisbet, Lord, Sunley, Bannister, Stewart.
Att: 3,110
Group D
Aug 13 v Oldham Athletic (h) 1-1
Grimes
Wealands; Nisbet, de Vries, Roberts(Sunley), Dobson, Haigh, Grimes, Galvin, Hawley, Bannister, Stewart.
Att: 1,618

1980-81
Group A
Jul 28 v Grimsby Town (h) 1-0
Deacy
Norman; Nisbet, Horswill, Booth, D.Roberts, Haigh, Norrie(Bennyworth), G.Roberts, Edwards, McClaren(Moss), Deacy.
Att: 5,056
Group A
Aug 2 v Sheffield United (a) 1-2
Moss
Norman; Nisbet, Horswill, Moss, D.Roberts, Haigh, Marwood, G.Roberts, Edwards, Norrie(Swann), Deacy(Richards).
Att: 5,454
Group A
Aug 5 v Chesterfield (a) 1-1
Haigh
Norman; Nisbet, Haigh, Moss, D.Roberts(Bennyworth), Richards, Norrie, Marwood, Edwards, McClaren, Deacy(Swann).
Att: 4,945
On no occasion did the Tigers progress beyond the preliminary group games.

Football League Group Cup

1981-82
Group B
Aug 15 v Bradford City (a) 1-2
Whitehurst
Norman; Hoolickin, Booth, Richards, Eccleston, Horswill, Marwood(Edwards), G.Roberts, Whitehurst, Norrie, Ferguson.
Att: 2,148
Group B
Aug 18 v Rotherham Uuited (h) 0-1
Norman; Hoolickin, Booth, Richards, Eccleston, Horswill, Marwood, G.Roberts, Whitehurst(Edwards), Norrie(Deacy), Ferguson.
Att: 2,205
Group B
Aug 22 v Hartlepool United (h) 1-0
Edwards
Norman; McNeil, Booth, Richards, Eccleston, Horswill, Edwards, G.Roberts, Whitehurst, Deacy(Norrie), Ferguson.
Att: 1,621

Football League Trophy

1982-83
Group D
Aug 14 v Hartlepool United (a) 2-1
Marwood, Whitehurst
Norman; McNeil, Thompson, D.Roberts, Skipper, Booth(Davis), Marwood, McClaren, Whitehurst, Mutrie(Flounders), G.Roberts.
Att: 962
Group D
Aug 17 v Halifax Town (a) 0-1
Norman; McNeil, Thompson, D.Roberts, Skipper, Booth, Marwood, Davis, Whitehurst, Mutrie, G.Roberts(McClaren).
Att: 1,323
Group D
Aug 21 v Bradford City (h) 0-0
Norman; Swann, Thompson, D.Roberts, Skipper, Booth, Marwood, Davis, Whitehurst, Mutrie, McClaren(Flounders).
Att: 3,202

Associate Members' Cup

1983-84
Round 1
Feb 21 v York City (a) 2-1
McClaren, Taylor
Norman; McNeil, Hollifield, Swann, Skipper, Booth, Marwood, McClaren, Whitehurst, Taylor(Flounders), Askew(G.Roberts).
Att: 5,837

Round 2
Mar 13 v Bury (h) 1-0
McEwan
Norman; McNeil, Swann, D.Roberts, Skipper, Askew, Marwood, McEwan, Flounders(Massey), Taylor, G.Roberts.
Att: 4,072
Round 3
Mar 20 v Preston North End (h) 3-0
G.Roberts 2, Taylor
Norman; McNeil, Swann, D.Roberts, Skipper, McEwan, Marwood, McClaren, Whitehurst, Taylor, G.Roberts.
Att: 4,227
Quarter-final
May 2 v Sheffield United (h) 1-0
Olsson
Blackburn; Olsson, Hollifield, Davis, Cockin, Booth, McClaren, Massey, Whitehurst, Askew, Taylor.
Att: 3,680
Semi-final
May 18 v Tranmere Rovers (h) 4-1
Taylor 2, G.Roberts 2
Norman; D.Roberts, Swann, Hollifield, Skipper, McEwan, Marwood, McClaren(Askew), Whitehurst, Taylor, G.Roberts.
Att: 4,678
Final
May 24 v Bournemouth (h) 1-2
McNeil
Norman; McNeil, Swann, D.Roberts(Askew), Skipper, McEwan, Marwood, McClaren, Whitehurst, Taylor(Flounders), G.Roberts.
Att: 6,197

1984-85
Round 1 (lst Leg)
Jan 22 v Mansfield Town (h) 2-2
Whitehurst, Calderwood (og)
Norman; McNeil, Pearson, Swann, Skipper, McEwan, Flounders(Massey), McClaren, Whitehurst, Askew, Ring(G.Roberts).
Att: 2,310
Round 1 (2nd Leg)
Feb 6 v Mansfield Town (a) 1-2
Askew
Norman; Brentano, Hollifield, Horton, Skipper, D.Roberts, Flounders(Massey), McClaren, Whitehurst, Askew, Williams(Ring).
Att: 2,086
Mansfield won 4-3 on aggregate.

Full Members' Cup

1985-86
Round 1
Oct 23 v Bradford City (h) 4-1
Bunn 2, McEwan, Whitehurst
Norman; Brentano, Swann, Doyle(Skipper), Jobson, McEwan, Williams, Flounders(Bunn), Whitehurst, Askew, Roberts.
Att: 2,177

Quarter-final
Nov 5 v Middlesbrough (h) 3-1 (aet)
Whitehurst 2, Bunn
Norman; Jobson, Swann, Doyle, Skipper, McEwan, Williams, Bunn(Saville), Whitehurst, Askew(Flounders), Roberts.
Att: 2,637
Semi-final (1st Leg)
Nov 26 v Manchester City (h) 2-1
McEwan, Bunn
Norman; Jobson, Swann(Pearson [Saville]), Doyle, Skipper, McEwan, Williams, Bunn, Whitehurst, Askew, Brentano.
Att: 5,213
Semi-final (2nd Leg)
Dec 11 v Manchester City (a) 0-2
Norman; Jobson, Swann, Doyle, Skipper, McEwan, Williams, Bunn, Saville, Askew, Roberts.
Att: 10,180
Manchester City won 3-2 on aggregate.

1986-87
Round 1
Oct 21 v Grimsby Town (a) 3-1
Flounders 2, Curran
Norman; Williams, Heard, Jobson, Skipper, McEwan, Curran, Saville, Flounders, Askew, Roberts.
Att: 2,460
Round 2
Nov 25 v Southampton (a) 1-2
Parker
Skipper; Jobson, Heard, Parker, Bunn, McEwan, Williams, Saville(Jenkinson), Flounders, Corkain, Roberts.
Att: 4,158

1987-88
Round 1
Nov 10 v Charlton Athletic (a) 1-1 (aet)
Roberts
Kelly; Palmer, Heard(Daniel), Jobson, Skipper, Parker, Roberts, Bunn(Thompson), Saville, Askew, Williams.
Att: 1,338
Charlton won 5-4 on penalties.

1988-89
Round 1
Nov 8 v Portsmouth (a) 1-2
Warren
Norman; Palmer, Jacobs, Warren, Jobson, Terry, Roberts, De Mange, Moore, Edwards, Jenkinson.
Att: 2,784

Other Matches

This section contains details of all those first-team games not included in the various categories of competitive fare. Some of these did have trophies at stake, such as the Hospital Cup games or the several contests for silverware around the globe in which the Tigers have participated. In view of the wide-ranging nature of matches in this section, they have been listed chronologically rather than attempting to classify them by type. Included are nine matches which began as competition fixtures but were abandoned due to the weather. The use of 'XI' after a team name indicates a select rather than a club side. Attendances are given where known.

1904
Pre-season friendly
Aug 29 v District XI (h) 5-0
Howe 2, Wolfe, Spence, H.Wilkinson
Pearce; Wilkinson, Alston, Martin, Wolfe, Raisbeck, McKiernan, Rushton, Howe, Spence, H.Wilkinson.
Att: 2,000

1905
FA Cup Third Qualifying Round
Nov 18 v Leeds City (h) 0-0
Spendiff; Langley, Jones, Browell, Robinson, Gordon, Manning, Wilson, Joe Smith, Jack Smith, Raisbeck.
Att: 3,000
Abandoned due to fog.

Friendly
Dec 30 v Wigan Town (a) 7-5
Spence 2, Spendiff, Browell, Manning, Rushton, Jack Smith
Spendiff; Romig, Jones, Browell, Martin, Raisbeck, Manning, Spence, Rushton, Jack Smith, Joe Smith.
Att: 6,000
This was the first match played by Wigan Town.

1906
Friendly
Apr 30 v Stanley (a) 3-5
Jack Smith 2, Joe Smith
Horton; Goodin, Hedley, Browell, Robinson, Gordon, Jack Smith, Simmon, Joe Smith, Howe, Lavery.
Att: 2,500

Benefit for dependants of D.Wilson
Nov 19 v Leeds City (a) 3-3
Howe 2, Jack Smith
Spendiff; Davies, McQuillan, Browell, Robinson, Raisbeck, Jack Smith, Joe Smith, Howe, Gordon, Neve.
Att: 4,000
Dave 'Soldier' Wilson, of Leeds and formerly Hull City died, in the course of Leeds' match against Burnley in October 1906.

1907
Friendly
Feb 23 v Sheffield United (h) 0-1
Spendiff; Hedley, McQuillan, Browell, Robinson, Gordon, Manning, Joe Smith, Jack Smith, Pearson, Wright.
Att: 8,000

Friendly
Oct 5 v York and District XI (a) 4-3
Temple 2, Gordon, Hunter
Roughley; Nevins, McQuillan, Browell, E.Hall, Gordon, Joe Smith, Hunter, Temple, Martin, Neve.
Att: 1,000

1908
Jack Manning Transfer Match
Mar 26 v Bradford (h) 1-2
Sloman
Spendiff; Hedley, Stephenson, Browell, E.Hall, Gordon, Joe Smith, Morrison, Sloman, Temple, Wright.
Att: 3,000

Tour Match
May 3 v Bruges (a) 3-1
Robinson, Shaw, Temple
Roughley; Stephenson, McQuillan, Browell, Robinson, Martin, Joe Smith, Jack Smith, Shaw, Temple, Neve.
Att: 3,000

Tour Match (at Bruges)
May 4 v Belgian XI (a) 3-2
Temple 2, Shaw
Roughley; Stephenson, McQuillan, Browell, Robinson, Martin, Simmon, Gordon, Temple, Shaw, Neve.
Att: 4,000

Tour Match
May 6 v The Hague (a) 3-0
Jack Smith, Joe Smith, Neve
Roughley; Stephenson, McQuillan, Browell, Robinson, Gordon, Simmon, Jack Smith, Temple, Joe Smith, Neve.
Att: 3,000

Friendly
Oct 12 v The Pilgrims (h) 4-1
Thistleton 3, Temple
Storey; Stephenson, McQuillan, G.Browell, A.Browell, D.Gordon, W.Wright, Taylor, Temple, Thistleton, Neve.
Att: 3,000
The Pilgrims were an amateur side on similar lines to the Corinthians.

Friendly
Oct 28 v Lincoln City (a) 1-0
E.Gordon
Storey; Stephenson, McQuillan, G.Browell, A.Browell, Martin, W.Wright, Taylor, E.Gordon, Morrison, Neve.
Att: 300

1909
Friendly
Feb 6 v Notts County (h) 1-1
Gilberthorpe
Roughley; Stephenson(J.Hall), McQuillan, G.Browell, Morrison, D.Gordon, Joe Smith, Gilberthorpe, Temple, Taylor, Neve.
Att: 6,000

Norwich Hospital Cup
Apr 19 v Norwich City (a) 0-0 (aet)
Roughley; Temple, McQuillan, G.Browell, A.Browell, D.Gordon, Joe Smith, Jack Smith, Toward, W.Smith, Neve.
Att: 6,900

Tour match (in Gothenburg)
May 15 v Southampton (n) 5-0
Jack Smith 2, Toward 2, G.Browell
Roughley; Temple, McQuillan, G.Browell, A.Browell, D.Gordon, W.Wright, Jack Smith, Toward, W.Smith, Neve.
Att: 4,000

Tour Match
May 18 v Stockholm (a) 2-0
Musgrave, Toward
Roughley; Temple, McQuillan, G.Browell, Martin, D.Gordon, W.Wright, Musgrave, Toward, W.Smith, Neve.
Att: 3,000

Tour Match (in Stockholm)
May 20 v West Bromwich Albion (n) 1-2
W.Smith
Roughley; Temple, McQuillan, G.Browell, A.Browell, D.Gordon, W.Wright, Jack Smith, Toward, W.Smith, Neve.
Att: 9,000

Tour Match
May 22 v Örgryte IS (a) 6-0
Toward 2, G.Browell, D.Gordon, W.Wright, Jack Smith
Roughley; Temple, McQuillan, G.Browell, A.Browell, D.Gordon, W.Wright, Jack Smith, Toward, W.Smith, Neve.
Att: 3,000

Tour Match (in Gothenburg)
May 25 v West Bromwich Albion (n) 4-3
A.Browell, W.Smith, D.Gordon, Neve
Roughley; Temple, McQuillan, G.Browell, A.Browell, Martin, W.Wright, Musgrave, W.Smith, D.Gordon, Neve.
Att: 4,000

1910
Norwich Hospital Cup
Apr 25 v Norwich City (a) 1-0 (aet)
Joe Smith
Roughley; Dan Gordon, Nevins, G.Browell, A.Browell, Davy Gordon, Joe Smith, Jack Smith, Temple, Musgrave, Neve.
Att: 10,000

Tour Match (in The Hague)
May 14 v Solingen (n) 16-0
Temple 6, Joe Smith 3, G.Browell 2, Dan Gordon, Davy Gordon, Jack Smith, Musgrave, Neve.
Roughley; Dan Gordon, McQuillan, G.Browell, A.Browell, Davy Gordon, Joe Smith, Temple, Jack Smith, Musgrave, Neve.
Att: 4,000

Tour Match
May 16 v Sparta Rotterdam (a) 4-1
Joe Smith 2, Roughley, A.Browell
Roughley; Dan Gordon, McQuillan(Simmon), G.Browell, A.Browell, Davy Gordon, Joe Smith, Temple, Jack Smith, Musgrave, Neve.
Att: 3,000

Friendly
Sep 20 v Grimsby Town (a) 2-2
Joe Smith, Neve
Hendry; McIntosh, McQuillan, G.Browell, A.Browell, Davy Gordon, Joe Smith, Taylor, Jack Smith, Musgrave, Neve.
Att: 300

Friendly
Oct 11 v Newcastle United (h) 1-3
G.Wright
Hendry; Dan Gordon, McQuillan, G.Browell, McIntosh, Davy Gordon, Joe Smith, Temple, E.Smith, W.Smith, G.Wright.
Att: 9,000

1911
Hull Hospital Cup
Apr 27 v Sheffield Wednesday (h) 3-1
T.Browell 3
Roughley; Nevins, McQuillan, W.Wright, McIntosh, Davy Gordon, Joe Smith, Temple, T.Browell, W.Smith, Neve.
Att: 5,000

De Decker Cup (at Brussels)
May 7 v Swindon Town (n) 1-0
Chapman
Roughley; Nevins, McQuillan, W.Wright, Houghton, Davy Gordon, Townend, Chapman, Temple, W.Smith, Neve.
Att: 8,000

Hull Hospital Cup
Nov 18 v Norwich City (h) 3-0
Chapman 2, A.Browell
Roughley; Nevins, McQuillan, W.Wright, A.Browell, Gordon, Best, Chapman, T.Browell, Temple, Neve.
Att: 6,000

1912
De Decker Cup (at Brussels)
May 12 v Tottenham Hotspur (n) 2-0
Best, Fazackerley
Roughley; Houghton, McQuillan, W.Wright, Chapman, McIntosh, Best, Goode, Temple, Fazackerley, Neve.
Att: 4,000

Tour Match
May 28 v Trondheim & District XI (a) 16-1
Fazackerley 11, Best 3, O'Connell, Temple
Roughley; Houghton, McQuillan, W.Wright, O'Connell, Fenwick, McDonald, Best, Temple, Fazackerley, Neve.
Att: 5,000

Tour Match
May 30 v Trondheim & District XI (a) 15-1
Temple 5, Fazackerley 4, Best 3, O'Connell, Fenwick, McDonald
Roughley; Houghton, McQuillan, W.Wright, O'Connell, Fenwick, McDonald, Best, Temple, Fazackerley, Neve.
3,000

Tour Match
Jun 2 v Trondheim & District XI (a) 9-0
Fazackerley 5, Temple 2, Houghton, Best
Roughley; Houghton, McQuillan, W.Wright, O'Connell, Fenwick, McDonald, Best, Temple, Fazackerley, Neve.
Att; 3,000

Tour Match
Jun 5 v Gothenburg XI (a) 1-0
Fazackerley
Roughley; Houghton, McQuillan, W.Wright, O'Connell, Fenwick, McDonald, Best, Temple, Fazackerley, Neve.

Tour Match
Jun 7 v Gothenburg XI (a) 4-0
Temple 2, Stevens, Fazackerley
Roughley; Houghton, McQuillan, W.Wright, O'Connell, Fenwick, McDonald, Stevens, Temple, Fazackerley, Neve.

Tom Browell Transfer Match
Oct 10 v Everton (h) 4-7
Fazackerley 3, Goode
Hendry; Houghton, Potts, Fenwick, McIntosh, Gordon, Best, Goode, O'Connell(Briggs), Fazackerley, Shaw.
Att: 10,000

1913
Division Two
Jan 4 v Glossop (h) 0-0
Hendry; Houghton, McQuillan, W.Wright, O'Connell, McIntosh, McDonald, Boyton, Fazackerley, Goode, G.Wright.
Att: 4,000
Play halted after 75 minutes due to bad light and waterlogged pitch.

Hull Hospital Cup
Apr 24 v Leeds City (h) 4-2 (aet)
Fenwick 2, McDonald, Stevens
Hendry; Nevins, McQuillan, W.Wright, McIntosh, Gordon, McDonald, O'Connell, Fenwick, Stevens, Hewitson.
Att: 3,000

De Decker Cup
May 11 v Racing Club Brussels (a) 6-0
Halligan 4, Gordon, W.Wright
Hendry; Nevins, McQuillan, Fenwick, O'Connell, McIntosh, McDonald, Gordon, Halligan, Stevens, W.Wright.

1914
Patsy O'Connell Transfer Match
Oct 12 v Manchester United (h) 3-2
Maw, Stevens, Halligan
W.Mercer; Pattison, Betts, Edelston, Deacey, Wright, Lee, Maw, Stevens, Halligan, Morgan.
Att: 3,000

1915
Division Two
Feb 13 v Lincoln City (h) 0-0
Hendry; Pattison, Betts, Edelston, Deacey, Morgan, D.Mercer, Cameron, Stevens, Halligan, Lee.
Att: 3,000
Abandoned after 54 minutes due to waterlogged pitch.

Friendly
Dec 27 v Lincoln City (a) 1-1
Lee
Edelston; Pattison, McQuillan, Voase, Gordon, Pace, Mercer, Lee, Slide, Percival, Salkeld.
Att: 4,000

1916
Friendly
Apr 21 v Durham Light Infantry (h) 4-0
Thistleton 2, D.Mercer, Slide
Hendry; Chaplin, Betts, Voase, Edelston, Sheridan, D.Mercer, Thistleton, Slide, Lee, Ford.
Att: 3,000

1917
Friendly
Mar 24 v Humber Garrison (h) 3-2
Jacketts, D.Mercer, Cleland
Hendry; Wigglesworth, Betts, Jacketts, W.Wright, Sheridan, D.Mercer, Edelston, Cleland, Pace, Isherwood.
Att: 1,000

Friendly
Apr 14 v Leicester Regiment (h) 4-2
D.Mercer, Cleland, Cookson, Pace
Hendry; Wigglesworth, Betts, Elvin, Edelston, Sheridan, D.Mercer, Jacketts, Cleland, Cookson, Pace.
Att: 1,000

Friendly
Apr 28 v Humber Garrison (h) 1-1
Sheridan
Hendry; Pattison, Betts, Jacketts, Edelston, Sheridan, D.Mercer, McManus, Cleland, Connelly, Pace.
Att: 1,000

Midland Section
Dec 25 v Grimsby Town (a) 1-0
Wallis
Hendry; Wigglesworth, Betts, Edelston, Deacey, Jacketts, Smith, D.Mercer, Wallis, Shaw, Hughes.
Att: 1,000
Abandoned after 11 minutes — blizzard obliterated pitch markings.

1918
Friendly
Mar 30 v Humber Garrison (h) 6-3
D.Mercer 3, Hughes 2, Osborn
Pattison; Wigglesworth, Betts, Jacketts, Edelston, Pace, Smith, D.Mercer, Osborn, Shaw, Hughes.
1,000

Friendly
Apr 20 v Rotherham County (h) 2-0
D.Mercer, Machin
Pattison; Pass, Betts, Harrison, Edelston, Jacketts, D.Mercer, Pace, Machin, Lee, Hughes.
Att: 2,000

1919
Midland Section
Jan 4 v Sheffield United (h) 6-1
D.Mercer 6
Hendry; Wigglesworth, Betts, Jacketts, Edelston, Pattison, Hughes, D.Mercer, Potter, McManus, Lee.
Att: 4,000
Notable for Mercer's record scoring contribution, this match was halted 10 minutes early due to bad light and waterlogged pitch. United's cause was not helped by having to play in borrowed kit.

Friendly
Apr 21 v Morton (h) 1-0
Potter
Hendry; Wigglesworth, Betts, Edelston, Deacey, Jacketts, D.Mercer, Potter, Rentoul, Lyon, Lee.
Att: 10,000

Friendly
Apr 28 v Hibernian (a) 3-3
Lyon 2, D.Mercer
Hendry; Wigglesworth, Inglis, Jacketts, Edelston, Wright, D.Mercer, Logan, Lyon, Bleakley, Lee.
Att: 500

Hull Hospital Cup
May 17 v Sheffield United (h) 0-2
Hendry; Wigglesworth, Betts, Edelston, Deacey, Jacketts, Hughes, D.Mercer, Potter, Wright, Lee.
Att: 7,500

1920
Friendly
Mar 6 v South Shields (a) 1-0
Stevens
W.Mercer; Betts, Barrass, Edelston, Deacey, Bleakley, Crawford, Wright, Stevens, Morrall, Hughes.
Att: 12,000

Friendly
Apr 5 v Hibernian (h) 2-0
Lyon 2
W.Mercer; Middlehurst, Barrass, Edelston, Lyon, Bleakley, Potter, Needham, Deacey, Morrall, Crawford.
Att: 10,000

Hull Hospital Cup
May 9 v Grimsby Town (h) 3-1
Brandon, Mills, Flood
W.Mercer; Barrass, Bell, Collier, Gilhooley, Bleakley, Crawford, Brandon, Mills, Flood, McKinney.
Att: 1,000

1921
Bill Inglis Benefit
Apr 27 v Raith Rovers (a) 1-3
McKinney
W.Mercer; Cheetham, Bell, Collier, Gilhooley, Bleakley, Crawford, Stoddart, Mills, Flood, McKinney.
Att: 8,000

Friendly
May 4 v Past Players (h) 2-0
McKinney, Charlesworth
W.Mercer; Cheetham, Barrass, Davies, McMurray, Bleakley, McKinney, Stoddart, Mills, Charlesworth, Harron.
Att: 3,000
Match arranged by Harry Simmon in aid of the North-East Railway's War Memorial Fund. The ex-Tigers lined up: Spendiff; Nevins, Pattison, F.Martin, Deacey, Edelston, Joe Smith, Simmon, Wadsworth, Jordan, Rose.

Hull Hospital Cup
May 9 v Grimsby Town (h) 3-1
Brandon, Mills, Flood
W.Mercer, Barrass, Bell, Collier, Gilhooley, Bleakley, Crawford, Brandon, Mills, Flood, McKinney.
Att: 1,000

1922
Tommy Spink Benefit
Apr 24 v Grimsby Town (a) 2-0
Flood 2
Mercer; Lodge, Bell, Collier, Kitchen, Bleakley, McKinney, Coverdale, Mills, Flood, Slater.
Att: 4,000

Hull Hospital Cup
Apr 27 v Leeds United (h) 2-1
Bleakley, Mills
Mercer; Lodge, Bell, Collier, Kitchen, Bleakley, Crawford, Coverdale, Mills, Flood, Hughes.
Att: 4,000

Bert Mills Transfer Match
May 1 v Barton Town (a) 2-1
Eccles, Mills
Briggs; Lodge, Blenkinsop, Collier, Garratt, Davies, McKinney, Proctor, Eccles, Mills, Stansfield.
Att: 2,000

1923
Friendly
Mar 24 v Newcastle United (a) 2-3
Coverdale, Martin
Mercer; Gibson, Bell, Collier, Bleakley, Coverdale, Crawford, McKinney, Martin, Kitchen, Thom.
Att: 6,000

Friendly
May 1 v Barton Town (a) 2-1
Mills 2
Mercer; Lodge, Bell, Collier, Bleakley, Middlemas, Crawford, Kitchen, Mills, Martin, Thom.
Att: 1,500

Hull Hospital Cup
May 3 v Bradford City (h) 4-1
Bleakley, Crawford, Mills, Martin
Mercer; Gibson, Bell, Collier, Bleakley, Coverdale, Crawford, McKinney, Mills, Martin, Thom.
Att: 3,500

1924
Friendly
Feb 2 v Doncaster Rovers (a) 1-2
Martin
Mercer; McGee, Bell, Johnson, Smailes, Bleakley, Richardson, Coverdale, Martin, Lewis, Thomas.
Att: 4,000

Hull Hospital Cup
May 1 v South Shields (h) 0-0
Mercer; McGee, Bell, Collier, Bleakley, Johnson, Thomas, Martin, Mills, Lewis, Thom.
Att: 2,000
City retained the Cup and South Shields won the toss for winners' medals.

Tour Match
May 18 v IF Kamraterna (Gothenburg) (a) 2-1
Owen, Martin
Mercer; McGee, Bell, Collier, Mitchell, Bleakley, Thomas, Mills, Owen, Martin, Thom.
Att: 12,419

Tour Match
May 21 v IFK Hälsingborg (a) 1-0
Martin
Mercer; Johnson, Bell, Collier, Adey, Bleakley, Thomas, Hamilton, Havelock, Martin, Robson.
Att: 3,500

Tour Match
May 23 v Gothenburg Alliance (a) 2-1
Owen, Martin
Mercer; Collier, Bell, Adey, Mitchell, Bleakley, Thomas, Hamilton, Owen, Martin, Thom.
Att: 8,345

Tour Match
May 25 v Gothenburg Alliance (a) 4-3
Hamilton 2, Havelock, Martin
Mercer; Johnson, Bell, Adey, Mitchell, Bleakley, Thomas, Hamilton, Havelock, Martin, Thom.
Att: 6,500

Tour Match
May 29 v AIK (Stockholm) (a) 3-0
Hamilton 3
Mercer; Johnson, Bell, Collier, Mitchell, Bleakley, Thomas, Hamilton, Havelock, Martin, Thom.
Att: 8,000

Tour Match
Jun 1 v IK Sleipner (Norrköping) (a) 1-0
Mills
Mercer; Adey, Bell, Collier, Mitchell, Bleakley, Thomas, Hamilton, Mills, Martin, Robson.
Att: 2,500

Tour Match
Jun 3 v Stockholm XI (a) 3-0
Hamilton, Mills, Martin
Mercer; Johnson, Bell, Collier, Mitchell, Bleakley, Thomas, Hamilton, Mills, Martin, Thom.
Att: 5,000

Friendly
Dec 29 v Corinthians (h) 1-4
Lewis
Dyke; Gray, McGee, Jordan, Mitchell, Johnson, Keen, Hamilton, Havelock, Lewis, Thomas.
Att: 4,000
Abandoned after 85 minutes when Corinthians' centre-forward Hilleary collided with Dyke and sustained a broken leg.

1925
Offside Trial
Apr 16 v Grimsby Town (h) 0-0
Iceton; Johnson, McGee, Jordan, Mitchell, Adey, Richardson, Hamilton, Havelock, Martin, Haworth.
Att: 1,000
Trial given to revised rule of only needing two defenders between attacker and goal (previously three).

Offside Trial
Apr 21 v Grimsby Town (a) 4-2
Hamilton 2, Adey, Goulden
Iceton; Johnson, McGee, Jordan, Mitchell, Adey, Keen, Hamilton, Goulden, Robson, Haworth.
Alternative proposal tried out of no offside in central third of field.

Billy Mercer Transfer Match
Apr 23 v Huddersfield Town (h) 0-3
Iceton; Johnson, McGee, Collier, O'Brien, Bleakley, Richardson, Martin, Goulden, Haworth, Thom.
Att: 4,000

Newland Orphanage Cup
Apr 28 v Past Players (h) 1-0
Mills
Iceton; Johnson, McGee, Blair, Mitchell, Bleakley, Keen, Jordan, Mills, Haworth, Thom.
Att: 2,000

Hull Hospital Cup
Apr 30 v Blackburn Rovers (h) 2-0
Mills 2
Maddison; Johnson, McGee, Mitchell, O'Brien, Bleakley, Richardson, Jordan, Mills, Haworth, Thom.
Att: 4,000

1926
Friendly
Mar 27 v Tottenham Hotspur (h) 5-0
Jones 3, Richardson, Martin
Maddison; McGee, Bell, Swan, O'Brien, Lee, Richardson, Martin, Jones, Wilkinson, Keers.
Att: 5,000

Hull Hospital Cup
Apr 8 v Leicester City (h) 1-2
Martin
Maddison; McGee, Bell, Swan, Garratt, Lee, Horne, Martin, Jones, Murray, Keers.
Att: 1,500

G.Martin (Norwich) Benefit
Apr 19 v Norwich City (a) 5-2
Whitworth 2, Maddison, Horne, Martin
Maddison; Gibson, Wilson, Mitchell, O'Brien, Bleakley, Horne, Martin, Whitworth, Lee, Thom.
Att: 5,500

Jimmy Carmichael Benefit
Apr 27 v Grimsby Town (a) 4-0
Horne 2, Martin 2
Maddison; Gibson, Wilson, Swan, O'Brien, Jordan, Horne, Martin, Hart, Lee, Thom.
Att: 4,000

Benefit for dependants of S.Hamilton
Sep 30 v Grimsby Town (h) 4-1
Horne, Swan, Cowan, McLaughlin
Gibson; Lloyd, Bell, Campbell, Morris, Lee, Horne, Swan, Cowan, McLaughlin, Brayson.
Att: 3,000
City forward Sammy Hamilton died in August 1925 after surgery for 'a nasal complaint'.

1927
Jock McGee and Syd Garratt Benefit
Apr 19 v St Mirren (h) 1-2
Howieson
Maddison; Gibson, Bell, 'Black', Watson, Lee, 'Thomas', Scott, Starling, Howieson, Horne.
Att: 7,500

Hull Hospital Cup
Apr 25 v Newcastle United (h) 3-0
Martin 2, Wyper
Maddison; Gibson, Bell, Swan, Bleakley, Sullivan, Wyper, Whitworth, Martin, Howieson, Taylor.
Att: 5,000

Grimsby Hospital Cup
May 3 v Grimsby Town (a) 1-3
Wyper
F.Gibson; Lloyd, Bell, Swan, Morris, Sullivan, Wyper, Alexander, Martin, Whitworth, Taylor.
Att: 2,500

1928
Friendly
Feb 18 v Hamilton Academical (h) 3-3
McKenzie, Wyper, Swan
Maddison; Lloyd, Bell, Sullivan, McKenzie, Bleakley, Wyper, Swan, Nelson, Howieson, Barraclough.
Att: 6,000

1929
Friendly
Jan 26 v Clyde (h) 1-3
Starling
Maddison; J.Gibson, Goldsmith, Dixon, Watson, Weaver, Alexander, Starling, McDonald, Walsh, Duncan.
Att: 5,000

1930
Hull Hospital Cup
Apr 28 v Leeds United (h) 2-2 (aet)
March, Starling
Basey; Bradford, Wilson, Walsh, Bleakley, Murray, Fawcett, Flannigan, March, Starling, Turner.
Att: 3,000
Leeds United won the trophy on the toss of a coin.

Friendly (at Driffield)
Oct 6 v Leeds United (n) 0-2
Gibson; Goldsmith, Watson, Gowdy, Cooke, Turner, Fawcett, A.Duncan, Alexander, Weldon, D.Duncan.
Att: 700

1931
Division Three North
Sep 2 v Wigan Borough (a) 1-3
Raleigh
Gibson; Rodgers, Goldsmith, Newton, Wrack, Gowdy, Barley, Mills, Raleigh, A.Duncan, D.Duncan.
Att: 3,035
Match deleted from Football League records on resignation of Wigan Borough in October 1931.

1932
Stan Denby Transfer Match
May 5 v Goole Town (a) 2-1
Shelton, Speed
Gibson; Goldsmith, Woodhead, Mills, Hill, Denby, Munnings, Allen, Shelton, Speed, Downes.
Att: 750

1934
George Goldsmith Benefit
Apr 23 v Grimsby Town (h) 2-4
McNaughton 2
Maddison; Quantick, Woodhead, Allen, Lawrence, Miller, Hubbard, Atkinson, McNaughton, Longden, Dodds.
Att: 3,000

1935
Friendly
Apr 29 v Folkestone (a) 1-4
Acquroff
Farquharson; Quantick, Woodhead, Longden, Tabram, Denby, Sims, Moore, Acquroff, Mackie, Thorley.
Att: 2,000

1938
Grimsby Hospital Cup
May 9 v Grimsby Town (a) 3-7
Hubbard, Fryer, Cumner
Goodall; Woodhead, Parker, Lawrence, Blyth, Hardy, Hubbard, Fryer, MacNeill, Davies, Cumner.
Att: 2,000

Football League Jubilee Fund Match
Aug 20 v York City (h) 1-1
Cunliffe
Ellis; Dowen, Woodhead, Hardy, Blyth, Robinson, Hubbard, White, MacNeill, Dickinson, Cunliffe.
Att: 3,500

1939
Willie Savage Benefit
Apr 19 v Queen of the South (a) 3-1
Robinson, Hubbard, Davies
Bly; Annables, Dowen, Treanor, Meens, Hardy, Huxford, Robinson, Hubbard, Davies, Cunliffe.
Att: 5,000

Cliff Woodhead Benefit
Apr 24 v Queen of the South (h) 2-3
Meens, Hubbard
Bly; Woodhead, Dowen, Treanor, Meens, Hardy, Huxford, Richardson, Hubbard, Davies, Cunliffe.
Att: 4,000

Football League Jubilee Fund Match
Aug 19 v York City (a) 2-2
G.Richardson, Lowe
Curnow; Woodhead, Watson, C.Robinson, Meens, Smith, Quigley, G.Richardson, Lowe, Davies, Cunliffe.
Att: 5,000

Friendly
Oct 7 v Bradford (h) 2-2
Prescott, Davies
Curnow; Woodhead, Watson, C.Robinson, Meens, Smith, Quigley, J.Robinson, Prescott, Davies, E.Richardson.
Att: 3,500

Friendly
Dec 16 v Notts County (h) 4-5
J.Robinson 2, Prescott 2
Curnow; Woodhead, Watson, Foster, Meens, Smith, J.Robinson, Stephenson, Prescott, Davies, E.Richardson.
Att: 3,500

Friendly
Dec 25 v Grimsby Town (a) 5-1
Prescott 3, Meens, Cunliffe
Curnow; Woodhead, Watson, Gilmore, Meens, Smith, E.Richardson, Davies, Prescott, Anderson, Cunliffe.
Att: 3,500

Friendly
Dec 26 v Grimsby Town (h) 0-0
Curnow; Woodhead, Watson, Gilmore, Meens, Smith, E.Richardson, Davies, Prescott, Stephenson, Cunliffe.
Att: 5,500

Friendly
Dec 30 v Rotherham United (a) 0-1
Curnow; Woodhead, Watson, C.Robinson, Meens, Smith, J.Robinson, Woods, Prescott, Davies, E.Richardson.
Att: 800

1940
Friendly
Mar 2 v Grimsby Town (h) 4-2
J.Robinson, Prescott, Anderson, Vincent (og)
Curnow; Woodhead, Watson, Gilmore, Meens, Smith, J.Robinson, Davies, Prescott, Anderson, Cunliffe.
Att: 3,000

1946
Friendly
May 2 v Hull Amateurs (a) 4-4
Knott 3, Jennings
Hannaby; Cottam, Cook, Goulding, Smith, S.Cook, Atkinson, P.Cook, Knott, Davies, Jennings.

Hull Hospital Cup
May 9 v Hull Amateurs (a) 3-0
Pridmore 2, Hutchinson
Hannaby; Stokes, Skidmore, P.Cook, Henson, Walters, Atkinson, Hutchinson, Pridmore, S.Cook, Jennings.
Both matches against the Amateurs were played on the Anlaby Road ground, which the latter had taken over.

Friendly
Nov 21 v Polish Army (h) 9-0
Tarrant 4, Peach 2, Shepherd, Davidson, Brownsword
Hannaby; Fowler, Hassall, Shepherd, Depear, Keen(A.N.Other), Davidson, Tarrant, Robinson, Peach, Brownsword.
Att: 6,000

1947
Friendly
Jan 25 v Fulham (h) 0-0
Carter; Watson, Fowler, Mills, H.Brown, Greenhalgh, Davidson, Peach, Lester, McGorrighan, T.Atkinson.
Att: 16,253

Bolton Crowd Disaster Fund
May 3 v Bolton Wanderers (h) 0-1
Hannaby; Fowler, Hassall, Greenhalgh, Meens, Mills, Major, Davies, Thompson, Harrison, Tootill.
Att: 19,000

East Riding Invitation Trophy
May 26 v Grimsby Town (h) 1-0
Thompson
P.Atkinson; Johnson, Hassall, Greenhalgh, Meens, Moore, Reagan, D.Smith, Thompson, Robertson, Major.
Att: 12,000

Friendly
Sep 25 v Rotterdam XI (h) 1-0
Thompson
Bly; Fowler, Hassall, Mellor, Meens, Greenhalgh, Reagan, Gallacher, Thompson, McGorrighan, Major.
Att: 15,000

1948
East Riding Invitation Trophy
May 3 v Grimsby Town (h) 1-3 (aet)
Murphy
Corbett; Fowler, Berry, Greenhalgh, Meens, Mellor, Bloomer, Conway, Murphy, Buchan, Durham.
Att: 18,000

Tour Match (at Aarhus)
May 9 v Jutland XI (a) 1-1
Moore
Bly; Fowler, Taylor, Greenhalgh, Meens, Berry, Bloomer, Conway, Moore(Murphy), Buchan, Durham.
Att: 6,300

Tour Match
May 12 v Kolding XI (a) 5-1
Conway 4, Mellor
Corbett; Taylor, Durham, White, Berry, Mellor, Bloomer, Buchan, King, Conway, Harrison.
Att: 5,000

Tour Match
May 15 v Malmö FF (a) 2-2
Buchan, Durham
Bly(Corbett); Fowler, Taylor, Greenhalgh, Berry, Mellor, Harrison, Conway, King, Buchan, Durham.
Att: 7,982

Division Three North
Aug 31 v Oldham Athletic (a) 1-0
Harrison
Bly; Fowler, Berry, Greenhalgh, Meens, Durham, Harrison, Carter, Moore, Conway, Burbanks.
Att: 10,725
Abandoned because of bad light after 86 minutes.

1949
East Riding Invitation Trophy
May 12 v Barnsley (h) 2-0
Harrison, Buchan
Bly; Hassall, Berry, Jensen, Seddon, Mellor, Bloxham, Harrison, Price, Buchan, Shepherd.
Att: 20,000

Tour Match
May 16 v Belfast Distillery (a) 5-3
Buchan 3, Jensen, Moore
Bly; Hassall, Taylor, Greenhalgh, Seddon, Mellor, Harrison, Jensen, Moore, Buchan, Shepherd.
Att: 3,500

Tour Match
May 19 v Portadown (a) 0-0
Robinson; Hassall, Berry, Jensen, Seddon, Durham, Bloxham, Carter, Price, Buchan, Shepherd.
Att: 7,500

Tour Match
May 24 v Cork XI (a) 3-1
Price 3
Robinson; Taylor, Durham, Greenhalgh, Seddon, Mellor, Harrison, Buchan, Price, Carter, Bloxham.

Tour Match
May 27 v Shelbourne (a) 6-1
Moore 2, Mellor, Harrison, Carter, Jensen
Bly; Taylor, Hassall, Greenhalgh, Seddon, Mellor, Harrison, Carter, Moore, Jensen, Shepherd.

1950
Friendly
Feb 11 v Stoke City (h) 0-1
Bly; Varney, Berry, Greenhalgh, Meens, Durham, Harrison, Smith, Jensen, Revie, Burbanks.
Att: 20,873

Friendly
Apr 27 v Clyde (h) 2-3
Smith, Lee
Bly; A.Gibson, Neal, Greenhalgh, Seddon, Jensen, Harris, Smith, Lee, Revie, Harrison.
Att: 10,850

Tour Match
May 13 v Hapoel Tel-Aviv (a) 1-0
Smith
Robinson; A.Gibson, Berry, Greenhalgh, Meens, Tarrant, Harrison, Smith, Lee, Carter, Shepherd.
Att: 9,000

Tour Match (at Tel-Aviv)
May 16 v Israel XI (n) 1-0
Shepherd
Robinson; A.Gibson, Berry, Greenhalgh, Meens, Tarrant, Hassall, Smith, Lee, Carter, Shepherd.
Att: 9,000

Tour Match
May 20 v Adana Demirspor (a) 4-0
Smith 2, Varney, Shepherd
Bly; A.Gibson, Berry, Greenhalgh, Meens(Seddon), Tarrant, Harrison, Smith, Lee(Varney), Carter, Shepherd.

Tour Match
May 21 v Gençlerbirliği (a) 3-1
Harrison 2, Shepherd
Bly; A.Gibson, Berry, Greenhalgh, Seddon, Tarrant, Hassall, Smith, Harrison, Carter, Shepherd.
Att: 7,000

Friendly
Sep 11 v Galatasaray (h) 2-0
Ackerman, Inwood
Robinson; Gibson, Jensen, Greenhalgh, Tarrant (Hassall), Durham, Harrison, Revie, Ackerman, Smith, Inwood.
Att: 13,000

1951
Friendly
Apr 18 v Scarborough (a) 2-0
Harrison, Carter
Bly; Hassall, Jensen, Tarrant, Franklin, Mellor, Harrison, Revie, Gerrie, Carter, Burbanks.
Att: 9,614

Benefit Match
Apr 23 v Peterborough United (a) 4-3
Harrison, Smith, Ackerman, Carter
Bly; Hassall, Jensen, Tarrant, Franklin, Mellor, Harrison, Smith, Ackerman, Carter, Fagan.
Att: 10,448
Beneficiaries were United's Bryan, Parrott and Wood.

Festival of Britain Match
May 9 v Partizan Belgrade (h) 2-3
Ackerman, Revie
Robinson; Hassall, Jensen, Tarrant, Franklin, Mellor, Harrison, Ackerman, Carter, Revie, Burbanks.
Att: 15,917

Festival of Britain Match
May 12 v Progres Niedercorn (h) 3-3
Revie 2, Burbanks
Bly; Hassall, Berry, Tarrant, Franklin, Mellor, Harrison, Ackerman, Gerrie(Gaynor), Revie, Burbanks.
Att: 16,665

Tour Match
May 24 v Atlético Madrid (a) 0-4
Bly; Berry, Hassall, Harris, Franklin, Jensen, Harrison, Revie, Durham, Ackerman(Mellor), Burbanks.
Att: 45,000

Tour Match
May 27 v Atlétic Bilbao (a) 0-2
Robinson; Hassall, Berry(Mellor [Meens]), Jensen, Franklin, Durham, Harris, Revie, Ackerman, Harrison, Burbanks.
Att: 20,000

Tour Match
Jun 3 v Barcelona XI (a) 3-5
Revie 2, Ackerman
Bly; Jensen, Meens, Tarrant, Franklin, Durham, Hassall, Harrison, Ackerman, Revie, Burbanks.
Att: 25,000

1952
Friendly
Feb 23 v Huddersfield Town (h) 5-0
Gerrie 3, Todd, Burbanks
Robinson; Hassall, Jensen, Harris, Berry, Durham, Fagan, Murray, Gerrie, Todd, Burbanks.
Att: 14,817

East Riding Invitation Trophy
Apr 28 v Sunderland (h) 2-2
Jensen, Duthie
Robinson; Hassall, Jensen, Harris, Berry, Tarrant, Fagan, Murray, Duthie, Carter, Burbanks.
Att: 29,274
Trophy shared. Sunderland won toss for winners' medals.

1953
Floodlit Friendly
Jan 19 v Dundee (h) 1-4
Hansen
Robinson; Feasey, Phillips, Harris, Davidson, Durham, Linaker, Gerrie, Hansen, Jensen, Cripsey.
Att: 31,702
First match played under floodlights at Boothferry Park.

Floodlit Friendly
Feb 16 v Hibernian (h) 2-3
Linaker, Cripsey
Robinson; Phillips, Jensen, Harris, Berry(Feasey), Durham, Linaker, Horton, Tarrant, Stephens, Cripsey.
Att: 28,000

Floodlit Friendly
Mar 2 v Wolverhampton Wanderers (h) 3-1
Gerrie 2, Horton
Bly; Phillips, Jensen, Harris, Berry, Durham, Linaker, Horton, Gerrie, Murray, Cripsey.
Att: 21,034

Floodlit Friendly
Mar 19 v Djurgårdens (h) 4-0
Jensen, Horton, Gerrie, Cripsey
Bly; Phillips, Jensen, Harris, Duthie, Durham, Fagan, Horton, Gerrie, Murray, Cripsey.
Att: 15,457

East Riding Invitation Trophy
May 7 v East Fife (h) 1-1
Christie (og)
Bly; Phillips, Neal, Harris, Berry, Jensen, K.Harrison, Horton, Duthie, Gerrie, Bulless.
Att: 11,133
Trophy shared. East Fife won toss for winners' medals.

Floodlit Friendly
Oct 6 v Fenerbahçe (h) 1-2
Murray
Forgan; F.Harrison, Neal, Harris(Smales), Franklin, Jensen, K.Harrison, Murray, Gerrie, Tarrant, Fagan.
Att: 13,366

Floodlit Friendly
Oct 26 v Portsmouth (h) 4-0
Crosbie 2, Gerrie, Ackerman
Bly; F.Harrison, Neal, Harris, Berry, Jensen, K.Harrison, Gerrie, Crosbie, Ackerman, Fagan.
Att: 14,582

Floodlit Friendly
Nov 9 v St Mirren (h) 5-2
Gerrie 2, Crosbie 2, Horton
Bly; F.Harrison, Neal, Harris, Berry, Jensen, K.Harrison, Gerrie, Crosbie, Horton, Fagan.
Att: 13,835

Floodlit Friendly
Nov 23 v Admira Wien (h) 1-2
Crosbie
Bly; F.Harrison, Neal(Durham), Harris, Berry, Jensen, K.Harrison, Gerrie, Crosbie, Ackerman, Fagan (Cripsey).
Att: 13,186

1954
Division Two
Jan 2 v Bury (a) 1-4
Ackerman
Bly; F.Harrison, Jensen, Harris, Berry, Durham, K.Harrison, Horton, Crosbie, Ackerman, Cripsey.
Att: 6,987
Abandoned after 75 minutes due to fog.

Floodlit Friendly
Mar 8 v Falkirk (h) 7-1
Crosbie 3, Atkinson 2, Ackerman, Cripsey
Bly(Forgan); F.Harrison, Jensen, Franklin, Berry, Porteous, Atkinson, Horton, Crosbie, Ackerman, Cripsey.
Att: 6,819

Floodlit Friendly
Mar 23 v Arsenal (h) 1-3
Ackerman
Forgan; F.Harrison, Jensen, Franklin, Berry, Porteous, Atkinson, Horton, Crosbie, Ackerman, Cripsey.
Att: 26,880

Friendly
Mar 30 v Falkirk (a) 0-1
Forgan; F.Harrison, Jensen, Porteous, Berry, Durham, Atkinson, Gerrie, Crosbie, Ackerman, Cripsey.
Att; 5,000

East Riding Invitation Trophy 1st Leg
Apr 26 v Grimsby Town (a) 0-1
Teece; F.Harrison, Jensen, Tulloch, Porteous, Durham, Atkinson, Gerrie, Crosbie, Ackerman, Bulless.
Att: 6,926

Challenge Shield
Apr 28 v Scunthorpe United (n) 2-2
Jensen, Gerrie
Teece; F.Harrison, Jensen, Tulloch, Porteous, Durham, Cawthorne, Gerrie, Smales, Atkinson, Bulless.
Att: 1,700
Played at Bridlington for Bridlington Central United's Jubilee Invitation Challenge Shield. The trophy was shared.

East Riding Invitation Trophy 2nd Leg
Apr 29 v Grimsby Town (h) 0-1
Teece; F.Harrison, Jensen, Franklin, Berry, Durham, Atkinson, Horton, Crosbie, Ackerman, Bulless.
Att: 4,264
Town won 2-0 on aggregate.

Tour Match
May 20 v EfB Esbjerg (a) 1-3
Dryburgh
Teece; F.Harrison, Jensen, Porteous, Berry, Durham, Atkinson, Horton, Crosbie, Ackerman, Dryburgh.
Att: 9,004

Tour Match (at Roskilde)
May 23 v Zealand League XI (n) 6-2
Duncan 2, Crosbie 2, Ackerman 2
Gagen; F.Harrison, Jensen, Porteous, Berry, Durham, Atkinson, Duncan, Crosbie, Ackerman, Dryburgh.

Tour Match
May 25 v Randers Freja (a) 6-0
Crosbie 5, Ackerman
Teece; F.Harrison, Jensen, Porteous, Berry, Durham, Atkinson, Ackerman, Crosbie, Horton, Bulless.
Att: 4,000

Tour Match
May 27 v Haderslev XI (a) 3-3
Atkinson, Crosbie, Horton
Teece; Whitnall, Jensen, Porteous, Berry, Durham, Cripsey, Atkinson, Crosbie, Horton, Dryburgh.
Att: 4,000

Floodlit Friendly
Oct 11 v Chelsea (h) 0-3
Bly; F.Harrison, Jensen, Horton, Franklin, Durham, K.Harrison, Downie, Crosbie, Ackerman, Dryburgh.
Att: 14,450

Floodlit Friendly
Oct 25 v Queen's Park Rangers (a) 2-0
Ackerman, Dryburgh
Bly; F.Harrison, Jensen, Porteous, Franklin, Durham, Crosbie, Horton, Gerrie, Ackerman, Dryburgh.
Att: 7,319

Floodlit Friendly
Nov 1 v Maccabi Tel-Aviv (h) 4-0
Ackerman 2, Horton, Downie
Bly; Berry, Jensen, Porteous, Franklin(Neal), Durham, Crosbie(Smith), Horton, Gerrie, Downie, Ackerman.
Att: 10,400

Floodlit Friendly
Nov 15 v Starlights (h) 7-1
Gerrie 2, Crosbie 2, Smith, Cripsey, Ackerman
Teece; F.Harrison, Jensen, Porteous, Franklin, Downie, Smith, Gerrie, Crosbie, Cripsey, Ackerman.
Att: 16,577

Floodlit Friendly
Nov 29 v EfB Esbjerg (h) 7-2
Ackerman 3, Dryburgh 2, Porteous, Horton
Teece; F.Harrison, Jensen, Porteous, Berry, Downie, K.Harrison, Horton, Ackerman, Atkinson, Dryburgh.
Att: 5,669

Floodlit Friendly
Dec 20 v Bradford City (a) 1-2
Downie
Teece; Whitnall, Neal, Tulloch, Franklin, Durham, Atkinson, K.Harrison, Davidson, Downie, Cripsey.
Att: 4,331

1955
Friendly
Jan 29 v Burnley (h) 1-2
Mannion
Bly; Dennison, Jensen, Downie, Franklin, Porteous, Atkinson, Horton, Ackerman, Mannion, Dryburgh.
Att: 8,970

East Riding Invitation Trophy
May 10 v York City (h) 0-0
Bly; Dennison, Jensen, Downie, Berry, Durham, Major, Duncan, Atkinson, Bulless, Cripsey.
Att: 8,598
Trophy shared.

Floodlit Friendly
Oct 17 v Vasas SC (h) 3-1
Bradbury 3
Fisher; Neal, Jensen, Martin, Franklin, Davidson (Atkinson), Smith, Bradbury(Major), Duncan, Bulless, Cripsey.
Att: 13,889

1956
Friendly
Jan 28 v Blackpool (h) 5-5
Mortensen 2, Clarke, Bradbury, Bulless
Bly; Neal, Jensen, Davidson, Berry, Porteous, Smith, Clarke, Mortensen, Bradbury, Bulless.
Att: 22,880

Friendly
Apr 18 v Spartak Subotica (h) 3-1
Bradbury, Clarke, Fraser
Fisher; Harrison, Jensen, Davidson, Feasey, Bulless, Smith, Stephens, Bradbury, Clarke, Fraser.
Att: 19,297

East Riding Invitation Trophy lst Leg
Apr 25 v York City (h) 4-2
Smith, Bradbury, Clarke, Fraser
Fisher; Harrison, Jensen, Davidson, Berry, Bulless, Smith, Stephens, Bradbury, Clarke, Fraser.
Att: 7,008

East Riding Invitation Trophy 2nd Leg
May 2 v York City (a) 0-5
Fisher; Harrison, Jensen, Davidson, Berry, Bulless, Stephens, Smith, Bradbury, Clarke, Fraser.
Att: 8,881
York City won 7-4 on aggregate.

Friendly
Oct 30 v Grimsby Town (h) 1-1
Clarke
Bly; Harrison, Jensen, Davidson, Feasey, Bulless, Stephens, Clarke, Mortensen, Gerrie, Cripsey.
Att: 3,650

1957
Friendly
Mar 13 v SV Werder Bremen (h) 5-0
Bradbury 2, Bulless 2, Stephens
Bly; Harrison, Durham, Collinson, Feasey, Davidson, Stephens, Clarke, Bradbury, Bulless, Cripsey.
Att: 10,952

Dick Conner Benefit
Mar 26 v Grimsby Town (a) 1-5
Collinson
Fisher; Harrison, Durham, Collinson, Feasey, Davidson, Stephens, Clarke, Bradbury, Bulless, Cripsey.
Att: 3,500

East Riding Invitation Trophy
May 6 v Sunderland (h) 1-2
Neilson
Bly; Harrison, Feasey, Collinson, Neilson, Davidson, Stephens, Clarke, Bradbury, Bulless, Cripsey.
Att: 7,525

1958
Friendly
Feb 15 v Lincoln City (a) 5-2
Coates 3, Clarke, Bulless
Bly; Hetherington, Durham, Bennion, Feasey, Davidson, Stephens, Clarke, Bulless, Coates, Cripsey.
Att: 2,123

Friendly
Apr 28 v Middlesbrough (h) 1-3
Smith
Fisher; Harrison, Durham, Bennion, Feasey, Davidson, Clarke, Bradbury, Smith, Bulless, Cripsey.
Att: 5,172

East Riding Invitation Trophy
Oct 20 v Hibernian (h) 4-0
Clarke, Collinson, Smith, Coates
Lord; Harrison, Durham, Bennion, Feasey, Garvey, Clarke, Collinson, Smith, Coates, Bowering.
Att: 10,829

1959
Friendly
Sep 29 v Baník Ostrava (h) 3-2
Collinson, Smith, Bradbury
Bly(Fisher); Harrison, Bulless, Bennion, Feasey, Davidson, Clarke, Collinson, Smith, Bradbury, Bowering.
Att: 11,023

1960
Friendly
Jan 30 v Leeds United (h) 0-1
Lord; Brown, Bulless, Collinson, Garvey, Stocks, Clarke, Sewell, Nicholson, Duncan, Shiner.
Att: 4,000

1963
Division Three
Jan 19 v Swindon Town (h) 0-0
Williams; Davidson, Sharpe, Collinson, Garvey, McMillan, Clarke, Henderson, Chilton, Cummins, McSeveney.
Att: 6,030
Frozen pitch caused play to be halted at half-time. The surface had been experimentally thawed out using ammonia.

Friendly
Mar 16 v Burnley (h) 1-1
McSeveney
Williams; Davidson, Bulless, Collinson, Garvey, McMillan, Henderson, King, Chilton, Cummins, McSeveney.
Att: 8,825

1965
Brian Bulless Testimonial
Apr 27 v All Star XI (h) 9-8
Wagstaff 3, Chilton 2, Houghton 2, McSeveney, I.Butler
Swan; Davidson, D.Butler, McMillan, Milner, Simpkin, McSeveney, Wagstaff, Chilton, Houghton, I.Butler.
Att: 6,329

1966

Pre-season Friendly

Aug 9 v Hibernian (h) 3-1

Wagstaff, Chilton, Houghton

Swan; A.Davidson, D.Butler, Jarvis, Milner, Simpkin, Henderson, Wagstaff, Chilton, Houghton, Young.

Att: 13,934

Pre-season Friendly

Aug 13 v Sunderland (h) 0-1

Swan; A.Davidson, D.Butler, Jarvis, Milner, Simpkin, Henderson, Wagstaff, Chilton, Houghton, Young.

Att: 15,135

Friendly

Nov 1 v Sofia XI (h) 2-2

Houghton 2

McKechnie; Beardsley, D.Butler(Collinson), Jarvis, Pettit, I.Davidson, Henderson, Wagstaff, Chilton, Houghton, Young.

Att: 11,109

1967

Friendly

Feb 17 v Slovan Bratislava (h) 1-2

Wagstaff

McKechnie(Swan); A.Davidson, D.Butler, Jarvis, Milner, Pettit, Henderson, Wagstaff, Chilton(Lill), Lord, I.Butler.

Att: 12,909

Friendly

Mar 10 v West Ham United (h) 1-4

Chilton

McKechnie; Greenwood, D.Butler, Jarvis, Milner, Simpkin, Henderson, Wagstaff, Chilton, Wilkinson, Young.

Att: 22,651

Pre-season Friendly

Aug 8 v Hearts (h) 4-0

Wagstaff 2, Chilton, I.Butler

Swan(McKechnie); A.Davidson(Greenwood), D.Butler, Jarvis, Milner, Simpkin, Heath, Wagstaff, Chilton, Houghton, I.Butler.

Att: 11,665

Pre-season Friendly

Aug 12 v Sunderland (h) 3-3

Heath, Chilton, Houghton

Swan; A.Davidson(Greenwood), Beardsley, Jarvis, Milner, Simpkin, Heath, Wagstaff, Chilton(Lord), Houghton, I.Butler.

Att: 8,713

1968

Trawler Disaster Fund Match

Feb 16 v Motherwell (h) 4-0

Chilton 2, Wagstaff, Heath

McKechnie; Banks, D.Butler(de Vries), Greenwood, Pettit, Simpkin, Young, Wagstaff, Chilton, I.Davidson(Lord), Heath.

Att: 6,799

Friendly

Mar 1 v Internacional ŽTS Bratislava (h) 2-0

Wilson, I.Butler

McKechnie; Banks, de Vries, Greenwood, Milner, Wilson, Young, Wagstaff, Chilton, Lord, I.Butler.

Att: 5,124

Pre-season Friendly

Jul 28 v Dundee (h) 0-1

McKechnie(White); Beardsley, D.Butler, Greenwood, Simpkin(Wilkinson), Jarvis(Barker), Lill, Wagstaff, Chilton(Lord), Houghton, McCunnell.

Att: 6,537

Pre-season Friendly

Aug 2 v Liverpool (h) 3-5

Wagstaff, Chilton, Houghton

McKechnie(Swan); Beardsley(Banks), D.Butler (Beardsley), Greenwood, Simpkin, Jarvis, Lill (Wilkinson), Wagstaff, Chilton, Houghton, Lord.

Att: 12,969

Pre-season Friendly

Aug 5 v Goole Town (a) 0-0

Swan(White); Banks, Beardsley, Greenwood, Barker, Simpkin, Jarvis(Lill), Wagstaff(Wilkinson), Chilton(O'Riley), Houghton, Lord(McCunnell).

Att: 1,490

1969

Andy Davidson Testimonial

Apr 1 v Manchester City (h) 2-0

Wagstaff 2

McKechnie; Banks(D.Butler), Beardsley(Blampey), Pettit, Barker, Simpkin, Greenwood, Lord, Wilkinson, Wagstaff, I.Butler.

Att: 13,027

Pre-season Friendly

Jul 29 v Kilmarnock (h) 2-2

Chilton 2

McKechnie; Banks, D.Butler, Greenwood, Pettit, Simpkin, Jarvis, Wagstaff, Chilton, Wilkinson, I.Butler, Sub used: Houghton.

Att: 4,833

Pre-season Friendly

Aug 2 v Newcastle United (h) 1-0

Simpkin

McKechnie; Banks, D.Butler, Greenwood(Barker), Pettit, Simpkin, Jarvis, Wagstaff, Wilkinson, Houghton(Lord), I.Butler.

Att: 8,559

Friendly

Dec 6 v Goole Town (a) 6-2

Chilton 3, Wilkinson 2, McCunnell

White; Smith, Beardsley, Pettit, Barker(de Vries), Wilkinson, Jarvis, Lord(Blampey), Chilton, Wagstaff, McCunnell(O'Riley).

Att: 250

1970
Barry Jackson Testimonial
Feb 23 v York City (a) 2-3
Houghton, Wagstaff
McKechnie; Banks, Beardsley(de Vries), Greenwood, Pettit, Simpkin, Jarvis, Houghton, Chilton, Wagstaff, I.Butler.
Att: 3,150

Jimmy Lodge Testimonial
Apr 8 v Derby County (h) 2-2
Houghton, Wagstaff
McKechnie; Greenwood, Beardsley, Pettit, Wilkinson, Simpkin, Jarvis, Houghton, Chilton(Lord), Wagstaff, I.Butler.
Att: 8,937

Pre-season Friendly
Aug 8 v Bradford City (a) 1-0
Houghton
Walters; Beardsley(Banks), de Vries(Greenwood), Wilkinson(Barker), Neill(Wilson), Simpkin(Pettit), Lord(Jarvis), Houghton(Holbrook), Pearson(Neill), Wagstaff(O'Riley), Butler.
Att: 3,542

1971
Division Two
Feb 16 v Blackburn Rovers (h) 2-0
Neill, Butler
McKechnie; Banks, de Vries, Wilkinson, Neill, Greenwood, Lord, Houghton, Chilton, Wagstaff, Butler.
Att: 24,846
Abandoned at half-time due to fog.

Chris Chilton Testimonial
May 3 v Leeds United (h) 7-6
Chilton 3, Wagstaff 3, McKechnie
Walters; Banks, Beardsley, Wilkinson(Greenwood), Neill(de Vries), Knighton, Lord(Holbrook), Houghton, Chilton, Wagstaff, Butler(McKechnie).
Att: 28,350

Tour Match
May 12 v Sarpsborg FK (a) 3-0
Chilton 2, Houghton
McKechnie; Banks, Beardsley, Wilkinson, Baxter, Knighton, Houghton, Lord, Chilton, Wagstaff, Butler.
Att: 4,000

Tour Match
May 16 v Clausenengen FK (a) 2-0
Houghton, Butler
McKechnie(Walters); Banks, de Vries, Wilkinson, Baxter(Pettit), Knighton, Greenwood, Houghton, O'Riley, Holbrook(Lord), Butler.
Att: 4,500

Tour Match
May 19 v HJK Helsinki (a) 6-2
O'Riley 4, Pearson, Holbrook
Walters; Banks(Greenwood), Beardsley, Wilkinson, Pettit, Knighton, Lord, Houghton, Pearson (Holbrook), O'Riley, Butler(Neill).
Att: 2,466

Tour Match
May 23 v Reipas Lahti (a) 5-0
O'Riley 2, Neill, Pettit, Pearson
Walters; Beardsley, de Vries, Neill, Pettit, Knighton(Holbrook), Banks, Greenwood, Pearson, O'Riley, Lord.
Att: 2,158

July Cup
Jul 19 v Sirius (n) 2-0
Houghton, Hansson (og)
McKechnie; Banks, de Vries, Wilkinson, Neill, Simpkin, Lord, Houghton, Pearson, Knighton (P.Greenwood), O'Riley.
Att: 600

July Cup
Jul 20 v IFK Stockholm (n) 1-0
Houghton
McKechnie; Banks, Beardsley, Wilkinson, Neill, Simpkin(P.Greenwood), Lord, Houghton, Pearson, Knighton, O'Riley.
Att: 3,000
All July Cup matches played at Västerhaninge, Stockholm. Final group positions were:

	P	*W*	*D*	*L*	*F*	*A*	*P*
1 Hull City	2	2	0	0	3	0	6
2 IFK	2	1	0	1	3	1	2
3 Sirius	2	0	0	2	2	6	0
1 Halmstad	2	2	0	0	8	2	4
2 Rasunda	2	1	0	1	3	5	2
3 Västerhaninge	2	0	0	2	2	6	0

July Cup Final
Jul 23 v Halmstad BK (n) 6-1
Wagstaff 3, Knighton, Lord, Pearson
McKechnie; Banks, Beardsley, Wilkinson, Pettit, Knighton, Lord, Houghton, Pearson, Wagstaff, Butler.
Att: 4,000

Tour Match
Jul 27 v Sandviken IF (a) 1-0
Pearson
Walters; Banks(Beardsley), de Vries, Wilkinson(Neill), Pettit, Simpkin(Butler), Lord, Houghton (P.Greenwood), Pearson, Wagstaff(O'Riley), Knighton.
Att: 3,000

Tour Match
Jul 29 v AIK Stockholm (a) 3-0
O'Riley 2, Knighton
Walters; Banks, Beardsley, Pettit, Neill, Knighton, Lord, Houghton, O'Riley, Wagstaff, Butler.
Att: 2,000

Friendly
Aug 4 v Japan XI (h) 5-0
O'Riley, Wagstaff, Butler, Ogi (og), Yanaguchi (og)
McKechnie; Banks, Beardsley, Wilkinson, Neill, Knighton, Lord, Houghton, O'Riley, Wagstaff, Butler.
Att: 10,627

1972
Friendly
Apr 11 v Inter Montevideo (h) 4-2
Kaye, Houghton, Pearson, R.Greenwood
McKechnie(Wealands); Banks, de Vries, Kaye, Baxter(Neill), Knighton(Wilkinson, Lord), McGill, Houghton, Pearson(R.Greenwood), O'Riley, Butler.
Att: 11,848

July Cup
Jul 15 v Hammarby IF (n) 5-0
Houghton 2, O'Riley 2, Pearson
McKechnie; Banks, de Vries, Kaye, Neill, Knighton, Wilkinson(Greenwood), Houghton, Pearson, O'Riley, Butler.
Att: 3,000

July Cup
Jul 20 v Manchester City (n) 0-1
McKechnie; Banks, de Vries, Kaye, Neill, Wilkinson, McGill, Lord, Pearson, O'Riley, Butler.
Att: 4,000
All July Cup matches played at Västerhaninge, Stockholm. Final group positions were:

	P	W	D	L	F	A	P
1 Manchester City	2	1	1	0	4	3	3
2 Hull City	2	1	0	1	5	1	2
3 Hammarby IF	2	0	1	1	3	8	1
1 Partick Thistle	3	3	0	0	16	1	6
2 Sirius	3	2	0	1	4	3	4
3 AIK	3	1	0	2	7	6	2
4 Västerhaninge	3	0	0	3	4	21	0

July Cup Third Place Match
Jul 22 v Sirius (n) 3-1
Knighton 2, O'Riley
Wealands; Banks, de Vries, Green, Neill, Knighton, McGill, Houghton, Holme(Wilkinson), Lord, Greenwood(O'Riley).
Att: 1,225

Pre-season Friendly
Jul 29 v Scarborough (a) 2-2
Banks, Greenwood
Wealands; Banks, Beardsley, Pettit, Green, Knighton, Lord, McGill, O'Riley, Greenwood, Butler(Wilkinson).
Att: 1,500

Pre-season Friendly
Aug 5 v 1.FC Kaiserslautern (h) 1-1
O'Riley
Wealands; Banks, de Vries, Kaye, Neill, Knighton, McGill, Lord, Holme, O'Riley(Greenwood), Wilkinson(Houghton).
Att: 4,654

Friendly
Dec 30 v Manchester United (a) 1-2
Wagstaff
McKechnie; Banks, McGill, Kaye, Neill, Knighton, Blampey, Houghton(Butler), Pearson, Wagstaff, Greenwood.
Att: 24,103

1973
Billy Wilkinson Testimonial
May 11 v West Ham United (h) 5-3
Lord 2, Greenwood 2, Pearson
McKechnie; Banks, de Vries, Croft, Wilkinson, Knighton, McGill, Lord, Pearson, Wagstaff, Greenwood.
Att: 2,853

Joe Stallard Benefit
Apr 16 v Brigg Town (a) 4-0
Pearson 3, Knighton
McKechnie; Banks, Beardsley, Kaye, Croft, Knighton, Grimes(Blampey), Lord, Pearson, Wagstaff(Hawley), Butler.
Att: 600

Tour Match (at Port of Spain)
May 23 v Trinidad & Tobago XI (a) 1-2
Knighton
McKechnie; Banks, de Vries, Kaye, Neill, Knighton, McGill, Houghton, Pearson, Lord(O'Riley), Greenwood.
Att: 4,000

Tour Match (at Port of Spain)
May 26 v Trinidad & Tobago XI (a) 2-0
Pearson 2
Wealands; Banks, de Vries, Kaye, Neill, Knighton, Lord, Hawley, Pearson, O'Riley, Greenwood.
Att: 5,000

Tour Match (at Linden)
May 30 v Upper Demerara XI (a) 7-0
Houghton 3, Beardsley, Knighton, O'Riley, Hemmerman
McKechnie; Banks, Beardsley, Kaye, Deere, Knighton, McGill, Houghton, Pearson, O'Riley, Hemmerman. Subs used: Lord, Blampey, Hawley, Greenwood, Croft.
Att: 1,000

Tour Match (at New Amsterdam)
Jun 1 v Berbice FA XI (a) 12-0
Knighton 3, Pearson 3, Hemmerman 2, O'Riley 2, Greenwood, McKechnie
Wealands; Banks, Beardsley, Kaye, Deere, Knighton, Lord, Houghton, Pearson, O'Riley, Greenwood. Subs used: McKechnie, Croft, Hawley, Hemmerman, Blampey.
Att: 1,000

Tour Match (at Georgetown)
Jun 3 v Guyana XI (a) 5-0
Pearson 2, Kaye, Lord, Greenwood
Wealands; Banks, de Vries, Kaye, Neill, Blampey, Lord, Knighton, Pearson, Hawley, Greenwood. Subs used: McGill, Houghton, Hemmerman.
Att: 5,000

Tour Match (at Georgetown)
Jun 6 v Caribbean XI (a) 1-1
Pearson
McKechnie; Banks, Beardsley, Kaye, Neill, Houghton, Lord, Knighton, Pearson, McGill, Greenwood. Subs used: Hawley, Hemmerman.
Att: 6,000

Tour Match (at Cayenne)
Jun 9 v French Guiana XI (a) 2-0
Hawley 2
Wealands; Banks, Beardsley, Kaye, Neill, Knighton, Lord, Hawley, O'Riley, Houghton, Greenwood. Subs used: de Vries, Croft, Deere, Hemmerman.
Att: 3,000

Tour Match (at Paramaribo)
Jun 10 v Robin Hood FC (a) 1-1
Greenwood
Wealands; Beardsley, de Vries, Deere, Neill, Houghton, Tisserand, Hawley, Pearson, Hemmerman, Greenwood. Subs used: Croft, Lord, O'Riley.
Att: 3,000

Tour Match
Aug 3 v Shamrock Rovers (a) 2-0
Wagstaff, Greenwood
Wealands(McKechnie); Banks, de Vries, Kaye(O'Riley), Deere, Galvin, McGill, Blampey, Pearson, Wagstaff, Greenwood.
Att: 2,000

Tour Match
Aug 5 v Finn Harps (a) 1-1
Wagstaff
Wealands; Banks, de Vries, Blampey, Deere, Galvin, McGill, Lord, Pearson, Wagstaff, Greenwood (Hawley).
Att: 3,000

Tour Match
Aug 7 v Cork Hibernians (a) 0-1
Wealands; Banks, de Vries, Kaye, Deere, Galvin, McGill, Lord, Pearson, Wagstaff, Greenwood (Hawley).
Att: 4,000

1974
Pre-season Friendly
Jul 27 v Falkirk (a) 1-1
Lord
Wealands; Daniel, McGill(de Vries), Kaye, Deere, Burnett, Grimes, Lord, Hawley(Fletcher), Wagstaff (Hemmerman), Greenwood.
Att: 1,200

Pre-season Friendly
Jul 31 v Hamilton Academical (a) 2-1
Hawley 2
Wealands; Daniel(Grimes), de Vries, Blampey, Deere, Burnett, Galvin(Hawley), Lord, Fletcher (Hemmerman), Wagstaff, Greenwood.
Att: 1,500

Pre-season Friendly
Aug 3 v Coventry City (h) 4-1
Lord, Hemmerman, Fletcher, Wagstaff
Wealands; Blampey, de Vries, Burnett, Deere, Lord, Grimes, Hawley, Hemmerman(Fletcher), Wagstaff, Greenwood.
Att: 2,691

Pre-season Friendly
Aug 6 v Grimsby Town (a) 0-1
Wealands; Blampey, de Vries, Burnett, Croft, Lord, Grimes, Hawley, Hemmerman, Wagstaff, Greenwood.
Att: 3,832

Pre-season Friendly
Aug 10 v Manchester United (h) 1-1
Hemmerman
Wealands; Blampey, de Vries, Burnett, Deere, Lord, Grimes, Hawley, Hemmerman, McGill, Greenwood.
Att: 8,303

1975
Pre-season Friendly
Jul 26 v Ayr United (a) 1-0
Wagstaff
Wealands; Banks, de Vries, Galvin(Staniforth), Croft, Roberts, Grimes, McGill, Wood, Wagstaff(Fletcher), Greenwood.
Att: 2,891

Pre-season Friendly
Jul 28 v Clyde (a) 3-2
Croft, Grimes, Fletcher
Wealands; Banks, Daniel, de Vries, Croft, Roberts, Grimes, McGill, Wood, Fletcher, Greenwood.
Att: 859

1976
Ken Wagstaff Testimonial
Apr 28 v Billy Bremner's XI (h) 4-6
Fletcher, Lyall, Wagstaff, Grimes
Wealands; Daniel, de Vries(Haigh), Roberts (Hemmerman), Galvin, Croft, Sunley(Fletcher), Lyall, Wood, Wagstaff, Grimes.
Att: 6,795

Pre-season Friendly
Aug 3 v York City (a) 2-1
Wood 2
Wealands(Blackburn); McGifford, Daniel, Croft (Dobson), Galvin, Haigh, Gibson(Staniforth), Lyall, Wood, Hawley(Hemmerman), Sunley(Stewart).
Att: 998

1977
Pre-season Friendly
Jul 30 v Scunthorpe United (a) 1-1
Hawley
Wealands(Blackburn); Daniel, de Vries(Gibson), Grimes(Hawker), Dobson, Haigh, Nisbet, Lord, Hawley(McDonald), Bannister, Galvin(Stewart).
Att: 1,331

1978
Pre-season Friendly
Aug 2 v SC Cambuur (h) 2-0
Dobson, Horswill
Wealands; Nisbet, de Vries(D.Holmes), Hawker, Dobson, Haigh, Hood(Marwood), Horswill, Bannister, McDonald, Farley.
Att: 1,504

Pre-season Friendly
Aug 7 v Newcastle United (h) 0-0
Wealands; Nisbet, de Vries, Croft, Dobson, Haigh, Hood(Hawker), Horswill, Bannister, McDonald, Farley.
Att: 2,960

1979

Tour Match

Jul 30 v VV Emmen (a) 5-0

Farley 2, Roberts, Hood, Bannister

Blackburn(Frankish); Nisbet, Skipper, Lord (Horswill), Dobson, Haigh, G.Roberts(Hood), Phillips(Hawker), Edwards, Bannister(McDonald), Farley.

Tour Match

Jul 31 v Haarlem (a) 1-1

Edwards

Blackburn; Nisbet, Skipper(Hood), Lord, McDonald(Dobson), Haigh, Hawker, Horswill (G.Roberts), Edwards, Bannister, Farley.

Tour Match

Aug 1 v SC Cambuur (a) 0-0

Blackburn; Nisbet, Hood, McDonald, Dobson, Hawker, G.Roberts, Horswill, Edwards(Norrie), Bannister, Farley(Lord).

Tour Match

Aug 2 v Bergum (a) 5-0

Edwards 4, Skipper

Blackburn(Frankish); Nisbet(Holt), Hood, Lord (Houghton), Skipper(Blackburn), Hawker, G.Roberts (McGuinness), Horswill, Edwards (Radcliffe), McDonald, Norrie.

Northern Professional Tournament

Aug 4 v SC Veendam (n) 2-0

Skipper, McDonald

Blackburn; Nisbet, Skipper, Hood, Dobson, Hawker, G.Roberts, Horswill, Edwards, Bannister, McDonald.

Att: 1,500

Northern Professional Tournament

Aug 5 v SC Heerenveen (n) 1-1

Hawker

Blackburn; Nisbet, Skipper, Dobson, Haigh, G.Roberts, Horswill, Hawker, Edwards, McDonald, Norrie.

Att: 1,500

Northern Professional Tournament Final

Aug 5 v FC Groningen (a) 0-1

Blackburn; Nisbet, Hood, Skipper, Haigh, Hawker, G.Roberts, Horswill, Edwards(Norrie), Bannister, McDonald.

Att: 2,500

All Northern Professional Tournament games played at Groningen. The final kicked off at 7pm — little more than two hours after the Tigers had completed their final group game.

Final group tables:

	P	W	D	L	F	A	P
1 Groningen	2	1	1	0	5	1	3
2 Cambuur	2	1	1	0	4	0	3
3 Emmen	2	0	0	2	1	9	0
1 Hull City	2	1	1	0	3	1	3
2 Heerenveen	2	0	2	0	2	2	2
3 Veendam	2	0	1	1	1	3	1

1981

Humber Bridge Festival Match

May 4 v Grimsby Town (h) 1-2

Horswill

Norman; Hoolickin, Booth, Richards, Eccleston, Horswill, Marwood(Moss), Swann, Whitehurst, Ferguson(Norrie), Mutrie(Edwards).

Att: 1,981

Malcolm Lord Testimonial

May 5 v Sunderland (h) 2-0

Chilton, Edwards

Norman(Fox); McNeil, Booth, Richards, Eccleston, Horswill, Swann, Lord(Marwood), Chilton(Mutrie), Pearson(Norrie), Edwards.

Att: 1,753

1982

Pre-season Friendly

Aug 3 v Scarborough (a) 3-2

Marwood, Swann, Flounders

Norman; McNeil, Thompson, Booth, Richards, Czuczman, Marwood, Swann, Flounders, Mutrie, G.Roberts.

Att: 1,251

Friendly

Nov 29 v Dinamo Kiev (h) 0-3

Davies(Findlay); McNeil, Askew(Thompson), D.Roberts(Richards), Skipper, Booth, Marwood, McClaren(Swann), Whitehurst(Flounders), Mutrie, G.Roberts.

Att: 6,901

1983

Stan Coombs Testimonial

Apr 25 v Ex-Tigers (h) 9-0

Whitehurst 2, Flounders 2, Mutrie 2, G.Roberts 2, Marwood

Norman(Davies); Hughes, Swann(McNeil), D.Roberts (Thompson), Skipper(Richards), Askew, Marwood (Booth), McClaren(Whitehurst), Flounders, Mutrie (Woof), G.Roberts.

Att: 1,551

The Ex-Tigers lined up: Wealands; Banks, Daniel, Wilson, Kaye, K.Houghton, Bremner, Lord, Chilton, Wagstaff, I.Butler. Subs used: McKechnie, Deere, Lyall, Barker, Sibborn, G.Houghton.

Harry Dunn Testimonial

May 4 v Scarborough (a) 1-1

Flounders

Davies(Norman); Hughes, Booth, D.Roberts(McNeil), Skipper, Askew(Ward), Marwood, McClaren(Swann), Flounders(Whitehurst), Woof(Saville), G.Roberts.

Att: 900

Friendly

May 9 v Newcastle United (h) 3-2

Mutrie 2, Marwood

Davies; McNeil, Booth, D.Roberts, Skipper, Askew, Marwood, McClaren, Whitehurst, Mutrie, G.Roberts.

Att: 5,431

Friendly
May 10 v Gateshead (a) 6-1
Richards, Marwood, McClaren, Mutrie, G.Roberts, Dixon(og)
Norman; McNeil, Hughes, Thompson, Richards, Askew, Marwood, McClaren(Swann), Woof, Mutrie (Chilton), G.Roberts(Flounders).
Att: 500

Stagnetto Cup (at Gibraltar)
May 19 v Real Balompedica Linense (n) 3-1
Marwood, Flounders, G.Roberts
Norman; McNeil, Swann, D.Roberts, Skipper, Booth, Marwood, Whitehurst(Richards), Flounders, Askew, G.Roberts.
Att: 2,200

Stagnetto Cup
May 21 v Gibraltar FA XI (a) 3-1
Marwood, Whitehurst, Askew
Davies; McNeil, Thompson, D.Roberts, Richards, Booth, Marwood, McClaren(Flounders), Whitehurst, Askew, G.Roberts.
Att: 5,000
Gibraltar FA drew their match with Real Balompedica Linense, leaving Hull City winners of the competition.

Pre-season Friendly
Aug 1 v Goole Town (a) 2-1
McClaren, Massey
Norman; McNeil, Wassell, D.Roberts, Skipper, Askew, Marwood, McClaren, Whitehurst, Massey, G.Roberts. Sub used: Flounders.
Att: 346

Pre-season Friendly
Aug 3 v Wisbech Town (a) 6-1
Whitehurst 3, Marwood 2, Massey
Davies(Norman); McNeil, Booth(Kemp), D.Roberts, Skipper, Askew(Turkington), Marwood, McClaren (Condon), Whitehurst, Massey(Flounders), G.Roberts.
Att: 400

Pre-season Friendly
Aug 8 v Bentley Victoria W (a) 5-0
Condon 2, Askew, Whitehurst, Staniforth
Davies; McNeil, Booth, D.Roberts, Skipper, Askew, Marwood, McClaren, Whitehurst, Flounders, G.Roberts. Subs used: Cockin, Kemp, Staniforth, Condon, Olsson, Massey.
Att: 125

Pre-season Friendly
Aug 13 v Derby County (h) 0-0
Norman; McNeil, Swann(Kamara), D.Roberts, Skipper, Booth, Marwood, McClaren, Whitehurst, Massey, Askew.
Att: 3,448

Pre-season Friendly
Aug 15 v Middlesbrough (h) 2-2
D.Roberts, Massey
Norman; McNeil, Wassell, D.Roberts, Skipper, Booth(Swann), Marwood, McClaren, Whitehurst (Mutrie), Massey, Askew.
Att: 2,857

Pre-season Friendly
Aug 19 v Sheffield Wednesday (h) 1-0
G.Roberts
Norman; McNeil, Hollifield(Kamara), D.Roberts, Skipper, Booth(Swann), Marwood, McClaren, Whitehurst, Massey(Mutrie), G.Roberts.
Att: 3,230

Pre-season Friendly
Aug 22 v Ipswich Town (h) 2-2
Skipper, Mutrie
Norman(Davies); McNeil, Askew(Swann), D.Roberts (Cockin), Skipper, Booth, Marwood(Flounders), McClaren, Whitehurst, Massey(Mutrie), G.Roberts.
Att: 5,123

1984

Friendly
Feb 1 v Scarborough (a) 1-2
Askew
Norman; McNeil, Hollifield, Swann, Skipper, Booth, Marwood, McClaren(Askew), Massey, Taylor, G.Roberts.
Att: 202

Friendly
Feb 18 v Grimsby Town (h) 2-3
Marwood 2
Norman; McNeil, Hollifield, Swann, Skipper, Booth, Marwood, McClaren, Whitehurst, Taylor, Askew (G.Roberts).
Att: 3,108

Anglo-American Cup lst Leg
Apr 8 v Tampa Bay Rowdies (h) 3-0
McClaren, Massey, G.Roberts
Blackburn; Olsson, Kemp, D.Roberts, Cockin, Booth, Taylor(Saville), McClaren(Corkain), Massey, Davis, G.Roberts(Tomlinson).
Att: 5,861

Tour Match
Jun 6 v Fort Lauderdale Sun (a) 1-0
G.Roberts
Davies; McNeil, Swann, Hollifield(D.Roberts), Skipper, McEwan, Flounders, McClaren, Whitehurst(Davis), Askew, G.Roberts.
Att: 1,565

Anglo-American Cup 2nd Leg
Jun 13 v Tampa Bay Rowdies (a) 0-1
Norman; McNeil, Swann, D.Roberts(Hollifield), Skipper, McEwan, Flounders, McClaren(Davis), Whitehurst, Askew, G.Roberts.
Att: 4,922
Hull City won 3-1 on aggregate.

North Ferriby United Golden Jubilee Match
Jul 31 v North Ferriby United (a) 2-0
McEwan, Massey
Davies(Norman); McNeil(Williams), Hollifield, Horton(Swann), Skipper, D.Roberts(McEwan), Askew(Pearson), McClaren(Davis), Flounders, Massey, G.Roberts.
Att: 500

Pre-season Friendly
Aug 3 v Goole Town (a) 1-0
Flounders
Norman(Davies); Williams(McNeil), Swann (Hollifield), Horton(Booth), Skipper(D.Roberts), McEwan, Massey, McClaren, Flounders, Askew, G.Roberts.
Att: 365

Pre-season Friendly
Aug 7 v Scarborough (a) 4-0
Ring 2, Askew, G.Roberts.
Davies(Norman); McNeil(D.Roberts), Hollifield (Swann), Horton, Skipper, McEwan, Ring, McClaren(Williams), Whitehurst(Massey), Askew, G.Roberts.
Att: 497

Pre-season Friendly
Aug 15 v Barnsley (h) 1-0
Whitehurst
Norman(Davies); D.Roberts(McNeil), Pearson, Horton(Booth), Skipper, McEwan, Ring(Massey), Williams, Whitehurst, Askew, G.Roberts.
Att: 1,120

Pre-season Friendly
Aug 18 v Scunthorpe United (a) 2-3
Whitehurst, Ring
Davies(Norman); D.Roberts, Pearson, Horton, Skipper, McEwan, Massey(Flounders), Williams (Olsson), Whitehurst, Askew(Ring), G.Roberts.
Att: 808

1985
Tour Match
May 23 v Gibraltar FA (a) 1-1
Whitehurst
Davies; Jobson, Pearson, Swann, Skipper, McEwan(McNeil), Flounders(Brentano), McClaren (Olsson), Whitehurst, Askew, Massey.
Att: 2,000

Billy Bly Trophy
Jul 29 v North Ferriby United (a) 4-0
Whitehurst 2, Bunn, Roberts
Norman; Brentano, Pearson(McNeil), Swann, Skipper, McEwan, Corkain(Williams), Bunn, Whitehurst, Ring(Flounders), Roberts.
Att: 500

Pre-season Friendly
Jul 31 v Scunthorpe United (a) 1-1
Bunn
Norman(Davies); Brentano, Swann, Corkain, Skipper, McEwan, Williams, Bunn, Whitehurst, Ring (Flounders), Olsson.
Att: 743

Pre-season Friendly
Aug 3 v Scarborough (a) 3-0
Jobson, Bunn, Whitehurst
Norman(Davies); Jobson, Pearson, Swann, Skipper, McEwan, Williams(Ring), Bunn, Whitehurst, Askew(Flounders), Corkain(Olsson).
Att: 777

Pre-season Friendly
Aug 6 v Manchester City (h) 2-1
Bunn, Askew
Norman; Jobson, Pearson, Swann, Skipper, McEwan, Williams, Bunn(Flounders), Whitehurst, Askew, Roberts.
Att: 3,144

Pre-season Friendly
Aug 10 v Watford (h) 2-0
Swann, Bunn
Norman; Jobson, Pearson, Swann, Skipper, McEwan, Williams, Bunn, Whitehurst, Askew, Roberts.
Att: 3,500

1986
Pre-season Friendly
Jul 31 v Brigg Town (a) 5-1
Parker 2, Payton, Bunn, Flounders
Kelly; Brentano(Jobson), Pearson(Skipper), Olsson, Swann, Corkain, Daniel(Payton), Bunn(Saville), Flounders, Parker, Roberts.
Att: 150

Billy Bly Trophy
Aug 2 v North Ferriby United (a) 1-0
Saville
Norman; Jobson, Heard, Doyle, Skipper, McEwan, Williams(Payton), Bunn, Saville(Flounders), Askew(Swann), Roberts(Pearson).
Att: 650

Pre-season Friendly
Aug 4 v Scarborough (a) 0-1
Norman; Swann(Williams), Heard, Doyle, Jobson, McEwan(Skipper), Parker, Bunn(Saville), Flounders, Askew(Daniel), Roberts.
Att: 736

Pre-season Friendly
Aug 6 v Doncaster Rovers (a) 1-0
Roberts
Norman; Jobson, Heard, Doyle(Williams), Skipper, McEwan, Parker, Swann, Flounders, Saville, Roberts.
Att: 405

Pre-season Friendly
Aug 11 v Scunthorpe United (h) 6-2
Flounders 3, Bunn, Saville, Daniel
Norman; Jobson, Swann(Pearson), Heard, Skipper, McEwan, Parker, Bunn(Saville), Flounders, Askew(Daniel), Roberts.
Att: 950

Pre-season Friendly
Aug 16 v Sheffield Wednesday (h) 2-2
Jobson, Bunn
Norman; Jobson, Swann(Pearson), Heard(Payton), Skipper, McEwan, Parker, Bunn, Flounders(Saville), Daniel(Askew), Roberts.
Att: 2,138

1987
Billy Bly Trophy
Jul 29 v North Ferriby United (a) 6-0
Dyer 5, Bunn
Norman; Palmer, Heard, Parker, Skipper(Jobson), McEwan, Dyer, Bunn, Saville(Daniel), Askew, Roberts(Williams).
Att: 700

Pre-season Friendly
Aug 1 v Wrexham (a) 1-0
Bunn
Norman; Palmer, Heard, Parker, Jobson, McEwan, Roberts, Bunn, Dyer, Askew, Daniel.
Att: 514

Pre-season Friendly
Aug 4 v Scarborough (h) 0-0
Norman; Palmer, Heard, Parker, Jobson, McEwan(Skipper), Daniel, Bunn(Saville), Dyer, Askew, Williams(Roberts).
Att: 1,160

Pre-season Friendly
Aug 5 v Whitby Town (a) 5-1
Bunn 2, Dyer 2, Saville
Norman(Kelly); Palmer(Williams), Heard(Daniel) Jobson, Skipper, McEwan, Parker(Corkain) Bunn(Saville), Dyer(Brown), Askew, Roberts.
Att: 267

Pre-season Friendly
Aug 7 v Luton Town (h) 1-1
Bunn
Norman; Palmer, Heard(Daniel), Jobson, Skipper, McEwan, Parker, Bunn, Dyer, Askew, Roberts.
Att: 1,038

Friendly
Oct 12 v Pontefract Collieries (a) 3-2
Payton, Thompson, Saville
Kelly; Palmer(Buckley), Heard, Jobson, Skipper, Parker, Roberts(Payton), Thompson(Brown), Saville, Askew, Williams.
Att: 800
First match under Pontefract Collieries' floodlights.

1988
Jeff Radcliffe Testimonial
Apr 15 v Tottenham Hotspur (h) 2-1
Saville, De Mange
Norman; Palmer, Daniel, Jobson, Skipper, Payton, Roberts, Saville, Radcliffe(Hotte), De Mange, Williams.
Att: 2,077

Friendly
May 11 v Kilham (n) 10-0
Saville 2, Edwards 2, Norman, Jobson, Payton, Roberts, De Mange, Daniel.
Norman; Brown, Jacobs(Heard), Jobson, Skipper, Payton, Roberts(De Mange), Saville, Edwards (Buckley), Daniel, Jenkinson(Thompson).
Att: 450
Played at Rudston in aid of All Saints Church (Kilham) Restoration Appeal. Bad light halted play after 76 minutes.

Tour Match
May 17 v Real Balompedica Linense (a) 1-0
Saville
Norman; Brown(Buckley), Jacobs, Jobson, Skipper, Hotte, Roberts, Saville, Edwards, De Mange, Jenkinson(Askew).

Billy Bly Trophy
Jul 30 v North Ferriby United (a) 3-0
Edwards 3
Norman; Jobson, Daniel, De Mange, Skipper, Terry, Payton, Roberts, Moore(Hotte), Edwards, Dyer.
Att: 720

Pre-season Friendly
Aug 4 v Harrogate Town (a) 4-0
Edwards 2, Dyer, Moore
Norman; Palmer, Jacobs, De Mange, Terry, Jobson, Dyer, Roberts, Moore, Edwards, Daniel(Jenkinson).
Att: 550

Pre-season Friendly
Aug 9 v Bridlington Trinity (a) 4-0
Edwards 2, Saville, Moore
Norman; Palmer(Brown), Jacobs, Buckley, Skipper, Dyer, Roberts, Saville, Moore, Edwards, Daniel(Hotte).
Att: 400

Pre-season Friendly
Aug 12 v Mansfield Town (a) 3-2
Dyer, Moore, Edwards
Norman; Palmer, Jacobs, Terry, Skipper, Smith, Dyer, Roberts, Moore, Edwards, Daniel.
Att: 1,100

Pre-season Friendly
Aug 15 v Seattle Storm (h) 2-2
De Mange, Edwards
Norman; Palmer, Jacobs, De Mange, Skipper, Jobson, Dyer, Roberts, Moore, Edwards, Daniel(Jenkinson).
Att: 754

Pre-season Friendly
Aug 17 v Middlesbrough (h) 2-2
Jobson, Dyer
Norman; Palmer, Jacobs(Buckley), Jobson, Skipper(Smith), Terry, Dyer, Roberts, Moore, Edwards, Saville.
Att: 1,214

Pre-season Friendly
Aug 22 v Aston Villa (h) 1-1
Saville
Norman; Palmer(Smith), Jacobs, Jobson, Skipper, Terry, Dyer, Roberts, Moore, Edwards, Saville.
Att: 1,297

Tour Match
Dec 15 v Dandy Town (a) 6-1
Payton 2, Edwards, De Mange, Jobson, Palmer
Norman; Palmer, Daniel, Warren, Jobson (Buckley), Terry, Payton, Roberts, Saville, Edwards, De Mange.
Att: 1,000

Tour Match
Dec 17 v Pembroke Hamilton Club (a) 3-0
Jobson 2, Palmer
Norman; Palmer, Daniel, Warren(Jenkinson), Jobson, Buckley, Payton, Smith(Jacobs), Saville(Moore), Edwards, De Mange.
Att: 500

Tour Match
Dec 19 v Bermuda XI (a) 0-0 *
Norman; Palmer, Daniel, Warren, Jobson, Buckley, Payton, Roberts (Smith), Saville, Moore, De Mange (Jenkinson).
Att: 1,000
*Match abandoned after 84 minutes due to floodlight failure.
All three matches in Bermuda played at the Warwick Bowl, Hamilton.

Tigers Against Other League Clubs

Hull City have played 104 clubs in the Football League since 1905. Below is the Tigers' record against each club. Some clubs changed their names (eg Small Heath became Birmingham then Birmingham City) and some clubs modified their titles (eg Leicester Fosse became Leicester City). In all cases the current name used by each club covers all games under previous names.

		HOME					*AWAY*				
	P	W	D	L	F	A	W	D	L	F	A
Accrington Stanley	24	9	2	1	31	13	8	3	1	20	10
AFC Bournemouth	24	9	2	1	30	12	2	4	6	14	26
Aldershot	4	0	1	1	3	4	2	0	0	5	1
Arsenal	4	1	0	1	2	2	0	1	1	1	2
Aston Villa	16	4	2	2	12	7	1	3	4	8	21
Barnsley	82	20	9	12	84	45	11	10	20	52	78
Barrow	22	8	3	0	26	4	6	1	4	14	12
Birmingham City	46	11	5	7	37	19	3	7	13	27	51
Blackburn Rovers	40	5	6	9	25	29	2	4	14	15	39
Blackpool	78	20	10	9	60	40	11	14	14	48	63
Bolton Wanderers	32	6	8	2	21	15	1	5	10	11	27
Bradford	34	8	4	5	34	22	2	2	13	17	43
Bradford City	56	15	7	6	46	29	5	6	17	28	50
Brentford	36	14	3	1	39	9	4	6	8	29	34
Brighton & Hove Albion	16	7	1	0	17	5	1	3	4	9	13
Bristol City	62	18	8	5	60	33	4	8	19	30	62
Bristol Rovers	28	7	2	5	24	12	4	3	7	18	26
Burnley	36	8	5	5	33	22	5	5	8	18	30
Burton United	4	1	1	0	4	1	2	0	0	5	1
Bury	56	16	3	9	55	31	6	5	17	23	48
Cambridge United	2	1	0	0	2	1	1	0	0	3	1
Cardiff City	34	4	11	2	22	16	6	4	7	21	30
Carlisle United	54	15	6	6	61	25	8	9	10	29	32
Charlton Athletic	28	2	6	6	18	26	5	1	8	19	28
Chelsea	26	4	3	6	15	17	0	2	11	2	28
Chester City	28	10	3	1	25	8	2	5	7	15	27
Chesterfield	28	11	3	0	26	9	7	3	4	21	14
Colchester United	20	4	3	3	17	10	3	3	4	11	16
Coventry City	28	8	4	2	28	14	5	3	6	17	21
Crewe Alexandra	28	11	2	1	31	11	7	3	4	25	20
Crystal Palace	32	8	5	3	31	14	6	5	5	19	22
Darlington	30	8	4	3	28	20	8	3	4	27	20
Derby County	40	9	9	2	34	16	6	4	10	24	43
Doncaster Rovers	32	8	4	4	39	19	5	3	8	20	31
Everton	6	2	0	1	3	3	1	0	2	2	7
Exeter City	12	4	2	0	16	7	3	1	2	13	9
Fulham	68	19	8	7	59	28	7	11	16	21	56
Gainsborough Trinity	14	4	1	2	18	10	3	2	2	9	8
Gateshead	40	10	4	6	30	19	5	3	12	21	37
Gillingham	14	2	4	1	6	4	2	0	5	5	8
Glossop	20	8	1	1	23	6	3	2	5	18	17
Grimsby Town	46	11	5	7	50	32	6	7	10	21	29
Halifax Town	34	11	3	3	47	13	6	4	7	23	23
Hartlepool United	26	10	3	0	37	7	4	6	3	23	24
Hereford United	6	2	1	0	5	2	0	1	2	2	5
Huddersfield Town	34	6	5	6	26	24	6	2	9	22	26
Ipswich Town	14	4	3	0	12	6	0	2	5	5	14
Leeds City	22	7	3	1	25	14	3	3	5	13	17

		HOME					AWAY				
	P	W	D	L	F	A	W	D	L	F	A
Leeds United	32	9	2	5	23	18	2	4	10	12	31
Leicester City	52	12	10	4	56	38	9	6	11	33	41
Leyton Orient	62	19	8	4	64	28	8	12	11	29	36
Lincoln City	52	15	7	4	51	27	12	3	11	38	36
Liverpool	6	0	1	2	3	5	0	0	3	4	10
Luton Town	30	5	3	7	23	24	5	4	6	22	23
Manchester City	12	3	2	1	11	8	0	2	4	4	13
Manchester United	16	4	2	2	13	8	0	1	7	4	22
Mansfield Town	30	9	4	2	37	14	3	5	7	20	26
Middlesbrough	32	6	7	3	26	22	3	2	11	14	32
Millwall	48	16	6	2	45	17	3	6	15	17	47
Nelson	4	2	0	0	6	1	1	1	0	3	1
New Brighton	18	7	2	0	28	5	2	4	3	10	12
Newcastle United	4	0	1	1	3	4	0	0	2	3	10
Newport County	12	4	1	1	16	5	3	1	2	8	9
Northampton Town	10	4	0	1	13	2	1	2	2	5	9
Norwich City	22	5	3	3	13	8	4	1	6	10	16
Nottingham Forest	52	13	3	10	40	32	6	4	16	20	49
Notts County	52	14	6	6	47	22	4	8	14	22	54
Oldham Athletic	64	20	5	7	68	23	5	12	15	27	61
Oxford United	28	5	3	6	12	11	3	6	5	17	21
Peterborough United	16	3	4	1	12	9	1	1	6	9	22
Plymouth Argyle	44	12	4	6	40	28	8	6	8	35	43
Portsmouth	38	8	6	5	33	23	3	8	8	21	28
Port Vale	52	18	5	3	49	19	7	3	16	26	48
Preston North End	38	9	7	3	38	20	2	2	15	19	42
Queen's Park Rangers	30	10	3	2	37	15	2	7	6	20	26
Reading	32	6	5	5	20	15	3	5	8	15	29
Rochdale	28	8	5	1	27	14	4	2	8	20	29
Rotherham United	52	12	6	8	41	35	7	10	9	27	29
Scunthorpe United	16	4	2	2	12	9	2	3	3	11	15
Sheffield United	38	5	8	6	27	28	3	5	11	20	51
Sheffield Wednesday	32	4	10	2	20	17	1	4	11	12	40
Shrewsbury Town	22	7	3	1	27	14	3	4	4	16	17
Southampton	40	8	9	3	28	15	3	6	11	22	44
Southend United	20	6	2	2	11	6	2	3	5	10	17
Southport	22	11	0	0	40	9	4	1	6	11	15
Stockport County	58	18	7	4	71	29	7	10	12	41	51
Stoke City	38	9	5	5	31	21	3	6	10	15	32
Sunderland	22	5	3	3	17	11	3	2	6	8	13
Swansea City	38	11	5	3	41	28	3	2	14	14	39
Swindon Town	32	6	7	3	14	11	1	6	9	9	22
Torquay United	8	3	0	1	11	4	1	1	2	5	7
Tottenham Hotspur	14	5	1	1	9	4	0	3	4	4	14
Tranmere Rovers	30	11	1	3	30	10	5	3	7	24	28
Walsall	22	7	3	1	20	8	4	4	3	18	14
Watford	22	7	3	1	21	10	2	5	4	15	22
West Bromwich Albion	30	9	4	2	30	13	3	5	7	14	26
West Ham United	28	6	5	3	22	14	1	6	7	13	24
Wigan Athletic	6	2	0	1	4	3	0	2	1	3	4
Wigan Borough	2	0	1	0	0	0	0	0	1	1	3
Wimbledon	8	1	3	0	4	3	2	0	2	9	8
Wolverhampton W	42	13	3	5	52	19	6	4	11	27	48
Workington	8	2	1	1	11	6	1	0	3	8	11
Wrexham	28	9	2	3	30	15	3	0	11	13	35
York City	34	8	4	5	29	21	7	3	7	22	25

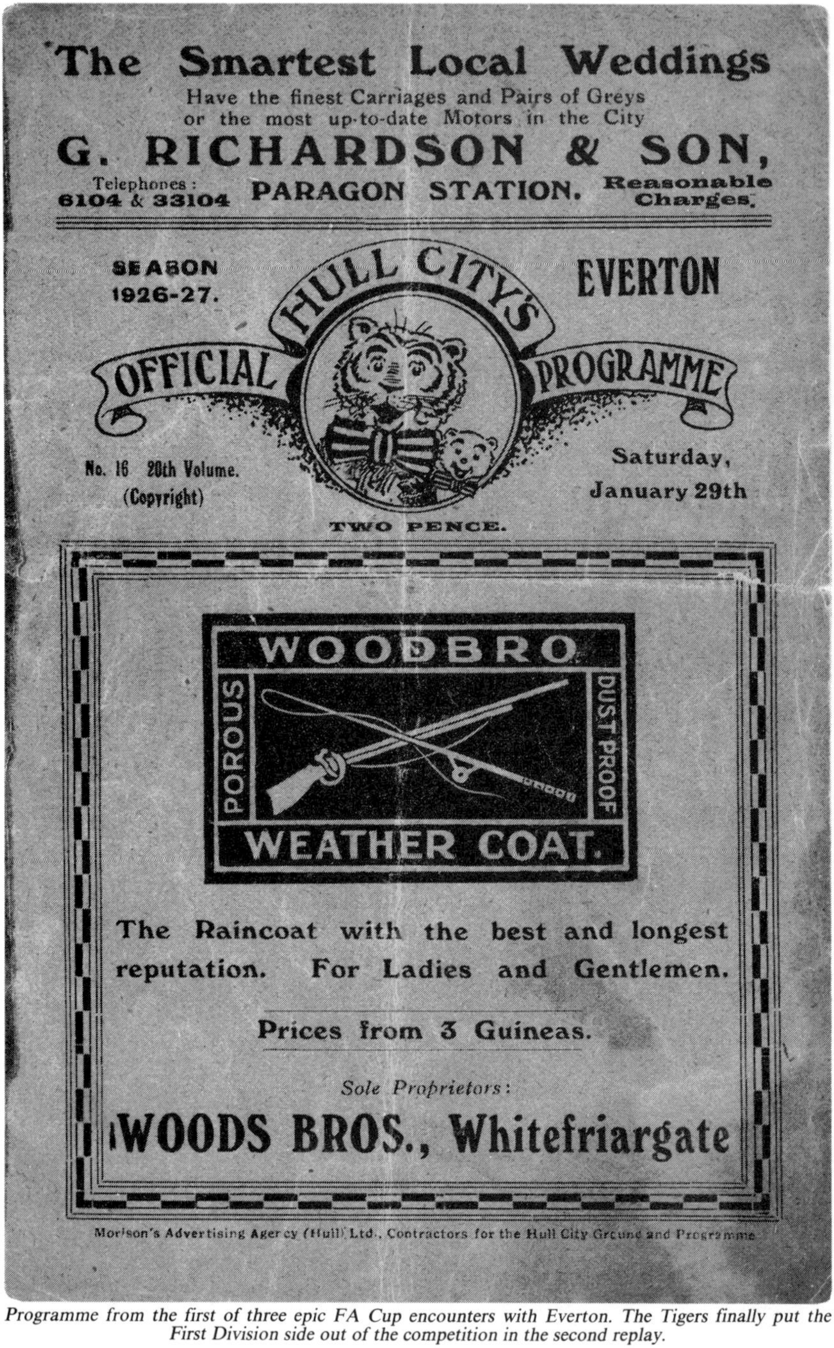

Programme from the first of three epic FA Cup encounters with Everton. The Tigers finally put the First Division side out of the competition in the second replay.

Tigers' Club by Club Record in Other Matches

	FA CUP						OTHER COMPS						OTHER MATCHES					
	P	W	D	L	F	A	P	W	D	L	F	A	P	W	D	L	F	A
Accrington Stanley	1	1	0	0	3	1	-	-	-	-	-	-	-	-	-	-	-	-
AFC Bournemouth	-	-	-	-	-	-	1	0	0	1	1	2	-	-	-	-	-	-
All Star XIs	-	-	-	-	-	-	-	-	-	-	-	-	3	2	0	1	20	15
Army Service Corps	-	-	-	-	-	-	-	-	-	-	-	-	1	1	0	0	5	1
Arsenal	4	1	2	1	6	4	3	0	0	3	2	10	1	0	0	1	1	3
Aston Villa	4	0	1	3	2	9	-	-	-	-	-	-	1	0	1	0	1	1
Ayr United	-	-	-	-	-	-	-	-	-	-	-	-	1	1	0	0	1	0
Barnsley	2	1	1	0	3	1	12	5	0	7	20	32	3	3	0	0	5	1
Barton Town	-	-	-	-	-	-	-	-	-	-	-	-	2	2	0	0	4	2
Bath City	1	1	0	0	3	0	-	-	-	-	-	-	-	-	-	-	-	-
Bentley Victoria W	-	-	-	-	-	-	-	-	-	-	-	-	1	1	0	0	5	0
Birmingham City	1	0	0	1	0	2	6	0	0	6	5	17	-	-	-	-	-	-
Blackburn Rovers	6	2	2	2	7	10	-	-	-	-	-	-	2	2	0	0	4	0
Blackpool	3	2	0	1	6	3	-	-	-	-	-	-	1	0	1	0	5	5
Blyth Spartans	3	1	2	0	5	4	-	-	-	-	-	-	-	-	-	-	-	-
Bolton Wanderers	5	1	1	3	6	12	2	0	1	1	1	5	1	0	0	1	0	1
Boston Town	-	-	-	-	-	-	-	-	-	-	-	-	1	1	0	0	4	2
Bradford	3	1	1	1	5	6	16	7	2	7	23	30	2	0	1	1	3	4
Bradford City	2	1	0	1	2	3	20	9	2	9	41	45	4	2	0	2	6	5
Brentford	5	3	2	0	10	5	1	0	0	1	0	3	-	-	-	-	-	-
Bridlington Trinity	-	-	-	-	-	-	-	-	-	-	-	-	1	1	0	0	4	0
Brigg Town	-	-	-	-	-	-	-	-	-	-	-	-	2	2	0	0	9	1
Brighton & Hove Albion	2	0	0	2	2	4	-	-	-	-	-	-	-	-	-	-	-	-
Bristol City	2	0	1	1	1	2	-	-	-	-	-	-	-	-	-	-	-	-
Bristol Rovers	4	1	1	2	4	7	1	1	0	0	1	0	-	-	-	-	-	-
Burnley	1	1	0	0	3	0	1	0	0	1	1	2	2	0	1	1	2	3
Burton United	-	-	-	-	-	-	-	-	-	-	-	-	1	1	0	0	3	1
Bury	2	0	1	1	1	2	2	2	0	0	5	3	1	0	0	1	1	4
Cardiff City	1	1	0	0	2	1	-	-	-	-	-	-	-	-	-	-	-	-
Carlisle United	5	1	2	2	6	10	-	-	-	-	-	-	-	-	-	-	-	-
Charlton Athletic	2	2	0	0	6	1	1	0	1	0	1	1	-	-	-	-	-	-
Chelsea	7	0	3	4	5	11	-	-	-	-	-	-	1	0	0	1	0	3
Cheltenham Town	1	1	0	0	4	2	-	-	-	-	-	-	-	-	-	-	-	-
Chester	2	0	1	1	2	3	-	-	-	-	-	-	-	-	-	-	-	-
Chesterfield	-	-	-	-	-	-	5	2	1	2	10	12	1	0	0	1	1	2
Clyde	-	-	-	-	-	-	-	-	-	-	-	-	3	1	0	2	6	8
Coldstream Guards	-	-	-	-	-	-	-	-	-	-	-	-	1	1	0	0	10	3
Corinthians	-	-	-	-	-	-	-	-	-	-	-	-	1	0	0	1	1	4
Coventry City	2	1	0	1	1	3	4	2	0	2	5	5	1	1	0	0	4	1
Crewe Alexandra	3	2	1	0	7	3	-	-	-	-	-	-	1	0	1	0	1	1
Crook Town	1	1	0	0	5	4	-	-	-	-	-	-	-	-	-	-	-	-
Crystal Palace	2	2	0	0	5	2	-	-	-	-	-	-	-	-	-	-	-	-
Darlington	6	2	4	0	8	4	4	1	1	2	8	15	2	1	1	0	8	4
Denaby United	1	1	0	0	2	0	-	-	-	-	-	-	-	-	-	-	-	-
Denton	-	-	-	-	-	-	-	-	-	-	-	-	1	1	0	0	2	1
Derby County	-	-	-	-	-	-	5	1	1	3	11	14	3	1	2	0	5	4
Doncaster Rovers	1	1	0	0	1	0	5	1	0	4	10	20	3	2	0	1	5	2
Dundee	-	-	-	-	-	-	-	-	-	-	-	-	2	0	0	2	1	5
Durham Lt Infantry	-	-	-	-	-	-	-	-	-	-	-	-	1	1	0	0	4	0
East Fife	-	-	-	-	-	-	-	-	-	-	-	-	1	0	1	0	1	1
East Riding XI	-	-	-	-	-	-	-	-	-	-	-	-	1	0	1	0	2	2
Everton 'A'	-	-	-	-	-	-	-	-	-	-	-	-	1	1	0	0	2	0

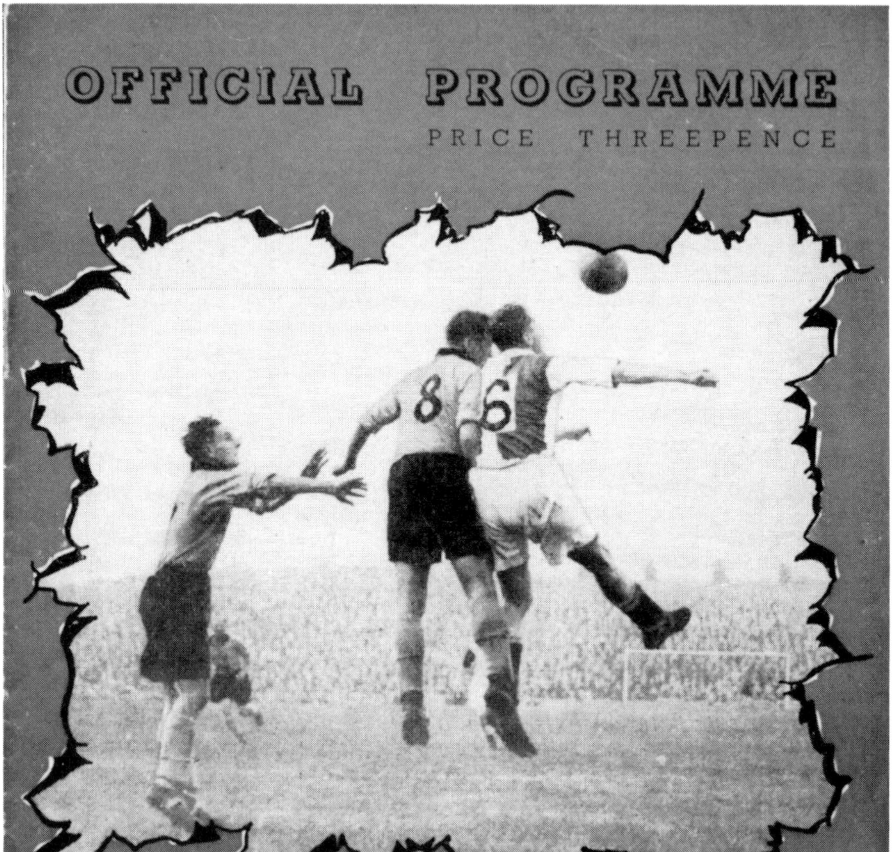

1 September 1949, the first Second Division match played at Boothferry Park.

	FA CUP						OTHER COMPS						OTHER MATCHES					
	P	W	D	L	F	A	P	W	D	L	F	A	P	W	D	L	F	A
Everton	6	2	3	1	10	8	-	-	-	-	-	-	1	0	0	1	4	7
Exeter City	1	1	0	0	2	1	1	1	0	0	1	0	-	-	-	-	-	-
Falkirk	-	-	-	-	-	-	-	-	-	-	-	-	3	1	1	1	8	3
Folkestone	-	-	-	-	-	-	-	-	-	-	-	-	1	0	0	1	1	4
Fulham	5	1	2	2	5	9	2	1	0	1	2	2	1	0	1	0	0	0
Gainsborough Reserves	-	-	-	-	-	-	-	-	-	-	-	-	1	0	0	1	1	2
Gainsborough Trinity	-	-	-	-	-	-	2	2	0	0	5	2	1	0	0	1	2	3
Gateshead (1)	3	2	0	1	9	2	2	0	0	2	3	8	2	1	1	0	1	0
Gateshead (2)	-	-	-	-	-	-	-	-	-	-	-	-	1	1	0	0	6	1
Glossop	-	-	-	-	-	-	-	-	-	-	-	-	2	1	1	0	2	1
Goole Town	-	-	-	-	-	-	-	-	-	-	-	-	5	4	1	0	11	4
Grimethorpe United	1	1	0	0	8	1	-	-	-	-	-	-	-	-	-	-	-	-
Grimsby Town	1	1	0	0	3	2	27	14	7	6	51	46	25	10	4	11	47	44
Halifax Town	1	1	0	0	2	1	10	6	2	2	17	8	-	-	-	-	-	-
Hamilton Academical	-	-	-	-	-	-	-	-	-	-	-	-	2	1	1	0	5	4
Harrogate Town	-	-	-	-	-	-	-	-	-	-	-	-	1	1	0	0	4	0
Hartlepool United	1	1	0	0	2	0	6	2	1	3	8	11	-	-	-	-	-	-
Heart of Midlothian	-	-	-	-	-	-	-	-	-	-	-	-	1	1	0	0	4	0
Hibernian	-	-	-	-	-	-	-	-	-	-	-	-	5	3	1	1	14	7
Huddersfield Town	1	0	0	1	1	3	13	4	1	8	16	20	2	1	0	1	5	3
Hull Amateurs	-	-	-	-	-	-	-	-	-	-	-	-	2	1	1	0	7	4
Hull District XI	-	-	-	-	-	-	-	-	-	-	-	-	1	1	0	0	5	0
Humber Garrison	-	-	-	-	-	-	-	-	-	-	-	-	3	2	1	0	10	6
Ipswich Town	-	-	-	-	-	-	-	-	-	-	-	-	1	0	1	0	2	2
Kidderminster Harriers	1	1	0	0	4	1	-	-	-	-	-	-	-	-	-	-	-	-
Kilham	-	-	-	-	-	-	-	-	-	-	-	-	1	1	0	0	10	0
Kilmarnock	-	-	-	-	-	-	-	-	-	-	-	-	1	0	1	0	2	2
Leeds City	2	1	1	0	3	2	11	3	4	4	12	16	6	4	0	2	17	9
Leeds United	-	-	-	-	-	-	9	1	2	6	13	28	5	2	1	2	11	12
Leicester City	4	0	1	3	2	6	11	5	3	3	24	22	2	1	0	1	3	2
Leicester Regiment	-	-	-	-	-	-	-	-	-	-	-	-	1	1	0	0	4	2
Leyton Orient	2	0	1	1	1	3	1	0	0	1	0	1	-	-	-	-	-	-
Lincoln City	2	0	1	1	2	4	32	13	7	12	51	57	6	3	3	0	10	5
Liverpool	1	0	0	1	2	3	3	0	1	2	1	6	2	0	0	2	5	11
Luton Town	-	-	-	-	-	-	-	-	-	-	-	-	1	0	1	0	1	1
Manchester City	4	1	1	2	5	8	3	1	0	2	2	6	4	2	1	1	4	2
Manchester City Reserves	-	-	-	-	-	-	-	-	-	-	-	-	1	0	0	1	0	1
Manchester United	2	1	0	1	2	1	3	0	1	2	1	7	3	1	1	1	5	5
Mansfield Town	1	1	0	0	4	1	4	1	1	2	7	6	1	1	0	0	3	2
Middlesbrough	5	1	2	2	9	7	8	4	2	2	15	16	3	0	2	1	5	7
Middlesbrough Reserves	-	-	-	-	-	-	-	-	-	-	-	-	2	0	1	1	4	5
Morton	-	-	-	-	-	-	-	-	-	-	-	-	1	1	0	0	1	0
Motherwell	-	-	-	-	-	-	-	-	-	-	-	-	1	1	0	0	4	0
New Brighton	3	2	1	0	6	1	-	-	-	-	-	-	-	-	-	-	-	-
Newcastle United	6	1	2	3	5	12	7	2	1	4	9	21	6	3	1	2	10	8
Northampton Town	1	1	0	0	2	1	-	-	-	-	-	-	-	-	-	-	-	-
North Ferriby United	-	-	-	-	-	-	-	-	-	-	-	-	5	5	0	0	16	0
Norwich City	1	1	0	0	3	0	2	1	0	1	2	2	4	3	1	0	9	2
Nottingham Forest	2	1	0	1	2	3	8	3	0	5	15	20	-	-	-	-	-	-
Notts County	-	-	-	-	-	-	9	2	2	5	10	16	3	0	2	1	7	8
Oldham Athletic	4	2	1	1	4	3	2	1	1	0	3	1	1	1	0	0	1	0
Past Players	-	-	-	-	-	-	-	-	-	-	-	-	3	3	0	0	12	0
Penrith	1	1	0	0	2	0	-	-	-	-	-	-	-	-	-	-	-	-
Peterborough United	-	-	-	-	-	-	4	2	0	2	6	3	1	1	0	0	4	3
Pilgrims	-	-	-	-	-	-	-	-	-	-	-	-	1	1	0	0	4	1
Plymouth Argyle	5	3	2	0	12	7	-	-	-	-	-	-	-	-	-	-	-	-

The largest League attendance at Boothferry Park, 50,103, watched this clash between two of the Second Division's promotion contenders.

	FA CUP						OTHER COMPS						OTHER MATCHES					
	P	W	D	L	F	A	P	W	D	L	F	A	P	W	D	L	F	A
Pontefract Colls	-	-	-	-	-	-	-	-	-	-	-	-	1	1	0	0	3	2
Portsmouth	3	0	2	1	4	6	1	0	0	1	1	2	1	1	0	0	4	0
Port Vale	4	1	2	1	8	9	-	-	-	-	-	-	1	0	0	1	1	2
Preston North End	2	0	1	1	0	1	2	2	0	0	7	2	2	0	1	1	4	5
Prince of Wales Hussars	-	-	-	-	-	-	-	-	-	-	-	-	1	1	0	0	1	0
Queen of the South	-	-	-	-	-	-	-	-	-	-	-	-	2	1	0	1	5	4
Queen's Park Rangers	-	-	-	-	-	-	3	0	0	3	2	10	1	1	0	0	2	0
Raith Rovers	-	-	-	-	-	-	-	-	-	-	-	-	1	0	0	1	1	3
Reading	3	1	1	1	2	2	-	-	-	-	-	-	-	-	-	-	-	-
Rhyl	1	1	0	0	5	0	-	-	-	-	-	-	-	-	-	-	-	-
Rochdale	3	1	2	0	5	4	-	-	-	-	-	-	-	-	-	-	-	-
Rotherham United	3	2	0	1	7	3	12	5	3	4	22	22	2	1	0	1	2	1
St Mirren	-	-	-	-	-	-	-	-	-	-	-	-	2	1	0	1	6	4
Scarborough	-	-	-	-	-	-	-	-	-	-	-	-	11	6	3	2	23	8
Scunthorpe United	1	1	0	0	4	0	-	-	-	-	-	-	5	1	3	1	12	9
Sheffield FC	-	-	-	-	-	-	-	-	-	-	-	-	2	2	0	0	7	2
Sheffield United	2	0	1	1	1	3	19	8	3	8	22	27	5	3	0	2	11	5
Sheffield Wednesday	1	0	0	1	3	4	12	4	3	5	19	20	3	2	1	0	6	3
Shrewsbury Town	1	1	0	0	2	1	1	0	0	1	0	1	-	-	-	-	-	-
Southampton	3	2	1	0	7	2	3	0	1	2	5	7	1	1	0	0	5	0
Southend United	-	-	-	-	-	-	2	0	1	1	1	3	-	-	-	-	-	-
Southport	5	3	2	0	11	3	2	1	1	0	3	2	1	0	1	0	1	1
Stafford Rangers	1	1	0	0	2	1	-	-	-	-	-	-	-	-	-	-	-	-
Stalybridge Celtic	1	1	0	0	8	2	-	-	-	-	-	-	-	-	-	-	-	-
Stanley	-	-	-	-	-	-	-	-	-	-	-	-	1	0	0	1	3	5
Stockport County	5	1	2	2	2	3	1	1	0	0	4	1	-	-	-	-	-	-
Stockton	2	0	1	1	4	7	-	-	-	-	-	-	1	0	1	0	2	2
Stoke City	4	1	0	3	5	10	1	0	0	1	0	2	1	0	0	1	0	1
Sunderland	3	0	0	3	2	9	1	0	0	1	1	2	5	1	2	2	8	8
Sutton Town	1	1	0	0	3	0	-	-	-	-	-	-	-	-	-	-	-	-
Swansea City	1	1	0	0	1	0	-	-	-	-	-	-	-	-	-	-	-	-
Swindon Town	-	-	-	-	-	-	-	-	-	-	-	-	2	1	1	0	1	0
Tottenham Hotspur	6	0	3	3	1	6	-	-	-	-	-	-	3	3	0	0	9	1
Tranmere Rovers	1	1	0	0	3	0	1	1	0	0	4	1	-	-	-	-	-	-
Watford	3	0	2	1	3	4	-	-	-	-	-	-	1	1	0	0	2	0
Wellingborough	-	-	-	-	-	-	-	-	-	-	-	-	1	1	0	0	3	2
West Bromwich Albion	3	2	0	1	3	3	1	0	0	1	1	2	2	1	0	1	5	5
West Ham United	2	1	0	1	3	3	1	0	0	1	0	1	2	1	0	1	6	7
West Hartlepool	-	-	-	-	-	-	-	-	-	-	-	-	1	1	0	0	3	1
Whitby Town	-	-	-	-	-	-	-	-	-	-	-	-	1	1	0	0	5	1
Wigan Athletic	1	0	0	1	0	3	-	-	-	-	-	-	-	-	-	-	-	-
Wigan Borough	-	-	-	-	-	-	-	-	-	-	-	-	1	0	0	1	1	3
Wigan Town	-	-	-	-	-	-	-	-	-	-	-	-	1	1	0	0	7	5
Wisbech Town	-	-	-	-	-	-	-	-	-	-	-	-	1	1	0	0	6	1
Wolverhampton W	4	1	1	2	3	5	-	-	-	-	-	-	1	1	0	0	3	1
Workington	1	1	0	0	2	0	-	-	-	-	-	-	-	-	-	-	-	-
Wrexham	1	1	0	0	2	0	-	-	-	-	-	-	1	1	-	-	1	0
York & District League	-	-	-	-	-	-	-	-	-	-	-	-	1	1	0	0	4	3
York City	2	1	0	1	4	6	13	5	2	6	24	26	7	2	3	2	11	14
York Garrison	-	-	-	-	-	-	-	-	-	-	-	-	1	1	0	0	7	1

Notes:

Abandoned matches, shown in the third set of figures, are included in the result column corresponding to the score at the time of abandonment.

Gateshead (1) is the former Football League club, once known as South Shields, whilst Gateshead (2) was formed in 1977, playing in the Alliance and Northern Premier Leagues.

Country by Country Record Against Foreign Opposition

Country	Club	P	W	D	L	F	A
AUSTRIA	Admira Wien	1	0	0	1	1	2
BELGIUM	Belgian XI	1	1	0	0	3	2
	Brugge XI	1	1	0	0	3	1
	Racing Club de Bruxelles	1	1	0	0	6	0
BERMUDA	Bermuda XI	1	0	1	0	0	0
	Dandy Town	1	1	0	0	6	1
	Pembroke Hamilton Club	1	1	0	0	3	0
BULGARIA	Sofia XI	1	0	1	0	2	2
CANADA	Seattle Storm	1	0	1	0	2	2
CZECHOSLOVAKIA	Banik Ostrava	1	1	0	0	3	2
	Internacional ŽTS Bratislava	1	1	0	0	2	0
	Slovan Bratislava	1	0	0	1	1	2
DENMARK	EfB Esbjerg	2	1	0	1	8	5
	Haderslev XI	1	0	1	0	3	3
	Jutland XI	1	0	1	0	1	1
	Kolding XI	1	1	0	0	5	1
	Randers Freja	1	1	0	0	6	0
	Zealand XI	1	1	0	0	6	2
FINLAND	HJK Helsinki	1	1	0	0	6	2
	Lahden Reipas	1	1	0	0	5	0
FRENCH GUIANA	French Guiana XI	1	1	0	0	2	0
GIBRALTAR	Gibraltar FA XI	2	1	1	0	4	2
GUYANA	Berbice FA XI	1	1	0	0	12	0
	Caribbean XI	1	0	1	0	1	1
	Guyana XI	1	1	0	0	5	0
	Upper Demerara XI	1	1	0	0	7	0
HOLLAND	Bergum	1	1	0	0	5	0
	SC Cambuur	2	1	1	0	2	0
	VV Emmen	1	1	0	0	5	0
	FC Groningen	1	0	0	1	0	1
	Haarlem	1	0	1	0	1	1
	The Hague XI	1	1	0	0	3	0
	SC Heerenveen	1	0	1	0	1	1
	Rotterdam XI	1	1	0	0	1	0
	Sparta Rotterdam	1	1	0	0	4	1
	SC Veendam	1	1	0	0	2	0
HUNGARY	Vasas SC	1	1	0	0	3	1
ISRAEL	Hapoel Tel-Aviv	1	1	0	0	1	0
	Israel XI	1	1	0	0	1	0
	Maccabi Tel-Aviv	1	1	0	0	4	0
ITALY	Bari	1	0	1	0	0	0
	Fiorentina	1	0	0	1	0	1
	Lazio	1	1	0	0	2	1
	Verona	1	1	0	0	2	1
JAPAN	Japan XI	1	1	0	0	5	0
LUXEMBOURG	Progres Niedercorn	1	0	1	0	3	3
NORTHERN IRELAND	Distillery	1	1	0	0	5	3
	Portadown	1	0	1	0	0	0
NORWAY	Clausenengen FK	1	1	0	0	2	0
	Trondheim & District XI	3	3	0	0	40	2
	Sarpsborg FK	1	1	0	0	3	0
POLAND	Polish Army XI	1	1	0	0	9	0

Country	Club	P	W	D	L	F	A
REPUBLIC OF IRELAND	Cork XI	1	1	0	0	3	1
	Cork Hibernians	1	0	0	1	0	1
	Finn Harps	1	0	1	0	1	1
	Shamrock Rovers	1	1	0	0	2	0
	Shelbourne	1	1	0	0	6	1
SPAIN	Atlétic Bilbao	1	0	0	1	0	2
	Atlético Madrid	1	0	0	1	0	4
	Barcelona XI	1	0	0	1	3	5
	Real Balompedica Linense	2	2	0	0	4	1
SURINAM	Robin Hood	1	0	1	0	1	1
SWEDEN	AIK	2	2	0	0	6	0
	Djurgårdens IF	1	1	0	0	4	0
	Gothenburg XI	4	4	0	0	11	4
	Halmstads BK	1	1	0	0	6	1
	Hammarby IF	1	1	0	0	5	0
	Hälsingborg IF	1	1	0	0	1	0
	IFK Stockholm	1	1	0	0	1	0
	Kamraterna	1	1	0	0	2	1
	Malmö FF	1	0	1	0	2	2
	Örgryte IS	1	1	0	0	6	0
	Sandviken IF	1	1	0	0	1	0
	Sirius	2	2	0	0	5	1
	IK Sleipner	1	1	0	0	1	0
	Stockholm XI	2	2	0	0	5	0
TRINIDAD	Trinidad & Tobago XI	2	1	0	1	3	2
TURKEY	Adana Demirspor	1	1	0	0	4	0
	Fenerbahçe	1	0	0	1	1	2
	Galatasaray	1	1	0	0	2	0
	Gençlerbirliği	1	1	0	0	3	1
URUGUAY	Inter Montevideo	1	1	0	0	4	2
USA	Fort Lauderdale Sun	1	1	0	0	1	0
	Tampa Bay Rowdies	2	1	0	1	3	1
USSR	Dinamo Kiev	1	0	0	1	0	3
WEST GERMANY	1.FC Kaiserslautern	1	0	1	0	1	1
	Union Solingen	1	1	0	0	16	0
	SV Werder Bremen	1	1	0	0	5	0
YUGOSLAVIA	Partizan Beograd	1	0	0	1	2	3
	Spartak Subotica	1	1	0	0	3	1

The Tigers owed their election to the League in 1905 to Charles Sutcliffe's motion to increase the size of the divisions. In the original re-election vote they lost out. Leeds City (25 votes), Burslem Port Vale (21), and Chelsea (20) filled the three vacancies, whilst Hull City (18), Burton United (10), Doncaster Rovers (4), Stockport County (3) and Clapton Orient (1) had to await the outcome of the second vote for the four newly-created places. It resulted in favour of Burton United (36), Hull City (36), Clapton Orient (26) and Stockport County (26), with Doncaster Rovers (20) the unfortunate ones.

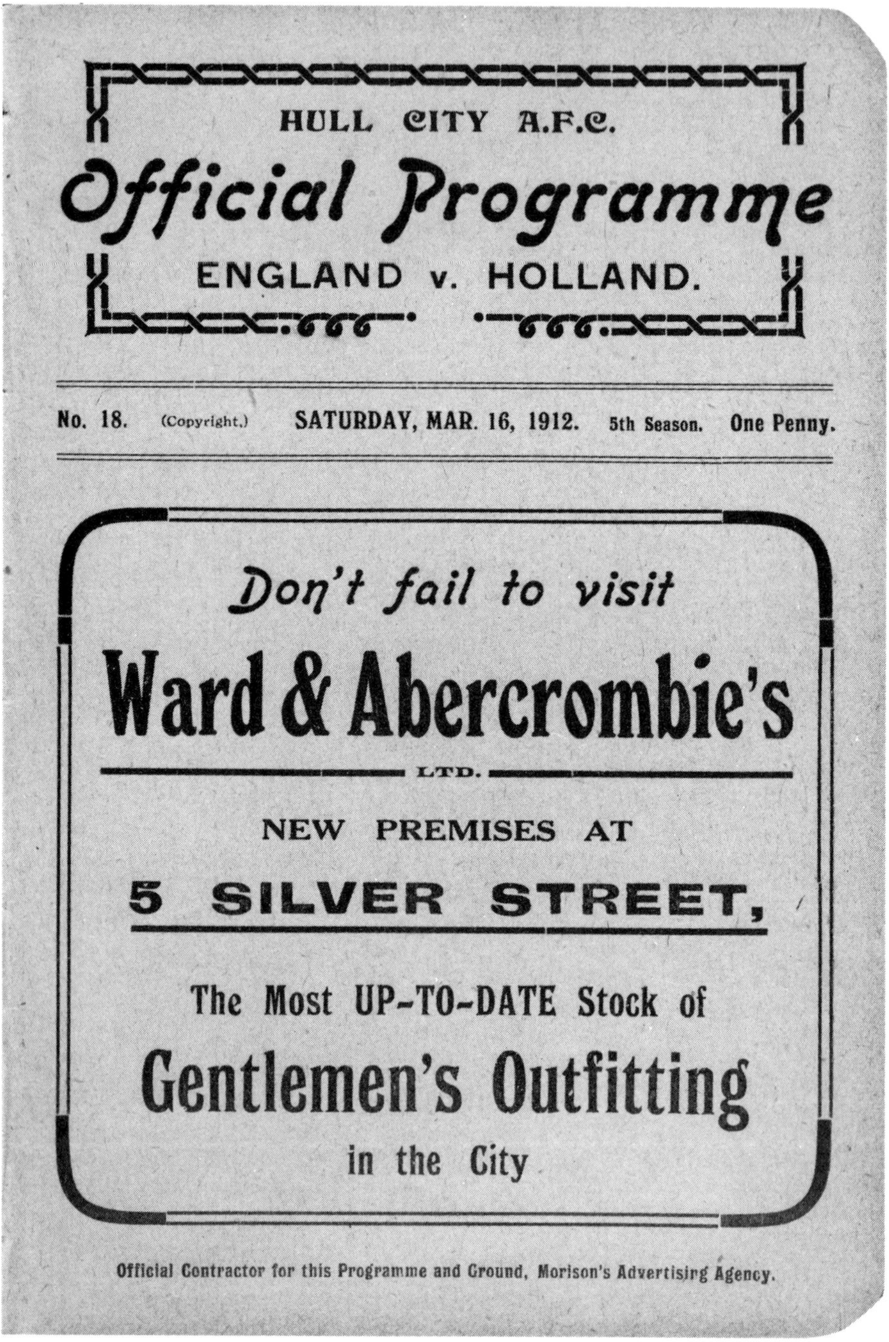

HULL CITY A.F.C.

Official Programme

ENGLAND v. HOLLAND.

No. 18. (Copyright.) SATURDAY, MAR. 16, 1912. 5th Season. One Penny.

Official Contractor for this Programme and Ground, Morison's Advertising Agency.

REPRESENTATIVE MATCHES

Anlaby Road 1906-1939

16 Nov 1909	England	7	Sweden	0	Amateur International
16 Mar 1912	England	4	Holland	0	Amateur International
15 Nov 1913	England	2	Holland	1	Amateur International

After Hull City's relegation from the Second Division in 1930, the Hull Hospital Cup was competed for by the Hull Boys team. The results were as follows:

21 Apr 1931	Hull Boys	1	York Boys	0
28 Apr 1932	Hull Boys	2	York Boys	1
25 Apr 1933	Hull Boys	3	York Boys	2
3 May 1934	Hull Boys	6	York Boys	1
2 May 1935	Hull Boys	2	York Boys	1
23 Apr 1936	Hull Boys	1	Doncaster Boys	0
3 May 1937	Hull Boys	0	Doncaster Boys	2
26 Apr 1938	Hull Boys	1	Doncaster Boys	1
8 May 1939	Hull Boys	1	Doncaster Boys	2

Boothferry Park 1946-1989

4 Mar 1950	England	0	Scotland	0	Amateur International
11 May 1950	Hull Boys	1	Doncaster Boys	1	E Riding Invitation Trophy
15 Feb 1951	FA Amateur XI	2	UAU XI	1	Representative Match
15 Nov 1952	England	2	Holland	2	Amateur International
1 Mar 1958	England	2	Scotland	0	Youth International
27 Oct 1965	Football League	5	League of Ireland	0	Inter-League Match*
20 Mar 1967	Leeds United	2	Sunderland	1	FA Cup round 5, 2nd Replay
10 May 1967	England	3	Austria	0	Under-23 International
30 Apr 1968	England	1	West Germany	4	Schools International
11 Nov 1970	England	2	Sweden	0	Under-23 International
24 Apr 1971	England	2	Wales	1	Schools International
16 Feb 1972	Northern Ireland	1	Spain	1	European Championship
28 Apr 1977	England	9	Switzerland	1	Women's International
12 Oct 1977	England	8	Finland	1	European Under-21 Cham
13 Sep 1979	England	2	Denmark	2	Women's International

*Hull City beat the Football League side 2-0 in a 60-minute training match the previous day. The Tigers' line up was: Swan; Davidson, D.Butler, Jarvis, Milner, Simpkin, Henderson, Wagstaff, Chilton, Houghton, I.Butler. Goalscorers were: Chris Chilton and George Cohen (own-goal).

On 8 January 1946, Harold Needler and Dick Smith visited the Secretary of the Football Association, Stanley Rous, to discuss their take-over of Hull City. A wide-ranging conversation ensued. Perhaps the most surprising item on the agenda was the securing of international and representative matches for a ground which they had not started to put in order. The pair also sought the Secretary's suggestions for a suitable team manager.

TIGERS INTERNATIONALS

The following list includes only those players who won international and representative honours whilst playing for Hull City. The Republic of Ireland first played as a separate nation in 1924 but Eire-born players appeared for Northern Ireland until after World War Two.

ENGLAND

FULL INTERNATIONALS

Wright, Gordon (1)	v Wales	19 March 1906

AMATEUR INTERNATIONALS

Ainsworth, Edgar (2)	v Wales	21 January 1933
	v Ireland	18 February 1933
Wright, Gordon (20)	v Ireland	7 December 1907
	v France	23 March 1908
	v Holland	12 April 1909
	v Belgium	19 April 1909
	v Switzerland	20 May 1909
	v France	22 May 1909
	v Sweden	6 November 1909
	v Wales	19 February 1910
	v Wales	18 February 1911
	v Belgium	4 March 1911
	v France	23 March 1911
	v Germany	14 April 1911
	v Holland	17 April 1911
	v Denmark	21 October 1911
	v Ireland	18 November 1911
	v Wales	17 February 1912
	v Hungary	16 March 1912
	v Belgium	8 April 1912
	v Finland	2 July 1912
	v Belgium	9 November 1912

UNDER-21 INTERNATIONALS

Daniel, Peter (7)	v Scotland	27 April 1977
	v Finland	26 May 1977
	v Norway	1 June 1977
	v Finland	12 October 1977
	v Italy	5 April 1978
	v Yugoslavia	19 April 1978
	v Yugoslavia	2 May 1978
Haigh, Paul (1)	v Norway (sub)	1 June 1977
Parker, Garry (5)	v Italy	9 April 1986
	v Italy	23 April 1986
	v Sweden	9 September 1986
	v Yugoslavia (sub)	11 November 1986
	v Spain	18 February 1987

YOUTH INTERNATIONALS

Dale, Mike	1969	**Harrison, Frank**	1949
Fisher, Andy	1969	**Healey, Graham**	1963
Goodwin, Ray	1953	**Hunt, Les**	1971
Greendale, Mike	1970	**Saunders, Roy**	1948

FA TOURISTS

Alexander, Stan	to Canada	1931
Chilton, Chris	to Australia	1971
Mercer, David	to South Africa	1920
Wagstaff, Ken	to Australia	1971

FA REPRESENTATIVE TEAMS

Chilton, Chris (2)	v Guernsey FA	10 September 1968
	v Republic of Ireland	24 May 1971
Moore, Norman (1)	v Oxford University	24 November 1949
Wagstaff, Ken (1)	v Republic of Ireland	24 May 1971

FOOTBALL LEAGUE

Carter, Raich (1)	v League of Ireland	14 April 1948
Smith, Jackie (1)	v Scottish League	29 February 1908

NORTHERN IRELAND (and Ireland before 1924)

FULL INTERNATIONALS

Bowler, Gerry (3)	v Scotland	1 October 1949
	v England	6 November 1949
	v Wales	8 March 1950
Gowdy, Bill (1)	v Scotland	19 September 1931
McKinney, Danny (1)	v Scotland	26 February 1921
Neill, Terry (15)	v Spain	11 November 1970
	v Cyprus	3 February 1971
	v USSR	22 September 1971
	v USSR	13 October 1971
	v Spain	16 February 1972
	v Scotland	20 May 1972
	v England	23 May 1972
	v Wales	27 May 1972
	v Bulgaria	18 October 1972
	v Cyprus	14 February 1973
	v Portugal	28 March 1973
	v Cyprus	8 May 1973
	v England	12 May 1973
	v Scotland	16 May 1973
	v Wales	19 May 1973

O'Brien, Mick (4)	v England	22 October 1924
	v Scotland	28 February 1925
	v Wales	18 April 1925
	v Wales	13 February 1926

O'Connell, Patsy (3)	v Wales	19 January 1914
	v England	14 February 1914
	v Scotland	14 March 1914
Stewart, David (1)	v Belgium	16 November 1977

VICTORY INTERNATIONALS

Halligan, Billy (2)	v Scotland	22 March 1919
	v Scotland	19 April 1919

SCOTLAND

FULL INTERNATIONALS

Gilhooley, Mike (1)	v Wales	4 February 1922

WALES

FULL INTERNATIONALS

Jarvis, Alan (3)	v Scotland	22 October 1966
	v England	16 November 1966
	v Northern Ireland	12 April 1967
Norman, Tony (5)	v Republic of Ireland (sub)	26 March 1986
	v Uruguay	21 April 1986
	v Canada	10 May 1986
	v Malta	1 June 1988
	v Italy	5 June 1988
Roberts, Dave (11)	v Luxembourg	1 May 1975
	v Northern Ireland	23 May 1975
	v Scotland	6 May 1976
	v Northern Ireland	14 May 1976
	v Yugoslavia	22 May 1976
	v England (sub)	31 May 1977
	v Northern Ireland	3 June 1977
	v Kuwait	6 September 1977
	v Kuwait (sub)	20 September 1977
	v Scotland	17 May 1978
	v Northern Ireland	19 May 1978

UNDER-23 INTERNATIONALS

Stephens, Johnny (1)	v England	23 April 1958

REPUBLIC OF IRELAND

FULL INTERNATIONALS

De Mange, Ken (1)	v Tunisia (sub)	19 October 1988

UNDER-23 INTERNATIONALS

De Mange, Ken (1)	v Northern Ireland (sub)	11 April 1989

Maurice Swan, the Tigers' Irish-born goalkeeper who joined them from Cardiff City in July 1960 and went on to make over 100 League appearances. Swan was capped for the Republic of Ireland in 1960 when he was with Drumcondra.

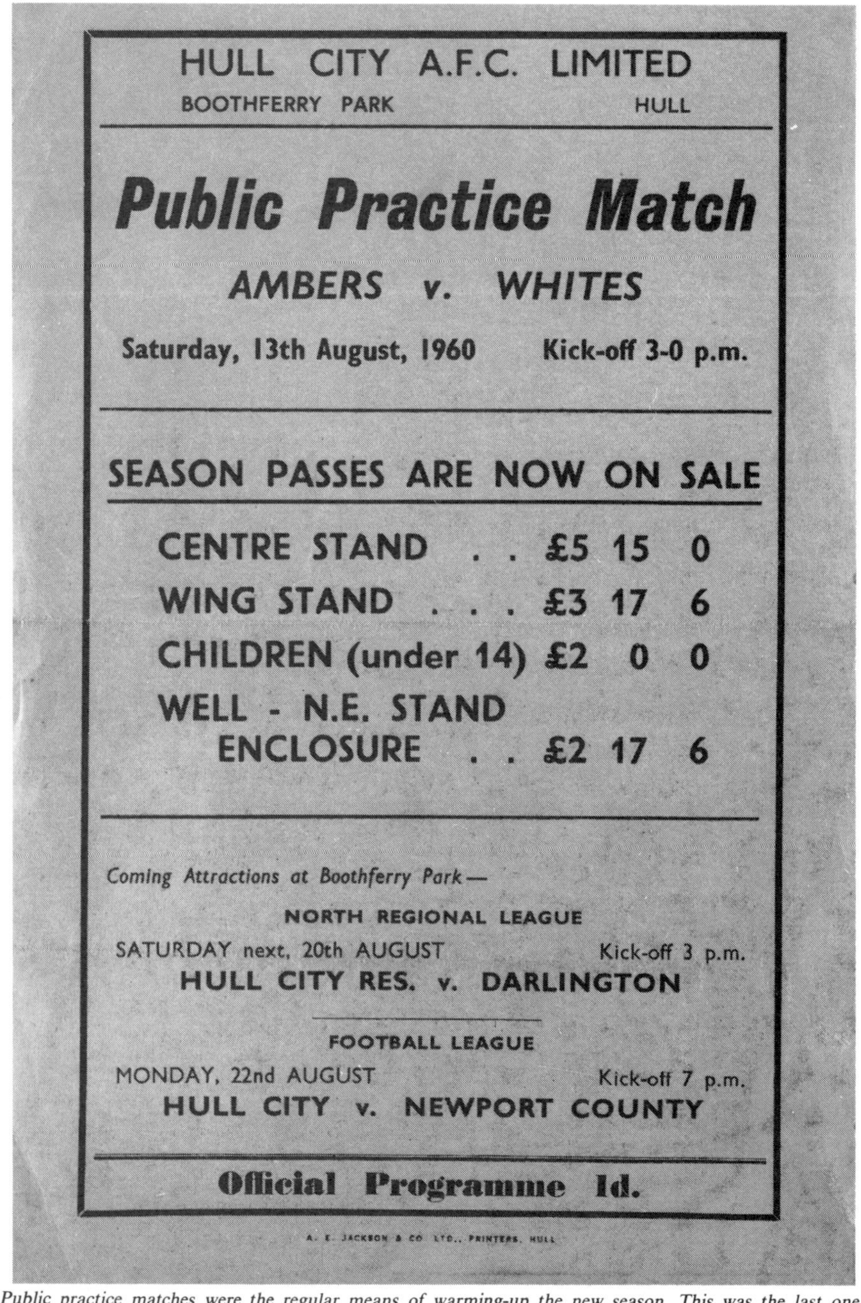

HULL CITY A.F.C. LIMITED

BOOTHFERRY PARK HULL

Public Practice Match

AMBERS v. WHITES

Saturday, 13th August, 1960 Kick-off 3-0 p.m.

SEASON PASSES ARE NOW ON SALE

CENTRE STAND . .	£5	15	0
WING STAND . . .	£3	17	6
CHILDREN (under 14)	£2	0	0
WELL - N.E. STAND ENCLOSURE . .	£2	17	6

Coming Attractions at Boothferry Park—

NORTH REGIONAL LEAGUE

SATURDAY next, 20th AUGUST Kick-off 3 p.m.

HULL CITY RES. v. DARLINGTON

FOOTBALL LEAGUE

MONDAY, 22nd AUGUST Kick-off 7 p.m.

HULL CITY v. NEWPORT COUNTY

Official Programme 1d.

A. E. JACKSON & CO. LTD., PRINTERS, HULL

Public practice matches were the regular means of warming-up the new season. This was the last one staged at Boothferry Park. The following year the club did not have enough professionals to field two teams.

Hull City Reserves

Final League Placings 1905-89

Season	*Pld*	*W*	*D*	*L*	*F*	*A*	*Pts*	*Pos*
EAST RIDING COUNTY LEAGUE								
1905-06	18	18	0	0	113	21	36	1
MIDLAND LEAGUE								
1906-07	38	15	4	19	66	75	34	11
1907-08	38	15	9	14	56	48	39	7
1908-09	38	17	7	14	79	66	41	7
1909-10	42	27	3	12	113	65	57	2
1910-11	38	20	9	9	105	63	49	4
1911-12	36	9	7	20	53	66	25	17
1912-13	38	17	3	18	67	71	37	12
1913-14	34	11	5	18	37	55	27	15
1914-15	38	8	2	28	39	105	18	19
1915-16*	East Riding League							
1916-19	Friendly Matches Only							
1919-20	34	16	2	16	74	59	34	9
1920-21	38	12	9	17	52	68	33	15
1921-22	42	10	8	24	55	83	28	20
1922-23	42	14	13	15	63	63	41	12
1923-24	42	19	8	15	70	48	46	9
MIDLAND COMBINATION								
1924-25	22	9	5	8	44	45	23	6
1925-26	24	12	5	7	70	50	29	4
1926-27	24	20	3	1	77	29	43	1
1927-28	40	22	5	13	92	52	49	2
MIDLAND LEAGUE								
1928-29	50	26	10	14	101	84	62	4
1929-30	50	20	7	23	109	105	47	16
1930-31	46	20	11	15	105	88	51	8
1931-32	46	17	7	22	76	112	41	17
1932-33	44	17	4	23	104	131	38	16
1933-34	32	15	3	14	74	70	33	6
1934-35	38	13	5	20	73	91	31	16
1935-36	40	12	8	20	63	99	32	20
1936-37	42	19	6	17	64	62	44	12
1937-38	42	17	4	21	73	83	38	17
1938-39	42	15	3	24	76	90	33	18
1939-40†	3	3	0	0	10	4	6	3
1939-46	Did not play							
1946-47	42	12	7	23	68	108	31	17
1947-48	42	19	6	17	86	71	44	13
1948-49	42	16	12	14	86	67	44	9
1949-50	46	22	11	13	91	64	55	5
1950-51	42	11	10	21	67	74	32	20
1951-52	42	21	8	13	80	54	50	4
1952-53	46	22	15	9	101	62	59	4
1953-54	46	23	8	15	103	71	54	6
1954-55	46	26	8	12	102	60	60	4
1955-56	46	19	8	19	105	85	46	13
1956-57	46	12	11	23	84	116	35	22
1957-58	46	16	10	20	78	84	42	16
NORTH REGIONAL LEAGUE								
1958-59	36	21	6	9	89	61	48	3
1959-60	42	22	6	14	85	69	50	6
1960-61	40	20	7	13	92	66	47	6
1961-62	28	7	5	16	33	51	19	14
1962-63	32	11	7	14	57	61	29	12
1963-64	32	20	4	8	67	43	44	3
1964-65	32	24	4	4	95	26	52	1
1965-66	32	23	4	5	89	30	50	1
1966-67	20	11	6	3	37	22	28	2
1967-68	16	11	3	2	42	17	25	1
NORTH MIDLANDS LEAGUE								
1968-69	26	11	9	6	46	34	31	3
1969-70	28	18	6	4	51	21	42	2
1970-71	26	15	4	7	53	28	34	2
1971-72	28	14	8	6	55	30	36	4
1972-73	28	16	7	5	72	34	39	3
1973-74	28	15	7	6	52	30	37	3
1974-75	28	18	5	5	71	38	41	4
1975-76	24	11	6	7	48	34	28	5
1976-77	22	10	3	9	35	26	23	6
1977-78	28	14	8	6	61	33	36	3
1978-79	30	14	8	8	48	40	36	5
1979-80	28	17	6	5	70	31	40	2
1980-81	28	8	11	9	40	41	27	7
1981-82	24	11	6	7	36	27	28	5
1982-83	16	13	1	2	37	10	27	1
1983-84	Friendly matches only							
CENTRAL LEAGUE DIVISION TWO								
1984-85	34	20	8	6	68	26	68	2
CENTRAL LEAGUE DIVISION ONE								
1985-86	34	15	4	15	52	53	49	8
1986-87	34	10	6	18	47	69	36	14
1987-88	34	12	6	16	53	61	42	15
CENTRAL LEAGUE DIVISION TWO								
1988-89	34	25	3	6	82	38	78	1st

Notes: * The 1915-16 emergency competition began with ten teams. By February 1916 the number had been reduced to seven and it is not certain whether the programme was completed. From the surviving records, Hull City Reserves lost only one match and were neck-and-neck with Beverley Barracks for the championship.

† The 1939-40 competition was abandoned upon the outbreak of World War Two.

East Riding Senior Cup

Hull City have participated in the premier local cup competition since 1905-06, with the exception of seasons 1920-21 to 1925-6 and 1963-4 to 1972-3. Through the years the club has been represented by a variety of reserve and junior line-ups but has reached the Final more than 30 times, as listed below. On each occasion the Tigers staged the Final on their own ground. The replays of 1930 and 1939 took place on the ground of their opponents.

Season	*Opponent*	*Result*	
1906-07	Beverley Old	W	7-0
1910-11	Reckitts	W	3-1
1919-20	Shiphams	W	4-0
1926-27	Bridlington Town	W	5-0
1927-28	Beverley White Star	W	2-1
1929-30	York City Reserves	D	5-5
	York City Reserves	L	1-2
1930-31	Bridlington Town	L	0-2
1931-32	Selby OCO	W	5-1
1932-33	Reckitts	W	5-0
1933-34	Bridlington Town	L	0-1
1934-35	Bridlington Town	W	3-0
1935-36	Bridlington Town	W	3-0
1936-37	Bridlington Town	W	4-1
1937-38	Marfleet	W	2-1
1938-39	Bridlington Town	D	1-1
	Bridlington Town	W	2-1
1946-47	Brunswick Institute	W	3-1
1948-49	Hall Road Athletic	W	3-2
1949-50	Bridlington Cental Utd	W	6-0
1950-51	Brunswick Institute	W	3-1
1951-52	Long Riston	W	3-1
1953-54	Market Weighton United	W	6-0
1954-55	Endike Athletic	W	3-0
1958-59	Willerby Old Boys	W	3-2
1959-60	Willerby Old Boys	W	2-1
1962-63	Bridlington Trinity	W	6-0
1974-75	Bridlington Town	W	2-1
1976-77	North Ferriby United	L	1-2
1979-80	Wolfreton	W	5-3
1980-81	Bridlington Trinity	W	2-1
1983-84	Schultz Youth Club	L	0-1
1984-85	North Ferriby United	W	3-2
1986-87	Bridlington Town	W	3-1
1987-88	Bridlington Town	W	2-0
1988-89	Bridlington Town	L	0-1

George Maddison's goalmouth antics added a wealth of lore to the Anlaby Road chronicle. One bitterly cold day he was on duty for the Reserves in an East Riding Cup tie. The Reserves outclassed most of the local sides, reaching every final in the thirties, and Geordie, fearing an afternoon of relative inactivity, emerged from the dressing-room with a brazier, which he placed in his goalmouth — until the referee made him move it to behind the goal-line.

In 1947 the Tigers recorded their first maximum-point Easter since 1923. After completing the double over Carlisle on the Monday, ten of the side found themselves turning out in the Reserves in the evening. It was not a mark of Major Buckley's dissatisfaction, rather a result of the conditions of the day. The second string had travelled to Scunthorpe in the afternoon for a Midland League fixture. They should have returned to Boothferry Park in time to take on Filey Town in the East Riding Cup. Unfortunately they were delayed en route, so the first team, with the exception of Ron Brown, had an extra 90 minutes. His replacement, Denis Thompson, scored five times in an 8-2 romp.

Hull City at the start of the 1979-80 season. Back row (left to right): D.Leadbeater, C.Norrie, D.Hood, R.McDonald, F.Skipper, S.Croft, M.Horswill. Middle row: T.Phillips, B.Marwood, P.Haigh, W.Boyd, E.Blackburn, I.Dobson, S.McClaren, M.Lord. Front row: K.Edwards, D.Hawker, B.Bannister, G.Nisbet, R.de Vries, G.Roberts, J.Farley.

The Hull City squad which began the 1981-2 season. Back row (left to right): S.Hoolickin, R.McNeil, B.Ferguson, W.Whitehurst, L.Mutrie, S.Eccleston. Third row: C. Chilton (reserve-team manager), D.Roberts, N.Deacy, A.Norman, R.Brown (youth coach), J.Davies, S.Richards, C.Norrie, J.Radcliffe (physiotherapist). Second row: K.Edwards, D.Kynman, S.McClaren, B.Marwood, M.Horswill, M.Smith (manager), C.Lea (assistant manager), G.Roberts, D.Booth, P. Moss, G.Swann. Front row: A.Hurst, M.Gray, I.Davis, A.Flounders, M.Davies.

LEADING GOALSCORERS

All the players listed are those who have scored over 50 League goals for the club.

1. Chris Chilton 193
2. Ken Wagstaff 173
3. Paddy Mills 101
4. Jack Smith 98
5. Keith Edwards 86
6. Sammy Stevens..................84
7. Bill Bradbury.....................82
8. Doug Clarke 79
   Ken Houghton 79
10. Arthur Temple 77
11. Ian Butler 66
12. John McSeveney 60
13. Syd Gerrie 59
14. Raich Carter 57
    Bill McNaughton 57
16. Cliff Hubbard 56
17. George Martin 55
18. Andy Flounders 54
    Ray Henderson..................54
20. Billy Whitehurst 52
21. Viggo Jensen 51
    Brian Marwood 51

Other claimants to inclusion in the table, whose contribution in the Leagues of 1915-19 takes their career totals above the 50 mark, are:

David Mercer
26 in Div 2 + 48 in WW1 = 74

Joe Smith
46 in Div 2 + 4 in WW1 = 50

Goals scored in consecutive League games:

Les Mutrie — 9 in Division 4 — 13 February to 20 March 1982

Viggo Jensen — 7 in Division 2 — 17 September to 29 October 1949

HIGH SCORES AND SCORERS

The record books rightly give the club's highest score as the 11-1 trouncing of Carlisle United in the Division Three North match in January 1939. There are a number of occasions in friendly games when the Tigers have bettered this total:

16-0 v Solingen in The Hague, 14 May 1910
16-1 v Trondheim & District in Trondheim, 28 May 1912
15-1 v Trondhiem & District in Trondheim, 30 May 1912
12-0 v Berbice FA in New Amsterdam, 1 June 1973

In competitive games the Reserves have run up several scores in excess of 11:

14-0 v Driffield White Star (a) East Riding County League, 30 September 1905
13-0 v Filey Town (h) East Riding Senior Cup, 9 January 1932
13-1 v Holderness Athletic (h) Hull Charity Cup, 2 December 1905
13-3 v Gainsborough Trinity Res (h) Midland League, 29 January 1910
12-2 v Kingston Recs (h) East Riding Senior Cup, 3 March 1934

A similar situation appertains as far as individual scoring feats are concerned. Ken McDonald (v Bristol City in the Second Division, November 1928) and Simon Raleigh (v Halifax Town in Division Three North, December 1930) claim the honours with five goals, but the following have exceeded that number:

Stan Fazackerley – 11 v Trondheim & District, Tour Match, 28 May 1912
Jackie Smith – 7 v Driffield White Star, East Riding County League, 30 September 1905
Tommy Burdett – 7 v Doncaster Rovers Res, Midland League, 19 April 1935

Ron Young – 7 v Gateshead, North Regional League, 4 November 1967
Arthur Temple – 6 v Solingen, Tour Match, 14 May 1910
David Mercer – 6 v Sheffield United, Midland Section, 4 January 1919

The ultimate scoreline, one suspects, occurred not so long ago. In October 1983, a selection of Hull City's Junior and Minor teams took on the combined might of the Under-15s of Sport Verein Millingen and the Wolds FA. The Tigers mauled their opponents to the tune of 20-0, with Andy Story scoring eight times, Mark Slater five, Paul Olsson four, Andy Tomlinson two and Neil Shepherd the other.

MOST LEAGUE APPEARANCES

The players listed are those who have played in 250 or more League games for the club.

1. Andy Davidson 520
2. George Maddison 430
3. Chris Chilton...............415
4. Billy Bly 403
5. Matt Bell 393
6. Ken Wagstaff 374/4
7. Tony Norman 372
8. Tommy Bleakley 368
   Doug Clarke 368
10. Garreth Roberts............365/5
11. Brian Bulless 326
12. Roger de Vries 314/4
13. Viggo Jensen 308
14. Cliff Woodhead 305
15. Ian Butler 300/5
16. Les Collinson 296/1
17. Peter Skipper 286/2
18. Frank Banks 284/4
19. Chris Simpkin..............284/1
20. Tom Berry 275
    Davy Gordon 275
22. Malcolm Lord..............271/27
23. Paul Feasey 271
24. Paddy Mills 269
25. Denis Durham 267
26. Ian McKechnie.............255
27. Ken Houghton 253/11

Other candidates for inclusion by virtue of their contribution in wartime Leagues are:

Jack McQuillan
239 in Div 2 + 31 in WW1 = 270

Nick Hendry
140 in Div 2 + 115 in WW1 = 255

Consecutive League appearances:

Tony Norman — 226 — 27 August 1983 to 20 September 1988

David Mercer — 218 — 18 April 1914 to 2 April 1920

Andy Davidson — 177 — 3 March 1962 to 1 January 1966

In December 1913 the Tigers beat Wolves 7-1. It restored a measure of respectability after the record defeat inflicted by the Molineux outfit two years earlier. Billy Halligan, who did the hat-trick for Wolves in the first game, bagged four of the Tigers' seven. It was a great day for the forward, whose wife presented him with a son. A blessing that it was not the other way round from a numerical point of view, was Patsy O'Connell's post-match quip.

THE HULL CITY ASSOCIATION FOOTBALL CLUB LIMITED

Accounts for the period 28 June 1904 to 31 July 1905

PROFIT AND LOSS ACCOUNT

EXPENDITURE	£	s	d
Wages, transfer fees, players' bonuses	1,757	6	0
Guarantees paid to visiting teams	663	2	11
Advertising	136	6	7
Travelling expenses	131	0	4
Hotel expenses	88	17	5
Rent	114	4	8
Entrance fees	11	15	0
Outfits	41	4	11
Ground outfits	21	16	11
Drugs and medical assistance	5	9	7½
Referees and linesmen	18	11	9
Repairs, washing	5	18	1½
Police and gatemen	68	12	0
Secretary's salary	36	15	0
Printing	67	1	0
Postages and telegrams	23	17	1
Insurances	17	5	6
Room for meetings	3	1	6
Bank interest	13	15	0
Cheque book	1	5	9
Compensation	25	0	0
	£ 3,252	7	1

INCOME	£	s	d
Gate receipts, guarantees received	1,350	4	8
Donations received	33	12	0
Passes	10	16	0
Discount received		11	9
Loss for the year	1,857	2	8
	£ 3,252	7	1

BALANCE SHEET

LIABILITIES AND CAPITAL	£	s	d
Capital:			
Authorised 4,000 shares of 10s each (since increased to 16,000)	2,000	0	0
Issued 3,094 shares, fully paid	1,547	0	0
Issued 150 shares, 5s paid	37	10	0
Issued 612 shares, 2s 6d paid	76	10	0
	1,661	0	0
Less calls in arrears	3	5	0
	1,657	15	0
Barclay and Company Limited	202	18	9
Cash due to secretary		8	10
Sundry loans	62	17	6
Sundry creditors	20	5	10
	£ 1,944	5	11

ASSETS	£	s	d
Preliminary expenses	81	11	6
Suspense account: Value of unexpired Telephone rent and Telegraphic Address	5	11	9
Debit balance on profit and loss account	1,857	2	8
	£ 1,944	5	11

PROFIT AND LOSS

The following table shows how the club has fared financially over the years.

Accounting period	Profit £	Loss £	Accounting period	Profit £	Loss £
28 Jun 04 - 31 Jul 05	-	1857	17 Aug 47 - 16 Aug 48	-	2897
1 Aug 05 - 30 Apr 06	76	-	17 Aug 48 - 16 Aug 49	20086	-
1 May 06 - 30 Apr 07	635	-	17 Aug 49 - 16 Aug 50	7384	-
1 May 07 - 30 Apr 08	1306	-	17 Aug 50 - 16 Aug 51	11924	-
1 May 08 - 30 Apr 09	250	-	17 Aug 51 - 16 Aug 52	15679	-
1 May 09 - 30 Apr 10	34	-	17 Aug 52 - 16 Aug 53	-	5037
1 May 10 - 30 Apr 11	-	415	17 Aug 53 - 16 Aug 54	9305	-
1 May 11 - 30 Apr 12	707	-	17 Aug 54 - 16 Aug 55	-	1894
1 May 12 - 30 Apr 13	-	322	17 Aug 55 - 16 Aug 56	-	12587
1 May 13 - 30 Apr 14	-	1323	17 Aug 56 - 30 Apr 57	-	3524
1 May 14 - 30 Apr 15	-	1687	1 May 57 - 30 Apr 58	-	6794
1 May 15 - 30 Apr 16	-	209	1 May 58 - 30 Apr 59	2366	-
1 May 16 - 30 Apr 17	-	638	1 May 59 - 30 Apr 60	-	14289
1 May 17 - 30 Apr 18	-	512	1 May 60 - 30 Apr 61	41	-
1 May 18 - 30 Apr 19	555	-	1 May 61 - 30 Apr 62	-	6068
1 May 19 - 31 May 20	-	8	1 May 62 - 30 Apr 63	-	4138
1 Jun 20 - 31 May 21	2159	-	1 May 63 - 30 Apr 64	-	58951
1 Jun 21 - 31 May 22	2963	-	1 May 64 - 30 Apr 65	-	150581
1 Jun 22 - 31 May 23	-	774	1 May 65 - 30 Apr 66	30218	-
1 Jun 23 - 21 May 24	-	4714	1 May 66 - 30 Apr 67	52082	-
22 May 24 - 21 May 25	125	-	1 May 67 - 30 Apr 68	4260	-
22 May 25 - 21 May 26	231	-	1 May 68 - 30 Apr 69	-	6415
22 May 26 - 21 May 27	-	2086	1 May 69 - 30 Apr 70	30032	-
22 May 27 - 21 May 28	-	2089	1 May 70 - 30 Apr 71	-	53942
22 May 28 - 21 May 29	153	-	1 May 71 - 30 Apr 72	53958	-
22 May 29 - 21 May 30	977	-	1 May 72 - 30 Apr 73	-	15381
22 May 30 - 21 May 31	-	2582	1 May 73 - 30 Apr 74	-	69670
22 May 31 - 21 May 32	40	-	1 May 74 - 30 Apr 75	-	9416
22 May 32 - 21 May 33	93	-	1 May 75 - 30 Apr 76	42622	-
22 May 33 - 21 May 34	2088	-	1 May 76 - 30 Apr 77	-	133591
22 May 34 - 21 May 35	1914	-	1 May 77 - 30 Apr 78	-	89303
22 May 35 - 21 May 36	-	7905	1 May 78 - 30 Apr 79	65879	-
22 May 36 - 21 May 37	-	755	1 May 79 - 30 Apr 80	-	491888
22 May 37 - 21 May 38	2108	-	1 May 80 - 30 Apr 81	-	131395
22 May 38 - 21 May 39	3704	-	1 May 81 - 31 Dec 81	37397	-
22 May 39 - 21 May 40	-	2459	1 Jan 82 - 31 Jul 82	-	309388
22 May 40 - 21 May 41	-	787	1 Aug 82 - 31 Jul 83	10347	-
22 May 41 - 21 May 42	-	164	1 Aug 83 - 31 Jul 84	40687	-
22 May 42 - 21 May 43	-	89	1 Aug 84 - 31 Jul 85	92085	-
22 May 43 - 21 May 44	-	31	1 Aug 85 - 31 Jul 86	107018	-
22 May 44 - 21 May 45	1407	-	1 Aug 86 - 31 Jul 87	7447	-
21 May 46 - 16 Aug 47	6656	-	1 Aug 87 - 31 Jul 88	26593	-

The take-over cost the syndicate £10,500 for Boothferry Park, and any fixtures and fittings left from the Anlaby Road ground, together with 'subsisting rights, privileges and goodwill', including the registrations of 24 players. They also undertook to pay off the £2,420 outstanding on the loan from the FA to buy the new ground, £300 worth of sundry creditors and £2,000 towards the £5,087 in loans made by the old company's directors.

THE COMPANIES ACT 1929.

COMPANY LIMITED BY SHARES.

Articles of Association

OF

Kingston Upon Hull Association Football Club Limited.

PRELIMINARY.

1. The provisions contained in Table A in the First Schedule to the Companies Act, 1929, shall, except in so far as they are modified or varied by these Articles, apply to the Company.

COMMENCEMENT OF BUSINESS

2. The Company shall forthwith enter into an agreement with Harold Needler, Kenneth Percival and William Richard Smith in the terms of the draft which has, for the purpose of identification, been signed by the first three of the subscribers to the Memorandum of Association of the Company and the Directors shall carry the same into effect, with or without modification as they may think fit. The basis on which the Company is established is that the Company shall acquire the property comprised in the said Agreement on the terms therein set forth, subject to any such modifications (if any) as aforesaid, and that the parties therein named as Vendors are to be the first Directors of th eCompany; accordingly it shall be no objection to the said agreement that the Vendors as promoters and directors stand in a fiduciary position towards the Company, or that they do not in the circumstances constitute an independent quoram or part thereof, or that an ind … regarding the

How close the club came to being renamed the Kingston Upon Hull AFC is shown by this draft of the Articles of Association for the new administration in 1946.

ADVERTISEMENT

HULL CITY SUPPORTERS

OPEN LETTER FROM TERRY NEILL

Dear Supporters,

One of the reasons which clearly influenced my thinking when accepting the appointment of Team Manager at Hull was the threefold potential — team, ground facilities and crowd potential.

Since my arrival in the city I have been very much impressed with the genuine desire for success. This is not unnatural; everyone wants success, YOU want it and I want it. Unfortunately, I can offer no guarantees, but I do pledge that I will do everything within my power to help Hull City achieve the success they deserve.

People make football — without the fans the game is dead, so WE need YOU. In saying that, I couldn't ask you to come along and support us if we were not providing good entertainment. Again I assure you that it will be the aim of myself and everyone connected with the Club to provide you with football of the highest quality.

In acquiring my services, the Club has overspent the special "Action Fund" set up for this purpose, and cash resources at my disposal for further team strengthening are of very limited dimensions. I cannot wait, nor, I believe, do you wish me to wait a further year or so for the Development side to accumulate another acceptable total — we need it NOW.

I believe the present squad is a very good one indeed, but football being what it is, one should always be able to strengthen and improve even the strongest of teams. I am asking, therefore, for your financial help.

Somehow, and this is the only way I know, I must accrue sizeable finances for the plans and projects I have in mind.

This letter, therefore, launches my own appeal — the "Terry Neill Appeal." To all Hull City supporters, past, present and future, help me achieve as quickly as possible the "big time" this city has never known . . . PLEASE GIVE ME £1.

Yes, I'm begging, and I'll borrow, too — anything in fact to MAKE this club successful.

If I could GUARANTEE First Division soccer next season, half the Riding would probably beat a path to my door right now! Regrettably, I can guarantee nothing except one helluva try, but one thing's for sure, a response of such magnitude today would guarantee every donor his money's worth this coming season. That I WILL promise!

If you cannot afford to give £1, will you please LEND me one? (State "loan" and claim back at end of season if not satisfied) — I can't be more fair than that.

Names of all donors will be shown throughout the season in match programmes, and ALL monies received will be earmarked expressly for "team strengthening."

The cheek of the Irish? Well, it's hardly the way to win friends and influence people I admit (though that is my chief aim), but I need some tools and thinking small, acting small, and indeed ASKING small, is no way to tackle a mammoth problem which, in this city, has defied solution for 60-odd years. TOGETHER we can solve this problem.

Cheques or Orders should be made payable to "Terry Neill Appeal," and when you have saved your £1 will you please send your donation and your name to:—

"TERRY NEILL APPEAL,"
HULL CITY A.F.C.,
BOOTHFERRY PARK, HULL

Thank you, and if I promise a different season, here's hoping it will be a successful one, too.

Sincerely,

This begging letter inaugurated Terry Neill's reign as Hull City manager.

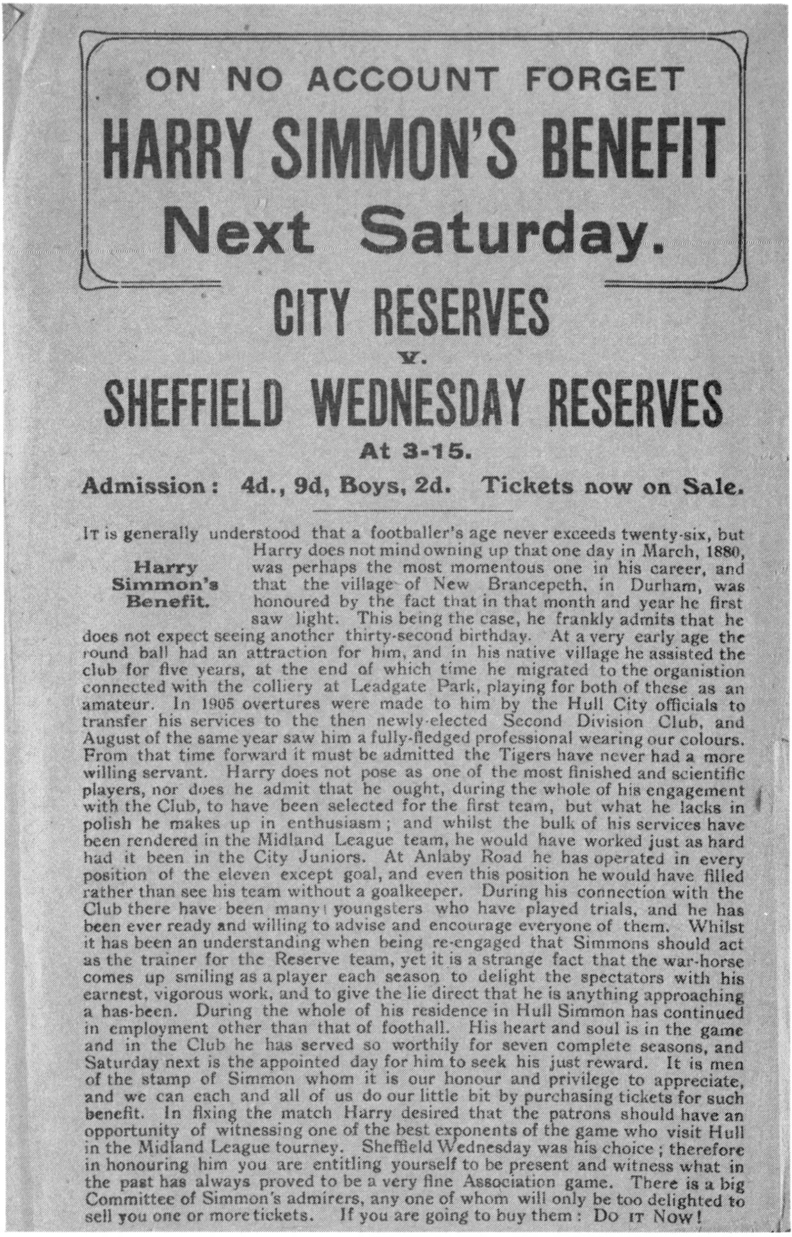
ON NO ACCOUNT FORGET

HARRY SIMMON'S BENEFIT

Next Saturday.

CITY RESERVES

v.

SHEFFIELD WEDNESDAY RESERVES

At 3-15.

Admission: 4d., 9d, Boys, 2d. Tickets now on Sale.

Harry Simmon's Benefit.

IT is generally understood that a footballer's age never exceeds twenty-six, but Harry does not mind owning up that one day in March, 1880, was perhaps the most momentous one in his career, and that the village of New Brancepeth, in Durham, was honoured by the fact that in that month and year he first saw light. This being the case, he frankly admits that he does not expect seeing another thirty-second birthday. At a very early age the round ball had an attraction for him, and in his native village he assisted the club for five years, at the end of which time he migrated to the organistion connected with the colliery at Leadgate Park, playing for both of these as an amateur. In 1905 overtures were made to him by the Hull City officials to transfer his services to the then newly-elected Second Division Club, and August of the same year saw him a fully-fledged professional wearing our colours. From that time forward it must be admitted the Tigers have never had a more willing servant. Harry does not pose as one of the most finished and scientific players, nor does he admit that he ought, during the whole of his engagement with the Club, to have been selected for the first team, but what he lacks in polish he makes up in enthusiasm; and whilst the bulk of his services have been rendered in the Midland League team, he would have worked just as hard had it been in the City Juniors. At Anlaby Road he has operated in every position of the eleven except goal, and even this position he would have filled rather than see his team without a goalkeeper. During his connection with the Club there have been many youngsters who have played trials, and he has been ever ready and willing to advise and encourage everyone of them. Whilst it has been an understanding when being re-engaged that Simmons should act as the trainer for the Reserve team, yet it is a strange fact that the war-horse comes up smiling as a player each season to delight the spectators with his earnest, vigorous work, and to give the lie direct that he is anything approaching a has-been. During the whole of his residence in Hull Simmon has continued in employment other than that of football. His heart and soul is in the game and in the Club he has served so worthily for seven complete seasons, and Saturday next is the appointed day for him to seek his just reward. It is men of the stamp of Simmon whom it is our honour and privilege to appreciate, and we can each and all of us do our little bit by purchasing tickets for such benefit. In fixing the match Harry desired that the patrons should have an opportunity of witnessing one of the best exponents of the game who visit Hull in the Midland League tourney. Sheffield Wednesday was his choice; therefore in honouring him you are entitling yourself to be present and witness what in the past has always proved to be a very fine Association game. There is a big Committee of Simmon's admirers, any one of whom will only be too delighted to sell you one or more tickets. If you are going to buy them: DO IT NOW!

Handbill advertising Harry Simmon's benefit match, the Midland League fixture against Sheffield Wednesday Reserves on 12 October 1912. The match ended 1-1.

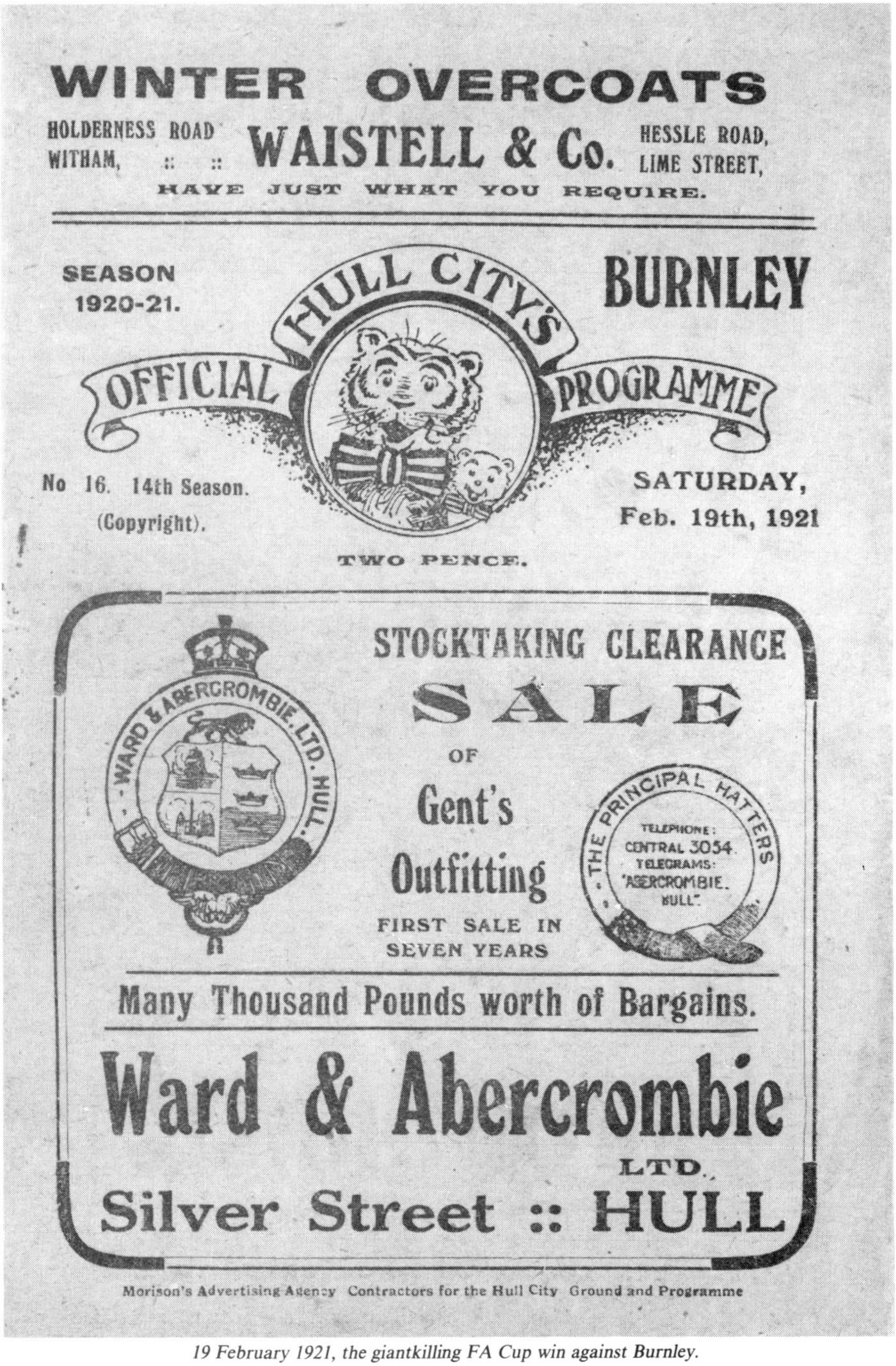

19 February 1921, the giantkilling FA Cup win against Burnley.

1 May 1933, the match which gave the Tigers the Third Division North Championship.

31 August 1935. This season saw Hull City play in a blue and white strip but the campaign turned out to be one of the worst in the club's history and the old colours were restored for the next season.

30 April 1938, the promotion showdown with Tranmere. Defeat cost Hull City promotion.

On 30 April 1949, a 6-1 demolition of Stockport brought the Northern Section title back to Hull.

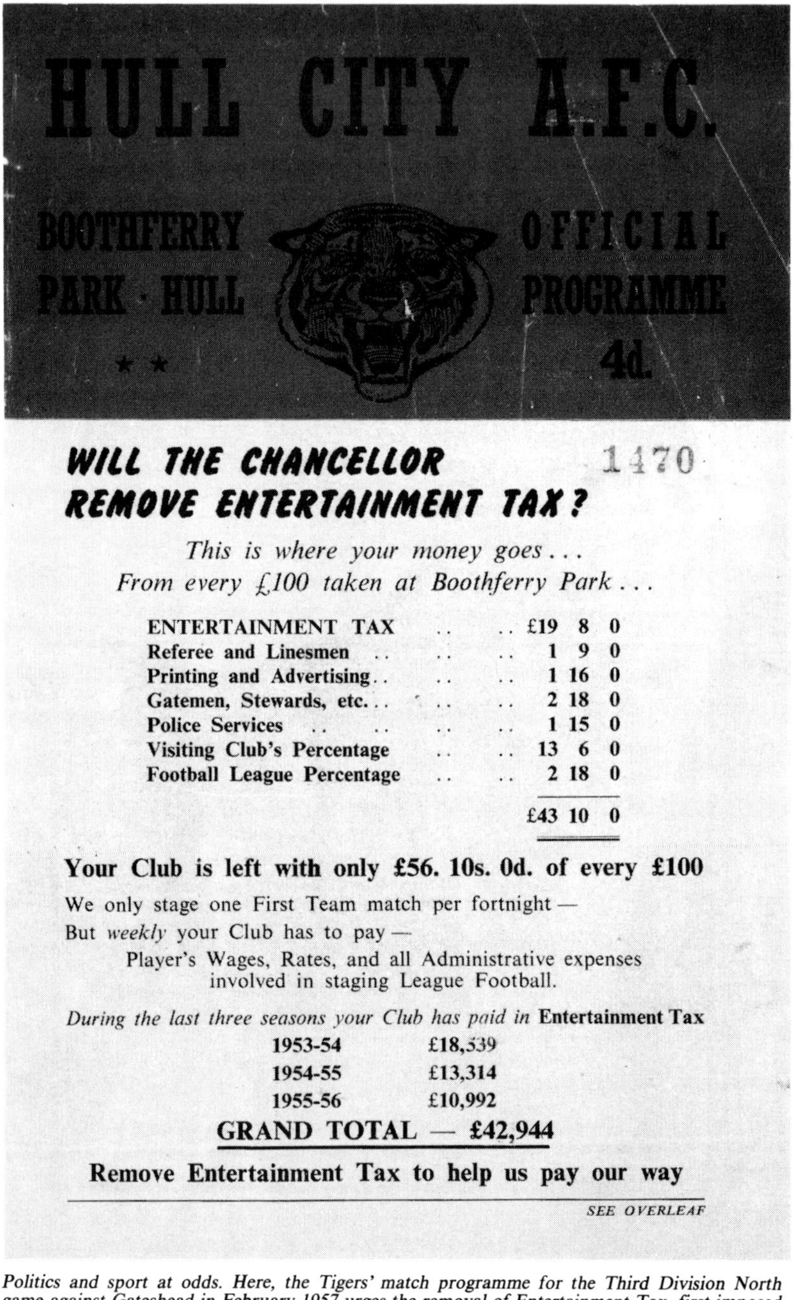

HULL CITY A.F.C.

BOOTHFERRY PARK · HULL

OFFICIAL PROGRAMME 4d.

WILL THE CHANCELLOR REMOVE ENTERTAINMENT TAX? 1470

This is where your money goes . . .
From every £100 taken at Boothferry Park . . .

ENTERTAINMENT TAX	£19 8 0
Referee and Linesmen	1 9 0
Printing and Advertising..	1 16 0
Gatemen, Stewards, etc...	2 18 0
Police Services	1 15 0
Visiting Club's Percentage	13 6 0
Football League Percentage	2 18 0
	£43 10 0

Your Club is left with only £56. 10s. 0d. of every £100

We only stage one First Team match per fortnight —
But *weekly* your Club has to pay —
Player's Wages, Rates, and all Administrative expenses involved in staging League Football.

During the last three seasons your Club has paid in **Entertainment Tax**

1953-54	**£18,539**
1954-55	**£13,314**
1955-56	**£10,992**

GRAND TOTAL — £42,944

Remove Entertainment Tax to help us pay our way

SEE OVERLEAF

Politics and sport at odds. Here, the Tigers' match programme for the Third Division North game against Gateshead in February 1957 urges the removal of Entertainment Tax, first imposed on football clubs during World War One.

10 April 1956, the first Football League match played under lights at Boothferry Park.

On 3 November 1962, the Tigers came close to defeat against non-League Crook Town. The cover design ran for four seasons, 1960-61 to 1963-4, the longest used of any post-war programme cover.

20 May 1966, the match which clinched the Third Division Championship.

Official
Programme 5p

LEEDS UNITED
A.F.C.
TOKEN

SPURS
2
1971-72

LEEDS UNITED

versus TOTTENHAM HOTSPUR

Wednesday, 25th August, 1971 Kick-off 7.30 p.m.
at BOOTHFERRY PARK, Hull

Leeds United

Colours :
WHITE SHIRTS, WHITE SHORTS

1. GARY SPRAKE
2. PAUL REANEY
3. TERRY COOPER
4. BILLY BREMNER
5. JACK CHARLTON
6. NORMAN HUNTER
7. PETER LORIMER
8. ALAN CLARKE
9. ROD BELFITT
10. JOHNNY GILES
11. PAUL MADELEY

Sub. ....

Spurs

Colours :
WHITE SHIRTS, BLUE SHORTS

1. PAT JENNINGS
2. JOE KINNEAR
3. ANTHONY WANT
4. ALAN MULLERY
5. MIKE ENGLAND
6. PHILIP BEAL
7. RALPH COATES
8. STEPHEN PERRYMAN
9. MARTIN CHIVERS
10. MARTIN PETERS
11. ALAN GILZEAN

Sub. ....

REFEREE :
Mr. D. A. CORBETT, Wolverhampton
LINESMEN :
Mr. R. MAXFIELD, Rotherham
RED FLAG
Mr. J. JOHNSON, Doncaster
YELLOW FLAG

25 August 1971, Leeds v Spurs — the only First Division match played at Boothferry Park. United's ground had been closed due to crowd trouble.

The first 'Sports Mail Football Annual', *published in 1919, looked forward to the Tigers achieving their goal of First Division football when League soccer resumed after the war. Seventy years later the ambition remains unfulfilled.*

Hull City supporter (after Swedish Tour in which the team won all its seven matches)—"Its a pity you can't play all your games in Sweden, you would soon win promotion!"

Following the club's successful tour of Sweden in 1924.

The Tiger's Handicap—
he could run without it!

The financial problems of the 1920s graphically captured.

A "MOVING" SCENE.

Owing to a portion of Hull City's ground being required for the proposed Scheme for the abolition of Level Crossings in Hull, the Tigers will have to find a new lair.

The issue for 1925-6 saw the club on the move some 20 years before they actually left the Anlaby Road ground.

Pride comes before a fall. This cartoon appeared in Manchester United's match programme prior to their third round FA Cup match against the Tigers in 1952. United were second in the First Division, but City, next to bottom in the Second Division, sprang a major upset by winning 2-0.

Lining up in readiness for the 1987-8 season. Back row (left to right): L.Thompson, A.Dyer, P.Heard, L.Jenkinson, N.Buckley, N.Brown, G.Parker, C.Palmer, M.Smith. Middle row: T.Wilson (reserve-team manager), F.Bunn, G.Kelly, S.McEwan, P.Skipper, A.Norman, R.Jobson, A.Saville, J.Radcliffe (physiotherapist). Front row: S.Corkain, N.Williams, G.Roberts, B.Horton (manager), W.Askew, R.Daniel, D.Booth (assistant manager).

Hull City Reserves prior to the 1987 East Riding Senior Cup Final. Back row (left to right): T.Wilson (reserve-team manager), N.Buckley, N.Brown, G.Kelly, L.Jenkinson, G.Parker, L.Thompson, A.Saville, R.Daniel. Front row: L.Pearson, S.Corkain, P.Olsson, M.Smith, N.Story.

That colourful Scot, Tommy Docherty, had a brief spell at Boothferry Park as assistant manager to Terry Neill. The Doc returned from Portugal in the summer of 1971, and Neill hoped his appointment would lighten the load whilst he was still playing. Within a couple of months the Scottish FA had put Docherty in charge of their national side, and when he won both his trial games, the Scots gave him a permanent full-time post.

There is nc record of the first throat to emit the cry 'Now, the Tigers!' nor of the precise occasion on which it happened. The first reference in print to the 'Tigers' appears in the Hull Daily Mail *in March 1905. Before that date the nearest to a nickname was the 'Citizens', popularly shortened to the 'Cits'. The city's two Rugby League clubs both had ornithological appelations. Hull Kingston Rovers were established as the 'Redbreasts', whilst Airlie Street, in close proximity to the Hull FC ground was exercising the sports cartoonists' imagination in trying to depict the mythical 'Airlie Bird'. Why not, suggested the* Mail *reporter, complete the trio with the another member of the animal kingdom, the tiger? With suitable exposure in their columns, the nickname caught on.*

When Leeds City came to Anlaby Road in January 1918 George Jacketts, attempting a clearance, kicked so strongly that the ball burst. The coincidence was that in the previous season's fixture the leather had also burst, and at almost the identical spot on the field.

In 1919 the Football League was expanded from 40 to 44 clubs. Chelsea, victims of match-fixing in 1915, were spared relegation, and a vote was taken for the extra club to make the First Division up to 22. Arsenal (18 votes) won the contest, whilst the Tigers (1 vote) missed out, along with Tottenham (8), Barnsley (5), Wolves (4), Nottingham Forest (3) and Birmingham (2).

Amongst the social changes in the years after World War One was a growth in the power of trade unions. When a reduction in railway workers' wages was proposed in September 1919, the whole railway network ground to a halt. The strike came on the eve of the Tigers' visit to Bury. Instead of crossing into Lancashire by train, the team spent 11 hours in the most uncomfortable of motor coaches to avoid the wrath of authority for not fulfilling the fixture. Little wonder they lost after that ordeal. The only consolation was that the strike lasted long enough to affect Bury's trip to Anlaby Road the following Saturday.

The great close season talking point of 1925 was how Jack Holt and Lou Harris would shape up in the Tigers' colours. The pair were crack three-quarters with Hull Kingston Rovers, who were Rugby League champions in 1924-5. Both had expressed a desire to try the dribbling code. Harris, though, had second thoughts during the break. Holt did turn out on the right wing in one of the annual public practice matches, but promptly returned to his first love.

The visit of Wolves in December 1925 provided the crowd with a spot of fun. In the second half the Tigers were awarded a penalty which Mick O'Brien took and hit the post. Fortunately for O'Brien, the referee ordered it to be retaken and the Irishman quickly handed over the responsibility to Paddy Mills. The former Bartonian did the necessary, but again the official was not satisfied. Undeterred, Mills once more planted the ball in the back of the net, and this time the goal stood. Price subsequently equalized, but it took just five minutes for Mills to restore City's advantage. Then, towards the close, Mills was bearing down on goal once more, until Wanderers' Fox fouled him. Yet again the referee awarded a penalty. Mills would have eagerly accepted the chance of a hat-trick, but for the effects of the full-back's challenge. George Whitworth took the kick but the referee spotted an infringement and Whitworth made the game safe at the second attempt. Five spot-kicks in one afternoon!

Controversy raged ten minutes from the end of the Tigers' visit to Middlesbrough in September 1928. 'Boro's Millar went down with blood pouring from his arm. The referee, a Mr Hull, investigated, and found City's centre-half, Arthur Childs, to be the culprit. A nail in Childs' boot had worked loose until protruding dangerously. The official sent the City pivot off, and Childs went, under the impression that a change of footwear would allow his return to the fray, but such were the rules of the day that any dismissal was final. The incident led to calls for a revision of the laws, and the FA took note. Two years later the same official dismissed the centre-half for retaliation in a match against Wigan.

Jack Hill made his City debut at Rochdale. The Lancashire side, managed by ex-Tiger Billy Cameron, languished at the foot of the Northern Section. After their last defeat a young actress from the town had threatened that, if the side fared no better against the Tigers, she would sign on and show them how it should be done. The record books show that Hill's men won 6-3, but one looks in vain for the debut of Miss Gracie Fields.

In 1946 the new regime wanted to break completely with the past. They envisaged orange shirts trimmed with blue, bearing the civic crest of three crowns on the breast. White shorts and orange and blue socks completed the rig-out. However, the Board of Trade refused to release the necessary dyes, so the team had to settle for pale-blue shirts and white shorts. Occasionally, for big matches and colour clashes, the old stripes were brought out. The following summer the board's inability to sever the tradition of four decades was confirmed with a compromise of amber shirts emblazoned with a tiger motif and black shorts.

In January 1913 a combination of failing light and a waterlogged pitch caused the abandonment of the Tigers' Second Division match with Glossop. It was City's first abandoned League fixture. One player, though, did his best to keep the crowd entertained. Defender Jack Houghton went full length in the mud, and when the crowd roared with laughter he promptly treated them to a repeat performance.

Hull City senior squad taken prior to the 1977-8 season. Back row (left to right): D.Stewart, R.McDonald, V.Grimes, P.Daniel, D.Sunley, E.Blackburn, J.Wealands, G.Nisbet, J.Hawley, P.Haigh, I.Dobson. Front row: D.Gibson, C.Galvin, G.Lyall, M.Lord, W.Bremner, S.Croft, R.de Vries, B.Bannister, D.Hawker.

Manager Ken Houghton (second from right) with his management team of (left to right) Andy Davidson (chief scout), Wilf McGuinness (coach) and Chris Chilton (youth coach).

The Tigers captured during a mid-season break at Scarborough in October 1982. Back row (left to right): W.Askew, L.Mutrie, W.Whitehurst, S.Richards, J.Davies, A.Norman. Middle row: S.McClaren, A.Flounders, D.Roberts, R.McNeil, N.Thompson, P.Skipper, C.Appleton (manager). Front row: D.Booth, B.Marwood, G.Roberts, G.Swann.

Hull City squad for the 1985-6 season. Back row (left to right): A.Flounders, G.Swann, A.Saville, P.Olsson, L.Pearson, A.Tomlinson. Middle row: D.Booth (coach), S.McEwan, P.Skipper, J.Davies, W.Whitehurst, A.Norman, R.Jobson, F.Bunn, J.Radcliffe (physiotherapist). Front row: N.Williams, S.Corkain, G.Roberts, B.Horton (player-manager), W.Askew, S.Brentano, M.Ring.

Bob Jackson's attempts to strengthen his side took a singular twist when the club sought to register a second Dane in November 1952. Jens-Peter Hansen came to Hull for a holiday with Viggo Jensen. He asked to turn out for the Tigers, who submitted the necessary amateur registration forms. Hansen had actually left for Southampton, all set to make his debut, when the League rang Boothferry Park to insist that he should not play. The club protested at length, but to no avail. Hansen did turn out for the Reserves, scoring four goals against Scarborough with a display of shooting power which would have been the ideal tonic for the first team.

In March 1957 the left-wing pair of Brian Bulless and Brian Cripsey caused the statisticians a headache with a curio of a goal against Hartlepools. They both scored it! Elusive Johnny Stephens swung over a centre and both Brians shouted for the other to leave it. They both stuck a foot out at the ball and appeared to connect simultaneously. The pair were good friends off the field and not inclined to argue the point in the after-match inquest. Cripsey deferred to his inside partner's claim: "I think what happened was that Brian hit the ball and I hit his foot."

One of the more unusual postponements was the Tigers' Third Division fixture with Notts County scheduled for 21 October 1961. It was called off due to an outbreak of polio in the city.

The Tigers should have been Queen's Park Rangers' first opponents after Rangers' move to the White City, but with the rain pouring down and scarcely 2,000 of the anticipated 20,000 present, the referee decided there was too much water on the pitch for the game to go ahead. It was as well, because the Hull City squad was stuck in a traffic jam and did not reach the ground until after the scheduled starting time.

In January 1984 the team failed to arrive for the Third Division fixture at Burnley. Their coach was halted on the Pennines by blizzard conditions. The League fined the club £2,500, taking into account the 'extenuating circumstances', and hinting that deduction of points and even expulsion were not beyond their powers.

Throughout the summer of 1966 a major topic of conversation amongst City followers was their team's goalkeeping spot. The departure of Mike Williams to Aldershot left Maurice Swan as the only experienced 'keeper at the club. Speculation as to a new signing centred on Chelsea's Peter Bonetti. Countless people claimed to have seen him in the presence of one or other of the Tigers' players or management. He had agreed to sign for City after the World Cup and the clubs had even decided upon a £50,000 transfer fee. "Too silly for words," said Cliff Britton.

The Carter era at Boothferry Park is still remembered fondly by Tigers' fans fortunate enough to have enjoyed those heady days when City took the Third Division North title under the former Sunderland, Derby and England star (above). Another familiar sight in those days of the late 1940s was Roy Kirk and his 'Tiger' mascot (below).

The Hull Hospital Charity Cup, a magnificent trophy for which Hull City competed against invited clubs before and after World War One.

Hull City Career Records

The following list includes every player who has played in a first-team match for Hull City. Football League and FA Cup records are shown separately but for reasons of conciseness other matches of a competitive nature, including the Football League Cup, wartime leagues and cups, have been included in the third set of figures. The final column contains all friendly, charity and tour matches, together with abandoned games, and including the two Northern Section matches at the start of the 1939-40 season. C.H.G.O.B. refers to Old Boys of the local Central Higher Grade School. The abbreviation 'cs' means close season. A detailed list of the footnotes thus [1] is given at the end of this section.

Player	From	To	Former club	Next known club	League App	League Gls	FA Cup App	FA Cup Gls	Other comp App	Other comp Gls	Others App	Others Gls
ABBOT Harry	Oct 04	Oct 04	Hull T Thursday	Amateur	-	-	-	-	-	-	2	0
ABLETT Gary I.	Sep 86	Oct 86	Liverpool	Loan	5	0	-	-	-	-	-	-
ACKERMAN Alfred A.E.	Jul 50	Jul 51	Clyde	Norwich C								
	Oct 53	Mar 55	Norwich C	Derby C	92	49	11	2	-	-	24	18
ACQUROFF John	Nov 34	Oct 36	Folkestone	Bury	70	25	1	0	1	0	1	1
ADAMS Charles L.	Mar 45	Apr 45	Constable St OB	Guest	-	-	-	-	3	0	-	-
ADAMS P.	Apr 19	Apr 19	West Ham U	Trialist	-	-	-	-	1	0	-	-
ADEY Thomas W.	Apr 23	Aug 25	Bedlington U	Swindon T	16	0	-	-	-	-	6	1
AINSWORTH Edgar W.	Sep 31	Jul 33	Old Boulevardiers	York C								
	Sep 34	cs 36	York C	Released	2	0	-	-	-	-	-	-
AINSWORTH J.	Dec 15	Apr 16	Guest		-	-	-	-	2	0	-	-
ALBERRY W. Edward	Apr 47	cs 48	Leeds U	Gainsborough T	1	0	-	-	-	-	-	-
ALEXANDER R.M.	Nov 04	Nov 04	Old Hymerians	Amateur	-	-	-	-	-	-	1	0
ALEXANDER Stanley	Jun 26	Nov 31	Percy Main	Bradford C	98	41	10	5	-	-	3	0
ALLEN Mervyn J.	Jun 31	cs 34	Gilfach	Carlisle U	15	1	-	-	-	-	2	0
ALSTON	Aug 04	Aug 04	Hessle	Amateur	-	-	-	-	-	-	1	0
ANDERSON Norman	Nov 39	Apr 41	Goole T	Guest	-	-	-	-	41	20	2	1
ANDREWS Mark	Sep 04	Feb 05	Hessle	Goole T	-	-	-	-	-	-	8	0
ANNABLES Walter	Jun 36	Jun 39	Grimsby T	Carlisle U	62	1	1	0	3	0	1	0
ARCHER John W.	Aug 44	Oct 44	Plymouth A	Guest	-	-	-	-	5	0	-	-
ARMESON Lawrence R.	Jan 45	Mar 45	Coventry C	Guest	-	-	-	-	7	1	-	-
ASKEW William	Aug 82		Gateshead		215/6	18	18	0	23/2	1	34/3	5
ATKINSON Charles	May 50	Jul 56	Marist OB	Bradford	37	2	2	1	-	-	14/1	3
ATKINSON G. Arthur	Jun 33	Jun 34	Lincoln C	Mansfield T	5	0	-	-	-	-	1	0
ATKINSON Peter	May 47	cs 48	Billingham Synth	Released	6	0	-	-	-	-	1	0
ATKINSON Trevor	May 46	Aug 48	Hull Amateurs	Barnsley	2	0	-	-	-	-	3	0
ATKINSON W.	Oct 16	Oct 16	Guest		-	-	-	-	1	0	-	-
BALDRY George W.	May 36	cs 37	Grimsby T	Scunthorpe U	5	2	-	-	-	-	-	-
BANKS Francis S.	Aug 66	Mar 76	Southend U	Southend U	284/4	6	22	0	24	1	40/2	1
BANNISTER Bruce I.	Jun 77	Jul 80	Plymouth A	US Dunkerque	79/6	20	3/1	0	12	4	8	1
BARKER Geoffrey A.[1]	Sep 65	Jun 71	Ainthorpe HS	Darlington	29/1	2	-	-	2	0	3/3	0
BARLEY Henry F.	May 31	Aug 32	Grimsby T	New Brighton	13	2	-	-	-	-	1	0
BARNES Peter S.	Mar 88	May 88	Manchester C	Bolton W	11	0	-	-	-	-	-	-
BARRACLOUGH William	Jun 27	Sep 28	Dairycoates	Wolves								
	Oct 40	Apr 41	Doncaster R	Guest	9	0	-	-	19	2	1	0
BARRASS James	see LODGE											
BASEY James R.	Aug 29	cs 30		Released	-	-	-	-	-	-	1	0
BAXTER William A.[2]	Mar 71	May 72	Ipswich T	Northampton T	20/1	0	2	0	-	-	3	0
BEARDSHAW E. Colin	Sep 44	Mar 45	Bradford C	Guest	-	-	-	-	14	0	-	-
BEARDSLEY Donald T.[3]	Jul 62	Aug 73	Eastfield HS	Grimsby T	128/2	0	6	0	8	0	25/2	1
BEESON George	Sep 44	Mar 45	Walsall	Guest	-	-	-	-	20	1	-	-
BELL Albert [4]	Sep 15	Sep 15	Goole T	Hull OB	-	-	-	-	1	0	-	-
BELL Douglas	Mar 89	Apr 89	Shrewsbury T	Loan	4	0	-	-	-	-	-	-

Diminutive Billy Askew has proved a real live-wire in midfield since signing for Hull City in 1982.

The Hull City team in 1910-11. Back row (left to right): T.Nevins, W.Wright, F.Martin, H.Simmon, E.Gordon, T.Browell. Third row: Mr A.Langley (manager), E.Roughley, Dan Gordon, J.Houghton, A.Browell, J.McIntosh, G.Browell. Second row: Joe Smith, A.Temple, T.Pearce, David Gordon, John Smith, W.Smith, E.Neve. Front row: J.McQuillan, A.Musgrave, E.A.Smith, D.Taylor, N.Hendry.

Player	From	To	Former club	Next known club	League App	League Gls	FA Cup App	FA Cup Gls	Other comp App	Other comp Gls	Others App	Others Gls
BELL Ernest	Nov 35	May 38	Blundell St OB	Mansfield T								
	Aug 44	Aug 47	Aldershot	Scarborough	27	5	-	-	27	4	-	-
BELL Matthew	Aug 19	Aug 31	W Hartlepool	Nottingham F	393	1	30	0	-	-	23	0
BELL William T.	May 32	May 33	Grimsby T	Released	4	0	-	-	-	-	-	-
BENNETT Reuben M.	Jan 36	cs 36	Aberdeen EE	Queen of the South	3	0	-	-	-	-	-	-
BENNION John R.	Jun 57	Jul 60	Burnley	Stockport C	35	1	1	0	-	-	4	0
BENNYWORTH Ian R.	Sep 77	Jul 81	Cottingham HS	Gainsborough T	1	0	-	-	0/2	0	-	-
BENTLEY Keith J.	Aug 57	Jul 58	Hull Schools	Scarborough	4	0	2	0	-	-	-	-
BERRY Thomas	Jun 47	Oct 57	Great Harwood	Buxton	275	1	20	0	-	-	38	0
BEST Charles	May 11	cs 13	Eston U	Retired (injury)	35	4	2	1	-	-	7	8
BEST Jeremiah	Oct 36	cs 37	Darlington	Released	31	11	1	0	-	-	-	-
BETTS Arthur C.	May 14	Jun 20	Derby C	Scunthorpe U	51	0	6	0	109	0	14	0
BEW Daniel C.	May 22	cs 23	Sunderland	Swindon T	11	0	1	0	-	-	-	-
BIRCHAM Bernard	Nov 44	Nov 44	Sunderland	Guest	-	-	-	-	1	0	-	-
BLACKBURN Edwin H.	Mar 73	May 80	Houghton-le-S GS	York C	68	0	5	0	3	0	7/2	0
BLACKBURN Paul	Apr 84	May 84	Goole T	Loan	-	-	-	-	1	0	1	0
BLAIR George	Nov 24	cs 25	Port Glasgow A	Released	-	-	-	-	-	-	1	0
BLAMPEY Stuart L.	Oct 65	Nov 76	Hessle HS	Scarborough	61/11	1	0/1	0	4/1	0	8/5	0
BLEAKLEY Thomas	Oct 18	cs 30	Walkden Cen	Goole T	368	5	21	2	13	0	28	2
BLENKINSOP Ernest	Oct 21	Jan 23	Cudworth	Sheffield W	11	0	-	-	-	-	1	0
BLOOMER James	Feb 48	Jun 49	Strathclyde	Grimsby T	4	2	-	-	-	-	3	0
BLOXHAM J. Alexander	Oct 47	Aug 50	Ollerton Col	Boston U	33	2	5	0	-	-	3	0
BLY William	Aug 37	May 60	Walker Celtic	Weymouth	403	0	35	0	18	0	37	0
BLYTH James	Apr 37	May 39	Tottenham H	Hearts	72	0	6	0	2	0	2	0
BOOTH Dennis	May 80	May 89	Watford		121/2	2	12	0	16	0	17/3	0
BOUCH C.	Apr 05	Apr 05	C.H.G.O.B.	Amateur	-	-	-	-	-	-	1	0
BOWERING Michael	Aug 57	Jun 60	Local	Chesterfield	45	7	1	0	-	-	2	0
BOWLER Gerrard C.	Aug 49	Jun 50	Portsmouth	Millwall	38	0	4	0	-	-	-	-
BOWN Herbert A.	Jan 25	cs 25	Halifax T	Retired	4	0	1	0	-	-	-	-
BOYTON John	Nov 12	May 14	Kilsyth Emmet R	Linfield	13	1	1	0	-	-	1	0
BRADBURY John	Apr 15	Jan 16	Local	Guest	-	-	-	-	17	4	-	-
BRADBURY William	Oct 55	Feb 60	Birmingham C	Bury	178	82	12	7	-	-	10	9
BRADFORD Bernard	Jul 27	cs 30	Walker Park	Walsall	1	0	-	-	-	-	1	0
BRADLEY George J.	Oct 40	Mar 41	Newcastle U	Guest	-	-	-	-	11	0	-	-
BRAILSFORD Thomas	Dec 44	Dec 44	Guest		-	-	-	-	1	1	-	-
BRANDON Thomas	Jun 20	Jun 22	Bristol R	Bradford	56	3	5	2	-	-	1	1
BRATLEY George	Nov 40	Apr 41	Rotherham U	Guest	-	-	-	-	12	1	-	-
BRATTON William	Dec 40	Dec 40	Local	Guest	-	-	-	-	1	0	-	-
BRAYSON Joseph H.	Apr 26	cs 27	Scotswood	Released	3	0	-	-	-	-	1	0
BREMNER William J.	Sep 76	May 78	Leeds U	Doncaster R(mangr)	61	6	3	0	4	1	-	-
BRENNAN T.	Apr 19	Apr 19	Port Vale	Trialist	-	-	-	-	1	0	-	-
BRENTANO Stephen R.	Mar 82	May 87	North Ferriby U	Bridlington Town	11/1	0	2	0	3	0	3/1	0
BREWER Cyril	Oct 44	Nov 44	RAF	Guest	-	-	-	-	3	0	-	-
BRIDGES Ben	Aug 55	Jul 60	Setting Dyke YC	Scarborough	1	0	-	-	-	-	-	-
BRIGGS Arthur L.	May 21	Aug 24	Walker Celtic	Tranmere R	5	0	-	-	-	-	1	0
BRIGGS James	Aug 12	Nov 13	Craghead U	Released	2	0	-	-	-	-	0/1	0
BROOKS George	Nov 04	cs 07	East Hull Thurs	East Hull Thurs	-	-	1	0	-	-	24	1
BROWELL Anthony 'Andy' [5]	Dec 07	Mar 12	Newburn	Everton	101	5	8	0	-	-	12	3
BROWELL George	Sep 05	cs 11	West Stanley	Grimsby T	194	3	14	0	-	-	24	5
BROWELL Thomas	Apr 10	Dec 11	Newburn	Everton	48	32	4	0	-	-	2	3
BROWN Charles	Sep 04	Sep 04	Tottenham H	Reading	-	-	-	-	-	-	1	0
BROWN David	Dec 16	Apr 17	Dundee	Guest	-	-	-	-	2	2	-	-
BROWN George	Sep 44	Sep 44	Kingston Wolves	Guest	-	-	-	-	1	0	-	-
BROWN Henry S.	May 46	Jan 47	Wolves	Retired (injury)	22	0	5	0	-	-	1	0

Nick Brown

Brian Bulless

The Hull City team in July 1974. Back row (left to right): Mr W.Dixon (assistant manager), C.Galvin, G.Staniforth, P.Daniel, V.Grimes, J.Radcliffe (physiotherapist). Middle row: A.Davidson (trainer), S.Croft, J.Hawley, S,Deere, J.Wealands, P.Fletcher, D.Burnett, K.Wagstaff, Mr T.Neill (manager). Front row: J.Hemmerman, S.Blampey, J. McGill, J.Kaye, M.Lord, R.de Vries, R.Greenwood.

Player	From	To	Former club	Next known club	League App	Gls	FA Cup App	Gls	Other comp App	Gls	Others App	Gls
BROWN J.	Dec 16	Dec 16	Guest		-	-	-	-	1	0	-	-
BROWN Michael J.	Aug 54	Jul 67	Gloucester schools	Lincoln C	8	0	1	0	-	-	1	0
BROWN Nicholas L.	Sep 83		Hull GS		22/2	0	4	1	-	-	2/3	0
BROWN Ronald	Feb 47	cs 47	Plymouth A	Linfield	7	3	-	-	-	-	-	-
BROWN W.	Feb 18	Feb 18	Gainsborough T	Guest	-	-	-	-	1	0	-	-
BROWNSWORD N. John	Sep 46	cs 47	Frickley Col	Scunthorpe U	10	0	1	0	-	-	1	1
BUCHAN William R.M.	Jan 48	Nov 49	Blackpool	Gateshead	40	12	6	1	-	-	8	5
BUCKLEY Neil A.	Aug 84		Schultz HS		14	0	3	0	-	-	3/5	0
BULLESS Brian	Aug 49	May 64	Clifton St School	Retired (injury)	326	30	24	6	7	0	20	4
BULLOCK Arthur	Aug 32	Dec 34	Southcoates La Sch	York C	18	3	-	-	-	-	-	-
BUNN Frank S.	Jul 85	Dec 87	Luton T	Oldham A	89/6	23	5	1	10/2	6	15	13
BUNTING Alan	Oct 44	Oct 44	Brigham's	Guest	-	-	-	-	1	0	-	-
BURBANKS W. Edwin	Jun 48	Jul 53	Sunderland	Leeds U	143	21	10	1	-	-	10	2
BURDETT Thomas	Jun 33	Jun 35	Wheatley Hill	Fulham								
	Aug 40	Oct 40	Bury	Guest	3	0	-	-	7	5	-	-
BURNETT Dennis H. [6]	Oct 73	Aug 75	Millwall	Brighton & HA	46	2	5	0	1	0	5	0
BURSELL J. Clifford	cs 50	Jul 56	Newland YC	Goole T	2	2	-	-	-	-	-	-
BURTON Edmund	Apr 16	Apr 16	Bristol C	Guest	-	-	-	-	1	1	-	-
BUTCHER Reginald	Mar 41	Apr 41	Chester	Guest	-	-	-	-	2	0	-	-
BUTLER Dennis M.	Jun 63	Dec 69	Chelsea	Reading	215/2	0	20	0	9	0	12/1	0
BUTLER Ian	Jan 65	Jul 73	Rotherham U	York C	300/5	66	22	4	12	0	24/2	6
BYRNE Andrew	Jun 13	Dec 13	Shelbourne	Rtnd to Ireland	3	0	-	-	-	-	-	-
CALVERT Mark	May 87		Co Durham Schls		5	0	-	-	-	-	-	-
CAMERON Kenneth	Jun 35	Aug 36	Bolton W	Queen's Park R	30	12	-	-	-	-	-	-
CAMERON William S.	Feb 14	cs 19	Bury	Bury	47	10	5	2	3	0	1	0
CAMPBELL Austin F.	Nov 35	Sep 36	Huddersfield T	Darwen	11	0	-	-	-	-	-	-
CAMPBELL Joseph	May 25	May 27	Walker Park	Bradford C	11	0	-	-	-	-	1	0
CAPEWELL Ronald	Jul 54	Jul 55	Sheffield W	King's Lynn	1	0	-	-	-	-	-	-
CARNEY M.	Apr 04	Sep 06	Beverley Barracks	Amateur	-	-	1	0	-	-	1	0
CARTER Horatio S.	Mar 48	Apr 52	Sunderland	Cork A	136	57	14	5	-	-	12	3
CARTER Joseph	Jun 46	Mar 47	Notts C	Bournemouth & BA	5	0	1	0	-	-	1	0
CARTWRIGHT Phillip	Jun 29	May 30	Bradford	Lincoln C	20	0	1	0	-	-	-	-
CASSIDY Joseph	May 35	cs 37	Glasgow Ashfield	Released	8	1	-	-	-	-	-	-
CAWTHORNE Charles H.	May 52	May 54	Endike Lane OB	Amateur	-	-	-	-	-	-	1	0
CHADWICK Clifton	Sep 46	Jul 47	Middlesbrough	Darlington	23	7	4	1	-	-	-	-
CHAPLIN George	Jan 16	Apr 16	Bradford C	Guest	-	-	-	-	15	0	1	0
CHAPMAN Henry	Apr 11	Sep 12	Sheffield W	Retired (injury)	32	7	2	0	-	-	3	3
CHARLES F.	Jan 18	Jan 18	Sheffield U	Guest	-	-	-	-	1	0	-	-
CHARLESWORTH Arthur L.	Oct 18	cs 21	Local	Worksop T	15	7	-	-	1	0	1	1
CHARLTON William	Nov 34	Jan 35	Southampton	Yorkshire W	3	1	1	1	-	-	-	-
CHEETHAM Samuel	May 20	Nov 21	Thatto Heath	Bradford C	28	1	5	0	-	-	2	0
CHILDS J. Arthur	Apr 28	Jun 31	Darlington	Exeter C	74	8	10	0	-	-	-	-
CHILTON Christopher [7]	Aug 59	Aug 71	Bilton	Coventry C	415	193	39	16	23	13	23/1	20
CHRISTMASS John	Feb 15	Mar 18	Atkins FC	Bridlington Town	-	-	-	-	7	4	-	-
CLARK Sydney D.	Dec 44	Dec 44	Guest		-	-	-	-	1	0	-	-
CLARK William	Mar 20	Mar 20	Notts C	Released	1	0	-	-	-	-	-	-
CLARKE Douglas	Nov 55	Jun 65	Bury	Torquay U	368	79	31	6	12	2	14	6
CLELAND James A.	Apr 15	Oct 17	Beverley Barracks	Amateur	1	0	-	-	7	1	3	2
CLUBLEY T. Raymond	Aug 38	Oct 47	Beverley W Star	Beverley U	-	-	-	-	2	0	-	-
COATES David P.	Oct 52	Mar 60	Shiny Row	Mansfield T	62	13	1	0	-	-	2	4
COCKIN Neil	cs 81	May 84	Sth Hunsley Sch	North Ferriby U	-	-	-	-	2	0	1/2	0
CODDINGTON A.S.	Aug 15	Oct 16	Local	Guest	-	-	-	-	1	0	-	-
COLLIER John C.	Jun 20	Jul 26	Inverkeithing U	Queen's Park R	168	0	14	0	-	-	16	0
COLLIER Thomas	Dec 44	Jan 45	Halifax T	Guest	-	-	-	-	5	0	-	-

Frank Bunn

Chris Chilton

Hull City in 1937-8. Back row (left to right): E.Bell, Lawrence, Annables, Goodall, Parker, Hardy, J.Beck (trainer). Front row: Hubbard, Fryer, MacNeill, Mr E.Blackburn (manager), Davies, Cumner, Blyth.

Player	From	To	Former club	Next known club	League App	Gls	FA Cup App	Gls	Other comp App	Gls	Others App	Gls
COLLINSON Leslie	Aug 53	Feb 67	Local	York C	296/1	14	26	0	9	2	8/1	3
CONDON Michael	Jul 83	Aug 83	Middlesbrough	Trialist	-	-	-	-	-	-	0/2	2
CONNELLY	Apr 17	Apr 17	Guest		-	-	-	-	-	-	1	0
CONWAY Andrew	Jun 47	Aug 49	North Shields	Dartford	6	5	-	-	-	-	5	4
COOK	May 46	May 46	Trialist	Released	-	-	-	-	-	-	1	0
COOK George W.	Jan 05	Aug 16	Brunswick Wes	Amateur	-	-	1	0	-	-	2	0
COOK Peter H. [8]	May 46	Aug 48	Kingston Wolves	Scarborough	5	0	2	1	-	-	2	0
COOK S.	May 46	May 46	Trialist	Released	-	-	-	-	-	-	2	0
COOKE Albert	Feb 30	Jul 32	Scunthorpe U	Halifax T	35	0	-	-	-	-	1	0
COOKSON Samuel	Mar 17	Apr 17	Manchester U	Guest	-	-	-	-	5	3	1	1
COOPER W.	Feb 05	Feb 05	Bridlington A	Amateur	-	-	-	-	-	-	1	0
CORBETT Alexander M.	Jan 48	Aug 49	New Brighton	Dartford	8	0	-	-	-	-	2/1	0
CORKAIN Stephen	Aug 83	May 88	Schools	Billingham	5	1	-	-	1	0	4/2	0
CORNER J. Norman	Aug 62	Oct 67	Horden Col Wel	Lincoln C	5	4	1	0	2	0	-	-
COTTAM Alfred	Sep 41	May 46	Lincoln C	Guest	-	-	-	-	2	0	1	0
COVERDALE Robert	Apr 16	Nov 16	Sunderland	Guest								
	May 21	Aug 24	Sunderland	Grimsby T	63	5	3	2	5	0	5	1
COWAN William	Sep 25	May 27	High Fell	Blackpool	11	8	1	1	-	-	1	1
CRAWFORD E.	Oct 39	Oct 39	Clapton O	Guest	-	-	-	-	1	0	-	-
CRAWFORD John F.	Mar 20	May 23	Jarrow T	Chelsea	126	9	8	4	-	-	9	1
CRAWSHAW Cyril B.	Jun 46	Oct 46	Stalybridge C	Stalybridge C	2	2	-	-	-	-	-	-
CRICKMORE Charles A.	Aug 57	Jun 62	Hull Schools	Bournemouth & BA	53	13	2	0	3	1	-	-
CRIPSEY Brian	Nov 51	Sep 58	Brunswick Inst	Wrexham	145	19	14	1	-	-	19/1	4
CROFT Stuart D.	Oct 70	Mar 81	Pegswood Jun	Portsmouth	187/3	4	12	2	13	0	8/4	1
CROFTS Ernest W.	Apr 45	Apr 45	Notts minor soccer	Guest	-	-	-	-	2	0	-	-
CROSBIE Robert C.	Oct 53	Jul 55	Bradford	Grimsby T	61	22	7	4	-	-	17	18
CROWTHER H.	Oct 16	Oct 16	Guest		-	-	-	-	1	0	-	-
CROZIER James	Jun 27	cs 28	Glasgow Ashfield	Derry C	3	0	-	-	-	-	-	-
CUBIE Neil G.	Jul 57	Jul 58	Bury	Scarborough	4	0	-	-	-	-	-	-
CUMMINS George P.	Nov 62	Feb 65	Cambridge C	Retired	21	2	3	0	1	0	2	0
CUMNER R. Horace	Jan 38	May 38	Margate	Arsenal	12	4	-	-	-	-	1	1
CUNLIFFE Arthur	Jun 38	cs 46	Burnley	Rochdale	42	20	3	1	32	10	9	2
CURNOW Jack	May 39	cs 45	Tranmere R	Tranmere R	-	-	-	-	55	0	9	0
CURRAN Edward 'Terry'	Oct 86	Nov 86	Panionios(Greece)	Sunderland	4	0	-	-	2	1	-	-
CUTTS E.	Jan 17	Dec 18	Sheffield U	Guest	-	-	-	-	2	0	-	-
CZUCZMAN Mychaljo	Aug 82	Dec 82	York C	Skegness T	-	-	-	-	-	-	1	0
DAGNALL William	May 06	May 07	St Helens Rec	St Helens Rec	8	2	-	-	-	-	-	-
DALEY Alan J.	Jul 47	cs 48	Mansfield T	Bangor C	7	0	-	-	-	-	-	-
DANIEL Peter W.	Oct 69	May 78	Andrew Marvel HS	Wolves	113	9	8	0	7	0	6	0
DANIEL Raymond C.	Jun 86		Luton T		55/3	3	0/1	0	1/1	0	14/5	2
DARLING Benjamin S.	Jun 38	cs 39	South Shields	Released	2	0	1	0	-	-	-	-
DAVIDSON Andrew	Mar 47	Jul 68	Douglas Water Th	Retired (injury)	520	18	43	1	16	0	22	0
DAVIDSON David C.	Nov 46	Aug 48	Douglas Water Th	Scarborough	22	4	1	0	-	-	2	1
DAVIDSON Ian [9]	Jul 63	Jun 69	Goole U	York C	5/1	1	-	-	-	-	2	0
DAVIES David D. 'Dai' [10]	Aug 35	Sep 48	Aberaman A	Scunthorpe U	141	30	8	3	40	7	14	3
DAVIES George A.	Mar 20	cs 22	Prescot	Merthyr T	11	0	-	-	-	-	2	0
DAVIES Harry J.	Mar 05	cs 07	Doncaster R	Leicester F	34	0	4	0	-	-	8	0
DAVIES John G. [11]	Feb 80	May 87	Cardiff C	Retired (injury)	24	0	2	0	1	0	11/6	0
DAVIN Martin	Nov 30	cs 31	Bolton W	Yeovil & Petters U	8	1	-	-	-	-	-	-
DAVIS Ian	Sep 80	Mar 85	Riley HS	Scarborough	25/3	1	-	-	3/1	0	1/3	0
DAWSON Daniel	May 40	Nov 40	Queen of the Sth	Hamilton A	-	-	-	-	9	3	-	-
DEACEY Charles	May 14	Dec 20	West Brom A	Grimsby T	75	4	6	1	16	2	8	0
DEACY Nicholas S.	Feb 80	Apr 82	Vitesse Arnheim	Happy Vly(H/K)	80/7	7	12	1	5/1	1	-	-
DEERE Stephen H. [12]	May 73	Mar 76	Scunthorpe U	Bridlington Town	65/1	2	3/3	0	12	0	10/1	0

Les Collinson

Steve Corkain

The Reserves' match at Doncaster in January 1926 came to a premature end ten minutes into the second half. The fog was so thick that City 'keeper Jacob Iceton was unaware of the decision, and remained in his goal until his teammates went back to look for him.

The Tigers FA Cup team of 1930. Back row (left to right): Mr W.McCracken (manager), Bell, Gibson, Childs, Maddison, Mills, Joe Beck (trainer). Front row: Starling, Howieson, Walsh, Gowdy, Duncan, Alexander, Rogers, Goldsmith. On ground: Bleakley, Taylor.

Player	From	To	Former club	Next known club	League App	League Gls	FA Cup App	FA Cup Gls	Other comp App	Other comp Gls	Others App	Others Gls
DE MANGE Kenneth J.P.P.	Mar 88		Leeds U		27/14	1	3	0	2	0	8/1	4
DENBY Stanley	Apr 32	cs 37	Goole T	Guildford C	124	3	6	0	-	-	2	0
DENNISON C. Robert	May 51	Jul 58	Bolton W	Scarborough	24	1	1	0	-	-	2	0
DEPEAR E. Roly	Nov 46	Nov 46	Boston U	Trialist	-	-	-	-	-	-	1	0
DE VRIES Roger S.	Aug 66	Jun 80	Wolfreton School	Blackburn R	314/4	0	12	0	32	1	30/6	0
DIAMOND John J.	Sep 31	Mar 32	Beverley W Star	Newark	1	0	-	-	-	-	-	-
DICK Harry W.	Feb 17	Feb 17	Reckitts	Guest	-	-	-	-	1	0	-	-
DICKINSON Peter	Sep 44	Dec 44	Constable St OB	Guest	-	-	-	-	4	0	-	-
DICKINSON William	May 38	cs 39	Southend U	Released	18	5	-	-	1	0	1	0
DIMBLEBY Stanley	Aug 35	Jun 37	Sth Killingholme	Port Vale	20	0	-	-	-	-	-	-
DIXON Edward	Mar 07	cs 07	Lincoln C	Released	3	0	-	-	-	-	-	-
DIXON E. Stanley	May 26	cs 30	Blackburn R	East Riding Ams	99	3	8	0	-	-	1	0
DIXON John T.	Nov 44	Nov 44	Aston Villa	Guest	-	-	-	-	1	1	-	-
DOBSON Ian	Jul 74	Jun 80	Riley HS	Hereford U	86/6	7	4	0	10	0	7/2	1
DODDS Leslie S.	Mar 34	Jun 35	Grimsby T	Torquay U	20	4	-	-	-	-	1	0
DON Robert P.	May 35	cs 37	Perthshire Juniors	Released	21	0	-	-	-	-	-	-
DOWEN John S.	Jun 38	Jun 39	Wolves	Wolves (trainer)								
	Oct 44	Oct 44	Wolves	Guest	39	0	3	0	2	0	3	0
DOWLING Joseph R.	Dec 44	Dec 44	RAF	Guest	-	-	-	-	1	0	-	-
DOWNES Percy	Feb 32	Aug 32	Blackpool	Stockport C	11	3	-	-	-	-	1	0
DOWNIE John D.	Jan 45	Jan 45	Bradford	Guest								
	Jul 54	Jul 55	Luton T	King's Lynn	27	5	1	0	1	0	7	2
DOYLE Dermot P.	Apr 22	cs 23	Pontypridd	Released	6	0	-	-	-	-	-	-
DOYLE Robert	Aug 85	May 87	Portsmouth	Retired (injury)	43	2	3	0	7	0	3	0
DREYER Gordon	Jun 35	cs 36	Hartlepools U	Hartlepools U	5	0	-	-	-	-	-	-
DRUMMOND Andrew	Oct 44	Oct 44	Scottish Junior	Guest	-	-	-	-	1	0	-	-
DRYBURGH Thomas J.D.	May 54	Jul 55	Leicester C	King's Lynn	23	3	1	0	-	-	7	4
DUNCAN Andrew	Jun 30	Mar 35	Renton Thistle	Tottenham H	105	31	9	0	-	-	2	0
DUNCAN Douglas	Aug 28	Mar 32	Aberdeen Richd	Derby C	111	47	11	3	-	-	3	0
DUNCAN James R.	Jul 53	Jun 60	Southcoates HS	Bradford C	26	3	-	-	-	-	4	2
DUNNE Leo	Jun 35	cs 36	Manchester C	Drumcondra	8	0	-	-	-	-	-	-
DURHAM R. Denis	Apr 47	Jul 60	East Halton U	Bridlington Town	267	7	22	0	-	-	36/1	1
DUTHIE James	Jun 51	May 53	Grimsby T	Southend U	17	3	-	-	-	-	3	1
DYER Alexander C.	Feb 87	Nov 88	Blackpool	Crystal P	59/1	14	4	1	2	0	12	10
DYER Reginald H.	Nov 39	Nov 39	Scarborough	Guest	-	-	-	-	1	0	-	-
DYKE Harry	Dec 24	cs 25	Hull OB	Amateur	-	-	-	-	-	-	1	0
EATHERINGTON Harry A.	Apr 45	Apr 45	Guest		-	-	-	-	2	1	-	-
ECCLES Thomas E.	Sep 22	cs 23	Hargreaves FC	Bridlington Town	9	2	-	-	-	-	1	1
ECCLESTON Stuart I.	Jan 81	cs 82	Stoke C	Port Vale	22/1	0	-	-	5	0	2	0
EDELSTON Joseph	Mar 13	Jun 20	St Helens Rec	Manchester C	109	0	8	0	135	1	17	1
EDWARDS Edmund C.	May 36	cs 37	Clapton O	Mossley	10	1	-	-	1	1	-	-
EDWARDS Keith	Aug 78	Sep 81	Sheffield U	Sheffield U								
	Mar 88		Aberdeen		183/2	86	13	8	16/2	3	19/1	18
ELLIOTT Harvey	Nov 46	cs 47	Manchester junior	Mossley	4	0	-	-	-	-	-	-
ELLIS John	May 38	cs 39	Bristol R	Clapton O	32	0	2	0	1	0	1	0
ELVIN Robert	Aug 16	Sep 18	Brunswick Inst	Hull FC	-	-	-	-	2	0	1	0
FAGAN Fionan	Mar 51	Dec 53	Transport(Dublin)	Manchester C	26	2	-	-	-	-	8	0
FAIRCLOUGH S.	Oct 16	Oct 16	Guest		-	-	-	-	1	0	-	-
FARLEY John D.	May 78	Aug 80	Wolves	Bury	59/1	5	3/1	0	3	0	5	2
FARQUHARSON Hugh	Sep 34	Jun 36	Renfrew Juns	Dunfermline A	7	0	-	-	-	-	1	0
FAWCETT Robert E.	May 29	cs 31	Unsworth Col	Released	6	0	-	-	-	-	2	0
FAZACKERLEY Stanley N.	Apr 12	Mar 13	Accrington S	Sheffield U	29	19	3	1	-	-	8	26
FEARNLEY E.	Oct 17	Oct 17	Bradford C	Guest	-	-	-	-	1	0	-	-
FEASEY Paul C.	Aug 49	Jul 66	York Railway Inst	Goole T	271	0	25	0	8	0	10/1	0

Player	From	To	Former club	Next known club	League App	League Gls	FA Cup App	FA Cup Gls	Other comp App	Other comp Gls	Others App	Others Gls
FENWICK Alfred R.	Sep 11	cs 14	Craghead U	West Ham U	17	7	-	-	-	-	8	3
FERGUSON J. Brian	Dec 80	Aug 82	Newcastle U	Goole T	24/4	2	3	0	5	1	1	0
FINCH A. Roy	Oct 44	Nov 44	West Brom A	Guest	-	-	-	-	3	2	-	-
FINDLAY Len	Aug 81	Feb 83	Bridlington Town	Bridlington Trin	-	-	-	-	-	-	0/1	0
FISHER J. Bernard	Aug 55	Jul 63	York Junior	Bradford C	126	0	11	0	5	0	6/1	0
FLANNIGAN Thomas	May 29	cs 30	Stoke C	Loughboro' Cor	2	0	-	-	-	-	1	0
FLETCHER Peter	May 74	May 76	Manchester U	Stockport C	26/10	5	2/1	1	5	2	2/4	3
FLINTON Walter	Dec 44	Apr 45	Scarborough	Guest	-	-	-	-	16	3	-	-
FLOOD Charles W.	Aug 20	May 22	Plymouth A	Bolton W	54	25	2	0	-	-	4	3
FLOUNDERS Andrew J.	Jun 78	Mar 87	Hull Schools	Scunthorpe U	126/33	54	10/3	4	12/7	5	15/12	10
FORD Bert	Jan 16	Jan 17	Goole T	Guest	-	-	-	-	30	2	1	0
FORD Jack	Oct 04	Jan 05	Hessle	Goole T	-	-	-	-	-	-	5	2
FORGAN Thomas C.	May 49	Jun 54	Sutton Est (Mbro)	York C	10	0	1	0	-	-	3/1	0
FORRESTER H.	Feb 05	Feb 05	Botanic Swifts	Amateur	-	-	-	-	-	-	1	0
FORWARD Frederick J.	Jul 32	Aug 33	Portsmouth	Bath C	39	6	4	2	-	-	-	-
FOSS F.	Dec 18	Jan 19	Lancashire Fus	Guest	-	-	-	-	2	0	-	-
FOSTER George	Aug 39	Dec 39	Brunswick Inst	Amateur	-	-	-	-	-	-	1	0
FOSTER Thomas	May 31	cs 38	Ranks FC	Released	25	1	1	0	1	0	-	-
FOWLER H. Norman	Sep 46	Nov 49	Middlesbrough	Gateshead	52	0	1	0	-	-	8	0
FOX Kevin	Mar 81	May 81	Lincoln C	Loan	-	-	-	-	-	-	0/1	0
FRANKISH Paul	Jul 78	cs 80	Wolfreton HS	Scarborough	-	-	-	-	-	-	0/2	0
FRANKLIN Cornelius	Feb 51	Feb 56	Stoke C	Crewe Alexandra	95	0	1	0	-	-	18	0
FRASER David M.	Feb 53	Jul 58	Arniston Rangers	Mansfield T	11	7	-	-	-	-	3	2
FRENCH John L.	Mar 41	Mar 41	Old Hullensians	Guest	-	-	-	-	1	0	-	-
FROST Benjamin S.	Oct 04	Oct 04	Hessle	Amateur	-	-	-	-	-	-	1	0
FROST Walter J.	Aug 05	Oct 06	Hessle	Amateur	1	0	1	0	-	-	-	-
FRYER John L.	May 37	Jun 38	Wrexham	Nottingham F	40	23	3	1	1	1	1	1
GAGEN Colin A.	Sep 51	May 54	Hull Police BC	Amateur	-	-	-	-	-	-	1	0
GALLACHER Constantine	Jun 47	Mar 48	Middlesbrough	Rochdale	18	3	3	1	-	-	1	0
GALLOWAY Andrew	Dec 44	Dec 44	Guest		-	-	-	-	1	0	-	-
GALVIN Christopher [13]	Jul 73	Apr 79	Leeds U	Stockport C	132/11	11	9	1	19/1	2	8	0
GARDNER Thomas	May 32	Feb 34	Grimsby T	Aston Villa	66	2	7	0	-	-	-	-
GARRATT Sydney	Nov 19	cs 27	Local	Goole T	8	0	-	-	-	-	2	0
GARVEY Brian	Aug 53	Jun 65	Local	Watford	232	3	17	0	9	0	4	0
GAYNOR Leonard A.	May 48	Jun 51	Eastwood Col	Bournemouth & BA	2	0	-	-	-	-	0/1	0
GERRIE Sydney	Nov 50	May 57	Dundee	Retired (injury)	146	59	6	3	-	-	18	12
GIBSON Alexander	Mar 50	Jul 51	Clyde	Stirling Albion	21	0	-	-	-	-	6	0
GIBSON David	Jul 74	Jul 78	Seaham Schools	Scunthorpe U	19/5	0	-	-	4	0	1/1	0
GIBSON Frederick W.	Aug 26	Nov 32	Dinnington Coll.	Middlesbrough	101	0	9	0	-	-	5	0
GIBSON John R.	May 22	Mar 29	Sunderland	Sheffield U	210	0	8	0	-	-	7	0
GIBSON Robert H.	Oct 49	Aug 50	Aberdeen	Ashington	12	5	-	-	-	-	-	-
GILBERTHORPE Alfred E.	Jun 08	cs 10	Chesterfield	Released	18	4	2	0	-	-	1	1
GILHOOLEY Michael	Jul 20	Mar 22	Clydebank	Sunderland	65	1	7	0	-	-	2	0
GILL Gary	Dec 83	Jan 84	Middlesbrough	Loan	0/1	0	-	-	-	-	-	-
GILLETT J.T.	Nov 18	Nov 18	Birmingham	Guest	-	-	-	-	1	0	-	-
GILMORE H. Patrick	Dec 34	Jul 35	Shotton Col Welf	Mansfield T								
	May 39	cs 46	Queen's Park R	Released	-	-	-	-	26	0	4	0
GLAISTER George	Aug 44	Feb 45	Blackburn R	Guest	-	-	-	-	18	6	-	-
GLAVES Arthur	Apr 05	Apr 05	C.H.G.O.B.	Amateur	-	-	-	-	-	-	1	0
GOBEY Ernest	Nov 44	Nov 44	Guest		-	-	-	-	1	0	-	-
GOLDSMITH George	Dec 28	Jun 34	Loftus Albion	Tottenham H	172	0	18	0	-	-	4	0
GOODALL Edward I.	May 37	May 38	North Shields	Bolton W	26	0	3	0	1	0	1	0
GOODE Herbert J.	May 12	May 13	Aston Villa	Wrexham	28	10	2	0	-	-	3	1
GOODFELLOW S.	Sep 17	Sep 17	Portsmouth	Guest	-	-	-	-	3	0	-	-

How local cartoonist Ern Shaw viewed the Tigers' giantkilling sixth round FA Cup success against Newcastle United in 1930.

Ray Daniel

Andy Davidson

The Hull City line-up which won promotion to the Second Division in 1958-9. Back row (left to right): F.Harrison, J.Davidson, C.Smith, W.Bly, B.Garvey, D.Durham. Front row: D.Clarke, W.Bradbury, P.Feasey, D.Coates, B.Bulless.

Player	From	To	Former club	Next known club	League App	League Gls	FA Cup App	FA Cup Gls	Other comp App	Other comp Gls	Others App	Others Gls
GOODIN William	Apr 05	Apr 06	Beverley Barracks	Amateur	1	0	-	-	-	-	2	0
GORDON Daniel	Apr 10	cs 11	Bradford	Southampton	11	0	-	-	-	-	4	1
GORDON David S.	Jun 05	cs 14	Leith A	Leith A	274	17	21	0	2	0	27	5
GORDON Edward	Jul 08	cs 11	Dundee Bainfield	Hull OB								
	Dec 15	Apr 18	Local	Guest	-	-	-	-	1	0	2	1
GOULDEN John T.	Sep 24	cs 26	Needlers	Raith R	2	0	-	-	-	-	2	1
GOULDING B.	May 46	Sep 46	Local	Goole T	-	-	-	-	-	-	1	0
GOWDY William A.	Jul 29	Dec 31	Ards	Sheffield W								
	Aug 40	Sep 40	Aldershot	Guest	65	1	8	0	3	0	2	0
GRANGER Michael	Jul 62	Jul 63	York C	Halifax T	2	0	-	-	-	-	-	-
GRAY Douglas H.	Dec 24	Jan 25	Aberdeen Mug'oss	Trial (ltr Rangers)	-	-	-	-	-	-	1	0
GREAVES S. William	Jan 45	Jan 45	Keighley	Guest	-	-	-	-	1	0	-	-
GREEN Leslie	Aug 60	Jul 62	Atherstone T	Nuneaton Bor	4	0	-	-	-	-	-	-
GREEN Melvin [14]	Sep 67	Jun 74	Hull Schools	Cambridge U	10	0	-	-	-	-	2	0
GREEN Reginald	Dec 40	Dec 40	Guest		-	-	-	-	1	0	-	-
GREENHALGH James R.	Aug 46	Nov 50	Newton Hth Loco	Bury	148	5	19	2	-	-	18	0
GREENWOOD Patrick G.	Jul 62	Nov 71	Ainthorpe HS	Barnsley	137/12	3	7/1	0	4/1	0	14/8	0
GREENWOOD Roy T.	Aug 68	Jan 76	Pudsey Juniors	Sunderland	118/8	24	11	0	18	6	21/4	8
GRIMES Vincent [15]	Aug 70	Jan 78	Scunthorpe Schls	Scunthorpe U	84/5	9	5	1	10	1	9/1	2
GRIMSHAW William	Sep 16	Dec 16	Bradford C	Guest	-	-	-	-	18	6	-	-
GUBBINS Ralph G.	Oct 59	Mar 61	Bolton W	Tranmere R	45	10	6	2	2	1	-	-
GUYAN George W.	Dec 26	cs 28	South Shields	Connah's Quay	19	9	3	2	-	-	-	-
HAIGH Paul	Jul 74	Nov 80	Schultz YC	Carlisle U	179/1	8	7	1	22	3	8/1	0
HALL Joseph E.	Aug 08	cs 09	Jarrow	Released	-	-	-	-	-	-	0/1	0
HALL Ellis	Jan 06	cs 08	Sheffield area	Stoke								
	Mar 16	Apr 16	Goole T	Guest	8	0	-	-	2	0	2	0
HALL George	Apr 22	Sep 23	Errington Swifts	Released	12	4	-	-	-	-	-	-
HALL Harry	Jan 06	cs 07	Sheffield area	Rotherham T	2	0	-	-	-	-	-	-
HALLIGAN William	May 13	Jul 19	Wolves	Preston NE	65	28	7	0	4	0	3	5
HAMILTON Samuel	Aug 23	Aug 25	Belfast jnr soccer	Deceased	27	7	4	1	-	-	9	8
HAMILTON Thomas	Dec 23	Jan 24	Llanelly	Contract cancelled	2	0	-	-	-	-	-	-
HANNABY Cyril	May 46	Feb 48	Wolves	Halifax T	17	0	2	0	-	-	4	0
HANSEN Jens-Peter	Nov 52	Jan 53	Esbjerg EfB	Amateur	-	-	-	-	-	-	1	1
HARDY John H.	Jul 37	cs 39	Chesterfield	Lincoln C	65	0	6	0	2	0	4	0
HARNBY Donald R.	Nov 44	Nov 44	Newcastle U	Guest	-	-	-	-	1	0	-	-
HARRIS Albert	May 30	cs 31	Herrington Swifts	Blackhall Col	5	0	-	-	-	-	-	-
HARRIS James B.	Aug 44	Apr 45	West Ham U	Guest	-	-	-	-	34	1	-	-
HARRIS William C.	Mar 50	Mar 54	Llanelly	Middlesbrough	131	6	14	1	-	-	15	0
HARRISON Jack	Nov 18	Nov 18	Rotherham C	Guest	-	-	-	-	1	0	-	-
HARRISON Francis J.	May 48	Jul 60	Hull GS	Margate T	199	0	15	0	-	-	28	0
HARRISON G.	Apr 18	Aug 18	Hull Kingston R	Guest	-	-	-	-	-	-	1	0
HARRISON Kenneth	Apr 47	Mar 55	Billingham Synth	Derby C	238	47	25	4	-	-	30	7
HARRON Joseph	Aug 20	Jan 21	Langley Park	Northampton T	2	0	-	-	-	-	1	0
HART James	Jun 25	Mar 27	Vale of Clyde	Flint	2	0	-	-	-	-	1	0
HARTNELL Samuel	Oct 17	Oct 17	Sunderland	Guest	-	-	-	-	2	1	-	-
HARVEY A.	Mar 17	Mar 17	Guest		-	-	-	-	1	1	-	-
HARVEY George K.	Oct 44	Jan 45	Brigham & Cowan's	Guest	-	-	-	-	6	0	-	-
HASSALL Wilfred	Jun 46	cs 53	R.M.Alsager	Worcester C	141	3	16	-	-	-	19/1	0
HAVELOCK P. Henry W.	Oct 23	Jun 25	16th Hussars	Lincoln C								
	May 31	Jun 32	Crystal P	Folkestone	9	2	-	-	-	-	5	1
HAWKER David	Jul 75	Mar 80	Schultz YC	Darlington	33/2	2	3/1	0	2/1	0	7/3	1
HAWKSWORTH Ernest	Oct 16	Oct 16	Rochdale	Guest	-	-	-	-	1	0	-	-
HAWLEY	Dec 16	Dec 16	Guest		-	-	-	-	1	0	-	-

John Davies

Bobby Doyle

The Tigers in 1972. Back row (left to right): D.Beardsley, R.Greenwood, P.Holme, M.Green, R.Pettit. Middle row: K.Wagstaff, K.Houghton, I.McKechnie, S.Pearson, J.Wealands, P.O'Riley, J.Kaye, T.Neill. Front row: I.Butler, F.Banks, R.de Vries, K.Knighton, W.Wilkinson, J.McGill, M.Lord.

Player	From	To	Former club	Next known club	League App	League Gls	FA Cup App	FA Cup Gls	Other comp App	Other comp Gls	Others App	Others Gls
HAWLEY John E.	Sep 70	May 78	Hodgsons	Leeds U								
	Dec 82	Dec 82	Arsenal	Loan	104/13	23	5	1	15/3	2	10/7	5
HAWORTH Ronald	Jun 24	May 26	Blackburn R	Manchester U	36	10	1	0	-	-	5	0
HAY William E.	Sep 04	Sep 04	Hessle	Amateur	-	-	-	-	-	-	1	0
HAYWOOD	Nov 16	Nov 16	Luton T	Guest	-	-	-	-	1	0	-	-
HEAD Michael	Dec 53	Jul 55	Brid Central U	King's Lynn	3	0	-	-	-	-	-	-
HEARD T. Patrick	Mar 86	Jul 88	Middlesbrough	Rotherham U	79/1	5	5	0	8	0	11/1	0
HEATH R. Terence	May 64	Mar 68	Leicester C	Scunthorpe U	27/6	1	3	3	0/1	0	3	2
HEDLEY Foster	May 28	Jun 29	Jarrow	Nelson	2	0	-	-	-	-	-	-
HEDLEY G. Thomas Tot	Mar 06	Apr 08	Hearts	Leicester F	78	2	6	0	-	-	3	0
HEDLEY Thomas	Jan 12	cs 12	Jarrow Cal	Released	2	0	-	-	-	-	-	-
HEDLEY Ralph B.	Oct 23	Dec 24	Newburn	Crystal P	9	0	-	-	-	-	-	-
HEELBECK Leslie W.	Sep 40	Oct 40	Scarborough	Guest	-	-	-	-	3	0	-	-
HELSBY Thomas	May 34	Jun 35	Swindon T	Newport C	22	0	1	0	-	-	-	-
HEMMERMAN Jeffrey L. [16]	Jul 71	Jun 77	Kingston HS	Port Vale	45/14	10	3	1	1/2	0	5/8	5
HENDERSON Raymond	Jun 61	Oct 68	Middlesbrough	Reading	226/3	54	22/1	6	12	1	7	0
HENDRY C. Nicholson	Apr 10	cs 21	Darlington	York C	140	0	11	0	120	0	16	0
HENSON	May 46	May 46	Trialist	Released	-	-	-	-	-	-	1	0
HENZELL William H.	May 20	cs 21	Walker Celtic	Retired (injury)	2	1	-	-	-	-	-	-
HERDMAN Henry	Aug 40	Aug 40	Rotherham U	Guest	-	-	-	-	1	0	-	-
HESFORD Iain	Dec 88		Sunderland		22	0	3	0	-	-	-	-
HETHERINGTON Alan	Sep 57	cs 58	Chelsea	Sittingbourne	-	-	-	-	-	-	1	0
HEWICK Alfred E.	Mar 40	Sep 44	RAF	Guest	-	-	-	-	5	0	-	-
HEWITSON Robert	Apr 13	Sep 13	Newburn	Released	1	0	-	-	-	-	1	0
HICKTON John	Jan 77	Feb 77	Middlesbrough	Loan	6	1	-	-	-	-	-	-
HIGGINS Alexander	Sep 16	Dec 16	Newcastle U	Guest	-	-	-	-	6	3	-	-
HIGGINS William	Jun 34	cs 35	Rutherglen G	Released	5	0	-	-	-	-	-	-
HILL John H.	Nov 31	cs 34	Bradford C	Retired	94	2	8	2	-	-	1	0
HOBSON Bert	Apr 15	Oct 16	Sunderland	Guest	-	-	-	-	3	0	-	-
HODSON W.	Apr 05	Apr 05	Manchester area	Trialist	-	-	-	-	-	-	1	0
HOLAH Eric T.	Aug 58	Jul 61	Malet Lambert OB	Bradford C	1	1	-	-	-	-	-	-
HOLBROOK Stephen	May 68	Jun 72	Richmond Co Sch	Darlington	2/1	0	-	-	-	-	1/4	1
HOLLIFIELD Michael	Aug 83	cs 85	Wolves	Tranmere R	45	1	2	0	6	0	6/2	0
HOLLIS Harry	Dec 44	Apr 45	Chester	Guest	-	-	-	-	8	0	-	-
HOLME Philip C.	Jul 72	Jul 74	Swansea C	Retired (injury)	29/9	11	4/2	0	4/1	3	2	0
HOLMES David	Aug 76	Aug 79	Hessle HS	Bridlington Trin	-	-	-	-	-	-	0/1	0
HOLMES Maxey M.	May 35	Jul 37	Grimsby T	Mansfield T	29	10	1	0	-	-	-	-
HOLT Glenn	Aug 79	Aug 79	Tour coach driver	Guest	-	-	-	-	-	-	0/1	0
HOOD Derek	Aug 77	Feb 80	West Bromwich A	York C	20/4	0	4	0	3	0	6/2	1
HOOLICKIN Stephen	Dec 80	Mar 82	Carlisle U	Retired (ill-health)	31	0	2	0	3	0	1	0
HOPE Charles	Nov 44	Nov 44	Guest		-	-	-	-	1	0	-	-
HOPKINS V.	Sep 18	Sep 18	Derby C	Guest	-	-	-	-	2	0	-	-
HORNE Alfred	May 25	May 27	Stafford Rangers	Southend U	25	2	1	0	-	-	5	4
HORSWILL Michael F.	Jul 78	Apr 82	Plymouth A	Happy Vly(H/K)	82/2	6	3	0	13	0	10/1	2
HORTON Brian	Jun 84	Apr 88	Luton T	Oxford U(asst man)	38	0	4	0	5	0	5	0
HORTON J. Kenneth	Oct 52	Jul 55	Preston NE	Barrow	76	16	10	4	-	-	17	6
HORTON V.	Oct 04	Oct 06	Botanic Swifts	Amateur	-	-	-	-	-	-	5	0
HOTTE Timothy A. [17]	Sep 87	Mar 89	North Ferriby U	Goole T	1/4	0	-	-	-	-	1/3	0
HOUGHTON John	May 10	May 13	Wallsend Pk Villa	Fulham	28	3	-	-	-	-	9	1
HOUGHTON Kenneth [18]	Jan 65	Jun 73	Rotherham U	Scunthorpe U	253/11	79	22/1	9	15/2	3	34/4	20
HOULT Alan J.	Jan 78	Mar 78	Leicester C	Loan	3	1	-	-	-	-	-	-
HOWE Leslie F.	Feb 45	Apr 45	Tottenham H	Guest	-	-	-	-	9	5	-	-
HOWE Peter	Jul 04	cs 07	Reading	Released	32	15	5	4	-	-	40	29
HOWIE David	Oct 16	Oct 16	Bradford	Guest	-	-	-	-	1	0	-	-

Highly-rated Richard Jobson, the Tigers' captain during 1988-9 and a consistent performer either in defence or midfield.

The Hull City squad taken prior to the start of the 1973-4 season. Back row (left to right): T.Neill (manager), F.Banks, K.Knighton, D.Beardsley, I.McKechnie, J.Wealands, S.Blampey, R.de Vries, P.O'Riley. Front row: J.Kaye, J.McGill, S.Pearson, P. Holme, K.Wagstaff, M.Lord, R.Greenwood, S.Deere.

Player	From	To	Former club	Next known club	League App	League Gls	FA Cup App	FA Cup Gls	Other comp App	Other comp Gls	Others App	Others Gls
HOWIESON James	Mar 27	cs 28	St Mirren	New Bedford (USA)								
	Aug 29	Jun 30	New York Giants	Shelbourne	67	12	7	2	-	-	3	1
HUBBARD Clifford	May 33	Apr 39	Scunthorpe U	West Ham U								
	Sep 44	Jan 45	West Ham U	Guest	183	56	12	5	8	1	5	3
HUDSON Tom	Jan 16	Mar 16		Guest	-	-	-	-	1	0	-	-
HUGHES Emlyn W.	Mar 83	cs 83	Rotherham U	Mansfield T	9	0	-	-	-	-	3	0
HUGHES Robert	Aug 17	May 22	Northampton T	Sheffield U	66	9	3	0	62	31	7	2
HUNTER William	May 07	cs 08	Sunderland EE	Lincoln C	-	-	-	-	-	-	1	1
HUTCHINSON James A.	Apr 45	May 46	Sheffield U	Guest	-	-	-	-	1	0	1	1
HUTCHISON Duncan	Jul 34	cs 35	Derby C	Dundee U	38	8	1	0	-	-	-	-
HUXFORD Harold	May 38	cs 39	Grimsby T	Boston U								
	Feb 45	Mar 45	Grimsby T	Guest	10	1	1	0	3	0	2	0
ICETON Jacob	Apr 25	cs 26	Cockburn	Fulham	-	-	-	-	-	-	4	0
INGLIS William	Apr 19	Apr 19	Raith R	Guest	-	-	-	-	-	-	1	0
INWOOD Gordon F.	May 50	cs 52	West Brom A	Kettering	3	0	-	-	-	-	1	1
IREMONGER Albert	Jan 17	Jan 17	Notts C	Guest	-	-	-	-	1	0	-	-
IREMONGER James	Dec 24	Dec 24	Clifton Col	Trialist	1	0	-	-	-	-	-	-
ISHERWOOD R.	Mar 17	Apr 17	Bradford	Guest	-	-	-	-	6	0	1	0
JACKETTS George A.	Feb 14	Jul 20	Hull Tivoli	Ebbw Vale	2	0	-	-	95	3	10	1
JACOBS Wayne G.	Mar 88		Sheffield W		39	0	3	0	2	0	8/1	0
JARVIS Alan L.	May 64	Mar 71	Everton	Mansfield T	148/11	12	12	0	5/1	0	15/1	0
JENKINSON Leigh	Aug 84		Thorne GS		8/6	1	-	-	1/2	0	2/4	0
JENNINGS	May 46	May 46	Trialist	Boston U	-	-	-	-	-	-	2	1
JENSEN H. Viggo	Oct 48	Nov 56	Esbjerg EfB	Esbjerg EfB	308	51	27	3	-	-	48	5
JOBSON John W.	Nov 30	cs 31	Hatfield Main	Released	2	0	-	-	-	-	-	-
JOBSON Richard I.	Feb 85		Watford		172/2	15	12	1	18	0	25/2	7
JOHNSON Herbert M.	Sep 44	Sep 44	Guest		-	-	-	-	1	1	-	-
JOHNSON Joseph	Dec 44	Feb 45	Southport	Guest	-	-	-	-	9	0	-	-
JOHNSON K.	Feb 45	Feb 45	Guest		-	-	-	-	1	0	-	-
JOHNSON Laurence	Oct 04	Oct 04	Hessle	Amateur	-	-	-	-	-	-	1	0
JOHNSON Samuel	May 47	Aug 48	Northwich V	Scarborough	10	0	1	0	-	-	1	0
JOHNSON William	Dec 19	Oct 20	Beverley Barracks	Bridlington Town	5	0	-	-	-	-	-	-
JOHNSON William	May 23	cs 26	Seaton Delaval	Released	46	0	2	0	-	-	12	0
JONES Ellis	May 25	cs 26	Spennymoor U	Annfield Plain	8	1	-	-	-	-	2	3
JONES Glanville	Jun 46	Jun 47	Merthyr T	Bournemouth & BA	7	0	-	-	-	-	-	-
JONES James M.	May 47	May 47	Manchester junior	Trialist	1	0	-	-	-	-	-	-
JONES John T.	Dec 44	Dec 44	Northampton T	Guest	-	-	-	-	1	0	-	-
JONES Thomas	Jul 04	cs 06	West Brom A	Wigan T	27	2	7	0	-	-	40	1
JORDAN	Feb 18	Feb 18	Guest		-	-	-	-	1	0	-	-
JORDAN Alfred R.	Jun 24	cs 26	Stoke	Bristol R	9	0	-	-	-	-	6	0
JORDAN David	Sep 32	Jun 36	Ards	Wolves	24	15	1	0	-	-	-	-
KAMARA Alan	Jul 83	Aug 83	Darlington	York Railway Inst	-	-	-	-	-	-	0/2	0
KAYE John	Nov 71	Aug 74	West Brom A	Retired (injury)	71/1	9	5	0	10	0	16	2
KEEN Errington R.L.	Nov 46	Dec 46	Derby C	Trialist	-	-	-	-	-	-	1	0
KEEN James F.	Jul 24	cs 25	Queen's Park R	Darlington	17	0	-	-	-	-	3	0
KEERS John M.	May 25	cs 26	Tow Law	Annfield Plain	8	1	-	-	-	-	2	0
KELLY Gavin	Aug 84		Headlands School		3	0	-	-	1	0	2/1	0
KEMP Neal	Jul 81	May 84	Sydney Smith HS	Released	-	-	-	-	-	-	1/2	0
KILGALLON Mark C.	Aug 80	Mar 81	Ipswich T	Released	0/1	0	-	-	-	-	-	-
KING David J.	Aug 57	Jul 63	Hull Schools	King's Lynn	65	24	1	1	1	0	1	0
KING George	Mar 48	Apr 49	Newcastle U	Port Vale	3	0	-	-	-	-	2	0
KINGWELL Leonard E.	Aug 44	Nov 44	Torquay U	Guest	-	-	-	-	2	0	-	-
KIRMAN Harold [19]	Jun 48	May 57	Francis Askew YC	Released	2	0	-	-	-	-	-	-
KITCHEN Joseph E.	Sep 21	Aug 23	Sheffield U	Scunthorpe U	30	5	-	-	-	-	4	0

Stan McEwan, a fiercely competitive defender and noted taker of free-kicks and penalties.

Hull City in 1908-09. Back row (left to right): E.G.D.Wright, J.McQuillan, E.Roughley, David Gordon. Third row: Mr A.Langley (manager), F.Martin, J.Morrison, G.Browell, J.Lindley, W.S.Robinson, A.Browell, T.Tildsley. Second row: J.Taylor, Joe Smith, John Smith, J.Shaw, A.Temple, E.Neve, A.Pace, W.Leach (trainer). Front row: E.Gordon, A.E.Gilberthorpe, T.Nevins, W.Stephenson, J.E.Hall.

ayer	From	To	Former club	Next known club	League App	League Gls	FA Cup App	FA Cup Gls	Other comp App	Other comp Gls	Others App	Others Gls
TCHEN Norman	Oct 35	Jul 36	Eden Col	Southport	4	1	-	-	-	-	-	-
IGHTON Kenneth	Mar 71	Aug 73	Blackburn R	Sheffield W	79/1	9	5	0	7	3	26	10
IOTT Herbert	Oct 40	Feb 47	Brierley Hill	Released	6	1	1	0	22	25	1	3
FFMAN S. Jack	Jun 46	Sep 46	Manchester U	Oldham A	4	-	-	-	-	-	-	-
NMAN David J.	Jul 78	Aug 82	Orchard Park U	Schultz YC	11	0	-	-	-	-	-	-
MB George	Nov 44	Nov 44	Gateshead	Guest	-	-	-	-	2	0	-	-
NDLES John A.S.	Oct 44	Oct 44	Guest		-	-	-	-	1	0	-	-
NGLEY Ambrose	Apr 05	cs 06	Sheffield W	Retired	13	0	2	0	-	-	1	0
VERY Patrick	Jul 05	cs 06	Gateshead	Released	2	0	1	0	-	-	1	0
WRANCE Raymond S.	Dec 33	Jun 36	Gainsborough T	Newport C	34	1	-	-	-	-	1	0
WRENCE Matthew	Sep 37	cs 39	Wrexham	Released	25	1	-	-	1	0	1	0
E James	Oct 48	Feb 51	Wolves	Halifax T	3	1	-	-	-	-	4	1
E John	Apr 13	Jan 20	Bird in Hand	Chelsea	75	19	8	3	71	28	9	1
E Patrick F.	Jun 25	cs 27	Vale of Clyde	Accrington S	25	6	1	0	-	-	6	0
ES Norman [20]	Sep 65	Jun 71	Schools	Darlington	4/1	0	-	-	1	0	-	-
IGH A. Sydney	Nov 16	Dec 17	Derby C	Guest	-	-	-	-	8	2	-	-
IPER Joseph	Aug 04	Oct 04	Motherwell	Aberdare	-	-	2	0	-	-	4	0
STER A. Benjamin	Sep 46	Jan 48	Selby T	Lincoln C	27	17	4	2	-	-	1	0
WIS Harry	Oct 23	Jan 25	Liverpool	Released	36	5	2	0	-	-	3	1
LL David A.	Aug 63	Oct 69	Schools	Rotherham U	16/2	2	-	-	-	-	2/2	0
NAKER John E.	Oct 51	Jun 53	York C	York C	26	3	1	0	-	-	3	1
NDLEY J.	Nov 18	Nov 18	Birmingham	Guest	-	-	-	-	1	0	-	-
TTLE Thomas S.C.	Mar 19	Mar 19	Bradford	Guest	-	-	-	-	1	0	-	-
VINGSTONE Allan	Mar 22	cs 24	Dumbarton Harp	Crewe Alexandra	1	-	-	-	-	-	-	-
EWELLYN George L.	May 36	cs 37	Caerphilly	Scarborough	4	0	-	-	1	0	-	-
OYD Charles F.	Aug 26	cs 28	Percy Main	Southend U	7	0	-	-	-	-	3	0
OYD Edward H.	Jun 33	Aug 35	Stockport C	Carlisle U	1	0	-	-	-	-	-	-
DGE James W.	Jan 20	Jul 24	Newburn	Halifax T	81	0	2	0	-	-	9	0
GAN Peter	Apr 19	Apr 19	Bradford C	Guest	-	-	-	-	-	-	1	0
NGDEN Eric	Oct 30	Feb 31	Leeds U	Blackpool								
	Dec 32	cs 35	Blackpool	Scarboro' (coach)	88	12	5	0	-	-	2	0
RD Barry	Oct 54	May 61	Goole Buchanan	Goole U	5	0	-	-	-	-	2	0
RD Malcolm	Aug 64	Feb 80	Beverley GS	Retired (injury)	271/27	24	14	0	19/3	2	42/10	6
UGHRAN James	May 22	Jul 24	Easington Col	Barrow	4	0	-	-	-	-	-	-
WE Richard E.	May 39	cs 46	Sheffield U	Released	-	-	-	-	-	-	3	3
CAS William H.	Sep 40	Oct 40	Swindon T	Guest	-	-	-	-	6	0	-	-
ALL George	Dec 75	Jan 78	Nottingham F	Scarborough	42	5	5	0	4	1	2	1
ON John	Oct 13	Jul 20	Prescot	Leeds U	37	6	2	0	15	7	3	4
ON Samuel	Dec 12	Jun 14	Prescot	Barnsley	6	1	-	-	1	3	-	-
AINSH James	Dec 33	cs 34	Clackmannan	Gateshead	7	0	-	-	-	-	-	-
CLAREN Steven	Jun 77	Jul 85	York Schools	Derby C	171/7	16	16	3	18/3	1	22	3
CORRY Henry	Apr 13	cs 14	Newburn	Chesterfield	10	4	-	-	2	0	-	-
COURTY W.	Oct 16	Oct 16	Guest		-	-	-	-	1	0	-	-
CUNNELL Barry	Sep 65	Jun 70	Endike Lane	Barton T	0/1	0	-	-	-	-	2/1	1
CURDIE James	Dec 40	Dec 40	Glasgow junior	Guest	-	-	-	-	1	0	-	-
DONALD Kenneth	Jun 28	Mar 30	Bradford	Halifax T	41	29	2	2	-	-	1	0
DONALD Robert R. [21]	Jul 75	Aug 80	Hull GS	Wageningen(Holland)	17/8	2	-	-	3	0	8/2	1
DONALD William	Feb 12	May 14	Craghead U	Chesterfield	69	5	5	0	3	0	8	2
DOWELL Charles	Nov 44	Dec 44	RAF	Guest	-	-	-	-	5	4	-	-
EWAN Stanley	Mar 84	Dec 87	Exeter C	Wigan A	113	25	6	1	21	5	22/1	1
GEE John	Mar 22	cs 28	Harrogate	Retired (injury)	70	0	10	0	-	-	11	0
GIFFORD Grahame L.	May 76	Jun 77	Huddersfield T	Port Vale	1	0	-	-	1	0	1	0
GILL James M.	Oct 71	Feb 76	Huddersfield T	Halifax T	141/6	2	11	1	18/1	1	17/1	0

The Tigers in 1909-10. Back row (left to right): J.McQuillan, A.E.Gilberthorpe, J.Morrison, T.Nevins, A.Browell, (inset): Gordon Wright. Third row: A.Musgrave, David Gordon. G.Browell, E.Storey, E.Roughley, D.Taylor, W.Leach (trainer). Second row: Joe Smith, W.Stephenson, John Smith, A.Temple, W,Smith, E.Neve, A.Toward. Front row: F.Martin, W.Wright, A.Pace, E.Gordon, H.Simmon.

Hull City during the 1927-8 season. Back row (left to right): R.Starling, A.Richards, B.Bradford, N.Sullivan, H.Scott, G.G.Wilson, E.Mooney, G.Guyan. Third row: Mr W.McCracken (manager), C.Swan, R.Mackenzie, C.F.Lloyd, F.Gibson, Mr J.Lodge (assistant trainer), G.Maddison, S.Dixon, J.Watson, J.Murray, Mr J.Beck (trainer). Second row: J.R.Gibson, G.S.Martin, T.Bleakley, M.Bell, G.Whitworth, J.Howieson, W.Taylor, T.Wyper. Front row: J.W.Alexander, J.Maloney, S.Alexander, J.Crozier.

Player	From	To	Former club	Next known club	League App	League Gls	FA Cup App	FA Cup Gls	Other comp App	Other comp Gls	Others App	Others Gls
McGORRIGHAN Francis O.	Aug 46	Feb 47	Carlisle U	Blackburn R								
	Sep 47	Jul 48	Blackburn R	Southport	26	1	7	1	-	-	2	0
McGUINNESS Wilfred	Aug 79	Aug 79	Club coach	Sub on tour	-	-	-	-	-	-	0/1	0
MACHIN Edward	Apr 18	cs 20	Stockport C	Hull OB	-	-	-	-	2	0	1	1
McINTOSH James B.	May 10	Aug 14	Glasgow Celtic	Released	92	2	4	0	2	0	8	0
McINTOSH James W.	Mar 76	Jul 77	Nottingham F	Dundee U	20	1	0/1	0	0/1	0	-	-
MACKAY William	May 37	cs 38	Swansea T	Released	12	0	-	-	2	0	-	-
MacKENZIE George D.	Nov 33	Aug 34	Queen's Park	Stockport C	9	4	1	0	-	-	-	-
MACKIE John	May 34	Oct 35	Bridgeton Wav	Bradford C	14	2	-	-	-	-	1	0
MACKRILL Henry W.	Oct 04	Oct 04	Hull & ER (RU)	Amateur	-	-	-	-	-	-	1	0
MACKRILL Oscar W.	Sep 04	Sep 04	Old Hymerians	Amateur	-	-	2	1	-	-	4	0
McKECHNIE Ian H.	Aug 66	May 74	Southend U	Goole T	255	0	17	0	12	0	28/4	2
McKENZIE Roy	May 27	cs 28	Newcastle U	South Shields	-	-	-	-	-	-	1	1
McKIERNAN	Aug 04	Sep 04	Brighton & HA	Released	-	-	-	-	-	-	2	0
McKINNEY Daniel	Oct 20	Jul 23	Belfast Celtic	Bradford C	55	12	5	0	-	-	7	2
McLAUGHLIN George	Jun 26	May 27	Glasgow Celtic	Accrington S	8	2	1	0	-	-	1	1
McMANUS T.	Dec 11	cs 20	National Radiator	Local	-	-	-	-	9	2	2	0
McMILLAN Eric	Jun 60	Jul 65	Chelsea	Halifax T	150	3	14	1	10	0	3	0
McMURRAY Campbell	Dec 20	cs 22	Strathclyde	York C	4	0	-	-	-	-	1	0
McNAUGHTON William F.	Jun 32	Oct 34	Gateshead	Stockport C	85	57	7	2	-	-	1	2
McNEIL Robert M.	Jul 79	Aug 85	Scottish Schools	Lincoln C	135/3	3	17	0	13	1	20/6	0
MacNEILL H. John	May 37	Feb 39	Ayr U	Bury	52	27	6	2	2	0	2	0
McPARLAND Ian J.	Mar 89		Notts C		11	1	-	-	-	-	-	-
McPHEAT John	Sep 35	cs 36	Rutherglen G	Released	9	0	-	-	-	-	-	-
McQUILLAN John	Oct 06	Jul 14	Jarrow	Leeds C								
	Sep 15	Feb 17	Leeds C	Guest	239	2	18	1	32	2	32	0
McSEVENEY John	Jul 61	Jun 65	Newport C	Retired	161	60	12	8	10	2	3	2
MADDISON George	Jun 24	cs 38	Tottenham H	Retired (injury)	430	0	24	0	2	0	10	1
MAJOR John L.	Mar 47	Sep 47	Hull Amateurs	Sunderland								
	Jun 55	Jul 57	Bishop Auckland	Goole T	13	0	-	-	-	-	4/1	0
MALKINSON T.	Apr 18	Apr 18	Guest	later Grimsby T	-	-	-	-	1	0	-	-
MANNING John T.	Apr 05	Aug 07	Boston T	Bradford	54	9	8	0	-	-	4	1
MANNION Wilfred J.	Dec 54	Sep 55	Middlesbrough	Poole T	16	1	1	0	-	-	1	1
MARCH Herbert	Nov 29	Sep 30	Army football	Lincoln C	8	0	-	-	-	-	1	1
MARSHALL James M.	Dec 20	cs 21	St.Peters Albion	Preston Col	1	0	-	-	-	-	-	-
MARTIN Frank	Jan 07	Aug 11	Gateshead Rod	Grimsby Town	29	1	3	0	-	-	6	0
MARTIN George S.	Oct 22	Mar 28	Hamilton A	Everton	204	55	14	3	-	-	20	15
MARTIN Harry	Jan 17	Feb 17	Sunderland	Guest	-	-	-	-	2	0	-	-
MARTIN James J.	Apr 34	cs 36	Bacup Borough	Released	4	1	-	-	-	-	-	-
MARTIN Thomas	Jun 55	Sep 57	Nottingham F	Rothes	32	2	-	-	-	-	1	0
MARTIN William J.T.	Aug 04	cs 06	Millwall	Clapton O	4	0	3	0	-	-	44	5
MARWOOD Brian	Jun 76	Jun 84	Seaham Schools	Sheffield W	154/4	51	16	1	16/1	1	18/2	10
MASON Thomas E.	Aug 19	Nov 20	Army football	Rotherham T	3	0	-	-	-	-	-	-
MASSEY Stephen	Jul 83	Jul 85	Northampton T	Cambridge U	34/8	9	2	1	5/4	1	12/3	5
MATTHEWS J.	Mar 17	Mar 17	Local	Guest	-	-	-	-	1	0	-	-
MAW	Sep 14	Feb 15	Cottingham	Released	-	-	-	-	-	-	1	1
MAYSON John D.	May 36	May 37	Clapton O	Tranmere R	23	8	1	1	1	0	-	-
MEDCALF James T.	Aug 14	Sep 14	Notts C	Released	2	0	-	-	-	-	-	-
MEENS Harold	Sep 36	May 54	Shepherd's Road	Retired (injury)	146	0	15	0	49	3	22/1	2
MEESE Albert E.	Mar 45	Mar 45	Yorkshire Schools	Guest	-	-	-	-	1	0	-	-
MELLOR J. Allan	Jun 47	Oct 52	Ashton U	Retired (injury)	104	4	13	0	-	-	12/2	2
MELVILLE David	Feb 14	Mar 15	Arthurlie	Clyde	5	0	-	-	-	-	-	-
MELVILLE James	Dec 33	Jun 34	Blackburn R	Northampton T	14	1	2	0	-	-	-	-
MERCER David W.	Jan 14	Dec 20	Skelmersdale U	Sheffield U	91	26	6	0	144	48	14	14

Paul Olsson

Andrew Payton

Hull City FC in August 1973. Back row (left to right): Chris Galvin, Stuart Blampey, John Kaye, John Hawley, Don Beardsley, Roy Greenwood. Middle row: Jeff Hemmerman, Stuart Croft, Mel Green, Ian McKechnie, Jeff Wealands, Phil Holme, Steve Deere, Paul O'Riley. Front row: Frank Banks, Roger de Vries, Jim McGill, Terry Neill (manager), Ken Wagstaff, Stuart Pearson, Malcolm Lord.

Player	From	To	Former club	Next known club	League App	Gls	FA Cup App	Gls	Other comp App	Gls	Others App	Gls
MERCER William H.	Sep 14	Nov 24	Prescot A	Huddersfield T	193	0	10	0	4	0	21	0
METCALFE Victor	Jun 58	Feb 60	Huddersfield T	Retired (injury)	6	3	-	-	-	-	-	-
MEYNELL Thomas	Jan 16	Jan 16	Goole T	Guest	-	-	-	-	1	0	-	-
MIDDLEHURST James H.	Aug 14	cs 20	St Helens Rec	Released	9	0	-	-	-	-	1	0
MIDDLEMAS John R.	Mar 22	cs 23	Herrington Swifts	York C	10	0	1	0	-	-	1	0
MILLER Alforth H.	Dec 33	May 35	Gainsborough T	Barrow	4	0	-	-	-	-	1	0
MILLER David	Aug 44	Mar 45	Middlesbrough	Guest	-	-	-	-	16	0	-	-
MILLS Bert R.	Sep 20	Mar 26	Barton T	Notts C								
	Dec 29	cs 33	Birmingham	Scunthorpe U	269	101	22	9	-	-	16	11
MILLS James	Oct 46	Dec 47	Rotherham U	Halifax T	42	1	5	0	-	-	2	0
MILNER A.	Apr 18	Apr 18	Guest		-	-	-	-	1	0	-	-
MILNER Michael	Aug 55	cs 68	Hull Schools	Stockport C	160	0	12	0	4	0	8	0
MITCHELL Andrew	Jun 33	Dec 33	Manchester U	Northampton T	8	0	-	-	-	-	-	-
MITCHELL Rowland	May 24	May 26	Liverpool	Nelson	27	1	-	-	-	-	12	0
MONTGOMERY Stan.W.J.	Sep 44	Sep 46	Romford	Southend U	5	0	-	-	10	4	-	-
MOONEY Edward Peter	Jan 27	cs 28	Newcastle U	Scunthorpe U	11	0	-	-	-	-	-	-
MOORE Alan	Jul 51	Jan 52	Chesterfield	Nottingham F	13	4	-	-	-	-	-	-
MOORE John [22]	Jun 88	May 89	Sunderland	FC Utrecht	11/3	1	-	-	2/1	0	8/1	3
MOORE John E.	Apr 34	Jun 36	Hebburn Col	Gateshead	5	0	-	-	-	-	1	0
MOORE Norman W.	May 47	Mar 50	Grimsby T	Blackburn R	81	46	11	7	-	-	5	4
MOORE T. Roy	Dec 44	Dec 44	Grimsby T	Guest	-	-	-	-	1	0	-	-
MORDUE Thomas	Sep 23	cs 24	Herrington Swifts	Horden A	6	0	-	-	-	-	-	-
MORGAN Douglas	May 13	Jan 17	Inverkeithing U	Killed in war	52	0	6	0	4	1	2	0
MORRALL George A.	Apr 19	Sep 20	Blackheath T	Grimsby T	37	17	1	0	2	1	3	0
MORRIS Christopher	Jan 57	May 61	Schools	York C	17	4	-	-	-	-	-	-
MORRIS John	Jun 26	May 27	Newarthill Thistle	Bradford C	1	0	-	-	-	-	2	0
MORRISON John	Mar 08	cs 09	Jarrow	Swindon T	4	0	-	-	-	-	3	0
MORTENSEN Stanley H.	Nov 55	Feb 57	Blackpool	Southport	42	18	4	2	-	-	2	2
MOSS Paul M.	Oct 79	Sep 81	Wolves	Scunthorpe U	53/1	7	2/1	0	4/1	1	0/1	0
MUDD Paul	May 86		Sydney Smith HS		1	0	-	-	-	-	-	-
MUNNINGS C. Edward	Aug 31	Jul 32	Swindon T	Swindon T	31	7	3	2	-	-	1	0
MURPHY George	Dec 47	Aug 48	Bradford C	Scunthorpe U	15	9	1	1	-	-	1/1	1
MURRAY Joseph	Feb 26	Aug 31	Dairycoates	Lincoln C	17	1	-	-	-	-	2	0
MURRAY Malcolm	Mar 89		Hearts		6/2	0	-	-	-	-	-	-
MURRAY Terence	Oct 51	Mar 54	Dundalk	Bournemouth & BA	32	6	1	0	-	-	5	1
MURRAY Thomas	Feb 14	cs 14	Bradford C	Retired (injury)	2	0	-	-	-	-	-	-
MUSGRAVE Archibald	May 09	cs 11	Workington T	Grimsby T (trial)	7	0	-	-	-	-	6	2
MUTRIE Leslie A. [23]	Dec 80	Jan 84	Blyth Spartans	Colchester U	114/1	49	8	1	8/1	0	6/4	6
NAISMITH E.	Mar 16	Apr 16	Guest		-	-	-	-	3	1	-	-
NEAL John	Aug 49	Jul 56	Silksworth Juniors	King's Lynn	60	1	2	0	-	-	9/1	0
NEARY John	Oct 40	Aug 44	Rochdale	Guest	-	-	-	-	3	0	-	-
NEEDHAM John	Mar 20	cs 21	Wolves	Released	18	1	-	-	-	-	2	1
NEILL W.J. Terence	Jun 70	cs 73	Arsenal	Retired	103	4	11	0	8	0	19/3	2
NEILSON Norman F.	Apr 57	Jul 58	Bury	Corby T	25	0	3	0	-	-	1	1
NEISH John	Aug 35	Oct 35	Partick Thistle	Rtnd to Scotland	1	0	-	-	-	-	-	-
NELSON Alf	Aug 27	cs 29	Sheffield W'house	Scarborough	21	8	1	0	-	-	1	0
NEVE Edwin	May 06	Aug 12	St Helens Rec	Derby C	102	12	2	0	-	-	27	4
NEVIN John	Oct 16	Mar 18	Ayr U	Guest	-	-	-	-	13	0	-	-
NEVINS Thomas	May 07	cs 14	Washington A	Blyth Spartans	130	0	10	0	2	0	7	0
NEWMAN S.	Dec 04	Jan 05	Withernsea	Amateur	-	-	-	-	-	-	3	0
NEWTON A.	Dec 18	Dec 18	Stalybridge C	Guest	-	-	-	-	2	1	-	-
NEWTON R.	Jan 05	Jan 05	Old Hymerians	Amateur	-	-	-	-	-	-	3	2
NEWTON William	Jul 31	Sep 32	Stockport C	Stockport C	24	0	3	0	-	-	1	0
NICHOLSON Peter W.	Sep 59	Feb 61	Kingburn A	Barton T	1	0	-	-	-	-	1	0

Lawrence Pearson

Garreth Roberts ➧

Andrew Saville

Player	From	To	Former club	Next known club	League App	Gls	FA Cup App	Gls	Other comp App	Gls	Others App	Gls
NICKLAS Charles	Nov 50	May 53	Silksworth CW	Darlington	6	1	-	-	-	-	-	-
NICOL John C.	Feb 36	Jul 36	Burton T	York C	6	2	-	-	-	-	-	-
NISBET Gordon J.M.	Sep 76	Dec 80	West Brom A	Plymouth A	190/3	1	10	1	17	0	10	0
NORMAN Anthony J.	Feb 80	Dec 88	Burnley	Sunderland	372	0	26	0	44	0	45/5	1
NORRIE Craig T.	Aug 76	Feb 82	Boulevard U	Wageningen(Holland)	22/9	4	7/1	2	7/1	0	2/4	0
NORTON Horace	Feb 17	Feb 17	Bradford C	Guest	-	-	-	-	1	0	-	-
O'BRIEN Michael T.	Jun 24	May 26	Leicester C	Brooklyn W(USA)	74	0	6	1	-	-	5	0
O'CONNELL Patrick	May 12	May 14	Sheffield W	Manchester U	58	1	5	0	2	0	9	2
OLSSON Paul [24]	Dec 80	May 87	Kelvin HS	Exeter C	-	-	-	-	1	1	3/4	0
O'RILEY Paul J. [25]	Aug 66	Jul 74	Schools	Barnsley	19/11	2	0/1	0	2/1	0	16/8	16
OSBORN Frederick	Mar 17	Nov 18	Preston NE	Guest	-	-	-	-	14	7	1	1
OWEN Gordon	Dec 87	Jan 88	Bristol C	Mansfield T	3	0	-	-	-	-	-	-
OWEN Griffith L.	May 24	cs 25	Liverpool	Chester	2	0	-	-	-	-	2	2
PACE Arthur	Nov 07	Jul 10	Hebburn A	Rotherham T								
	Sep 15	Nov 18	Worksop T	Guest	5	0	-	-	25	-	6	1
PALMER Charles A.	Feb 87	Feb 89	Derby C	Notts C	69/1	1	3	0	5	0	16	2
PARKER Garry S.	Feb 86	Mar 88	Luton T	Nottingham F	82/2	8	4	0	7	1	11	2
PARKER W. David	Jun 37	Aug 38	Liverpool Marine	Wolves	30	0	3	0	1	0	1	0
PARKINSON Keith J.	Nov 81	Dec 81	Leeds U	Loan	0/1	0	-	-	-	-	-	-
PARR J.	Sep 18	Sep 18	Bradford	Guest	-	-	-	-	1	0	-	-
PASS G.	Apr 18	Apr 18	Watford	Guest	-	-	-	-	-	-	1	0
PATRICK Albert	Mar 05	Mar 05	Yorks Lt Infantry	Amateur	-	-	-	-	-	-	1	0
PATTERSON George T.	Oct 52	Jul 56	Silksworth CW	King's Lynn	7	1	-	-	-	-	-	-
PATTISON John M.	Mar 13	Aug 19	Bedlington	Scunthorpe U	48	0	3	0	49	0	7	0
PAYTON Andrew P.	Jul 85		Burnley		29/22	6	6	0	1/2	0	6/4	5
PEACH John	Nov 46	Sep 47	Barnsley	Queen's Park R	19	2	4	1	-	-	2	2
PEACH R.	Sep 18	Sep 18	Sheffield W	Guest	-	-	-	-	1	0	-	-
PEACOCK Terence	May 50	Aug 56	St Andrews HS	Queen's Park R	2	0	-	-	-	-	-	-
PEARCE James D.	Aug 04	cs 06	C.H.G.O.B.	Botanic Swifts	-	-	-	-	-	-	1	0
PEARCE Thomas H.	Dec 09	Dec 11	London junior	Portsmouth	3	0	-	-	-	-	-	-
PEARS John	Jun 37	Jun 38	Swansea T	Rochdale	30	8	3	3	2	0	-	-
PEARSON Frank	Oct 06	May 07	Chelsea	Luton T	13	6	-	-	-	-	1	0
PEARSON Lawrence	May 84	May 87	Gateshead	Bristol C	58/1	0	6	0	9/1	0	8/4	0
PEARSON J. Stuart [26]	May 65	May 74	Local	Manchester U	126/3	44	7	0	13/1	1	24	18
PEPPER H.	Jan 17	Jan 17	Bradford C	Guest	-	-	-	-	1	0	-	-
PERCIVAL Charles	Apr 15	Dec 15	Grimsby T	Released	-	-	-	-	11	3	1	0
PETTIT Raymond J.	Aug 63	Sep 72	Ainthorpe HS	Barnsley	78/1	0	1	0	4	0	15/2	1
PHILLIPS Ernest	Nov 51	Jun 54	Manchester C	York C	42	0	3	0	-	-	5	0
PHILLIPS Trevor	Jun 79	Mar 80	Rotherham U	Chester	22	3	-	-	2	0	1	0
PINKERTON Henry	Feb 34	May 35	Dunipace Juniors	Port Vale	2	1	-	-	-	-	-	-
PORTEOUS J.W.	Mar 41	Mar 41	Hearts	Guest	-	-	-	-	1	0	-	-
PORTEOUS Trevor	Apr 49	Jun 56	Endike Lane	Stockport C	61	1	2	0	-	-	15	1
POTTER Cecil B.	Aug 18	cs 20	Norwich C	Hartlepools U	10	0	-	-	22	7	4	1
POTTS Joseph	Mar 12	cs 14	Ashington	Portsmouth	5	0	-	-	-	-	1	0
PRESCOTT John	Aug 44	Oct 44	Everton	Guest	-	-	-	-	4	0	-	-
PRESCOTT John R.	May 39	Jun 40	Cardiff C	Released	-	-	-	-	21	16	6	7
PRICE A.J. William	Jan 49	Nov 49	Reading	Bradford C	8	5	-	-	-	-	3	3
PRICE T. Dudley	Sep 60	Jul 63	Southend U	Bradford C	76	26	8	3	6	1	-	-
PRIDMORE Arnold J.	May 46	May 46	Grimsby T		-	-	-	-	-	-	1	2
PRIESTLEY Joe	Nov 17	Nov 17	Bradford	Guest	-	-	-	-	1	0	-	-
PRINCE Arthur	Jun 28	cs 29	Sheffield W	Walsall	5	0	-	-	-	-	-	-
PRITCHARD Thomas H.	Mar 41	Mar 41	Guest		-	-	-	-	1	0	-	-
PROCTOR E.	May 22	May 22	Bridlington GS	Amateur	-	-	-	-	-	-	1	0
QUANTICK John H.	Jun 33	cs 37	West Bromwich A	Worcester C	88	1	2	0	-	-	2	0

The Hull City squad prior to the 1936-7 season. Back row (left to right): Yorke, Quantick, Annables, Pearson, Maddison, Tabram, Simpson, Dimbleby. Middle row: Mr Menzies (secretary-manager), Llewellyn, Don, Foster, Woodhead, Denby, Edwards, Gray, J.Lodge (assistant trainer), J.Beck (trainer). Front row: Baldry, Mayson, Hubbard, Acquroff, Holmes, Spivey, Bell, Davies, Cassidy.

Player	From	To	Former club	Next known club	League App	League Gls	FA Cup App	FA Cup Gls	Other comp App	Other comp Gls	Others App	Others Gls
QUIGLEY Dennis	May 39	Oct 39	Grimsby T	Released	-	-	-	-	-	-	4	0
RADCLIFFE Jeffrey	Aug 79		Club Physio		-	-	-	-	-	-	1/1	0
RAFFERTY Ronald	Jul 63	Jun 66	Grimsby T	Aldershot	16	6	-	-	-	-	-	-
RAISBECK Andrew	Aug 04	Apr 08	Liverpool	Emgtd to Canada	47	5	7	1	-	-	42	3
RALEIGH Simon	Aug 30	cs 32	Huddersfield T	Gillingham	31	21	2	0	-	-	1	1
RANBY Sam	Dec 20	Feb 21	Gilberdyke	Reckitts	1	0	-	-	-	-	-	-
RAYNOR George	Dec 40	Dec 40	Aldershot	Guest	-	-	-	-	1	0	-	-
READ Stanley	Oct 44	Oct 44	Guest		-	-	-	-	1	0	-	-
REAGAN C. Martin	May 47	Feb 48	York C	Middlesbrough	18	1	4	2	-	-	2	0
REEVE Eric P.	Jun 40	Dec 40	Brunswick Inst	Guest	-	-	-	-	2	0	-	-
RENTOUL Robert	Apr 19	Apr 19	Edinburgh area	Trialist	-	-	-	-	1	1	1	0
REVIE Donald G.	Nov 49	Oct 51	Leicester C	Manchester C	76	12	6	1	-	-	9	5
RHODES Brian	Nov 44	Nov 44	Local	Guest	-	-	-	-	1	0	-	-
RICHARDS Stephen C.	Jul 78	cs 83	Snaith Schools	Goole T	55/3	2	4	0	7/1	0	5/3	1
RICHARDSON David	Nov 44	Jan 45	Bradford C	Guest	-	-	-	-	2	0	-	-
RICHARDSON Ernest	Oct 39	Feb 40	Aldershot	Guest	-	-	-	-	9	1	5	0
RICHARDSON George [27]	Nov 38	Jun 48	Sheffield U	Bangor C	36	15	5	4	10	0	4	1
RICHARDSON George E.H.	Dec 23	cs 26	Huddersfield T	Bradford C	40	2	6	0	-	-	5	1
RICHES William	Jan 38	Dec 44	Hull Co-op Thurs	Batley RLFC	-	-	-	-	3	0	-	-
RIDSDALE J.	Dec 04	Dec 05	Botanic Swifts	Amateur	-	-	-	-	-	-	1	2
RILEY H.	Feb 18	Feb 18	Bradford	Guest	-	-	-	-	1	2	-	-
RING Michael P. [28]	Jul 84	May 86	Ballymena U	Aldershot	17/7	2	3/1	1	3/3	1	4/2	3
RINTANEN Mauno	Sep 56	Oct 56	HJK (Helsinki)	Amateur	4	0	-	-	-	-	-	-
ROBERTS David F.	Feb 75	Aug 78	Oxford U	Cardiff C	86	4	3	0	9	0	3	0
ROBERTS Garreth W.	Jul 77		Wolfreton School		365/5	47	27	5	42/2	7	54/3	12
ROBERTS J. Dale	Feb 80	Apr 85	Ipswich T	North Ferriby U	149/4	6	10	0	19	1	18/3	1
ROBERTS John G.	Aug 80	Jun 81	Wrexham	Oswestry	26	1	3	0	2	0	-	-
ROBERTSON Leonard V.	May 47	Mar 48	Watford	Scunthorpe U	9	2	-	-	-	-	1	0
ROBINSON	Nov 46	Nov 46	Trialist	Released	-	-	-	-	-	-	1	0
ROBINSON A.	Apr 17	Apr 17	Guest		-	-	-	-	1	0	-	-
ROBINSON Charles	Jun 37	cs 46	Plymouth A	Released	68	4	6	0	4	0	6	1
ROBINSON E.	Oct 04	Oct 04	C.H.G.O.B.	Amateur	-	-	-	-	-	-	1	0
ROBINSON John	May 39	cs 46	Sheffield U	Released	-	-	-	-	46	0	4	3
ROBINSON Joseph	Feb 49	Jul 53	Blackpool	Wisbech T	70	0	7	0	-	-	11	0
ROBINSON William S.	Jun 05	Feb 09	Manchester C	Bolton W	119	6	12	1	-	-	7	1
ROBSON C. Leslie	cs 48	May 53	North Hull Junrs	Darlington	3	1	-	-	-	-	-	-
ROBSON Fred	Feb 05	Feb 05	Hessle	Amateur	-	-	-	-	-	-	1	0
ROBSON J. Cecil	Mar 23	Aug 25	NE minor soccer	Reading	1	0	-	-	-	-	3	0
ROBSON William	Jan 11	cs 12	Hebburn A	Released	8	0	-	-	-	-	-	-
RODGERS Arthur	Jan 29	Jul 33	Denaby U	Doncaster R	67	0	3	0	-	-	1	0
ROGERS William	Sep 40	Sep 40	Guest		-	-	-	-	1	0	-	-
ROMIG George E.	Dec 05	Sep 06	Beverley Barracks	Amateur	-	-	-	-	-	-	1	0
ROSS Albert C.	Sep 40	Mar 41	Chester	Guest	-	-	-	-	16	0	-	-
ROTHERY Harry	Apr 45	Apr 45	Bournemouth & BA	Guest	-	-	-	-	3	1	-	-
ROUGHLEY Edward	May 06	May 14	St Helens Rec	Chesterfield	157	0	9	0	-	-	23	1
ROUND Leonard F.	Jun 57	Jul 58	Ayr U	Sittingbourne U	17	0	-	-	-	-	-	-
RUMNEY John	Jan 23	May 24	Preston Col	Chesterfield	13	4	-	-	-	-	-	-
RUSHTON George	Jul 04	May 07	Burslem Port Vale	Swindon T	29	14	9	1	-	-	43	30
RYLEY Henry S.	May 21	May 21	Barrow	Released	1	0	-	-	-	-	-	-
SALKELD David	Dec 15	Dec 15	Lincoln C	Guest	-	-	-	-	-	-	1	0
SALVIDGE George B.	Dec 35	cs 39	Beverley W Star	Burton T	4	1	-	-	-	-	-	-
SARGEANT Charles	May 32	Mar 34	Bristol C	Chester	60	16	6	2	-	-	-	-
SARGENT Fred A.	Aug 44	Sep 44	Tottenham H	Guest	-	-	-	-	2	2	-	-
SAUNDERS J.	Dec 15	Jan 16	Guest		-	-	-	-	5	2	-	-

Player	From	To	Former club	Next known club	League App	League Gls	FA Cup App	FA Cup Gls	Other comp App	Other comp Gls	Others App	Others Gls
SAVAGE John A.	Aug 50	Mar 52	RAF	Halifax T	4	0	-	-	-	-	-	-
SAVILLE Andrew V.	Sep 81	Mar 89	Malet Lambert HS	Walsaa	74/27	18	3/2	1	10/2	1	13/8	10
SCORER Robert	Apr 22	cs 23	Felling on Tyne	Bristol R	5	0	-	-	-	-	-	-
SCOTT Henry	Nov 26	Jun 28	Wolves	Bradford	29	8	5	2	-	-	1	0
SEDDON Frank O.	May 47	Jan 51	Notts C	Halifax T	3	0	-	-	-	-	7/1	0
SELBY William A.	Mar 41	Mar 41	Ranks FC	Guest	-	-	-	-	1	0	-	-
SERGEAUNT Harry	Oct 20	cs 22	Felling Col	Brighton & HA	19	8	5	1	-	-	-	-
SEWELL John	Oct 59	Apr 61	Aston Villa	City of Lusaka	44	8	5	1	1	0	1	0
SHARP Alexander	Oct 35	Sep 36	Blackburn R	Falkirk	18	4	1	0	-	-	-	-
SHARPE Leonard T.	May 62	Sep 66	Scunthorpe U	Goole T	58	4	7	0	6	0	1	0
SHAW Alan	Aug 61	Apr 64	Hamilton Steelers	Rtrnd to Canada	15	1	3	1	-	-	-	-
SHAW Frederick E.	Dec 11	May 13	Wallsend	Portsmouth	9	1	-	-	-	-	1	0
SHAW Joseph F.	May 07	Oct 09	Sunderland	Grimsby T	46	20	2	2	-	-	2	2
SHAW P.	Aug 17	Nov 18	Local	Guest	-	-	-	-	8	2	2	0
SHEEN John	Jun 46	Oct 46	Sheffield U	Kettering	5	1	-	-	-	-	-	-
SHELTON Thomas	Mar 32	cs 34	Mansfield junior	Released	5	1	-	-	-	-	1	1
SHEPHARD George	Oct 44	Oct 44	Sheffield U	Guest	-	-	-	-	1	0	-	-
SHEPHERD Ernest	Mar 49	Jul 50	West Bromwich A	Queen's Park R	15	3	-	-	-	-	8	3
SHEPHERD Harry	Nov 46	cs 47		Goole T	-	-	-	-	-	-	1	1
SHERIDAN James	Aug 15	Nov 17	Local	Guest	-	-	-	-	72	2	4	1
SHERWOOD Clifford H.	Jun 38	cs 39	Wolves	Released	4	0	-	-	-	-	-	-
SHERWOOD George W.	Feb 40	Sep 44	Stockport C	Guest	-	-	-	-	7	0	-	-
SHINER Roy A.J.	Nov 59	Jul 61	Sheffield W	Cheltenham T	22	8	1	0	-	-	1	0
SIMMON Henry	Jul 05	May 19	Leadgate Park Col	Retired	17	-	1	0	11	2	3/1	0
SIMPKIN Christopher	Sep 59	Oct 71	Ainthorpe HS	Blackpool	284/1	19	18	1	11	1	19/1	1
SIMPSON A.	Mar 16	Apr 16	Guest		-	-	-	-	2	0	-	-
SIMS Sydney	Dec 34	cs 35	Thorne Col	Scarborough	3	0	-	-	-	-	1	0
SINGLETON Edward A.	Sep 44	Sep 44	Southend U	Guest	-	-	-	-	1	0	-	-
SKIDMORE William	Apr 45	May 46	Wolves	Guest	-	-	-	-	1	0	1	0
SKIPPER Peter D. [29]	Sep 78	May 80	Schultz YC	Darlington								
	Aug 82	Oct 88	Darlington	Oldham A	286/2	19	17	1	32/1	1	50/3	3
SLATER Harold	Mar 22	cs 23	Harrogate	Released	3	0	-	-	-	-	1	0
SLIDE Robert	Sep 14	Apr 16	Brunswick Inst	Brunswick Inst	-	-	-	-	20	7	2	1
SLOMAN	Feb 08	cs 08	Joint Dock FC	Goole T	-	-	-	-	-	-	1	1
SMAILES Matthew	Feb 24	May 24	Langley Park	later Blackburn R	-	-	-	-	-	-	1	0
SMALES Kenneth	May 53	cs 58	Brunswick Inst	Scarborough	1	0	-	-	-	-	1/1	0
SMITH Alan	Sep 46	Sep 46	Trialist	Released	1	0	-	-	-	-	-	-
SMITH Augustus	Oct 04	Aug 05	Stockport C	Goole T	-	-	-	-	-	-	34	17
SMITH Dennis	May 46	Oct 47	Frickley Col	Accrington S	15	0	-	-	-	-	2	0
SMITH Edwin A.	May 10	Dec 11	Brierley Hill	Crystal P	9	0	-	-	-	-	1	0
SMITH E. Colin	Dec 56	Jun 60	Army Police	Rotherham U	65	39	1	0	-	-	3	3
SMITH F.	Nov 18	Nov 18	Birmingham	Guest	-	-	-	-	1	0	-	-
SMITH Frederick A.	Oct 49	May 51	Aberdeen	Sheffield U	17	1	-	-	-	-	8	5
SMITH H. Raymond	May 51	Jul 56	Local	Peterborough U	23	2	-	-	-	-	6/1	2
SMITH Ian	Apr 20	Sep 22	Hull OB	Amateur	1	0	-	-	-	-	-	-
SMITH John	Jun 05	Nov 10	Hebburn A	Sheffield U	156	98	12	4	-	-	15	9
SMITH John	Nov 44	Nov 44	Guest		-	-	-	-	1	1	-	-
SMITH Joseph E.	Sep 05	Mar 12	West Stanley	Everton								
	Oct 16	Apr 18	Bury	Guest	213	46	18	6	34	4	19	9
SMITH Kenneth R.	Apr 45	Apr 45	Brough	Guest	-	-	-	-	1	1	-	-
SMITH Michael K.	Mar 85		Sydney Smith HS		9/3	1	-	-	1	0	2/3	0
SMITH Robert M.S.	Sep 67	Sep 71	Local	Grimsby T	-	-	-	-	-	-	1	0
SMITH Samuel J.W.	Jun 28	May 29	Port Vale	Millwall	14	2	-	-	-	-	-	-
SMITH Thomas F.	Jun 39	cs 46	Dundee	Released	-	-	-	-	24	0	9	0

Centre-forward Roy Shiner, (above left) a former Sheffield Wednesday star, was brought to Boothferry Park in 1959 in an attempt to keep the Tigers out of the Third Division.

Maurice Swan (above right), a former Republic of Ireland international whose goalkeeping helped Hull City to capture the Third Division championship in 1966.

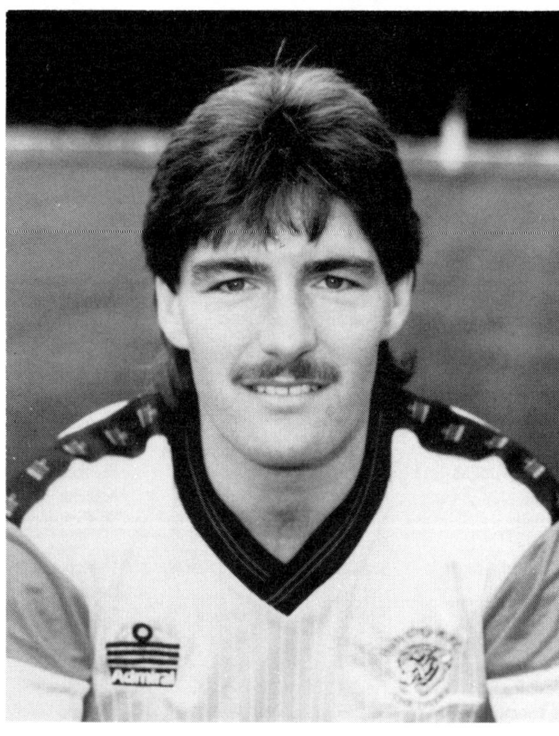

Gary Swann (right) was equally at home in defence or midfield in the City side which climbed from the Fourth to the Second Division in the early eighties.

Player	From	To	Former club	Next known club	League App	League Gls	FA Cup App	FA Cup Gls	Other comp App	Other comp Gls	Others App	Others Gls
SMITH Thomas P.	Jun 23	cs 24	Merthyr T	Hartlepools U	8	2	-	-	-	-	-	-
SMITH Wallace	Mar 09	cs 12	Leicester F	Worksop	91	32	6	0	-	-	9	2
SMITH William	Feb 05	Feb 05	C.H.G.O.B.	Amateur	-	-	-	-	-	-	1	0
SOMMERSCALES W.	Apr 05	Apr 05	Albany	Amateur	-	-	-	-	-	-	1	0
SPEED Frederick	Feb 31	Jul 34	Newark	York C	49	15	3	3	-	-	1	1
SPENCE George	Jul 04	Jun 06	Southampton	Clyde	19	2	4	2	-	-	42	18
SPENCER Ernest	Nov 44	Nov 44	RAF	Guest	-	-	-	-	1	1	-	-
SPENDIFF Martin N.	May 05	Apr 08	Grimsby T	Bradford C	104	0	11	0	-	-	5	1
SPIVEY Richard	Mar 35	Jul 37	Southc'tes La OB	Torquay U								
	Oct 39	Apr 41	Southport	Guest	21	5	-	-	17	2	-	-
STABLES A.	Mar 17	Mar 17	Guest		-	-	-	-	1	0	-	-
STAINFORTH Andrew	cs 81	Mar 85	Malet Lambert HS	Released	-	-	-	-	-	-	0/1	1
STANIFORTH Gordon	Nov 70	Dec 76	Greatfield HS	York C	7/5	2	-	-	-	-	0/2	0
STANSFIELD John	Jan 22	cs 22	Castleford T	Castleford T	12	1	-	-	-	-	1	0
STARLING Ronald W.	Apr 26	May 30	Washington Col	Newcastle U	78	13	8	1	-	-	3	2
STEPHENS W. John	Aug 51	Jun 58	Cardiff junior	Swindon T	94	20	9	2	-	-	9	1
STEPHENSON Eric	Nov 39	Dec 39	Leeds U	Guest	-	-	-	-	1	0	2	0
STEPHENSON William	May 07	Aug 10	Whitburn	Tottenham H								
	Aug 19	Jun 20	Tottenham H	Hartlepools U	64	0	2	0	-	-	7	0
STEVENS Samuel	Feb 12	Jul 20	Cradley Heath	Notts C	150	84	11	9	35	26	7	4
STEVENSON	Apr 18	Apr 18	Guest		-	-	-	-	1	0	-	-
STEWART David C.	Jul 74	May 79	Bangor	Chelsea	46/5	7	3	0	8/1	0	0/2	0
STOCKS Joseph R.	Aug 57	Aug 61	Hull Schools	Millwall	9	1	1	0	-	-	1	0
STODDART George G.	Nov 20	cs 21	Raith R	Released	7	0	-	-	-	-	2	0
STOKES Archer	Apr 37	cs 39	Hull Nomads	Released	1	0	-	-	-	-	-	-
STOKES Ernest	Nov 44	May 46	Southend U	Guest	-	-	-	-	10	0	1	0
STONE John	Sep 44	Apr 45	Sheffield U	Guest	-	-	-	-	6	0	-	-
STOREY Ernest	Oct 08	cs 10	Birtley	Spennymoor U	3	0	-	-	-	-	2	0
STOTT George R.B.	May 32	cs 33	Bradford C	Released	4	0	-	-	-	-	-	-
SUDDES Fred	Oct 18	Mar 19	Aston Villa	Guest	-	-	-	-	5	1	-	-
SULLIVAN Cornelius	May 26	May 29	Newburn	Bradford	65	3	5	0	-	-	3	0
SULLIVAN Maurice	Dec 40	Dec 40	Mansfield T	Guest	-	-	-	-	1	0	-	-
SUMMERS Gerald T.F.	Apr 64	Oct 65	Sheffield U	Walsall	59	1	3	1	3	0	-	-
SUMMERS J.	Feb 18	Feb 18	Bradford	Guest	-	-	-	-	1	0	-	-
SUNLEY David	Jan 76	Jun 78	Sheffield W	Lincoln C	58/11	11	3	0	9/2	0	2	0
SURREY Thomas H.	Oct 29	cs 30	Scotswood	Released	1	0	-	-	-	-	-	-
SWAN Christopher	Jul 25	May 29	Stockport C	Crystal P	73	8	4	0	-	-	7	2
SWAN Maurice M.G.	Jun 63	Nov 68	Cardiff C	Dundalk	103	0	14	0	5	0	6/2	0
SWAN Peter H.	Mar 89		Leeds U		11	1	-	-	-	-	-	-
SWANN Gary	Jul 78	Nov 86	York Schools	Preston NE	176/10	9	11	1	20/3	0	22/9	2
SYKES Harry	Apr 45	Apr 45	Guest		-	-	-	-	1	1	-	-
SYMONS John [30]	Dec 44	cs 47	Local	Released	-	-	-	-	12	0	-	-
TABRAM William D.	May 34	cs 37	Port Vale	North Shields	106	5	3	0	1	0	1	0
TAIT Michael P.	Sep 79	May 80	Carlisle U	Portsmouth	29/4	3	1	1	-	-	-	-
TALBOT F. Leslie	Aug 44	Jan 45	Cardiff C	Guest	-	-	-	-	7	3	-	-
TARRANT J. Edward	Jun 46	Dec 53	Doncaster Schools	Walsall	30	2	-	-	-	-	14	4
TAYLOR Alan D.	Dec 83	Jun 84	Vancouver W'caps	Burnley	13/1	3	-	-	6	4	3	0
TAYLOR Arthur M.	Apr 62	Jun 63	Goole T	Halifax T	1	0	-	-	-	-	-	-
TAYLOR David W.	Apr 09	cs 11	Newcastle EE	Released	-	-	-	-	-	-	1	0
TAYLOR John	Aug 07	cs 09	Parkhead FC	New Brompton	9	3	-	-	-	-	3	0
TAYLOR John	Jul 47	May 50	Norwich C	Weymouth	72	0	14	0	-	-	6	0
TAYLOR William	Jun 26	Jun 31	Aberdare A	Norwich C	152	17	13	1	-	-	2	0
TEASDALE Thomas	May 47	May 47	Trialist	Released	1	0	-	-	-	-	-	-
TEECE David A.	Feb 52	Jun 56	Hyde U	Oldham A	25	0	-	-	-	-	9	0

Neil Williams (above) won England Youth caps with his previous club Watford. At Boothferry Park he demonstrated considerable versatility in clocking up over 100 first-team appearances for Hull City.

> *Hull City's first strip consisted of amber and black striped shirts with black shorts. In the 1920s white shorts replaced black, but early the following decade there was a suggestion of changing to an England-style strip of white shirts and navy shorts. By 1935 the 'change your colours, improve your luck brigade' had won the day. That August the team stepped out in ultramarine shirts and white shorts. The result? The worst season in the club's history up to that point. The original strip was brought back the very next season.*

Defender Tom Wilson (right) concluded his League career with the Tigers. For close on a decade he assisted Goole Town, and then returned to Boothferry Park as a member of the coaching staff.

Player	From	To	Former club	Next known club	League App	League Gls	FA Cup App	FA Cup Gls	Other comp App	Other comp Gls	Others App	Others Gls
TEMPLE G. Arthur	Jul 07	cs 14	Wallsend Pk Villa	Blyth Spartans	173	77	11	4	-	-	26	22
TERRY Steve G.	Jun 88		Watford		33	1	-	-	3	0	6	0
THISTLETON James H.	Sep 08	cs 09	Central A	Released	-	-	-	-	-	-	1	3
THISTLETON Mark	Mar 16	Apr 17	Local	Guest	-	-	-	-	3	1	1	2
THOM Alexander	Sep 22	Jun 26	Airdrieonians	Swindon T	131	18	9	0	-	-	14	0
THOMAS Alfred C.	Jun 23	cs 25	Merthyr T	South Shields	36	4	2	0	-	-	10	0
THOMAS Ronald W.	Nov 44	Apr 45	RAF	Guest	-	-	-	-	8	0	-	-
THOMPSON Denis	Mar 47	Jan 48	Whitburn Welfare	NE minor soccer	9	8	-	-	-	-	3	2
THOMPSON James W.	Oct 31	Dec 31	Fulham	Tunbridge Wells R	1	0	-	-	-	-	-	-
THOMPSON Leslie [31]	Apr 86		Grimsby T		11/3	2	-	-	2/1	0	1/1	1
THOMPSON Neil	Oct 81	Sep 83	Nottingham F	Scarborough	29/2	0	-	-	3	0	3/2	0
THOMSON Robert	Jul 34	cs 35	Newcastle U	Racing Club de Paris	4	0	-	-	-	-	-	-
THORLEY Ernest	Nov 34	cs 36	Sunderland	Kidderminster H	34	5	2	0	-	-	1	0
THORNTON William	Feb 05	cs 07	Doncaster R	Denaby U	1	0	1	0	-	-	14	1
THORPE Tom	Sep 18	Sep 18	Sheffield W	Guest	-	-	-	-	1	0	-	-
TICKLE J.	Oct 18	Oct 18	Huddersfield T	Guest	-	-	-	-	1	0	-	-
TISSERAND Alain	Jun 73	Jun 73	French Guiana	Guest	-	-	-	-	-	-	1	0
TODD Paul R.	Oct 51	May 53	Blackburn R	King's Lynn	27	3	3	0	-	-	1	1
TOMLINSON Andy	Sep 84	May 86	Greatfield HS	Doncaster R	-	-	-	-	-	-	0/1	0
TOOTILL	May 47	May 47	Trialist	Released	-	-	-	-	-	-	1	0
TOWARD Alfred V.	Dec 08	Dec 09	Leadgate Park Col	Oldham A	10	6	-	-	-	-	5	5
TOWNEND H. Vincent	Sep 09	cs 12	Selby T	Goole T	12	1	-	-	-	-	1	0
TRAYNOR Laurence	Jan 05	cs 06	Brunswick Wes	Amateur	-	-	-	-	-	-	1	0
TREANOR James L.	Sep 36	cs 39	Accrington S	Released	44	1	1	0	1	0	2	0
TULLOCH Roland	Dec 53	cs 55	S African soccer	Rtrnd to S Africa	3	0	-	-	-	-	3	0
TURKINGTON Mark	Jul 83	Aug 83	Chelsea	Trialist	-	-	-	-	-	-	0/1	0
TURNER Albert	Mar 29	Aug 31	Denaby U	Walsall	19	2	-	-	-	-	2	0
TURNER Henry	Feb 14	cs 15	Wallsend Elm Villa	Released	6	3	-	-	-	-	-	-
TURNER John	Oct 04	Feb 05	Stockport C	Released	-	-	-	-	-	-	7	0
TURNER Robert F.	May 30	cs 32	Cockfield	Southport	1	0	-	-	-	-	-	-
TWELLS Donald	Dec 40	Apr 41	St Mirren	Guest	-	-	-	-	7	0	-	-
VARNEY John F.	Aug 49	May 51	Oxford C	Lincoln C	9	0	1	0	-	-	1/1	1
VAUGHAN Edward	Feb 45	Apr 45	Northum Ams	Guest	-	-	-	-	9	1	-	-
VAUX Edward	Feb 45	Feb 45	Chelsea	Guest	-	-	-	-	2	0	-	-
VEALE W.	Aug 16	Sep 16	Irish amateur	Guest	-	-	-	-	1	0	-	-
VICKERS John	Mar 28	cs 29	Bishop Auckland	Darlington	2	0	-	-	-	-	-	-
VOASE Frank N.	Dec 15	Apr 16	Local	Guest	-	-	-	-	5	0	2	0
WADSWORTH Eric A.	Aug 19	cs 20	Local amateur	Hornsea T	1	0	-	-	-	-	-	-
WAGSTAFF Kenneth	Nov 64	May 76	Mansfield T	G Cross (Austral)	374/4	173	29	14	26/1	10	39	26
WAINSCOAT W. Russell	Oct 31	cs 34	Leeds U	Retired	79	42	6	8	-	-	-	-
WALDEN George	Oct 09	Sep 10	London minor club	Rotherham T	2	1	-	-	-	-	-	-
WALDEN Harold	Oct 17	Mar 19	Bradford C	Guest	-	-	-	-	25	11	1	1
WALE L.	Feb 17	Feb 17	Guest		-	-	-	-	2	0	-	-
WALKER Frederick	Mar 45	Mar 45	Sheffield W	Guest	-	-	-	-	1	0	-	-
WALKER Frederick A.	Apr 45	Apr 45	Guest		-	-	-	-	3	0	-	-
WALKER J. William	Jul 23	cs 24	Langley Park	Released	5	1	-	-	-	-	-	-
WALLIS H.			see Walden									
WALSH James A.	Jun 28	Aug 31	Liverpool	Colwyn Bay	82	9	7	0	-	-	2	0
WALTERS H.	Jan 16	Feb 16	Goole T	Guest	-	-	-	-	3	0	-	-
WALTERS Harry	May 46	May 46	Wolves	Walsall	-	-	-	-	-	-	1	0
WALTERS Peter L. [32]	Jul 70	May 73	NE junior soccer	Corby T	2	0	-	-	-	-	6/1	0
WARBOYS Alan	Sep 77	Jul 79	Fulham	Doncaster R	44/5	9	1	0	-	-	-	-
WARD Phillip	Sep 81	Feb 85	Wolfreton HS	Goole T	-	-	-	-	-	-	0/1	0
WARD Thomas E.G.	Oct 44	Oct 44	Mansfield T	Guest	-	-	-	-	1	0	-	-

Player	From	To	Former club	Next known club	League App	League Gls	FA Cup App	FA Cup Gls	Other comp App	Other comp Gls	Others App	Others Gls
WARREN Lee A.	Aug 88		Rochdale		27/1	0	-	-	3	1	3	0
WASSELL Kim D.	Aug 83	Sep 83	Australian soccer	Bradford C	1	0	-	-	-	-	2	0
WATERS Dennis	Mar 45	Mar 45	Hull Forge	Guest	-	-	-	-	1	0	-	-
WATSON Arthur E.	Jun 39	May 47	Chesterfield	Retired	35	2	5	0	25	0	10	0
WATSON John I.	Apr 27	Oct 30	Aberdeen Rich	Suspended *sine die*	47	0	1	0	-	-	3	0
WEALANDS Jeffrey A.	Feb 72	Jul 79	Darlington	Birmingham C	240	0	11	0	31	0	23/1	0
WEAVER Samuel	Apr 28	Nov 29	Sutton T	Newcastle U	48	5	2	0	-	-	1	0
WELDON Anthony	Jun 30	Jun 31	Everton	West Ham U	31	6	1	0	-	-	1	0
WELSH C.T.	Jan 05	Feb 05	Barton St Chad's	Amateur	-	-	-	-	-	-	3	0
WEST Henry	Aug 06	cs 07	Army	Cottingham	1	0	-	-	-	-	-	-
WHEELDON J.	Jan 16	Apr 16	Local	Guest	-	-	-	-	1	0	-	-
WHITCHURCH Stanley	Mar 45	Apr 45	Guest		-	-	-	-	4	0	-	-
WHITE Barry J.	Mar 64	Jun 70	Willerby School	Halifax T	-	-	-	-	-	-	1/2	0
WHITE Kenneth	Nov 47	cs 49	Selby T	Scarborough	1	0	-	-	-	-	1	0
WHITE Lionel S.	Sep 44	Mar 45	C.D.Holmes FC	Guest	-	-	-	-	3	0	-	-
WHITE William W.	Jun 38	cs 39	Lincoln C	Released	2	0	-	-	-	-	1	0
WHITEHOUSE James	Jul 04	cs 05	Third Lanark	Southend U	-	-	2	0	-	-	38	0
WHITEHURST William	Oct 80	Dec 85	Mexborough T	Newcastle U								
	Dec 88		Sunderland		197/17	52	13	5	27/1	12	24/2	13
WHITFIELD Norman	Mar 16	Apr 16	Leicester F	Guest	-	-	-	-	3	0	-	-
WHITNALL Brian	cs 48	May 56	Bentley Schools	Scunthorpe U	2	0	-	-	-	-	2	0
WHITTINGHAM Harry	Oct 17	Nov 17	Derby C	Guest	-	-	-	-	2	0	-	-
WHITWORTH George	Nov 25	cs 28	Sheffield W	Peterborough U	67	31	5	1	-	-	3	2
WIENAND George	Oct 38	cs 39	Huddersfield T	Rtrnd to S Africa	15	3	-	-	-	-	-	-
WIGGLESWORTH Arthur [33]	Aug 16	cs 20	Goole T	Doncaster R	7	0	-	-	101	0	8	0
WILDE R.	Jan 17	Feb 17	Bradford C	Guest	-	-	-	-	2	0	-	-
WILKINSON	Aug 04	Aug 04	Nelson	Trialist	-	-	-	-	-	-	1	0
WILKINSON Graham J.	cs 50	cs 60	Welton HS	Bridlington Trin	3	0	-	-	-	-	-	-
WILKINSON Harry	Aug 04	cs 05	Manchester U	West Ham U	-	-	2	0	-	-	36	9
WILKINSON Jack	Oct 36	cs 37	Sunderland	Scunthorpe U	17	2	1	0	-	-	-	-
WILKINSON Norman	Aug 44	Aug 44	Stoke C	Guest	-	-	-	-	1	0	-	-
WILKINSON Norman F.	Nov 52	May 54	RAF	York C	8	3	-	-	-	-	-	-
WILKINSON Thomas	Nov 24	cs 26	Durham minor club	Everton	4	2	-	-	-	-	1	0
WILKINSON William	Aug 61	Nov 72	Stockton	Rotherham U	208/15	34	16/1	5	12	2	21/6	2
WILLIAMS Emlyn	Jun 29	cs 30	Clapton O	Merthyr T	1	0	-	-	-	-	-	-
WILLIAMS Michael J.	Aug 60	Jul 66	Francis Askew HS	Aldershot	88	0	6	0	6	0	2	0
WILLIAMS Neil J.F.	Jul 84	May 88	Watford	Preston NE	75/16	9	7	1	14/1	0	11/7	0
WILLIAMS Trevor	Sep 04	Oct 04	Grimsby T	Grimsby Rangers	-	-	-	-	-	-	3	1
WILSON A.	Oct 15	Sep 17	Guest		-	-	-	-	2	0	-	-
WILSON David	May 05	Dec 05	Hearts	Leeds C	10	3	2	2	-	-	1	0
WILSON David M.	Mar 41	Apr 41	Scottish junior	Guest	-	-	-	-	2	0	-	-
WILSON Gordon G.	Apr 26	Jun 31	Scotswood	Luton T	28	1	-	-	-	-	3	0
WILSON Henry	Sep 20	Jul 21	Glenavon	Charlton A	30	2	5	3	-	-	-	-
WILSON Thomas	Nov 67	Jul 71	Millwall	Goole T	60	1	5	0	1	0	1/1	1
WOLFE Frederick	Aug 04	Aug 05	Everton	Chelsea	-	-	2	0	-	-	27	3
WOOD Alfred E.H.	Nov 74	Oct 76	Millwall	Middlesbrough	51/2	10	5	2	8	2	4	2
WOOD James L.	Dec 21	cs 23	Methley	Released	2	2	1	0	-	-	-	-
WOODHEAD Clifford	May 30	Apr 41	Denaby U	Goole T	305	0	18	0	52	0	15	0
WOODLAND Arthur	Jan 17	Jan 17	Notts C	Guest	-	-	-	-	1	0	-	-
WOODS Cyril	May 39	cs 46	Hartlepools U	Released	-	-	-	-	4	1	1	0
WOOF William [34]	Oct 82	May 83	Cardiff C	Hartlepool U	9/2	3	-	-	-	-	2/1	0
WOOTTON James	Nov 18	Nov 18	Birmingham	Guest	-	-	-	-	1	0	-	-
WRACK Charles	May 31	cs 32	Grimsby T	Boston	3	0	1	0	-	-	1	0
WRIGHT David	Jul 34	May 35	Liverpool	Bradford	32	11	1	0	-	-	-	-

Player	From	To	Former club	Next known club	League App	League Gls	FA Cup App	FA Cup Gls	Other comp App	Other comp Gls	Others App	Others Gls
WRIGHT E. Gordon D.	Dec 05	Aug 13	Portsmouth	Went to S Africa	152	14	16	0	-	-	4	1
WRIGHT Frederick	Nov 30	cs 31	Grantham	Released	2	0	-	-	-	-	-	-
WRIGHT George A.	Jun 46	Feb 47	Cardiff C	Released	4	1	-	-	-	-	-	-
WRIGHT James	Nov 15	cs 19	Hull Tivoli	Guest	-	-	-	-	1	0	-	-
WRIGHT John B.	Sep 47	Aug 49	Tyne Dock U	Dartford	1	0	1	0	-	-	-	-
WRIGHT William 'Tim'	Oct 08	cs 21	Withernsea	Retired	153	5	13	0	82	15	24	2
WYPER H. Thomas	Feb 27	Sep 28	Accrington S	Charlton A	40	2	-	-	-	-	3	3
YORKE Robert	Jun 35	Sep 37	Dundee U	Dundee U	9	0	-	-	1	0	-	-
YOUNG Harry	Nov 39	Nov 39	Goole T	Guest	-	-	-	-	1	0	-	-
YOUNG Robert T.	Apr 16	Apr 16	Sunderland	Guest	-	-	-	-	1	0	-	-
YOUNG Ronald	Aug 63	Sep 68	NE minor soccer	Hartlepools U	24/2	5	1	0	1	0	6	0
			Unnamed trialists		-	-	-	-	-	-	2	0
			Unnamed substitutes		-	-	-	-	-	-	0/2	0
			Short-handed		-	-	-	-	2	-	-	-
			Own-goals		-	69	-	5	-	7	-	7

REFERENCES

[1] On loan to Southend United, Dec 70-May 71.
[2] On loan to Watford, Oct-Dec 71.
[3] On loan to Doncaster Rovers, Mar-May 72.
[4] Assistant trainer for a spell during the 1920s.
[5] Also played in Reserves' first Yorkshire Midweek League match, Sep 22.
[6] On loan to Millwall, Mar-Apr 75.
[7] Figures include friendly games played during subsequent spell on coaching staff.
[8] On loan to Scarborough from Feb 47.
[9] On loan to Scunthorpe United, Sep 68-May 69.
[10] On loan to Scarborough, Nov 47-Sep 48.
[11] On loan to Notts County, Mar-May 86.
[12] On loan to Barnsley, Oct-Nov 75 and Stockport County, Dec 75-Jan 76.
[13] On loan to York City, Dec 76-Apr 77.
[14] On loan to Drogheda, Feb-Apr 74.
[15] On loan to Bradford City, Dec 77-Jan 78.
[16] On loan to Scunthorpe United, Sep-Oct 75.
[17] On loan to York City, Sep-Oct 1988.
[18] Figures include friendly game played during subsequent spell as manager.
[19] On loan to Gillingham, Jul 52-Jan 55.
[20] On loan to Hartlepool, Dec 70-May 71.
[21] On loan to SC Cambuur, Feb-May 80.
[22] On loan to Sheffield United, Mar-May 89.
[23] On loan to Doncaster Rovers, Dec 83-Jan 84.
[24] On loan to Exeter City, Mar-Apr 87.
[25] On loan to Scunthorpe United, Mar-May 71.
[26] Figures include guest appearance in friendly.
[27] On loan to Ransome & Marles for most of World War Two, until Aug 47.
[28] On loan to Bolton Wanderers, Mar-Apr 86.
[29] On loan to Scunthorpe United, Jan-Mar 80.
[30] Also assisted Reserves in mid-1930s.
[31] On loan to Scarborough, Dec 88-Jan 89.
[32] On loan to Darlington, Feb-May 72.
[33] Also played for Juniors and Reserves prior to Mar 12.
[34] Assisted Happy Valley (Hong Kong), Nov 82-Jan 83.

Players' Career Records 1899-1903

*Denotes played later in first or reserve team for professional club.

		League		Cups		Others	
		App	Gls	App	Gls	App	Gls
ANDREWS M*	1901-03	11	4	23	5	19	2
BAGSHAW T	1900-01	2	1	0	0	0	0
BAINBRIDGE	1902-03	2	0	1	0	3	1
BARLOW E	1901-03	12	0	20	7	7	2
BARNES Frank	1902-03	0	0	2	1	0	0
BEACOCK A	1901-02	0	0	0	0	1	0
BLYTHE Tommy	1900-01	1	2	0	0	0	0
BOLTON A	1902-03	0	0	0	0	1	0
BROMLEY Ted	1900-01	2	0	0	0	0	0
BROWN G	1901-02	0	0	0	0	1	0
BURRIDGE C	1900-01	0	0	0	0	3	0
CLIFFE E	1902-03	12	5	11	1	6	0
COCKERILL C	1899-1901	10	1	3	2	5	3
COLLINGWOOD T	1900-01	0	0	0	0	1	0
CROMPTON Ben	1899-1902	4	0	1	0	0	0
DAWSON AH	1900-02	0	0	0	0	3	0
DICKINSON E	1899-1901	2	0	0	0	0	0
FOGGIN FG	1899-1902	11	0	2	0	11	0
FROST Ben*	1902-03	0	0	0	0	1	0
FROST EL	1899-1901	14	0	4	0	9	0
GIBBS	1900-01	0	0	1	0	0	0
GREENFIELD H	1902-03	4	0	0	0	2	1
HAMPTON C	1901-02	0	0	1	0	5	0
HAY Harry	1899-1903	15	3	16	6	21	12
HAY Will*	1899-1903	25	11	27	15	26	10
HEATON GW	1899-1900	0	0	0	0	1	3
HOBBIS James	1901-03	10	6	22	10	18	4
HOWDEN F	1899-1901	12	11	2	1	10	6
HUTCHINSON JE	1899-1901	7	0	2	0	8	1
JACKSON	1901-02	0	0	0	0	1	0
JOHNSON Laurie*	1899-1903	19	0	23	0	27	0
KELSEY G	1902-03	0	0	0	0	1	0
KERSHAW Leo	1899-1900	0	0	0	0	1	0
KIDDLE J†	1899-1900	0	0	0	0	1	1
KIDDLE J†	1901-02	0	0	0	0	1	0
LEVITT Fred	1899-1903	27	0	23	0	27	0
McCALL R	1900-01	1	0	0	0	0	0
McDOUGALL DJG	1901-02	0	0	5	4	7	6
MACHIN H	1902-03	1	1	0	0	0	0
MACKAY R	1899-1900	0	0	0	0	3	0
MACKRILL Henry*	1901-03	0	0	5	3	1	0
MASSEY S*	1900-03	14	3	8	3	16	1
METHAM Dick	1901-02	0	0	4	1	7	3

†The second Kiddle was a guest player from Scunthorpe. It is open to conjecture as to whether he is the same player as formerly assisted Hull Comet.

		League		Cups		Others	
		App	Gls	App	Gls	App	Gls
MILTON L	1899-1900	1	3	0	0	5	0
MOSS C	1900-01	0	0	1	0	0	0
MOODY Fred	1901-02	0	0	0	0	1	0
MOXLEY E	1900-01	4	4	1	0	0	0
MOXLEY L	1900-01	2	1	1	0	0	0
NEWMAN S*	1902-03	0	0	0	0	2	0
NEWTON WR	1901-02	0	0	0	0	1	0
PARKER AW	1900-01	1	1	0	0	0	0
PATON Geordie	1901-02	0	0	5	4	4	3
PEARCE James*	1901-02	0	0	0	0	1	0
PURVIS J	1902-03	7	1	1	0	2	1
REEVE A	1901-03	2	1	4	1	5	0
RICHMOND Frank	1900-01	0	0	1	0	0	0
RIDSDALE J*	1900-03	19	11	27	15	20	4
RIPPON PJ	1902-03	0	0	0	0	1	0
ROBINSON E*	1900-03	14	2	24	3	22	3
ROBINSON F	1899-1900	8	4	1	0	6	1
ROBSON Fred*	1902-03	0	0	0	0	1	0
ROGERS Tommy	1900-02	4	0	3	0	13	0
ROGERSON HM	1899-1900	3	2	0	0	3	1
RUSSELL J	1901-02	0	0	0	0	3	0
RUSSELL W	1899-1900	3	4	0	0	3	0
SANDERSON EJ	1899-1900	0	0	0	0	1	0
SELLARS E	1899-1900	1	0	1	0	1	0
SHAKESPEARE A	1899-1900	1	0	0	0	0	0
SHAW Walt	1902-03	0	0	0	0	1	1
SMITH Syd	1902-03	1	0	0	0	3	0
SMITH W	1901-02	0	0	1	0	5	0
TIPLADY H*	1901-02	0	0	0	0	6	0
TRAYNOR Laurie*	1899-1903	9	1	11	1	14	3
TYSON E	1899-1900	0	0	0	0	1	0
WATTS H	1902-03	0	0	7	8	1	0
WHARTON A	1901-02	0	0	10	1	16	11
WHITE W	1899-1900	0	0	0	0	1	0
WILKINSON Charlie	1899-1903	16	1	8	0	19	0
WILKINSON W	1899-1901	1	0	1	0	1	0
WILSON LM	1899-1900	1	0	0	0	0	0
WRIGHT Arnold	1899-1901	12	3	4	0	13	4
WRIGHTSON P	1901-02	0	0	0	0	2	0
Short-handed		2	-	1	-	2	-
Substitutes		0	0	0	0	5	1
Own-goals		-	2	-	2	-	0
Untraced		0	2	0	2	22	7

SUBSCRIBERS

Presentation Copies
1 Hull City Association Football Club
2 The Football League • 3 The Football Association

4 Chris Elton
5 Don Robinson
6 Raich Carter
7 Bill Walker
8 John Treleven
9 James Herbert Sharp
10 Leslie Alan Wilson
11 Andrew James Wilson
12 J B Cook
13 Stephen Pearson
14 Bernard Shaw
15 Stephen Terry Sutton
16 Nicholas David Perry
17 George Burns
18 Nicholas Gloster
19 Paul Geoffrey Bray
20 P A Thompson
21 Carl Bemrose
22 Michael John Breasley
23 D J Fitches
24 Stephen Driffill
25 Gary Clark
26 Christian Taylor
27 Malcolm MacPhee
28 Ian Westray
29 Stella Forward
30 Ernest Adcock
31 Peter Allen
32 Ian Johnson
33 Mike Cook
34 Paul Collier
35 Jeff & Jacky Baldry
36 Martin R Smith
37 Jean Proctor
38 James Jordan
39 Charles Edward Harrison
40 Stephen Claxton
41 Arthur Claxton
42 Richard Claxton
43 R C Milner
44 H H West
45 Robert Edwards
46 Barry Shears
47 John Tate
48 Frank Hansford
49 Eric E Smithson
50 W E Quine
51 Jeffrey W Maddison
52 Bernard Watson
53 A E Broadbank
54 Joseph Henry Ball
55 Paul Drant
56 John Earl
57 George Rhodes
58 Simon Wyke
59 Michael J Naylor
60 J M McGrath
61 Philip & Stewart Mays
62 I A Tichias
63 John C Kelly
64 Ian Rowe
65 P J Goforth
66 Raymond Walsh
67 Glenn Seager
68 G S Cross
69 Gary Bennett
70 Lawrence Fallon
71 John R Wood
72 Steven Woomble
73 Joe Prothero
74 Captain Graham J Botterill
75 John Manchester
76 Richard Netherton
77 Ian Milner
78 Trevor Anthony Richardson
79 G Cooper
80 Raymond Friston
81 Andrew Dixon
82 Michael Armstrong
83 Steven Ellerington
84 Michael W Richards
85 P Buxton
86 Alan Riby
87 C R L Wells
88 Ian Lees
89 Susan Goodrick
90 C H Catterick
91 Shaun Fairburn
92 Stephen Boville
93 Paul A Green
94 Ian Dale
95 Andrew J Dougill
96 M C Wilburn
97 Colin Johnson
98 N Rennard
99 Colin Leslie Lancaster
100 Philip Williamson
101 Kevin Parker
102 S F P Easingwood
103 Patrick Plumb
104 W A Renshaw
105 David Scott
106 Jenny Clark
107 G H Fletcher
108 Tony Appleton
109 Hughie Sizen
110 Thomas F Downing
111 David Wright
112 Paul Chapman
113 Gary Davis
114 John G Wilson
115 Carl Dulling
116 A Thompson
117 Jeff, Ann & Andrew Leighton, Gilberdyke
118 Andrew P Netherton
119 Michael Peter Willingham
120 Hugh & Michele McAllister
121 Ian Pashby
122 Gavin Bennett
123 Bryan Henry Fussey
124 Philip Smith
125 Peter F Lincoln
126 John Rhodes
127 Mrs J M Foster
128 K Peck
129 Miss J Dickson
130 Mrs J Drake

131 F S R Gray
132 Alan Appleby
133 Michael Grange
134 Alan Slight
135 Kevin Baxter
136 David Andrews
137 Michael John Sykes
138 G R A Conley
139 C Gleadell
140 D Turner
141 Peter G Johnson
142 S Buttery
143 Peter Higham
144 Darran Lee Turner
145 David A Woodford
146 David Philipson
147 Gordon Lawson
148 Simon Rees
149 Dorothy Margaret Arnott
150 John Grayson
151 Ian Strodder
152 John Reed
153 Edwin T Bacon
154 Jack Close
155 Peter Holmes
156 Paul Bainbridge
157 Adrian Harper
158 S C Brown
159 Paul Ibbotson
160 Barry Ibbotson
161 J G Dunnett
162 R Cowburn
163 Helen Coyle
164 William Rands
165 A K Kirby
166 Angela Shimells
167 Mark Shimells
168 Michael Cole
169 Jean Stone
170 Kevin G Willerton
171 Katie Dealey
172 R Ballard
173 David M Baron
174 Colin Davenport
175 B L & K B Jackson
176 S Hare
177 Philip Ian Beaumont
178 Paul Heathcote
179 Albert Robinson
180 Brendan Lewis
181 D T Bryant
182 J A Harris
183 Brian H Hobbs
184 J S Pyke
185 Gerald Hill
186 A P J M Otten
187 Christopher Minchin
188 Esa Kautonen
189 Geir Juva
190 Lars-Olof Wendler
191 P W Stevenson
192 Simons Martin
193 Harald Lohr
194 Surapot Saengchote
195 Kåre M Torgrimsen
196 I Watts
197 David J Godfrey
198 M Swart
199 A Young
200 Keith Lowe
201 Claude Bugg
202 T Bugg
203 Trevor Bugg
204 R G Woolman
205 Richard Stocken
206 Gordon Small
207 John Motson
208 S P Tomlin
209 P H Whitehead
210 Phil Soar
211 G D Painter
212 Brian Rolfe
213 John Parkin
214 Gordon Mason
215 R K Haith
216 George Ian Fenwick
217 M D Brogden
218 Michael R Thomson
219 Peter H Thomson
220 Stephen Garner
221 Andrew Garner
222 D G Shephard
223 D G Shephard
224 David Bryan Temple
225 Josephine Wright
226 G W Mowforth
227 Michael James Ball
228 Valerie Boys
229 Anthony Trevor Daniels
230 Harry Kay
231 Derek Hyde
232 Geoff Allman
233 R J Gamble
234 B H Standish
235 David Keats
236 Moira & Frederick Furness
237 Fred Lee
238 Graham & Janet Carter
239 Donald Noble
240 Peter Lunn
241 D A R H Webster
242 R D N Wells
243 David Robert Earnshaw
244 Dave Hillam
245 Colin Cameron
246 R A Kelly
247 Mark C Hughes
248 Philip Mark Raleigh
249 Roger A Kirby
250 Thomas A Craven
251 Andy Walker
252 R W Beacroft
253 A J Ounsworth
254 K W & C W Warkup
255 Peter Simon
256 Stephen Fielder
257 Peter Baxter
258 Peter Pickup
259 Ian Willott
260 R B Dalziel
261 Nick Burton
262 David Bryan Simms
263 Gary R Miles
264 Christopher Paul Bell
265 A J Hindley
266 Eric Heesom
267 Anders Johansson
268 J Gardiner
269 Ingvar Thomas
270 Ian Griffiths
271 W D Phillips
272 Harry Thompson
273 Dave Helliwell
274 George Quinn
275 Charlie Peck
276 David Potter
277 Angus W Rodger
278 Andrew Anderson
279 Anthony W Conway
280 Paul Cullingworth
281 Andrew Barber

282 Andrew Growns
283 David Goodman
284 L J Ransome
285 M W Ransome
286 Raymond Shaw
287 Robert Pratt
288 David Jepson
289 Stewart John Elvidge
290 Les Gold
291 C R Williamson
292 P Williamson
293 David & Robert Lee
294 J Ringrose
295 J L Elvidge
296 Simon N Jackson
297 Simon N Jackson
298 Malcolm Ferguson
299 Dean Banyard
300 Colin Farmery
301 Mike Purkiss
302 Trond Isaksen
303 David M Lovell
304 Neal Southwick
305 L M Penn
306 Harry Downes
307 Harold W Laverack
308 Keith Drury
309 Sports Marketing (Australia)
310 Michael K Williams
311 David Collinson
312 Christopher Norrie
313 J Lathan
314 David L Close
315 Mark N Peacock
316 Anthony Wright
317 David Gardham
318 Roger Wash
319 Brian Tabner
320 Rob Winn
321 P Winstanley
322 Stephen Phineas Musgrave
323 Steve Johnson
324 Dr C J Morton
325 Stanley A Robinson
326 Wayne Bemrose
327 G S Briggs
328 David Moore
329 Paul Yates
330 David Downs
331 Norman Green
332 Tom & Joe Atkinson
333 Aiden Stradling
334 Alan Collins
335 Michael Beckett
336 Charles White
337 C Peers
338 Paul Jerome
339 T Ellis
340 Alan Wilson
341 Trevor Island